Information Technology Control and Audit

Fourth Edition

Information Technology Control and Audit

Fourth Edition

Sandra Senft • Frederick Gallegos • Aleksandra Davis

CRC Press
Taylor & Francis Group
Boca Raton   London   New York

CRC Press is an imprint of the
Taylor & Francis Group, an **informa** business
AN AUERBACH BOOK

Contents

SECTION II   AUDITING IT PLANNING AND ORGANIZATION

SECTION III IT ACQUISITION AND IMPLEMENTATION

SECTION IV   IT DELIVERY AND SUPPORT

SECTION V   ADVANCED TOPICS

Preface

This book is designed to meet the increasing need for information technology (IT) and audit professionals to understand IT governance and the controls required to manage this key resource. This book can be used by IT and audit professionals to gain an understanding of IT governance, controls, and audit practices. This book aligns to and supports the Control Objectives for Information and Related Technology (COBIT) model and assists in preparation for the Certified Information Systems Auditor (CISA) exam. Exhibit P.1 provides a map of this text to the CISA exam.

Exam (%)	CISA Examination Content Areas to Model Curriculum (Undergraduate) — Title and Description	IT Audit and Control	IT Planning and Organization	IT Acquisition Implementation	IT Delivery and Support	Advanced Topics
14	*The IS audit process* Provides IS audit services in accordance with IS audit standards, guidelines, and best practices to assist the organization in ensuring that its IT and business systems are protected and controlled	X				
14	*IT governance* Provides assurance that the organization has the structure, policies, accountability, mechanisms, and monitoring practices in place to achieve the requirements of corporate governance of IT	X	X			
19	*Systems and infrastructure life-cycle management* Provides assurance that the management practices for the development/acquisition, testing, implementation, maintenance, and disposal of systems and infrastructure will meet the organization's objectives		X	X		

Exhibit P.1   Mapping text to CISA exam.

23	*IT service delivery and support* Provides assurance that the IT service management practices will ensure the delivery of the level of services required to meet the organization's objectives		X	X	X	
30	*Protection of information assets* Provides assurance that the security architecture (policies, standards, procedures, and controls) ensures the confidentiality, integrity, and availability of information assets		X	X	X	X

Exhibit P.1   **(Continued) Mapping text to CISA exam.**

Acknowledgments

We have many to thank for the support we received in the preparation of this book. We have a combined total of over 50 years of information systems (IS) audit, control, and security experience that includes four books, over 200 professional articles, and 200 presentations in this field. This book is designed for those who wish to learn and possibly select this field as their profession and those who wish to retool and enhance their audit tool kit with new experiences and techniques. In essence, we have collected our past experiences, successes, and lessons learned. We hope you will profit from this book and share it with your colleagues.

We wish to thank the IS Audit and Information Assurance Faculty worldwide who have been in the trenches to teach this profession to the many who want to learn what it is all about. The research and writings of Professors A. Faye Borthick, Ron Weber, Roger Jamieson, John Wyber, Alan Friedberg, Dan Kneer, Nils Kandelin, Tommie Singleton, Sokratis Katsikas, Damaso Lopez, Howard Kanter, Karen Forcht, Alan T. Lord, Joe Gelinas, Kil C. Kim, Hiroshi Yoshida, Josef Vyskoc, Gordon B. Davis, Elsie Jancura, Corey Schou, Carol Sledge, Peter Best, Jim Gau, Jai Mehta, Anna M. Berta, Tony Coulson, Mo Beheshti, and many more have been so helpful and contributed to the advancement of information technology audit, control, and security. This book is dedicated to the memory of the earlier professionals who paved the way: Jae Up Kim, Gary McCombs, Joseph Wasserman, Harold J. Highland, Wayne Snipes, Keagle Davis, Stan Halper, Francis Langlinais, and Donald C. Scantlebury. This book is in honor of those professionals who continue the search for excellence in this field: John Lainhart IV, Robert B. Parker, Michael Cangemi, Steven Ross, Steven Jue, Art Foreman, David Irvin, Nick Horsky, William Perry, Bill Mair, Donald Wood, Carl Pabst, John Kuyers, Dana "Rick" Richardson, Belden Menkus, Robert Roussey, Akira Matsuo, Paul Williams, Fred Lilly, Michael Parkinson, John Beveridge, Donn Parker, Michael Villegas, Hugh H. Peri-Williams, Hugh Parkes, John Tongren, and many, many more.

We also thank our earlier and current employers for giving us the opportunity to experience this challenging environment and excel in our IS audit careers: the U.S. Government Accountability Office (formerly General Accounting Office), Mercury Insurance, Farmers Insurance, and Zurich Financial Services. Finally, we appreciate the involvement and experience of the professional associations worldwide that support this field; they are mentioned in this book for their many contributions, especially those members of the Information Systems Audit and Control Association (ISACA) Model Curriculum Task Force and Academic Relations Committee and their initial product, which was issued in March 1998, and the Follow-On Model Revision Task Force effort led by Dr. Alan Lord and issued in 2005.

We also thank our colleagues, alumni, and students for their participation and contributions to the writings and editing of this work. We thank Professors Steven Powell, Louise Soe, Koichiro

Isshiki, Drew Hwang, Larisa Preiser-Houy, Steven Curl, Ida Masouris, Ruth Guthrie, Ward Testerman, Dan Manson, Carol Heins-Gonzales, Anna Carlin for their written contributions. We thank our former MSBA-IS Audit and CIS alumnis who have worked or are currently working in the Information Assurance field—Loida Tison-Dualan, Ken Le, Kevin Fried, Bill Liao, Debbie Newman, Don Fergus, Paul King, Isabelle Prieve-Theisen, Mattie Woods, Scott Kandel, Roin Nance, Matt Touquet, Karen Seketa, Kevin Powell, Dan Dow, Amin Leiman, Larry Lam, Richard Leonard, Ron Proulx, Harry Soo, John Barger, Thomas Halsell, Mariska Handoyo, Charles Bent, Tessa Rogge, Albert Kim, Cindy Kubis, Rita Leung, Ron Lim, Erin Manalo, Isreal Perez Carin Ruiz, Marlow Sabanegh, Daniel Smith, Elysa Soedharma, Tina Soedjak, Joel Sothern, David Wright, Lana Nino, Karen Nelson, Tom Burns, Gerald Morris, Henry Townsend, John Carvala, Hala Alhasan, Imelda Armantha, Ania Briscoe, Stephan Barnes, Christine Kartawidjaja, Lidya Kartawidjaja, Heru Subroto, Raymond Cheung, Tom Duffy, Haydee Durant, David Freed, Larry Himmel, Jim Turner, Vincent Turner, Andy Marzo, Ammar Massoud, Michelle McCullough, Matt Meyers, Anita Montgomery, Michael Miller, Sinta Muljadi, Naz Nageer, Will Nguyen, Yvonne Guan Zheng, Chuong Tran, Martin Tuggorono, Silvia Widyawati-Chiu, Roehl Amante, Charles Bogguess, Larry Carter, Matt Case, Jonathan Chan, Jason Chow, Jeffery Cowherd, Cameron Doherty, Rodney Dor, Michael Du, Julia Francis, Unity Gwanzura, Anthony Hacha, Todd Hayashibara, Sherrie Simmons, Christopher Stathis, Doug Bieber, Audie Suhandinata, Ronil Tataria, Irwin Tjan, Ralph Velasco, Dean West, Kathleen Tang, Steven Tanner, Meta Setiawan, Tommy Ng, Janet Zhu, Nurullah Askan, Gatu Prihartoyo, Kim Phelps-Keough, Paul Wan, Boulton Fernando, Waberyn Wambugi, Sally Xu, Rosina Liu, Seth Cox, Randy Coneby, Lorne Dear, Jerry Sadowski, Jason Patterson, Andrew Rios, Darren Ross, Nathan Mawby, Pedro R. Garcia, Kim Ho, Ken Jiang, Elmo Ju, Linda Jung, Jennifer Lao, Violet Shay, Cristy Shum, Michael Wong, Walter Wyckoff, Sherman Yang, Ali Zia, Sherman Hung, Stephen Sha, Luke Kwo, James Koh, Mary Keung, Lisa Kinyon, Ray Krzystofiak, Khoa Le, Daniel Lee, Sherman Hung, Minal Shah, Ryan Andrews, David Dear, Mesiagh Sobhanian, Tom Calabrese, Maribel Tomenis, Linda Tsai, Evan Tsai, Dennis Tye, Christina Tsang-Reveche, Doan Vinh, Cathy Wang, Mary Michaels, Anupama Sahni, Phoung Quach, Benny Hsu, Amanda Xu, Edson Gin, Matt Smith, Kevin Butscher, Rodney Kocot, Miccal Jackson, Michael Sundareson, Alex Li, Genemar Lazo, Stephen Sun, Sean Liu, Arthur Estillore, Martin Rojas, Allison Delpit, Adi Dzaferovich, Brandon Brown, Kendrick Tse, Suwandi Chandra, Charles Chu, Sheryl Benedict, Charles Chantakrivat, Michael Vong, Romeo Garcia, Garrett Martel, Irina Kessinger, and over 300 others whom we have placed into the IS audit profession.

We thank our earlier students and now information assurance colleagues/educators and special thanks to Dr. Dan Manson, Dr. Carol Heins-Gonzales, Mohammad Al-Abdullah, Stephanie Doda, Edson Gin, and Steven Tanner for their assistance and support in the first and second editions. We wish to thank our faculty support staff Kathleen Von Velasco, Martha Guarnett, Fritzi Taylor, and Victoria Galvez for their support of the first and second editions.

This work is a combined effort of the many we have worked with, the many we have shared with, and the many we have taught to go on into this profession worldwide. We hope you will use it and add to it in your professional development in this exciting field.

Authors

Sandra Senft is an executive with more than 30 years combined experience in auditing, financial management, insurance, and IT. During her career in IT, her responsibilities included finance, process improvement, project management, quality management, service management, sourcing, and vendor management.

Senft developed an extensive understanding of the IT and financial disciplines in her role as the global chief financial officer for Group IT within Zurich Financial Services in Zurich, Switzerland. Prior to that she was the assistant vice president for IT Support Services at Farmers Insurance in Los Angeles, California, where she was responsible for the project management office, IT finance, quality assurance, sourcing and vendor management, service management, and asset management.

During her career as an IS auditor and IS audit manager, she specialized in auditing systems development projects as well as general control audits of mainframe and distributed systems, information security, disaster recovery, and quality assurance. She was also responsible for defining and developing the audit risk methodology, audit methodology, automated audit workflow system, and training audit staff.

She was a faculty member at California State Polytechnic University, Pomona, California, from 1997 to 2000, where she taught undergraduate and graduate courses in IT and IS auditing. She has also presented IS auditing topics at seminars, conferences, and CISA review courses specializing in systems development auditing. She has authored and coauthored several articles on IT controls and audit for Auerbach Publications.

Senft graduated from California State Polytechnic University, Pomona, California, with a master of science in business administration option in IS auditing and a bachelor of science in accounting. She is a nonpracticing Certified Information Systems Auditor (CISA) and Certified Internal Auditor (CIA). She served as president, treasurer, director of research and academic relations, and spring conference chair for the Los Angeles Chapter of ISACA.

Frederick Gallegos has expertise in IT audit education, IS auditing, security, and control of information systems; legal environment of information systems; local area and wide area network security and controls; and computer ethics, management information systems, executive support systems, and Internet as an audit resource. He has more than 35 years of teaching and practical experience in the field, published four books, and authored and coauthored more than 200 articles in the aforementioned subjects. He received a BS and an MBA from the California State Polytechnic University, Pomona, California. He has a California Community College Instructor Credential, and taught for the Computer Information Systems Department, College of

Business at Cal Poly, Pomona, California, from 1976 to 1996 (part-time) and full-time from 1996 to 2006. After 30 years of teaching, he retired in September 2006 and received lecturer emeritus status from the university in May 2007. In February 2008, he received the Computer Information Systems (CIS) Lifetime Achievement Award from the CIS Department at Cal Poly, Pomona, California. He continues to maintain contact and provides consulting services with his past undergraduate and graduate students and alumni of the CIS Department's Information Assurance programs from Cal Poly, Pomona, California.

Before teaching full-time at Cal Poly, Gallegos worked for the Government Accountability Office (GAO)–Los Angeles Regional Office (1972–1996) and advanced within GAO to serve as manager, Management and Evaluator Support Group. He managed staff involved in office automation, computer audit support, computer audit, training, human resource planning and staffing, technical information retrieval, and security/facilities management. He retired from the GAO in 1996 with 26 years of federal and military service. He is a recipient of several service awards from the GAO, *EDP Audit, Control, and Security Newsletter* (EDPACS), and Information Systems Audit and Control Association (ISACA), which recognized his past contributions to the field and his efforts in the establishment of formal university courses at his alma mater in IS auditing, control, and security at the undergraduate level in 1979 with the implementation of the Association to Advance Collegiate Schools of Business (AACSB) accredited graduate-level Master of Science in business administration degree program in IS auditing since 1980. (The AACSB was founded in 1916 to accredit schools of business worldwide.) Gallegos has spoken widely on topics related to the IS audit, control, and security field, and served in a number of assignments and positions with the ISACA in the past. They are as follows:

ISACA Foundation. Member of the Standards Board and Committee (1984–1996), involved in the issuance of general standards for the EDP audit profession and named as contributor for the general standards and nine IS audit standards

ISACA. Member of the History Committee (1986–2006), involved in writing the history of EDP Auditors Association for the 25th anniversary, editorial board member for *ISACA Journal* (1995–2006), member of the Academic Liaison Committee (1984–1990, 1995–1997), Chair, President's Task Force ISACA for the development of curricula for undergraduate and graduate education in IS auditing (May 1995—issued March 1998) and member of the second task force for the revision of the ISACA Model, issued 2004

Aleksandra Davis has over 15 years combined experience in auditing, financial management, insurance, and risk management. Currently, she is an IT audit principal at a leading insurance company in California.

Throughout her career, Davis has spearheaded several compliance programs, including SOX 404, and continues to incorporate improvements to ensure sustainability of the programs. She also consults on key company initiatives to help ensure that adequate controls are considered and provides audit and other consulting services, including Enterprise Risk Management (ERM), Business Continuity/Disaster Recovery (BC/DR), and Quality Assessment and Improvement Program (QAIP). Davis also facilitates communication to help increase internal controls awareness and is a liaison to external auditors.

Davis graduated from California State Polytechnic University, Pomona, California, with a master of science in business administration option in IS auditing. As a past president of the Los Angeles Chapter of ISACA, Davis has been an active chapter volunteer and supporter since she was in her graduate program. Her graduate paper on IS audit training needs was awarded the first prize at the ISACA LA Best Paper Contest. It was later published in *Issues in Information Systems* and accepted for presentation and publication at the International Association for Computer Information Systems (IACIS) Conference, where it was selected by IACIS for the Best Research Paper Award. Davis is a Certified Information Systems Auditor (CISA), Certified Internal Auditor (CIA), and Certified Public Accountant (CPA).

A FOUNDATION FOR IT AUDIT AND CONTROL

1

Chapters 1 through 7

The first part of this text examines the foundation for information technology (IT) audit and control. This foundation has evolved through the recognition of the need for strong IT controls by professional organizations, business, and government. For the novice IT auditor, it provides a prospective as to how far the evolution of IT control guidance and techniques has come. This section examines the emerging issues in IT auditing today and in the future. It focuses on the legal environment, its impact on information reviews, and the important roles IT auditors will play in examination of issues from IT contracts to compliance with Internet law. Other major areas for IT auditors are the issues of security and privacy of IT. Demand by the public and governments have generated concern for the protection of individual rights and corporate information. Thus, career planning has become an important element for IT auditors and management. Development of the knowledge, skills, and abilities is a continuous challenge for the IT audit professional. Finally, we provide an outlook for the information systems (IS) audit profession, a view of the future.

Chapter 1 presents the IT environment today and discusses why issues involving IT control and audit are so important. It briefly discusses what IT auditing involves and the development of guidance by a number of organizations worldwide to deal with IT control and auditability issues. Information integrity, reliability, and validity are extremely important in today's competitive business world. Also, with the increased demand for IT have come growing legal issues of concern to the CEO, CIO, and IT professional. The IT auditor must keep pace with legal issues that may impact business processes and profitability. Control and audit are global concerns, especially in areas such as electronic funds transfer, electronic payment systems, and wireless technology.

Chapter 2 provides an overview of the legal environment and the IT auditor's role in assisting management and legal counsel. Much has happened in our world and changed our views and outlook. The events of September 11, 2001 have made us more security conscious. The financial disasters of Enron, WorldCom, and others have generated the call for new laws and federal regulation. With the services industry expanding, the importance of financial responsibility, contract compliance, and monitoring has grown proportionally, exceeding the abilities of the organization to successfully identify problems and alert management to take action before they become business disasters or frauds and end up in the courts. Recent rulings and laws have hastened organizations to examine corporations' use of electronic mail, intranets, extranets, and the Internet itself. Government's concern for protection of individual rights has generated a frenzy worldwide and global positioning for information control and dissemination. The Homeland Security Act and the Sarbanes–Oxley Act will have tremendous impact on the audit, control, and security of IT in business and our lives.

Chapter 3 discusses the process of audit and review and its IT role. Who are IT auditors? What are their roles? What do they do? What are their Standards of Practice? What level of knowledge or skills should an IT auditor possess and how do they obtain them? Again, this discussion provides the novice IT auditor and IT audit manager/supervisor with important baseline information to help in the training and preparation of the IT auditor.

Chapter 4 covers the IT audit process for the auditing of IT and the demands it will place on the profession in the years ahead. IT auditing is both basic and complex. This chapter discusses its basics and beginnings and its evolution. With the evolution, professional associations and government have taken an active role in generating guidance for the practitioner. Worldwide, all of these efforts have contributed to the IT audit process and the array of tools and techniques being used by practitioners today.

Chapter 5 discusses the use of computer-assisted audit tools and techniques in auditing. This chapter discusses the planning steps necessary for use and application of computer-assisted tools and techniques. The various types of tools and techniques available for the auditor to use are described along with their advantages and disadvantages. Recognition and selection of the tools and techniques available to the auditor is an important step in the audit process.

Chapter 6 discusses IT audit career planning and development. As we move into the next millennium with the growth of IT services, the continued advances of new IT into business processes, and the generation of global IT competition, management must be ready to deal with the multitude of current and future IT-related control issues they will face. IT audit career planning and development will play a key role in development of new resources to meet the challenge and the retooling or advanced training of current resources. As new information technologies are integrated and become commercially profitable, so too must the skills of the IT auditor be at a level to meet the challenge and comply with professional practice standards.

Chapter 7 discusses IT auditing and provides the student and practitioner a view of the IT auditor's role in the years ahead. The audit profession has a long history of standardizing methods and techniques used in the review of operations. Although the process of performing the audit will change little, the tools to do it with and the rapidity of reporting with follow-up of management actions will change to be profitable, competitive, efficient, effective, and economic.

Chapter 1

Information Technology Environment: Why Are Controls and Audit Important?

The role of information technology (IT) control and audit continues to be a critical mechanism for ensuring the integrity of information systems (IS) and the reporting of organization finances to avoid and hopefully prevent future financial fiascos such as Enron and WorldCom. Unfortunately, the fiascos continue as we have seen in the recent financial crisis. Global economies are more interdependent than ever and geopolitical risks impact everyone. Electronic infrastructure and commerce are integrated in business processes around the globe. The need to control and audit IT has never been greater.

Initially, IT auditing (formerly called electronic data processing [EDP], computer information systems [CIS], and IS auditing) evolved as an extension of traditional auditing. At that time, the need for an IT audit function came from several directions:

- Auditors realized that computers had impacted their ability to perform the attestation function.
- Corporate and information processing management recognized that computers were key resources for competing in the business environment and similar to other valuable business resource within the organization, and therefore, the need for control and auditability is critical.
- Professional associations and organizations, and government entities recognized the need for IT control and auditability.

The early components of IT auditing were drawn from several areas. First, traditional auditing contributes knowledge of internal control practices and the overall control philosophy. Another contributor was IS management, which provides methodologies necessary to achieve successful design and implementation of systems. The field of behavioral science provided such questions and analysis to when and why IS are likely to fail because of people problems. Finally, the field of computer science contributes knowledge about control concepts, discipline, theory, and the formal models that underlie hardware and software design as a basis for maintaining data validity, reliability, and integrity.

IT auditing continues to be an integral part of the audit function because it supports the auditor's judgment on the quality of the information processed by computer systems. Initially, auditors with IT audit skills are viewed as the technological resource for the audit staff. The audit staff often looked to them for technical assistance. As you will see in this textbook, there are many types of audit needs within IT auditing, such as organizational IT audits (management control over IT), technical IT audits (infrastructure, data centers, data communication), application IT audit (business/financial/operational), development/implementation IT audits (specification/requirements, design, development, and postimplementation phases), and compliance IT audits involving national or international standards. The IT auditor's role has evolved to provide assurance that adequate and appropriate controls are in place. Of course, the responsibility for ensuring that adequate internal controls are in place rests with the management. The audit's primary role, except in areas of management advisory services, is to provide a statement of assurance as to whether adequate and reliable internal controls are in place and are operating in an efficient and effective manner. Therefore, whereas management is to ensure, auditors are to assure.

Today, IT auditing is a profession with conduct, aims, and qualities that are characterized by worldwide technical standards, an ethical set of rules (Information Systems Audit and Control Association [ISACA] Code of Ethics), and a professional certification program (Certified Information Systems Auditor [CISA]). It requires specialized knowledge and practicable ability, and often long and intensive academic preparation. In-house training and professional development have emerged as tools to employers filling the needs for needed training in specialized areas. Most accounting, auditing, and IT professional societies have made improvements in research and education curriculum to provide an IT auditor with better theoretical and empirical knowledge base to perform the IT audit function. Education obtained at the university level is one resource to be merged with in-house and external training resources. The need to maintain proficiency and currency in this dynamic field is critical.

The breadth and depth of knowledge required to audit IT systems are extensive. For example, IT auditing involves

- Application of risk-oriented audit approaches
- Use of computer-assisted audit tools and techniques
- Application of standards (national or international) such as ISO/IEC 27000, ISO 9000/3, and ISO 17799 to improve and implement quality systems in software development and meet IT security standards
- Understanding of business roles and expectations in the auditing of systems under development as well as the purchase of software packaging and project management
- Assessment of information security and privacy issues which can put the organization at risk
- Examination and verification of the organization's compliance with any IT-related legal issues that may jeopardize or place the organization at risk
- Evaluation of complex systems development life cycles (SDLC) or new development techniques (e.g., prototyping, end-user computing, rapid systems, or application development)
- Reporting to management and performing a follow-up review to ensure actions taken at work

The auditing of complex technologies and communications protocols involves the Internet, intranet, extranet, electronic data interchange, client servers, local and wide area networks, data communications, telecommunications, wireless technology, integrated voice/data/video systems, and the software and hardware that support these processes and functions.

IT Today and Tomorrow

High-speed information processing has become indispensable to organizations' activities. For example, Control Objectives for Information and Related Technology (COBIT) emphasizes this point and substantiates the need to research, develop, publicize, and promote up-to-date internationally accepted IT control objectives. The primary emphasis of COBIT (issued by Information Systems Audit and Control Foundation, 1996) is to ensure that information needed by businesses is provided by technology and the required assurance qualities of information are both met. COBIT, fourth edition and now entering its fifth edition, has evolved and improved in its guidance to incorporate the essential elements of strategic management, value delivery, resource management, risk management, and performance management.

Around the world, reports of white-collar crime, information theft, computer fraud, information abuse, penetration, and information theft occurring in major financial institutions and other information/technology control concerns continue to be heard in the press and major television networks. Thanks to surveys and reports by SANS (SysAdmin, Audit, Network, Security) Institute, U.S. Government Accountability Office (GAO), Federal Bureau of Investigation (FBI), Federal Trade Commission (FTC), Computer Security Institute (CSI), Computer Emergency Response Teams (CERT), The Committee on National Security Systems (CNSS), and other information assurance-oriented organizations, businesses, and Governments have been warned of the threats and losses as a result of poor controls over IS.

Today, more than ever, organizations are more information dependent and conscious of the pervasive nature of technology across the business enterprise. The increased connectivity and availability of systems and open environments have proven to be the lifelines of most business entities. IT is used more extensively in all areas of commerce around the world. Owing to the rapid diffusion of computer technologies and the ease of information accessibility, knowledgeable and well-educated IT auditors are in great demand. They ensure that effective IT controls are in place to maintain data integrity and manage access to information.

Private industry, professional associations, and organizations such as International Federation of Information Processing (IFIP), Association for Computing Machinery (ACM), Association of Information Technology Professionals (AITP), Information Systems Security Association (ISSA), and others have recognized the need for more research and guidance as identified in Appendix III. Control-oriented organizations such as the American Institute of Certified Public Accountants (AICPA), the Canadian Institute of Chartered Accountants (CICA), Institute of Internal Auditors (IIA), Association of Certified Fraud Examiners (ACFE), and others have issued guidance and instructions and supported studies/research in this area. Since 1996, The Colloquium for Information Systems Security Educators (CISSE) has been a leading proponent for implementing the course of Instruction in Information Security (InfoSec) and Information Assurance in education.

The need for improved control over IT, especially in business/commerce, has been advanced over the years in earlier and continuing studies by many national and international organizations. Essentially, technology has impacted three significant areas of the business environment:

■ Technology has impacted what can be done in business in terms of information and as a business enabler. It has increased the ability to capture, store, analyze, and process tremendous amounts of data and information, which has increased the empowerment of the business decision maker. Technology has also become a primary enabler to various production and service processes. It has become a critical component to business processes. There is a residual effect in that the increased use of technology has resulted in increased budgets, increased successes and failures, and increased awareness of the need for control.

■ Technology has significantly impacted the control process. Although control objectives have generally remained constant, except for some that are technology specific, technology has altered the way in which systems should be controlled. Safeguarding assets, as a control objective, remains the same whether it is done manually or is automated. However, the manner by which the control objective is met is certainly impacted.

■ Technology has impacted the auditing profession in terms of how audits are performed (information capture and analysis, control concerns) and the knowledge required to draw conclusions regarding operational or system effectiveness, efficiency and integrity, and reporting integrity. Initially, the impact was focused on dealing with a changed processing environment. As the need for auditors with specialized technology skills grew, so did the IT auditing profession.

Information Integrity, Reliability, and Validity: Importance in Today's Global Business Environment

Organizations today operate in a dynamic global multienterprise environment with team-oriented collaboration and place very stringent requirements on the telecommunications network. The design of such systems is complex and management can be very difficult. Organizations are critically dependent on the timely flow of accurate information. A good way to view how stringent the network requirements are is to analyze them in terms of the quality of the telecommunications service. Perhaps, two examples of the world's dependency on IT come as a result of two reported events in the past where IT failure impacted world commerce and communications. In 1998, an AT&T major switch failed due to two software errors and a procedural error, causing communications at that switch to become overloaded and making customers using credit cards unable to access their funds for 18 hours. In another 1998 event, a communication satellite went into an uncontrollable rotation causing pager communication systems worldwide to be "useless," and those companies using this technology for E-account transaction and verification were unable to process credit card information for 24 hours, thus causing their customers to pay cash for their transactions. The disruption of the paging services caused severe impact to services provided by both private and governmental organizations that depended on this communication. Even today, these types of events are repeated over and over again where organizations dependent on technology encounter failure and disruption to services and business. In August 2003, the northeast quadrant and part of Canada were still recovering from a massive power outage to the area that shut down ATMs and all electrical services (elevators, phone service, street signals, subways, etc.).

Most telecommunication experts believe the network must be able to reach anyone anywhere in the world and be capable of supporting the sharing of a wide range of information, from simple voice, data, and text messages to cooperative transactions requiring the information updating of a variety of databases. The chief executive officer (CEO) and chief information officer (CIO) want to meet or exceed their business objectives and attain maximum profitability through an extremely high degree of availability, fast response time, extreme reliability, and a very high level of security.

This means that the products for which IT provides consumer feedback will also be of high quality, rich in information content, and come packaged with a variety of useful services to meet the changing business conditions and competition. Flexible manufacturing and improvement programs such as Just-In-Time (JIT) and Lean Manufacturing, and Total Quality Management (TQM) will enable low-cost production. Flexible manufacturing will permit products to be produced economically in arbitrary lot sizes through modularization of the production process.

The unpredictability of customer needs and the shortness of product life cycles will cause the mix of production capabilities and underlying resources required by the organization to change constantly. Organizations must be capable of assembling its capabilities and resources quickly, thereby bringing a product to market swiftly. To achieve the high degree of organizational flexibility and value-chain coordination necessary for quick market response, excellent product quality, and low cost, the organization will employ a network, team-oriented, distributed decision-making organizational approach rather than a more traditional hierarchical, vertically integrated, command-and-control approach.

Organizations will possess a dynamic network organization synthesizing the best available design, production, supply, and distribution capabilities and resources from enterprises around the world and linking them and the customers together. A multienterprise nature will enable organizations to respond to competitive opportunities quickly and with the requisite scale, while, at the same time, enabling individual network participant's cost and risk to be reduced. The network will be dynamic because participant identities and relationships will change as capabilities and resources required change. The global scope of the network will enable organizations to capitalize on worldwide market opportunities. Work will be performed by multidisciplinary, multienterprise teams, which will work concurrently and, to reduce production time, be granted significant decision-making authority. Team members will be able to work collaboratively regardless of location and time zone. Openness, cooperativeness, and trust will characterize the relationships among the organizations in the network and their personnel.

Aside from reach, range, and service responsiveness, the network must be highly interconnective so that people, organizations, and machines can communicate at any time, regardless of location. Also, the network must be very flexible because the organization is constantly changing. Finally, the network must be cost effective because low cost is one of the ingredients in the mass-customization strategy. In addition, a control structure, which provides assurances of integrity, reliability, and validity, must be designed, developed, and implemented.

So how can this be accomplished? The ability to reach anyone anywhere in the world requires global area networks. Clearly, the Internet and global carrier services will be crucial. Also, because the intended receiver need not be in the office or even at home, wireless networks will play a major part. This will be true on-premise, such as with the use of wireless private branch exchanges (PBXs) or local area networks (LANs), and off-premise, with the use of cellular networks (iPad, iPhone, etc.), global satellite networks such as Iridium, and Personal Communications Networks. To support the sharing of a wide range of voice, data, and video information, bandwidth on demand will be required all the way to the desktop as well as the mobile terminal and hand-held devices. Also, various collaborative service platforms such as Microsoft and Unix will be necessary. Finally, perfect service will have to be designed into the network. Speed can be achieved through broadband networking: locally via fast Ethernet, gigabit, and asynchronous transfer mode (ATM) LANs, and over a wide area via switched multimegabit data services (SMDS) and ATM services, and reliability through quality hardware/software and proven wired and wireless solutions where possible.

Control and Audit: A Global Concern

We can point to the events of September 11, 2001, the collapse of trust in the financial reports of private industry (Enron, WorldCom, etc.) and most recently the collapse of the mortgage market and the follow-on recession have caused much reflection and self-assessment within the business world. The evolution of the economic society parallels the evolution of exchange mechanisms because advancement in the latter allows the facilitation of the former. Society started with the primitive use of the barter system. In this way, individuals were both consumers and producers because they brought to market that commodity which they had in excess and exchanged it directly for a commodity for which they were in need. Simply, society exercised an exchange of goods for goods. Owing to its numerous inefficiencies and societies' demands to accommodate for the increased population, production, communication, and trading areas, this system was soon replaced by a modified barter exchange mechanism. In the modified barter exchange system, a common medium of exchange was agreed upon. This allowed the time and effort expended in trying to find a trading partner with the need for one's product to be reduced. In the early stages of economic development, precious metals such as gold and silver gained widespread acceptance as exchange media. Precious metals characterized acceptability, durability, portability, and divisibility, but it gradually played the role of money. Thus, when emerging central governments began minting or coinage of these metals to begin the money-based exchange system, its monetary role was even more strengthened.

As economies became more commercial in nature, the influential mercantile class shaped the new society. The needs of the mercantilists, which included the promotion of exchange and accumulation of capital, led to the development of money warehouses that served as depositories for the safekeeping of funds. A receipt would be issued for those who opened a deposit account, and upon presentation of the receipt, the warehouse would return the specified amount to the depositor. These warehouses represented an elementary banking system because, like banks of today, they collected fees to cover their costs as well as earned profits for their owners. Soon the warehouses began issuing bills of exchange or their own drafts because of the idea that not all depositors would withdraw their funds at the same time. This created the fractional reserve banking system in which banks used the deposits not only to back up the receipts that they issued but also to extend credit. The coin, currency, and demand deposit payment mechanism flourished for many decades because of its convenience, safety, efficiency, and widespread acceptance by the public. However, another major change is now at hand for payment mechanisms: electronic funds transfers (EFTs).

E-Commerce and Electronic Funds Transfer

Electronic-commerce (E-commerce) and EFT open the next chapter for payment systems. They have been around since the 1960s. The banking industry is considered to be one of the forerunners in the use of computers. The industry started with mechanizing bookkeeping and accounting tasks, automating transaction flows, implementing magnetic ink character recognition (MICR) technology, and finally, utilizing online terminals to update depositor's account and record receipt or disbursement of cash. The advancement of both computer and communication technologies has spurred the phenomenal growth of EFT systems in the past 20 years. As more consumers become familiar and trust electronic financial transactions, EFTs will continue to be more widely used. Today, EFTs have already gone beyond the banking industry and can be seen in almost all retail establishments such as convenience stores (7–11, a.m./p.m., etc.), supermarkets, clothing stores, gas stations, and even amusement parks. EFTs allow the convenience of paying for goods and services without having to use checks or currency. In today's society of ever more computer-literate individuals, a transition is being witnessed from the traditional cash and check system to electronic payment systems.

Future of Electronic Payment Systems

The increased used of the Internet has brought with it a new form of exchange: virtual commerce. The cashless society that futurists have long forecasted is finally at hand, and it will replace today's paper money, checks, and even credit cards. Virtual commerce involves a new world of electronic cash (e-cash). Virtual transactions work very much like physical cash but without the physical symbols.

Although the use of e-cash has its positive aspects such as more convenience, flexibility, speed, cost savings, and greater privacy than using credit cards or checks on the Internet, it also has negative ramifications. Uncontrolled growth of e-cash systems could threaten bank and government-controlled payment systems, which would fuel the growth of confusing and inefficient systems. Also, current technology has not yet deemed e-cash to be more secure than bank money because money stored in a personal computer (PC) could be lost forever if the system crashes. In addition, e-cash could permit criminal activity such as money laundering and tax evasion to hide behind cyber dollars. Counterfeiters could also design their own mints of e-cash that would be difficult to differentiate from real money. Finally, criminals such as computer hackers could instantaneously pilfer the wealth of thousands of electronic consumers.

Therefore, many companies have been compelled to develop electronic payment systems that will solve these consumer concerns. In 2000, it represented about 40% of the online population. This grew to 63% by 2006. Today, even the Social Security Administration is phasing out hard-copy checks by 2012 in favor of electronic payment to your banking account. Both the federal government and many states are pushing citizens to file their income taxes electronically. There is a definite need for the security and privacy of payments made over the Internet, as millions of transactions occur daily and will be increasing at a rapid pace in the future. With this increase of E-commerce, the likelihood of fraud increases as well. E-commerce depends on security and privacy because, without them, neither consumers nor businesses would have an adequate level of comfort in digital transmission of transaction and personal data. In the newly revolutionized economy, it is a necessity for companies to conduct business online and reach out to customers through the Internet. The primary areas of concern with E-commerce are confidentiality, integrity, nonrepudiation, and authentication. These areas are addressed through several ways such as encryption, cryptography, and the use of third parties.

In addition, the credit card industry has been motivated to find secure technology for E-commerce. The National Institute of Standards and Technology (NIST) has done some extensive work in this area under its Information Technology Laboratory, devoting an emphasis to Smart Card Standards and Research at http://smartcard.nist.gov/. Organizations like these are only a fraction of the massive experiments that will transform the way people think about money. This is a worldwide commerce movement, and not just a U.S. movement. e-cash is the next inevitable payment system for an increasingly wired world. Economic history has once again reached another crossroad. Just as the mercantile class transformed the money exchange system to one of money warehouses, E-commerce (trade on the Internet) will be a revolutionary opportunity for global society to transform today's traditional system of exchange into a system of electronic payments. Thus, the need for auditability, security, and control of IT has become a worldwide issue.

Legal Issues Impacting IT

The Sarbanes–Oxley Act was created as the result of public demand for the new legislation to prevent, detect, and correct such aberrations. In addition to this legislation, the advancements in network environments technologies have resulted in bringing to the forefront issues of security and privacy that were once only of interest to the legal and technical expert but which today are topics that affect virtually every user of the information superhighway. The Internet has grown exponentially from a simple linkage of a relative few government and educational computers to a complex worldwide network that is utilized by almost everyone from the terrorist who has computer skills to the novice user and everyone in between. Common uses for the Internet include everything from marketing, sales, and entertainment purposes to e-mail, research, commerce, and virtually any other type of information sharing. Unfortunately, as with any breakthrough in technology, advancements have also given rise to various new problems that must be addressed, such as security and privacy. Use of the Internet for nonbusiness purposes on company time has caused several organizations (public and private) embarrassment. These problems are often being brought to the attention of IT audit and control specialists due to their impact on public and private organizations. Hence, security and privacy legislation will be discussed in Chapter 2, as they relate to the networked environment and the Internet. Current legislation and government plans will affect the online community and, along with the government's role in the networked society, will have a lasting impact in future business practices.

Federal Financial Integrity Legislation

It has been more than a decade since the Enron–Arthur Andersen LLP financial scandal but it still continues to plague today's financial market as the trust of the consumer, the investor, and the government to allow the industry to self-regulate have all been violated. The reminder of the Enron fiasco is today's scandals in the mortgage and mortgage investment market and the domino effect it has had on government, private industry, and the public.

Therefore, the Sarbanes–Oxley Act of 2002 will be a vivid reminder of the importance of due professional care. The Sarbanes–Oxley Act prohibits all registered public accounting firms from providing audit clients, contemporaneously with the audit, certain nonaudit services including internal audit outsourcing, financial-information-system design and implementation services, and expert services. These scope-of-service restrictions go beyond existing Security and Exchange Commission (SEC) independence regulations. All other services, including tax services, are permissible only if preapproved by the issuer's audit committee and all such preapprovals must be disclosed in the issuer's periodic reports to the SEC.

The act requires auditor (not audit firm) rotation. Therefore, the lead audit partner and the concurring review partner must rotate off the engagement if he or she has performed audit services for the issuer in each of the five previous fiscal years. The act provides no distinction regarding the capacity in which the audit or concurring partner provided such audit services. Any services provided as a manager or in some other capacity appear to count toward the 5-year period. The provision starts as soon as the firm is registered, therefore, absent guidance to the contrary, the audit and concurring partner must count back 5 years starting with the date in which Public Company Accounting Oversight Board registration occurs. This provision has a definite impact on small accounting firms. The SEC is currently considering whether or not to accommodate small firms in this area; currently, there is no small-firm exemption from this provision.

This act is a major reform package mandating the most far-reaching changes Congress has imposed on the business world since the Foreign Corrupt Practices Act of 1977 and the SEC Act of the 1930s. It seeks to thwart future scandals and restore investor confidence by, among other things, creating a public company accounting oversight board, revising auditor independence rules, revising corporate governance standards, and significantly increasing the criminal penalties for violations of securities laws.

Federal Security Legislation

The IT auditor should recognize that the U.S. federal government has passed a number of laws to deal with issues of computer crime and security and privacy of IS. Private industry has in the past been reluctant to implement these laws because of the fear of the negative impact it could bring to a company's current and future earnings and image to the public. The passage of the Homeland Security Act of 2002 and the inclusion of the Cyber Security Enhancement Act will have a substantial impact on private industry. An example of a number of past laws in place is as follows.

Computer Fraud and Abuse Act

The Computer Fraud and Abuse Act (CFAA) was first drafted in 1984 as a response to computer crime. The government's response to network security and network-related crimes was to revise the act in 1994 under the Computer Abuse Amendments Act to cover crimes such as trespassing (unauthorized entry) into an online system, exceeding authorized access, and exchanging information on how to gain unauthorized access. Although the act was intended to protect against attacks in a network environment, it does also have its fair share of faults. More details may be found in Chapter 2. The IT auditor must be aware of it significance.

Under this act, penalties are obviously less severe for "reckless destructive trespass" than for "intentional destructive trespass." The reasoning behind this is that reckless attackers may not necessarily intend to cause damage, but must still be punished for gaining access to places that they should not have access to. However, the impact of such terminology appears to possibly create some confusion in prosecuting the trespasser because it resides in such a "gray area." In *Morris v. United States*, it was determined that "intent" applied to access and not to damages. The implication here would be that if the "intentional" part of the violation was applied to access and not the damage, then the culprit could possibly be prosecuted under the lesser sentence.

For example, if an individual intentionally intended to release a virus over a network, it would seem difficult for prosecutors to prove the motive for the violation. What if the individual stated that he or she was conducting some type of security test (as Morris contested) and "accidentally" set off a procedure that released a virus over the network? Intentional could refer to access to a system but it may not apply to damage. In this case, the lesser penalty of "reckless destructive trespass" may be applied. Within the courts, this is a matter that must be contemplated on a case-by-case basis, observing the facts of each individual case. In some instances, however, it would appear that even "intentional" trespass could be defended by claims that the violation was due to negligence and therefore falls under the less severe of the two circumstances.

This legislation has been helpful as a legal tool for prosecuting crimes involving some of the aforementioned intruders and violators of system security, but it also seems to have a loophole in certain cases. Unfortunately, this loophole may be large enough for a serious violator of the act to slip through and be prosecuted under a lesser penalty by virtue of having to prove intent. All states have closed a portion of that loophole through statutes prohibiting harassment or stalking, including "e-mail." This act has been amended several times since 1984 to keep it current.

Computer Security Act of 1987

Another act of importance is the Computer Security Act of 1987, which was drafted due to congressional concerns and public awareness on computer security-related issues and because of disputes on the control of unclassified information. The general purpose of the act was a declaration from the government that improving the security and privacy of sensitive information in federal computer systems is in the public interest. The act established a federal government computer security program that would protect sensitive information in federal government computer systems. It would also develop standards and guidelines for unclassified federal computer systems and facilitate such protection.

The Computer Security Act also assigned responsibility for developing government-wide computer system security standards, guidelines, and security training programs to the National Bureau of Standards. It further established a Computer System Security and Privacy Advisory Board within the Commerce Department, and required federal agencies to identify computer systems containing sensitive information and develop security plans for those systems. Finally, it provided periodic training in computer security for all federal employees and contractors who managed, used, or operated federal computer systems.

The Computer Security Act, as discussed in Chapter 2, is particularly important because it is fundamental to the development of federal standards of safeguarding unclassified information and establishing a balance between national security and other nonclassified issues in implementing security and privacy policies within the federal government. It is also important in addressing issues concerning government control of cryptography, which, as can be seen in Chapter 20, has recently become a hotly contested topic.

Privacy on the Information Superhighway

Now that some issues associated with computer security have been reviewed, how the issue of privacy is impacted when computer security is breached will be examined. As is well known, there is a tremendous amount of information that companies and agencies are able to retrieve on any individual. People, corporations, and government are active in trading personal information for their own gain. In Virginia, a resident filed suit in the state court against *U.S. News & World Report*, challenging the right of the magazine to sell or rent his name to another publication without his express written consent. It is known that individuals share private information on a daily basis, but how has it affected the network world and the Internet? This issue will be analyzed in the following section.

The large number of users on the Internet has resulted in the availability of an enormous amount of private information on the network. This information unfortunately seems to be available for the taking by anyone who might be interested. A person's bank balance, Social Security number, political leanings, medical record, and much more is there for anyone who may want it. Information identity theft has been one of the fastest-growing crimes, and use of the IS highway has been a key component of such crimes. In 2003, it was revealed that a hacker penetrated the State of California payroll system and gained access to personal information. This information potentially could be put up for sale to anyone who might be interested in it. Someone has been collecting information and making it available for use, and a large number of these individuals seem to be refusing to follow any sort of fair information practice. In another 2003 incident, all it took was a phone call for Internet hijackers to steal 65,000 Web addresses belonging to the County of Los Angeles. The addresses were then sold and used to send pornographic material and junk e-mail and to try to hack into other computers.

Fortunately, the FTC has been very active in providing the public alerts to the various ongoing scams, and by visiting its Website at www.ftc.gov, people can be helped by the information it can provide if they become victims. This activity is a cause of alarm for everyone and the question is asked—Is it entitled to one's information? What is the government's policy regarding privacy of an individual and keeping a strong security policy? Ideally, citizens would like to limit the amount of monitoring that the government is allowed to do on them, but is the government in a position to monitor communications on the information superhighway? How will this affect one's right to privacy as guaranteed by the U.S. Constitution? The focus of the following section will then be to address these issues, paying especially close attention to the security-based measures that have affected the ideal of individual right to privacy.

Privacy Legislation and the Federal Government Privacy Act

In addition to the basic right to privacy that an individual is entitled to under the U.S. Constitution, the government also enacted the Privacy Act of 1974. The purpose of this is to provide certain safeguards to an individual against an invasion of personal privacy. This act places certain requirements on federal agencies, which include the following:

- Permits an individual to determine what records pertaining to him or her are collected and maintained by federal agencies
- Permits an individual to prevent records pertaining to him or her that were obtained for a particular purpose from being used or made available for another purpose without consent
- Permits an individual to gain access to information pertaining to him or her in federal agency records and to correct or amend them
- Requires federal agencies to collect, maintain, and use any personal information in a manner that assures that such action is for a necessary and lawful purpose, that the information is current and accurate, and that safeguards are provided to prevent misuse of the information

Although the Privacy Act is an important part of safeguarding individual privacy rights, it is important for the IT auditor to recognize that there are many exemptions under which it may be lawful for certain information to be disclosed. This could, in some cases, for various agencies, both federal and nonfederal, allow the means by which they can obtain and disclose information on any individuals simply because they may fall under one of the many exemptions that the Privacy Act allows. For example, the subsequent Freedom of Information Act provides the federal government a way to release historical information to the public in a controlled fashion. The Privacy Act has also been updated over time through the amendment process.

Electronic Communications Privacy Act

In the area of computer networking, the Electronic Communications Privacy Act is one of the leading early pieces of legislation against violation of private information as applicable to online systems. Before analyzing some of the implications that the act has had on the network community, let us briefly analyze some of the provisions defined by the act, as it seems to be quite complicated in giving privacy protection in some instances and not others.

Communications Decency Act of 1995

The Communication Decency Act (CDA) bans the making of "indecent" or "patently offensive" material available to minors through computer networks. The act imposes a fine of up to $250,000 and imprisonment for up to 2 years. The CDA does specifically exempt from liability any person who provides access or connection to or form a facility, system, or network that is not under the control of the person violating the act. Also, the CDA specifically states that an employer shall not be held liable for the actions of an employee unless the employee's conduct is within the scope of his or her employment. More recent application of this law has been used to protect minor's use of social networks and falling prey to predators/stalkers.

Health Insurance Portability and Accountability Act of 1996

On August 21, 1996, President Clinton signed the Health Insurance Portability and Accountability Act (HIPAA) into law. The original purpose of the law was to make it easier for Americans to maintain their health insurance when they switch jobs and restrict the ability of insurers to reject them based on preexisting health conditions. Unfortunately, the digital age added the provision of "administrative simplifications" to the law. According to the U.S. Department of Health,

> The "administrative simplifications" provisions require the adaptation of national standards for electronic health care transactions. By ensuring consistency throughout the industry, these national standards will make it easier for health plans, doctors, hospitals, and other healthcare providers to process claims and other transactions electronically. The law also required security and privacy standards in order to protect personal information.

The provisions for administrative simplification came "At the time when hospitals and insurers used more than 400 different software formats to transmit healthcare data. These covered everything from the headers on insurance forms to the codes describing diseases and medication." Many in the healthcare industry have viewed the "administrative simplification" component of the laws to be the most expensive and most difficult to implement. Part of the reason for the difficulty in implementation involves the issue of privacy. According to *InfoWorld*, "Medical organizations will need to invest in some of the new technologies currently available in other industries. Technologies like digital certificates, authentication, and biometric standards are needed to ensure that those authorized to view something are the only ones that have access." The cost and difficulty of implementing these new technologies to meet the requirements of HIPAA can be both time consuming and expensive, especially for smaller hospitals and clinics with little or no IT support. This is a challenge for internal and external auditors of the U.S. health care industry. Noncompliance by organizations can face stiff fines and penalties. Recent guidance issued by NIST and support of professional associations such as ISSA, IIA, ISACA, and Association of Health Internal Auditors have helped to make internal control improvements to this area.

Security, Privacy, and Audit

In summary, it appears that traditional as well as new security methods and techniques are simply not working. Although many products are quite efficient in securing the majority of attacks on a network, no single product seems to be able to protect a system from every possible intruder. Current security legislation, although addressing the issues of unwanted entry into a network, may also allow for ways by which some criminals can escape the most severe penalties for violating authorized access to a computer system. Moreover, some legislation, in effect, does not require periodic review, thus allowing for various policies and procedures to get outdated. The computer networking industry is continually changing. Because of this, laws, policies, procedures, and guidelines must constantly change with it; otherwise, they will have a tendency to become outdated, ineffective, and obsolete.

On the subject of privacy, it has been seen that in the online world, private information can be accessed by criminals. Some of the legislation passed in recent years does protect the user against invasion of privacy. However, some of the laws observed contain far too many exceptions and exclusions to the point that their efficacy suffers. In addition, the government continues to utilize state-of-the-art techniques for the purpose of accessing information for the sake of "national security" justified currently under the Homeland Security Act. New bills and legislation continue to attempt to find a resolution to these problems, but new guidelines, policies, and procedures need to be established, and laws need to be enforced to their full extent if citizens are to enjoy their right to privacy as guaranteed under the constitution.

Thus, if security products are not safe from every attack, and if current laws may not always be efficient in addressing the problem correctly, is there anything a user might be able to do? Although there is nothing at this time that will guarantee a system's security, a good starting point might be the establishment and implementation of a good computer security policy and Institutional Governance of Information Technology. A good policy can include

- Specifying required security features
- Defining "reasonable expectations" of privacy regarding such issues as monitoring people's activities
- Defining access rights and privileges and protecting assets from losses, disclosures, or damages by specifying acceptable use guidelines for users and also, providing guidelines for external communications (networks)
- Defining responsibilities of all users
- Establishing trust through an effective password policy
- Specifying recovery procedures
- Requiring violations to be recorded
- Acknowledging that owners, custodians, and clients of information need to report irregularities and protect its use and dissemination
- Providing users with support information

A good computer security policy will differ for each organization, corporation, or individual depending on security needs, although such a policy will not guarantee a system's security or make the network completely safe from possible attacks from cyberspace. With the implementation of such a policy, helped by good security products and a plan for recovery, perhaps the losses can be targeted for a level that is considered "acceptable" and the leaking of private information can be minimized. The IT auditor is part of an institutional team that helps create shared governance over the use, application, and assurance over IT within the organization.

Conclusion

Because IT and information security are integral parts of the IT's internal controls, we have discussed earlier the Internal Control Integrated Framework publication by COSO in 1997, which specifically includes IT controls. Also addressed are the IIA's SAC and ISACA's COBIT, which are both directly related to the frameworks identified by COSO in their reports. These are standards of practice, mentioned earlier, to help guide business in its IT strategic planning process, discussed in a Chapter 9. This chapter has provided guidance and examples of how critical these components are in setting the direction for what will follow.

The computer is changing the world. Business operations are also changing, sometimes very rapidly, because of the fast continuing improvement of technology. Events such as September 11, 2001, and financial upheavals from corporate scandals such as Enron and Global Crossing, to the more recent mortgage and mortgage investment scandals have resulted in increased awareness by the public and global business market. Yes, IT controls are very important. Today, people are shopping around at home through networks. People use "numbers" or accounts to buy what they want via shopping on computers and smart phones. These "numbers" are "digital money," the modern currency in the world. Digital money will bring us benefits as well as problems. One major benefit of digital money is its increased efficiency. However, it will also create another problem for us. "Security" is perhaps the biggest factor for individuals interested in making online purchases by using digital money. Also, it must be remembered that vigilance needs to be maintained over those who use the Internet for illegal activities, including those who are now using it for scams, crime, and covert activities that could potentially cause loss of life and harm to others. IT control and security is everyone's business.

Many people still fear giving their credit card numbers, phone numbers, or other personal information to strangers. They are afraid that people will be able to use these to retrieve their private or other valuable information without their consent. Unfortunately the magnetic strip on the

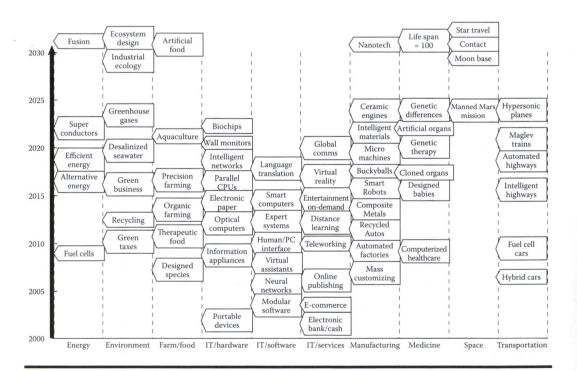

Exhibit 1.1   George Washington University Forecast of Emerging Technology. (From George Washington University, http://www.GWForecast.edu.)

back of your credit or debit card has become a target for skimmers who can extract the personal information electronically. Reports from the Federal Trade Commission have stated that identity theft and fraud are on the rise, much care is needed in the protection, security, and control of such information. Even banks like Wells Fargo are marketing support systems as E-Defense to protect your personal electronic financial transactions. Security, indeed, is the biggest risk in using digital money on the Internet. Besides the problem of security, privacy is a significant factor in some electronic payment systems. To encourage people to use digital money, these electronic payment systems should ensure that personal and unrelated information is not unnecessarily disclosed.

For the IT auditor, the need for audit, security, and control continue to be critical in the areas of IT and will be the challenge of this millennium. Perhaps, George Washington University said it best in its Forecast of Emerging Technologies and their impact on society and industry (see Exhibit 1.1). There are many challenges ahead; everyone must work together to design, implement, and safeguard the integration of these technologies in the workplace.

Review Questions

1. What is IT auditing? What does it involve?
2. Briefly, what are the skills needed to audit IS? Are they technical or nontechnical?
3. List five professional associations or organizations that support the needs of IT auditors today.
4. List at least three studies or documents issued that discuss the need for improved IT control.
5. Technology has impacted the business environment in three areas. What are those areas?
6. Why is IT control and auditability so important in today's virtual environment?
7. List and explain three U.S. federal laws which impact IT auditors.
8. What are some of the major concerns regarding control and auditability of IT in today's global environment?
9. What is EFT and what are its areas of vulnerability?
10. What is e-cash? What are the IT control concerns associated with e-cash?

Multiple-Choice Questions

1. One reason why IT auditing evolved from traditional auditing was that
   a. Auditors realized that computers had impacted their ability to perform the attestation function
   b. Computers and information processing were not a key resource
   c. Professional associations such as AICPA and ISACA did not recognize the need
   d. Government did not recognize the need
2. IT auditing may involve
   a. Organizational IT audits
   b. Application IT audits
   c. Development/implementation IT audits
   d. All of the above
3. The breadth and depth of knowledge required to audit IT and systems are extensive and may include
   a. Application of risk-oriented audit approaches

b. Reporting to management and performing follow-up review to insure action taken

c. Assessment of security and privacy issues that can put the organization at risk

d. All of the above

4. COBIT stands for
   a. A computer language
   b. A federal agency
   c. Control Objective for Information and Related Technology
   d. None of the above

5. ISACA stands for
   a. Information Systems Security Association
   b. Institute of Internal Auditors
   c. Information Systems Audit and Control Association
   d. International Association for Computer Educators

6. ISO is
   a. A government organization
   b. A private company
   c. The International Organization for Standardization
   d. None of the above

7. The federal law now being used against child predators/stalkers on the Internet is called
   a. FIP 102 Computer Security and Accreditation
   b. National Strategy for Securing Cyberspace
   c. Computer Decency Act of 1995
   d. Privacy Act of 1974

8. The Sarbanes–Oxley Act of 2002
   a. Does not affect the attestation function
   b. Applies only to the Big Four accounting firms
   c. Requires auditor rotation
   d. Does not apply to small accounting/audit firms

9. Which is the most recent federal law that addresses computer security or privacy?
   a. Computer Fraud and Abuse Act
   b. Computer Security Act
   c. Homeland Security Act
   d. Electronic Communications Privacy Act

10. Which act has a provision where punishment can be up to life in prison if electronic hackers are found guilty of causing death to others through their actions?
    a. Computer Fraud and Abuse Act
    b. Freedom of Information Act
    c. Communications Decency Act
    d. Homeland Security Act

Exercises

1. List and explain five Websites you can go to for information about IT auditing.
2. List and explain five Websites you can go to for information about IT security and privacy issues.

3. List and explain five Websites you can go to for information about recent U.S. or World Court laws or court cases involving IT issues.
4. You are asked by your IT audit manager to do a background search on auditing IT disaster recovery planning. List and summarize five Websites where information can be obtained to help you in your background research.
5. You are asked by your IT audit manager to obtain studies and articles on conducting performing control self-assessment reviews. List five articles or Websites that can provide such information.

Answers to Multiple-Choice Questions

1—a; 2—d; 3—d; 4—c; 5—c; 6—c; 7—c; 8—c; 9—c; 10—d

Further Reading

1. Basel Committee on Banking Supervision, Sound practices for the management and supervision of operational risk, bank for international settlements, December 2001, http://www.bis.org/publ/bcbs86.htm.
2. COBIT Steering Committee and The IT Governance Institute, *COBIT*, 3rd Edition, Information Systems Audit and Control Foundation, Rolling Meadows, IL, 2002.
3. Gallegos, F. and A. Carlin, IT audit: A critical business process, *Computer Magazine*, pp. 87–89, Vol. 40, No. 7, IEEE, July 2007.
4. Gallegos, F., *Federal Laws Affecting IS Auditors*, EDP Auditing Series, #72-10-23, Auerbach Publishers, Boca Raton, FL, January 2001, pp. 1–24.
5. Gallegos, F., Electronic funds transfer: Control issues in a cashless, checkless society, *Inf. Strategy Executive's J.*, 17(2), 36–39, 2001.
6. Gallegos, F., Due professional care, *Inf. Syst. Control J.*, 2, 25–28, 2002.
7. George Washington University, *Forecast of Emerging Technology*, 2002.
8. The IT Governance Institute and the IT Control Practices Committee of ISACA, *IT Control Practice Statement for the COBIT High-Level Control Objective PO-9 Assess Risks*, IT Governance Institute, Rolling Meadows, IL, 2001.
9. ISO, ISO 27KStandards (ISO/IEC 27000 series), http://www.iso27001security.com/.
10. Miccolis, J., Enterprise risk management in the financial services industry, from concept to management process, IRMI, November 2000, http://www.irmi.com/Expert/Articles/2000/Miccolis11.aspx.

Chapter 2

The Legal Environment and Its Impact on Information Technology

IT auditing, control, and security constitute one of the fastest-growing fields in technology today. The advancements in IT have resulted in bringing to the forefront public concern on issues of security and privacy that were once only of interest to the legal and technical expert but today are topics that affect virtually every user of IT. With this concern has come federal and international laws which businesses and the public must comply with. Therefore, business must not only comply with organizational policies and procedures but any governing laws which they must be in compliance with as a part of doing business locally or globally. As an auditor, we monitor for compliance with organization policies and procedures but we must also be cognizant of laws that protect and govern our business.

The Internet has grown exponentially from a simple linkage of a relatively few government and educational computers to a complex worldwide network that is used by businesses, governments, and the public—almost everyone from the computer specialist to the novice user and everyone in between. Today, common uses for the Internet include everything from marketing, sales, and entertainment purposes to e-mail, research, and commerce, and virtually any other type of information sharing. Unfortunately, as with any breakthrough in technology, advancements have also given rise to various new problems that must be addressed. These problems are often being brought to the attention of the IT audit and control specialist. Hence, this chapter focuses on legislation that governs the use and misuse of IT, including security and privacy. We believe that federal legislation (current and past) has had a lasting impact on the online community (government, business, and the public). It is something that those entering the IT audit and information assurance profession should be knowledgeable of.

IT Crime Issues

The IT explosion has opened up many new gateways for criminals. Since the integration of computers into business, organizations have had to safeguard their intellectual assets against computer crime. The 2009 Internet Crime Report states that "From January 1, 2009, through December 31, 2009, the Internet Crime Complaint Center (IC3) Website received 336,655 complaint submissions. This was a 22.3% increase as compared to 2008 . . . the total dollar loss from all referred cases was $559.7 million . . . up from $264.6 million in 2008 FBI and NCCC reports indicate that less than 10 percent of computer fraud crimes are reported." This is largely due to the public embarrassment companies face and potential negative press such incidences receive. Just a glance at the U.S. Department of Justice Website for a list of recent computer crimes gives a sense of vulnerability (Exhibit 2.1).

As you can see from Exhibit 2.1, there are three main categories of crimes involving computers. These crimes may be committed as individual acts or concurrently. The first of these is where

■ New Hampshire Man Pleads Guilty to Computer Intrusion into Former Employer's Computer Systems (July 13, 2011)
■ Romanian Man Sentenced to 48 Months in Prison for Role in International Fraud Scheme Involving Online Auction Websites (June 29, 2011)
■ Final Defendant Sentenced to 7 Years in Federal Prison for Participating in Child Pornography Distribution Ring (June 27, 2011)
■ Lead Defendant in International Computer Hacking Ring Sentenced in Two Cases to 13 Years in Federal Prison (June 27, 2011)
■ Belarusian National Is Sentenced to 41 Months in Prison for Participating in International Online Scheme to Steal U.S. Tax Refunds (June 22, 2011)
■ Department of Justice Disrupts International Cybercrime Rings Distributing Scareware (June 22, 2011)
■ Computer Programmer Sentenced to Federal Prison for Unauthorized Computer Access (May 19, 2011)
■ Charges Filed against College Student for Creating and Disseminating Counterfeit Online Coupons over the Internet (May 11, 2011)
■ Attempt to Hack Houston ATMs Nets North Carolina Resident a Prison Term (May 9, 2011)
■ Former Montgomery County Police Officer Pleads Guilty to Illegally Accessing a Government Computer to Obtain Information (April 27, 2011)
■ Hacker Pleads Guilty to Identity Theft and Credit Card Fraud Resulting in Losses of More Than $36 Million (April 21, 2011)
■ Michigan Woman Pleads Guilty to Selling More Than $400,000 in Counterfeit Business Software (April 20, 2011)
■ United States Enters Domain-Name Use Agreements with Two Online Poker Companies (April 20, 2011)

Exhibit 2.1 Computer crimes from August 2, 2011. (From U.S. Department of Justice, http://www.justice.gov/criminal/cybercrime/cc.html.)

the computer is the target of the crime. Generally, this type of crime involves the theft of information that is stored in the computer. This also covers unauthorized access or modification of records. Two specific crimes that can result directly from targeting the computer are techno-vandalism and techno-trespass. Damage resulting from unauthorized access is commonly called techno-vandalism. Techno-trespass occurs when the unauthorized access occurs. The most common way to gain unauthorized access is for the criminal to become a "super-user" through a backdoor in the system. The backdoor in the system is there to permit access should a problem arise. Being a super-user is equivalent to being the system's manager and it allows the criminal access to practically all areas and functions within the system. This type of crime is of the greatest concern to industry.

The next general type of computer crime occurs when the computer is used as an instrument of the crime. In this scenario, the computer is used to assist the criminal in committing the crime. This category covers fraudulent use of automatic teller machine (ATM) cards and machines and identity, credit card, telecommunications, and financial fraud from computer transactions. Until 2001, the most publicized example of this type of crime was the cloning of cellular phone numbers. This crime is committed by capturing computerized billing codes during cellular transmissions. The code is then transmitted into a portable computer, and a program then allows the criminal to bill his or her cellular phone calls to other cellular phone customers. In this scenario, the computer is an instrument in two facets. First, the computer is used to illegally capture information. Then, a program inside the computer manipulates the data to further the crime. In this category, the computer is necessary to commit the crime. Fraudulent, inaccurate financial reporting continues to plague the financial community. Just when we thought the financial fiascos of 2001–2002 involving companies like Enron and WorldCom were behind us, we have the more recent mortgage banking and other mortgage investment scandals. These events have cast doubts on the integrity of financial statements and the word of chief financial officer (CFO) and CEO. With the equity funding fraud of the 1970s, the rise of the Foreign Corrupt Practices Act of 1976–1977, and industry's promise that they can self-regulate, we have come full circle again to misreporting and financial integrity and the lack of due professional care by the accounting profession. We enter the era of Sarbanes–Oxley, Public Law 107-204.

In the third category, the computer is not necessary to commit the crime. The computer is incidental and is used to commit the crime faster, process greater amounts of information, and make the crime more difficult to identify and trace. The most popular example of this crime is child pornography. Owing to increased Internet access, child pornography is more widespread, easier to access, and harder to trace. IT helps law enforcement prosecute this crime because the incriminating information is often stored in the computer. This makes criminal prosecution easier. If the criminal is savvy, the computer is programmed to encrypt the data or erase the files if it is not properly accessed. Thus, the field of computer forensics and computer security are opening new job opportunities for audit and security professionals who use their skills to capture the evidence.

Organizations such as the International Technology Law Association (www.itechlaw.org), Association of Certified Fraud Examiners (www.acfe.com), American College of Forensic Examiners (www.acfei.com), and International High Technology Crime Investigation Association (www.htcia.org) provide a source for those looking at career opportunities in the law and IT field. In their book, Gerald R. Ferrera et al. state that cyberlaw is the law governing the use of computers and the Internet. The authors agree and believe that cyberlaw not only encompasses a combination of state and federal statutory, decisional, and administrative laws, but also international laws arising out of the use of the Internet as well.

Protection against Computer Fraud

In light of the lack of effective legislation in place currently, the best defense against computer fraud is a good offense. IT auditors should alert their clients to the dangers that are present, and there are several ways they can protect their clients from computer fraud. This is generally in the form of controls, firewalls, or encryption. The combined use of these methods will certainly help to reduce the risk of unauthorized access to the IS.

The FBI's National Computer Crime Squad has the following advice to help protect against computer fraud:

- Place a log-in banner to ensure that unauthorized users are warned that they may be subject to monitoring.
- Turn audit trails on.
- Consider keystroke level monitoring if adequate banner is displayed. Request trap and tracing from your local telephone company.
- Consider installing caller identification.
- Make backups of damaged or altered files.
- Maintain old backups to show the status of the original.
- Designate one person to secure potential evidence. Evidence can consist of tape backups and printouts. These pieces of evidence should be documented and verified by the person obtaining the evidence. Evidence should be retained in a locked cabinet with access limited to one person.
- Keep a record of resources used to reestablish the system and locate the perpetrator.
- Encrypt files.
- Encrypt transmissions.
- Use one-time password (OTP) generators.
- Use secure firewalls.

The explosion of the information age has created many opportunities for improving business. It has also created more opportunities for criminals. Six years ago, the International Trade Commission reported that computer software piracy is a $4 billion-a-year problem worldwide. Three years ago, experts believe that software piracy costs the computer industry more than $11 billion a year and software thefts drain the U.S. economy of jobs and wages. Others estimate that there is one illegal copy of each computer software program for every two legitimate copies. Organizations such as the Business Software Alliance, Software Publishers Association, Institute of Internal Auditors, and the Information Systems Audit and Control have been instrumental in raising the awareness to this type of crime.

In addition to the IT auditor's primary function of auditing the use and application of IT by business, he or she has obtained the additional responsibility of the security of the system. The federal government has passed laws and continues improving existing ones to help combat computer crimes. However, the greatest aid to the safety of the information is a combination of scrutiny controls, firewalls, and encryption. The IT auditor's role is constantly expanding, and security of the data is an important concern.

Computer Fraud and Abuse Act

The CFAA was first drafted in 1984 as a response to computer crimes. The government's response to network security and network-related crimes was to revise the act in 1994 under the Computer

Abuse Amendments Act to cover crimes such as trespass (unauthorized entry) into an online system, exceeding authorized access, and exchanging information on how to gain unauthorized access. Although the act was intended to protect against attacks in a network environment, it does also have its fair share of faults.

The act requires that certain conditions needed to be present for the crime to be a violation of the CFAA. Only if these conditions are present will the crime fall under violation of the CFAA. The three types of attacks that are covered under the act and the conditions that have to be met include

- *Fraudulent trespass.* This is when a trespass is made with the intent to defraud that results in both furthering the fraud and the attacker obtaining something of value.
- *Intentional destructive trespass.* This is a trespass along with actions that intentionally cause damage to a computer, computer system, network, information, data, or program, or results in denial of service and causes at least $1000 in total loss in the course of a year.
- *Reckless destructive trespass.* This is when there is the presence of trespass along with reckless actions (although not deliberately harmful) that cause damage to a computer, computer system, network, information, data, or program, or results in denial of service and causes at least $1000 in total loss in the course of a year.

Each of these three types of definitions is geared toward a particular type of attack. Fraudulent trespass was a response against crimes involving telephone fraud that is committed through a computer system, such as using a telephone company computer to obtain free telephone service. This condition helps prosecute individuals responsible for the large financial losses suffered by companies such as American Telephone & Telegraph (AT&T) as mentioned earlier. Telephone toll fraud has snowballed into over a billion dollars a year problem for the phone companies.

The other two usually apply to online systems and have been implemented to address problems of hackers or crackers, worms, viruses, and virtually any other type of intruder that can damage, alter, or destroy information. The two attacks are similar in many ways, but the key in differentiating the two are the words "intentional," which would, of course, mean a deliberate attack with the intent to cause damage, whereas "reckless" can cover an attack in which damage was caused due to negligence. Penalties under Section 1030(c) of the CFAA vary from 1 year imprisonment for reckless destructive trespass on a nonfederal computer to up to 20 years for an intentional attack on a federal computer where the information obtained is used for "the injury of the United States or to the advantage of any foreign nation" (i.e., cases of espionage).

The penalties are obviously less severe for "reckless destructive trespass" than for "intentional destructive trespass." The reasoning behind this is that the reckless attacker may not necessarily intend to cause damage but must still be punished for gaining access to places that they should not have access to. However, the impact of such terminology appears to possibly create some confusion in prosecuting the trespasser as it resides in such a gray area. In *Morris v. United States*, it was determined that "intent" applied to access and not to damages. The implication here would be that if the "intentional" part of the violation was applied to access and not to the damage, then the culprit could possibly be prosecuted under the lesser sentence. For example, if an individual intentionally intended to release a virus over a network, it would seem difficult for prosecutors to prove the motive for the violation. What if the individual stated that he or she was conducting some type of security test (like Morris contested), and "accidentally" set off a procedure that released a virus over the network? Intentional could refer to access to a system, but it may not apply to damage. In this case, the lesser penalty of reckless destructive trespass may be applied. Obviously, this is a matter that must be contemplated on a case-by-case basis, observing the facts of each individual case. In some instances, however, it would appear that even intentional trespass could be defended by claims that the violation was due to negligence and therefore falls under the less severe of the two circumstances.

This legislation has been helpful as a legal tool for prosecuting crimes involving some of the aforementioned intruders and violators of system security, but it also seems to have a loophole in certain cases. Unfortunately, this loophole may be large enough for a serious violator of the act to slip through and be prosecuted under a lesser penalty by virtue of having to prove intent. All states have closed a portion of that loophole through statutes prohibiting harassment or stalking including e-mail.

Computer Abuse Amendments Act

A more specific crime that is often prosecuted is trespass. The Computer Abuse Amendments Act of 1994 qualified trespass as including "unauthorized entry onto an online system, exceeding authorized access and exchanging information on gaining authorized access." Included in the act are three kinds of trespass and the conditions that must be met for the crime to be a violation of the act. Fraudulent trespass is trespass with the intent to defraud; the fraud is pursued during the trespass and the trespasser procures information that is of value. This definition of fraud was a "response to telephone fraud committed through a computer system." The other two types of trespasses were introduced to criminally prosecute the trespasser who damages, alters, or destroys information. Intentional destructive trespass is fraudulent trespass with the additional criterion of intentional action to cause damage to the computer and resulting in damages worth at least $1000 in the course of the year. This is a deliberate act with the intent to cause damage. Penalties for this crime can be up to 20 years in prison. Reckless destructive trespass is the same as intentional destructive access without the intent to damage, alter, or destroy information. Reckless actions occur that cause at least $1000 in damage to the computer system. The penalties for this crime are not as stiff. It is important to note that for intentional destructive trespass, the intent of the crime is related to the intent to damage the system, not the intent to illicitly access the system. If prosecutors can only prove intentional unauthorized access of the system, then reckless destructive trespass applies.

Sarbanes–Oxley Act (Public Law 107-204)

The world of financial auditing has changed dramatically over the past decade and will continue to rapidly change as more and more companies rely on IT to achieve their business objectives. Certainly, the passage of the Sarbanes–Oxley Act of 2002 (Public Law 107-204) will have a major impact on the internal and external auditor. Also, the IT auditor will play an integral role in assuring compliance with this act.

It is no longer acceptable for auditors to audit around the computer, as was once the case. With the increase of fraud and ceaseless corporate scandals over the past 2 years, it is even more imperative now than ever before that auditors have a full understanding of both manual and automated internal control processes. The assessment of both the manual and automated internal controls of any system can provide the needed assurance auditors can use to base their professional judgment on as far as the quality of the information derived off the system. This judgment is a key element in the risk analysis process that the auditor must perform during the planning stages of any audit.

Today, external financial auditors are relying more on the process approach rather than on the traditional transaction approach. The results of an evaluation of an organization's manual and automated internal controls can either increase or reduce the amount of transaction testing needed to render an opinion on financial statements.

For internal auditors, internal controls are also very important. One of the main functions of an internal auditor is to provide assurances to the management that their approved internal controls are in place and are working effectively and efficiently, and if in fact there are problems, they are being addressed and corrected.

It is important for both the manual and automated internal controls to be operational and effective because management will base their business decisions on the financial results generated from the IS.

It is also important to external auditors that manual and automated internal controls are operational and effective because this will provide assurance to external auditors that information generated from the system is valid, accurate, and complete. Based on this assurance from the system, auditors can then place the appropriate level of reliance on the internal controls of the IS.

If the necessary controls are not in place, or if they are in place but not being applied effectively and as management intended, then the integrity of the data and information generated from the system should be called into question by both external and internal auditors.

Although it is essential that manual controls be in place and are working effectively and efficiently to produce accurate data output, due to the broadness of the subject matter, this chapter focuses on auditors' reliance on automated internal controls and the effects of this reliance on the auditors' judgment in assessing business risk related to the integrity of information generated from the system.

As mentioned in Chapters 1 and 3 and this chapter, the Sarbanes–Oxley Act has provided the needed muscle to internal auditors to do their jobs better and added accountability to management to take action on whatever auditors may identify. Once again, financial fraud has come to the forefront of the audit community as a result of the financial scandals of Enron, Global Crossing, and others during this time period. Just as the Equity Funding scandal of 1973 gave rise to the development of strong state and federal regulation of the insurance industries, corporate creative accounting of oil companies and the aerospace industry provided support for the development and enactment of the Foreign Corrupt Practices Act of 1977 more than 25 years before the Sarbanes–Oxley Act.

Perhaps now the Sarbanes–Oxley Act of 2002 will be a vivid reminder of the importance of due professional care and financial integrity. This act is a major reform package mandating the most far-reaching changes Congress has imposed on the business world since the Foreign Corrupt Practices Act of 1977 and the SEC Act of the 1930s. It seeks to thwart future scandals and restore investor confidence by, among other things, creating a Public Company Accounting Oversight Board, revising auditor independence rules, revising corporate governance standards, and significantly increasing the criminal penalties for violations of securities laws.

Major Points from the Sarbanes–Oxley Act of 2002

The act discusses requirements for the board, including composition and duties. The board must (1) register public accounting firms; (2) establish or adopt, by rule, auditing, quality control, ethics, independence, and other standards relating to the preparation of audit reports for issuers; (3) conduct inspections of accounting firms; (4) conduct investigations and disciplinary proceedings, and impose appropriate sanctions; (5) perform such other duties or functions as necessary or appropriate; (6) enforce compliance with the act, the rules of the board, professional standards, and the securities laws relating to the preparation and issuance of audit reports and the obligations and liabilities of accountants with respect thereto; and (7) set the budget and manage the operations of the board and the staff of the board.

The Sarbanes–Oxley Act of 2002 focuses on the importance of due professional care. It prohibits all registered public accounting firms from providing to audit clients, contemporaneously with the audit, certain nonaudit services including internal audit outsourcing, financial IS design and implementation services, and expert services (e.g., tax consulting, systems design, and special studies). These scope-of-service restrictions go beyond existing SEC independence regulations. All other services, including tax services, are permissible only if preapproved by the issuer's audit committee, and all such preapprovals must be disclosed in the issuer's periodic reports to the SEC.

The act requires auditor (not audit firm) rotation. Therefore, the lead audit partner or the concurring review partner must rotate off the engagement if he or she has performed audit services for the issuer in each of the 5 previous fiscal years. The act provides no distinction regarding the capacity in which the audit or concurring partner provided such audit services. Any services provided as a manager or in some other capacity appear to count toward the 5-year period. The provision starts as soon as the firm is registered; therefore, absent guidance to the contrary, the audit and concurring partner must count back 5 years starting with the date in which Public Company Accounting Oversight Board registration occurs. This provision has a definite impact on small accounting firms. The SEC is currently considering whether or not to accommodate small firms in this area; currently, there is no small-firm exemption from this provision.

To audit a public company, a public accounting firm must register with the board. The board shall collect a registration fee and an annual fee from each registered public accounting firm in amounts that are sufficient to recover the costs of processing and reviewing applications and annual reports. The board shall also establish a reasonable annual accounting support fee to maintain the board.

Annual quality reviews must be conducted for firms that audit more than 100 issuers; all others must be conducted every 3 years. The SEC and the board may order a special inspection of any firm at any time. The board of a firm can impose sanctions if it fails to reasonably supervise any associated person with regard to auditing or quality control standards. The act also includes foreign accounting firms that audit a U.S. company for registrations with the board. This would include foreign firms that perform some audit work, such as in a foreign subsidiary of a U.S. company, which is relied on by the primary auditor.

It is unlawful for a registered public accounting firm to provide any nonaudit service to an issuer during the same time with the audit, including

- Bookkeeping or other services related to the accounting records or financial statements of the audit client
- Financial IS design and implementation
- Appraisal or valuation services, fairness opinions, or contribution-in-kind reports
- Actuarial services
- Internal audit outsourcing services
- Management functions or human resources
- Broker or dealer, investment adviser, or investment banking services
- Legal services and expert services unrelated to the audit
- Any other service that the board determines, by regulation, is impermissible

The board may, on a case-by-case basis, exempt from these prohibitions any person, issuer, public accounting firm, or transaction, subject to review by the commission. However, the SEC has oversight and enforcement authority over the board. The board, in its rulemaking process, is to be treated as if it were a registered securities association.

It will not be unlawful to provide other nonaudit services if the audit committee preapproves them in the following manner. The act allows an accounting firm to engage in any nonaudit service, including tax services that are not listed previously, only if the audit committee of the issuer preapproves the activity. The audit committee will disclose to investors in periodic reports its decision to preapprove nonaudit services. Statutory insurance company regulatory audits are treated as an audit service, and thus do not require preapproval.

The preapproval requirement is waived with respect to the provision of nonaudit services for an issuer if the aggregate amount of all such nonaudit services provided to the issuer constitutes less than 5% of the total amount of revenues paid by the issuer to its auditor (calculated on the basis of revenues paid by the issuer during the fiscal year when the nonaudit services are performed). Such services were not recognized by the issuer at the time of the engagement to be nonaudit services, and are promptly brought to the attention of the audit committee and approved before completion of the audit. The authority to preapprove services can be delegated to one or more members of the audit committee, but any decision by the delegate must be presented to the full audit committee.

For independence acceptance, the lead audit or coordinating partner and the reviewing partner must rotate off of the audit every 5 years. Also, the accounting firm must report to the audit committee all critical accounting policies and practices to be used, all alternative methods to Generally Accepted Accounting Principles (GAAP) that have been discussed with the management, and ramifications of the use of such alternative disclosures and methods.

Another audit independence compliance issue is that the CEO, controller, CFO, chief accounting officer, or person in an equivalent position cannot be employed by the company's audit firm during the 1-year period preceding the audit. The CEO and the CFO of each issuer shall prepare a statement to accompany the audit report to certify the appropriateness of the financial statements and disclosures contained in the periodic report, and that those financial statements and disclosures fairly present, in all material respects, the operations and financial condition of the issuer. A violation of this section must be knowing and intentional to give rise to liability. It shall be unlawful for any officer or director of an issuer to take any action to fraudulently influence, coerce, manipulate, or mislead any auditor engaged in the performance of an audit for the purpose of rendering the financial statements materially misleading.

The act penalizes executives for nonperformance. If an issuer is required to prepare a restatement due to material noncompliance with financial reporting requirements, the CEO and the CFO must reimburse the issuer for any bonus or other incentive or equity-based compensation received during the 12 months following the issuance. It prohibits the purchase or sale of stock by officers and directors and other insiders during blackout periods. Any profits resulting from sales in violation of this will be recoverable by the issuer.

Each financial report that is required to be prepared in accordance with GAAP shall reflect all material-correcting adjustments that have been identified by a registered accounting firm. Each annual and quarterly financial report shall disclose all material off-balance sheet transactions and other relationships with unconsolidated entities that may have a material current or future effect on the financial condition of the issuer.

The SEC shall study off-balance sheet disclosures to determine the (1) extent of off-balance sheet transactions (including assets, liabilities, leases, losses, and the use of special-purpose entities) and (2) whether generally accepted accounting rules result in financial statements of issuers, reflecting the economics of such off-balance sheet transactions to investors in a transparent fashion and make a report containing recommendations to Congress. Generally, it will be unlawful for an issuer to extend credit to any director or executive officer. Consumer credit companies may make home improvement and consumer credit loans and issue credit cards to its directors and executive officers if it is done in the ordinary course of business on the same terms and conditions made to the general public. Also, directors, officers, and 10% owners must report designated transactions by the end of the second business day following the day on which the transaction was executed.

The act requires each annual report of an issuer to contain an internal control report. The SEC shall issue rules to require issuers to disclose whether at least one member of its audit committee is a financial expert. Also, the issuers must disclose information on material changes in the financial condition or operations of the issuer on a rapid and current basis.

Criminal Intent

The act identifies as a crime for any person to corruptly alter, destroy, mutilate, or conceal any document with the intent to impair the object's integrity or availability for use in an official proceeding or to otherwise obstruct, influence, or impede any official proceeding, such a person being liable for up to 20 years in prison and a fine. Also, the SEC is authorized to freeze the payment of an extraordinary payment to any director, officer, partner, controlling person, agent, or employee of a company during an investigation of possible violations of securities laws. Finally, the SEC may prohibit a person from serving as an officer or director of a public company if the person has committed securities fraud.

Penalties and Requirements under Title VIII of the Act

- It is a felony to knowingly destroy or create documents to "impede, obstruct, or influence" any existing or contemplated federal investigation.
- Auditors are required to maintain "all audit or review work papers" for 5 years.
- The statute of limitations on securities fraud claims is extended to 5 years from the fraud and 2 years after the fraud was discovered, from 3 years and 1 year, respectively.
- Employees of issuers and accounting firms are extended "whistleblower protection" that would prohibit the employer from taking certain actions against employees who lawfully disclose private employer information to, among others, parties in a judicial proceeding involving a fraud claim. Whistleblowers are also granted a remedy of special damages and attorney's fees.

Penalties and Requirements under Title IX of the Act

- Maximum penalty for mail and wire fraud increased from 5 to 10 years.
- The CEO and CFO must certify financial statements filed with the SEC. The certification must state that the financial statements and disclosures fully comply with the provisions of the Securities Exchange Act and that they fairly present, in all material respects, the operations and financial condition of the issuer. Maximum penalties for willful and knowing violations of this section are a fine of not more than $5 million and imprisonment of up to 20 years.

Remedies and Effectiveness

Computer-related crimes are relatively new in law enforcement and prosecution. Criminal prosecution continues to lag behind the wave of precedence set by civil courts. Currently, individuals and companies can obtain civil or criminal justice to varying degrees of effectiveness. Some of the new aggressive remedies and financial penalties recognized by Congress are injunctive relief, seizure, impoundment, and destruction of goods. As discussed earlier in the passage of the Sarbanes–Oxley Act, these monetary and nonmonetary remedies are designed to prevent further wrongful activity.

Injunctive relief is available to both federal and state courts. Parties found in violation of an injunction are in contempt of court and are subject to fines or jail time. The federal courts have specific criteria for issuing an injunction:

- The movant's (party asking for injunction) likelihood of prevailing on the merits
- Lack of adequate remedy at law (irreparable harm in the absence of injunctive relief)
- Balance of hardships between movant and respondent
- Public interest

The plaintiff must start the injunctive procedures within a reasonable time period of discovering the crime. If not, the courts will deny the injunction.

Two of the most common types of injunctions are permanent and preliminary. A permanent injunction is granted after the case has been adjudicated and the court has found for the plaintiff. Preliminary injunctions are granted before the final adjudication. Before a preliminary injunction is granted, a hearing is normally held so that the defendant may oppose the motion. The purpose of a preliminary injunction is to prevent irreversible harm to the plaintiff while the case is being decided. Another type of injunction available to the courts is *ex parte*. In this situation, the defendant does not need to be present to oppose the plaintiff's motion for an injunction. This is especially useful in Internet fraud cases. An example of this type of injunction is a temporary restraining order. A temporary restraining order forces the defendant to cease the harmful activity until a hearing can be held to determine whether a preliminary injunction will be granted. If the court grants a preliminary injunction or a temporary restraining order, the movant must post a bond for the payment of damages incurred by the defendant in the case of wrongful injunction or seizure.

Another aggressive remedy within the court system is the seizure, impoundment, and destruction of property used to commit or facilitate the crime. This is much more difficult to obtain than injunctive relief as courts are much less likely to grant it. Congress determined that counterfeiters could easily destroy evidence of their crime and amended the 1984 Lanham Act. This amendment provides for seizure of goods without the presence of the defendant at the hearing. The *ex parte* provision is available when the property can be easily destroyed or erased. This is especially prevalent in cases involving Internet crime.

As always, there are concerns about constitutional violations whenever these remedies are enacted. Some argue that freedom of speech as provided by the First Amendment is violated by injunctions, usually injunctions involving copyright infringement cases. The Fourth, Fifth, and Fourteenth Amendments are scrutinized when the seizure of property by the courts has been authorized. The Fourth Amendment does not allow search or seizure of another's property without a warrant. It also qualifies that the warrant must specify the place to be searched and the items to be seized. This poses a unique problem for law enforcement, as it is difficult to identify a specific computer that committed a crime just by looking at it. The Fifth and Fourteenth Amendments specify that neither the federal nor state governments may seize property without due "process of law." Due process of law usually requires that an individual be given notice and an opportunity to be heard before he is deprived of his property. Therefore, *ex parte* orders are argued to be a constitutional violation. The Supreme Court has formed criteria for *ex parte* seizure orders to continue to allow them to be a useful tool for law enforcement.

Legislation Providing for Civil and Criminal Penalties

In the past 30 years, Congress has become very active in passing legislation providing penalties for computer fraud. Recently, the Sarbanes–Oxley Act has changed the audit process to ensure the practice of due professional care, integrity, and validity. Various pieces of legislation have provided essential tools in the fight against computer crime. However, as with most new laws, there are a lot of problems. Most of the laws currently in effect, with the exception of the Sarbanes–Oxley Act and the Homeland Security Act, are either not specific enough or provide enough loopholes so that it is difficult to convict. Other problems materialize with the courts implementing the laws. In some instances, the courts ignore the mandated legislation and follow their own law. For the fight against computer fraud to become more effective, useful and effective laws must be passed and adhered to.

The 1976 Copyright Act grants civil courts the authority to grant injunctions as well as orders for impoundment and destruction of articles used in committing the fraud in disputes involving copyright infringement. This act also provides the definition of infringement for criminal prosecution. It requires that a person willfully infringe on a copyright for the purposes of personal or commercial financial gain. A party found guilty of criminal copyright infringement is subject to the forfeiture of profits from the criminal activity as well as the destruction of property used in the activity. The Copyright Act has not proven useful in court cases involving Internet fraud. In *United States v. LaMacchia*, an MIT student set up a Website that uploaded programs from visitors to the site. Others could then go to another site and download free applications. This is clearly a violation of the spirit of the Copyright Act but because the premise is not clearly addressed in the legislation, the Supreme Court did not believe the student to be guilty. The 1984 amendments to the Lanham Act are similar to those provided under the civil remedies of the Copyright Act. The Lanham Act allows the courts to grant injunctions and allows seizures in cases of trademark counterfeiting.

The Federal Trademark Dilution Act signed in 1996 addresses a new form of intellectual property—domain names. Under this act, domain names are now subject to trademark law. Many lawsuits have been filed in this area and to date few have gone to trial. Generally, a large corporation has sued a small business or individual and the individual cannot afford the legal costs of the battle. Out-of-court settlements usually result in the large corporation getting rights to the domain name they want. This issue has now come up at a major International Internet Conference and for a potential World Court involvement on the issue of Internet governance.

The few cases that have been adjudicated have resulted in the courts finding the defendant in violation of the Federal Dilution Act. In *Intermatic Inc. v. Toeppen*, the court demanded that the domain name "intermatic.com" be turned over to Intermatic. There are some inconsistencies in the courts' decisions. "The federal antidilution of law only calls for the remedy of an order that a party cease and desist from its diluting activity. In rare cases it might allow for damages, attorney fees or the destruction of the offending goods. It does not specify that the prevailing trademark owner actually get to take possession of the diluting goods." These types of inconsistencies show that there are still many issues that need to be addressed in the field of computer legislation.

The Industrial Espionage Act is another piece of legislation to address fraud concerning intellectual property. This act provides monetary and criminal penalties for theft, misappropriation, or copying of proprietary information. If convicted, the criminal must forfeit all the monetary proceeds from the conduct and the computer equipment used to commit the crime. The proceeds and equipment confiscated are turned over to the government, not to the parties harmed by the misconduct.

Criminal prosecution for information crimes is growing rapidly. There are associated benefits and problems with criminally prosecuting information crimes. Some of the benefits are earlier trials, greater deterrence due to the criminal penalties, and criminal penalties, including incarceration. The downside to criminal prosecution is that it is not a high priority for law enforcement officials. Some see it as a victimless crime because no physical injury is caused. Another issue is that computer crimes are difficult to prove and evidence is easy to destroy. It is difficult to prove which person out of the numerous people who had access to the computer actually committed the crime. Also, the evidence on a computer is very easily erased. By the time law enforcement arrives with the proper warrants, the criminals have ample time to destroy all evidence of the crime. The legislation providing for the criminal penalties is usually poorly written; therefore, it is easy for the defendant's lawyers to find loopholes for their clients.

Computer Security Act of 1987

The Computer Security Act of 1987 was drafted due to congressional concerns and public awareness on computer security-related issues and because of disputes on the control of unclassified information. The general purpose of the act was a declaration from the government that improving the security and privacy of sensitive information in federal computer systems is in the public interest.

The act established a federal government computer-security program that would protect sensitive information in federal government computer systems. It would also develop standards and guidelines for unclassified federal computer systems and facilitate such protection.* The Computer Security Act also assigned responsibility for developing government-wide computer system security standards, guidelines, and security training programs to the National Bureau of Standards (now the National Institute of Standards and Technology [NIST]) by amending the act of March 3, 1901, and the Federal Property and Administrative Services Act of 1949.† It further established a Computer System Security and Privacy Advisory Board within the Commerce Department and required federal agencies to identify those computer systems containing sensitive information and develop security plans for those systems. Finally, it provided periodic training in computer security for all federal employees and contractors who managed, used, or operated federal computer systems.

The Computer Security Act is particularly important because it is fundamental to the development of federal standards of safeguarding unclassified information and establishing a balance between national security (as well as other issues in implementing security) and privacy policies within the federal government. It is also important in addressing issues concerning government control of cryptography, which as we will learn later, has recently become a hotly contested topic.

---

* Office of Technology Assessment, Issue Update on Information Security and Privacy in Networked Environments, p. 105.
† House of Representatives, Computer Security Act of 1987, Public Law 100-235 (H.R. 145).

The act was also a legislative response to overlapping responsibilities for computer security among several federal agencies. Some level of federal computer security responsibility rests with the Office of Management and Budget (OMB), the General Services Administration (GSA), and the Commerce Department (particularly NIST), and the National Telecommunications and Information Administration (NTIA). The OMB maintains overall responsibility for computer security policy. The GSA issues regulations for physical security of computer facilities and oversees technological and fiscal specifications for security hardware and software. The National Security Administration (NSA) is responsible for security of information that is classified for national security purposes.* Such overlapping responsibilities were found to impede the development of one uniform federal policy regarding the security of unclassified information. The act gives authority to NIST for developing standards and guidelines (see Appendixes II and III). Again, government roles and responsibilities for cybersecurity changed with the passage of the Homeland Security Act of 2002 and the USA Patriot Act.

Homeland Security Act of 2002

With the event of September 11, 2001 fresh in our minds and the Department of Homeland Security releasing its "National Strategy for Securing Cyberspace" in 2002, it may be time for educational entities at all levels to begin rolling up their sleeves and bringing the process of establishing courses and curriculum to educate the masses in protecting its information and infrastructure. This is a tall order to begin establishing such coursework at the university level, not to mention extending this to the community colleges and K–12. The passage of the Homeland Security Act of 2002 and the inclusion of the Cyber Security Enhancement Act within that act makes the need to be aware and practice cyber security or information assurances everyone's business (private and public).

The Cyber Security Enhancement Act (H.R. 3482) was incorporated into the Homeland Security Act of 2002. The act demands life sentences for those hackers who recklessly endanger lives. Also, the act included provisions that seek to allow Net surveillance to gather telephone numbers, Internet Protocol (IP) addresses, and universal resource locaters (URLs) or e-mail information without recourse to a court where an "immediate threat to a national security interest" is suspected. Finally, Internet Service Providers (ISPs) are required to hand over users' records to law enforcement authorities, overturning current legislation that outlaws such behavior.

The Homeland Security Act added additional phrasing that seeks to outlaw the publication anywhere of details of tools such as Pretty Good Privacy (PGP), which encode e-mails so that they cannot be read by snoops. This provision allows police to conduct Internet or telephone eavesdropping randomly with no requirement to ask a court's permission first. As mentioned earlier, this law has a provision that calls for punishment of up to life in prison for electronic hackers who are found guilty of causing death to others through their actions. Any hacker convicted of causing injuries to others could face prison terms up to 20 years under cyber crime provisions, which are in Section 225 of the Cyber Security Enhancement Act provision of the Homeland Security Act.

The Homeland Security Act of 2002 was created to prevent terrorist attacks within the United States and reduce the vulnerability of the United States to terrorism. It plays a major role in the security of cyberspace because it enforces many limitations and restrictions to users of the Internet.

---

* Office of Technology Assessment, Issue Update on Information Security and Privacy in Network Environments, p. 108.

For example, one goal of the act is to establish an Internet-based system that will only allow authorized persons the access to certain information or services. Owing to this restriction, the chances for vulnerability and attacks may decrease. The impact of this act will definitely contribute to the security of cyberspace because its primary function is to protect the people of the United States from any form of attack, including Internet attacks.

Section 214 of the Homeland Security Act is titled "Protection of Voluntarily Shared Critical Infrastructure Information." This section states that the act "[Protects] critical infrastructure information accompanied by an express statement protecting its disclosure ... [It] protects systems, which include physical systems, computer-based virtual systems, and information that affect national security." This section is similar to "The National Strategy for Securing Cyberspace," which is discussed later; both promote security of the nation's infrastructures. Overall, with the implementation of these strategies, it is hoped that the United States will gradually reduce its vulnerability and, most importantly, be protected from threats and attacks. In the future, the Internet will become one of the most important assets to many companies. With this in mind, it is very important that a strong security is established today so that tomorrow's security will be indomitable.

Privacy on the Information Superhighway

Now that we have had an opportunity to view some issues associated with computer security, we need to examine how the issue of privacy is impacted when computer security is breached. As we all know, there is a tremendous amount of information that companies and agencies are able to retrieve on any individual. People, corporations, and government are active in trading personal information for their own gain. Thankfully, the FTC, an agency within the federal government, has increased its monitoring and review of the Internet for consumer fraud and identity theft. Unfortunately, understaffed for this assignment, their Website should be one to bookmark for current information about such issues at www.ftc.gov.

Online identity theft is a major concern regarding E-commerce security. Over 10 million Americans are victims of identity theft each year according to a 2010 report by the U.S. Department of Justice. Identity theft is carried out when someone uses another's name or personal information (such as a credit number) in a fraudulent manner and without the other's consent. Such action can be carried out on purchasing products, taking out loans, accessing bank accounts, and much more. The most common way personal information is stolen is through stealing business records, but other ways such as "dumpster diving" or stealing information found in the trash, stealing mail, and simply snatching someone's wallet or purse have been found as tools to gain private information. Other tools include IP spoofing and spoofing or spam e-mail soliciting donations, funds, and deals.

This type of crime is a big threat and a growing concern for Internet users. A Federal Trade Commission 2006 survey found that some victims of identity theft can spend more than 130 hours reconstructing their identities (e.g., credit rating, bank accounts, reputation, etc.) following an identity crime. Credit card information theft accounts for the major portion (over 50%) of identity theft with an estimated annual cost of $53 billion. Identity theft is the fastest-growing crime in the United States. Many of the reported vulnerabilities were due to people errors, credit card skimming, and laptop theft. Coupled with the increased number of hacker attacks, the need for increased security has never been greater.

The large number of users on the Internet has resulted in the availability of an enormous amount of private information on the network. This information unfortunately seems to be available for the taking by anyone who might be interested. A person's bank balance, social security number, political leanings, and an individual's medical record and much more are there for anyone who may want it. These are some examples:

- *Cellular telephones.* Your calls can be intercepted and your access number cribbed by eavesdroppers with police scanners.
- *Registering to vote.* In most states, voter registration records are public and online. They typically list your birth date, phone number, and address.
- *Supermarket scanners.* Many grocery stores let you register for discount coupons that are used to track what you purchase.
- *Browsing on the Web.* Many sites mark visitors with "magic cookies" that record what you have been looking for and when you do it.

Are they entitled to your information? What is the government's policy regarding privacy of an individual and keeping strong security policy? Ideally, we would like to limit the amount of monitoring that the government is allowed to do on us, but is the government in a position to monitor our communications on the information superhighway? How will this affect our right to privacy as guaranteed by the U.S. Constitution? The focus of the following section will then be to address these issues paying especially close attention to the security-based measures that have affected the ideal of individual right to privacy. Later in this chapter, new and emerging laws that impact such issues are discussed.

National Strategy for Securing Cyberspace

Over the years, the government has drastically changed its operations, and businesses have not been able to function the way they used to. These activities now rely on IT infrastructures called cyberspace. Over the years, cyberspace threats have increased dramatically. However, securing cyberspace is not a simple task. It involves a coordinated effort by the government, businesses, and individual users. Exhibit 2.2 represents some of the roles and responsibilities in securing cyberspace.

In April 2011, the Whitehouse released The National Strategy for Trusted Identities in Cyberspace (NSTIC or Strategy) which charts a course for the public and private sectors to collaborate to raise the level of trust associated with the identities of individuals, organizations, networks, services, and devices involved in online transactions.

As technology continues to emerge, new vulnerabilities emerge as well. The number of vulnerabilities and incidents has continued to increase exponentially. The number of vulnerabilities reported increased from 171 in 1995 to over 8000 in 2006 (CERT, Carnegie Mellon University). The strategy to eliminate all threats and vulnerabilities is almost impossible these days. Although it is difficult to eliminate these occurrences, another strategy would be to reduce them. The United States plans to

- Reduce threats and deter malicious hackers through effective programs to identify and punish them
- Identify and remediate those existing vulnerabilities that could create the most damage to critical systems if exploited
- Develop new systems with less vulnerability and assess emerging technologies for vulnerabilities

	Priority 1	Priority 2	Priority 3	Priority 4	Priority 5
	National Cyberspace Security Response System	*National Cyberspace Security Threat and Vulnerability Reduction System*	*National Cyberspace Security Awareness and Training Program*	*Securing Government's Cyberspace*	*National Security and International Cyberspace Security Corporation*
Home user/small business		X	X		
Large enterprises	X	X	X	X	X
Critical sectors/ infrastructures	X	X	X	X	X
National issues and vulnerabilities	X	X	X	X	
Global					X

Exhibit 2.2 Roles and responsibilities in securing cyberspace. (From U.S. Government, author unknown, Cyberspace threats and vulnerabilities, http://www.whitehouse.gov/pcipb/ case_for_action.pdf.)

Methods That Provide for Protection of Information

Multiple pieces of legislation have been passed that allow for the protection of information. Through amendments to the original legislation, intellectual property rights and computer-related issues have been addressed. The acts that are currently included in law fall into two applications: commercial and government. Some of the acts provide criminal penalties but are only applicable if the criminal accessed a federal computer or entered a federal system. These acts tend to have stiffer penalties, as all the information in a federal computer is deemed "sensitive."

The Trade Secrecy and Protection Act established security for sensitive information in federal government computer systems. This act only covers information on federal computers but is viewed as a precursor to the same type of law for a commercial setting. The Computer Security Act of 1987 and the Computer Security Enhancement Act of 1997 enhance the Trade Secrecy and Protection Act by establishing minimum security standards for guarding federal systems. Few of the acts applicable to commercial purposes allow criminal penalties. Generally, civil prosecution is the only remedy allowed. The Identity Theft and Assumption Deterrence Act of 1998 criminalizes the unauthorized use or transfer of identification and extended the definition of victims to include individuals whose identity was compromised. The Identity Theft Penalty Enhancement Act (HR 1731) established penalties for aggravated identity theft and increased penalties for employees who gain access to information at work used in identity theft crimes.

Web Copyright Law

The Copyright Law pertains to violations of copyright infringement. To prosecute a successful claim in court, it must be proven that the material was copied from a Website or computer and that the owner has ownership of a valid copyright. Penalties for infringement of copyright valued of at least $1000 include fines ranging from $100,000 to $250,000. For infringements against property valued at more than $2500, an additional sentence may include a jail term of up to 3 years. Repeated offenses may result in a jail term of up to 6 years and fines.

The Copyright Law allows intellectual property to be copyrighted and is subject to all the same privileges and penalties that tangible property is provided under this law. The Electronic Communications Privacy Act prohibits the interception and divulgence of wire, oral, or electronic communications or the use of these intercepted communications as evidence. The Encrypted Communications Privacy Act provides encryption as a legal form of data transmission and authorized criminal and civil penalties to a party releasing the key to the code without consent. This act also permits the sale of encryption within the United States. These acts and other pending legislation attempt to curb the crime wave that is infecting IS technology.

Privacy Legislation and the Federal Government Privacy Act

One of the major pieces of federal legislation to come out of the 1970s to augment the basic right to privacy that an individual is entitled to under the U.S. Constitution is the Privacy Act of 1974. The purpose of this act is to provide certain safeguards for an individual against an invasion of personal privacy. This act places certain requirements on federal agencies, some of which include*

- Permitting an individual to determine what records pertaining to him or her are collected and maintained by federal agencies
- Permitting an individual to prevent records pertaining to him or her obtained for a particular purpose from being used or made available for another purpose without consent
- Permitting an individual to gain access to information pertaining to him or her in federal agency records and to correct or amend them
- Requiring federal agencies to collect, maintain, and use any personal information in a manner that assures that such action is for a necessary and lawful purpose, that the information is current and accurate, and that safeguards are provided to prevent misuse of the information

In light of the provision mentioned earlier, it would seem that the Privacy Act would protect many individuals against distribution of private information on the part of any agency. This, however, may not be the case as the act outlines various general and specific exemptions. Because of these exemptions, it would seem that law enforcement agencies as well as other commercial agencies may have some rights to private information according to the act.

Under Section (j), "General Exemptions," information maintained by agencies such as the Central Intelligence Agency (CIA) is exempt from the above provision for national security reasons. In addition to the CIA, information maintained by an agency that performs any activity pertaining to the enforcement of criminal laws is also exempt from the provisions of the act. This seems to implicate that these agencies can make inquiries for the sake of national security

---

* CSR Privacy/Information Archive, Privacy Act of 1974 and Amendments.

whenever they wish. Section (k), "Special Exemptions," further makes exempt from the provision certain information in regard to positions, appointments, and promotions in federal service jobs or positions in the armed forces.

The point of this seems to be that although the Privacy Act is an important part of safeguarding individual privacy rights, there are many exemptions under which it may be lawful for certain information to be disclosed. This could in some cases allow for various agencies, both federal and nonfederal, means by which they can obtain and disclose information on any individual simply because they may fall under one of the many exemptions that the Privacy Act allows.

Electronic Communications Privacy Act

The Electronic Communications Privacy Act is one of the leading legislations against violation of private information applicable to online systems. Before analyzing some of the implications that the act has had on the network community, let us briefly analyze some of the provisions defined by the act as they seem to be quite complicated in giving privacy protection in some instances and not others.

Section 2511 of the act makes interception and disclosure of wire, oral, or electronic communications prohibited, and prohibits the manufacture and possession of intercepting devices prohibited under Section 2512. Section 2516, however, seems to transcend these two as it authorizes and makes exceptions for the interception of wire or electronic communications under certain circumstances. Despite the exceptions under Section 2516, Section 2515 prohibits the use of intercepted wire or oral communications as evidence. Although evidence is intercepted and collected, it would seem that agencies cannot introduce this evidence in court! Does that make sense?

To continue with our analysis, we come to a very important provision in the sense of government intervention in online privacy. Under Section 2701, it is unlawful for anyone (including the government) to access stored communications without proper authority (i.e., a warrant). Once again, however, an exception is made in this provision. Under Section 2701(c)(a)(1), it is stated that the person or entity providing a wire or electronic communications service can intercept communications with prior user consent. Under Section 2702(b)(6)(B) on disclosure, such a person can then report the information to a law enforcement agency if such contents appear to pertain to the commission of a crime (again with prior consent). On reading this, most people may think that clearly anyone desiring privacy would not give prior consent. But what about cases where consent is given when the contract is agreed upon? Some services will include fine print on the terminal screen at the time the user first joins the service, which indicates the role of the system operator or system administrator. This can contain statements regarding privacy rights as they apply to that specific service. If people do not scrutinize the fine print closely enough, then they may be setting themselves up and having their private information intercepted by and disclosed to others. For these reasons, one must take special care to read the policy guidelines when signing up for an online service.

The point of seizure of private information stored on computer without a warrant was made clear in the landmark case of *Steve Jackson Games Inc. v. U.S. Secret Service*.* Secret Service officials raided the office of Steve Jackson Games as part of a nationwide investigation of data piracy in 1990. The agents first violated privacy rights by searching and seizing messages without proper authority and without a warrant. It was found when the gaming company did receive a copy of the Secret Service warrant affidavit that it was unbelievably flimsy. It seems as though the author of the game GURPS Cyberpunk was suspected to be guilty by "remote association!" The author had corresponded with a

---

* *Steve Jackson Games v. U.S. Secret Service*, 36F. 3d 457 (5th Cir. 1994).

variety of people, from computer security experts to computer hackers. That was enough to put him on a federal list of "dangerous hoodlums."* More than 3 years later, a federal court awarded damages over $50,000, plus over $250,000 in attorney's fees, ruling that the raid had been careless, illegal, and completely unjustified. This was an important case on the topic because it was the first step toward establishing that online speech is entitled to constitutional protection and that law enforcement agents cannot seize and hold a Bulletin Board Service (BBS) with impunity.

In summary, the Electronic Communications Privacy Act, although very good in its intentions to protect privacy rights, may have too many exceptions to be fully effective. This would hold true for the user and law enforcement agencies alike. Ideally, we would like to keep any information regarding our private affairs from being shared by others, but as we have observed, this is not always easy to do. In addition, although law enforcement officials may get access to private information, it would appear to be difficult at times for authorities to base their prosecution solely on electronic communication.

Communications Decency Act of 1995

Another act passed by Congress, the CDA, bans the making of "indecent" or "patently offensive" material available to minors through computer networks. The act imposes a fine of up to $250,000 and imprisonment for up to 2 years. The CDA does specifically exempt from liability any person who provides access or connection to or from a facility, system, or network that is not under the control of the person violating the act. Also, the CDA specifically states that an employer shall not be held liable for the actions of an employee unless the employee's conduct is within the scope of his or her employment.

Children's Online Privacy Protection Act

This is another act passed by Congress following the CDA, effective April 2000. This act applies to the online collection of personal information from children under 13. The new rules spell out what a Website operator must include in a privacy policy, when and how to seek verifiable consent from a parent, and what responsibilities an operator has to protect children's privacy and safety online. Operators or owners of a commercial Website or an online service directed to children under 13 years that collect personal information from children or if you operate a general audience Website and have actual knowledge that you are collecting personal information from children, you must comply with the Children's Online Privacy Protection Act.

■ To determine whether a Website is directed to children, the FTC considers several factors, including the subject matter; visual or audio content; the age of models on the site; language; whether advertising on the Website is directed to children; information regarding the age of the actual or intended audience; and whether a site uses animated characters or other child-oriented features.

■ To determine whether an entity is an "operator" with respect to information collected at a site, the FTC will consider who owns and controls the information; who pays for the collection and maintenance of the information; what the preexisting contractual relationships are in connection with the information; and what role the Website plays in collecting or maintaining the information.

---

* *Steve Jackson Games v. U.S. Secret Service*, 36F. 3d 457 (5th Cir. 1994).

In 2008, Congress amended this act and included it as Title II "Protecting the Children" of the Broadband Data Improvement Act of 2008, Public Law 110-385—October 10, 2008. The act specifically defines personal information for a child. Personal information is defined as individually identifiable information about a child that is collected online, such as full name, home address, email address, telephone number, or any other information that would allow someone to identify or contact the child. The act and rule also cover other types of information—for example, hobbies, interests and information collected through cookies or other types of tracking mechanisms—when they are tied to individually identifiable information.

Encrypted Communications Privacy Act of 1996

This act contains a general declaration that the use of encryption by a U.S. person, domestically or abroad, regardless of algorithm selected, with or without key escrow function, and with or without third-party key escrow holder is lawful. The act provides for criminal penalties and civil liabilities for a key holder (escrow agent) who releases the key to other than either the consent of the key owner or to authorized investigative or law enforcement officers. Another provision would make all sales of encryption within the United States legal, no matter how strong the technology.

Health Insurance Portability and Accountability Act of 1996

The first-ever federal privacy standards to protect patients' medical records and other health information provided to health plans, doctors, hospitals, and other healthcare providers took effect on April 14, 2003. Developed by the Department of Health and Human Services (HHS), these new standards provide patients with access to their medical records and more control over how their personal health information is used and disclosed. They represent a uniform, federal floor of privacy protections for consumers across the country. State laws providing additional protections to consumers are not affected by this new rule.

The HIPAA of 1996 calls for stringent security protection for electronic health information, both while maintained and while in transmission. For IT directors, complying with HIPAA's privacy requirements is primarily a matter of computer security protecting the privacy and confidentiality of medical patient information and standardizing the reporting and billing processes for all health and medical-related information.

National standards for electronic healthcare transactions will encourage electronic commerce in the healthcare industry and ultimately simplify the processes involved. This will result in savings from the reduction in administrative burdens on healthcare providers and health plans. Today, healthcare providers and health plans that conduct business electronically must use many different formats for electronic transactions. For example, about 400 different formats exist today for healthcare claims. With a national standard for electronic claims and other transactions, healthcare providers will be able to submit the same transaction to any health plan in the United States and the health plan must accept it. Health plans will be able to send standard electronic transactions such as remittance advices and referral authorizations to healthcare providers. These national standards will make electronic data interchange (EDI) a viable and preferable alternative to paper processing for providers and health plans alike.

HIPAA Compliance

- Any connection to the Internet or other external networks or systems occurs through a gateway or firewall.

- Strong authentication is used to restrict the access to critical systems or business processes and highly sensitive data.
- Assessments of vulnerability, reliability, and the threat environment are made at least annually.

The U.S. Health and Human Services Department has given the healthcare industry until August 2002 (October 2003 for small health plans) to comply and set substantial penalties for noncompliance. In response, NIST has released guidance to help the medical industry and organizations to comply with IT control issues associated with HIPAA.

Risk Assessment and Communications Act of 1997

This act coordinates federal information policy including privacy and information access under open network management (ONM), develops privacy and computer security policies and standards, and creates a Government Information Locator Service (GILS).

Gramm–Leach–Bliley Act of 1999

The Gramm–Leach–Bliley Act, which signed into law on November 12, 1999 requires financial institutions to assess risk, manage and control risk, oversee service providers, and adjust security programs as needed based on changing risk. One specific provision requires the business to "identify reasonably foreseeable internal and external threats that could result in unauthorized disclosure, misuse, alteration, or destruction of customer information or customer information systems."

USA Patriot Act of 2001

The purpose of the USA Patriot Act is to deter and punish terrorist acts in the United States and around the world, to enhance law enforcement investigatory tools, and other purposes, some of which include

- To strengthen U.S. measures to prevent, detect, and prosecute international money laundering and financing of terrorism
- To subject to special scrutiny foreign jurisdictions, foreign financial institutions, and classes of international transactions or types of accounts that are susceptible to criminal abuse
- To require all appropriate elements of the financial services industry to report potential money laundering
- To strengthen measures to prevent use of the U.S. financial system for personal gain by corrupt foreign officials and facilitate repatriation of stolen assets to the citizens of countries to whom such assets belong

Internet Governance

At the annual convention of the Internet Society held in Geneva, more than 1500 participants attended representing nearly every country in the world. This conference has produced some controversy and debate, focusing mostly on reforming the way the Internet domain names are created and registered. For example, recently, a Canadian firm was ordered to relinquish the "avery.net" and "dennison.net" domain names to business supplies maker Avery Dennison Corporation by a U.S. district judge. Legal experts say the decision could have a far-reaching impact on the way the trademark law is applied to the Internet. Other countries expressed dissatisfaction with the U.S. dominance in assigning domain names and have argued for this function being assigned to a non-profit international governance board. Legal experts say that these cases and a growing number like them underscore future issues, which may ultimately end up in the World Court as international giants battle for the right to domain names.

Perhaps, the most far-reaching was the fact that the ISO issued its Standard 17799 and other follow-on amendments (such as ISO/IEC 27K series) and the Organization for Economic Cooperation and Development (OECD) (see www.OECD.org) has provided guidance for providing Internet security.* Also, the International Federation of Accountants (IFAC) and the International Association of Supreme Audit Organizations (INTOSAI) have issued their directive and guidance for Internet governance and controls. These early efforts have paved the way for Information Technology governance (IT governance) to become a major issue with organizations. This issue continues to be a very important one in the coming years. Internationally, especially in Europe, privacy of personal information has been a very important and sensitive issue since the end of World War II. In the United Kingdom, the Data Protection Act of 1998 provides very firm guidance to organizations wishing to do business in the country. The act has financial and criminal penalties for violation.

Conclusion

In summary, it appears that traditional as well as new security methods and techniques are simply not working. Although many products are quite efficient in securing the majority of attacks on a network, no single product seems to be able to protect a system from every possible intruder. Current security legislation, although addressing the issues of unwanted entry onto a network, may also allow for ways by which some criminals can escape the most severe penalties for violating authorized access to a computer system. Moreover, some legislation in effect does not require periodic review, thus allowing for various policies and procedures to become outdated. The computer networking industry is continually changing. Because of this, laws, policies, procedures, and guidelines must constantly change with it; otherwise, they will have a tendency to become outdated, ineffective, and obsolete.

On the subject of privacy, we have seen that in the online world, private information has begun to leak out of systems as though it were a running faucet. Although some of today's legislation does protect the user against invasion of privacy, some of the laws we have observed contain far too many exceptions and exclusions to the point that their efficiency suffers. In addition, the government continues to utilize state-of-the-art techniques for the purpose of getting to our information for the sake of national security. New bills and legislation continue to attempt to find a resolution to these problems, but new guidelines, policies, and procedures need to be established, and laws need to be enforced to their full extent if we are to enjoy our right to privacy as guaranteed under the constitution.

For the IT auditor, the need to keep updated on the current new laws and changes in the existing laws and cyberlaw is critical. They can provide leverage in helping organizations understand the risks they face and the potential for consequences. Such consequences could even be decided

---

* Privacy Online: OECD Guidance on Policy and Practice, November 14, 2003.

at the international level as IT issues such as Internet governance begin to appear before the World Court. The potential for lawsuit through computer crime, invasion of privacy, copyright, patent and trademark infringement, and IT contract nonperformance is very high. The cost is even greater in dollars and resources if the case goes to court and the company, business, or industry receives negative exposure from the incident.

Review Questions

1. What advice does the FBI provide in protecting against computer fraud?
2. What is software piracy? How big a problem is it? Who is the Software Publishers Association or the Business Software Alliance?
3. What is the CFAA?
4. What is "reckless destructive trespass"?
5. What is the Sarbanes–Oxley Act?
6. What is the Copyright Act? How is this being used in IT issues?
7. What impact has the Federal Trademark Dilution Act had on corporate users of the Internet?
8. What is the Computer Security Act? Who does it impact? What problems has the act encountered?
9. What is the Homeland Security Act? Can hackers who cause injury or death to others be prosecuted under this act?
10. What is the Privacy Act? What does it protect?
11. What is the Electronic Communications Privacy Act? What does it protect?
12. What is the Patriot Act? What does it protect?
13. What is the recent U.S. plan for securing cyberspace?
14. Why is it important for IT auditors to know about the legal environment of information systems?

Multiple-Choice Questions

1. According to Department of Justice 2010 report, how many people each year were victims of identity theft?
   a. 1 million
   b. 5 million
   c. 8 million
   d. 10 million
2. Cyberlaw is
   a. State law
   b. Federal law
   c. Law governing use of the computer and the Internet
   d. International law
3. Software piracy costs the computer industry more than
   a. $1 billion per year
   b. $4 billion per year
   c. $9 billion per year
   d. More than $10 billion dollars per year

4. The CFAA covers
    a. Fraudulent trespass
    b. Intentional destructive trespass
    c. Reckless destructive trespass
    d. All of the above
5. The Sarbanes–Oxley Act requires that the board of an organization must
    a. Register public accounting firms
    b. Establish or adopt, by rule, auditing, quality control, ethics, independence, and other standards related to preparation of the audit reports for issuers
    c. Conduct inspections of accounting firms
    d. All of the above
6. The Cyber Security Enhancement Act as incorporated into the Homeland Security Act of 2002
    a. Demands life sentences for those hackers who recklessly endanger lives
    b. Does not require ISPs to hand over records
    c. Does not outlaw publications such as details of PGP
    d. None of the above
7. The 2009 Internet Crime report states that the reported total dollar loss from incidents/cases reported
    a. 100 million dollars
    b. 200 million dollars
    c. 400 million dollars
    d. More than 500 million dollars
8. A federal agency that protects consumers and has increased its monitoring and review of the Internet for consumer fraud and identity theft is the
    a. NSA
    b. CIA
    c. FTC
    d. None of the above
9. The National Strategy for Securing Cyberspace
    a. Applies only to defense area
    b. Applies only to medical records
    c. Provides a framework for protecting the nation's infrastructures that is essential to the economy, security, and the way of life
    d. None of the above
10. Which act is the first-ever federal privacy standard to protect patient's medical records?
    a. Encrypted Communications Privacy Act of 1996
    b. Privacy Act of 1974
    c. HIPAA of 1996
    d. All of the above

Exercises

1. Using an Internet Web browser, perform a search on the topic "computer crime." Examine five Websites and summarize the information they provide.
2. Using an Internet Web browser, perform a search on the topic "computer privacy." Examine five Websites and summarize the information they provide.

3. Using an Internet Web browser, perform a search on the topic "computer law." Examine five Websites and summarize the information they provide.

4. Using an Internet Web browser, perform a search on the topic "Computer Security Act." Examine five Websites and summarize the information they provide.

5. Using the Internet Web browser, look up the Software Publishers Association. Who are they? What help or assistance can they provide?

6. Answer Case 8 in Appendix I, OhMY Corporation.

Answers to Multiple-Choice Questions

1—d; 2—c; 3—d; 4—d; 5—d; 6—a; 7—d; 8—c; 9—c; 10—c

Further Reading

1. Author unknown, Cyberspace threats and vulnerabilities, http://www.whitehouse.gov/pcipb/case_for_action.pdf.

2. Author unknown, A national cyberspace security threat and vulnerability reduction, http://www.whitehouse.gov/pcipb/priority_2.pdf.

3. Author unknown, A letter from the president, http://www.whitehouse.gov/pcipb/letter.pdf.

4. Author unknown, National Strategy for Trusted Identities in Cyberspace; Enhancing online choice, efficiency, security and privacy, April 2011, http://www.whitehouse.gov/sites/default/files/rss_viewer/NSTICstrategy_041511.pdf.

5. Author unknown, Cyberspace policy review: Assuring a trusted and resilient information and communications infrastructure. The White House, May 2009, p. 33, http://www.whitehouse.gov/assets/documents/Cyberspace_Policy_Review_final.pdf.

6. Author unknown, Federal Identity, Credential, and Access Management (FICAM) Roadmap and Implementation Guidance, Federal Chief Information Officers Council and the Federal Enterprise Architecture, June 2, 2010, http://www.idmanagement.gov/documents/FICAM_Roadmap_Implementation_Guidance.pdf.

7. Author unknown, 2009 Internet Crime Report, Internet Crime Complaint Center IC3, March 12, 2010, p. 14, June 2, 2010, http://www.ic3.gov/media/annualreport/2009_IC3Report.pdf.

8. Author unknown, The Department of Justice's Efforts to Combat Identity Theft, US Department of Justice Office of the Inspector General, March 2010, June 2, 2010, http://www.justice.gov/oig/reports/plus/a1021.pdf.

9. Ferrera, G.R., M.E.K. Reder, R.C. Bird, J.J. Darrow, J.M. Aresty, J. Klosek, and S.D. Lichtenstein, *CyberLaw: Text and Cases*, 3rd Edition. South-Western, Independence, KY, 2011.

10. Gallegos, F., *Federal Laws Affecting IS Audit and Control Professionals*, EDP Auditing Series #72-10-20, Auerbach Publishers, Boca Raton, FL, 2001, pp. 1–20.

11. Graff, M.G., Sleepless in 2021: The future of the Internet, http://www.tnty.com/newsletter/futures/archive/v01-02technology.html.

12. Keyes, J., *Internet Management*, CRC Press LLC, Boca Raton, FL, 2000.

13. Overview of 104th Congress: Electronic Privacy and Civil Liberties Legislation, compiled by the Electronic Privacy Information Center, 1995, http://www.epic.org/privacy/.

14. Privacy Act of 1974 and Amendments, Document from the CPSR privacy/information archive, http://www.epic.org/privacy/laws/privacy–act.html.

15. Privacy Guidelines for NII Review of Proposed Principles of the Privacy Working Group, compiled by Electronic Privacy Information Center, http://www.epic.org.

16. Synovate. Federal Trade Commission—2006, Identity Theft Survey Report, November 2007.

16. The Copyright Act, 18 USC 506.

17. The Lanham Act, 15 USC 105.
18. U.S. Congress, Computer Security Act of 1987, compiled by Electronic Privacy Information Center, http://www.epic.org/crypto/csa.
19. U.S. General Accounting Office, U.S. General Accounting Office, GAO-02-766, Identity Theft: Greater Awareness and Use of Existing Data Are Needed, July 2002.
20. United States Government Accountability Office, Testimony before Congressional Subcommittees on Information Security, February 14, 2008.
21. United States Government Accountability Office, Report to Congressional Requesters on Personal Information, June 2007.
22. Xie, J., Summary of the Homeland Security Act of 2002, Copyright 2002, http://www.uslawnet.com/Englishhome/News/messages/35.htm.

Other Internet Sites

1. Author unknown, 2006 Identity Theft Survey Report, Federal Trade Commission, November 2007, p. 6, June 2, 2010, http://www.ftc.gov/os/2007/11/SynovateFinalReportIDTheft2006.pdf.
2. Author unknown, US Department of Justice CyberCrime, http://www.justice.gov/criminal/cyber-crime/cc.html.
3. Author unknown, Credit card theft, www.theftlibrary.com/tl.nsf/htm1/cctheft.html.
4. Author unknown, US Patriot Act, http://www.fincen.gov/statutes_regs/patriot/index.html.
5. Author unknown, October 2007, www.cert.org/stats/fullstats.html.
6. CERT Statistics, http://www.cert.org/stats/cert_stats.html.
7. CIPHER—Electronic Newsletter of the Technical Committee on Security and Privacy, A Technical Committee of the Computer Society of the IEEE, http://www.ieee-security.org/cipher.html.
8. Computer Security Spending Statistics, http://www.securitystats.com/sspend.html.
9. Cornell Law Review, http://organizations.lawschool.cornell.edu/clr/.
10. Economic Crimes Policy Team, Identity Theft, United States Sentencing Commission, December 1999, http://www.ussc.gov/identity/identity.pdf.
11. Forum of Incident Response and Security Teams, http://csrc.ncsl.nist.gov/.
12. Griffiths, A., Cost of hacking, http://dag.unifiedcomputing.com/costs.pdf.
13. House of Representatives Internet Law Library, http://www.lawguru.com/ilawlib/home.htm.
14. Organisation for Economic Co-Operation and Development (OECD), http://www.oecd.org/.
15. Houle, K.J. and G.M. Weaver, Trends in denial of service attack technology, http://www.cert.org/archive/pdf/DoS_trends.pdf.
16. Medical Privacy—National Standards to Protect the Privacy of Personal Health Information, http://www.hhs.gov/ocr/hipaa/.
17. Rutgers University Computing Services, http://www-ns.rutgers.edu/index.php.
18. The Web Copyright Law, U.S. Copyright Office, http://www.copyright.gov/title17/circ92.pdf (provides a full text version of the Copyright Law).
19. U.S. Department of Health and Services, Office for Civil Rights—HIPAA, http://aspe.hhs.gov/admnsimp/pL104191.htm and http://www.hhs.gov/ocr/hipaa.
20. U.S. Department of Justice, Overview of the Privacy Act of 1974, May 2004, http://www.usdoj.gov/oip/04_7_1.html.
21. Westlaw Legal Directory, http://directory.westlaw.com/.

Chapter 3

Audit and Review: Their Role in Information Technology

For the IT manager, or any manager, the words "audit" and "auditor" send chills up and down the spine. Yes, the auditor or the audit has been considered an evil that has to be dealt with by all managers. In the IT field, auditors in the past had to be trained or provided orientation in IS concepts and operations to evaluate IT practices and applications. IT managers cringed at the auditor's ability to effectively and efficiently evaluate the complexities and grasp the issues.

In today's environment, organizations must integrate their IT with business strategies to attain their overall enterprise objectives, get the most value out of their information, and capitalize on the technologies available to them. Where IT was formerly viewed as an enabler of an enterprise's strategy, it is now regarded as an integral part of that strategy to attain profitability and service.

As computerized applications are penetrating nearly all business functions and processes, organizations are mixing hardware platforms from different vendors with a combination of commercially available software and in-house-developed software. Issues such as IT governance, international information infrastructure, E-commerce, security, and privacy and control of public and enterprise information have driven the need for self-review and self-assurance.

The Situation and the Problem

Computers have been in use commercially since 1952. Computer-related crimes were reported as early as 1966. However, it was not until 1973, when the significant problems at Equity Funding Corporation of America (EFCA) surfaced, that the auditing profession looked seriously at the lack of controls in computer IS. In 2002, almost 30 years later, another major fraud was uncovered, which brought skepticism and downfall to the financial markets. This time, neither the major accounting firms nor the security- and exchange-regulated businesses in major exchanges were able to avoid the public outrage, lack of investor confidence, and increased government regulation that befell the U.S. economy. And again, in 2008, the U.S. economy suffered as mortgage banking and mortgage investment companies (such as Countrywide, IndyMac, etc.) defaulted from unsound lending strategies and poor risk management.

When EFCA declared bankruptcy in 1973, the minimum direct impact and losses from illegal activity were reported to be as much as $200 million. Further estimates from this major financial fraud escalated to as much as $2 billion, with indirect costs such as legal fees and depreciation included. These losses were the result of a "computer-assisted fraud" in which a corporation falsified the records of its life insurance subsidiary to indicate the issuance of new policies. In addition to the insurance policies, other assets, such as receivables and marketable securities, were recorded falsely. These fictitious assets should have been revealed as nonexistent during the corporation's regular year-end audits but were never discovered. As the computer was used to manipulate files as a means of covering the fraud, the accounting profession realized that conventional, manual techniques might not be adequate for audit engagements involving computer application.

In 1973, the AICPA, in response to the events at EFCA, appointed a special committee to study whether the auditing standards of the day were adequate in such situations. The committee was requested to evaluate specific procedures to be used and the general standards to be approved. In 1975, the committee issued its findings. Another critical review of the existing auditing standards was started in 1974, when the AICPA created its first standards covering this area. Then, 29 years later, the Enron–Arthur Andersen fiasco of 2002 took us back to 1973.

The issue of "due professional care" has come to the forefront of the audit community at the beginning of this decade as a result of the financial scandals and poor management of Enron, Global Crossing, and more recently Countrywide, IndyMac, and others. The EFCA scandal of 1973 led to the development of strong state and federal regulation of the insurance industries and corporate creative accounting in the aerospace industry, which provided support for the Foreign Corrupt Practices Act (FCPA) of 1977. Perhaps today, the Sarbanes–Oxley Act of 2002 will be a vivid reminder of the importance of due professional care. This act is a major reform package, mandating the most far-reaching changes Congress has imposed on the business world since the FCPA of 1977 and the Securities and Exchange Commission (SEC) Act of 1934. It seeks to thwart future scandals and restore investor confidence by creating a Public Company Accounting Oversight Board, revising auditor independence rules, revising corporate governance standards, and significantly increasing the criminal penalties for violations of securities laws.

Before the end of 2002, there were several public frauds that focused public attention on all aspects of financial reporting. The frauds and financial misreporting at companies such as Global Crossing, Adelphia, and Tyco were just the beginning. The Enron and the WorldCom collapse shook the financial community with reports of fraud up to billions of dollars. As a result of these frauds and the events that followed, and the pressures brought on Congress by the public, including investors, pensioners, and taxpayers, the Sarbanes–Oxley Act was passed on July 30, 2002. This law supports efforts to increase public confidence in capital markets by seeking to improve corporate governance, accountability, and audit quality. The act will result in more attention being given to financial versus operational controls. Thus, internal audit will be a more critical resource for management and cause IT auditors to extend their work. There will be rework needed on corporate governance (especially the role and independence of audit committees).

Audit Standards

The AICPA committee, charged with the responsibility of reviewing auditing standards as a result of EFCA's collapse, stated that "generally accepted auditing standards are adequate and no changes are called for in the procedures commonly used by auditors." However, the Sarbanes–Oxley Act will have a dramatic effect on public accounting. Section 404—Management Assessment of Internal Controls of the Act states that the companies that are affected will be required to

- State the responsibility of the management for establishing and maintaining an adequate internal control structure and procedures for financial reporting
- Prepare an assessment at the end of the issuer's fiscal year of the effectiveness of the internal control structure and procedures of the issuer for financial reporting

These requirements will have a major impact on the internal and IT auditors, as they most probably have to complete this work as well as evaluate, assess, and report on internal controls for management's report required by Sarbanes–Oxley.

The AICPA has responded to these audit failures and financial frauds in Enron, WorldCom, Adelphia, etc. by changing the previously issued SAS 82. SAS 99—"Consideration of Fraud in a Financial Statement Audit" deals with brainstorming the risk of fraud and increasing professional views that it could happen here; use of unpredictable audit tests; and responding to management override controls by requiring on every audit certain procedures to detect management override.

Similarities

It appears that whenever the audit process has a breakdown, new auditing standards are required for the examination of financial statements based on computer-generated records. Generally, the standards of fieldwork are the same as those applied to manually generated records. Also, the basic elements of adequate internal control remain the same. The main purposes of the study and evaluation of internal control still are to provide evidence for an opinion and determine the basis for the scope, timing, and extent of future audit tests.

Differences

With computer-based financial reporting systems, new auditing procedures must be continually developed and improved. The computations performed, addition or deletion of records or fields within records, and assurances that the transactions were authorized must be done through the computer in concert with the transaction flow. As one can experience, there are significant differences in the techniques of maintaining adequate internal control in computer-based processes. Also, there is some variation in the manner in which the study and evaluation of internal control is made. A major difference is that people have been removed from some phases of internal accounting control and reliance due to computer-generated validation processes and procedures.

Importance of Audit Independence

Audit independence is a very critical component if a business wishes to have an audit function; it can add value to the organization. The audit report and opinion must be free of any bias or influence if the integrity of the audit process is to be valued and recognized for its contribution to the organization's goals and objectives. A number of professional organizations (such as AICPA, the IIA, the ISACA, formerly EDP Auditors Association, Association of Government Accountants [AGA], and others) have addressed this point in very clear context and language. Governmental organizations such as the U.S. GAO and the International Organization of Supreme Audit Organizations have also reviewed this area in depth.

The Sarbanes–Oxley Act of 2002 will be a vivid reminder of the importance of due professional care. The Sarbanes–Oxley prohibits all registered public accounting firms from providing audit clients, contemporaneously with the audit, certain nonaudit services such as internal audit outsourcing, financial IS design and implementation services, and expert services. These scope-of-service restrictions go beyond existing SEC independence regulations. In addition, all other services, including tax services, are permissible only if preapproved by the issuer's audit committee and all such preapprovals must be disclosed in the issuer's periodic reports to the SEC.

The act also requires auditor (not audit firm) rotation. The lead audit partner or the concurring review partner must rotate off the engagement if he or she has performed audit services for the issuer in each of the five previous fiscal years. There is no distinction regarding the capacity in which the audit or concurring partner provided such audit services. Accordingly, services provided as a manager or in any other capacity appear to count toward the 5-year period. In addition, the provision applies as soon as the firm is registered. Therefore, without guidance to the contrary, the audit and concurring partner must count back 5 years, starting from the date on which Public Company Accounting Oversight Board registration occurs. This provision is particularly important because of its potential impact on small accounting firms. The SEC is considering whether or not to accommodate small firms in this area; currently, there is no small-firm exemption from this provision.

As mentioned earlier, this act is a major reform package, mandating the most far-reaching changes Congress has imposed on the business world since the FCPA of 1977 and the SEC of 1934. It seeks to thwart future scandals and restore investor confidence by creating a Public Company Accounting Oversight Board, revising auditor independence rules, revising corporate governance standards, and significantly increasing the criminal penalties for violations of securities laws.

Past and Current Accounting and Auditing Pronouncements

The AICPA Statements on Auditing Standards (SASs) are the professional standards for Certified Public Accountants (CPAs). These standards are an interpretation of generally accepted auditing standards (GAAS), and the AICPA requires its members to adhere to the statements or be prepared to justify any departure from them. Appendix III identifies several major AICPA SASs.

AICPA Pronouncements: From the Beginning to Now

The accounting profession began addressing the topic of internal control of IT systems officially in 1974 when the AICPA issued SAS 3, "The Effects of EDP on the Auditor's Study and Evaluation of Internal Control." SAS 3 was concerned with the evaluation of internal control of clients who processed significant records using a computer system. The growing use of computer-based financial systems created a need for auditors to go beyond matters of internal control in audits of financial statements. Consequently, in 1984, the AICPA superseded SAS 3 with SAS 48, "The Effects of Computer Processing on the Examination of Financial Statements." SAS 48 requires auditors to consider the effects of computer processing throughout the whole audit process, and not just during the evaluation of internal control. SAS 48 amended other SASs to synchronize audit practice with the increased use of computer-based processing in client financial systems.

SAS 48 provides the basic framework for the auditing procedures necessary in examining the financial statements of entities that use computer accounting applications. The pronouncement describes the basic procedures and areas of concern with which the auditor should be familiar. The pronouncement specifically covers the following topics:

- How the audit is affected by the following:
    - Extent of computer use in each significant accounting application
    - Complexity of the organization's computer operations
    - Organizational structure of IT activities
    - Availability of data for audit use
    - Use of computer-assisted audit techniques (CAAT) to increase the efficiency of audit procedures (AU Sec. 311.09)
- Need for auditors with specialized expertise in IT (AU Sec. 311.10)
- Influence of internal control procedures on the methods an organization uses to process significant data
- Characteristics distinguishing computer processing from manual processing are
    - Abbreviated life of transaction trails
    - Greater uniformity of processing, which decreases processing errors but increases vulnerability to programming errors
    - Potential for concentration of incompatible functions
    - Increased chance for errors and irregularities due to ease of gaining unauthorized access to systems and files
    - Potential for increased management supervision
    - Automatic initiation of processing functions
    - Interdependence of manual and automated controls (AU Sec. 320.33)
- Interdependence of control procedures (AU Sec. 320.57)
- Adequacy of general and application controls. General controls relate to several computer-based activities such as control over system development. Application controls are application-specific controls (AU Sec. 320.58)
- Need to obtain reasonable assurance for the reliability of the operation of programmed controls (AU Sec. 320.65-66)
- Unchanging nature of audit objectives, although evidence collection methods may vary (AU Sec. 326.12)

SAS 48 represents the current position of the AICPA on audit of computer-based financial systems. In addition, the following supportive SASs were issued:

- SAS 55, "Consideration of the Internal Control Structure in a Financial Statement," 1988
- SAS 70, "Requirements and Guidance for Service Auditor" moved to Statement on Standards for Attestation Engagements (SSAE) No. 16 "Reporting on Controls at a Service Organization," 2011
- SAS 78, "Amendment to SAS 55," 1990 and SAS 82, "Consideration of Fraud in Financial Statements," 1996

■ SAS 94, "The Effect of Information Technology on the Auditor's Consideration of Internal Control in a Financial Statement Audit," 2001 (note this SAS amends SAS 55)
■ SAS 99, "Consideration of Fraud in a Financial Statement," 2002

Several auditing standards apply in general to IT auditing and are mentioned in detail in Appendix III. For example, SAS 16, "The Independent Auditor's Responsibility for the Detection of Errors or Irregularities" (AU Sec. 327) is general in nature and applies to both manual and computerized systems. It defines the auditor's responsibility for detecting errors and irregularities in an accounting system. AU Sec. 327.05 states:

> Under GAAS the independent auditor has the responsibility, within the inherent limitations of the auditing process, to search for errors or irregularities that would have a material effect on the financial statements, and to exercise due skill and care in the conduct of that examination.

A limitation, however, is placed on the auditor's responsibility. Paragraph 13 states:

> The auditor is not an insurer or guarantor; if his examination was made in accordance with GAAS, he has fulfilled his professional responsibility.

From this emerged other AICPA standards to address the changes in technology that impact the audit process and the financial statements. SAS 94 was issued in and has been effective from June 2001. This supplementary audit standard was issued to provide guidance to auditors concerning the appropriate types of assessment vehicles, which can be used in the evaluation of internal controls within IT systems. The auditing standard states that CAATs, which is discussed in depth in Chapter 5, are needed to test certain types of IT controls in certain types of IT environments. Before this, the auditing standards (SAS 48, 55, and 78) were the major standards relevant and applied to computer-based audits. Unfortunately, as mentioned earlier, a large percentage of auditors using these standards assessed control risk at the maximum and performed only substantive tests of account balances and transactions to gather evidence of financial statement assertions. SAS 94 states that this past approach may not be viable in complex IT environments.

In the case of SAS 70, prior to the issuance of SSAE No. 16, the requirements and guidance for service auditors and user auditors was included in SAS No. 70, Service Organizations (AU Sec. 324). The AICPA's Auditing Standards Board, as part of its project to converge audit, attest, and quality control standards with those of the International Auditing and Assurance Standards Board (IAASB), decided that the guidance for service auditors in AU Section 324 of Statements on Auditing Standards should be moved to the SSAEs, and the guidance for user auditors should be retained in AU Section 324. This change was effective June 2011.

Another announcement has to do with the newly created Certified Information Technology Professional (CITP) credential created and supported by the AICPA. The CITP is a CPA recognized for his or her unique ability to provide business insight by leveraging knowledge of information relationships and supporting technologies. Unlike other certifications that recognize on a wide scope of skills, the CITP credential is an accounting professional that focuses on information assurance and management, making a CPA among the most trusted business advisor. The CITP credential holder possesses a breadth of business and technology experience. The CITP Body of Knowledge represents the qualifying areas of information assurance and management knowledge for both business experience and life-long learning. The CITP Examination questions are based on the five fundamental dimensions of

- Risk assessment
- Fraud considerations
- Internal control and IT general controls
- Evaluate, test, and report
- Information management and business intelligence

Other Standards

Other standards-setting organizations have also issued guidelines. For example, the IIA, ISACA, and the GAO have been quite active in providing audit-related guidelines. Another such organization is the National Institute of Standards and Technology (NIST)—a division of the U.S. Department of Commerce. NIST issues the Federal Information Processing Standards (FIPS) Publication Series. FIPS that focus on computer security and related publications are listed in Appendixes II and III.

Although the FIPS standards are not considered GAAS by the accounting profession, they do provide valuable guidelines on specific topics not addressed by the AICPA. Also, those companies engaged in providing services or support to the federal government through contracts or subcontracts are required to comply with FIPS if they do not have the equivalent in place.

Internal auditors are not required to follow the GAAS in the performance of their audits. However, most internal auditors are familiar with the standards and use them as general guidelines. Again, with Sarbanes–Oxley, this may change soon.

Professional associations such as IIA and the ISACA and their foundations have issued their own professional guidelines. In 1978, the IIA issued its Standards for the Professional Practice of Internal Auditing and subsequently issued the Statements on Internal Auditing Standards (SIAS), which has now evolved to Standards Related to Performance and Attributes. In 1991, with a revision in 1994, the IIA Foundation's Systems Auditability and Control (SAC) was issued and offered assistance to internal auditors on the control and audit of IS and IT.

In 1984, the ISACA issued its "EDP Control Objectives—Update 1984," a set of EDP control standards to replace the original Control Objectives issued in 1975. There have been four sets of updates to the Control Objectives. Recently, the Information Systems Audit and Control Foundation issued COBIT, which is a framework providing a tool for business owners to efficiently and effectively discharge their control responsibilities. Today, the fourth edition is the most current and provides an extensive look at internal control infrastructure in a business environment with the fifth edition currently in review stage. Chapters 8 through 22 will provide an application of those techniques and methodologies.

The federal government has issued standards for internal auditors in the private sector in its announcement of the Sarbanes–Oxley Act of 2002. Before this, federal laws such as the FCPA had provided strength to the need for internal controls. Up until the Enron scandal, the SEC personnel had alluded to the importance of the internal auditor's role. The Sarbanes–Oxley Act provides greater support for the SEC's position of having internal auditors review internal control, as an important part of an organization's plan to devise and maintain an adequate control system, as discussed in Chapter 2. Ten years before the Sarbanes–Oxley Act, the Committee of Sponsoring Organizations of the Treadway Commission (CSOTC) issued its "Internal Control–Integrated

Framework" report, also known as the COSO Report. This report makes specific recommendations to management on how to evaluate, report, and improve control systems. COSO completed a study of 200 fraud cases from the 300 filed with the SEC from 1989 to 1999. These cases were studied for trends and "red flags." It was found that 83% of these cases of financial fraud involved a CEO, CFO, or both.

One way of evaluating an organization's internal audit function is to measure it against the audit standards issued by the GAO. The "Yellow Book" or Government Auditing Standards, which GAO has issued, are audit standards that must be followed in audits of federal organizations, programs, activities, and funds received by contractors, nonprofit organizations, and other external organizations (such as companies with federal contracts). In addition, it has recently released a supplement that provides auditor guidance in the use of computer-generated information in reports. GAO reports, publications, and references in this area are identified in Appendixes II and III.

These standards relate to the scope and quality of the audit effort and the characteristics of professional and meaningful audit reports. The three elements of expanded auditing covered in the standards are finance and compliance, economy and efficiency, and program results. Also, federal legislation requires that the inspectors general in federal agencies follow these standards.

Financial Auditing

Financial auditing encompasses all activities and responsibilities concerned with the rendering of an opinion on the fairness of financial statements. The basic rules governing audit opinions indicate clearly that the scope of an audit covers all equipment and procedures used in processing significant data.

Financial auditing, as carried out today by the independent auditor, was spurred by legislation in 1933 and 1934 that created the SEC. This legislation mandated that companies whose securities were sold publicly be audited annually by CPAs. CPAs, then, were charged with attesting to the fairness of financial statements issued by companies that reported to the SEC. The AICPA issued in 1993 a document called "Reporting on an Entity's Internal Control Structure over Financial Reporting (Statement on Standards for Attestation Engagements 2)" to further define the importance of internal control in the attestation engagement.

Within the CPA profession, two groups of standards have been developed that affect the preparation of financial statements by publicly held companies and the procedures for their audit examination by CPA firms: GAAP and GAAS.

Generally Accepted Accounting Principles

GAAP establishes consistent guidelines for financial reporting by corporate managers. As part of the reporting requirement, standards are also established for the maintenance of financial records on which periodic statements are based. An auditor, rendering an opinion indicating that financial statements are stated fairly, stipulates that the financial statements conform to GAAP. These accounting principles have been formulated and revised periodically by private-sector organizations established for this purpose. The present governing body is the Financial Accounting Standards

Board (FASB). Implementation of GAAP is the responsibility of the management of the reporting entity.

Generally Accepted Auditing Standards

The major national professional organization of CPAs is the AICPA. In 1949, the AICPA adopted standards for audits, known as GAAS. These standards cover three categories:

- *General standards* relate to professional and technical competence, independence, and due professional care.
- *Fieldwork standards* encompass planning, evaluation of internal control, sufficiency of evidential matter, or documentary evidence upon which findings are based.
- *Reporting standards* stipulate compliance with all accepted auditing standards, consistency with the preceding account period, adequacy of disclosure, and, in the event that an opinion cannot be reached, the requirement to state the assertion explicitly.

These standards provide broad guidelines, but not specific guidance. The profession has supplemented the standards by issuing statements of authoritative pronouncements on auditing. The most comprehensive of these is the SAS series. SAS publications provide procedural guidance relating to many aspects of auditing. In 1985, the AICPA released a codification of the SAS 1-49. Today, the number of statements exceeds 119.

As a result, business risk increases. IT auditing is needed to evaluate the adequacy of IS to meet processing needs, evaluate the adequacy of internal controls, and ensure that assets controlled by those systems are adequately safeguarded. Situations such as those at Enron, WorldCom, Countrywide, IndyMac, and others give weight to the need for audit and independence. The passage in the United States of the Sarbanes–Oxley Act of 2002 provides the needed support for organizations to clean up their act and rely on their internal audit capability.

Today, even in these economic times, the demand for qualified IT auditors exceeds the supply. IT governance has created vast opportunities for the IT auditor.

IT Auditing: What Is It?

The evaluation of IS and IT by auditors has generated the term "IT auditing." IT auditing is the evaluation of IT, practices, and operations to assure the integrity of an entity's information. Such evaluation can include assessment of the efficiency, effectiveness, and economy of computer-based practices. This involves the use of the computer as an audit tool. The evaluation should also determine the adequacy of internal controls within the IT environment to assure valid, reliable, and secure information services.

The computer auditor's evaluation of systems, practices, and operations may include one or both of the following:

- Assessment of internal controls within the IT environment to assure the validity, reliability, and security of information
- Assessment of the efficiency and effectiveness of the IT environment in economic terms

As for the IT auditors of today, their advanced knowledge and skills will progress in two ways. One direction is continued growth and skill in this profession, leading the way in computer audit research and development and progressing up the external and internal audit career paths. The other direction involves capitalizing on a thorough knowledge of organizational systems and moving into more responsible career areas in general management.

Need for IT Audit Function

Organizations continue to rely heavily on computer technology. With the increased reliance on computers to perform daily transactions and with the higher risks associated with new technology, management needs assurance that the controls governing its computer operations are adequate. Management looks toward the audit function to provide this assurance. However, because of the rapidly changing technology and the new risks associated with that technology, specialists are needed to perform these control assessments. The EDP auditors of the past have evolved into the IT auditors of today and the future. Exhibit 3.1 lists the top 10 reasons for the start of IT auditing.

There have been many changes in the way enterprises address IT issues, resulting in a new framework called IT governance. CEOs, CFOs, chief operating officers (COOs), CTOs, and chief information officers (CIOs) agree on the founding principles of IT governance, which focus on strategic alignment between IT and enterprise objectives. This, in turn, creates changes to tactical and day-to-day operational management of IT in the organization.

In simple terms, IT governance is the process by which an enterprise's IT is directed and controlled. Effective IT governance helps ensure that IT supports business goals, maximizes business

1.	Auditing around the computer was becoming unsatisfactory for the purpose of data reliance.
2.	Reliance on controls was becoming highly questionable.
3.	Financial institutions were losing money due to creative programming.
4.	Payroll databases could not be relied on for accuracy due to sophisticated programmers.
5.	The security of data could no longer be enforced effectively.
6.	Advancements occurred in technology.
7.	Internal networks were being accessed by employees' desktop computers.
8.	Personal computers became accessible for office and home use.
9.	Large amounts of data required advanced software programs to audit them, known as CAATs (computer-assisted audit technique).
10.	The tremendous growth of corporate hackers, either internal or external, warranted the need for IT auditors.

Exhibit 3.1   The top 10 reasons for the start-up of IT auditing. (From Singleton, T. and D.L. Flesher, *IS Audit Control J.*, IV, 38, 1994.)

investment in IT, and appropriately manages IT-related risks. IT governance also helps ensure achievement of critical success factors (CFSs) by efficiently and effectively deploying secure, reliable information, and applied technology.

Learning new ways of auditing is always a priority of internal and external IT auditors. Most auditors want tools or audit methodologies that will aid them in accomplishing their task faster and easier. Almost every large organization or company has some sort of IT audit function or shop that involves an internal audit department. Today, the "Big Four" CPA firms have designated special groups that specialize in the IT audit field. PriceWaterhouseCoopers LLP, Ernst & Young LLP, Deloitte LLP, and KPMG LLP have staff that perform IT audits.

Most of these groups assist the financial auditors in establishing the correctness of financial statements for the companies in which they audit. Others focus on special projects such as Internet security dealing with penetration studies, firewall evaluations, bridges, routers, and gateway configurations. Some other areas in which IT audit skills are needed are listed in Exhibit 3.2.

No.	Subject	Description
1.	Performance of general controls	Internal and external shop operations
2.	Preparation of application assessments	Featured on mainframe, UNIX, Windows NT, and other operating systems
3.	Transfer control protocol/ Internet protocol (TCP/IP)	Internet-related data security practice
4.	Asynchronous transfer method (ATM)	Telecommunications
5.	Electronic funds transfer (EFT)	Telecommunications
6.	Database management systems (DBMS)	Knowledge of Oracle, Access, and other DBMS
7.	Business continuity planning (disaster recovery planning)	The planning and recommended implementation of a corporate disaster recovery plan
8.	Systems under change	The use of system development methodology, security and control design, and postimplementation reviews
9.	Audit integration services	Working with financial auditors to make assertions on a company's financial statements
10.	Information security services	Internet penetration studies using Internet Security Systems (ISS), Security Administrator Tool for Analyzing Networks (SATAN), and a large-scale Constrained Optimization Problem Set (COPS), and other Internet security tools of trade. Working with a computer forensics specialist on evidence collection and documentation

Exhibit 3.2   Skills related to IT auditing.

Auditors Have Standards of Practice

As a manager at any level, you must remember that auditors, whether internal or external, have standards of practice that they are supposed to follow. Like IT professionals, auditors may belong to one or more professional associations and have code of ethics and professional standards of practices and guidance that help them in performing their evaluations/audits. Some of the organizations that produced such standards of practice are the AICPA, IIA, IFAC, CICA, and ISACA. Even government auditors have standards of practice. The GAO, the watchdog of congressional spending, has for many years influenced government auditing standards worldwide. Appendix III provides an overview of these standards.

Anyone who wants to impress the audit committee or the auditors they are working with should ask for their credentials. If they are seen not performing their work to "standards of practice" for their profession, they know they could be open to a potential lawsuit or even "decertified." Understand that auditors as the IT professionals take their work seriously and try to do their best to provide a quality effort.

Auditors Must Have Independence

Audit independence is a very critical component if a business wishes to have an audit function that can add value to the organization. The audit report and opinion must be free of any bias or influence if the integrity of the audit process is to be valued and recognized for its contribution to the organization's goals and objectives. A number of professional organizations (such as AICPA, IIA, ISACA, AGA, and others) have addressed this point in very clear context and language. Governmental organizations such as the GAO and the International Organization of Supreme Audit Organizations have also addressed this area in depth.

The Sarbanes–Oxley Act of 2002 will be a vivid reminder of the importance of due professional care. The Sarbanes–Oxley prohibits all registered public accounting firms from providing audit clients contemporaneously with the audit; certain nonaudit services including internal audit outsourcing, financial information system design and implementation services, and expert services. These scope-of-service restrictions go beyond existing Security and Exchange Commission (SEC) independence regulations. All other services, including tax services, are permissible only if preapproved by the issuer's audit committee and all such preapprovals must be disclosed in the issuer's periodic reports to the SEC.

The act requires auditor (not audit firm) rotation. Therefore, the lead audit partner or the concurring review partner must rotate off the engagement if he or she has performed audit services for the issuer in each of the five previous fiscal years. The act provides no distinction regarding the capacity in which the audit or concurring partner provided such audit services. Any services provided as a manager or in some other capacity appear to count toward the 5-year period. The provision starts as soon as the firm is registered; therefore, absent guidance to the contrary, the audit and concurring partner must count back 5 years starting with the date in which Public Company Accounting Oversight Board registration occurred. This provision has a definite impact on small accounting firms. The SEC is currently considering whether or not to accommodate small firms in this area; currently, there is no small-firm exemption from this provision.

This act is a major reform package, mandating the most far-reaching changes Congress has imposed on the business world since the FCPA of 1977 and the Security & Exchange Commission

Act of 1934. It seeks to thwart future scandals and restore investor confidence by, among other things, creating a Public Company Accounting Oversight Board, revising auditor independence rules, revising corporate governance standards, and significantly increasing the criminal penalties for violations of securities laws.

High Ethical Standards

For one to act as an auditor, one must have a high standard of moral ethics. The term *auditor* is Latin for one that hears complaints and makes decisions or acts like a judge. To act as a judge, one definitely must be morally ethical or it defeats the purpose. Ethics are a very important basis for our culture as a whole. If the auditor loses favor in this area, it is almost impossible to regain the trust the auditor once had with audit management and auditees.

Trust is the mainstay thrust upon all auditors as they enter into the position. Whether an auditor is ethical in the beginning or not, they should all start off with the same amount of trust and good favor from the client or auditee. If the bond is not broken, the auditor establishes a good name as someone who can be trusted with sensitive material.

In today's world economy, trust is an unheard-of word. No one can trust anyone these days and for this reason it is imperative that high ethics are at the top of the manager's list of topics to cover with new staff. Times are changing and so are the clients requesting our services. Most managers will tell you that they cherish this aspect called ethics because it distinguishes them from others without it.

For example, say a budget calls for numerous hours. It is unethical to put down hours not worked. It is also unethical to overlook something during the audit because the client says it is not important.

> One has to be objective, one has to be fair, and one has to be ethical. If I have to stress one thing above all with respect to Due Professional Care, it's ethics. Sometimes, our wants and desires to succeed and produce the best profit margin for our company get in the way of our ethical standing. I think at times we use gray areas with ethics. It's black, it's white, it's right or it's wrong. So, if there is one message I can give, it's to have a high standard of ethics.*

A fine line exists between what is ethical and what is legal. Something can be ethically wrong but still legal. However, with that being said, some things initially thought to be unethical become illegal over time. If there is a large enough population opposed to something ethically incorrect, you will see legislation introduced to make it illegal.

When IT auditors attain their CISA certification, they also subscribe to a Code of Professional Ethics. This code applies to not only the professional conduct but also the personal conduct of IT auditors. It requires that the ISACA standards are adhered to, confidentiality is maintained, any illegal or improper activities are reported, the auditor's competency is maintained, due care is used

---

* Truglio, T., Best Practices of IS Audit Management, ISACA International Conference, Universal Sheraton Hotel, 1995.

in the course of the audit, the results of audit work is communicated, and high standards of conduct and character are maintained.*

Auditor: Knowledge, Skills, and Abilities

Traditionally, there have been three commonly accepted sources of obtaining an IT auditing education:

- ◾ The first source is to participate in a mixture of on-the-job training and in-house programs. These are most appropriate where the technology presented has been adopted and implemented by the organization.
- ◾ The second source is to participate in seminars presented by professional organizations or vendors. These are valuable in presenting information that is new or for exploring various approaches to IS auditing problems. In the seminar environment, a peer group can share perspectives not available from a single instructor. However, seminars involve costs, not only for the program, but also for travel, accommodations, and loss of time at work. Also, some seminars do not provide the in-depth technical hands-on competence required in IS auditing.
- ◾ The third source is found in the traditional university academic environment. Past studies have shown that as much as 70% of audit training is on the job, compared to only 8% learned in school. Thus, one of the purposes of proposing a model curriculum for undergraduate and graduate education in IT auditing is to increase the level of education received in this field. Further, a model curriculum provides a framework for universities in structuring or restructuring their courses as well as developing new courses that meet the needs of employers of their graduates.

In the information-based business environment, business professionals who are technically competent in IT or IT specialists who understand the accounting, commerce, and financial operations are in high demand for IT auditing careers. The IT specialist and the IT auditor must continuously receive education to upgrade their knowledge, skills, and abilities. Universities, with the appropriate curriculum, can generate employable candidates for the IT audit, security, and control profession. A university-sponsored proactive IT auditing curriculum at the undergraduate and graduate levels is very desirable to those professionals wishing to change their career path or upgrade their skills for job enhancement. The ISACA "Model Curricula for IS Auditing Education at the Undergraduate and Graduate Levels" was developed and issued in March 1998 and later updated in 2005. The undergraduate and graduate model curricula provide a goal for universities worldwide to strive toward meeting the demand for IT auditing, security, and control education. Under the direction of Task Force Chairperson, Dr. Alan Lord, a new update of this model was created and is being used today.

In the Information Assurances Community, information security (InfoSec) has made significant strides in gaining support from the U.S. universities. The National InfoSec Education and Training

---

* ISACA, The Code of Professional Ethics, Information Systems Audit Control Association Website, www.isaca. org.

Program (NIETP) operates under national authority and its initiatives provide the foundation for a dramatic increase in the population of trained, professionally competent security experts. Activities in this area directly support government efforts to develop professionally competent and certified system administrators and associated network positions in security practices and procedures. There is no single vehicle to accomplish this task. NIETP initiatives are multifaceted and strive to address all aspects of its role in education, training, and awareness by creating partnerships among government, academia, and industry. Through these partnerships, the NIETP can assess current offerings in InfoSec courses from a variety of sources to identify gaps and determine how to fill those gaps. To date, more than 145 U.S. universities and colleges have been identified as National Centers of Academic Excellence in Information Assurance 2-Year Education, National Centers of Academic Excellence in Information Assurance Education, or National Centers of Academic Excellence in Information Assurance Research and have their courses certified to meet federal standards. The U.S. Department of Homeland Security (DHS) and the National Security Agency (NSA) are continuing in their leadership role with national-level programs via the National Security Telecommunications and Information Systems Security Committee (NSTISSC) for assuring the very finest preparation of professionals entrusted with securing the national security systems.

A major supporter of the Information Assurance Education effort has been the Colloquium for Information Systems Security Education (CISSE). Since 1996, this group has worked with U.S. NSA and later U.S. DHS to help develop support for InfoSec education and research in many U.S. universities. One of the outcomes was the establishment of National Information Assurance Training and Education Center (NIATEC) supported by Idaho State University and under the direction of Dr. Corey Schou. Today, the colloquium supports a regional and national CyberSecurity Defense contest engaging information assurance students to secure mock corporate networks from cyber attacks.

These models and efforts by CISSE can also serve those who are interested in obtaining an IT auditing or information assurance education or in educational institutions worldwide that are developing curricula in IT auditing or information assurance. The sample syllabi of courses identified are offered as examples of what content and requirements courses may include or contain. Universities that have been successful in starting and maintaining such programs at the undergraduate and graduate levels have shared or provided their syllabi to other educational units. Non-U.S. educational institutions may substitute sequence, courses, and content due to government or educational requirements/restrictions imposed within their environment.

Finally, in August 2011, the cybersecurity arm of the United Nations has endorsed the Global CyberLympics, a new initiative by the EC-Council to foster stronger international cooperation on information security issues and to improve cybersecurity training and awareness in developing nations and third-world countries. Created by EC-Council, the Global CyberLympics is a series of ethical hacking games comprised of both offensive and defensive security challenges that will take place starting from September across six continents. Teams will vie for regional championships, followed by a global hacking championship round to determine the world's best cybersecurity team. The EC-Council is sponsoring over $400,000 worth of prizes at the CyberLympics. The Global CyberLympics is supported by the International Multilateral Partnership Against Cyber Threats (IMPACT), the cybersecurity executing arm of the United Nations' specialized agency—the International Telecommunications Union (ITU). With this support, the Global CyberLympics hopes to be able to promote its mission to 136 partner countries with the world's first hacking contest around the globe.

Broadest Experiences

Experience in IT management is a definite must, and this is equally true with regard to IT audit management. Nothing in this world can compare to actual on-the-job, real-world experiences. Theory is also valuable, and for the most part an IT auditor should rely on theory to progress through an audit. For example, if IT auditors wish to demonstrate their commitment and knowledge level of the field, they can select an area to be tested. A number of professional certifications exist that can benefit the auditor. In the IT audit area, to pass the CISA exam, one must know, understand, and be able to apply the theory of modern IT auditing to all exam questions posed. In other situations, certifications such as the CPA, Certified Chartered Accountant (CA), Certified Internal Auditor (CIA), Certified Computer Professional (CCA), Certified Government Financial Manager (CGFM), Certified Information Systems Security Professional (CISSP), Certified Information Security Manager (CISM), CITP, and Certified Fraud Examiner (CFE) are some examples of certifications that may be very useful to one's career and future plans.

The understanding of theory is definitely essential to the successful IT auditor. However, theory can only take one so far. This textbook and others available should be viewed as a guide. In this field, due to the technology complexity and situation, there comes a time when an IT auditor has to rely on experience to confront a new never before encountered situation. Experience in the field is a definite plus, but having experience in a variety of other fields can sometimes be more beneficial. For example, if you are working for a Big Four public accounting firm as an IT audit manager, you are going to be exposed to a wide variety of IT audit situations and scenarios. The experience you receive will help broaden your horizons and further your knowledge in the IT audit field.

This textbook is designed for the professional and those who wish to learn about the Information Systems Audit and Control community as well as those aspiring to enter the profession. It can be used as a resource for training and learning about this field.

Certainly, support for education and the need to share experiences in this area has been recognized and training materials provided for many years by accounting, auditing, and information security professional societies such as the AICPA, the IIA, ISACA, Information Systems Security Association, and the Institute for Management Accountants. The Association of Information Technology Professionals (AITP), formerly Data Processing Management Association (DPMA), in the issuance of its Model Curriculum for Undergraduate Computer Information Systems Education in 1981, included the need for an elective course on IT auditing. This course is still in their most recent model curriculum. From an international perspective, organizations such as the IFAC and IFIP/WG11.8 (Information Security Education and Training; where IFIP—International Federation for Information Processing) have published documents advocating the need for university-developed training in IT auditing, security, and control.

Direct entry into the profession, as is the situation today, may change with entry-level requirements, including experience in business processes, systems, and technology, as well as sound knowledge of general auditing theory supplemented by practical experience. In addition, IT auditors may require specific industry expertise such as telecommunications, transportation, or finance and insurance to adequately address the industry-specific business/technology issues. This book provides current information and approaches to this complex field, which can help the practitioners and those wanting to learn more.

Individuals seeking entry into this profession must understand that experiences in auditing IT applications and operations will provide exposure to languages such as JAVA, C++, a 4GL or

Cobol, or others that are relevant. Also, exposure to computer-based communications networks, for example, can include additional technical or programming work such as object-oriented programming or general knowledge of operating systems/programming issues. IT-related experiences provide both exposure to and awareness of the complexities of Computer Forensics, IT operations, and the management of IT. For example, the experience may include discussion on IT project management, IT risk management, and recognizing success and failure factors in IT-related projects. Universities worldwide can provide such exposure, experiences, and training in their coursework.

A measure of success is the fact that employers for this career field continuously seek candidates from these universities. Such employers are active in providing speakers and funding for joint research/education. The following courses were suggested and cover 11 areas in the IFAC study "The Impact of Information Technology on the Accountancy Profession" and the follow-up discussion paper, "Minimum Skill Levels in Information Technology for Professional Accountants." Thus, the blend of accounting, business, and IT education at the graduate level can enrich a person with the basic skills to perform in the area of IT auditing. The 11 areas are

1. IT and its application
2. Systems analysis, design, development, and implementation
3. Internal controls and documentation of IS
4. Data structures, database concepts, and management
5. IS applications and processing cycles
6. Management of IS and technology
7. Computer programming languages and procedures
8. Computer communications and networks
9. Model-based systems (decision support and expert systems)
10. Systems security and disaster recovery planning
11. Auditing of IT and its role in business

A program beyond the bachelor's degree should be designed to satisfy the following eight technical proficiency requirements*:

1. Proficiency as an auditor
2. Ability to review and evaluate IT internal controls and recommend the extent of audit procedures required
3. Understanding of IT system design and operations
4. Knowledge of programming languages and techniques and the ability to apply CAAT and assess their results
5. General familiarity with computer operating systems and software
6. Ability to identify and reconcile problems with client datafile format and structure
7. Ability to bridge the communications gap between the auditor and the IT professional, providing support and advice to management
8. Knowledge of when to seek the assistance of an IT professional (network security specialist, cryptography specialist, computer forensics specialist, etc.)

---

* Myers, J., Chair of the Accounting Department, Woodbury University, Burbank, CA, 1994.

Supplemental Skills

In addition to the experience and technical skills, effective IS auditors possess a variety of skills that enable them to add value to their organizations and clients. The finest technical training does not fully prepare auditors for the communication and negotiation skills, among others, that are required for success.

Many of the nontechnical or supplemental skills are concerned with gathering information from and, of comparable importance, presenting information to, people. As such, these supplemental skills are readily transferable to other disciplines, for example, finance, management, and marketing. The final product auditors create is the information presented in their audit report. If this information is not effectively and efficiently delivered via solid oral and written communication skills, all value accruing from the audit process could potentially be lost.

Experience comes with time and perseverance, as is well known, but auditors should not limit themselves to just one industry, software, or operating system. They should challenge themselves and broaden their horizons with a multitude of exposure in different environments, if possible. The broader and more well rounded the IT auditor is, the better the chance for a successful audit career. The auditor can pull on experiences in other fields, software packages, or even operating systems to act as a mental guide during the audit.

Note

Having a well-rounded diverse background never hurts when one is working with an auditee. For example, a junior auditor was recently conducting an audit in which she was faced with a client/auditee that was not very cooperative.

During the questioning process, the junior auditor established a rapport with the client by using people skills or "soft skills." The role of an auditor is not an easy one when we are asked to review and question the work of others. Many times, the auditee must have a clear understanding of our role and that the auditor's focus is not to be critical of the individual but of the organizational policies, procedures, and process. The audit objectives focus on the organization's goals and objectives.

Trial and Error

Some of the best learning comes from the mistakes of others and one's own errors. Errors committed by a simple oversight teach the auditor to become thorough and exact before releasing the work papers to upper management. No one is perfect in this world. Everyone makes mistakes. It is for this reason that most audit managers realize the importance of error and the valuable lessons that can be learned from such errors. Nobody wants to be a failure. However, it is inevitable, and, for that matter, inconceivable, to believe that employees are not going to make mistakes. The key to success in any business environment is the individual employee. An efficient auditor will learn from errors and improve productivity so that the same error is never committed again.*

Most IT audit managers will admit that they all have done things on audits as an inexperienced staff member that they would like to forget. The thing to remember here is that all IT audit

---

* Kneer, D., J. Vyskoc, D. Manson and F. Gallegos, Information systems audit education, *IS Audit Control J.*, 4, 1–20, 1994.

professionals who are successful have learned from their mistakes and have built a solid foundation on which to grow.

Committing errors will always happen in day-to-day life. That is just a fact, and anyone who believes otherwise is just fooling himself. Learn to accept that perfection is not possible and that faults must be worked on to enhance productivity and quality of work.

Role of the IT Auditor

The auditor evaluating today's complex systems must have highly developed technical skills to understand the evolving methods of information processing. Contemporary systems carry risks such as noncompatible platforms, new methods to penetrate security through communication networks (e.g., the Internet), and the rapid decentralization of information processing with the resulting loss of centralized controls.

Auditing the processing environment is divided into two parts. The first and most technical part of the audit is the evaluation of the operating environment, with major software packages (e.g., the operating and security systems) representing the general or environmental controls in the automated processing environment. This part is usually audited by the IT audit specialist. The second part of the processing environment is the automated application, which is audited by the general auditor who possesses some computer skills.

As the use of IT in organizations continues to grow, auditing computerized systems must be accomplished without many of the guidelines established for the traditional auditing effort. In addition, new uses of IT introduce new risks, which in turn require new controls. IT auditors are also in a unique position to evaluate the relevance of a particular system to the enterprise as a whole. Because of this, the IT auditor often plays a role in senior management decision making.

The role of IT auditor can be examined through the process of IT governance and the existing standards of professional practice for this profession. As mentioned earlier, IT governance is an organizational involvement in the management and review of the use of IT in attaining the goals and objectives set by the organization.

Because IT impacts the operation of an entire organization, everyone should have an interest and role in governing its use and application. This growing awareness has led organizations to recognize that, if they are to make the most of their IT investment and protect that investment, they need a formal process to govern it.

Reasons for implementing an IT governance program include

- Increasing dependence on information and the systems that deliver the information
- Increasing vulnerabilities and a wide spectrum of threats
- Scale and cost of current and future investments in information and IS
- Potential for technologies to dramatically change organizations and business practices to create new opportunities and reduce costs

As long as these factors remain a part of business, there will be a need for effective, interdependent systems of enterprise and IT governance.

An open-standard IT governance tool that helps nontechnical and technical managers and auditors understand and manage risks associated with information and related IT was developed by the IT Governance Institute and the Information Systems Audit and Control Foundation.

COBIT is a comprehensive framework of control objectives that helps IT auditors, managers, and executives discharge fiduciary responsibilities, understand their IT systems, and decide what level of security and control is adequate. COBIT provides an authoritative, international set of generally accepted IT practices for business managers and auditors.

COBIT can be downloaded on a complimentary basis from www.isaca.org. It includes a publication containing detailed management guidelines to bridge the gaps among business risks, control needs, and technical issues. These new tools help businesses monitor processes by using CSFs, key goal indicators (KGIs), key performance indicators (KPIs), and maturity models (MMs). Additional resources and information are available at www.ITgovernance.org.

IT Auditor as Counselor

In the past, users have abdicated responsibility for controlling computer systems, mostly because of the psychological barriers that surround the computer. As a result, there are few checks and balances, except for the IT auditor. Therefore, auditors must take an active role in developing policies on auditability, control, testing, and standards. Auditors also must convince users and IT personnel of the need for a controlled IT environment.

An IT audit staff in a large corporation can make a major contribution to computer system control by persuading user groups to insist on a policy of comprehensive testing for all new systems and all changes to existing systems. By reviewing base-case results, user groups can control the accuracy of new or changed systems by actually performing a complete control function.

Insisting that all new systems be reviewed at predefined checkpoints throughout the system's development life cycle can also enhance control of IT. The prospect of audit review should prompt both user and systems groups to define their objectives and assumptions more carefully. Here, too, IT auditors can subtly extend their influence.

IT Auditor as Partner of Senior Management

Although the IT auditor's roles of counselor and skilled technician are vital to successful company operation, they may be irrelevant if the auditor fails to view auditing in relation to the organization as a whole. A system that appears well controlled may be inconsistent with the operation of a business.

Decisions concerning the need for a system traditionally belonged to senior management, but because of a combination of factors (mostly the complex technology of the computer), computer system audits were not successfully performed. When allocating funds for new systems, management has had to rely on the judgment of computer personnel. Although their choices of new and more effective computer systems cannot be faulted, computer personnel have often failed to meet the true business needs of the organization.

Management needs the support of a skilled computer staff that understands the organization's requirements, and IT auditors are in such a position to provide that information. They can provide management with an independent assessment of the effect of IT decisions on the business. In addition, the IT auditor can verify that all alternatives for a given project have been considered, all risks have been accurately assessed, the technical hardware and software solutions are correct, business needs will be satisfied, and costs are reasonable.

IT Auditor as Investigator

As a result of increased legislation and the use of computer evidence within the courts, the ability to capture and document computer-generated information related to criminal activity is critical for purposes of prosecution. The awareness and use of computer-assisted tools and techniques in performing forensic support work have provided new opportunities for the IT auditor, IT security personnel, and those within law enforcement and investigation. For the IT audit professional, computer forensics is an exciting, developing field. The IT auditor can work in the field of computer forensics or work side by side with a computer forensics specialist, supplying insight into a particular system or network. The specialists can ask the IT audit professionals questions pertaining to the system and get responses faster than having to do research and figure everything out on their own. Although the specialist is highly trained and can adapt to almost any system or platform, collaboration can make the jobs of the forensic specialist and the IT professional easier and more efficient.

Since its birth in the early 1970s, computer forensics has continuously evolved into what is now a very large field. New technologies and enhancements in protocols are allowing engineers and developers to create more stable and robust hardware, software, and tools for the specialist to use in computer-related criminal investigations. As computers become more advanced and more abundant, so do criminal activities. Therefore, the computer forensics niche is also in constant progression along with the technological advancements of computers.

With new complex advancements, there are also complicated challenges. One of these challenges facing the field of computer forensics is the advancement of encryption. As encryption standards rise and the algorithms become more complex, it will be more difficult and more time consuming for specialists to decrypt and then piece together encrypted files into meaningful information. Another major challenge is maintaining credible certifications and industry standards in the field. Currently, there are a few cardinal rules that specialists tend to follow to ensure that no forensic evidence is damaged, destroyed, or otherwise compromised by the procedures used during the investigation: (1) never work on the original evidence, (2) establish and maintain a continuing chain of custody, and (3) document everything. These rules are especially important because they help ensure that the data gathered will be done so in a structured manner although there is no solid set of standards now. Currently, the NIST creates the various standards for the technology industry. More standards need to be adopted for this field to make the gathered evidence and the compiled information used in court more credible in the eyes of the judge, jury, and opposing attorneys. Once better standards are addressed and adopted, information gathered by specialists will be more reliable in court and for the general public.

At times, individuals might attempt to hide data that contain incriminating information that they do not want others to find. One method that is commonly used to hide data is to rename a file of a particular type to another, thus, changing the extension of a file. One of the most challenging aspects of a forensic analysis of a computer is the possibility of data being intentionally hidden by your suspect. For example, an individual might be keeping child pornography pictures on his computer, but he does not want others to find it; therefore, it is possible that he might change the .jpg extension to .xls for Microsoft Excel. Renaming the file makes it nearly impossible for someone to search through and determine the correct file type. In cases such as this, EnCase can be utilized to flag suspicious file types. Using tools to run a HASH analysis of the hard drive will interpret the file headers and mark them as containing incorrect header information. Thus, after the file has been flagged, the analyst can read the file header information and make a determination of the correct file type.

Computer forensic specialists gather evidence against the individual who has committed a crime in several ways. They can image a hard drive or other types of media that the illegal information might be stored on. Data can come on a variety of media such as data tapes, zip disks, CD-ROM disks, and memory cards (Vacca 2002). For example, if the attacker has saved the database and formatted the disk, the specialist can most probably retrieve the illegal data from the drive. Specialists can decrypt and crack passwords that have been imposed on files, as criminals might encrypt their files and set passwords to inhibit others from gaining access to their illegal files.

The science of computer forensics is meticulous and requires a tremendous amount of patience and dedication. Some have been called in to work round the clock to investigate, gather, identify, and document their findings. Specialists must be extremely careful to preserve the original file or device for that is all that they have to work with. Therefore, it is extremely important to first create exact images of the information and examine that information on a different type of media. Forensic specialists work hard to find vital information, and aim toward gathering enough evidence for prosecution or disciplinary action.

Often, these specialists investigate under extreme secrecy so that other individuals do not know exactly what they are doing or what information they have gathered. Once they have thoroughly gathered all the information and evidence that they can, specialists compile a report to be used in court. At times, the specialists themselves have testified in court when an independent opinion is needed on complex technical issues as these individuals are specially trained, have an extensive background in working with computers and dealing with technical issues, and are, of course, familiar with gathered information and the methods used to acquire that information.

Types of Auditors and Their Duties, Functions, and Responsibilities

There are two types of audit functions that exist today. They have very important roles in assuring the validity and integrity of financial accounting and reporting systems. They are the internal and external audit functions.

Internal Audit Function

The internal audit function is a control function within a company or organization. The primary purpose of the internal audit function is to assure that management-authorized controls are being applied effectively. The internal audit function, although not mandatory, exists in most private enterprise or corporate entities, and in government (such as federal, state, county, and city governments). The mission, character, and strength of an internal audit function vary widely within the style of top executives and traditions of companies and organizations. IT audits is one of the newer, emerging areas of support for internal audit.

The internal audit group, if appropriately staffed with the resources, performs the monitoring and testing of IT activities within the control of the organization. Of particular concern to private corporations is the processing of data and the generation of information of financial relevance or materiality.

As mentioned in the following section, management has a very large part to play in the effectiveness of an internal audit function. Their concern with the reliability and integrity of computer-generated information from which decisions are made is critical. In organizations where management shows and demonstrates concern about internal controls, the role of the internal audit grows in stature. As the internal audit function matures through experience, training, and career development, the external audit function and the public can rely on the quality of the internal auditor's work. With a good, continuously improving internal audit management and staff, corporate management is not hesitant to assign reviews, consultation, and testing responsibilities to the internal auditor. These responsibilities are often broader in scope than those of the external auditor.

Within the United States, internal auditors from government agencies often come together to meet and exchange experiences through conferences or forums. For example, the Intergovernmental Audit Forum is an example of an event where auditors come together from city, county, state, and federal environments to exchange experiences and provide new information regarding audit techniques and methods. The IIA holds a national conference that draws an auditor population from around the world, both private and government, to share experiences and discuss new audit methods and techniques.

External Auditor

The external auditor evaluates the reliability and the validity of systems controls in all forms. The principal objective in their evaluation is to minimize the amount of substantial auditing or testing of transactions required to render an opinion on a financial statement.

External auditors are provided by public accounting firms and also exist in government as well. For example, the GAO is considered an external reviewer because it can examine the work of both federal and private organizations where federal funds are provided. The Watchdogs of Congressional Spending provide a service to the taxpayer in reporting directly to Congress on issues of mismanagement and poor controls. Interestingly, in foreign countries, an Office of the Inspector General or Auditor General's Office within that country prepares similar functions. Also, the GAO has been a strong supporter of the International Audit Organization, which provides government audit training and guidance to its international audit members representing governments worldwide.

From a public accounting firm standpoint, firms such as Deloitte, Ernst & Young, PriceWaterhouseCoopers (formerly Price Waterhouse and Coopers & Lybrand), and KPMG have provided these types of external audit services worldwide. The external auditor is responsible for testing the reliability of client IT systems and should have a special combination of skills and experience. Such an auditor must be thoroughly familiar with the audit attest function. The attest function encompasses all activities and responsibilities associated with the rending of an audit opinion on the fairness of the financial statements. Besides the accounting and auditing skills involved in performing the attest function, these external auditors also must have substantial IT audit experience. The Sarbanes–Oxley Act of 2002 now governs their role and limits of services that can be offered beyond audit.

Legal Implications

In the pre-Sarbanes–Oxley years, the establishment of "limited liability partnerships" came as a result of a "Big Five" organization being taken to court by a client. The client, who selected a support system based on the firm's recommendation, failed to perform in the manner recommended and caused the company financial loss. The courts held the Big Five firm liable for not exercising "due professional care" in the conduct of their work performed. The company sought the protection of a limited liability partnership with its auditee.

Today, we now have a Big Four due to the Enron scandal and the demise of Arthur Andersen LLP. The guidance the courts used to evaluate the issues of this case was issued by the AICPA. Because the firm held itself and its professionals compliant with AICPA's governing standards and guidance, the courts used this guidance as a basis for evaluating the evidence of the case and their professional conduct. Arthur Andersen LLP was the first major international accounting firm taken to court and successfully convicted for lack of due professional care in the destruction of client documents and obstructing justice. A jury on June 16, 2002, found Arthur Andersen LLP guilty of obstructing justice, all but sealing the fate of this accounting firm.

After a month-and-a-half trial and 10 days of deliberations, jurors convicted Andersen for obstructing justice when it destroyed Enron Corp. documents while on notice of a federal investigation. Andersen and its lawyers had claimed that the documents were destroyed as part of its housekeeping duties and not as a ruse to keep Enron documents away from the regulators.

Conclusion

The audit function, whether internal or external, is part of the corporate environment. It is a process to objectively validate, verify, and substantiate a process, activity, function, system, subsystem, or project within an organization. In this chapter, we have provided the major points of IT audit evolution. IT auditors have a unique set of skills and abilities that allows them to evaluate varied issues and environments. They also have standards of professional practice that they follow, depending on their level of qualifications (knowledge, skills, and abilities) and any certifications they may have attained. IT Audit is a profession that requires continuous education and development.

Assessment of strategic and operational events is not beyond their scope as well as their ability to assess issues involving efficiency, effectiveness, and economic resources. As an auditor, the use of this scarce, highly valued resource can be helpful and cost effective. Corporate management can successfully use this resource to help them manage a very complex environment and work toward achieving the organizational goals and objectives. In addition, several career path studies have shown that IT auditors at some point in time in their career path move into other parts of the organization. Therefore, as managers, the IT auditor with their corporate overview, communication skills, analytical skills, and technology skills may be candidates for operational or support positions within IT.

Review Questions

1. List and explain three reasons for the start up of an IT audit function.
2. What are the skills related to IT auditing? List and describe three areas.
3. List some examples of the auditor's standards of practice. Which organizations have issued standards or guidance to the auditor?
4. What is SAS 1 and why is it important to the audit process today?
5. Why are the Equity Funding event and the Enron event of 2002 so important to computer auditing?
6. What are the differences in "auditing through the computer" versus the more traditional book and records audit?

7. What are SAS Nos. 48, 55, 78, 94, and 99? Why are these important to external and internal auditors?
8. Who are the IIA, ISACA, GAO, AICPA, and IFAC? Why are they important to internal or external auditors and IT auditors?
9. Why are GAAP and GAAS important to the IT auditor?
10. What and where are the resources available to train auditors, especially IT auditors?
11. What are the basic skills needed to perform in the area of IT auditing?
12. For education in IT auditing beyond the bachelor's degree, what technical proficiency areas are suggested?
13. What are some supplemental skill development areas for auditors?
14. What are external auditors? What are their roles and responsibilities? Provide and discuss two examples of external auditors.
15. What are internal auditors? What are their roles and responsibilities?
16. What is computer forensics? Where and how would an IT auditor use this resource?

Multiple-Choice Questions

1. Which of the following is not one of the top 10 reasons for the start up of IT audit?
   a. Auditing around the computer was becoming unsatisfactory for the purposes of database reliance
   b. Accessibility of personal computers for office and home use
   c. Very little advancement in technology
   d. The growth of corporate hackers
2. Professional associations that have standards of practice:
   a. IIA
   b. ISACA
   c. AICPA
   d. All the above
3. A federal agency that develops and issues government auditing standards is
   a. GSA
   b. GAO
   c. Federal Bureau of Investigation (FBI)
   d. Federal Trade Commission (FTC)
4. A special condition is one where an auditor must be free of any bias or influence, and have
   a. IT skills
   b. Good writing skills
   c. Professional development
   d. Independence
5. Which federal law was developed and passed by U.S. lawmakers in reaction to the recent financial frauds such as Enron?
   a. FCPA
   b. SEC Act
   c. Sarbanes–Oxley Act
   d. Computer Fraud and Abuse Act
6. In the author's opinion, an auditor must have
   a. High ethical standards

b. Limited training
c. Poor communication skills
d. Poor time management skills

7. GAAS was developed and issued by
   a. NIST
   b. AICPA
   c. FTC
   d. NSA

8. Certifications that may be helpful to an IT auditor:
   a. CISA
   b. CFE
   c. CISSP
   d. All of the above

9. An auditor who works for Bank of America directly and is on its audit staff is considered to be
   a. An external auditor
   b. An internal auditor
   c. A consultant
   d. None of the above

10. Computer forensic specialists are experts who
    a. Investigate under extreme secrecy so that other individuals do not know exactly what they are doing or what information they have gathered
    b. May testify in court where an independent opinion is needed on complex technical issues
    c. Have an extensive background working with computers and dealing with technical issues, and are, of course, familiar with gathered information and the methods used to acquire that information
    d. All of the above

Exercises

1. Visit the Websites of four external audit organizations: two private and two government sites. Provide a summary of who they are and their roles, function, and responsibilities.

2. Visit the Websites of two internal audit organizations: two private and two government sites (federal, state, county, or city). Provide a summary of who they are and their roles, functions, and responsibilities.

3. You are asked by your audit supervisor to identify national colleges or universities that provide training or education in the internal audit or IT auditing area. List five colleges or universities that can provide that type of training worldwide.

4. You are asked by your audit supervisor to obtain a list of professional certifications and organizations that would be helpful for the audit staff to take or join and become involved in. Provide a list of five professional certifications and state why you think membership would be helpful. Provide a list of five professional organizations and tell why it would be beneficial to join or become involved with them.

5. Your audit supervisor has asked you to study the area of control self-assessment and business continuity planning. Provide five articles or Websites that can provide your supervisor useful information on these current topics.

Answers to Multiple-Choice Questions

1—c; 2—d; 3—b; 4—d; 5—c; 6—a; 7—b; 8—d; 9—b; 10—d

Further Reading

1. American Institute of Certified Public Accountants (AICPA) 1987, Statement on Auditing Standard 48 and Statement on Auditing Standard 55, Consideration of the Internal Control Structure in a Financial Statement, April 1988. Statement on Auditing Standard 78, Amendment to SAS 55, and Statement on Auditing Standard 82, Consideration of Fraud in Financial Statements, 1996 and Statement on Auditing Standard 94, The Effect of Information Technology on the Auditor's Consideration of Internal Control in a Financial Statement Audit, 2001 and Statement on Auditing Standard 99, Consideration of Fraud in a Financial Statement Audit, 2002.
2. American Institute of Certified Public Accountants (AICPA), Overview of the Certified Information Technology Professional, 2010, http://www.aicpa.org/InterestAreas/InformationTechnology/Membership/Pages/Overview%20of%20The%20Certified%20Information%20Technology%20Professional%20Credential.aspx.
3. American Institute of Certified Public Accountants (AICPA), 2011 Top Technology Initiatives, http://www.aicpa.org/InterestAreas/InformationTechnology/Resources/TopTechnologyInitiatives/Pages/2011TopTechInitiatives.aspx.
4. American Institute of Certified Public Accountants (AICPA), *The Effect of Information Technology on the Auditor's Consideration of Internal Control in a Financial Statement Audit (SAS 94)*, 2001.
5. American Institute of Certified Public Accountants (AICPA), *Consideration of Fraud in a Financial Statement Audit (SAS 99)*, 2002.
6. CEO Task Force for Securing Cyberspace, www.technet.org.
7. Cerullo, M.V. and M.J. Cerullo, Impact of SAS No. 94 on Computer audit techniques, *Inf. Syst. Control J.*, 1, 53–57, 2003.
8. Committee of Sponsoring Organizations of the Treadway Commission (COSO), *Report to SEC of 200 Actual Fraud Cases*, 2001.
9. Gallegos, F., IT auditor careers: IT governance provides new roles and opportunities, *IS Control J.*, 3, 40–43, 2003.
10. Gallegos, F., Due professional care, *Inf. Syst. Control J.*, 2, 25–28, 2002.
11. Gallegos, F., Maintaining IT audit proficiency: The role of professional development planning, *IS Control J.*, 6, 20–23, 2002.
12. Gallegos, F., IT audit career development plan, *IS Control J.*, 2, 16, 17, 2003.
13. Gallegos, F. and A. Carlin, IT audit: A critical business process, *Computer Magazine*, pp. 87–89, Vol. 40, No. 7, IEEE, July 2007.
14. Gallegos, F., R. Richardson, and F. Borthick, *Audit and Control of Information Systems*, Thomson Corporation–South-Western, Cleveland, OH, 1987.
15. High Technology Crime Investigation Association, HTCIA.org.
16. Information Systems Audit and Control Association, *2003 CISA Examination Domain*, ISACA Certification Board, Rolling Meadows, IL, 2002.
17. The ISACA Model Curriculum Task Force, *Model Curricula for Information Systems Auditing at the Undergraduate and Graduate Levels*, 2nd Edition, Information Systems Audit and Control Foundation, Carol Stream, IL, 2005.
18. Kruse, W. G. and J. G. Heiser. *Computer Forensics. Incident Response Essentials*, Addison-Wesley, Boston, 2001.
19. Looho, A. and F. Gallegos, IS audit training needs for the 21st century: A selected assessment, *J. Comput. Inf. Syst., Int. Assoc. Computer Inf. Sys.*, 41(2), 9–15, 2000–2001.
20. Menkus, B. and F. Gallegos, *An Introduction to IT Auditing*, Auerbach EDP Auditing Series, 71-10-10.1, CRC Press LLC, New York, 2001, pp. 1–14.

21. Nelson, B., A. Phillips, and C. Steuart. *Guide to Computer Forensics and Investigations*, Course Technology, Cengage Learning, Boston, MA, 2010.
22. The Comprehensive National CyberSecurity Initiative, 2012, http://www.whitehouse.gov/cybersecurity/comprehensive-national-cybersecurity-initiative.
23. National Strategy for Trusted Identities in Cyberspace; Enhancing Online Choice, Efficiency, Security and Privacy April 2011, http://www.whitehouse.gov/sites/default/files/rss_viewer/NSTICstrategy_041511.pdf.
24. Singleton, T., The ramifications of the Sarbanes–Oxley, *IS Control J.*, 3, 11–16, 2003.
25. Smith, M. and F. Gallegos, Red teams: An audit tool, techniques and methodology for information assurance, *Inf. Sys. Control J.*, 2, 51–56, 2006.
26. U.S. Department of Defense, Department of defense: Computer forensics laboratory, 2003, http://www.dcfl.gov/DCFL/aboutdcfl.asp.
27. U.S. General Accounting Office, *Government Audit Standards, Exposure Draft*, 2002.
28. Vacca, J.R., *Computer Forensics: Computer Crime Scene Investigation*, Charles River Media Inc, Hingham, MA, 2002.
29. U.S. Department of Justice, *Prosecuting Computer Crimes*, 2nd Edition, 2010, http://www.justice.gov/criminal/cybercrime/ccmanual/index.html.

Chapter 4

Audit Process in an Information Technology Environment

Whether the IT audit reviews operations or applications, the controls applied in these areas need to be verified. The IT auditor's function complements that of the internal auditor by providing reasonable assurance that assets are safeguarded, information is timely and reliable, and all errors and deficiencies are discovered and corrected promptly. Equally important objectives of this function are better control, complete audit trails, and compliance with organizational policies. For example, in 2009, GAO issued *Federal Information System Controls Audit Manual* (FISCAM) as a guide to help IT control specialist conduct information system control audits within the federal government.

This chapter looks at the audit process for IT and the demands that will be placed on the profession in the future. IT auditors must prepare for and move into a world that literally depends on large, heavily integrated computer systems. These systems may be characterized by the use of emerging technologies such as distributed processing, local area networking, client/server, Internet/intranet, microtechnology, firmware, satellite transmissions, and others.

Today's IT auditor is faced with many concerns about the exposure of computer information systems to a multitude of risks. From these concerns arise the objectives for the audit process and function. Achieving these objectives requires the support and involvement of all the participants described in this chapter.

Audit Universe

One of the best practices for an audit function is to have an audit universe. The audit universe is an inventory of all the potential audit areas within an organization. Building an audit universe documents the key business processes and risks of an organization. Incorporating enterprisewide risk assessments into audit plans has emerged as a best practice for organizations. The IIA's Standard 2010 encourages the establishment of risk-based plans to determine the priorities for internal audit activity. An audit universe includes the organization's objectives, the processes that support those objectives, risks of not achieving those objectives, controls that mitigate the risk, and audit objectives for each audit area. Tying the audit universe to organization objectives, links the entire audit process to business objectives and risks, making it easier to communicate the impact of control deficiencies.

The audit universe is also an essential building block to a properly risk-based internal audit process. Typically, audit groups prepare annual audit schedules along with the annual planning process to determine the number of hours available and the number of audits that can be performed. The audit universe and audit planning process is an ongoing process as an organization changes, new risks arise or existing risks change, and new regulations are introduced. Audit organizations can either remove lower-priority audits from the schedule or hire external auditors to supplement internal staff.

IT audit will have IT-specific processes to include in the audit universe. COBIT provides a comprehensive list of critical IT processes, which can be used as a starting point. The COBIT processes can then be customized to the organizations' environment. IT audit can also help audit management identify the applications associated with the critical business and financial processes.

The general objective is to verify those processes and controls that are necessary to make the area being audited free from significant exposures to risk. This objective also encompasses validating adherence of the systems under examination to appropriate standards (e.g., financial accounting should conform to GAAP).

Once the audit universe has been developed, the next step in the planning process is to perform a risk assessment for each universe item. The risk assessment will analyze exposures and help prioritize audit projects.

Risk Assessment

Risk assessment is the foundation of the audit function. It determines what audits/projects are to be performed. Risk assessment assists the audit function in developing the audit schedule and the process for planning individual audit projects. It also improves the quality, quantity, and accessibility of planning data such as risk areas, past audits and results, and project budget information.

Risk assessment is a technique used to examine potential projects in the audit universe and choose projects that have the greatest risk exposure. Risk assessment is important in that it provides a framework for allocating audit resources to achieve maximum benefits. Given that there are an unlimited number of potential audit projects, but a limited amount of audit resources, it is important to focus on the right projects. The risk assessment approach provides explicit criteria for systematically evaluating and selecting audit projects.

In today's environment, it is difficult to keep pace with organization and regulatory changes to provide timely information on internal controls. Change increases the audit universe, the number of business partners (i.e., vendors), and the number of projects where an objective and independent perspective is needed. An effective planning process allows auditing to be more flexible and efficient to meet the needs of a changing organization. These steps include

- Quickly identifying changes in organization risk areas
- Quickly identifying new risk areas as they arise

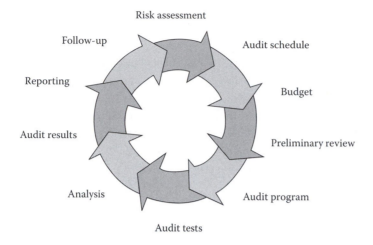

Exhibit 4.1   Cyclical process of auditing.

- Efficiently accessing current regulatory and legal information
- Taking advantage of information gathered during the audit process to improve risk assessment

Audit areas can be evaluated using a weighted scoring mechanism. However, audit management must evaluate the results using their knowledge of the organizational objectives and environment to make sure the priorities reflect reality. Audit areas may also be grouped to improve audit efficiency when reviewing similar processes.

Auditing is a cyclical process that uses historical and current information for risk assessment, analysis of controls, reporting to management, and then incorporating audit results into risk assessment (see Exhibit 4.1).

Audit Plan

Under its charter, the audit function should formulate both long-range and annual plans. Planning is a basic function necessary to develop the Annual Audit Schedule and perform individual audits. Such plans describe what must be accomplished, include budgets of time and costs, and state priorities according to organizational goals and policies. The objective of audit planning is to optimize the use of audit resources. To effectively allocate audit resources, internal audit departments must obtain a comprehensive understanding of the audit universe and the risks associated with each universe item. Failure to select appropriate items can result in missed opportunities to enhance controls and operational efficiencies. Internal audit departments that develop and maintain audit universe files provide themselves with a solid framework for audit planning. At a minimum, an IT audit plan should

- Define scope
- State objectives
- Structure an orderly approach
- Provide for measurement of achievement

- Assure reasonable comprehensiveness
- Provide flexibility in approach

At this level, the computer audit plan is stated in general terms. The intent is to provide an overall approach within which audit engagements can be conducted. Plans for specific audit engagements are then carried out to sufficient levels of detail to prepare budgets and actual work assignments. There is, however, another rationale for conceptualizing the computer audit plan at a general level; both the systems in development and the state of the art in computer technology are undergoing constant, dynamic change. Detailed plans at the functional level cannot hope to anticipate the pattern of such change. Thus, they would quickly become obsolete and ineffective.

A computer audit plan partitions the audit of IT into discrete segments. These segments describe a computer systems audit as a series of manageable audit engagements and steps. At the detailed planning or engagement level, these segments will have objectives that are custom-tailored to implement organizational goals and objectives within the circumstances of the audit.

Thus, computer auditing does not call for "canned" approaches. There is no single series of detailed steps that can be outlined once and then repeated in every audit. The computer audit plan, therefore, is an attempt to provide an orderly approach within which flexibility can be exercised.

A professional IT audit environment supports a professional staff by maximizing the effect of special skills and abilities and minimizing redundant activity. Key prerequisites for a professional environment are a firm management commitment to discipline and orderly planning and a structured methodology for auditing.

Once estimated audit hours and other factors have been considered, audit management should be able to arrange the audit schedule. The next step in the process is the creation of the annual schedule.

Developing an Audit Schedule

Auditing departments create annual audit schedules to gain agreement from the board on audit areas, communicate the audit areas with the functional departments, and create a project/resource plan for the year. The audit schedule should be linked to current business objectives and risks based on their relative cost in terms of potential loss of goodwill, loss of revenue, or noncompliance with laws and regulations.

Annual schedule creation is the process of determining the total audit hours available, then assigning universe items to fill the available time. As mentioned previously, to maximize the risk assessment process, "high risk" universe items should be given top audit priority. Schedule creation should be performed in conjunction with the annual risk assessment process; this will enable internal audit departments to account for the changes in risk rankings and make any necessary additions or deletions to the audit universe. Once the available audit hours are determined, audit management can prepare the audit plan.

Planning and scheduling are ongoing tasks as risks and priorities change or resources and timelines change. When this happens, it is important to communicate the change to the audit committee/board and impacted functional departments.

Audit Budget

Ideally, the audit budget should be created after the audit schedule is determined. However, most organizations have budget and resource constraints. An alternative approach may be necessary when building the audit schedule. After determining the audit priorities, audit management would determine the number of available hours to determine how many audits they can complete in a year. If this is the case, audit management needs to clearly communicate to the audit committee/board the high-priority audits that will not be completed and the additional cost to complete these audits. This allows the audit committee/board to make informed decisions on the audit schedule and budget.

Budget Coordination

Before the first question is ever asked, first inquiry made, or an observation commenced, a well-thought-out budget must be completed and adhered to by the IT audit manager. The managers must know the capabilities of the staff at their disposal. The importance of knowing the associates involved is extremely vital when one is working with sensitive material, a sensitive auditee, or technologically complex software and systems. Most managers know that in today's market, personnel resources for this field are scarce. When negotiating the audit, the manager should consider adding a little more time for training and error-correction purposes. After all, if the manager trains the staff right the first time, the staff will eventually become another added bonus to the audit team. Most, if not all, audits the auditors have conducted involved some sort of training, and the time allotted to that training was given.

Audit Preparation

Audit preparation is composed of all the work that is involved in initiating an audit. The functions include audit selection, definition of audit scope, initial contacts and communication with auditees, and audit team selection. In preparation for the audit, for example, the auditor should become familiar with prior audit reports on the financial accounting systems to be audited.

Audit Scope Objectives

The scope of the audit defines the area to be reviewed. It should clearly state the process areas, controls, geographic or functional area, time period, and other specifics to delineate the area to be reviewed.

Audit objectives are formal statements that describe the purposes of the audit. By defining appropriate objectives at the outset, management can ensure that the audit will verify the correct functioning and control of all key audit areas. The objectives are derived from control objectives pertinent to the audit scope and the purpose of the application, activity, or installation under review. For example, to define the audit objective, the auditor should examine the organization's control objectives with regard to systems development projects.

Objective and Context

The objective and context of the work one is to perform is a key element in any audit environment and should not be overlooked. It is the basis by which all audits should be approached.

The *objective* is what we are trying to accomplish. The *context* is the environment in which we perform our work. Thus, everything ultimately depends on both our objective and the context of the work we are to perform. That is to say, the decisions we make about the scope, nature and timing of our work depends on what we're trying to do (i.e., gain assurance of an A/R balance, gain assurance that a Website is secure, gain assurance that a new application will work correctly when implementation is complete, gain assurance that a business is prepared to continue functioning after a riot) and that the environment we are working in (i.e., a big company versus a small company, a domestic organization with a centralized common systems versus a multinational organization with multiple divisions using a variety of disparate applications on a multitude of computer platforms, an organization based in Los Angeles or New York versus an organization based in Fargo, North Dakota or Portland, Oregon). Keep in mind what works well for one organization, may not work as well in another, based on many combinations of objective and context.

For example, if the auditor has a General Controls Assessment, the audit objectives may be to verify that all controls related to the data center, the building in which the data center is located, Accounts Receivable (A/R), Accounts Payable (A/P), are adequate. Therefore, the IT auditor needs to verify the controls because the financial auditors were relying on the computer system to provide them with the correct financial information. The context is where the auditor's true analytical skills come into play. Here, the environment is for the most part always different from shop to shop. The auditor must assess the context for which he or she has entered and make a decision as to how the environment should be addressed (i.e., big company, small company, large staff, and small staff).

Using the Plan to Identify Problems

The IT audit objectives, charter, and plan provide the guidance for auditing the organization's integral processes. The organization and its management must participate in and support this effort fully. Commitment can be gained if participants recognize that a good plan can help pinpoint problems in a highly dynamic, automated IT environment. Thus, it should be the responsibility of all participants not only to help pinpoint such problems, but also to assist in the measurement and quantification of problems.

Identifying, measuring, and quantifying problems in the IT area are difficult. The IT field is technologically complex and has a language of its own. Participants in the formulation of the IT audit plan, and particularly the IT auditors themselves, must have sufficient experience and training in technical matters to be able to grasp key concepts and abstractions about systems. For example, abstractions about IT might include significant aspects that are susceptible to naming, counting, or conceptualizing. Understanding the systems at this level can lead to the identification of major problem areas. Audit concentration, then, may be directed to the major problem areas most likely to yield significant results.

Based on this identification of problems, the auditor determines what additional data might be required to reach evaluation decisions. The audit process, therefore, must be flexible enough to combine skilled personnel, new technology, and audit techniques in new ways to suit each situation. However, this flexibility of approach requires documentation in planned, directed steps. Systems that are understood poorly (or that have been designed without adequate controls) can result in lost revenues, increased costs, and perhaps disaster or fraud.

Modern management accounting has an obligation in this new environment. Fulfilling this obligation can be addressed in two fundamental steps. First, the management must encourage and support the development of professional audit teams. Second, the management must assure more vigorous and effective accounting participation in the development and evaluation of systems controls.

Audit Process

The time-honored method of using the general ledger as the starting point for audits is not enough in examinations of modern computer systems. However, the experienced auditor or financial manager recognizes the value of having a consistent, logical, audit, or management approach that accommodates both manual and computerized methods. Although auditing computer systems requires changes from the traditional general-ledger approach, any new audit approach should be applicable universally.

For example, we mentioned that GAO issued its FISCAM. The revised FISCAM reflects changes in (1) technology used by government entities, (2) audit guidance and control criteria issued by the NIST, and (3) generally accepted government auditing standards (GAGAS), as presented in Government Auditing Standards (also known as the "Yellow Book"). The FISCAM provides a methodology for performing IS control audits in accordance with GAGAS, where IS controls are significant to the audit objectives. However, at the discretion of the auditor, this manual may be applied on other than GAGAS audits. As defined in GAGAS, IS controls consist of those internal controls that are dependent on information systems processing and include general controls and application controls. This manual focuses on evaluating the effectiveness of such general and application controls. This manual is intended for both (1) auditors to assist them in understanding the work done by IS controls specialists and (2) IS controls specialists to plan and perform the IS controls audit. The FISCAM is not intended to be used as a basis for audits where the audit objectives are to specifically evaluate broader IT controls (e.g., enterprise architecture and capital planning) beyond the context of general and business process application controls.

Such universal approaches that apply equally to manual and computerized systems were formalized for the public accounting profession in the Statement on Auditing Standards (SAS 1). This standard has the effect of mandating a uniform, process-oriented approach to audit engagements. The approach depicted is a true process technique. That is, audit engagements follow a series of logical, orderly steps, each designed to accomplish specified end results. During implementation, initial efforts in the audit examination center are on gaining a basic understanding of the accounting systems. The IIA and ISACA standards provide similar guidance on the audit process. The difference in an IT audit is the specialized approach to the audit work and the skills needed to understand technology and the IT control environment.

The process continues to increase in depth in the study and examination of the applications that develop financially significant data for inclusion in financial statements. Exhibit 4.2 illustrates the steps involved and the workflow in the audit process.

Although schematic diagrams tend to indicate distinct steps, actual audit processes are less rigid. The phases of auditing activities typically overlap and involve some reassessment and retracing of procedures performed earlier. Typical phases of an audit engagement include

- Preliminary review
- Preliminary evaluation of internal controls
- Design audit procedures
- Test controls

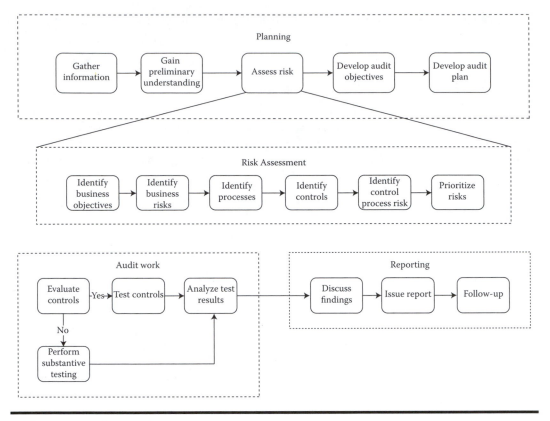

Exhibit 4.2   Audit workflow.

- ■ Final evaluation of internal controls
- ■ Substantive testing
- ■ Documenting results

Note that the scope of each type of testing depends on the outcome of the previous step. This relationship is discussed further in the following text.

The final, necessary phase of each audit engagement is reporting. However, reporting is not affected by the introduction of computers into a client's financial system and, thus, is not treated separately in the following discussion. This chapter discusses the phases of audit execution: audit planning, communication, and reporting.

Preliminary Review

In this step, the auditor should obtain and review summary-level information and evaluate it in relation to the audit objectives. The purpose of the preliminary review phase of an audit engagement is to gather information as a basis for formulating an audit plan, which is the end product of this phase. During preliminary review, the auditor will gather general information on the processes and systems under review. The auditor conducts this preliminary review at a general level, without examining details of individual applications and the processes involved.

General Data Gathering

The auditor begins the examination process by becoming acquainted, generally, with the company, its line of business, and its financial systems. Typically, an external auditor would tour the client company's plant and observe general business operations that bear upon customer service as well as on strictly financial functions.

Given this familiarity, the next level of general data gathering would include the accumulation or preparation of organization charts, particularly those for the accounting and IT functions. These audit requirements are no different from those for manual systems.

Should adequate organization charts be unavailable, the auditor must develop them. Once drawn, the charts should be reviewed with the client to secure an agreement that they represent the actual organization structure. This verification would be done through interviews and discussions with key executives in the accounting and IT areas. In addition, during these interviews, the auditor would secure copies of the company's chart of accounts and an accounting standards manual, if available.

For systems in which the client company uses computers to process financially significant data, the auditor would also gather a number of other specific items of evidential matter, including

- An overall narrative or an overview flowchart of the major applications subsystems and their interrelationships, including inputs and outputs
- Descriptions of the make and model of equipment units in the client's computer installation
- Programming languages, data processing standards, and procedures manuals used in the computer system
- Data control procedures
- Assurance that an uninterruptible power supply is in place or that an alternate power source is available
- Procedures and provisions for backup, recovery, and restart of operations in the event of equipment failure or accidental destruction of data
- Data and source statement library procedures
- Procedures for job setup and operations within the data center
- The installation's documentation standards manual or such documentation standards as exist
- Descriptions of physical security control transactions

Methods applied in gathering these data are chiefly interviews and reviews of documentation. Physical inspection techniques are used both to gather data and to validate existing documents or representations made during the interviews. For example, a single visit to the computer center can provide both data gathering and validation opportunities for determining equipment configurations, library procedures, operating procedures, physical security controls, and data control procedures.

Many of these procedures are substantially the same regardless of whether the accounting system is computerized or not. Differences associated with the audit of computerized systems center around changes in controls, documentation, audit techniques, and technical qualifications required by audit staff members.

Fact Gathering

Fact gathering is composed of all activities that help the auditor understand the audit subject. Such audit activities include a review of computer information systems and human interface practices, procedures, documents, narratives, flowcharts, and record layouts. Fact gathering requires observing, interviewing, flowcharting, and documenting each activity. If the auditor is using an electronic document management support system, how well this support tool is used to capture facts gathered should be determined.

Preliminary Evaluation of Internal Controls

In this step, the auditor determines which controls are essential to the overall audit objectives. This includes building a detailed understanding of the area being audited. To complete the understanding, the auditor interviews key personnel to determine policies and practices, and prepares supplemental audit information as required.

Design Audit Procedures

In this step, the auditor must prepare an audit program for the area being audited, select the verification techniques applicable to each area, and prepare the instructions for their performance.

An audit program is a formal plan for reviewing and testing each significant audit subject area disclosed during fact gathering. The auditor should select subject areas for testing that have a significant impact on the control of the application, activity, or installation and those that are within the scope defined by the audit objectives. IT audit areas are very specific to the type of audit. Following are some examples of the types of audits conducted in IT. More detailed information on how to audit IT processes, applications, and operations are discussed in Chapters 8 through 22.

Types of IT Audits

For IT controls, COBIT is a good starting point as it lists the key controls, objectives, and risks. This information then has to be customized to the particular organization objectives, processes, and technology.

Reviewing Information System Policies, Procedures, and Standards

Today, the auditor, especially the new breed of IT auditors, has the level of knowledge, skills, and abilities to do a quality job and provide a quality assessment. But how can the IT manager better utilize the IT auditor to assist in providing objective, value-added contributions to their work? Techniques such as risk assessment, participation in corporate audit planning, developing IT audit skill and capability, and holding auditors to their standards of practice are ways of accomplishing this goal.

The techniques mentioned previously could work if supported by top management and IT management. The support of top management is essential. It is precisely the managerial initiatives that provide the opportunity for reducing threats of carelessness, corruption, and incompetence. It is equally essential to gain the support of all members of the organization and design security systems so that they are as unobtrusive in the workplace as possible. These managerial initiatives to reduce risk can be combined with the more traditional defensive strategies and tactics of IS security to provide the best (most cost effective) approach to protecting corporate information assets.

IT Audit Support of Financial Audits

Once the auditor has gained a general familiarity with the client's accounting procedures, specific areas of audit interest must be identified. The auditor must decide what applications or subsystems will have to be examined at a more detailed level. As a basis for preparation of the audit plan, the auditor must also determine, in general, how much time will be required; what types of people and skills will be needed to conduct the examination; and, roughly, what the schedule will be.

This requirement applies even if the client is not using a computer. If computers are being used for financially significant applications, the auditor must determine their sophistication and extent of use. This preliminary study goes just deep enough for the auditor to evaluate the complexity and sophistication of the systems and determine the procedures to be followed in evaluating internal control. During the preliminary review phase, it is not necessary to go into detailed analysis, such as flowcharting of applications, be they manual or computerized.

Findings are formal statements that identify and describe inaccurate, inefficient, or inadequately controlled audit subjects. For example, an auditor found that changes made to an application were implemented without authorization. The auditor then discovered that the organization's procedures manual did not include instructions to seek management permission before making changes to applications.

Identifying Financial Application Areas

The identification of financial application areas is often referred to as areas of interest. This can be accomplished with the auditor gaining familiarity with the organization's accounting procedures and processes. Through the preliminary review of these applications and subsystems, the auditor will decide which applications need to be reviewed in detail. These audit steps contribute to the audit plan. As mentioned earlier, the audit plan provides the auditor with more in-depth information on how to accomplish the audit tasks and the time and resources needed.

The process of identifying financial application areas applies to all computer and noncomputer applications that are part of the financial process. With computerized applications, the importance of determining the financially significant applications has to be derived through preliminary analysis. The assessment of the sophistication of the application, its complexity, and extent of use are factors that come into play in deciding whether to select it and how one might evaluate it. The preliminary study/review phase is a critical step in the audit process that examines an organization's financial systems and provides the auditor with a basis for selecting audit areas for more detailed analysis and evaluation whether they are manual or computerized.

Auditing Financial Applications

Auditors involved in reviewing information systems should focus their concerns on the system's control aspects. They must look at the total systems environment—not just the computerized segment. This requires their involvement from the time a transaction is initiated until it is posted to the organization's general ledger. Specifically, auditors must ensure that provisions are made for

■ An adequate audit trail so that transactions can be traced forward and backward through the system

- The documentation and existence of controls over the accounting for all data (e.g., transactions) entered into the system and controls to ensure the integrity of those transactions throughout the computerized segment of the system
- Handling exceptions to, and rejections from, the computer system
- Unit and integrated testing, with controls in place to determine whether the systems perform as stated
- Controls over changes to the computer system to determine whether the proper authorization has been given and documented
- Authorization procedures for system overrides and documentation of those processes
- Determining whether organization and government policies and procedures are adhered to in system implementation
- Training user personnel in the operation of the system
- Developing detailed evaluation criteria so that it is possible to determine whether the implemented system has met predetermined specifications
- Adequate controls between interconnected computer systems
- Adequate security procedures to protect the user's data
- Backup and recovery procedures for the operation of the system and assurance of business continuity
- Ensuring technology provided by different vendors (i.e., operational platforms) is compatible and controlled
- Adequately designed and controlled databases to ensure that common definitions of data are used throughout the organization, redundancy is eliminated or controlled, and data existing in multiple databases is updated concurrently

This list affirms that the auditor is primarily concerned with adequate controls to safeguard the organization's assets and that the Sarbanes–Oxley Act of 2002 will ensure that quality and independence are maintained in this review process.

Management of IT and Enterprise Architecture

IT management must develop an organizational structure and procedures to ensure a controlled and efficient environment for information processing. This plan should also specify the computers and peripheral equipment required to support all functions in an economic and timely manner. With enterprise systems being very critical to medium-size and large businesses today, the need to monitor and validate operational integrity of an enterprise resource planning system (ERPS) is an important process. IT audit plays an important role in maintaining and monitoring the enterprise architecture.

Computerized Systems and Applications

The audit should verify that systems and applications are appropriate to the users' needs, efficient, and adequately controlled to ensure valid, reliable, timely, and secure input, processing, and output at current and projected levels of system activity.

Information Processing Facilities

The information processing facility must be controlled to ensure timely, accurate, and efficient processing of applications under normal and potentially disruptive conditions.

Systems Development

An IT audit should ensure that systems under development meet the objectives of the organization, satisfy user requirements, and provide efficient, accurate, and cost-effective systems and applications. The audit should also ensure that these systems are written, tested, and installed in accordance with generally accepted standards for systems development.

Client/Server, Telecommunications, Intranets, and Extranets

Many companies are decentralizing their traditional mainframe information processing facilities into LANs, wide area networks (WANs), value-added networks (VANs), virtual private networks (VPNs), and client/server and Internet/intranet/extranet systems. In a client/server environment, all applications that can be dedicated to a user are put on the client. All resources that need to be shared are put on the server. Auditors must ensure that controls are in place on the client (computer-receiving services) as well as the server (computer-providing services) and on the network (i.e., the supporting WANs and VANs) connecting clients and servers. In an Internet/intranet/extranet environment, the networks provide both applications and data to clients from the intranet or extranet server. Auditors must provide the same level of control assurance in an Internet/intranet/extranet environment as in the client/server environment with emphasis on two key intranet protocols: Transmission Control Protocol/Internet Protocol (TCP/IP) and Hypertext Transfer Protocol (HTTP).

Fieldwork and Implementing Audit Methodology

There are seven basic steps that can assist an auditor in the review of a computer-based system. These steps are valid regardless of computer environment, audit area, or system complexity. For each audit, the steps must be understood clearly, planned, and coordinated with the organizational objectives set for the audit function.

1. *Define objectives.* The auditor defines the general objectives to verify those processes and controls necessary to make the area being audited free from significant exposures to risk. This objective also encompasses validating adherence of the systems under examination to appropriate standards; for example, financial accounting should conform to GAAP.
2. *Build a basic understanding of the area being audited.* The auditor obtains and reviews summary-level information and evaluates it in relation to the audit objectives.
3. *Build a detailed understanding of the area being audited.* The auditor interviews key personnel to determine policies and practices, and prepares supplemental audit information as required to complete the understanding.
4. *Evaluate controls, strengths, and weaknesses.* The auditor determines which controls are essential to the overall audit objectives.
5. *Design the audit procedures.* The auditor prepares an audit program for the area being audited, selects the verification techniques applicable to each area, and prepares the instructions for their performance.
6. *Test the critical controls, processes, and apparent exposures.* The auditor performs the necessary testing by using documentary evidence, corroborating interviews, and personal observation.

7. *Evaluate the results.* In the final step, the auditor evaluates the results of the work and prepares a report on the findings.

These are seven basic steps that constitute the computer auditor's review.

Test Controls

Test the critical controls, processes, and apparent exposures. The auditor performs the necessary testing by using documentary evidence, corroborating interviews, and personal observation.

Validation of the information obtained is prescribed by the auditor's work program. Again, this work program is the organized, written, and preplanned approach to the study of the IT department. It calls for validation in several ways as follows:

- Asking different personnel the same question and comparing the answers
- Asking the same question in different ways at different times
- Comparing checklist answers to work papers, programs, documentation, tests, or other verifiable results
- Comparing checklist answers to observations and actual system results
- Conducting mini-studies of critical phases of the operation

Such an intensive program allows an auditor to become informed about the operation in a short time.

Final Evaluation of Internal Controls

The auditor performs the necessary testing by using documentary evidence, corroborating interviews, and personal observation.

Validation of Work Performed

Documentary evidence may consist of a variety of forms of documentation on the system under review. Examples could include notes from meetings on subject system, programmer notes, systems documentation, user manuals, and change control documentation from any system or operation changes since inception, and a copy of the contract if third parties involved. Many of these examples of documentary evidence after review may require the auditor to ask questions of the user, developer and managers, and help the auditor establish the appropriate test criteria to be used. It also helps in identifying the critical systems and processes to be tested.

Corroborating interviews and personal observations are also part of the testing controls process as the documentary evidence must be validated. For example, in interviewing a programmer for the system under review, the programmer states that the system has undergone recent changes not reflected in the current documentation. It is very important to identify what those changes were if those areas of the application or system were to be selected for control testing.

If we were examining a disaster recovery exercise, we could use personal observations of such an event to determine whether personnel followed appropriate procedures and processes. Through personal observations, one can observe and assess if personnel is following its operating procedures and plans, and is adequately prepared for the disaster simulated.

The quality of the auditor's fieldwork, audit methodology used, and testing of controls will rest with the validation techniques used, applied, and discussed in the next section.

Substantive Testing

Where controls are determined not to be effective, substantive testing may be required to determine whether there is a material issue with the resulting financial information. In an IT audit, substantive testing is used to determine the accuracy of information being generated by a process or application. Audit tests are designed and conducted to verify the functional accuracy, efficiency, and control of the audit subject. During the audit of an IS application, for example, the auditor would build and process test data to verify the processing steps of an application.

Auditing through the computer involves some additional steps in addition to those mentioned previously. Programs are run on the computer to test and authenticate application programs that are run in normal processing. Usually, the audit team will select one of the many GAS packages such as SAS, SPSS, qzCAATT, TopCAATs, or CA-Easytrieve(T) and determine what changes are necessary to run the software at the installation. The auditor will use this software to do sampling, data extraction, exception reporting, summarize and foot totals, and other tasks. Also, the auditor via microcomputer or client/server support can use packages such as Microsoft Access or Excel, IDEA, or ACL to perform in-depth analysis and reporting capability.

Computer audit teams increasingly are using such audit packages. Many large installations already have GAS installed for their internal auditors. Reasons include the fact that auditors are becoming qualified technically to alter programs and the facility's job control procedures so that packages may run successfully or similar support software may be integrated into the client/server environment. Also, better and easier to use audit tools are available for use in both environments. However, the auditor must be aware that each installation is unique in its own scheduling and eccentricities. Also, the installation may have to disrupt its normal processing schedule to accommodate these testing procedures.

The auditor selects and uses computer-aided audit tools to gather information and conduct the planned audit tests. The appropriate selection of audit tools and their effective and accurate uses are essential to adequate audit testing. For example, if the performance of an application requires analysis, a computer program analyzer or instrumentation package would be an appropriate choice for use as an audit tool. In addition, if the audit staff uses an electronic document management system to capture their audit work (e.g., interviews, electronic documents, and schedules), how well does the auditor use this support tool? Audit tools are discussed in more detail in Chapter 5.

Documenting Results

The final step involves evaluating the results of the work and preparing a report on the findings. The audit results should include the audit finding, conclusions, and recommendations.

Audit Findings

Audit findings should be formally documented and include the process area audited, the objective of the process, the control objective, the results of the test of that control, and a recommendation in the case of a control deficiency. An audit finding form serves the purpose of documenting both control strengths and weaknesses and can be used to review the control issue with the responsible

IT manager to agree on corrective action. This information can then be used to prepare the formal audit report and corrective action follow-up.

Analysis

Interviews and functional tests provide the raw materials for drafting the audit report. It cannot be emphasized enough that the design and performance of audit tests and interviews is essential to producing a quality audit report. If care is not taken, it becomes a classic case of garbage in, garbage out. Analysis is the most important factor in converting raw data into a finished product ready for inclusion in an audit report. Complete analysis of test information should provide the auditor with all the necessary information to write an audit report. Thorough analysis includes a clear understanding of

- The standards
- The cause of the deviation
- The control weakness that led to the deviation
- The materiality and exposure involved
- When possible, recommendations for corrective action

Analysis of the results of tests and interviews should occur as soon as possible after they are completed. Too often, the bulk of audit analysis occurs when the auditor sits down and writes the audit report. Timely analysis enables the auditor to determine the causes and exposures of findings early in the audit. This gives the auditor time to conduct further testing when necessary and allows everyone more time to create corrective actions. It also promotes the better use of audit time by determining findings and exposures with a minimum of testing. One of the purposes of the current work paper guidelines is to provide documentation of this analysis process. Four analysis steps may be needed:

- Reexamine the standards and the facts
- Determine the cause of the deviation
- Determine the materiality and exposure of the deviation
- Determine possible recommendations for corrective action

Although these are referred to as steps, they are not necessarily performed in chronological order. Likewise, completion of one step is not always necessary to complete later steps. As in all other areas of auditing, analysis requires judgment. Following is a discussion of each of the four steps in more detail. The terms finding, deficiency, problem, and issues are basically synonymous and mean the auditor identified a situation where controls or efficiencies can be improved. The situation, if acted upon, could result in enhanced productivity; the deterrence of fraud; or the prevention of monetary loss, personal injury, or environmental damage.

Reexamination

This is the most essential step in performing analysis. From this step, the auditor has the requisite data to make a judgment and formulate an opinion. The two factors under consideration are a standard (for comparison to the facts) and the facts (to compare to the standard). Step one reviews the standard, the facts, and whether a discrepancy actually exists between the two.

Standards

Standards are the procedures, operating guidelines, regulations, good business practices, or other predefined methodologies that define how an operation under audit should function. The standard establishes the viewpoint used by the auditor to evaluate test information. Where one stands determines what one sees.

With a standard you can audit anything. Conversely, without a standard you cannot make a judgment. Standards should be identified and evaluated at the beginning of the audit, and decisions on the appropriateness of standards should be addressed at the time the audit tests are created. Performance of the audit may give the auditor additional data to use in developing more appropriate standards.

The standard used must be clearly understood by the auditor and there must be sufficient confidence that the correct standard is used. Although the standard is a written, published procedure, it may be outdated, redundant, or not appropriate. Using the wrong standard can lead to incorrect or incomplete findings. Critical evaluation of a standard can also lead to the identification of inefficient practices. Four situations may occur while evaluating standards:

1. No standard exists either explicitly or implicitly (this may imply a high degree of risk since no standard is present to guide how a function should perform).
2. A standard exists but is not formal (i.e., good business practices).
3. The standard is formal and published but is redundant, not cost effective, no longer necessary, or no longer appropriate in some other manner.
4. The standard is formal and is appropriate for evaluating the work performed.

Facts

After reviewing the standard, the auditor must evaluate the gathered facts. The auditor should re-verify that deviations found are representative of the current control environment, have adequate support (photocopies or other hard evidence if possible), and, whenever possible, have an agreement with the audit client that deviations exist. To ensure that findings are accurate and descriptive of the population, samples should be

■ Large enough to reflect the behavior of the population from which they were drawn
■ Representative of all types of individual members in the population, and representative of the current control practices (timely)

If the sample fails to meet these characteristics, the deviation might not be the basis for a useful finding. To remedy this, it may be necessary to add to the sample or select an entirely new sample.

Verification

Finally, the auditor must again compare the findings to the reexamined standards to determine if a valid discrepancy still exists. If not, there is no issue and nothing to report. If the discrepancy is still apparent, then the analysis of the finding continues.

Cause

Once the auditor is sure of his or her understanding of the standard, the next step is to identify the cause of the deviation. This is based on the reexamination of the standards involved. Determining the cause of a deviation is answering the who, what, why, where, and when of a particular asset, transaction, or event. The answers provide the raw material to help make judgments about the control system currently in place. Determining the cause helps identify the exposures and aids in formulating recommendations.

Exposure and Materiality

This step examines the potential consequences of deviations. It answers the question, "Why does this need correction?" To answer this, the auditor must understand exposure and materiality.

Exposure results from subjecting an asset to potential loss, harm, damage, theft, improper or inefficient use, or neglect. Assets are tangible (money, buildings, computers) or intangible (an account, data, good will), human or nonhuman. The risk is posed by people (theft, neglect, misuse) or by the environment (fire or weather). The degree of exposure is related to the proximity and severity of the risk.

Proximity of the risk refers to how available the asset is to the person or environmental factor posing the risk. For example, there is less proximity to risk for small physical assets with high dollar values (e.g., computers) when there is limited access; inventory controls such as identification numbers and inventory lists; and a physical comparison of the asset to the list. The fewer controls in place, the greater the likelihood or more proximate the possibility of greater risk.

Severity of the risk refers to the potential amount of loss for each deviation. The greater the value of the asset exposed to risk and the closer the proximity to risk, the higher the potential loss for each deviation.

Materiality is a qualitative judgment about whether a deviation's frequency of occurring and degree of exposure are significant enough for the deviation to be corrected and included in the final audit report.

Frequency refers to how often an event will occur. It is the combination of the likelihood an individual transaction will deviate from the standard and the total number of transactions.

- With this understanding of exposure and materiality, answers to the following questions help identify why corrections should take place.
- What happened or can happen (exposure) because of the identified deviation? Remember the big picture. Start with the deviation found and expand outward to get to the big picture. Be specific regarding what assets, transactions, and business entities are affected. Name the risk(s) that the asset or transaction is exposed to.
- How serious (materiality) is this consequence in terms of some standard of value (money, time, personal injury, or ill will)? Identify which standard(s) of value apply to the deviation analyzed. Make measurements of the severity of the exposure. If extrapolating, use a statistically sound method of estimation.
- How often (frequency) has the deviation occurred or is it expected to occur?

Upon completing this step of analysis, the auditor should have a complete understanding of

- The standard used to measure the deviation
- Why the standard is an appropriate measure (or model) of how an asset/transaction should be handled or controlled
- The substantial, significant, compelling audit evidence (proof) that a deviation has occurred
- What caused the deviation to occur in terms of the department/person responsible for controlling the asset/transaction, what controls were not in place or not followed that allowed

the deviation to occur, and the effectiveness of management's review process and corrective action over the area under audit
■ The degree of exposure and the materiality of the deviation

Based on this, the auditor will have sufficient data to make an informed judgment about the state of controls and the efficiency of operations in the area under audit.

Conclusions

Conclusions are auditor opinions, based on documented evidence, that determine whether an audit subject area meets the audit objective. All conclusions must be based on factual data obtained and documented by the auditor as a result of audit activity. The degree to which the conclusions are supported by the evidence is a function of the amount of evidence secured by the auditor.

Recommendations

Recommendations are formal statements that describe a course of action that should be implemented to restore or provide accuracy, efficiency, or adequate control of audit subjects. A recommendation must be provided for each audit finding for the report to be useful to the management.

Examples of situations in which recommendations can be quantified are (1) unnecessary rework occurring due to a control flaw that, once changed or corrected, resulted in staff resources assigned to that issue being reduced and fewer complaints from both customers and employees and (2) identifying an error in a computer algorithm that causes reordering or inventory problems. In the first situation, the staff time spent in handling the existing problem can be quantified in terms of salary and overhead costs. Savings can be expressed as cost avoidance per month or per annum. In the next situation, computational processing errors, if caught in production, can be traced historically to show how much the company lost per month or per annum. In these two examples, loss can be shown in projected terms.

Working Papers

Working papers are the formal collection of pertinent writings, documents, flowcharts, correspondence, results of observations, plans for tests, results of tests, the audit plan, minutes of meetings, computerized records, data files or application results, and evaluations that document the auditor activity for the entire audit period. Typically, the final audit report is included in the working papers. A complete, well-organized, cross-referenced, and legible set of working papers is essential to support the findings and recommendations as stated in the audit report and achieve concurrence by audit management. Again, a review of electronic document organization and maintenance can be used to support this process.

Audit Report

The value of an audit can be immediate, and its effects can be short- or long term. The value can be quantifiable in tangible or intangible terms. The follow-up process is often ignored because of time or resource constraints. For example, IT audit recommendations might involve the change of a process or implementation of a control that can help the company monitor a problem area more effectively, results of which could be immediate, or it may take time to collect the necessary data to determine the effect as a result of the audit recommendations.

The value of an audit depends, in large part, on how effectively the results of the audit are communicated. The formal communication issued by the audit department describing the results of the audit is called an audit report. The report should include (at a minimum) the audit scope and objectives, a description of the audit subject, a narrative of the audit work activity performed, conclusions, findings, and recommendations. To be effective, audit reports must be timely, credible, readable, and have a constructive tone. No one element is more important than the others. They all work together to provide a professional report that is accepted and acted upon.

On receipt of the formal report by the IT department staff, IT management and affected staff should review the document immediately. Those items not already completed should be handled. Within a relatively short time, the fact that all discrepancies have been corrected should be transmitted to the audit staff in a formal manner. These actions are noted in the audit files, and such cooperation reflects favorably in future audits.

Follow-Up of Audit Recommendations

It is important to track corrective action to verify that control weaknesses have been remediated. This requires a formal process to track audit findings, corrective action, target date, and status for reporting to IT management and the audit committee/board. Audit support systems can make this an integral process by looking at an early example of the GAO's Status of Open Recommendation Support System (see Exhibit 4.3).

Director: Randolph C. Hite, (202) 512–6256
Information Technology
Business Systems Modernization: IRS Needs to Better Balance Management Capacity with System Acquisition Workload GAO-02-356 February 28, 2002
Recommendations for Executive Action
Recommendation: To address the escalating risks facing the Internal Revenue Service (IRS) on its Business Systems Modernization (BSM) program, the Commissioner of IRS should reconsider the planned scope and pace of the BSM program as defined in the fifth expenditure plan, with the goal of better balancing the number of systems acquisition projects under way and planned with IRS's capacity to manage this workload. At a minimum, the Commissioner's reconsideration should include (1) slowing ongoing projects and delaying new project starts to reduce BSM Office resource demands, (2) making correcting modernization management weaknesses a top priority and a matter of top management attention, and (3) reapplying resources—financial and human capital—available from slowed and delayed projects toward correction of control weaknesses.
Target: Department of the Treasury: Internal Revenue Service
Status: Open
Status Comments:
Recommendation: The Commissioner of IRS should address weaknesses in software acquisition management by immediately assessing critical BSM projects (i.e., Customer Account Data Engine, Security and Technology Infrastructure Release, and E-services) against the Software Engineering Institute's Software Acquisition Capability Maturity Model (SA-CMM) level 2 requirements.

Exhibit 4.3   GAO's status of open recommendation support system.

Target: Department of the Treasury: Internal Revenue Service
Status: Open
Status Comments:
Recommendation: The Commissioner of IRS should, based on this assessment, develop a plan for correcting identified weaknesses for these projects, including having an independent SA-CMM evaluation performed on them before submission of the next BSM expenditure plan.
Target: Department of the Treasury: Internal Revenue Service
Status: Open
Status Comments:
Recommendation: The Commissioner of IRS should submit, with the next expenditure plan, the results of this independent evaluation, along with a plan for ensuring that all BSM projects that have passed milestone 3 will meet SA-CMM level 2 requirements.
Target: Department of the Treasury: Internal Revenue Service
Status: Open
Status Comments:
Recommendation: The Commissioner of IRS should require all projects that did not pass milestone 3 as of December 31, 2001, to be assessed as SA-CMM level 2, and have a plan for correcting any project weaknesses found as a condition of milestone 3 approval.
Target: Department of the Treasury: Internal Revenue Service
Status: Open
Status Comments:
Recommendation: The Commissioner of IRS should, for configuration management, risk management, enterprise architecture implementation, human capital strategic management, integrated program scheduling, and cost and schedule estimating, ensure that commitments discussed herein for addressing residual weaknesses are implemented as planned, and report any deviations from these planned commitments to IRS's appropriations subcommittees.
Target: Department of the Treasury: Internal Revenue Service
Status: Open
Status Comments:
Recommendation: The Commissioner of IRS should, until contractor quality assurance weaknesses are corrected, increase the level of IRS oversight, scrutiny, and quality assurance of contractor activities.
Target: Department of the Treasury: Internal Revenue Service
Status: Open

Exhibit 4.3   (Continued) GAO's status of open recommendation support system.

This is a great example which shows how an organization can track and follow up on prior audit recommendations made in previous reports. The specific recommendations made to the organization and their status, the responsible GAO official contact, and the report and date of report are shown.

Communication Strategy

Good client/auditee relations are a necessity for productive and efficient audit results to occur. Conduct and professionalism are primary attributes, with respect to the auditee, even when they are difficult to work with. The main impression the auditor wants to give his or her client/auditee is that the auditor is there to help and not to find all their mistakes. Nobody enjoys being told they are wrong, especially from an outsider who is just visiting for a short while.

Speaking from experience, if auditors have a client/auditee that is reluctant to help them through the audit, it may become harder for the auditors to meet all the demands of their audit managers. It will also be equally difficult to meet the desired budget set for the audit engagement. If an auditor encounters such a problem, he or she should contact the audit manager as soon as possible. The manager will appreciate the alert and will most likely take care of the situation for the auditor.

To meet the needs of our changing customer base, our goal is to develop an effective strategy for communicating with our customers throughout the audit process. We will also address the identification of reportable issues, the method to be used to report audit issues, the point(s) during the audit process when issues will be communicated, and who will receive audit communications. A communication strategy should encompass the criteria for

- Identifying reportable issues
- Measuring the severity of the issues
- Determining the frequency of reporting issues
- Defining the point(s) during the audit process when issues are communicated
- Identifying the levels of management to which the issues are communicated

During the audit planning phase, the IT audit manager should meet with the CIO and senior members of IT management to gain their input and concurrence with the preliminary risk assessment of the IT processes in the audit universe. If there is an IT steering committee, the audit universe should be reviewed with it as well. This will help ensure alignment between IT, business, and audit on the key risk areas.

The next checkpoint will be a review of the annual audit schedule. As IT will be impacted by the audit activities, it is important to gain their agreement with the audits and dates to ensure support during the audit process. Of course, the audit schedule will also need to be agreed with the audit committee as part of the overall audit planning process.

At the beginning of each audit, it is important to meet with the CIO and impacted IT managers to introduce the audit staff and communicate the scope, objectives, schedule, budget, and communication process to be used throughout the engagement. This is also an opportunity for an open discussion of IT management's perception of risk areas, significant changes in the area under review, and identification of appropriate contacts in IT. It is important to communicate any changes in the scope, objectives, schedule, or staffing to IT management.

During the audit, communicate via interim status reports or meetings any items requiring immediate attention, scope changes, and audit progress. This is particularly important for long audit engagement (e.g., systems development reviews).

At the conclusion of audit tests, it is best to communicate the findings with IT management to gain their agreement on the finding and begin any corrective action. This will allow them to start working on the corrective action immediately and maybe even have the issue resolved before the conclusion of the audit. It will also save time during the reporting process, as the information is already prepared. A standard form can be developed that includes

- The control issue or risk area
- The problem (be sure to include quantifiable findings and impact wherever possible as this helps set context for the priority of the finding)
- Recommendations
- Management's response
- Target implementation date
- Responsibility for implementation

At the close of the audit, issue a draft report for review by all impacted parties. The review process will go much faster if the findings have already been agreed during the testing phase. After the audit report has been finalized, it is a good practice to schedule an exit meeting with the CIO to review the audit objectives and ask for feedback on the performance of the audit team. This meeting will provide valuable feedback into the performance of the audit staff and lessons learned for improving future engagements.

Postaudit communication includes reviewing open and completed corrective action. It is also a good practice to test the completion of corrective action to validate that the control is functioning as intended.

Conclusion

Over decades, the computer has been used to support daily operations, especially in science and business environments. Most companies find that they must use computer technology effectively to remain competitive. The nature of technology, however, continues to change rapidly. As a result, companies continue to integrate their accounting systems and operations. Diverse operating units are becoming computerized and end-user computing (EUC) is growing rapidly. The audit profession has made these adjustments as well. Worldwide, professional organizations have issued useful guidance and instruction to assist managers and the audit professionals.

Auditors are entrusted with a unique public service. The profession is increasingly called on to perform expanded services for its clients and the public at large. To maintain this high public image, auditors' services must be performed at the highest level of technical competence and integrity. Computers can be helpful in many ways, but auditors are also faced with certain problems when they must audit complexities.

The nature of auditing will undoubtedly continue to undergo substantial change as the level of technology improves. A proliferation in the number of computers and workstations (desktop to handheld) is also expected in the next millennium. Today's auditor must be able to identify important auditing controls available with computers and determine the impact of those controls on the company's overall structure. Auditors must understand the design of the client's computer system to carry out an efficient audit.

In brief, it is necessary to integrate computers into the audit process from project initiation to the final reporting stage. Full automation will enable auditors to make more efficient use of all available resources and enhance the credibility of the audit performed. Effective use of computer technology can empower auditors to conduct audits in today's highly automated environments.

Review Questions

1. What are the steps in planning the audit?
2. How can the audit plan help identify problems?
3. What is the preliminary review portion of an audit and why is it important?
4. What are the seven basic steps in reviewing computer-based systems?
5. The audit report and postaudit follow-up are important steps in the audit process, what are some of the major tasks that should be accomplished by the audit in these steps?

Multiple-Choice Questions

1. Which audit area involves definition of audit scope, initial contacts and communication with auditees, and audit team selection?
   a. Fact gathering
   b. Audit tests
   c. Audit preparation
   d. Audit objectives
2. Which audit area involves a formal plan for reviewing and testing each significant audit subject area disclosed during fact gathering?
   a. Audit objectives
   b. Audit program
   c. Audit tests
   d. Use of audit tools
3. Which IT audit area involves formal statements that describe a course of action that should be implemented to restore or provide accuracy, efficiency, or adequate control of audit subject?
   a. Audit tests
   b. Findings of the audit reports
   c. Recommendations of an audit report
   d. Conclusion of an audit report
4. At the minimum, an audit plan should include all but
   a. Definition of scope
   b. Objectives stated
   c. An orderly, structured approach
   d. A lack of flexibility in approach
5. The activities of a preliminary review may include
   a. General data gathering
   b. Identifying financial application areas
   c. Preparing the audit plan
   d. All of the above

6. The first step in conducting fieldwork and implementing audit methodology is
   a. Design audit procedures
   b. Define audit objectives
   c. Evaluate results
   d. Build a detailed understanding of area being audited
7. The purpose of follow-up is to
   a. Determine if the audit recommendations have been implemented
   b. Determine the progress made in implementing the audit recommendations
   c. Assess any potential savings/value added as a result of the recommendations
   d. All of the above
8. The advantage of tying the audit universe to organization objectives is that it
   a. Links the entire audit process to business objectives
   b. Improves management's understanding of the audit process
   c. Develops the communication plan for the audit
   d. None of the above
9. Audit risk assessment is an important step in the audit process because
   a. It leverages the abilities of audit staff and by minimizing redundant activity
   b. It provides a framework for communicating the audit results
   c. It provides a framework for allocating audit resources to achieve maximum benefit
   d. None of the above
10. Auditing is a cyclical process because
    a. Performing audit tests is an iterative process
    b. Audit results are used in subsequent risk assessments
    c. The audit universe is aligned to the business cycle
    d. All of the above

Exercises

1. You are an external auditor being asked to perform an application review of an end-user developed system. In this financial company, EUC development systems were causing a problem with the general ledger system due to the timing of the transfer of transactions. Data were transferred late, causing end of the month reports to be inaccurately stated. Managers who met to review reports of previous months' activity noticed a shortfall of $50,000 in some accounts. Prepare an audit plan for conducting an audit of this situation.
2. You are an internal auditor and you have been assigned an audit of the organization's software inventory. The Copyright Act of 1976 makes it illegal to copy computer programs except for backup or archival purposes. Any business or individual convicted of illegally copying software is liable for both compensatory and statutory damages of up to $100,000 for each illegal copy of software found on the premises. Software piracy is also a federal crime that carries penalties of up to 5 years in jail. Prepare a preliminary review for conducting this audit.

Answers to Multiple-Choice Questions

1—c; 2—b; 3—c; 4—d; 5—d; 6—b; 7—d; 8—a; 9—c; 10—b

Further Reading

1. Baker, N., *Under One Umbrella*. Internal Auditor. Institute of Internal Auditors, Altamonte Springs, FL, August 2007.
2. Benson, J., *The Importance of Monitoring*. Internal Auditor. Institute of Internal Auditors, Altamonte Springs, FL, August 2007.
3. Berry, L., *A Kinder, Gentler Audit*. Internal Auditor. Institute of Internal Auditors, Altamonte Springs, FL, October 2007.
4. Casas, E., *Tell It Like It Is*. Internal Auditor. Institute of Internal Auditors, Altamonte Springs, FL, October 2007.
5. Chaney, C. and K. Gene, *The Integrated Auditor*. Internal Auditor. Institute of Internal Auditors, Altamonte Springs, FL, August 2007.
6. Flipek, R., *IT Audit Skills Found Lacking*. Internal Auditor. Institute of Internal Auditors, Altamonte Springs, FL, June 2007.
7. Gallegos, F., The audit report and follow up: Methods and techniques for communicating audit findings and recommendations, *Inf. Syst. Control J.*, 4, 17–20, 2002.
8. Gallegos, F. and L. Preiser-Houy, *Reviewing Focus Database Applications*, EDP Auditing Series, 74-10-23, Auerbach Publishers, Boca Raton, FL, 2001, pp. 1–24.
9. Hyde, G., *Enhanced Audit Testing*. Internal Auditor. Institute of Internal Auditors, Altamonte Springs, FL, August 2007.
10. Institute of Internal Auditors Research Foundation (IIARF), *Systems Auditability and Control*, IIA, Altamonte Springs, FL, 1991, revised 1994.
11. ISACF, *COBIT: Control Objectives for Information and Related Technology*, 4.1 Edition, ISACF, Rolling Meadows, IL, 2009.
12. Manson, D. and F. Gallegos, *Auditing DBMS Recovery Procedures*, EDP Auditing Series, 75-20-45, Auerbach Publishers, Boca Raton, FL, September 2002, pp. 1–20.
13. Menkus, B. and F. Gallegos, *Introduction to IT Auditing*, #71-10-10.1, Auerbach Publishers, Boca Raton, FL, 2002, pp. 1–20.
14. Pareek, M., *Optimizing Controls to Test as Part of a Risk-based Audit Strategy*. Information Systems Audit and Control Association, Journal Online, 2006.
15. Singleton, T., The ramifications of the Sarbanes–Oxley Act, *Inf. Syst. Control J.*, 3, 11–16, 2003.
16. U.S. General Accounting Office, Assessing the Reliability of Computer Processed Data Reliability, External Version 1 October 2002.
17. U.S. General Accounting Office, *Federal Information System Controls Audit Manual (FISCAM)*, GAO-09-232G, February 2, 2009
18. U.S. General Accounting Office, *Government Auditing Standards, Exposure Draft*, 2010, http://www.gao.gov/yellowbook.
19. U.S. General Accounting Office, *Standards for Internal Control in the Federal Government*, November 1999, GAO/AIMD 00-21.3.1.

Chapter 5

Auditing IT Using Computer-Assisted Audit Tools and Techniques

Today's auditors work constantly with computerized records. It is likely that many audit clients either have eliminated or will eliminate a substantial portion of their paper documents and replace them with electronic documents filed only in computerized form. An auditor who is unable to use computerized audit tools effectively will be at a tremendous disadvantage. Therefore, today's auditor must be equipped with an understanding of alternative tools and approaches to test the operations of computerized systems and gather and analyze data contained in computerized files.

Computer technology has become an integral part of most organizational functions. Experts are forecasting continued improvement in the power and flexibility of computers and communication devices while costs are expected to decrease. Competitive factors have made it necessary for both auditors and clients to utilize new technological developments.

The computer is an important tool for many occupations. The auditing profession is particularly dependent on computers to perform most of the functions of the job. All types of audits and all types of auditors can take advantage of software tools and techniques to be more efficient and effective. This chapter describes software tools and techniques used in IT audits.

Audit productivity tools is software that help auditors to reduce the amount of time spent on administrative tasks by automating the audit function and integrating information gathered as part of the audit process.

Computer-assisted audit tools (CAATs) is software that help auditors evaluate application controls, and select and analyze computerized data for substantive audit tests.

Computer-assisted audit tools and techniques (CAATTs) is software and/or the methodology (such as data flow diagram or using SARF) applied to test or document selected IT processes and their integration within the IT environment.

This chapter examines the multitude of support tools available to the IT auditor, which assist him in auditing IT. As this chapter suggests, the auditor's toolkit is a critical component in conducting audits in today's complex environment. The chapter will provide examples of uses of CAATTs as a way of generating and documenting audit evidence (SAS 106 Audit Evidence). The chapter also introduces a fast-growing area of CAATTs, called computer forensics, supporting law enforcement, security, and audit professionals in computer forensics investigations. Also discussed is the use and application of Web analysis tools as audit tools for reviewing Web design, development, and usability.

Auditor Productivity Tools

The core of the audit process is analyzing controls to determine if they are adequate or need improvement. Many of the tasks associated with performing an audit, such as planning, developing, and documenting, although necessary, take time away from doing the actual analysis work. Thus, the need for automating the auditing functions. In addition, computer systems are highly complex and testing through the computer provides greater evidence of the functioning of controls.

Mainframe, client/server, and all forms of personal computers are an integral part of the audit processes. Technology is used as part of the audit process for the following activities:

- *Planning and tracking the annual audit schedule* using spreadsheets, database, and project management software
- *Documentation and presentations* using word processing, flowcharting, and graphics and video software
- *Communication and data transfer* using electronic connectivity and a centralized server or distributed resources
- *Resource management* using online work papers review and e-mail
- *Data management* using database, groupware, and intranet software
- *Reports and correspondence* using word processing, video software, conferencing software, collaborative writing, file sharing, and notation techniques

Audit Planning and Tracking

Risk assessment (such as those identified in SAS 106 (Audit Evidence) and SAS 107 (Audit Risk and Materiality in Conducting an Audit), audit schedule preparation and tracking, and budget preparations are necessary tasks in audit planning. Spreadsheets or database software can be used to record risk values such as those values required in SAS 107, develop an "audit universe," and prepare a budget. Project management software can be used to schedule audits and track the current status. Each of these solutions is a standalone. Their integration may not even be possible. Because planning tasks are interdependent, an integrated application would provide quicker update and ensure that all phases of planning are kept in sync. For example, the budget should provide sufficient costs to accomplish the audit schedule, or the audit schedule should not exceed the resources available.

Documentation and Presentations

The use of packages such as Microsoft Office suite provides "cut and paste" and linking functionality. These features facilitate the creation of consistent, accurate documents. For example, spreadsheet data containing functional testing results can be incorporated into a report document with a few clicks of a mouse. This same data can then just as easily be copied to a presentation slide and also be "linked," so that changes to the source documents will be reflected in any of the related documents. Software suite functionality saves time and ensures consistency and accuracy. Other support tools are the use of conferencing software to provide presentations to collaborators worldwide and the use of video capture capability to document audit evidence.

Communication

Because the auditor operates as part of a team, the need to share data as well as communicate with other members of the group is important. Providing immediate access to current data, electronic messaging, and online review capabilities allows staff to quickly communicate and gather research information for audits and special projects. In addition, auditors may occasionally need to operate from a host computer terminal, yet still have all the capability of a dedicated desktop processor. Therefore, it is necessary to have the required computer hardware, media hardware, protocol handlers, desired terminal software emulators, high-speed modems, and wireless connectivity at the audit site.

Electronic connectivity not only allows auditors to communicate but also provides access for audit clients to exchange information. For example, a member of senior management can be given access to the auditing risk universe database. This allows them to browse the database and suggest additions or changes to risk areas. Again, video conferencing capability allows meetings to be conducted and members to participate worldwide. They can see a spreadsheet, a graph, a video clip, receive live data feeds, and see responses from parties involved.

Data Management

Establishing electronic connectivity provides audit personnel with the capability to access and input data into a central data repository or knowledge base. The central data repository can archive historical risk, audit schedule, and budget data that can be accessed electronically by all authorized users throughout the audit group, regardless of physical location. Database applications can be developed to automatically consolidate data input electronically from all audit functions.

Through the use of databases, audit management can centrally monitor and have immediate access to critical activity such as audit schedule status, field audit status, fraud or shortage activity, and training and development progress. Database applications can automatically consolidate function-wide data and generate local and consolidated status and trending reports. Auditors can produce more effective products by leveraging off the knowledge of other auditors by having access to function-wide data. The database can contain information such as risk areas, audit programs, findings, corrective action, industry standards, best practices, and lessons learned. This information could be available for research whenever needed. Online storage of information will allow auditors to do text and word searches to find specific information in voluminous documents (e.g., insurance code).

It helps auditors to research an audit area to determine prior risk areas and functional testing approaches, identify related or interrelated areas, and review local or organization-wide corrective action. In addition to historical data, a repository provides a platform for interactive activities such as electronic bulletin boards. Audit personnel (and others, if authorized) can post new information or update old information.

A central repository provides immediate access to historical data (e.g., prior audit programs) so that time will not be wasted "reinventing the wheel." Building a central knowledge base facilitates applying lessons learned and increases the level of understanding about the business environment throughout the entire organization.

Resource Management

Another challenge for audit managers is to manage a remote workforce. Whether an auditor is working on a local audit or out in the field, managers need to be able to provide guidance and review work in progress. Managers need to provide feedback while the auditor is on location in case follow-up action is necessary.

A distributed workforce requires a very informed and responsive management team that can gather and disseminate information quickly. Important information can be rapidly gathered and disseminated function-wide through e-mail and internal electronic b-boards. Supervisors can provide immediate feedback and direction on audit projects through online review of electronic work papers.

Groupware

Groupware is a specialized tool or assembly of compatible tools that enables business teams to work faster, share more information, communicate more effectively, and do a better job of completing tasks. Groupware systems create a collaborative work environment. Today, we are seeing desktop conferencing, videoconferencing, coauthoring features and applications, e-mail and b-boards, meeting support systems, paging and voice applications, workflow systems, and group and subgroup calendars as examples of groupware products and support systems. A popular early groupware application is Lotus Notes. Lotus Notes is a client/server application development platform. It is designed to enhance group productivity by allowing users to share information, while also allowing individuals to customize private views of the information. Notes differ from traditional relational database software through its use of document-oriented databases. In Notes, a document is defined as an object containing text, graphics, video, and audio objects or any other kind of rich-text data. The ongoing work on Web 2.0 hopes to bring the next generation of groupware into use and practice.

Groupware is "a natural" for automating the audit function. These products use database features and workflow processing that can be used to store and integrate information gathered and used in the audit process. For example, risk assessment information feeds audit planning, and audit results feed audit reporting and update the risk assessment model. There are several products on the market that use groupware products such as Lotus Notes or Microsoft Office to automate the audit process.

Using Computer-Assisted Audit Tools in the Audit Process

As mentioned in Chapter 3, the American Institute of Certified Public Accountants (AICPA) issued the Statement on Audit Standard (SAS) 94, "The Effect of Information Technology on the Auditor's Consideration of Internal Control in a Financial Statement Audit." This SAS does not change the requirement to perform substantive tests on significant amounts but states, "It is not practical or possible to restrict detection risk to an acceptable level by performing only substantive tests." When assessing the effectiveness and integrity of the design and operation of controls, it is necessary for the auditor to test and evaluate these controls. The decision to test and evaluate is not related to the size of the firm but the complexity of the IT environment. Therefore, CAATTs play a very important role in the performance of audit work.

Of the more recent SASs, SAS 104 through SAS 111 require the auditor and the organization to carefully assess the risks of material misstatement (RMM) of the financial statements and what actions the organization is taking to reduce their risks. The AICPA's Information Technology membership sections developed their guide, "IT Considerations in Risked Based Auditing: A Strategic Overview" to help auditors implement these standards. These standards can help clients to identify control weaknesses and reduce the amount of substantive procedures required due to a greater reliance on controls and the use of CAATTs. Of these SASs (104-111), there is greater emphasis related to the impact of IT on five of them: 106, 107, 108, 109, and 110.

CAATTs can be used in a variety of ways to evaluate the integrity of an application, determine compliance with procedures, and continuously monitor processing results. Information systems auditors review application systems to gain an understanding of the controls in place to ensure the accuracy and completeness of the data. When adequate application controls are identified, the auditor performs tests to verify their effectiveness. When controls are not adequate, auditors must perform more extensive testing to verify the integrity of the data. To perform tests of applications and data, the auditor may use CAATTs. Many tools and techniques have been developed that offer significantly improved management control and reduced costs if properly applied. Automated techniques have proven to be better than manual techniques when confronted with large volumes of information. The auditor, by using automated techniques, can evaluate greater volumes of data and quickly perform analysis on data to gather a broader view of a process. Four software packages are ACL, CA-Easytrieve (T), SAS, and IDEA. These tools can be used to select a sample, analyze the characteristics of a data file, identify trends in data, and evaluate data integrity. In addition to auditing software, other software products can be used for analyzing data. For example, Access can be used to analyze data, create reports, and query data files. Excel can also be used to analyze data, generate samples, create graphs, and perform regression or trend analysis.

Also, as mentioned earlier, there may be situations where the auditor may be required to conduct tests and evaluate IT controls and perform substantive tests to obtain sufficient information and evidence regarding financial statement assertions. If the auditor is using SAS 107 (Audit Risk and Materiality in Conducting an Audit), the auditor will look at audit risk and materiality as the basis for the audit approach to be used. Examples of some of these situations can be

- Applications or systems involving electronic data interchange (EDI) and financial transactions
- Electronic payment systems that transmit electronic transactions from one company network to another
- Decision support systems that involve automatic reasoning or artificial intelligence or heuristic scenarios where they support decision making within the organization processes and have financial implications
- Applications that use technology such as neural network to assess financial conditions using ratio application in calculation of credit worthiness
- In systems where enterprise resource architecture is used to integrate the enterprise resource planning systems, blending legacy data with newer support systems
- In systems that provide electronic services of all types to customers, especially where the IT system initiates bills for services rendered and processes the billing transaction
- Computer programs that perform complex calculations involving money or resulting in a financial decision, present or future, such as reorder points, commissions, retirement or pension funds, and collection of accounts

A large part of the professional skills required to use computer-assisted auditing techniques lies in planning, understanding, and supervision (e.g., SAS 108—Planning and Supervision) in applying the appropriate audit tools/techniques and conducting the appropriate audit functions and tests. The computer has a broad range of capabilities. By way of illustration, four broad categories of computer auditing functions can be identified:

■ Items of audit interest
■ Audit mathematics
■ Data analysis
■ System validation

Items of Audit Interest

The auditor can use the computer to select material items, unusual items, or statistical samples of items from a computer-maintained file. The auditor has alternatives for the application of the computer to select items of audit interest. For example, the auditor can

■ Stipulate specific criteria for selection of sample items
■ State relative criteria and let the computer do the selection

An example of selection by specific criteria might be a specification that the computer identifies all transactions of $100,000 or more and prepares a report for audit review. However, the auditor could take a relative approach and instruct the computer to select the largest transactions that make up 20% of the total dollar volume for a given application.

This approach abridges manual audit procedures because the auditor can rely on the computer's selection of items of interest. If the computer were not used, the auditor would have to validate the selection process. Under traditional approaches, for example, it would be common for an auditor to ask client personnel to list all transactions of $100,000 or more. With the computer, the auditor can be satisfied that the selection program has looked at the total universe of accounts payable items. The validation of the selection process is inherent in the auditor's developing and accepting the computer-auditing application program.

Audit Mathematics

Performing extensions or footing can be a cost-effective payoff area for the application of computers in auditing—particularly if the calculations can be performed as a by-product of another audit function. For example, suppose the computer is being used to select significant items from an accounts receivable file. In the process of looking at this file, the computer can be programmed to extend and foot all invoicing transactions. Because of the speed of the computer, these calculations can be performed on 100% of the items in a file with no significant addition of time or cost for this processing.

By contrast, extensions and footings are both tedious and costly under conventional manual examination techniques. Typically, the auditor must limit examination of any given application to extension and footing of a judgmental sample covering a few short intervals of the period under examination. Clearly, reliance can be far higher when these verification calculations are performed on complete files.

Remember, however, that the computer has limitations in this area. Although it can be programmed to make many logical comparisons and tests, the computer cannot supplant human judgment in examining items to be tested.

Data Analysis

Using the computer for analysis of data represents a major opportunity for innovation by the auditor. The computer can compare and summarize data and can represent data in graphic form. Data analysis programs use techniques such as

- Histograms
- Modeling
- Comparative analysis

"Histograms" are bar charts showing graphic relationships among strata of data. In computer-assisted auditing, histograms typically are graphic representations of frequency distributions of records within data files. By picturing these relationships in graphic form, histograms give the auditor an improved perspective on the analysis of financial statements. The histogram is, in effect, a snapshot showing the substance, makeup, and distribution of data within an organization's accounting system.

With a histogram, auditors can apply their judgment in identifying and selecting appropriate testing techniques. By comparison, given a large collection of data about which such distribution data are not known, the auditor performs testing on a relatively blind basis. In such cases, the auditor cannot be sure of the significance of data until after testing is well along. With a histogram, items of significance for testing can be identified in advance because their relationship to the accounting universe is emphasized graphically.

"Modeling" is a technique by which the auditor can compare current data with a trend or pattern as a basis for evaluating reasonableness. For example, the auditor can develop a model based on several years of financial statements. Then the current year's total revenue can be put into the model. The computer can generate a *pro forma* financial statement based on past revenue or cost relationships. The *pro forma* statement is compared with the actual financial statements as a test of reasonableness.

Both techniques—histograms and modeling—add new content and dimensions of information to the audit process through the use of the computer. With these methods, the auditor is no longer restricted simply to validating data provided by applications personnel. With these automated techniques, the auditor generates figures or snapshots of financial data to test the reasonableness of representations under examination.

"Comparative analysis" is a proven, cost-effective application of computers within audit examination that involves the comparison of sets of data to determine relationships that may be of audit interest. For example, the computer may be used to compare the inventory files of the previous and current years. Wide variations in year-end balances could lead to reviews for possible obsolescence. A failure to match part numbers from the previous and current years might trigger testing procedures to determine whether old items have been dropped or new ones added.

Flowcharting Techniques

Emphasis on developing an understanding of client accounting systems is particularly appropriate during the application analysis phase of an audit engagement. It is important for the auditor to understand the relationship of each application to the conduct of the client company's business. Even where a computer plays a critical role, the auditor should avoid having audit activities become too technical and detailed too soon.

Another practice to be avoided is the tendency to treat manual and computerized elements of accounting systems as separate, distinct entities. Companies process data manually and on computers in a planned continuum. Manual and mechanized procedures usually are interdependent. The auditor should treat them accordingly. Thus, in walking through applications or subsystems, the auditor should include the entire manual and mechanized procedures that go into the preparation and presentation of information in client financial statements.

Where individual applications are concerned, the auditor concentrates on two primary functions:

1. Gathering samples of source documents, input forms, and output documents on reports. Documents should include both manually and computer-produced forms and reports.
2. Flowcharting each application in continuity. The relationship between manual and automated procedures and identification of control points, where applicable, should be included.

Auditors prepare application flowcharts using standard symbols and techniques. Flowcharts developed during the application analysis phase of an audit engagement are most useful if they distinguish processing according to department, function, or company area. There are some very good application support packages for flowchart development as well as the power of the word processor to build diagrams and illustrations of the process as illustrated in Exhibit 5.1.

Flowcharting as an Analysis Tool

As illustrated in Exhibit 5.2, for a computer auditor, flowcharts represent a method for identifying and evaluating control strengths and weaknesses within a system under examination. It can be time consuming to build an understanding of strengths and weaknesses within a system to be audited. However, identification of strengths and weaknesses often is crucial because the entire direction of the remainder of an audit is toward substantiating and determining the effect of identified control weaknesses.

For example, SAS 109 requires the auditor gain an understanding of the entity and its environment and determine those controls relevant to the audit. The auditor must have an understanding of the nature and complexity of the systems that are part of the control environment being audited. One way of gaining that understanding is through any existing documentation which may provide a visual illustration of the system under review and any interaction with other systems. Any existing documentation (flowcharts, systems charts, flow diagrams, etc.) provides a benchmark for the auditor's review.

As a step toward building the needed understanding of control weaknesses, the audit staff should develop a flow diagram of all information processed. The flow diagrams, or audit data flow diagrams, as depicted in Exhibits 5.1 and 5.2, should encompass all information processed, from source documents to final outputs. Either automated or manual techniques can be used in preparing these audit data flow diagrams. With either approach, the process leads to the evaluation of a number of elements of a system, including the following:

■ Quality of system documentation
■ Adequacy of manual or automated controls over documents
■ Effectiveness of processing by computer programs (i.e., whether the processing is necessary or redundant and whether the processing sequence is proper)
■ Usefulness of outputs, including reports and stored files

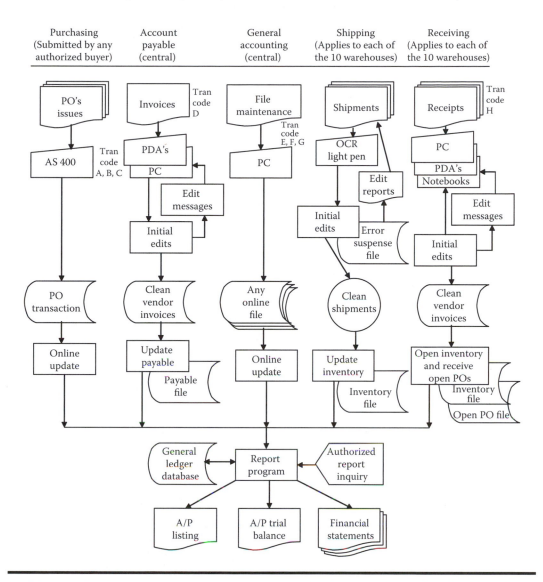

Exhibit 5.1 Database computer accounting system implementation under distributed processing concept.

Steps followed in the development of flowcharts and their use as audit evaluation tools include

- Understanding how data are processed by computers
- Identifying documents and their flow through the system
- Defining critical data
- Developing audit data flow diagrams
- Evaluating the quality of system documentation
- Assessing controls over documents
- Determining the effectiveness of processing under computer programs
- Evaluating the usefulness of reports

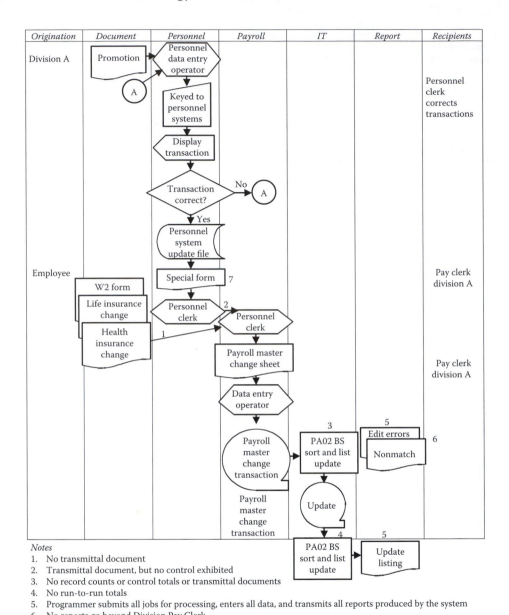

Exhibit 5.2 The payroll process from an auditor's control-oriented view.

Understanding How Computers Process Data

The auditor should build an understanding of how the system under examination generates its data. This understanding should encompass the entire scope of the system from preparation of source documents through to final distribution and use of outputs. While learning how the system works, the auditor should identify potential areas for testing, using familiar audit techniques such as

- Reviewing corporate documentation, including system documentation files, input preparation instructions, and users' manuals
- Interviewing organization personnel, including users, systems analysts, and programmers
- Inspecting, comparing, and analyzing corporate records

Identifying Documents and Their Flow through the System

To understand document flow, certain background information must be obtained through discussions with corporate officials, from previous audits or evaluations, or from system documentation files. Because this information may not be current or complete, it should be verified with the responsible programmer or analyst. The auditor will have to obtain

- Name (title) of the computer product
- Purpose of the product
- System name and identification number
- Date the system was implemented
- Type of computer used (manufacturer's model) and location
- Frequency of processing and type of processing (batch, online)
- Person(s) responsible for the computer application and database that generates the computer product

A user or member of the computer center staff may already have a document flow diagram that shows the origin of data and how it flows to and from the computer. (This diagram should not be confused with either a system flowchart that shows detailed computer processing of data or a program flowchart that describes a computer program.)

More often than not, the auditor will have to develop document flow diagrams in a format that is workable in a given situation, whether it is a narrative description, a block diagram using simple symbols, a flowchart using standard symbols, or some combination. The document flow diagram or narrative description should include

- Each source document, by title and identification number, with copies of the forms attached
- Point of origin for each source document
- Each operating unit or office through which data are processed
- Destination of each copy of the source document and the action applied to each copy (filed, audited, entered into a computer, etc.)
- Actions taken by each unit or office in which the data are processed (recorded in books of account, unit prices or extensions added, control numbers recorded and checked, etc.)
- Controls over the transfer of source documents between units or offices to assure that no documents are lost, added, or changed (controls include record counts, control totals, arithmetic totals of important data, etc.)
- Recipients of computer outputs

Document flow descriptions should not encompass actual computer processing that takes place within a portion of the system treated as a "black box." Processing details are beyond the scope of reliability assessment. If computer output is the product of more than one input, this condition should be noted clearly in the document flow description.

Defining Critical Data

The auditor must build a clear understanding of the data being recorded within the system under study. Therefore, the individual elements of data must be defined. Titles can be deceptive. For example, is a cost derived from the current period or is it cumulative? Is the cost accrued or incurred? What are the components of a cost? Has the composition of cost changed during the fiscal periods under review?

The organization's data element dictionary is a good source for such definitions. If a data dictionary is not available, a record layout may contain the needed definitions. In many instances, there is no one-to-one relationship between data elements and the data in a computer-processed report or file.

Developing Audit Data Flow Diagrams

Inputs from which data flow diagrams are prepared should include copies of the following:

- Narrative descriptions of all major application programs
- All manually prepared source documents that affect application processing as well as corresponding coding sheets and instructions for data transcription
- Record layouts for all major computer input and output records, computer master files, and work files (such as update or file maintenance tapes and computation tapes)
- All major outputs produced by the automated system
- Lists of standard codes, constants, and tables used by the system

These documents, along with the information developed in the previous tasks, should enable the audit staff to prepare an audit data flow diagram identifying

- Point of origin (title or individual) for all source documents
- All transfers of source documents from one person or office to another (make sure that all control points are identified)
- Transcriptions of source documents into a machine-readable format
- Computer processing of application data
- All major outputs created from the source documents
- Recipients of all essential outputs

Evaluating the Quality of System Documentation

On the basis of user and IT staff inputs, as well as on the degree of difficulty experienced in constructing an audit data flow diagram, the auditor should be able to comment on the quality of system documentation. There are two basic questions to answer: Is the documentation accurate? Is the documentation complete?

To illustrate, if a federal auditor were examining IT internal control issues at a U.S. Navy computer facility, he or she might use the *Federal Information Systems Controls Audit Manual* (FICAM) recently updated by the (U.S.) Government Accountability Office (GAO). This publication would provide a basis for assessing information system controls compliance to federal guidelines.

Assessing Controls over Documents

Control points identified during the preparation of the audit data flow diagram, along with information on controls developed in the background segment, should enable the auditor to identify system controls. With a diagram of this type, the auditor can determine whether the following controls are used:

- Turnaround documents (These documents [manual or automated] should be returned to the originator to make sure that all documents were received and none were added during transmittal.)
- Record counts (They [manual or system generated] should be maintained for all documents to make sure that none are added or lost.)
- Predetermined control totals (For payroll, predetermined control totals should be developed for important data items, such as hours worked, leave taken, hourly rates, gross pay, and deductions. The purpose is to make sure that records are not altered.)
- Run-to-run totals (These totals should be maintained to assure that no records are added or lost during steps in the computer processing sequence.)

Determining the Effectiveness of Processing under Computer Programs

The audit staff should identify any problem areas in the processing cycle including but not limited to

- Redundant processing of data or other forms of duplication
- Bottlenecks that delay processing
- Points in the operating cycle at which clerks do not have enough time to review output reports and make corrections

Evaluating the Usefulness of Reports

The audit staff should review the key or major outputs (such as edit listings, error listings, and control of hours listings) of the application system and determine if the outputs are

- Accurate
- Useful as intended

The auditor should confirm findings by interviewing the users of the output reports. One appropriate technique might be the completion of a questionnaire or survey, perhaps conducted by e-mail on user satisfaction with output reports.

Appropriateness of Flowcharting Techniques

A distinction should be noted between the use of systems flowcharts in computer auditing and in the broader field of systems analysis. In recent years, systems analysts have begun to favor other methods of modeling and documentation. Data flow diagrams, for example, are often preferred over systems flowcharts for purposes of analysis. The rationale is that data flow diagrams are process-oriented and emphasize logical flows and transformations of data. By contrast, systems flowcharts emphasize physical processing steps and controls. It is just this type of control-oriented view, however, that is the auditor's primary focus. Thus, although the use of systems flowcharting may be declining for systems development purposes, this modeling tool remains important for computer auditors.

Systems flowcharting is not necessarily always the most practical approach for the auditor. Existing documentation including data flow diagrams, narratives written in structured English, or descriptions of programs in pseudocode may be used as points of departure. Based on a review of existing documentation, the auditor can decide what additional modeling is needed to gain adequate understanding of the systems under examination.

The auditor should also be aware of the increasing use of automated tools in preparing flowcharts. Software packages are available, many of which run on mainframes and microcomputers that accept program source code as input and generate finished flowcharts. Also, microcomputer-based software packages now available can aid in documentation or verification of spreadsheets or database applications.

The technique for departmental segregation of processing in the preparation of flowcharts is important. For example, separate vertical columns on the flowchart can show processing by function or department. This representation is useful because one of the important controls the auditor evaluates is the segregation of duties within the accounting system. Structuring flowcharts in this way helps to discipline the auditor's thinking and identify any incompatible functions that may exist within accounting applications. Using this technique you are documenting the role of IT in the initiation, authorization, recording, processing, and reporting of transactions handled by the application or within the system of applications.

During the preliminary review and application analysis phases, the auditor should be accumulating notes to be considered for later inclusion as comments within a letter of recommendations to client management.

At the conclusion of the preliminary review and application analysis phases of the engagement, the audit team briefs audit firm partners and client managers associated with the audit. All responsible parties should have a clear understanding of the sources and procedures for the development of information reflected in the financial statements on which the audit firm will render an opinion.

On completing its preliminary review and application analyses, the audit team should have built an understanding that includes

- Establishing of sources for all financially significant accounting information
- Identifying processing steps, particularly of points within applications at which major changes in accounting information take place
- Determining and understanding processing results
- Analyzing the nature and progress of audit trails to the extent that they exist and can be followed within individual applications

Sampling

Some audit tools assist in defining sample size and selecting the sample. For example, ACL, an audit analysis tool, will automatically calculate the sample size and select a sample from the population, and spreadsheet applications will generate random numbers for selecting a sample. There are two types of sampling techniques:

Judgmental sampling: The sample is selected and the results evaluated are based on the auditor's experience. The judgment may be to select a specific block of time, geographic region, or function.

Statistical sampling: The sample is randomly selected and evaluated through the application of the probability theory.

Both methods allow the auditor to project to the population. However, only statistical sampling allows the auditor to quantify the risk that the sample is not representative of the population. The specific method selected for a sample will depend on the audit objectives and the characteristics of the population. Some of the techniques mentioned earlier in Exhibit 5.2 can be integrated with sampling techniques. For example, the sample audit review file (SARF) technique can apply a number of different sampling methodologies mentioned later in Exhibit 5.3. The appropriateness of the methodology selected should be reviewed for validity purposes by statistical or actuarial staff

Sampling Method	Description
Random number sampling	Items are randomly selected from a population so that each item has an equal chance of being selected.
Systematic sampling (interval sampling)	A method of random sampling that begins the sample by selecting a random starting point in a population and then selecting the remaining items at fixed intervals. This method should not be used for selection from a population that has a fixed pattern.
Stratified sampling	A method of random sampling that separates the population into homogeneous groups before selecting a random sample. This method should be used for selection from a population with wide variances in value.
Cluster sampling (block sampling)	A method of random sampling that separates the population into similar groups and then selects a random sample from the group.
Stop-or-go sampling (sequential sampling)	Minimizes the sample size by assuming a low error rate. It estimates the error rate of the population within a specified interval (e.g., plus or minus number).
Discovery sampling	Tests for a significant error or irregularity. It should not be used where there are known deviant conditions.
Dollar-unit sampling (probability proportional to size)	This method uses the dollar as a sampling unit, which increases the probability that larger dollar values will be selected. It primarily detects overpayments.
Mean per unit	The mean value of a sample is calculated and multiplied by the units in the population to estimate the total value of the population.
Difference estimation	The average difference between the audit value and book value for a sample unit is calculated. This difference is then multiplied by the population to estimate the total value.
Ratio estimation	The sample ratio to book value is multiplied by the population book value to estimate the total value.

Exhibit 5.3 Statistical sampling techniques.

that has expertise in this area. Also, the applied technique should be revisited and reassessed over time to see if there is any change to the characteristics or attributes of the population under review.

Random Attribute Sampling

Random attribute sampling is a statistical technique that tests for specific, predefined attributes of transactions selected on a random basis from a file. Attributes for which such testing is done could include signatures, account distribution, documentation, and compliance with policies and procedures. To perform attribute sampling, the auditor must specify three parameters that determine sample size:

1. Estimate the "expected error rate," or estimated percentage of exception transactions, in the total population
2. Specify the required "precision," or degree of accuracy desired, of the sample conclusion to be made
3. Establish an acceptable "confidence level" that the conclusion drawn from the sample will be representative of the population

The size of the sample will be determined by the combination of the precision, confidence level, and expected error rate parameters.

Variable Sampling Techniques

Variable sampling estimates the dollar value of a population or some other quantifiable characteristic. To determine the sample size, the auditor must specify four parameters:

1. Acceptable "confidence level" that the conclusion drawn from the sample will be representative of the population
2. Absolute value of the "population" for the field being sampled
3. "Materiality" or maximum amount of error allowable in the population without detection
4. "Expected error rate" or estimated percentage of exception transactions in the total population

The size of the sample will be determined by the combination of confidence level, population value, materiality, and expected error rate.

Exhibit 5.3 lists various statistical sampling techniques. Again, the auditor must watch for changes and updates to guidance in the use of sampling to perform audit work within his profession. A good example is SAS 111 (Amendment to the Statement on Auditing Standard No. 39, Audit Sampling). SAS 111 addresses the concepts of establishing "tolerable deviation rates" when sampling test of controls such as matching and authorization. It also defines the appropriate use of dual-purpose sampling.

System Validation

System validation is a method for testing the reliability of programs through simulation with either the test data or the actual data. With parallel simulation techniques, the auditor may be able to satisfy both compliance and substantive testing needs in one process.

Computer-Assisted Audit Tools and Techniques for Application Reviews

Auditing applications require specific and general knowledge about hardware and software. In addition, familiarity with system utilities helps in conducting control and substantive tests. For auditing applications and data integrity, there is a variety of auditing tools that are useful. There are tools that analyze spreadsheet logic and calculations for accuracy. There are tools that analyze a database application and produce a logical flowchart. Finally, generalized audit software can be used to analyze data produced from most applications. Again, all of the information generated by the use of CAATTs must be evaluated.

Generalized Audit Software

Use of generalized audit software makes it possible to perform required functions directly on application files. Audit software can be used to

- Analyze and compare files
- Select specific records for examination
- Conduct random samples
- Validate calculations
- Prepare confirmation letters
- Analyze aging of transaction files

IT auditors can also use the same software tools as the programming staff or additional tools used by auditors. There are a variety of query and analysis tools, as shown in Exhibit 5.4.

Application Testing

Once controls have been identified, the next step in an audit is to verify the control's effectiveness. This can be accomplished by

- Submitting a set of test data that will produce known results if the application functions properly
- Developing independent programs to reperform the logic of the application
- Evaluating the results of the application

In any case, the auditor will need to understand the processing logic of the application to simulate the application or evaluate the application's results.

Designing Tests of Controls

Reproducing an application can be very time consuming if the application being reviewed is fairly complex. The simulated application will need to be coded and tested before being able to rely on the results. Consider only partially duplicating the application logic to test key functions.

Data Analysis

Organizations develop a wealth of information from their transaction processing systems. Auditors can use this information to gain an overall understanding of an area to identify general trends and

Product	Features	Platform
Access	A database program that provides data selection, analysis, and reporting	Client/server, personal computers, notebooks, personal digital assistants (PDAs)
ACL	General audit software that reads files from most formats (e.g., EBCDC, TXT) and provides data selection, analysis, and reporting	Mainframe, client/server, personal computers, notebooks
Excel	Spreadsheet software that provides analysis, calculation, graphing, and reporting	Client/server, personal computers, notebooks, PDAs
CA-Examine	A programming language that provides data selection, analysis, and reporting	Mainframe
CA-Easytrieve	A programming language that provides data selection, analysis, and reporting	Mainframe and Unix
Vbasic, C, C++, JAVA, SQL, Perl	A programming language that provides data selection, analysis, and reporting	Mainframe, client/server, personal computers, notebooks
SAS, SPSS	A programming language that provides data selection, analysis, and reporting	Mainframe

Exhibit 5.4   Query and analysis tools.

decide where best to focus audit tests. For example, when performing an audit of accounts receivable, the auditor could quickly age payables or receivables and then look in more detail at items over a certain number of days or over a certain dollar value. CAATTs can also be used to scan for invalid values or combinations of values that indicate a breakdown in controls or potential fraud. They can also be used to join two files, identify sequence gaps in check or purchase order files, and check for duplicates.

Compliance Testing

Information systems auditors can help determine compliance with a particular procedure for operational and financial audits. This can be accomplished by developing programs to detect data outside of expected values or analyzing how exceptions or errors were handled. Were they in compliance with organization policy and procedures?

Application Controls

Auditors need to apply the same standards to their own applications as they recommend to others. Whether the application involves downloading a file from the mainframe to a spreadsheet or the creation of a department database, controls should be in place to ensure accurate results.

Spreadsheet Controls

Spreadsheets may seem to be relatively straightforward because of their widespread use. However, the risks presented are significant if the spreadsheet results are relied on for decision making. Lack of reliability, lack of auditability, and lack of modifiability are all risks that are associated with poor spreadsheet design. Auditors use spreadsheets for analyzing data and forming opinions. The risk of relying on inaccurate information for audit opinions can be professionally embarrassing. Controls should be implemented to minimize the risk of bad data and incorrect logic, particularly, if spreadsheets are reused. Some of the key controls that minimize the risks in spreadsheet development include

- *Analysis.* Understanding the requirements before building the spreadsheet
- *Source of data.* Assurances that data being used are valid, reliable, and can be authenticated to originating source
- *Design review.* Review by peers or system professionals
- *Documentation.* Formulas, macro command, and any changes to the application should be documented externally and within the application
- *Verification of logic.* Reasonableness checks and comparison with known outputs
- *Extent of training.* Formal training in spreadsheet or application design, testing, and implementation
- *Extent of audit.* Informal design review or formal audit procedures
- *Support commitment.* Ongoing application maintenance and support from IT personnel

Database Controls

Department databases should be protected with controls that prevent unauthorized changes to the data. In addition, once the database application is implemented, the application should be kept in a separate program directory and limited to "execute only." The database can also be protected by enabling "read-only" abilities to users for data that remain static. Access rights should be assigned to specific users for specific tables (access groups). The input screens should include editing controls that limit data entry to valid options. This can be accomplished by having a table of acceptable values for the data fields. Data accuracy can also be enhanced by limiting the number of free-form fields and providing key entry codes with lookup values for the full description. Database integrity controls can include

- *Referential integrity:* Prevent deleting key values from related tables
- *Transaction integrity:* Restore value of unsuccessful transactions
- *Entity integrity:* Create unique record identification
- *Value constraints:* Limit values to a selected range
- *Concurrent update protection:* Prevent data contention
- *Backup and recovery protection:* Ability to back up critical information and applications and restore to continue
- *Testing protection:* Perform tests at the systems, application, and unit level

There may be situations in this environment where auditing around the computer may be adequate when automated applications are relatively simple and straightforward. Unfortunately, SAS 94 does not eliminate the use of this technique. The major weakness of the auditing-around-the-computer approach is that it does not verify or validate whether the program logic is correct. Also, this method does not evaluate how the application and their embedded controls respond to various types of transactions (anomalies) that can contain errors. Therefore, the issuance of SAS 106 through 110 by the AICPA helps support the importance of CAATTs and its role in performing audit procedures in response to assessed risks and evaluating the audit evidence obtained.

Certainly, when audits involve the use of advanced technologies or complex applications, the IT auditor must draw upon techniques combined with tools to successfully test and evaluate the application. The techniques most commonly used are shown in Exhibit 5.5. Again, many of these techniques should be embedded into the application for use by auditors and security personnel. These techniques provide continuous audit and evaluation of the application or systems and

Technique	Description
Integrated test facility	Integrated test facilities are built-in test environments within a system. This approach is used primarily with large-scale, online systems serving multiple locations within the company or organization. The test facility is composed of a fictitious company or branch, set up in the application and file structure to accept or process test transactions as though it was an actual operating entity. Throughout the financial period, auditors can submit transactions to test the system.
Test data	This technique involves methods of providing test transactions to a system for processing by existing applications. Test data provide a full spectrum of transactions to test the processes within the application and system. Both valid and invalid transactions should be included in the test data as the objective is to test how the system processes both correct and erroneous transaction input. For a consumer credit card service, such transactions may be invalid account numbers, accounts that have been suspended or deleted, and others. If reliance is placed on program, application, or system testing, some form of intermittent testing is essential. Test data generators are very good tools to support this technique but should not be relied on entirely for extreme condition testing.
Parallel simulation	Parallel simulation involves the separate maintenance of two presumably identical sets of programs. The original set of programs is the production copy used in the application under examination. The second set could be a copy secured by auditors at the same time that the original version was placed into production. As changes or modifications are made to the production programs, the auditors make the same updates to their copies. If no unauthorized alteration has taken place, using the same inputs, comparing the results from each set of programs should yield the same results. Another way is for the auditor to develop pseudocode using higher-level languages (Vbasic, SQL, JAVA, etc.) from the base documentation following the process logic and requirements. For audit purposes, both software applications (test versus actual) would utilize same inputs and generate independent results that can be compared to validate the internal processing steps.

Exhibit 5.5 **Computer-assisted audit techniques for computer programs.**

Continuous monitoring or continuous assurance	These techniques require planning, design, development, implementation, and continuous monitoring and assurance if they are to be used and applied successfully. The application of statistical sampling, regression, and advanced analytics to identify anomalies (unusual events or situations). These anomalies can be extracted in real time through embedded audit modules or audit hooks designed into the application.
SARF	SARF selects transactions and processes through sampling techniques and places these into log files for evaluation by auditor and security personnel.
Systems control audit review file	Systems Control Audit Review File (SCARF) is another real-time technique that can collect specific transactions or processes that violate certain predetermined conditions or patterns. This may be enhanced by decision support software that alerts designated personnel (audit, security, etc.) of unusual activity or items out of the ordinary. Computer forensic specialists can collect data to log files for further review and examination.
Transaction tagging	This is the ability to follow a selected transaction through the entire application from input, transmission, processing, and storage to output to verify the integrity, validity, and reliability of the application under review. Some applications have a trace or debug function, which can allow one to follow the transaction through the application. This may be a way to ensure that the process for handling unusual transactions is followed within the application modules and code.
Snapshot	The ability to look at a selected execution of application code and variables used to validate the values going into the process and the values being generated by the process to ensure that they meet requirement.

Exhibit 5.5   (Continued) Computer-assisted audit techniques for computer programs.

provide management and the audit or security personnel assurances that controls are working as planned, designed, and implemented.

The techniques and the tools provide the auditor the mechanisms to perform their audit. Using technology to audit technology has long been a practice applied by the authors. They have used these tools and techniques to support the audit functions.

Computer-Assisted Audit Tools and Techniques for Operational Reviews

Earlier, we covered a number of tools and techniques used for performing tasks to support the audit of applications. Most of these tools can be used to support operational reviews as well as collect information about the effectiveness of general controls over IT operations. Exhibit 5.6 lists a sample of tools that can be used for different areas of review and support.

However, the use of tools need not be limited to specialized packages. Computer languages can be useful in performing operational tests and collecting information about the effectiveness of general controls. Even basic tools such as Access in MS Office can be used to take an imported data file of operational data (e.g., users' account information and file accesses, rights to number of file accesses), perform analysis on the file (histograms, frequencies, summaries), and then move

Name of Tool	Client/ Server Control	Computer- Assisted Audit Tools	Contingency Planning	Data Warehousing and E-Commerce
Control Compliance Suite, Electronic Discovery & Audit by Symantec, Inc., Cupertino, CA	X	X		
SQLsecure by Idera	X	X		
ACL by ACL Services Ltd., Vancouver, BC, Canada		X		
IDEA by Audimation Services, Inc., Houston, TX		X		X
Number-Audit Sampling by Linton Shafer Computer Services, Inc., Frederick, MD		X		
ADM Plus by Joseph Pleier & Associates, Mission Viejo, CA		X		
WizWhy™ and WizRule™ by Wizsoft Inc., Syosset, NY		X		
RecoveryPAC, RecoveryPAC Web, and RiskPac by HaXer LLC, the Netherlands			X	X
Software Asset Management (SAM) by Software One, New Berlin, WI	X		X	
Disaster Recovery System (DRS) by TAMP Computer Systems Inc., Merrick, NY	X		X	X
Informatica Identity Resolution by Informatica, Redwood City, CA		X		X
COD 32, Double Check, and Achieve by IPS of Boston, Middleboro, MA				X

Exhibit 5.6   List of selected operational audit tools and techniques.

data into MS Excel and visually portray information for management or even forecast trends with regard to workload, growth, and other IT operational areas.

Should the IT auditor have the technical capability to "design, develop, and implement" host routines to support audit function and activities, most fourth-generation languages offer full support. Exhibit 5.7 outlines the capability of the support available.

Product	Environment					Application-Generation Function														Human Factoring			Database Support			
	IBM Environment	Server Environment	Tool Available on PC	Micro-to-Mainframe Link	Full PC Implementation	Query Language	Report Generator	Screen Painter/Data Entry	Graphics Generator	Decision-Support Tools	Subset for End Users	IT Professionals	Procedural Language	Interface-to-Action Diagrams	Well-Structured Code	Provable Specifications	Heavy-Duty Computing	Full COBOL Replacement	Recommended for Information Centers	Help Facility	Computer-Aided Instruction	Computer-Aided Thinking	Support Database Management	Standard DBMS Package	Data Dictionary	Data-Modeling Tool
MS Office	×	×	×	×	×	×	×	×	×	×	×	×		×					×	×	×	×	×	×	×	×
SQL	×	×	×		×	×	×	×	×	×	×	×	×	×	×				×	×			×	×	×	×
Perl	×	×	×	×		×	×	×	×	×	×	×	×		×				×	×			×	×	×	×
SAP	×	×		×		×	×	×	×	×	×	×							×	×	×		×	×	×	
QBE	×					×	×	×			×								×				×	×		
QMF	×	×	×	×	×	×	×	×	×	×	×				×		×		×	×			×	×	×	×
ACL		×	×	×			×		×	×				×					×	×		×	×			
IDEA		×	×	×			×		×	×				×					×	×		×	×			
Oracle	×	×	×	×	×	×	×	×	×	×	×	×	×	×	×	×	×	×	×	×	×		×	×	×	

Exhibit 5.7 List of selected operational audit tools and techniques.

Product	IBM Environment	Server Environment	Tool Available on PC	Micro-to-Mainframe Link	Full PC Implementation	Query Language	Report Generator	Screen Painter/Data Entry	Graphics Generator	Decision-Support Tools	Subset for End Users	IT Professionals	Procedural Language	Interface-to-Action Diagrams	Well-Structured Code	Provable Specifications	Heavy-Duty Computing	Full COBOL Replacement	Recommended for Information Centers	Help Facility	Computer-Aided Instruction	Computer-Aided Thinking	Support Database Management	Standard DBMS Package	Data Dictionary	Data-Modeling Tool
	Environment					**Application-Generation Function**														**Human Factoring**			**Database Support**			
Webmetrics 3.0	×	×	×				×		×			×		×						×						
C++	×	×	×	×	×	×	×	×	×	×	×	×	×	×	×		×	×	×	×	×		×	×	×	×
SAS	×	×	×	×			×		×	×	×	×					×			×		×				×
VS-Basic	×	×	×	×	×	×	×	×		×	×	×	×	×	×		×	×	×	×			×	×	×	×
DMS	×		×			×	×	×			×	×					×						×	×	×	
SPSS	×	×	×				×		×		×	×					×		×	×		×				
Application Factory		×				×	×	×			×	×	×	×	×		×	×	×	×		×	×		×	
Asset	×	×	×		×		×			×		×							×							
JAVA	×	×	×		×			×				×	×		×		×		×	×	×					

Exhibit 5.7 (Continued) List of selected operational audit tools and techniques.

The methods or techniques in use for performing the reviews in the areas of systems maintenance, operating systems, client/server applications, and ISO 9001 will be discussed in Chapter 11. It should be kept in mind that the ability to perform these tasks (the techniques) is supported by tools to gather information that may help determine if controls are working.

Web Analysis Tools

On reviewing an organization's Website, IT auditors can measure download time, transaction time, and availability of the Website. In addition, IT auditors have to be aware of errors such as failed connection attempts, missing pages, missing page components, and broken links, which have to be tabulated. The IT auditor should evaluate the overall performance of the organization's Website by obtaining or preparing comparative Web performance statistics for several months. These statistics should be examined for significant issues and used in the assessment of the overall performance of the Website. Moreover, IT auditors should review the Web information to ensure that all posted data are current. It is impossible for IT auditors to manually perform a Website audit. Manually checking that all posted data are current will be time consuming. Discovering broken links, missing pages, and page components manually are almost impossible. Thus, IT auditors need CAATTs to assist them in performing this kind of audit. Web analysis software is appropriate to be one of the CAATs because it gives IT auditors the following advantages on audits of Websites:

- Reduces the time to complete audit analysis, test, and reports
- Increases audit coverage by reducing the amount of time spent on manual processes
- Provides quality audit services by having a standard set of audit tools and procedures
- Leverages the knowledge gathered as a result of audit projects to provide immediate metric/data quality feedback to management

Using Web analyst software as CAATs not only benefits the IT auditors but also the organizations. By having a good and effective Website, an organization will gain the following benefits:

- Reduced advertising costs
- Equal access to new markets
- Increased sales
- More opportunity for niche marketing
- Reduced delivery cost for goods that can be delivered electronically

Finally, IT auditors have to be aware that Web analysis software such as CAATs has its strength and weakness. It cannot be operated on all computer systems and platforms. Moreover, IT auditors should also consider a proper combination of manual techniques and Web analysis software while performing an audit of a Website.

Web Analysis Software as an Audit Tool

There are many Web analysis software tools and services for assessing the usability of a Website. One of the earliest of these Web analysis tools is "Webmetrics" (version 3.0) from NIST. Webmetrics is not sold in the market; it is still in development. However, NIST has made it available for use.

Webmetrics can be downloaded free from the NIST Web Metrics Testbed site at http://zing.ncsl. nist.gov/WebTools/.

ITL of NIST released the first Webmetrics 1.0 Tool Suite in August 1998. In January 2003, they released their latest version. Webmetrics is one of the research projects of ITL's Information Access Division (IAD). For more information about current and past research, products and tools, or other information about IAD, visit IAD's Website.

The objective of developing Webmetrics is to provide industries with the current state-of-the-art technology that will allow improved usability of Websites. Improved usability can dramatically increase the effectiveness and accessibility of a Website, and this is critical if the U.S. industry is to remain competitive in the global marketplace. Some of the earlier IT audit uses of this type of tool was looking at Web usability and compliance with Web development and testing standards.

Today, a number of products and companies are offering services that are available which could be used for audit support purposes providing Web analysis and security alert capability. Some examples are Clicktracks, SAS Web Analytics, Google Analytics, Site Catalyst by Omniture, and Nedstat. Clicktracks provides products and hosted services in the field of Website traffic analysis. SAS Analytics applies SAS Customer Intelligence software to online channels so that every customer interaction is captured and analyzed with a profile view of the customer. Google Analytics offers free Web analytic services with integrated analysis of Adwords. This product is based on Urchin which Google acquired in 2005. Site Catalyst by Omniture is a hosted application that offers a complete view of activity on a company's Website that includes historical (data warehouse) and real-time analysis and reporting. Nedstat is a provider of software solutions and services for monitoring Websites and reporting on Website visits.

Computer Forensics

Computer forensics is the examination, analysis, testing, and evaluation of computer-based material, conducted to provide relevant and valid information to a court of law. Computer forensics tools are increasingly used to support law enforcement, computer security, and computer audit investigations.

A good source for evaluating computer forensics tools is the Computer Forensics Tool Testing (CFTT) Project Website at http://www.cftt.nist.gov/. CFTT is a joint project of the NIST, the U.S. Department of Justice's National Institute of Justice (NIJ), the Federal Bureau of Investigation (FB), the Defense Computer Forensics Laboratory (DCFL), the U.S. Customs Service, and others to develop programs for testing computer forensics tools used in the investigation of crimes involving computers.

One tool recently reviewed by CFTT was EnCase Forensics by Guidance Software, Inc. EnCase enables "noninvasive" computer forensic investigations, allowing examiners to view relevant files including "deleted" files, file slack, and unallocated space. Other valuable resources for experience in the use of computer forensics tools and techniques would be those professional associations or organizations that support this area. Some of those would be The International High Technology Crime Investigators Association, Association of Certified Fraud Examiners, the Institute of Internal Auditors, Federal Government's Electronic Crimes Task Force, FBI Regional Computer Forensics Laboratory, and Colloquium for Information Systems Security Education. Note that when applying computer forensics techniques, one must be aware of the investigative methodology, processes, and procedures that must be followed to the letter to ensure that the evidence can be gathered successfully, documented, and not contaminated as evidential matter that could be used in court. Again, an excellent resource is the U.S. Department of Justice publication, *Prosecuting Computer Crimes* (2nd edition) published in 2010, as well as information provided by the High Tech Criminal Investigation Association (www.htcia.org).

Conclusion

The use of IT to audit IT is not a new idea. It is one of auditor innovation, knowledge, skills, and ability. The continued evolution of IT has placed advanced features of both hardware and software in the hands of IT auditors to apply in support of conducting, documenting, and executing the audit process. With the advancements in both hardware and software, we can see that even at the applications level, software tools and techniques exist for the auditor to apply innovative approaches to validating processes. IT has created new skills and new opportunities such as computer forensics.

Applications and systems have tools and techniques available to the auditor for use in auditing through the system. CAATs can be used efficiently, and effective tools in documenting audit work can be performed to validate application processing. We have provided an extensive look at the use of CAATs to support the audit process. The domain of CAATs extends from the workstation or notebook level to the client/server, mainframe, and network level. The IT audit professional must use due professional care in the application of CAATs to support the audit process and the possibility of computer forensics application if a crime has been committed in their organization.

Review Questions

1. What are CAATTs?
2. What role do CAATTs play in performing audit work?
3. What are audit query and analysis tools? List and explain two such tools.
4. What is transaction tagging? What is snapshot? How are these techniques used in application audits?
5. What are the critical areas that management needs to consider when introducing new technologies into the audit process? What are some of the typical phases an organization goes through?
6. Can software tools and techniques that IT professionals use for application design, development, testing, and maintenance be used for audit purposes as well? Please discuss the pros and cons, providing three examples in each area.
7. How can MS Office be used as a support tool in IT operational audits?
8. What capabilities does Oracle have as a support tool?
9. What is computer forensics?
10. Name some commonly used computer forensics tools.

Multiple-Choice Questions

1. Audit productivity tools can be used in

a. Planning and tracking
b. Documentation and presentations
c. Communications and data transfer
d. All of the above
2. Generalized audit software can
   a. Validate calculations
   b. Select specific records for examination
   c. Analyze and compare files
   d. All of the above
3. The task of examining a spreadsheet for reasonableness checks and comparison with known outputs is
   a. Documentation
   b. Extent of training
   c. Verification of logic
   d. Support commitment
4. Which is not a database integrity control?
   a. Value constraints
   b. Biometrics
   c. Backup and recovery protection
   d. Referential integrity
5. A testing approach used to validate processing by setting up a fictitious company or branch in an application for testing transaction processing is called
   a. Snapshot
   b. SARF
   c. Integrated test facility
   d. Transaction tagging
6. A technique used to follow a selected transaction through the entire application to verify the integrity, validity, and reliability is called
   a. Snapshot
   b. Transaction tagging
   c. Systems Control Audit Review File (SCARF)
   d. Test data
7. Which of the following are categories of computer audit functions?
   a. Items of audit interest
   b. Data analysis
   c. Systems validation
   d. All of the above
8. The histogram analysis technique allows the auditor to
   a. Apply judgment in identifying and selecting appropriate testing techniques
   b. Validate transmission of data
   c. Prepare the audit plan
   d. All of the above
9. Which automated technique can apply a sampling methodology to the collection of transactions or records?
   a. Test data
   b. Snapshot

c. SARF
d. None of the above
10. Computer forensic tools are increasingly used to
    a. Support law enforcement
    b. Support computer security investigations
    c. Support computer audit investigations
    d. All of the above

Exercises

1. List three software tools that IT professionals use which can be employed to audit the application. Explain their application.
2. List three software techniques that IT professionals use which can support the audit of an application. Explain their application.
3. What specific benefits can CAATs bring to the audit? Please list and explain four benefits.
4. Read Appendix 1, Case 1, Wooback City; solve Part 1 and Part 2.
5. Read Appendix 1, Case 2, Ready or Not Auto Insurance; complete the assignment.

Answers to Multiple-Choice Questions

1—d; 2—d; 3—c; 4—b; 5—c; 6—b; 7—d; 8—a; 9—c; 10—d

Further Reading

1. AICPA, Information Technology Considerations in Risk-Based Auditing: A Strategic Overview, AICPA Top Technology Initiatives 2007, June 26, 2007.
2. Barbin, D. and J. Patzakis, Cyber crime and forensics, *IS Control J.*, 3, 25–27, 2002.
3. Bates, T.J., Computer evidence—Recent issues, *Inf. Sec. Tech. Rep.*, 5(2), 15–22, 2000.
4. Cerullo, V.M. and M.J. Cerullo, Impact of SAS No. 94 on computer audit techniques, *IS Control J.*, 1, 53–57, 2003.
5. Computer Forensic Tool Testing (CFTT) Project Website, National Institute of Standards and Technology, http://www.cftt.nist.gov/.
6. Gallegos, F., *WebMetrics: Computer-Assisted Audit Tools*, EDP Auditing Series, #73-20-50, Auerbach Publishers, Boca Raton, FL, 2001, pp. 1–16.
7. Gallegos, F., *Personal Computers in IT Auditing*, EDP Auditing, #73-20-05, Auerbach Publishers, Boca Raton, FL, 2002, pp. 1–7.
8. Guidance Software, Inc., EnCase Enterprise, Pasadena, CA, 2008, http://www.guidancesoftware.com/products/ee_index.aspx.
9. Guidance Software, Inc., EnCase Information Assurance, Pasadena, CA, 2008, Product Information, http://www.guidancesoftware.com/products/IA_index.aspx.
10. Heiser, J. and W. Kruse, *Computer Forensics—Incident Response Essentials*, Addison-Wesley, Reading, MA, 2002.
11. Kaplin, J., Leverage the Internet, *Internal Auditor*, Institute of Internal Auditors, June 2007.
12. Kneer, D.C., Continuous assurance: We are way overdue, *IS Control J.*, 1, 30–34, 2003.
13. Morris C.A. Sr., What every auditor needs to know about e-commerce, *Internal Auditor*, June 2000, p. 60.

14. National Institute of Standards and Technology, NIST Web Metrics, Version 3.0, January 2003, http://zing.ncsl.nist.gov/Webtools/.
15. Protzman, K. and V. Raval. Concept mapping—A learning tool for the information systems audit profession, Information Systems Audit and Control Association, JournalOnline, 2006, http://www.isaca.org/Content/NavigationMenu/Members_and_Leaders/Publications/Journal/Information_Systems_Control_Journal_Home.htm.
16. Sarva, S. Continuous auditing through leveraging technology, Information Systems Audit and Control Association, JournalOnline, 2006, http://www.isaca.org/Content/NavigationMenu/Members_and_Leaders/Publications/Journal/Information_Systems_Control_Journal_Home.htm.
17. Sayana, S.A., Using CAATs to support IS audit, *IS Control J.*, 1, 21–23, 2003.
18. Singleton, T., Generalized audit software: Effective and efficient tool for today's IT audits, Information Systems Audit and Control Association, JournalOnline, 2006, http://www.isaca.org/Content/NavigationMenu/Members_and_Leaders/Publications/Journal/Information_Systems_Control_Journal_Home.htm.
19. U.S. Department of Justice, *Prosecuting Computer Crimes*, 2nd edition, 2010, http://www.justice.gov/criminal/cybercrime/ccmanual/index.html.

Chapter 6

Managing IT Audit

A career development plan is essential to developing and retaining IT auditing expertise in an organization. Career development planning involves an integrated consideration of the individual's and the organization's needs. An organization can successfully develop its own IT auditor through training and development of knowledge, skills, and abilities and provide a career path for this professional. This chapter presents a method for planning and establishing the career development process for the IT auditor and gives guidelines for formulating and implementing a career development plan to fit the needs of a particular organization.

A related key area is the quality of an IT auditor's performance. Managers are constantly searching for better methods of evaluating staff performance. Performance management, counseling, and career development planning require effective performance evaluation practices. Through total quality management, auditors are being challenged today to provide a more customer-oriented focus. Because of the complex technical nature of IT auditing, audit managers require effective methods for assessing individual and group performance. This chapter discusses techniques for assessing the quality of IT audits and the auditors conducting them.

The concept and purpose of "best practices" is the sharing of successful ideas and lessons learned from experiences among professionals in their own domain. For many years, professional associations have done this in roundtable forums or meetings dedicated to sharing experiences and best practices. This chapter presents some of the best practices of IT audit management that was expressed by managers to the authors over our years of service. Some ideas may help professionals develop much-needed policies, procedures, and practices for their organizations. New ideas can aid IT professionals in their quest to become more efficient and productive in their work.

IT Auditor Career Development and Planning

An IT auditor's career development is as important to the individual as to the company which commits training and resources to this position. A career development plan and path offers the professional such as an IT auditor the opportunity to grow and upgrade the level of services provided to an organization. If a career path and development program does not exist, the chances of poor performance and turnover are high. An organization must recognize that an IT auditor with the proper mix of training (formal and on the job), development of designated skills, and increased level of knowledge and abilities provides a valued resource for potential managerial positions in corporate, financial, and other operational areas.

Among the various types of incentives for a professional, career advancement is one of the most effective. In recent surveys, some professionals rank career advancement higher than a monetary reward. In the IT audit profession, a large percentage of the professionals who go into this field do so because they recognize the management visibility they receive from this position. Experience and exposure in the audit profession can often provide opportunities in management.

In today's environment, most organizations' career development planning for IT audit staff is insufficient. This is largely due to pressures of time and job performance. In most instances, individuals do not receive the appropriate mix of training and experience for them to adequately develop their knowledge, skills, and abilities and progress within the organization. Thus, the career ladder and options open to an individual are not planned or formally defined, resulting in turnover and losses to outside organizations. In a sample of 227 IT audit professionals from various companies (government and private), approximately 31% of the respondents indicated the lack of an established career path for IT auditors. Of these, many stated that they had considerable problems in the hiring and retaining of IT auditors.

How does an audit manager or organizational management design, develop, and implement a career development plan? The process of matching individual career paths with organizational objectives is not easy. Career development is an important element to any organization; it should not be overlooked. The key components of such a plan are a defined career path with experiential development, training, and expected knowledge, skills, and abilities to be achieved as a person progresses up the career ladder.

A key point that management needs to remember is that a career development plan must be a viable, workable, management-supported concept. It should not be another sales pitch to the potential employees or a false promise to the staff. Employee motivation and trust will be impacted in a negative manner if they find out that the plan, in reality, cannot be actualized. This is where organizational management can lose their credibility with their staff.

Establishing a Career Development Plan

A functional and fully successful career development plan consists of six major elements, which must be integrated into an established process within the organization. These elements are

- Career path planning with management support
- Definition of knowledge, skills, and abilities
- Performance assessment
- Performance counseling and feedback
- Training
- Professional development

Each of these elements becomes necessary components of an effective career development plan. Exhibit 6.1 displays more information on each of these elements as related to the IT auditor.

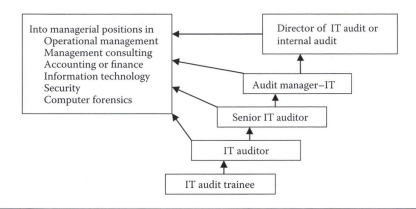

Exhibit 6.1   IT audit career path.

Career Path Planning Needs Management Support

The establishment of the career development planning process must begin with the support of the management in the organization. It requires a commitment from the management to acknowledge and define horizontal and vertical career path opportunities within the organization (see Exhibit 6.1). The IT audit career path, as illustrated, offers the professional tremendous diversity in their career. Management gains by supporting such diversity and job opportunity. Often, management can help infuse an organization with knowledge, skills, and abilities to implement change. Without management support, career opportunities will be viewed with mixed emotions and doubt by IT audit staff. This can cause the eventual loss of employees to outside concerns because the opportunities are similar. An example would be an IT audit professional that started with a Big Four CPA firm, then, after 4 years moved to an IT audit manager position in a private firm. Later, after potentially 3–4 years, the individual moved to an audit director position with another firm. Many external opportunities are present if the employee is not satisfied with his or her own career development or advancement. These opportunities can be in business operations, IT security, and IT. Also, another field of growing opportunity is computer forensics.

The organization must ask itself a very serious question. Can it continue to bring new staff into these critical positions, train, and develop them and then lose these resources to opportunities outside the organization? With a good career development plan, a company builds resources that are knowledgeable about the lifeblood systems of the organization and have strong skills in information technologies and auditing methods, as well as excellent communication and administrative skills. Such people are ideal candidates for managing and integrating new technology into the operating environment of an organization.

Knowledge, Skills, and Abilities

Definition of the level of knowledge, skills, and abilities needed at each position level is a key step to a career development plan. This establishes the organization's expectation for an employee's performance in specified areas of responsibility and duties. Also implied is the level of skill one must attain to perform at a proficient level. Usually, a job or position description identifies these critical elements; however, job descriptions in an organization tend to stagnate and do not adequately reflect the change in increased responsibilities and technology. Therefore, it is recommended that job descriptions be reassessed on an annual basis to ensure relevancy in the performance assessment process.

When an employee and supervisor sit down to develop a career development plan, the employee must be given specific objectives or goals from which his or her performance and acquisition/development of knowledge and abilities can be adequately assessed. Further, the plan should provide an integrated focus on both yearly performance and career aspirations beyond the immediate future. This will allow the staff to take a more active role in their own career progress within the organization.

Performance Assessment

The next step is to begin structuring a career development plan that integrates organizational goals and objectives. Keep in mind that an individual career development plan requires the participation of the individual and management. Further, the individual must understand that progression up the career path of IT audit (see Exhibit 6.2) does not guarantee horizontal or vertical movement within the organization. To advance, he or she must effectively demonstrate through strong performance and the successful attainment of knowledge, skills, and abilities the traits to successfully make the transition. The assessment must incorporate organization and individual goals, any deviations to those goals that occurred as a result of workload changes, and the individual's accomplishments and contribution.

Like the financial auditor, the IT auditor can go through a period of gaining knowledge about the entire audit function and process. Typically, in the later years of their career, they become more specialized, but some organizations allow transition across areas for purposes of career development and enriching traditional areas with new methods and techniques. Some of these staff who make such transitions may have multiple certifications such as Chartered Accountant (CA), Certified

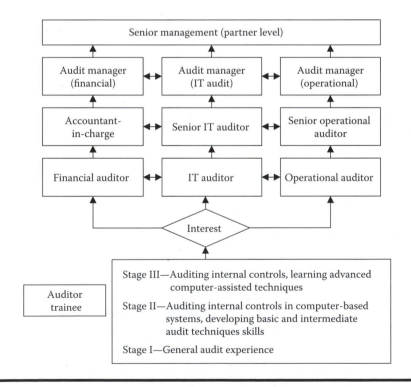

Exhibit 6.2 Career path for an IT auditor within an audit organization.

Public Accountant (CPA), Certified Information Systems Auditor (CISA), Certified Internal Auditor (CIA), Certified Information Security Manager (CISM), Certified Fraud Examiner (CFE), Certified Government Financial Manager (CGFM), Certified Information Systems Security Professional (CISSP), Certified in the Governance of Enterprise IT (CGEIT), Certified in Risk and Information Systems Control (CRISC), Certified Information Technology Professional (CITP), and others.

For new staff, they typically go through a learning and experience cycle in understanding the audit process and gaining experience in new computer-assisted audit methodologies and techniques. After a period of time, experience, and sustained performance level, they can choose the area in which they wish to concentrate, as Exhibit 6.2 illustrates.

For advancement to the next level or lateral movement into other areas, a determination of level of performance expected must be made. This assessment must incorporate organizational and individual goals, any deviation to those goals that resulted because of workload changes, the individual's accomplishments, and overall corporate contribution. However, if the organization does not provide the training and experience promised, IT auditors can move to another firm that has a need for the experience and skills they possess.

Performance Counseling/Feedback

Management feedback is a very important component of the career development process. Interim feedback on a quarterly or semiannual basis as well as the annual review will provide the necessary level of employee performance counseling to assess progress within the career path. If more training or experience is needed to better develop employee knowledge, skills, and abilities, it can be effectively planned for in this process.

Training

Training is another key component within the career development planning process. One of the major reasons given by IT auditors for leaving an organization is not receiving the training originally promised to them. A carefully staged, integrated, phased training program is very important to IT audit staff, both new and experienced.

The training plan should identify formal education to be given as progress is made along the career path. As depicted in Exhibit 6.3, the training plan identifies the specific types of training required to adequately develop IT auditors. Note that the program is modular to allow expansion, substitution, and ease in updating. Training focuses on audit methodology development, communication development, and technical development. If an individual has equivalent training or expertise in his or her prior education or through related work experience, then other relevant, developmental courses can be substituted, or training requirements can be identified as already met.

The formal training plan can be supplemented by specific on-the-job training. This type of training should be identified and integrated into the individual's career development plan. This will give IT audit supervisors and staff members guidance on how formal training may be applied to practical on-the-job experience. Of course, the training course selected for audit managers and supervisors will be at an advanced level to help them better prepare for technology changes or new IS audit methodologies, or concentrate on developing their managerial skills.

One problem that commonly occurs, especially with a small IT audit staff, is that the reality of assignment deadlines often overrides the need for training. Thus, the employee is either canceled out of the course or rescheduled for the course at "a later, more convenient time." The management must understand the consequences of not sending someone to a relevant, developmental training

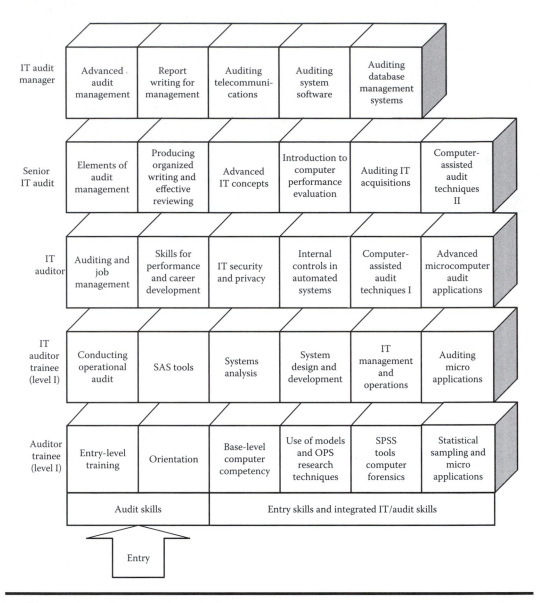

IT audit manager	Advanced audit management	Report writing for management	Auditing telecommunications	Auditing system software	Auditing database management systems
Senior IT audit	Elements of audit management	Producing organized writing and effective reviewing	Advanced IT concepts	Introduction to computer performance evaluation	Auditing IT acquisitions	Computer-assisted audit techniques II
IT auditor	Auditing and job management	Skills for performance and career development	IT security and privacy	Internal controls in automated systems	Computer-assisted audit techniques I	Advanced microcomputer audit applications
IT auditor trainee (level I)	Conducting operational audit	SAS tools	Systems analysis	System design and development	IT management and operations	Auditing micro applications
Auditor trainee (level I)	Entry-level training	Orientation	Base-level computer competency	Use of models and OPS research techniques	SPSS tools computer forensics	Statistical sampling and micro applications

Audit skills	Entry skills and integrated IT/audit skills

Entry

Exhibit 6.3   IT auditor model curriculum.

course, especially a course that is directly applicable to an ongoing work or may add to the staff's knowledge in future planned work. Before an audit team ever starts an assignment and milestones are agreed to, the management should plan for these developmental interruptions and allow for both on-the-job and formal training to take place as planned. A training chart (see Exhibit 6.4) can be extremely helpful to managers in identifying and minimizing potential conflicts.

Professional Development

Another component of any career development plan is continual professional development of the IT auditor. In IT auditing, there are a number of professional organizations that can support the

Name _____ Position _____ Certifications _____ Date of Plan _____

| Skill Category | Course | Month Offered | | | | | | | | | | | | Prerequisite | * | Accepted |
		J	F	M	A	M	J	J	A	S	O	N	D			
Basic																
Intermediate																
Advanced																

Exhibit 6.4 IT auditors development plan. *Needed for professional certification maintenance (check if applicable).

varied professional interests of the IT auditor. Also, many of these organizations support professional certification as a method of establishing measures of professional competence for a specific discipline (see Exhibit 6.5).

The IT auditor should be encouraged to continue his professional development and seek certification to enhance his professional status and development. This can be a developmental goal set between the management and individual as well as a performance goal. Once achieved, the staff member can be rewarded with a bonus or a quality step increase to present salary as a means of organizational recognition of a professional accomplishment.

Designation	Title	Professional Affiliate
CPA	Certified public accountant	American institute of certified public accountants
CA	Chartered accountant	Canadian institute of chartered accountants
CISA	Certified information systems auditor	Information systems audit and control association
CISM	Certified information security manager	Information systems audit and control association
CGEIT	Certified governance of enterprise IT	Information systems audit and control association
CCP	Certified computer professional	Association of information technology professionals
CIA	Certified internal auditor	Institute of internal auditors
CFE	Certified fraud examiner	Association of certified fraud examiners
CGFM	Certified government financial manager	Association of government accountants
CMA	Certified management accountant	Institute of management accountants
CSQA	Certified software quality analyst	Quality assurance institute
CBA	Certified bank auditor	Bank administration institute
CISSP	Certified information systems security professional	Information systems security association
CRISC	Certified in risk and information systems control	Information systems audit and control association
CITP	Certified information technology professional	American institute of certified public accountants

Exhibit 6.5 Professional certifications.

Besides certification, the individual might want to develop himself through continued education beyond the bachelor's degree level. Many local colleges and universities throughout the country offer post-bachelor certificate programs or advanced degrees at the master's or PhD level in business administration, accountancy, computer information systems (IS), and so on, which provide more formal development of a person's knowledge, skills, and abilities.

Several universities have offered training courses and curriculums in IT auditing, that is, a Master of Science in business administration (option—IT auditing) offered by California State Polytechnic University, Pomona, CA; Arizona State University; Bowling Green State University; Bentley College; Eastern Michigan University; Florida Atlantic University; and Georgia State University's master's degree in accounting (the latter with emphasis in IS auditing). In Europe, several academic institutions under European Community Action Scheme for the Mobility of University Students (ERASMUS) have joined together to offer a postgraduate program in IS security, safety, and dependability. Some of the non-U.S. universities active in educational offerings in this field are University of Queensland (Australia), Curtin University (Australia), National University (Singapore), and Chung-An University (South Korea). Such training-related goals should be part of a career development plan and performance contract. Such integration will provide accountability to both the individual and the company he works for.

Also, supportive organizations such as the Colloquium for Information Systems Security Educators have generated interest in the development of curriculum in the field of information assurance which encompasses the audit, control, and security of information technology. With the support of the U.S. National Security Agency and the Department of Homeland Security, more than 100 universities have been identified as Academic Centers of Excellence in information assurance education or Academic Centers of Excellence in Information Assurance Research or Academic Centers of Excellence in Information Assurance (2 year college programs). Universities such as Carnegie Mellon, Idaho State University, U.C. Davis, Georgia Tech, George Washington University, University of Maryland, West Point Military Academy, Naval Post Graduate School, and others have been identified for their educational offerings and research in the information assurance field. Support activities such as the NIATEC under Dr. Corey Schou have made a valuable wealth of training materials available to all colleges and universities interested in teaching in this field.

Finally, activity in professional associations is another measure of professional development. An individual's active commitment to serve on professional association boards and take an active role in the development of a professional association often goes unnoticed and is seldom rewarded. Again, a career development plan could include a requirement for enhancing the individual's professional knowledge, skills, and abilities through his involvement in external professional associations. Such involvement can be very beneficial to the individual as well as his company. For example, involvement in professional associations builds management skills and professional contacts that share information of mutual concern. For the company, an IT auditor who is amply recognized by an external professional organization for professionalism and expertise transfers that intangible benefit to the organizations he works for.

Evaluating IT Audit Quality

To ensure the value of audit assessments, audit management should implement a standard method for evaluating the quality of audits and auditors. Many companies have adopted TQM. In a TQM environment, internal auditors are measured against customer needs as well as traditional audit objectives. This section discusses the role of the auditor in defining specific control objectives and assessing whether the audit on completion has satisfactorily addressed those objectives. An assessment form is included as a tool for evaluating both the quality of the audit and the performance of the auditor; a list of suggested assessment criteria is provided for each audit area. How audit managers can use the assessment form as a tool to communicate audit results to senior management, evaluate audit methodology, and develop a training program for staff members has also been described.

Terms of Assessment

Senior management must be able to trust that the IT auditor's report and recommendations are based on a complete and thorough investigation. The findings must be documented in detail in the audit work paper files associated with the IT audit and audit report.

To ensure that audit results are accurate, each IT audit should be reviewed. The review must assess the completeness, accuracy, and pertinence of the audit conclusions, findings, and recommendations. The IT audit manager should review the results of the audit after the audit working papers and audit reports have been completed. This work must be done before authorization is given for the audit report to be issued and the closing meeting is to be held. Performing the review at this point allows identified weaknesses to be reviewed and corrected before audit conclusions are formally issued to the senior management of the organization being audited.

Any deviations from an acceptable audit product disclosed in the audit report and working papers must be resolved before the audit report is released. Effective communication between audit management and the auditor during this phase can be productive not only in ensuring an acceptable audit product but also in providing on-the-job training and career development.

Another important phase is the audit follow-up. This process may sometimes be conducted 6 months to a year after the audit report was issued. It is also important to conduct follow-up as a way for both management and the auditor to assess how successful the audit process has been.

IT Audit and Auditor Assessment Form

Exhibit 6.6 presents an assessment form that can be used for evaluating both the IT audit and the performance of the auditor in charge of that audit. The evaluation form is designed to be completed by both the audit management and the auditee—the auditor's primary customer. In a TQM environment, meeting customer needs from the customer's viewpoint is critical to the success of the audit function. The evaluation of the auditor should help to indicate the auditor's strengths and list the areas in which the auditor requires further training or improvement. In addition, this review should indicate the auditor's readiness for accepting more difficult audit assignments or other career path choices.

This form is designed for use with a variety of scoring systems. A simple binary system might be used to indicate whether a specific criterion was satisfied, and a more complex scoring system might be used if it is necessary to indicate how well or to what degree the criterion was satisfied. For example, a plus sign could be used to indicate that the audit work was done well, a blank space to mean the work was adequate, and a minus sign to indicate that the work was below an acceptable level of performance. The scoring method may also be adjusted to satisfy the requirements of the firm administering the evaluation. When further information is required to clarify a specific assessment, the evaluator should add a footnote to the score, referencing the additional information. These footnotes should be attached to the assessment form.

It is not necessary to score all assessment criteria for each audit area on the form. The evaluator should select only the degree of scoring required to produce a meaningful and complete appraisal. To a large extent, the scope and complexity of the audit determine the criteria to be assessed. The

(a)

Assessment Criteria

Audit Management Assessment

Audit Assessment: Completeness, Pertinence, Accuracy, Appropriateness of Recommendations, Audit Follow-Up

Auditor Assessment: Timely, Inquisitive, Decisive, Initiative, Resourceful, Communication Skills, Judgment, Tact, Auditing Knowledge

Auditee Assessment

Audit Assessment: Completeness, Pertinence, Appropriateness of Recommendations, Accuracy, Audit Follow-Up

Auditor Assessment: Timely, Inquisitive, Decisive, Initiative, Resourceful, Communication Skills, Judgment, Tact, Auditing Knowledge

Audit:

Audit Areas

Date Started:
Date Completed:
Assessment Date:

- Audit preparation
- Audit objective
- Fact gathering
- Audit program
- Audit tests
- Use of audit tools
- Conclusions
- Documented
- Supported
- Findings
- Documented
- Supported
- Recommendations
- Documented
- Supported
- Audit report
- Working papers
- Organization
- Cross-reference
- Readability
- Relations with auditee
- Relations with audit management

Exhibit 6.6   (a) Audit and auditor assignment form. (b) Auditor assessment footnotes.

(b)

Audit Statistics

Planned   Elapsed Time: _____ Months _____ Days

Actual Time: _____ Months _____ Days

Planned Staff Resources (Audit): _____ Staff Days

Actual Staff Resources (Audit): _____ Staff Days

Planned Follow-Up Date: ___/___/___

Actual Follow-Up Date: ___/___/___

Benefits

Check Applicable Boxes

Measurable

Estimated Savings _____ per annum

Cost Avoidance _____ per annum

Improved Control

Improved Efficiency, Effectiveness, and Economy

Follow-Up Analysis by Audit Management:

_____

_____

_____

_____

_____

Date: ___/___/___ Initials _____

Follow-Up Assessment by Auditee:

_____

_____

_____

_____

_____

Date: ___/___/___ Initials _____

Future Action: Reaudit Area   Reaudit in 2 Years   Reaudit in 4 Years

_____

Exhibit 6.6   (Continued) (a) Audit and auditor assignment form. (b) Auditor assessment footnotes.

following section of this chapter describes each audit area and assessment criterion that appears on the assessment form.

The second page of this form is used for the audit follow-up process (6 months to a year after the audit report). It allows the management or the auditor to perform a follow-up of the audit recommendations and assess their effect on operations. This must be done in an objective, independent manner. In some cases, quantitative measurements can be taken, such as improvements in productivity and dollar savings in staff time.

Criteria for Assessing the Audit

The audit methodology, supervisory review, and working papers are critical to the audit process. Working with evidence that is in transparent form (e.g., magnetic tapes, magnetic disks, and optical disks) requires complete, pertinent, and accurate reports. The audit and working papers should be evaluated on the basis of the following criteria:

- *Completeness*: An audit must cover every element of the audit subject. For example, the IT auditor should ensure that all applications currently in use by end users are examined during the audit.
- *Pertinence*: The audit should be free of extraneous or unnecessary elements. For example, the IT auditor should examine only key fields and records that directly relate to the audit objective.
- *Accuracy*: All elements of the audit must be precise and error free. The auditor must verify that all procedures and computerized processes produce correct results and that the measures used to evaluate these processes are error free. When developing computer-assisted audit routines, for example, the auditor must test and validate all program codes and algorithms before the routine is actually used.
- *Appropriate conclusions, findings, and recommendations:* The audit must present appropriate conclusions and findings that lead to recommendations reflecting cost-conscious, workable, and timely solutions to audit objectives.
- *Follow-up of findings and recommendations:* The value of the audit must be assessed to ensure that the findings and recommendations reflect that cost-conscious, workable, and timely solutions have been achieved in some manner.

Criteria for Assessing the Auditor

To objectively assess the performance of an IT auditor, the manager can use the standard criteria listed on the assessment form. The auditor can use this form to identify key performance areas and evaluation criteria; when the evaluation is complete, the form will help the auditor identify areas for improvement or further training. The following list explains the criteria shown in Exhibit 6.6 for the auditor assessment:

- *Timely:* The auditor is punctual and finishes work within time objectives.
- *Inquisitive:* The auditor questions, tests, and investigates to gain relevant facts and demonstrates a need to understand all aspects of the system under investigation.
- *Decisive:* The auditor is willing and able to make timely decisions.
- *Initiative:* The auditor is self-reliant and works well with minimal supervision.
- *Resourceful:* The auditor seeks alternative paths when initial plans are precluded or impeded.

- *Communication skills:* The auditor writes, speaks, and relates to others clearly and effectively.
- *Judgment:* The auditor chooses proper and timely courses of action and makes sound decisions based on the best data available.
- *Tact:* The auditor is helpful and respectful toward others and encourages their help and cooperation in the successful completion of audit tasks.
- *Auditing knowledge:* The auditor understands and conducts the audit according to generally accepted audit techniques and procedures.

Applying the Concept

The audit manager must address the challenge of effectively coordinating human skills and talents. The form presented in Exhibit 6.6 helps the audit manager assess specific audit areas. The manager can evaluate staff performance for these areas on the basis of both objective and subjective criteria. The second page of this form provides a mechanism to reexamine the audit recommendations and determine what effect the audit recommendations have had on organizational controls and processes over a specific period of time. Benefits from audits are not always immediate, but over time, they can be assessed and measured in different ways.

The manager can adjust or substitute audit areas and assessment criteria on this form to meet the special requirements of the audit environment. The manager may choose to adapt the assessment method so that it conforms to the mandates of the company's IT audit charter. Adjustments can also be made to accommodate areas of emphasis from senior management or the board of directors.

The finalized standard for measuring performance should be clearly communicated to staff members to ensure that they understand the process and can provide feedback. Any changes must also be communicated to staff members so that they know what is expected of them and understand how their performance will be measured. As part of this process of communication, managers should

- Gather and respond to feedback properly
- Prevent misconceptions about assessment policy and methods
- Maintain and continuously improve communications
- Develop an effective, participative assessment system

These characteristics are critical if the assessment process is to work effectively.

Evaluation of IT Audit Performance

As mentioned earlier, a variety of scoring methods can be used with this assessment form. A consistent application of the selected method, however, is important. The standards for assessment should be clearly communicated to those being evaluated.

The following example illustrates the application of an assessment. An organization requires as policy that, before an audit is conducted, the following tasks be performed:

- Define the audit objectives
- Prepare the audit program
- Conduct an initial meeting with managers responsible for the area under audit

Evaluation of the audit must assess that the audit work performed was in compliance with official company policy and governing audit standards and the audit work performed adequately supported the findings and recommendations reported. Compliance with organizational policy and procedures and governing audit standards used requires a yes-or-no evaluation. The managers conducting the evaluation must apply their own judgment, knowledge, skills, and experience to determine how well the work was done. It is recommended that this evaluation be based on the experience and work of a group rather than that of an individual.

In evaluating scores, the manager should be most concerned with poor scores, especially if they affect the conclusions, findings, and recommendations of the audit. On the basis of the evaluation, managers should develop training plans to improve the IT audit methodologies used and train the staff in proper audit techniques and tools. The follow-up of the audit recommendations is another way of assisting the evaluation process. Although the activity takes place at a later date, it may reconfirm an earlier evaluation and provide a basis for additional training requirements.

What Is a Best Practice?

What works well for others must work well for me! This is a misconception of some auditors and, unfortunately, this is not always the case. There are many subfactors that auditors must take into consideration before adopting a new set of auditing standards for their firms or businesses. First, what is the environment to be audited (i.e., entertainment, financial, and industrial)? Second, how big is the business that one is auditing (i.e., employees, assets, size, and locations)? Third, what are the policies and procedures generally accepted within the organization that is being audited (i.e., personnel rules and regulations, training memos, and organization charts)?

In the following, samples of the types of responses typically received from IT audit professionals in this field today regarding their interpretation of what best practices means to them are listed:

- The ability to choose and use the appropriate techniques and tools to accomplish a specific objective or set of objectives within a given circumstance or context
- The identification of those kinds of processes, procedures, and controls that will meet the business needs of an organization most effectively
- The methods that any organization uses to achieve its business objectives in the most effective and cost-efficient way while achieving the highest-quality product
- The integration of business processes with technology and people to provide a practice that is both efficient and effective and can provide value to the organization

As you will note, there are a variety of different answers to the same question. However, almost all professionals polled indicated that best practices should provide value-added concepts to the customer.

Why Is It Important to Learn about Best Practices?

There are many reasons why people should learn about best practices, some of which are as follows:

- To improve efficiency
- To add value to client/auditee or organization
- To aid in the advancement of technology
- For insight into learning how others are performing audits faster and more efficiently and easily

To keep up good relations with the client/auditee, an effective auditor will present some sound advice to the auditee on how to correct his problem. In a sense, a good auditor comes up with a solution to the problem.

Overview of Best Practices in IT Audit Planning

To succeed in auditing, IT audit managers must have a well-thought-out plan as to how they will conduct their audit. A well-thought-out plan gives the IT auditor a checklist of important issues that must be covered, thus, giving auditors their blueprints for a successful audit if, and only if, the checklist is correct. One of the most important steps in determining the correct approach in planning an audit of a large or small organization is to obtain an in-depth understanding of the area to be audited and its organization. The auditor's understanding should include IT environments, operating practices, and assigned responsibilities. Finally, the auditor should thoroughly understand the business issues associated with management risks.

The audit plan should have a purpose for each task that was to be completed in a sequential order. This provides an easy-to-use reference when it is time to present the findings and recommendations to the auditee or management. A well-thought-out plan can also be an answer to possible questions by the client/auditee.

There is nothing worse than going into a closing meeting with your client/auditee and having them ask you a question about your finding that you cannot answer. It is for this reason the audit manager or supervisor should insist that the audit is planned to a "T."

The audit manager or supervisor should make sure that all risks have been accounted for before the audit has started. With their audit experience, they may narrow down the objective and the context for which the audit will be performed. The scope of the audit should be consistent with the task at hand and the objective of the audit. All that is needed is adequate cooperation from the client/auditee. What this teaches is that every client/auditee is important, and the audit is a representation of the audit manager, the company, and the way in which job duties are performed.

Research

Another best practice technique used in IT audit planning and extremely valuable to IT audit managers is research. Everywhere one looks, someone is doing research. Research has become much easier now than ever before as Internet connectivity and search engines allow you to find what you are looking for on the information superhighway.

The Internet is a vast storehouse of knowledge with a wide range of information covering a massive variety of different areas and topics. Most IT audit managers understand the importance the Internet brings to the forum of IS auditing. With the use of the Internet, staff, senior auditors, and audit managers can locate information on a new client/auditee. This information becomes very important when one is competing to be the sole auditing firm of an organization or, as an internal auditor, seeks to know all about a company to make a good impression on management. Knowing the client/auditee or the company for whom one works for is a necessity in today's dynamically changing environment. It seems the world is getting smaller and smaller with technology. This is all the more the reason why IT auditors should research the company they are auditing to see if any mergers or buyouts are on the way which could impact financial statements.

The Internet, intranet, or extranet also offers auditors the ability to pose questions to people or persons they have never met or even heard of before. What makes this so advantageous is the capability given to auditors from around the world to communicate with one another on the latest techniques in IS auditing. This is all made possible by the use of electronic mail or chat rooms or online video conferencing provided on a local point-to-point carrier. Another added bonus is that it strengthens the use of best practices between IT audit managers around the world. A couple of buttons pushed, a password submitted, and a few words typed to compose a question and one is in business. Another good aspect of research is coming across benchmarks for the environment in which one is auditing.

Benchmarking

This is a practice that has been used to define what has worked well in other environments. This frequently mentioned tool is designed to present to individuals an idea of what to expect if they implement a certain concept into their audit approach. As defined in the dictionary, a benchmark is a point at which all measurements can be referenced back.

For example, the network security system is being audited and the goal is to verify that the service the security system is providing is adequate. One good way to measure such a task is to benchmark it against other leading brands (i.e., RACF, TOP Secret, ACF2) to see how it ranks in comparison to its leading competitors. One best practice, as shown in Exhibit 6.7, is where a partner of a computer audit group uses benchmarking to help aid him in the goals of his audits. In this example, the partner is looking at the types of audits being performed by staff to assess experience levels and complexity. Also, this illustrates that not all benchmarking has to be a comparison of performance.

Planning Memo

Another best practice technique mentioned is the planning memo. This document sets the tone or course of action IT audit managers plan to take with clients/auditees. The memo is good because it outlines for the client/auditee the areas in which one is most likely to spend time analyzing. This also gives a client/auditee the opportunity to voice concerns, if any. Most clients/auditees, whether internal or external, always have concerns that they address themselves, would like addressed, or are planning to address as soon as they get time. With a planning memo issued from the auditor, the client/auditee can prepare staff for a review of their operations. The clients/auditees can inform the staff to give full cooperation and assistance during the IT auditor's review of their system.

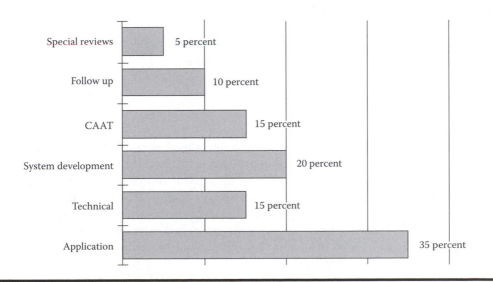

Exhibit 6.7 Benchmark planning guideline.

Planning memos serve the primary purpose of documenting plans. In some cases, this will serve as evidence of agreements among multiple parties about the nature, timing, and extent of work to be performed. In all cases, the plans provide a basis for measurement of results (i.e., Did you do what you intended to do, and did you get it done on time and on budget?). That is not to say that people cannot change their minds once they start an audit. The planning memo just helps document the original plans. Any change in plan would usually get documented in some sort of supplement to the planning memo.

Budget Coordination

Before the first question is ever asked, first inquiry made, or an observation commenced, a well-thought-out budget must be completed and adhered to by the IT audit manager. The managers must know the capabilities of the staff at their disposal. The importance of knowing the associates involved is extremely vital when one is working with sensitive material, a sensitive auditee, or technologically complex software and systems. Most managers know that in today's market, personnel resources for this field are scarce. When negotiating the audit, the manager should consider adding a little more time for training and error-correction purposes. After all, if the manager trains the staff right the first time, the staff will eventually become another added bonus to the audit team. Most, if not all, audits the authors have conducted involved some sort of training, and the time allotted to that training was given.

Risk Analysis

Another best practice found is that of risk analysis. Estimation of risk is a must in any business during any type of audit. Risk is so important to understand that the Information Systems Audit and Control Association asks questions relating to many IT audit, security, and control issues during the CISA Examination. Most IT audit managers complete what is called a risk analysis of the business to see what threats exist to the business, either externally or internally. Some of the techniques used to do this are listed in the following:

- Loss or corruption of information and IS assets
- Impaired and ineffective management decision making
- Disruptions to customer service and other critical operations
- Cost overruns, delays, and reduced quality in new systems development
- Loss of disclosure of confidential or proprietary information

For example, audit risk can be assessed in three areas: total exposure, risk, and time since last audit. Exhibit 6.8 displays a table with which to chart these areas. The total exposure component provides insight regarding the impact to the organization if control weaknesses exist. The risk component identifies the various factors that tend to increase the probability that control weaknesses may exist. The time since last audit component allows you to elevate the immediacy or lower the frequency of individual projects. To make sure that the risk analysis test is accurate, it is suggested that the factors used in the original risk analysis be verified with the organization's management personnel at the beginning of each project.

Business risk is a concern for all IT audit professionals, internal and external. What Exhibit 6.8 can do is help alleviate some of that concern, provided the auditor takes the time to examine all

Subject	Description	Low	Medium	High
1. Total exposure factor	Dollar value or equivalent controlled by system	0 = Low	1 = Medium	2 = High
A. Total asset value		Less than $2 million	$2–$9 million	More than $9 million
B. Transaction volume		Hundreds per month	Hundreds per week	Hundreds per day
C. Business impact		Minor business impact, company noncritical	Management focus, departmental critical	Legal/regulatory compliance, mission critical, potential impact to goodwill, reputation, public standing
2. Institutional or organizational risk factor				
A. Previous audit results	History of control weaknesses, system failure, operational problems	Few minor findings	Some medium control weaknesses or previously limited scope review	Many significant control weaknesses
B. Assets/ liabilities controlled by system		Fixed assets—not readily disposable	Confidential data or readily disposable assets	Financial Assets
C. System maturity		More than 5 years old	2–5 years old	Less than 2 years old
D. Enhancements/ changes to system	Program/ platform change, organizational restructure	Minor	Average	Major (include use of new technology, client/server)
E. System complexity	Consider: stand-alone, enterprise-wide, number of interfaces,	Small noncomplex or stand-alone	Moderately complex	Enterprise-wide system, complex operations or complicated database

Exhibit 6.8   Components of risk analysis.

Subject	Description	Low	Medium	High
	number of processes, technical operating environment			
F. Enterprise	Transactions	International	United States only	Small business
3. Time since last audit	Critical area? Audit follow-up?	More than 3 years	1–3 years	Less than 1 year

Exhibit 6.8 (Continued) Components of risk analysis.

steps thoroughly and exercises extreme caution when evaluating critical risks. Some risks, if not examined carefully, could bring a company to its knees. Thus, the theory of examining risks as part of the planning procedure has been a best practice for many auditors in the past.

As mentioned in the prior chapter, as guidance, the AICPA's issuance of SAS 104-111 recognizes the pervasiveness of IT in financial processes and that IT increasingly represents both a primary source of financial control risk and financial controls. These standards require the auditors to identify and assess risks of material misstatement at the financial statement level and the assertion level as a basis to perform further audit procedures (test of controls and substantive audit procedures). This means that under no circumstances can control risk be set to maximum as a default without considering internal controls.

Although most organizations and corporations view risks as being resident only in daily financial dealings, business risks live and lurk in all corners, waiting to strike and cripple. A risk must be redefined as any event or action that stops an organization from achieving its goals or business objectives. From the boardroom to the boiler room, proactive risk controls must be accepted for survival and should be embraced for success. As recognition of knowledge, skills, and abilities, the auditor as part of their career development plan may want to pursue the Certified in Risk and Information Systems Control (CRISC).

Kick-Off Meeting

Another best practice has to do with how one conducts the first meeting as an IT auditor with one's client/auditee. This is the most important aspect of the audit. From this meeting, the auditor will know if the audit will go as planned or if interruptions will supersede the progress of the audit. The first meeting sets the tone of the audit and establishes the auditor's rapport with the client/auditee. It is important to keep in mind that this is just as equally important between internal auditors as it is with external auditors.

Good client/auditee relations are a necessity for productive and efficient audit results to occur. Conduct and professionalism are primary attributes, with respect to the auditee, even when they are difficult to work with. The main impression the auditor wants to give his or her client/auditee is that the auditor is there to help and not to find all their mistakes. Nobody enjoys being told they are wrong, especially from an outsider who is just visiting for a short while.

From experience, if auditors have a client/auditee that is reluctant to help them through the audit, it may become harder for the auditors to meet all the demands of their audit managers. It will also be equally difficult to meet the desired budget set for the audit engagement. If an auditor encounters such a problem, the audit manager should be contacted as soon as possible. The manager will appreciate the alert and will most probably take care of the situation for the auditor.

Staff Mentoring

Again, part of the planning process is knowing when to be a mentor for one's staff and seniors to follow. This is a necessary duty that must be performed by all IT audit managements. After all, managers have to instruct their staff on the fine art of IT auditing and what better way to do that than to teach by example. In addition, the mentoring process provides the manager the opportunity to stay updated on new issues that pop up before the everyday staff or seniors working in the trenches. It also allows the manager to be more proactive when building a team from the ground up. Most managers like to mold their people to conform to their style of auditing and client/auditee relationships. Along with the concept of mentoring comes a new concept called coaching.

Coaching

Another best practice technique is coaching, which has been around since the early days of sports and probably before then. Time must be allocated to allow for coaching. The concept of coaching is relatively simple. The coach is someone who knows all about the subject and is willing to spend the time to pass on his or her knowledge. Often, managers are now reviewing the work of staff before the work is due to make sure all aspects of the audit are covered and are correctly stated. In the event the work is not correct, managers now take the time to explain in complete detail how they would approach the issue. This approach to auditing seems to be working because there are fewer and fewer review notes that are handed out after the engagements. Thus, the engagement runs more smoothly, accurately, and within budget.

Lunch Meetings

The lunch meeting has been around for years. This is a chance to meet with staff and supervisors and discuss issues and new developments. Managers frequently mention that they hold such a meeting once a month and name a supervisor or staff member to identify a topic to be covered and run the meeting. This facilitates sharing of information among members of the staff and generates new techniques or approaches to audits.

Managers often include members of the client's staff who might have a special interest or experience in an area. Audit managers take advantage of all opportunities they get to establish a greater rapport with their client/auditee. The times they work in are highly competitive and, therefore, their number one priority is their client/auditee and getting to know them as much as possible.

Understanding Requirements

Another critical process for the audit manager to understand, especially within audit planning, is the audit objectives and requirements. Clients/auditees for the most part are all the same; they all have needs and concerns for their businesses that must be addressed. Clients/auditees may come to IT auditors with concerns about a certain operating system or application. Although the concern is not within the scope of their audit, they must adhere to the client/auditee on a request. Most requests are simple and take but a few minutes to complete. The auditee will appreciate the communication of the potential delay and at the same time have more confidence in the auditor's ability to provide them with quality analytical skills, thus giving added value to a client/auditee.

Conclusion

The IT audit career development process should be institutionalized and supported by corporate management. The process itself involves (1) the establishment and integration of career path planning; (2) the definition of career path knowledge, skills, and abilities; (3) performance measurement; (4) performance counseling; (5) training; and (6) professional development. Each element requires institutional support and commitment to make it work. Like any process, it will require time, refinement, and improvement to make it work effectively.

The investment in establishing such a process in an organization is small compared to the long-range benefits it can bring. An example of such a benefit can be in the form of an experienced management cadre who can effectively understand, use, and manage the IS flows within the organization. This cadre was formerly IT auditors who were capable of developing their individual knowledge, skills, and abilities to successfully make the transition into a financial, operational, or corporate management position.

The IT auditor handles a great deal of responsibility within an organization. To develop controls that reduce the company's threat of exposure, IT auditors must understand the objectives of the audit, which is to conduct thorough, accurate, pertinent, and complete reviews that yield effective recommendations to senior management. To ensure that the audit and the auditor are meeting these goals, the audit management must provide evaluations regularly.

Evaluating audits and the auditors who perform them poses a substantial challenge to the audit management. For an evaluation to be effective, the management must be sure that every audit is reviewed and that its findings are clearly communicated to the auditor.

The IT audit and auditor assessment form can serve as a standardized testing system. It should indicate an auditor's strengths and weaknesses and provide guidance for career objectives. Scoring systems and assessment criteria can differ according to the level of detail required; however, it is essential that one scoring system and one set of criteria be consistently applied to every evaluation. Furthermore, evaluating IT audits should be an ongoing process to ensure audit quality and adjust to the organizational changes placed on the IT audit function.

Audit planning is a critical component of the audit process. A number of best practices that have been successfully used by audit management, supervisors, and staff in performing this process have been shared in this chapter. The audit plan itself is a guide to performing the steps of the audit process.

It has been shown how research, benchmarking, planning memos, budget coordination, risk analysis, kick-off meetings, staff mentoring and coaching, lunch meetings, and understanding requirements are all components of the planning process. Examples of these components have been provided as a way of showing how others have used them in being successful in their audit planning.

A best practice is a technique or method used that proves successful in practice. The ability to transfer these practices depends on the operating environment of the recipient. The sharing of best practices provides information to those who want to continue to improve their operations and are looking for those elements that help make others successful.

Review Questions

1. What is a career development plan? What is the IT audit career path? What options and alternatives does it provide?
2. How does an audit manager or organizational management design, develop, and implement a career development plan?
3. Why is performance assessment and performance counseling and feedback an important component within a career development plan?
4. What does professional development consist of?
5. Why is evaluating audit quality important?
6. What criteria can be developed for assessing the audit process? What are the critical steps in the audit process that can be evaluated?
7. What criteria can be developed for assessing the auditor? What are metrics?
8. What are two very important rules in the development of metrics?
9. How can audit follow-up assist in the evaluation process?
10. What is a best practice? Why should auditors learn about best practices?
11. What are some best practices in IT audit planning?
12. What are some of the major reasons for using risk analysis in audit planning?
13. What roles do mentoring or coaching play in audit planning best practices?
14. What are the skills needed to be an IT auditor? What skills do you have? What weaknesses do you need to build on?

Multiple-Choice Questions

1. Some of the following elements should be included in a career development plan:
    a. Career path planning with management support
    b. Definition of knowledge, skills, and abilities
    c. Performance assessment and counseling
    d. All of the above
2. Which professional certification can be helpful to an IT auditor's career?
    a. CISA
    b. CISSP
    c. CPA
    d. All of the above
3. Which IT audit area involves audit selection, definition of audit scope, initial contacts and communication with auditees and audit team selection?
    a. Fact gathering
    b. Audit tests
    c. Audit preparation
    d. Audit objectives
4. Which IT audit area involves a formal plan for reviewing and testing each significant audit subject area disclosed during the fact gathering?
    a. Audit objectives
    b. Audit program
    c. Audit tests
    d. Use of audit tools

5. Which IT audit area involves formal statements that describe a course of action that should be implemented to restore or provide accuracy, efficiency, or adequate control of an audit subject?
   a. Audit tests
   b. Finding of an audit report
   c. Recommendations of an audit report
   d. Conclusion of an audit report

6. IT audit assessment is very important and, at a minimum, consists of reviewing
   a. The completeness of the audit
   b. The pertinence of the information presented
   c. The accuracy of the audit work and supporting working papers
   d. All of the above

7. Some of the areas that one can assess for the IT auditor's individual performance are
   a. Communication skills
   b. Judgment
   c. Auditing knowledge
   d. All of the above

8. Why is it important to learn about best practices?
   a. Efficiency
   b. Add value to client/auditee or organization
   c. Advancement in technology
   d. All of the above

9. This best practice consists of a document that sets the tone or course of action you plan to take with your client/auditee:
   a. Benchmarking
   b. Planning memo
   c. Risk analysis
   d. None of the above

10. The reasons for risk analysis are
    a. Loss or corruption of information and IS assets
    b. Impaired and ineffective management decision making
    c. Disruption to customer service or other critical operations
    d. All of the above

Exercises

1. Interview an IT auditor and gather the following information:
   a. Position and company
   b. Number of years of experience in IT auditing
   c. Degree(s) and professional certifications
   d. Career path
   e. Why did he or she get into this field? What do they like about IT auditing? What do they dislike?
   f. What do they feel about the future of this field? Where do they see themselves in 5 years?

2. Using Web browsers, find general information about the IS Audit and Control Association.

3. Using a Web browser, find general information about the Institute of Internal Auditors.

4. Using a Web browser, find general information about the Association of Government Accountants.
5. Using a Web browser, find what universities offer graduate education in this field.

Answers to Multiple-Choice Questions

1—d; 2—d; 3—c; 4—b; 5—c; 6—d; 7—d; 8—d; 9—b; 10—d

Further Reading

1. Cangemi, M. and F. Gallegos, CIS auditing: A career plan, *New Accountant*, pp. 27–30, February 1991.
2. Carlin, A. and F. Gallegos, IT audit: A critical business process, *Computer Magazine*, pp. 87–89, Vol. 40, No. 7, IEEE, July 2007.
3. Curts, R.J. and D.E. Campbell, A Systems Engineering Approach to Information Assurance Operations, 2002 Command and Control Research and Technology Symposium, Conference Proceedings, Monterrey Naval Post Graduate School, CA, June 2002.
4. Gallegos, F., D.R. Richardson, and A.F. Borthick, *Audit and Control of Information Systems*, Thomson Corporation–South-Western Publishers, Cincinnati, OH, 1987.
5. Gallegos, F., Computer information systems audit career development, *CIS Auditors J.*, 1, 37–40, 1991.
6. Gallegos, F., *IS Audit Career Development Planning*, RIA/Auerbach Publishers, Boca Raton, FL, 1997.
7. Gallegos, F., Due professional care, *IS Control J.*, 2, 25–28, 2002.
8. Gallegos, F., Maintaining IT audit proficiency: The role of professional development planning, *IS Control J.*, 6, 20–23, 2002.
9. Gallegos, F., IT audit career development plan, *IS Control J.*, 2, 16–17, 2003.
10. Gallegos, F., IT auditor careers: IT governance provides new roles and opportunities, *IS Control J.*, 3, 40–43, 2003.
11. Gallegos, F. and A. Carlin, *Best Practices in Due Professional Care: An IT Audit Perspective*, #72-20-20.1, EDP Auditing Series, Auerbach Publishers, New York, 2003, pp. 1–13.
12. Information Systems Audit and Control Foundation, Model Curriculum for Undergraduate and Graduate Education in IS Auditing, Carol Stream, IL, March 1998.
13. Katsikas, S.K., *A Proposal for a Post-Graduate Curriculum in Information Security, Dependability and Safety*, ERASMUS New Technologies Publications, Greece, 1994.
14. Kneer, D. and F. Gallegos., Information systems audit education, *IS Audit Control J.*, 4, 1–10, 1994.
15. Looho, A. and F. Gallegos, IS Audit Training Needs for the 21st Century: A Selected Assessment, International Association for Computer Information Systems Conference, Las Vegas, NV, October 4–7, 2000, in *Information Systems*, 1, 147–153, 2000. (This paper was selected by IACIS as their Year 2000 recipient of the Best Research Paper Award.)
16. Lord, A.T. and F. Gallegos, ISACA model curriculum 2004: Continuing to invest in the future, *Inf. Syst. Control J.*, 6, 39–41, 2004.
17. Manson, D. and F. Gallegos, *Evaluating the Quality of an IS Audit*, RIA/Auerbach Publishers, Boca Raton, FL, 1997.
18. McIntosh, E., *Internal Auditing in a Total Quality Environment*, The Institute of Internal Auditors, Altamonte Springs, FL, 1992.
19. Sabroux-Rosenthal, C., The current state of IT audit education: A French perspective, *Journal Online*, ISACA, 2006.
20. Summers, S., Revised IASAC model curriculum for IS audit and control, *ISACA J.*, 5, 1–2, 2009.

Chapter 7

IT Auditing in the New Millennium

Chapters 1 through 6 provided our historical perspective as to how IT auditing originated and evolved. The impact of computer crime, the laws enacted and established to protect, the reaction of the audit, security and control profession to create and establish standards of practice, the practices, tools and techniques that have evolved, and the lessons learned in managing, performing, and reassessing the audit process were also dealt with. In this chapter, we will give you our glimpse of IT auditing in this new millennium and the challenges you will be facing.

With the passage of the Homeland Security Act, the Patriot Act, and the Sarbanes–Oxley Act, the role of the auditor (internal and external) will be more critical to the verification and validation of the financial infrastructure. The profession of IT auditing can provide a person with exposure to the way information flows in an organization and give its members the ability to assess its validity, reliability, and security. IT auditing involves people, technology, operations, and systems. It is a dynamic and challenging profession, a profession with a future. In addition, the field brings growth into new areas such as IT security and computer forensics.

Today, IT auditors interact with managers, users, and technicians from all areas of most organizations. They must have interpersonal skills to interact with multiple levels of personnel and technical skills to understand the variety of technology used in information processing activity—especially technology that impacts the company's financial statements. Also, he or she must gain an understanding of and a familiarity with the operational environment to assess the effectiveness of internal control. Finally, the IT auditor must understand the technological complexities of existing and future systems and the impact they have on operations and decisions at all levels.

IT auditing involves using computers to verify the integrity of computer-based systems. This process includes the examination, testing, and evaluation of internal controls within and around computer-based systems. The IT auditor is the technical expert who provides guidance to the audit staff or performs this function. Also, the IT auditor may be involved in assessing efficiency, effectiveness, and risks associated with the use of computers in the organization. IT auditing is a relatively new profession. IT audit employment opportunities are present in all sectors of private industry, public accounting, and government worldwide.

Nevertheless, what of tomorrow? What does the profession hold for us? What new challenges do we face? What controls will need to be in place? How will we educate the IT auditor of the future to deal with the changes the new millennium brings? How as information assurance professionals can we better educate and train the generations to come in practicing cybersecurity? This chapter intends to provide thoughts toward the future of an exciting field and profession.

IT Auditing Trends

Computing has become indispensable to the activities of organizations worldwide. The COBIT Framework (created in 1995 by the Information Systems Audit and Control Foundation) emphasizes this point and substantiates the need to research, develop, publicize, and promote up-to-date, internationally accepted IT control objectives. COBIT will be entering its 5th edition soon. In earlier documents such as the 1993 discussion paper "Minimum Skill Levels in Information Technology for Professional Accountants" and their 1992 final report "The Impact of Information Technology on the Accountancy Profession," the IFAC acknowledges the need for better university-level education to address growing IT control concerns and issues.

Reports of information theft, computer fraud, information abuse, and other information/technology control concerns are being heard more frequently around the world. Organizations are more information-conscious, people are scattered due to decentralization, and computers are used more extensively in all areas of commerce. Owing to the rapid diffusion of computer technologies and the ease of information accessibility, knowledgeable and well-trained IT auditors are needed to ensure that more effective controls are put in place to maintain data integrity and manage access to information. The need for better controls over IT has been echoed in the past by prior studies such as the AICPA COSO, ISO 9000, the IIA Systems Auditability and Control Report, Guidelines for the Security of IS by the OECD, and the U.S. President's Council on Integrity and Efficiency in Computer Audit Training curriculum. The most recent additions to these major studies are *Control Objectives for Information and Related Technology (COBIT): Framework*, now entering its 5th edition, the United States' National Strategy for Securing Cyberspace released in 2002, and ISO 17799 and 27000 and its follow-on amendments.

The AICPA's Assurance Services Executive Committee Trust Services/Data Integrity Task Force is responsible for updating and maintaining the Trust Services Principles and Criteria (TSPC) and creating a framework of principles and criteria to provide assurance on the integrity of information. Trust Services are a set of professional attestation and advisory services based on a core set of principles and criteria that address the risks and opportunities of IT-enabled systems and privacy programs. The following principles and related criteria are used by practitioners in the performance of Trust Services engagements:

- *Security*: The system is protected against unauthorized access (both physical and logical).
- *Availability*: The system is available for operation and use as committed or agreed.
- *Processing integrity*: System processing is complete, accurate, timely, and authorized.
- *Confidentiality*: Information designated as confidential is protected as committed or agreed.
- *Privacy*: Personal information is collected, used, retained, disclosed, and destroyed in conformity with the commitments in the entity's privacy notice and with criteria set forth in generally accepted privacy principles issued by the AICPA and CICA.

Following the Enron case and the demise of Arthur Andersen LLP, the AICPA's Assurance Services Executive Committee and the profession's legal environment have been impacted. The effect of the Sarbanes–Oxley Act will create change as far as the future of assurance service liability and limited liability partnership is concerned. This is an area that is very hard to predict with certainty. The opportunities basically fall into three areas: providing needed information to companies, providing assurances on new accountabilities including criteria for measurement, and providing intermediary services on behalf of the clients. The threats are in areas such as potential damage to the profession's image or reputation, increased competition, liability, and discontinuities caused by difficulty in adapting to new conditions.

Other areas mentioned for future growth are electronic commerce, healthcare performance measurement, elder care, policy compliance, outsourced internal audit, trading partner accountability, mergers and acquisitions, ISO 9000 and 27000, and World Wide Web assertions. These and the previously mentioned areas provide a glimpse of the impact of technology on business processes and the need for information assurances to audit, control, and secure. The AICPA has several reports well worth reading at www.aicpa.org.

The theory and methodologies of IT auditing are integrated from five areas: a fundamental understanding of business, traditional auditing, IT management, behavioral science, and IT sciences. Business understanding and knowledge are the cornerstones of the audit process. Traditional auditing contributes knowledge of internal control practices and overall control philosophy within a business enterprise. IS management provides methodologies necessary to achieve successful design and implementation of systems. Behavioral science indicates when and why IS are likely to fail because of people's problems. IT sciences contribute to knowledge about control theory and the formal models that underlie hardware and software designs as a basis for maintaining data integrity.

IT auditing is an integral part of the audit function because it supports the auditor's judgment on the quality of computer systems. IT auditors are the technological resource for the audit staff. The audit staff often looks to them for technical assistance. Within IT auditing, there are organizational IT audits (management control over IT), technical IT audits (infrastructure, data centers, data communication), application (business/financial) IT audits, and compliance IT audits involving national or international standards. Ever since the ISACA, formerly the EDPAA, was formed in Los Angeles in 1969, there has been a growing demand for well-trained and skilled IT audit professionals. The publication *The EDP Auditors Association: The First Twenty-Five Years* documents the early struggles of the association and evolution of IT audit practices in this field.

IT auditing is a profession with conduct, aims, and qualities that are characterized by worldwide technical and ethical standards. It requires specialized knowledge and often long and intensive academic preparation. Most accounting, auditing, and IT professional societies believe that improvements in research and education will definitely provide a "better-developed theoretical and empirical knowledge base for the IT audit function." They feel that emphasis should be placed on education obtained at the college level.

The breadth and depth of knowledge required to audit IT is extensive. For example, IT auditing involves the application of risk-oriented audit approaches; the use of computer-assisted audit tools and techniques (e.g., EnCase, CaseWare, Idea, ACL, Guardant, eTrust, CA-Examine); the application of standards (national or international) such as ISO 9000/3 and ISO 17799 and 27000 and related amendments to improve and implement quality systems in software development; the auditing of systems under development involving complex SDLC or new development techniques (e.g., prototyping, end-user computing, rapid systems development); and the auditing of complex technologies involving electronic data interchange, client servers, local and wide area networks, data communications, telecommunications, and integrated voice/data/video systems.

New Dimension: Information Assurance

Organizations increasingly rely on critical digital electronic information capabilities to store, process, and move essential data in planning, directing, coordinating, and executing operations. Powerful and sophisticated threats can exploit security weaknesses in many of these systems. Outsourcing technological development to countries that could have terrorists on their development staff causes speculation that the potential exists for code to be implanted that would cause disruption, havoc, embezzlement, theft, and so on. These and other weaknesses that can be exploited become vulnerabilities that can jeopardize the most sensitive components of information capabilities. However, we can employ deep, layered defenses to reduce vulnerabilities and deter, defeat, and recover from a wide range of threats. From an information assurance perspective, the capabilities that we must defend can be viewed broadly in terms of four major elements: local computing environments, their boundaries, networks that link them together, and their supporting infrastructure. The U.S. National Strategy for Securing Cyberspace is one of those initiatives.

The term "information assurance" is defined as information integrity (the level of confidence and trust that can be placed on the information) and service availability. In all contexts, whether business or government, it means safeguarding the collection, storage, transmission, and use of information. The ultimate goal of information assurance is to protect users, business units, and enterprises from the negative effects of corruption of information or denial of services. We believe the Department of Homeland Security and Supporting Organizations such as the NSA, FBI, and CIA have worked toward supporting this goal and the plan.

The extent of such examples can range from situations where the personnel data in a human resource database is valid in the sense that it could be but is not, in fact, correct, and there may be no negative impact on the IS but the enterprise may suffer when people get the wrong amount of money in their paychecks or when the money is sent to the wrong address. Similarly, if an order for an engine part in a supply and logistics system is lost in the part of the system that should have dictated which pallets get loaded onto which boat to which destination, the IS continues to operate but the supply service is denied to the person requiring the parts. Naturally, if the IS processing, storing, or communicating information becomes corrupt or unavailable, the enterprise may also be affected as a whole. However, simply protecting the systems without protecting the information, processing, and communication is not adequate.

As the nation's IS and their critical infrastructures are being tied together (government and business), the points of entry and exposure increase, and thus, risks increase. As mentioned earlier, the National Information Infrastructure (NII), the Government Information Infrastructure (GII), and the Corporate Information Infrastructure (CII) are overlapping in their domains. The technological advancement toward higher bandwidth communication and advanced switching systems has reduced the number of communications lines and further centralized the switching functions. Survey data indicates that the increased risk from these changes is not widely recognized. Since 9/11, we have seen more coordinated efforts have been made by U.S. defense organizations such as the Defense Information Systems Agency (DISA) to promulgate standards for the Defense Information Infrastructure (DII) and the Global Information Grid (GiG), which should have a positive impact on information assurance that will extend beyond the U.S. Department of Defense and impact all segments of the national economy. The NSA has drafted and produced standards for IT security personnel that not only impact federal agencies but also corporate entities who contract IT services in support of the federal government. NIST has generated security guidance for HIPAA compliance that impacts the medical profession and all corporations/business servicing the health field who handle medical information.

IT Audit: The Profession

IT auditing is a relatively new profession for a new generation. A profession is more than just an occupation. A profession has certain special characteristics: it is supported by a common body of knowledge, certification, continuing education, code of ethics and standards, an educational curriculum, and a professional association. Since 1975, there have been various studies identifying a common body of knowledge for the IT audit profession. With regard to certification, the CISA provides a level of accreditation for the profession. Certification requires continuing education so that those who are certified maintain a level of proficiency and continue their certification.

The audit profession, as shown in Appendix III, is supported by a code of ethics and professional standards that has been developed by several professional associations that support audit professionals. As mentioned in Chapter 6, there are a number of additional certifications that can benefit one seeking to enter the IT audit, control, and security field. A number of universities provide education in auditing computer systems and several are in the process of developing IT audit curricula and information assurances curricula. Finally, there are a number of professional associations involved in IT audit, control, and security community, as noted in Appendix III.

As for the future, the profession will continue as IT impacts the business process and shrinks our global communication structure. As several studies mentioned in earlier Chapter 3 have shown, new standards and practices will evolve. The terms mobility, flexibility, efficiency, effectiveness, and economy will be commonplace in the method of work. The ability to use technology in accomplishing assigned tasks and responsibilities, reporting, and follow-up will continue to evolve.

A Common Body of Knowledge

A common body of knowledge consists of clearly identified areas in which a person must attain a specific level of understanding and competency necessary to successfully practice within the profession. These areas are categorized into core areas. Organizations such as ISACA, AICPA, IIA, CICA, ISSA, InfoSec, and others around the world have issued major studies and papers on the topic of the knowledge, skills, and abilities needed to audit computers. Students, especially business and computer majors, receive a degree of base-level training in (1) auditing concepts and practices; (2) management concepts and practices; (3) computer systems, telecommunications, operations, and software; (4) computer information processing techniques; and (5) understanding of business on local and international scales. These are some of the major core areas of competency identified by the various independent studies for the individual who enters the IT audit, control, and security field.

Certification

Certification is a vital component of a profession. As you prepare for entry into your profession, whether it is accounting, IS, or other business fields, certification will be the measure of your level of knowledge, skills, and abilities in the profession. For example, attainment of the CPA designation is an important career milestone for the practicing accountant. In IT auditing, CISA, is the level of recognition and attainment.

A CISA must pass a rigorous written examination and have at least 5 years of experience and education. The CISA examination covers areas such as IS security and control practices;

IS organization and management; IS process; IS integrity, confidentiality, and availability; and IS development, acquisition, and maintenance. Thus, university education plays an important part in providing the groundwork toward the certification process.

Certification is important and a measure of skill attainment within the profession. Attainment of more than one certification will enhance your knowledge, skills, and abilities within the audit domain. Proficiency in skill application comes from experience and continuing education. The dynamic changes in business (commerce), IT, and world events continue to shape the future.

Continuing Education

Another critical element for the next millennium is continuing education. It is an important element for career growth. As graduates enter their profession, they will find that their academic education is the foundation for continued development of career-enhancing knowledge, skills, and abilities. A continuing education requirement exists to support the CISA program. The IT auditor of the twenty-first century will constantly face change with regard to existing systems and the dynamics of the environment (i.e., reorganization, new technology, operational change, and changing requirements).

Because the organizational environment in which the IT auditor operates is a dynamic one, it is important that new developments in the profession be understood so that they may be appropriately applied. Thus, the continuing education requirement helps the CISA attain new knowledge and skills to provide the most informed professional opinion. Training courses and programs are offered by a wide variety of associations and organizations to assist in maintaining the necessary skills that they need to continue to improve and evolve. Methods for receiving such training may even be global with video teleconferencing and telecommuting and with the Internet playing a major role in training delivery.

A Code of Ethics and Professional Standards

A code of ethics and professional standards provides the foundation for a profession even into the next millennium. Professional associations establish codes of ethics to guide the conduct of their members in their professional and personal activities. The image of a professional is an important characteristic in establishing creditability.

Professional standards determine how the profession should be practiced and the goals toward which the practitioner strives. As a professional of the future, you should become familiar with the code of ethics and professional standards of your profession. Further, IT audit professionals need to become involved in the development of those standards and best practices. Again, technology is a tool in the dissemination of lessons learned and best practices.

Educational Curricula

The academic communities both in the United States and abroad have incorporated portions of the common body of knowledge and the CISA examination domains into courses taught at the university level. Several recent studies indicate the growth of computer audit courses emerging in university curricula worldwide. A model curriculum for undergraduate and graduate education in

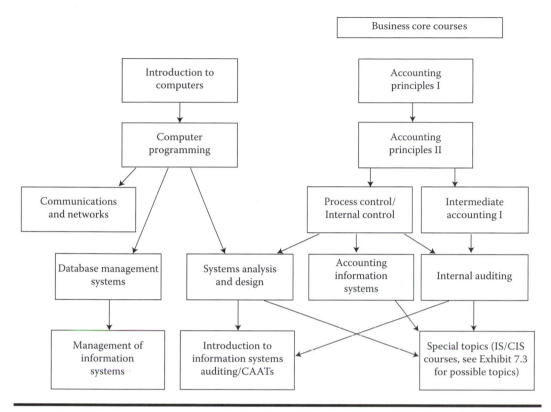

Exhibit 7.1   Structure of the model curriculum for an undergraduate program in IS auditing.

IS audit education was initially issued in March 1998 and updated in 2005 by the IS Audit and Control Association and Foundation (see Exhibits 7.1 through 7.4). In Exhibits 7.5 and 7.6, we look at how that model relates to areas of emphasis for the CISA exam.

Also, several universities have developed curricula tailored to support the profession of IT auditing. These prototypes exist at institutions such as Arizona State University, California State Polytechnic University (Pomona), the University of West Florida (Pensacola), the University of Houston, the University of Minnesota, Georgia State University, Florida Atlantic University, the University of Nagoya (Japan), Queensland University of Technology and Curtin University of Technology (Australia), and others. IT auditing is a profession that provides opportunity and challenge. As an important stepping-stone in one's career, it can open many opportunities.

Also, the area of information assurances has grown and evolved. As mentioned in the following section, InfoSec, through U.S. federal support, has developed criteria and training standards for IT security professionals. The United States in its passage of the Cyber Security Research and Development Act has pledged almost a billion dollars for the development of curriculum, research, and skills for future professionals needed in this field.

New Trends in Developing IT Auditors and Education

The IT audit training can be at two levels—development of professionals for entry and follow-up training for professionals in the field. At the entry level, universities have been responding

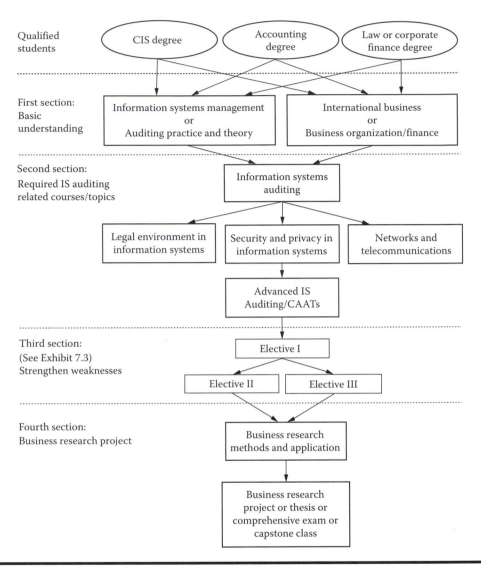

Exhibit 7.2   Structure of the model curriculum for IS auditing at the graduate level.

to the needs of the IT audit and information assurances profession. At the undergraduate level, IT courses have begun to be integrated into accounting programs and accounting or finance courses into IT programs. At the graduate level, several universities have successfully implemented and maintained IT audit programs. These universities have attempted to meet the growing demand for entry-level knowledge, skills, and abilities of the IT auditor and security personnel.

Currently under review, ISACA is currently in the process of updating its model curriculum. The first was published by ISACA in 1998. In 2005, under the direction of Dr. Alan T. Lord of Bowling Green University, an international Task Force updated this model is available

Rapid systems development

IS planning

Executive IS

Computer forensics

Encryption, cryptographic, and biometrics

Advanced systems analysis and design

Wide area/voice networks

Information assurance

Software quality assurance

Business systems analysis

Network management

Human factors in systems design

Business economics

Advanced office systems/directed study

Managerial accounting for decision making

Database design and processing

Executive development

Professional presentations using technology/directed study

Management science/directed study

Advanced financial management/directed study

Accounting for decisions and control/directed study

IS integrity, confidentiality, and availability

Exhibit 7.3   Sample undergraduate or graduate course topics for special topics or directed electives.

at ISACA Website. A partial list of such universities who met the criteria of the model have been recognized by ISACA can be found at www.isaca.org The *ISACA Model Curriculum for IS Audit and Control* was developed for use in universities and colleges by a task force of 11 academics and practicing professionals from 11 countries on five continents. Its aim is to develop the skills that businesses require to adequately govern, control, and audit information systems.

As stated at their academic Website, "The model curriculum is interdisciplinary, a format encouraged by most international accrediting bodies. The curriculum outlines the academic training needed to prepare candidates for entry-level positions in IS assurance, provides support for curriculum development and evolution, (and) discusses the research on current university offerings in the field."

In addition, ISACA issued in 2008 the *Model Curriculum for Information Security Management*. For those institutions interested in IS, the curriculum provides academic institutions with a basic

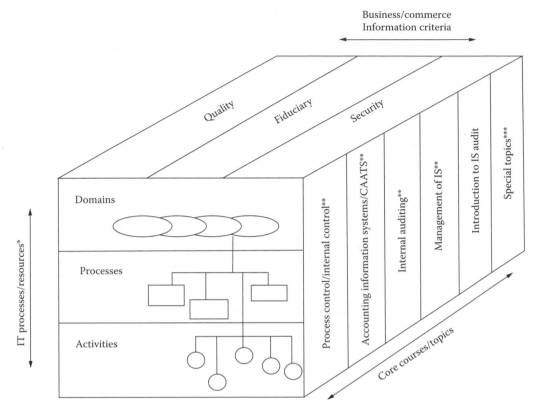

*IT resources involve people, application systems, technology, facilities, and data.
**Courses offered within most universities may have different name or course title.
***See Exhibit 7.3.

Exhibit 7.4   Relevance of undergraduate IS audit model.

framework of the education required to develop the knowledge, skills, and abilities needed to make students employable in the profession. The curriculum

- Is a set of comprehensive topics that should be included in the educational program for developing information security managers
- Provides a goal for colleges and universities worldwide to meet the demand for educating future information security management professionals
- Can serve those who are interested in obtaining an information security education and interested educational institutions worldwide that have already developed or are interested in developing a curriculum in information security

In the information assurances community, InfoSec has made significant strides in gaining support from the U.S. universities. The NIETP operates under national authority and its initiatives provide the foundation for a dramatic increase in the population of trained and professionalized security experts. Activities in this area directly support government efforts to professionalize and certify system administrators and associated network positions. There is no single vehicle to accomplish this task. NIETP initiatives are multifaceted and strive to address all aspects of its

Percent of Exam	CISA Examination Content Areas to Model Curriculum (Undergraduate) Title and Description	Process Control/Internal Control	Accounting Info Systems/CAATS	Internal Audit	Management of IS	Introduction to IS Auditing
14%	*The IS audit process* Provide IS audit services in accordance with IS audit standards, guidelines, and best practices to assist the organization in ensuring that its information technology and business systems are protected and controlled	X	X	X	X	X
14%	*IT governance* Provide assurance that the organization has the structure, policies, accountability, mechanisms, and monitoring practices in place to achieve the requirements of corporate governance of IT	X		X	X	X
19%	*Systems and infrastructure lifecycle management* Provide assurance that the management practices for the development/acquisition, testing, implementation, maintenance, and disposal of systems and infrastructure will meet the organization's objectives	X	X	X	X	X
23%	*IT service delivery and support* Provide assurance that the IT service management practices will ensure the delivery of the level of services required to meet the organization's objectives	X	X		X	X
30%	*Protection of information assets* Provide assurance that the security architecture (policies, standards, procedures, and controls) ensures the confidentiality, integrity, and availability of information assets	X	X	X	X	X

Exhibit 7.5   Relevance of IS audit undergraduate.

Domain	CISA Examination Domain to Model Curriculum (Graduate) Title and Description	IS Audit/CAATS	Legal Environment of IS	Security and Privacy of IS	Network/Telecommunication	Advanced IS Audit
14%	*The IS audit process* Provide IS audit services in accordance with IS audit standards, guidelines, and best practices to assist the organization in ensuring that its information technology and business systems are protected and controlled	X	X	X	X	X
14%	*IT governance* Provide assurance that the organization has the structure, policies, accountability, mechanisms, and monitoring practices in place to achieve the requirements of corporate governance of IT	X	X	X	X	X
19%	*Systems and infrastructure lifecycle management* Provide assurance that the management practices for the development/acquisition, testing, implementation, maintenance, and disposal of systems and infrastructure will meet the organization's objectives	X	X	X	X	X
23%	*IT service delivery and support* Provide assurance that the IT service management practices will ensure the delivery of the level of services required to meet the organization's objectives	X	X	X	X	X
30%	*Protection of information assets* Provide assurance that the security architecture (policies, standards, procedures, and controls) ensures the confidentiality, integrity, and availability of information assets	X	X	X	X	X

Exhibit 7.6   Relevance of IS audit graduate.

role in education, training, and awareness by creating partnerships among government, academia, and industry. Through these partnerships, the NIETP can assess current offerings in InfoSec courses, from a variety of sources to identify gaps and determine how to fill those gaps. As of 2011, more than 100 U.S. universities have been identified as centers of excellence in information assurances education (university and community colleges) or Academic Centers of Excellence in Information Assurance Research, and have had their courses certified to meet U.S. federal standards. The U.S. Department of Homeland Security and the U.S. National Security Agency are continuing a leadership role with national-level programs by the NSTISSC for ensuring the finest preparation of professionals entrusted with securing the U.S. National Security Systems.

In 2010, the U.S. CyberChallenge (USCC) was initiated. The mission of the USCC is to significantly reduce the shortage in the cyber workforce by serving as the premier program to identify, recruit, and place the next generation of cybersecurity professionals. USCC's goal is to find 10,000 of America's best and brightest to fill the ranks of cybersecurity professionals where their skills can be of the greatest value to the nation. The Cybercamps were originally launched in 2009 under the auspices of the Center for Strategic and International Studies, and the nonprofit Center for Internet Security. This public–private program enjoys the support of government agencies such as the Federal Chief Information Officers Council, the Department of Homeland Security's Science and Technology Directorate, and the Department of Defense; and private firms including Lockheed Martin, Microsoft, Booz Allen Hamilton, Secure Info, AFFIRM, the Women in Technology Educational Foundation, and others.

Although predicting future trends is always problematic, the need for qualified people to deal with these developments is critical. Some future trends could be as follows:

- More applications will be purchased or outsourced, and fewer applications will be developed in-house, including audit software.
- The use of communication facilities will increase, providing greater interaction between personnel and computers, migration to virtual corporations, and businesses as a whole. The global, national, and business information infrastructure must be secure.
- More sophisticated auditing techniques will emerge, permitting the auditor to make more use of the computer in auditing the computer.
- Quality assurance groups will become more effective in the performance of their responsibilities. As these groups become more effective, auditors will be able to rely on their work and perform fewer audit tasks.
- Organizations will begin to incorporate artificial intelligence and expert systems into day-to-day business processing. As this occurs, auditors will need to become more involved in ensuring the adequacy of controls in these systems. Tests of such controls will extend beyond the physical borders of the country because business (commerce) is global.
- Less reliance will be placed on the centralized information group to manage and control information within the organization.
- More use will be made of the exchange of information electronically throughout the organization in assessing and improving the totality and quality of business processes.
- There will be a rapid reduction in the cycle time of introducing both new technology and new business applications.

If most of these predictions are accurate, auditors, as representatives of management, will become more involved in the daily operations of the computer department. To build controls into the computer systems, IT auditor, control, and security personnel must develop a high degree of competence in IT and become involved in its complete life cycle.

Perhaps, the most revealing of trends is the work done at George Washington University and their "Forecast of Future Technology" and its impact on industry shown in Chapter 1. One looks at this forecast with apprehension, wondering how it will be possible to audit, control, and secure this technology and its application within business and society as a whole.

Finally, your authors believe that there is a very critical need to bring information assurance education into the K–12 domain. The reasons are quite clear with the threat and reports of information theft, cyberbullying, improper use of social networking, child pornography, child endangerment, and teen abuse appearing in news accounts. What is sad is that our young generation is not adequately prepared to handle and confront child exportation, cyberbullying, and intimidation, which has resulted in attempted suicides and even deaths. Social networking sites such as MySpace.com, Facebook.com, match.com, and others are creating traps for the innocent and unaware.

Cyberspace has created new domains of misuse and abuse toward fellow citizens. There is a drastic need to educate. We applaud the efforts of institutions such as Carnegie Mellon University who have seen this need and developed supportive sites such as MySecureCyberspace.com and federal agencies such as the U.S. Secret Service and Department of Justice who have produced CDs on such subjects for free distribution to K–12 schools who request them. The safety and education of our children in practicing cybersecurity are new goals and objectives for all of us in this field to work toward. The following section illustrates an approach, through a Regional Security Center, through which one might bring information assurance professionals and educators at the university, community college, and K–12 together to reach this common goal through collaborative support in Exhibit 7.7.

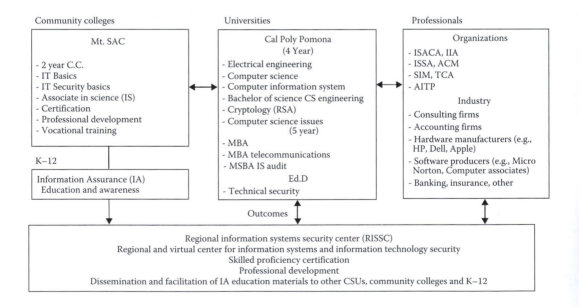

Exhibit 7.7 Model for collaborative development, dissemination, and adaptation of information assurance survivability curriculum.

Career Opportunities in the Twenty-First Century

IT audit, control, and security offer a variety of career opportunities. This profession can be a career in itself or it can lead to other careers that utilize the knowledge, skills, and abilities gained as an IT audit professional. Today's IT auditors are employed by public accounting firms, management consulting firms, private industries, and the government. The career path can be what one wants it to be. The IT auditor, IT security professional, and IT forensic professional for the twenty-first century will continue to be in demand. Internationally, the need is growing.

Public Accounting

Public accounting firms offer individuals an opportunity to enter into IT auditing and IT forensics. Although these firms may require such individuals to begin their careers in financial audits to gain experience in understanding the organization's audit methodologies, after initial audit experience the individual who expresses interest will be transferred to this specialty for further training and career development. Many who have taken this career path have been successful, and several have advanced to partnership level of the firm. The primary sources for most CPA firms are college recruitment and development within. However, it is not uncommon for a firm to hire from outside for specialized expertise (i.e., computer forensics, telecommunication, and database systems). As mentioned earlier in the AICPA report, opportunities exist in the assurance services marketplace.

Private Industry

Like public accounting, private industry offers entry-level IT audit and IT security professional positions. In addition, IT auditors gain expertise in more specialized areas (i.e., telecommunications, systems software, and systems design), which can make them candidates for IT operations, IT forensics, and security positions. Many chief executive officers view audit experience as a management training function. The IT auditor has particular strengths of educational background, practical experience with corporate IS, and understanding of executive decision making. Some companies have made a distinction between IT auditors and operational and financial auditors. Others require all internal auditors to be capable of auditing IT systems. The sources for persons to staff the IT audit function within a company generally may come from the following areas: college recruitment, internal transfers or promotions, and outside hiring.

Management Consulting

Another area of opportunity for IT audit, control, and security personnel is management consulting. This career area usually is available to IT auditors with a number of years' experience. Many management consulting practices, especially those that provide services in the computer IS environment, hire experienced IT audit, control, and security personnel. This career path allows these candidates to use their particular knowledge, skills, and abilities in diagnosing an array of computer and management information issues and then assist the organization in implementing the solutions. The usual resources for such positions are experienced personnel from CPA firms, private industries, and the government. IT forensics is another growing area in management consulting services.

Government

The government offers another avenue for one to gain IT audit experience. In the United States, federal, state, county, and city governments employ staffs that conduct IT audit-related responsibilities. Worldwide, governments employ staff that conduct IT audits. Such government positions offer training and experience to staff responsible for performing this function. The sources for government IT auditors are college recruits and employees seeking internal promotion or transfer. There are occasions when experienced resources may be hired from the outside as well.

As cited earlier, there are a number of career opportunities available to the individual seeking an opportunity in IT audit. For the college graduate with the appropriate entry-level knowledge, skills, and abilities, this career provides many paths for growth and development. Further, as a career develops and progresses, IT audit can provide mobility into other areas as well. Federal organizations such as the NSA, FBI, Department of Justice, and CIA employ personnel who have IT audit experience, computer security experience, and IT forensics experience. Career paths may vary substantially within different organizations and countries. The USCC demonstrates the Federal Government's interest in locating candidates with such skills for potential employment and follow-on training.

Role of the IT Auditor in IT Governance

It is time to revisit the role of the IT auditor mentioned in Chapter 3 of this book. The role of the IT auditor is critical to the success of IT governance and the audit, control, and security of IS of the future. Ensuring the quality, integrity, and authenticity of the information of tomorrow is of utmost importance. The auditor evaluating today's complex systems must have highly developed technical skills to understand the evolving methods of information processing. Contemporary systems carry risks such as noncompatible platforms, new methods to penetrate security through communication networks (e.g., the Internet), and the rapid decentralization of information processing with the resulting loss of centralized controls.

Auditing the processing environment is divided into two parts. The first and the most technical part of the audit is the evaluation of the operating environment with major software packages (e.g., the operating and security systems) representing the general or environmental controls in the automated processing environment. This part is usually audited by the IT audit specialist. The second part of the processing environment is the automated application, which is audited by the general auditor who possesses some computer skills.

As the use of IT in organizations continues to grow, auditing computerized systems must be accomplished without having in place many of the guidelines established for the traditional auditing effort. In addition, new uses of IT introduce new risks, which in turn require new controls. IT auditors are also in a unique position to evaluate the relevance of a particular system to the enterprise as a whole. Because of this, the IT auditor often plays a role in senior management decision making.

The role of an IT auditor can be examined through the process of IT governance and the existing standards of professional practice for this profession. As mentioned earlier, IT governance is an organizational involvement in the management and review of the use of IT in attaining the goals and objectives set by the organization.

Because IT impacts the operation of an entire organization, everyone should have an interest and role in governing its use and application. This growing awareness has led organizations to recognize that if they are to make the most of their IT investment and protect that investment, they need a formal process to govern it.

Reasons for implementing an IT governance program include

- Increasing dependence on information and the systems that deliver the information
- Increasing vulnerabilities and a wide spectrum of threats
- Scale and cost of current and future investments in information and IS
- Potential for technologies to dramatically change organizations and business practices, create new opportunities, and reduce costs

As long as these factors remain a part of business, there will be a need for effective, interdependent systems of enterprise and IT governance.

An open-standard IT governance tool that helps nontechnical and technical managers and auditors understand and manage risks associated with information and related IT was developed by the IT Governance Institute and the IS Audit and Control Foundation. COBIT is a comprehensive framework of control objectives, which helps IT auditors, managers, and executives discharge fiduciary responsibilities, understand their IT systems, and decide what level of security and control is adequate. COBIT provides an authoritative, international set of generally accepted IT practices for business managers and auditors.

COBIT can be downloaded on a complimentary basis from www.isaca.org. It includes a publication containing detailed management guidelines to bridge the gaps among business risks, control needs, and technical issues. These new tools help businesses monitor processes by using critical success factors (CSFs), key goal indicators (KGIs), key performance indicators (KPIs), and maturity models (MMs). Additional resources and information are available at www.ITgovernance.org.

IT Auditor as Counselor

In the past, users have abdicated responsibility for controlling computer systems mostly because of the psychological barriers that surround the computer. As a result, except for the IT auditor, there are few checks and balances. Therefore, auditors must take an active role in developing policies on auditability, control, testing, and standards. Auditors also must convince users and IT personnel of the need for a controlled IS environment.

An IT audit staff in a large corporation can make a major contribution to computer system control by persuading user groups to insist on a policy of comprehensive testing for all new systems and all changes to existing systems. By reviewing base-case results, user groups can control the accuracy of new or changed systems by actually performing a complete control function.

Insisting that all new systems be reviewed at predefined checkpoints throughout the system's development life cycle can also enhance the control of IT. The prospect of audit review should prompt both user and systems groups to define their objectives and assumptions more carefully. Here, too, IS auditors can subtly extend their influence.

IT Auditor as Partner of Senior Management

Although the IT auditor's roles of counselor and skilled technician are vital to successful company operation, they may be irrelevant if the auditor fails to view auditing in relation to the organization as a whole. A system that appears well controlled may be inconsistent with the operation of a business.

Decisions concerning the need for a system traditionally belonged to senior management, but because of a combination of factors (mostly the complex technology of the computer), computer system audits had not been successfully performed. When allocating funds for new systems, management has had to rely on the judgment of computer personnel. Although their choices of new and more effective computer systems cannot be faulted, computer personnel have often failed to meet the true business needs of the organization.

Management needs the support of a skilled computer staff that understands the organization's requirements, and IT auditors are in a position to provide that information. They can provide management with an independent assessment of the effect of IT decisions on the business. In addition, the IT auditor can verify that all alternatives for a given project have been considered, all risks have been accurately assessed, the technical hardware and software solutions are correct, business needs will be satisfied, and costs are reasonable.

Educating the Next Generation on IT Audit and Control Opportunities

Many have prospered from their experiences in the profession of IT auditing. Hopefully, more will choose to become involved in the future of IT auditing by the involvement of their organization in supporting research efforts at the university level and taking the time to be a "professor for a day" to share their experiences and knowledge level with faculty and students. This is a valuable opportunity to educate the next generation.

Many more opportunities in IT auditing will continue to open in this new millennium. Career profiles of alumni who have chosen IT auditing provide a good example of career paths. Also, professional associations such as the IIA, AGA, and ISACA chapters may have student-related activities and information. Typically, many ISACA chapters sponsor activities such as a "Student Night" and "Best Student Paper Contest" or provide speakers to colleges for discussing IT audit-related topics.

Other opportunities for students and those wishing to enter this field to demonstrate their knowledge skills and abilities come in the form of competition. For several years now, the Colloquium for Information Systems Security Educators has sponsored the Collegiate Cyber Defense Competition which has grown dramatically to the point where they now have regional competition with the winners going to a National Competition event. We expect the US Cyber Challenge (USCC) to continue in growing and generating interest in Cyber Security careers. A recent US National Science Foundation Grant in 2011 was awarded to establish Cyber Security Competition League at the collegiate level. And, as mentioned earlier, interest in the development of people with such skills is going global as the cybersecurity executing arm of the United Nations has endorsed the Global CyberLympics, a new initiative by the EC-Council to foster stronger international cooperation on information security issues and to improve cybersecurity training and awareness in developing nations and third-world countries.

Created by EC-Council, the Global CyberLympics is a series of ethical hacking games comprised of both offensive and defensive security challenges that will take place starting from September 2011 across six continents. Teams will vie for regional championships, followed by a global hacking championship round to determine the world's best cybersecurity team. The EC-Council is sponsoring over $400,000 worth of prizes at the CyberLympics.

The Global CyberLympics is supported by the International Multilateral Partnership against Cyber Threats (IMPACT), the cybersecurity executing arm of the United Nations' specialized agency—the International Telecommunications Union (ITU). With this support, the Global

CyberLympics hopes to be able to promote its mission to 136 partner countries with the world's first international team hacking contest around the globe.

Participation by the professional, faculty, and student is a necessary element in this process. Certainly, if one is interested in a profession, necessary steps should be taken to educate others about it. Many ISACA chapters provide students with opportunities to learn more about this dynamic and challenging profession. Also, such endeavors can help in the next step of educating K–12 in safe practices and do's and don'ts in the use of cyberspace.

Conclusion

Where there are computer systems and information generated by this technology to support decision making, there will be a need to assess the reliability, validity, and internal controls of such systems. There will be a need to secure them. Such technology affects everyone's future regardless of his or her profession—law, medicine, education, social work, and so on. As an IT auditor or IT control professional, one is and will continue to be on the forefront of this change and aid one's employer in successfully preparing for the business environment of the new millennium. This is a dynamic profession constantly facing change and challenges—a continuous learning environment.

Opportunity for careers in this challenging and dynamic field has never been better as the new millennium begins. IT governance, new technology, e-business, and legal issues have opened a new frontier and the need for new skills and common sense in applying good business practices. Corporate, institutional, and business integrity are under constant review by the public and government. Audit as an institutional process can be a major player in reestablishing the public's confidence in business. Thanks to the Sarbanes–Oxley Act, the audit report has more value today than ever before. As a result of the Homeland Security Act, the Patriot Act, and the U.S. National Strategy for Securing Cyberspace, information assurances (audit, control, and security) are now everyone's business.

As organizations rely more on IT for day-to-day processing and decision making, the need for auditor involvement will increase accordingly. The introduction of new IT brings with it new risks. Management, as part of the governance process, needs assurance that risks are under adequate control. Auditors, as part of the IT governance, must become involved in the introduction of new technology. In addition, the responsibility for IT is being distributed from IS personnel to end users. Thus, information assurances (audit, control, and security) will become a more important part of all audits.

Review Questions

1. What knowledge, skills, and abilities must an IT auditor have?
2. Where are IT auditors employed?
3. What is the role of the AICPA's Assurance Services Executive Committee Trust Services/ Data Integrity Task Force?
4. What professional standards and guidance exist for the auditor, IT auditor, and government auditor?
5. Will the audit profession continue? How will it keep pace with the change in technology, business practices, government regulation, and international events?
6. What is a common body of knowledge?

7. What professional certifications exist for the audit professional and IT auditor?
8. What are the CISA exam domains? What is the CISA exam?
9. The ISACA issued its "Model Curriculum for Graduate and Undergraduate Education in Information Systems Auditing." What guidance does this document provide?
10. Where are the career opportunities for an IT auditor in the future?

Multiple-Choice Questions

1. IT auditing involves
   a. People
   b. Technology
   c. Operations and systems
   d. All of the above
2. COBIT was developed and issued by
   a. AICPA
   b. IIA
   c. ISACA
   d. ACFE
3. The SAC reports were issued by
   a. IIA
   b. ISSA
   c. ISACA
   d. AICPA
4. Information assurance is defined as
   a. Information integrity
   b. The level of confidence and trust that can be placed on the information
   c. The level of trust and confidence that can be placed on service availability
   d. All of the above
5. Which U.S. federal act has pledged almost a billion dollars toward curriculum, research, and skill development in IT audit, control, security, and information assurances issues?
   a. Computer Fraud and Abuse Act of 1984
   b. Computer Security Act of 1987
   c. Cyber Security Research and Development Act
   d. HIPAA Act of 1996
6. Which organization operating under U.S. national authority and its initiatives provides the foundation for a dramatic increase in the population of trained and professionalized security experts?
   a. AICPA
   b. ISACA
   c. NIETP
   d. None of the above
7. Standards for information security officers have been issued by
   a. CIA
   b. FBI
   c. GAO
   d. NSTISSC

8. A new field of opportunity and career growth is
   a. Business systems analyst
   b. Computer forensic analyst
   c. Network administrator
   d. None of the above
9. The number of universities within the United States identified as Academic Centers of Excellence in Information Assurance Education or Research is
   a. 10
   b. 25
   c. 50
   d. Greater than 100
10. The IT auditor's role in IT governance can be as
    a. A counselor
    b. A partner of senior management
    c. An educator
    d. All of the above

Exercises

1. Do you believe that IT auditing is a career opportunity for you? If so, what are your strengths and do they match the knowledge, skills, and abilities needed to perform in this profession?
2. What do IT auditors do? What are their roles and areas of responsibilities?
3. Obtain five position announcements for IT auditors and summarize the five key skills wanted of them.
4. List three universities that provide graduate education in IT security, IT audit, and/or information assurances.

Answers to Multiple-Choice Questions

1—d; 2—c; 3—a; 4—d; 5—c; 6—c; 7—d; 8—b; 9—d; 10—d

Further Reading

1. Accounting Education Change Commission, Position Statement No. 1: Objectives of education for accountants, *Issues in Accounting Education*, Fall, 307–312, 1990.
2. American Institute of Certified Public Accountants (AICPA), Top Technology Initiatives 2007, Discussion Paper: Information Technology Considerations in Risk Based Auditing: A Strategic Overview, June 26, 2007.
3. American Institute of Certified Public Accountants (AICPA), Statement on Standards for Attestation Engagements No. 16, Reporting on Controls at a Service Organization, 2010.
4. American Institute of Certified Public Accountants (AICPA), *The Effect of Information Technology on the Auditor's Consideration of Internal Control in a Financial Statement Audit (SAS 94)*, 2001.
5. American Institute of Certified Public Accountants (AICPA), *Consideration of Fraud in a Financial Statement Audit (SAS 99)*, 2002.

6. American Institute of Certified Public Accountants (AICPA), Special Committee on Information Assurances, *MegaTrends Affecting Future Assurance Services*, April 2003.

7. American Institute of Certified Public Accountants (AICPA), Special Committee on Information Assurances, *Affect of Information Technology on the Assurance Services Marketplace*, April 2003.

8. Bess, J., *Sharing Best Practices for a World-Class Audit Function*, Protiviti Inc., New York, 2006.

9. Cerullo, V. and M.J. Cerullo, Impact of SAS No. 94 on computer auditing techniques, *IS Control J.*, 1, 53–57, 2003.

10. Gallegos, F., IT audit careers: IT governance provides new roles and opportunities, *IS Control J.*, 3, 40–43, 2003.

11. Gallegos, F., IT audit career development plan, *IS Control J.*, 2, 16–17, 2003.

12. Gallegos, F. and A. Carlin, IT audit: A critical business process, *Computer Magazine*, pp. 87–89, Vol. 40, No. 7, IEEE, July 2007.

13. Gallegos, F. and M. Smith, Red Teams: An audit tool, techniques and methodology for information assurance, *Inf. Syst. Control J.*, 2, 51–56, 2006.

14. Information Systems Audit and Control Foundation, COBIT, 5th Edition, Information Systems Audit and Control Foundation, Rolling Meadows, IL, 2012. Available at: http://www.isaca.org/Knowledge-Center/COBIT/Pages/Overview.aspx

15. Information Systems Audit and Control Association, *2011 CISA Examination Domain*, ISACA Certification Board, Rolling Meadows, IL, 2010.

16. Looho, A. and F. Gallegos, Audit training needs for the 21st century: A selected assessment, *J. Computer Inform. Syst.*, XXXXI(2), 9–15, 2000–2001.

17. Menkus, B. and F. Gallegos, *An Introduction to IT Auditing*, #71-10-10.1, Auerbach Publishers, Boca Raton, FL, 2002, pp. 1–16.

18. Singleton, T., What every IT auditor should know about cyberforensics, Information Systems Audit and Control Association, *JournalOnline*, 2006, http://www.isaca.org/Content/NavigationMenu/Members_and_Leaders/Publications/Journal/Information_Systems_Control_Journal_Home.htm.

19. Staley, B., I. Scott and M. Shapeero, From CSI to the classroom: Developing a computer forensics degree program, Information Systems Audit and Control Association, *JournalOnline*, 2006, http://www.isaca.org/Content/NavigationMenu/MembersandLeaders/Publications/Journal/Informations_Systems_Control_Journal_Home.htm.

20. Summers, S., Revised ISACA model curriculum for IS audit and control, *ISACA Journal*, 5, 1–2, 2009.

21. Wiederkehr, B., IT security programme, *IS Control J.*, 3, 30–33, 2003.

AUDITING IT PLANNING AND ORGANIZATION

Chapters 8 through 12

Effectively managing an IT organization requires a solid foundation of governance and control over IT resources. Governance guides the decision rights, accountability, and behaviors of an organization. This is controlled through a series of processes and procedures that identify who can make decisions, what decisions can be made, how decisions are made, how investments are managed, and how results are measured. This section covers the critical issues and best practices in governing and controlling IT resources. Key processes like project management and quality management ensure that investments made in IT deliver on their promised value.

In this section, the processes of the COBIT plan and organize domain (Exhibit II.1) and the monitor and evaluate domain (Exhibit II.2) are discussed in more detail and compared to other existing standards.

Plan and organize. This domain covers strategies and tactics, and concerns the identification of the way IT can best contribute to the achievement of the business objectives.

Monitor and evaluate IT performance. This domain addresses IT governance and performance management facilitated by reporting and measurement.

Chapter 8 covers the foundation for IT governance by aligning IT decisions with business strategy. This process is a very important step for management, auditors, and users, in that it sets a framework for accomplishing control objectives within the organization and allows active involvement of organization's stakeholders.

Chapter 9 covers IT strategic planning for aligning IT decisions with the business strategy. Alignment helps ensure that investment decisions are made that deliver value to the organization. Architectural processes and technology standards help ensure that applications are developed with an eye to delivering long-term flexibility and cost effectiveness.

PO1 Define a Strategic IT Plan
Control Objectives
1.1   IT value management
1.2   Business–IT alignment
1.3   Assessment of current performance
1.4   IT strategic plan
1.5   IT tactical plans
1.6   IT portfolio management
PO2 Define the Information Architecture
Control Objectives
2.1   Enterprise information architecture model
2.2   Enterprise data dictionary and data syntax
2.3   Data classification scheme
2.4   Integrity management
PO3 Determine Technological Direction
Control Objectives
3.1   Technological direction planning
3.2   Technological infrastructure plan
3.3   Monitoring of future trends and regulations
3.4   Technology standards
3.5   IT architecture board
PO4 Define the IT Organization and Relationships
Control Objectives
4.1   IT process framework
4.2   IT strategy committee
4.3   IT steering committee
4.4   Organizational placement of the IT function
4.5   IT organizational structure
4.6   Roles and responsibilities
4.7   Responsibility for IT quality assurance
4.8   Responsibility for risk, security, and compliance
4.9   Data and system ownership
4.10   Supervision

Exhibit II.1   **Processes for planning and organization.**

4.11	Segregation of duties
4.12	IT staffing
4.13	Key IT personnel
4.14	Contracted staff policies and procedures
4.15	Relationships

PO5 Manage the IT Investment

Control Objectives

5.1	Financial management framework
5.2	Prioritization within IT budget
5.3	IT budgeting process
5.4	Cost management
5.5	Benefit management

PO6 Communicate Management Aims and Direction

Control Objectives

6.1	IT policy and control environment
6.2	Enterprise IT control framework
6.3	IT policies management
6.4	Policy rollout
6.5	Communication of IT objectives and direction

PO7 Manage Human Resources

Control Objectives

7.1	Personnel recruitment and retention
7.2	Personnel competencies
7.3	Staffing of roles
7.4	Personnel training
7.5	Dependence upon individuals
7.6	Personnel clearance procedures
7.7	Employee job performance evaluation
7.8	Job change and termination

PO8 Manage Quality

Control Objectives

8.1	Quality management system
8.2	IT standards and quality practices

Exhibit II.1   (Continued) Processes for planning and organization.

| 8.3 Development and acquisition standards |
| 8.4 Customer focus |
| 8.5 Continuous improvement |
| 8.6 Quality measurement, monitoring, and review |
| **PO9 Assess and Manage IT Risks** |
| *Control Objectives* |
| 9.1 IT and business risk management alignment |
| 9.2 Establishment of risk context |
| 9.3 Event identification |
| 9.4 Risk assessment |
| 9.5 Risk response |
| 9.6 Maintenance and monitoring of a risk action plan |

Exhibit II.1 (Continued) Processes for planning and organization.

| **ME1 Monitor and Evaluate IT Performance** |
| *Control Objectives* |
| 1.1 Monitoring approach |
| 1.2 Definition and collection of monitoring data |
| 1.3 Monitoring method |
| 1.4 Performance assessment |
| 1.5 Board and executive reporting |
| 1.6 Remedial actions |
| **ME2 Monitor and Evaluate Internal Control** |
| *Control Objectives* |
| 2.1 Monitoring of internal control framework |
| 2.2 Supervisory review |
| 2.3 Control exceptions |
| 2.4 Control self-assessment |
| 2.5 Assurance of internal control |
| 2.6 Internal control at third parties |
| 2.7 Remedial actions |

Exhibit II.2 Processes to monitor and evaluate.

ME3 Ensure Regulatory Compliance	
Control Objectives	
3.1	Identification of laws and regulations having potential impact on IT
3.2	Optimization of response to regulatory requirements
3.3	Evaluation of compliance with regulatory requirements
3.4	Positive assurance of compliance
3.5	Integrated reporting
ME4 Provide IT Governance	
Control Objectives	
4.1	Establishment of an IT governance framework
4.2	Strategic alignment
4.3	Value delivery
4.4	Resource management
4.5	Risk management
4.6	Performance measurement

Exhibit II.2   (Continued) Processes to monitor and evaluate.

Chapter 10 discusses the risk management process. Risk management should be part of an organization's thinking, integrated into strategic planning, operational planning, project management, resource allocation, and other processes. The assessment and analysis of risk in any IT environment is not an easy process. This chapter examines the application of risk assessment and resources available to assist IT auditors and IT professionals in this area.

Chapter 11 discusses IT processes and quality assurance processes needed to ensure that the IT systems meet the stated objectives. Quality is a goal that enhances product and process. Mature processes help ensure quality that increases customer satisfaction and the ability to compete in a global market. Quality assurance includes measurement tools and techniques to assess and adjust the business processes. This information gives management a comfort that processes are working as intended or early warning of problem areas.

Chapter 12 discusses the financial management processes needed to ensure that investment decisions support business objectives. This is not an easy process in economic times where justification and priorities must be reconciled. There is a price for audit, control, and security and often one must be assured that this does not exceed the level of risk or potential loss the organization may face.

Chapter 8

IT Governance

IT governance has taken on greater importance in many organizations. With the globalization of many industries and financial markets, developed and developing economies are recognizing the importance of effective governance and controls to the success of organizations. Sarbanes–Oxley and COSO in the United States, the Combined Code on Governance in the United Kingdom, and the OECD Principles of Corporate Governance in Europe have set the bar for corporate governance. For IT, COBIT is becoming a global standard for IT governance and controls. COBIT provides a framework for implementing controls in IT to comply with Sarbanes–Oxley and other global governance standards. Organizations around the world are using the principles defined in COBIT to improve IT performance.

In a survey conducted by the IT Governance Institute in 2011, 94% of participating organizations considered IT to be quite or very important to the overall organization strategy. The same survey noted that the higher the level of IT governance maturity, the higher the return on IT investment. To achieve IT governance maturity and a higher return on IT investment requires a close partnership between IT and business management. Close alignment of the IT strategy with the business strategy is essential to the success of a well-functioning partnership. It is important for the IT organization to understand the business it supports and for the business to understand the IT it uses. For this to happen, the IT organization must have a seat at the table with the CEO and other business leaders.

Communicating with senior management is not an easy task as IT is only a small portion of the issues faced by organizations today. The IT leaders must be seen as valuable members of the team, and not just a service provider. For this to happen, the CIO and IT management must first seek to understand the business issues and offer proactive solutions to the organization's needs. IT management must also have a clear understanding of their current strengths and weaknesses and be able to honestly communicate this information to the business management.

IT governance provides the structure to achieve the alignment of the IT strategy with the business strategy, incorporate IT into the enterprise risk management (ERM) program, manage the performance of IT and ensure delivery of value, and ensure adequate internal controls and regulatory compliance.

IT Processes

The COBIT Monitor and Evaluate IT Performance domain (Exhibit 8.1) addresses IT governance and performance management facilitated by reporting and measurement.

Effectively managing an IT organization requires a solid foundation of governance and control over IT resources. Governance guides the decision rights, accountability, and behaviors of an organization. This is controlled through a series of processes and procedures that identify who can make decisions, what decisions can be made, how decisions are made, how investments are managed, and how results are measured. Implemented effectively, IT governance can improve organizational performance by

- Ensuring decisions and investments are aligned with organizational objectives
- Integrating IT into the ERM program

ME1 Monitor and Evaluate IT Performance
Control Objectives
1.1 Monitoring approach
1.2 Definition and collection of monitoring data
1.3 Monitoring method
1.4 Performance assessment
1.5 Board and executive reporting
1.6 Remedial actions
ME2 Monitor and Evaluate Internal Control
Control Objectives
2.1 Monitoring of internal control framework
2.2 Supervisory review
2.3 Control exceptions
2.4 Control self-assessment
2.5 Assurance of internal control
2.6 Internal control at third parties
2.7 Remedial actions
ME3 Ensure Regulatory Compliance
Control Objectives
3.1 Identification of laws and regulations having potential impact on IT
3.2 Optimization of response to regulatory requirements
3.3 Evaluation of compliance with regulatory requirements
3.4 Positive assurance of compliance
3.5 Integrated reporting

Exhibit 8.1 Processes to monitor and evaluate.

ME4 Provide IT Governance
Control Objectives
4.1 Establishment of an IT governance framework
4.2 Strategic alignment
4.3 Value delivery
4.4 Resource management
4.5 Risk management
4.6 Performance measurement
4.7 Independent assurance

Exhibit 8.1 (Continued) Processes to monitor and evaluate.

- Improving oversight and control of organizational requirements, process proposal decisions, as well as implementation planning and support
- Establishing a framework for managing IT to deliver value to the organization
- Ensuring adequate internal controls and regulatory compliance
- Defining roles and responsibilities across the organization to support the identification and assignment of appropriate resources for development, implementation, compliance, and management efforts

Delivering value from IT is a joint effort between business and IT to develop the right requirements, work together for successful delivery, and deliver the promised benefits of automation. To be effective, the board must understand the current state of IT and actively participate in establishing the future direction of IT.

Effectively communicating with the board about IT is not always easy. IT is a very complex environment, which is difficult to explain to non-IT professionals. In addition, many members of senior management will have their own issues and a vested interest in certain IT projects and services that may influence the decision-making process. Getting agreement up front on the measures of IT performance will go a long way toward focusing senior management on the key issues in managing IT. In addition, measuring both business and IT performance will help hold both parties accountable for the success of IT projects and service delivery.

Enterprise Risk Management

According to an article in the *Harvard Business Review*, the key to getting value from IT is to effectively manage risk. The COSO ERM Framework defines ERM as follows:

> Enterprise risk management is a process, effected by an entity's board of directors, management and other personnel, applied in strategy setting and across the enterprise, designed to identify potential events that may affect the entity, and manage risks to be within its risk appetite, to provide reasonable assurance regarding the achievement of entity objectives.*

---

* Unknown, Enterprise Risk Management—Integrated Framework. Committee of Sponsoring Organizations of the Treadway Commission. September 2004, p. 2. http://www.coso.org/documents/coso_erm_executivesummary.pdf

Mismanagement of risk can carry an enormous cost. In recent years, business has experienced numerous risk-associated reversals that have resulted in considerable financial loss, decrease in shareholder value, damage to organization reputations, dismissals of senior management, and, in some cases, the very dissolution of the business. This increasingly risky environment in which risk mismanagement can have dire consequences mandates that the management adopt a more proactive perspective on risk management.

What Is Enterprise Risk Management?

Over time, a business that cannot manage risk effectively will not prosper and will perhaps fail. For example, a product recall could be disastrous and the organization's end. Rogue traders without oversight and adequate controls have destroyed old, well-established institutions in a very short time. Historically, risk management in even the most successful businesses has tended to be in "silos"—the insurance risk, the technology risk, the financial risk, and the environmental risk—all managed independently in separate compartments. Coordination of risk management has usually been nonexistent, and identification of emerging risks has been sluggish.

At first glimpse, there is much similarity between ERM and other classes of risk (e.g., credit, market, and liquidity risk) and the tools and techniques applied to them. In fact, the principles applied are nearly identical. ERM must identify, measure, mitigate, and monitor risk. However, at a more detailed level, there are numerous differences, ranging from the risk classes themselves to the skills needed to work with operational risk.

ERM has become more widely accepted as a means of managing organizations. In a survey conducted by the Professional Risk Managers' International Association, over 90% of respondents believed that ERM is or will be part of their business processes. Should firms be able to develop successful ERM programs, the next step will be for these firms to integrate ERM with all other classes of risks into truly enterprise-wide risk management frameworks. See Exhibit 8.2 for an example of an ERM organizational structure representative of the banking industry.

There are many reasons for the establishment of ERM functions within organizations. The following are a few of them.

Organizational Oversight

In light of events surrounding corporate scandals and the increasing executive and regulatory focus on risk management, the percentage of companies with formal ERM methods is increasing, and audit committees are becoming more involved in corporate oversight. The United Kingdom and Canada have set forth specific legal requirements for audit committee oversight of risk evaluation, mitigation, and management, which are widely accepted as best practices in the United States. For example, in the United States, the AICPA took action to clarify the application of risk in the issuance of Statement on Auditing Standards 104-111.

Increasing Business Risks

The magnitude of loss and the impact of operational risk and losses to date are difficult to ignore. There is no better illustration of the failure to appropriately manage risk than the financial losses realized during the financial crisis of 2007–2009. In 2009, the Basel Committee published survey results of internal losses from 121 banks in 17 countries realized over 10 million incidence of loss

Performance Indicators	Measure	Standard
Organization Contribution		
Strategic contribution	Completion of strategic initiatives	Approved projects
Business value of IT projects	Business evaluation based on financial measures (return on investment [ROI])	Internal rate of return
Management of IT investment	Actual versus budgeted expenses	Industry comparison
Future Orientation		
Service capability improvement	Deliver internal projects to plan: • Internal process improvement • Organization development • Technology renewal • Professional development	Industry comparison and past performance
Staff management effectiveness	Staff metrics by function: • Utilization/billable ratios • Voluntary turnover by performance level • Percent of staff with completed professional performance plans	Industry comparison and past performance
Enterprise architecture evolution	Development/approval of enterprise architecture plan (EAP)	Industry or market comparison and past performance
	Systems adherence to EAP and technology standards	
Emerging technologies research	Percent of IT budget allocated to research of new and updated technologies	Comparison to selected competitors
Knowledge management	Completion of training courses	Past performance
	Percentage of positions with qualified backup	
Operational Efficiency and Effectiveness		
Process excellence	Process maturity rating	CMMI maturity level
	Process performance • Quality • Cost • Speed	

Exhibit 8.2   Example of IT performance measures.

Responsiveness	Process cycle time	Past performance
	Cycle time to market	
Backlog management and aging	Staff days of budgeted work in backlog status	Past performance
	Days outstanding of oldest budgeted work	
Internal cost of quality	Time/cost of process improvement and quality assurance initiatives per IT employee	Industry or market comparison and past performance
Security and safety	Absence of major issues in audit reports	Industry or market comparison and past performance
	Absence of major, unrecoverable failures or security breaches	
Customer Orientation (Customer Service)		
Customer satisfaction	Score on customer satisfaction survey	Past performance
IT/business partnership	Frequency of IT Business Group (ITBG) meetings	Schedule
	Index of IT involvement in generating new strategic applications	Past performance
	Index of user involvement in generating new strategic applications	Past performance
Application development performance	Delivery to customer expectations • Quality (user acceptance) • Cost (budget) • Speed (schedule)	Past performance
Service-level performance	Weighted percent of applications and operations services meeting service-level targets for availability and performance	Past performance

Exhibit 8.2 (Continued) Example of IT performance measures.

with a total of over 59.6 million Euros. These losses did not even include the losses from the financial meltdown. The highest frequency of loss occurred in the areas of execution, delivery, process management, and fraud.*

With the increasing speed of change for all companies in this new era, senior management must deal with many complex risks that have substantial consequences for the organization. A few forces currently creating uncertainty are

---

* Basel Committee on Banking Supervision, Sound Practices for the Management and Supervision of Operational Risk, consultative document, issued December 2010, pp. 10–11.

- Technology and the Internet
- Increased worldwide competition
- Free trade and investment worldwide
- Complex financial instruments
- Deregulation of key industries
- Changes in organizational structures from downsizing, reengineering, and mergers
- Increasing customer expectations for products and services
- More and larger mergers

Collectively, these forces are stimulating considerable change and creating an increasing risk in the business environment.

Regulatory Issues

The international regulators clearly intend to encourage banks to develop their own proprietary risk measurement models to assess regulatory as well as economic capital. In 2003, the Basel Committee on Banking Supervision submitted a paper "Sound Practices for the Management and Supervision of Operational Risk." In developing these sound practices, the committee recommended that banks have risk management systems in place to identify, measure, monitor, and control operational risks. Although the guidance in this paper is intended to apply to internationally active banks, plans are to eventually apply this guidance to those banks deemed significant on the basis of size, complexity, or systemic importance and smaller, less complex banks. Regulators will eventually conduct regular independent evaluations of a bank's strategies, policies, procedures, and practices, addressing operational risks. The paper indicates that an independent evaluation of operational risk will incorporate a review of the following six areas*:

- Process for assessing overall capital adequacy for operational risk in relation to its risk profile and its internal capital targets
- Risk management process and overall control environment effectiveness with respect to operational risk exposures
- Systems for monitoring and reporting operational risk exposures and other data quality considerations
- Procedures for timely and effective resolution of operational risk exposures and events
- Process of internal controls, reviews, and audit to ensure integrity of the overall risk management process
- Effectiveness of operational risk mitigation efforts

Market Factors

Market factors also play an important role in motivating organizations to consider ERM. Comprehensive shareholder value management and ERM are very much linked. Today's financial markets place substantial premiums for consistently meeting earnings expectations. Not meeting expectations can result in severe and rapid decline in shareholder value. Research conducted by

---

* Basel Committee on Banking Supervision. Sound Practices for the Management and Supervision of Operational Risk. June 2011, pp 10-11. http://www.bis.org/publ/bcbs195.pdf.

Tillinghast–Towers Perrin found that, with all else being equal, organizations that achieved more consistent earnings than their peers were rewarded with materially higher market valuations.* Therefore, for corporate executives, managing key risks to earnings is an important element of shareholder value management. The traditional view of risk management has often focused on property- and liability-related issues or internal controls. However, traditional risk events such as lawsuits and natural disasters may have little or no impact on destroying shareholder value compared to other strategic and operational exposures such as customer demand shortfall, competitive pressures, and cost overruns. One explanation for this is that traditional risk hazards are relatively well understood and managed today—not that they do not matter. Managers now have the opportunity to apply tools and techniques for traditional risks to all risks that affect the strategic and financial objectives of the organization.

For nonpublicly traded organizations, ERM is valuable for many of the same reasons. Rather than from the perspective of shareholder value, ERM would provide managers with a comprehensive overview of other important items such as cash flow risks or shareholder risks. Regardless of the organizational form, ERM can be an important management tool.

Corporate Governance

The strongest defense against operational risk and losses resides and flows from the highest level of the organization—the board of directors and executive management. The board, the management team that they hire, and the policies that they develop, all set the tone for an organization. As guardians of shareholder value, the board of directors must be acutely attuned to market reaction to negative news. In fact, they can find themselves castigated by the public if the reaction is severe enough. As representatives of the shareholders, board of directors are responsible for policy matters relative to corporate governance, including but not limited to setting the stage for the framework and foundation for ERM.

At present, ERM is a hot topic of discussion for regulators and in boardrooms across the globe. In 2010, the Basel Risk Management Committee issued updated guidance on managing operational risk that further highlights the importance of enterprise risk management. Meanwhile, shareholders are aware of operational risks that can add up to billions of dollars every year and include frequent, low-level losses and also infrequent but catastrophic losses that have actually wiped out firms. Regulators and shareholders have already signaled that they will hold directors and executives accountable for managing operational risk.

Best Practice

Senior managers need to encourage the development of integrated systems that aggregate various market, credit, liquidity, operational, and other risks generated by business units in a consistent framework across the institution. Consistency may become a necessary condition to regulatory approval of internal risk management models. An environment where each business unit calculates its risk separately with different rules will not provide a meaningful oversight of enterprise-wide risk. The increasing complexity of products, linkages between markets, and potential benefits offered by overall portfolio effects are pushing organizations toward standardizing and integrating risk management.

---

* Tillinghast–Towers Perrin, *Enterprise Risk Management: Trends and Emerging Practices*, The Institute of Internal Auditors Research Foundation, Altamonte Springs, FL, 2001, p. xxvi.

Future of Enterprise Risk Management

It seems clear that ERM is more than another management fad or academic theory. In the past decade, ERM has become part of the management process for organizations. Had these processes been in place during the previous two decades, a number of the operational risk debacles that took place may not have occurred or would have been of lesser magnitude.

The following improvements are already in progress and will continue to evolve as more organizations apply lessons learned to the process:

- Organizations will no longer view risk management as a specialized and isolated activity—for instance, the management of insurance or foreign exchange risks. The new approach will keep managers and employees at all levels sensitized to and concerned about risk management. Risk management will be coordinated with senior management oversight and everyone in the organization will view it as part of his or her job. The risk management process will be continuous and broadly focused. All business risks and opportunities will be covered.
- The use of bottom-up risk assessments will be a standard used to identify risks throughout the organization. Self-assessment will involve everyone in the organization and require individual units to focus and report on the threats to their business objectives. Through this, the organization will be able to understand loss potential and risk control by business, profit center, and product. The individual line manager will begin to understand the loss potential in his or her own processing system.
- The use of top-down scenario analysis will be another standard method used to identify risks throughout the organization. This analysis will determine the risk potential for the entire firm, business, organization, or portfolio of business. By its very nature, it is a high-level representation and cannot get into the bottom-up transaction-by-transaction risk analysis.

For example, Microsoft has a campus of more than 50 buildings in the quake-prone Seattle area, and therefore, earthquakes are a risk.* In the past, organizations looked at silos of risk. It would have looked at property insurance when considering the risks of an earthquake and how to protect equipment and buildings. However, using scenario analysis, it is now taking a more holistic perspective in considering the risk of an earthquake.

The Microsoft risk management group has analyzed this disaster scenario with its advisors and has attempted to quantify its real cost, taking into account how risks are correlated. In the process, the group identified risks in addition to property damage such as the following:

- Director and officer liability if some people think the management was not properly prepared
- Key personnel risk
- Capital market risk because of the firm's inability to trade
- Worker compensation or employee benefit risk
- Supplier risk for those in the area of the earthquake
- Risk related to loss of market share because the business is interrupted
- Research and development risks because those activities are interrupted and product delays occur
- Product support risks because the organization cannot respond to customer inquiries

---

* Crouhy, M., D. Galai, and R. Mark, *Making Enterprise Risk Management Payoff*, McGraw-Hill, New York, 2001, pp. 132–133.

By using scenario analysis, management has identified a number of risks that it might not have otherwise, and Microsoft is now in a better position to manage these risks. The future ERM tools such as risk assessment and scenario analysis will assist companies in identifying and mitigating the majority of these risks.

Organizations are using internal and external loss databases to capture occurrences that may cause loss to the organization and the extent of the loss. These data are used in quantitative models that will project the potential losses from the various risk exposures. It is used to manage the amount of risk an organization may be willing to take.

Organizations allocate capital to individual business units based on operational risk. By linking operational risk capital charges to the sources of that risk, individuals with risk-optimizing behavior will be rewarded and those without proper risk practices will be penalized.

Internal audit can become even more focused on how risks are managed and controlled throughout the organization on a continuous basis. Internal audit will be responsible for reporting on integrity, accuracy, and reasonableness of the organization's entire risk management process. In addition, internal audit can be involved in ensuring the appropriateness of the organization's capital assessment and allocation processes. Audit can also influence continual improvement of risk management and controls through the sharing of best practices.

Management will be looking for individuals who are skilled in risk management. Professional designations such as the Bank Administration Institute's Certified Risk Professional (CRP) and the Information and Audit and Control Association's CISM will demonstrate proficiency in the risk management area and will be in demand. In 2007, ISACA introduced a new certification in IT governance. The CGEIT is for individuals responsible for corporate IT governance, including risk management. ISACA recently announced the CRISC designation for IT professionals who have hands-on experience with risk identification, assessment, evaluation, response, monitoring, control design and implementation, and control monitoring and maintenance. The CRISC designation will not only certify professionals who have knowledge and experience identifying and evaluating entity-specific risk, but also aid them in helping enterprises accomplish business objectives by designing, implementing, monitoring, and maintaining risk-based, efficient, and effective controls.

Overall, organizations will be better positioned to deal with the broad scope of enterprise-wide risks. By implementing the ERM process, companies will begin to maximize their overall risk profile for competitive advantage.

Regulatory Compliance and Internal Controls

One of the key risks that organizations need to manage is compliance with laws and regulations. The sheer number of laws and regulations applicable to a global organization can be overwhelming (see Chapter 2). It can take a dedicated team to sift through all the financial, security, privacy, and industry-specific regulatory requirements to determine the impact on processes and information systems. Fortunately, many of the IT requirements are satisfied with the implementation of the controls outlined in COBIT.

There are tools that can help an organization identify laws and regulations and track the control processes implemented to address them.* There are also tools that can help with mapping controls to regulatory requirements (e.g., Sarbanes–Oxley Act). These tools provide key information for auditors, regulators, and user groups to determine where controls are effective for testing, and gaps that

---

* Filipek, R., Compliance automation, *Internal Auditor*, February 2007, pp. 27–29.

need to be filled. IT should work together with the organization's compliance officer to ensure that it is aware of new requirements and report on the resolution of existing requirements.

The implementation of Sarbanes–Oxley has created greater awareness and focus on IT controls. Although there is some debate on the value of SOX to enterprises, there is no doubt that it has increased investment in IT general controls and application controls in many organizations. SOX compliance has forced many organizations to review existing applications that process financial transactions with an eye to controlling these processes. This has created improved awareness and knowledge of IT, business, and financial professionals on the need to develop control requirements to build controls into applications during the development process.

Performance Measurement

Measuring IT performance is dependent on the strategy and objectives of the organization. However, it comes down to the value IT is delivering to the organization. In general, IT delivers value through delivering successful projects and keeping operations running. If an organization is looking for reduced costs, it may measure the cost of IT and the business function cost before and after automation. If an organization is focused on growing new markets, it may measure the time to market for new products. IT adds value to an organization through project and service delivery.

IT projects deliver business value by automating business processes. As these projects are enabled by technology, IT is adding value to the organization. Measuring the amount of benefit delivered from these projects is one way of representing the value of IT. Automating business processes typically results in higher IT costs and lower business costs (or higher revenue). The original project's business case made certain assumptions about the cost and benefit of the new application. Although the project's business case will be validated as part of the postimplementation review (see Chapters 10 and 11), it is important to continue measuring the ongoing costs over time. There may be a perception that IT costs are growing without the recognition that business costs should be dropping or revenue growing by a greater margin. It is important to keep this information in front of the board and senior management as a reminder of the value of IT. Delivering the promised value is the responsibility of both IT and the business functions. Reporting on the actual results holds both parties accountable for the expected results. Another measure of value is how quickly the organization can respond to new business opportunities. If IT has been successful at implementing flexible infrastructure, applications, and processes, it will be able to respond to business needs.

IT services deliver value by being available for the organization as needed. Organizations rely heavily on automated systems to function on a day-to-day basis. The failure of these systems results in loss of revenue or increased expense to the organization. A more positive perspective is the amount of revenue or productivity generated by these systems. As part of the strategic and operational planning process, an organization must decide the level of service required of IT. The service levels will depend on the type of organization, application portfolio, services provided by IT, and the objectives of the organization. An online auction house that depends on 24×7 service availability for its existence will have a different need than a grocery store.

Balanced Scorecard

IT governance, business alignment, internal controls, and performance can be measured by implementing a balanced scorecard. A balanced scorecard provides an overall picture of IT performance aligned to the objectives of the organization. A balanced scorecard is developed by listing the objectives of IT and establishing measurements that track performance against these objectives (Exhibit 8.2).

Metrics and Management

In today's complex environment, one way to effectively manage IT is to implement the measurement of key processes. Measurement is required to monitor key processes to track performance, detect control failures, and identify trends.

Developing a measurement process takes time and resources (time and money) to implement. To be successful, both the organization and IT management must be in full support. They should also be consulted as to the types of measurements they believe will benefit the organization. The areas to be measured should be closely aligned to the objectives of the organization. It makes no sense to measure something that no one cares about. Management will be most supportive when it sees the metrics applied to the areas that it feels are most in need of improvement. Typically, those areas that are being measured have a tendency to attract focus and improve over time. A critical metric set—the few key metrics that are critical to the successful management of the function—should be identified and applied to the environment.

Once the critical metric set has been identified, the individuals in the areas that are to be measured should be consulted, and a set of measurements that will provide meaningful data should be devised. The individuals responsible for doing the work should select the best means to measure the quality and productivity of their work. Metrics that are developed should only be applied to data that are both measurable and meaningful. The individuals in the area can best identify these areas. It is useless to waste time on developing measures on areas that do not fall within the critical metric set, as these measures will not satisfy the needs of management.

After the initial implementation of the first measurements, it is important to show the results. Data should be compiled over a predefined period, and results should be provided to management on a regular basis. As the metrics database grows, the reliability of the data will increase and the usefulness of the reports to management will increase.

Although it is quite an easy task to get management to support metrics if management is informed as to what metrics are and the impact they can have, it is difficult to get support from management if they have not been educated or if they are skeptical. In this situation, a different tack should be taken. First, management must be made to realize that it is next to impossible to manage what cannot be or is not measured. The easiest way to strengthen this argument is to back it up with some sample metrics.

Second, survey data from other organizations can be compiled and presented to encourage adoption of a metrics frame of mind. For sample metrics, identify several areas that can be measured and provide with a reports on these areas. Again, it is important to provide short-term payback to show results and continue to produce reports showing progress in those areas. Once management sees that the areas being measured are improving, they will be more likely to provide support for the process.

Metric Reporting

Once the data are gathered, it must be put in a format that is easy for the reader to understand. A combination of graphics and text is important to illustrate the context and performance trends.

The reports must stress the progress in those areas selected for measurement. This is a key point in that it shows short-term results in the long-term measurement process. Areas of improvement must be stressed to show that the process is working.

When management has accepted the concept of metrics, it is time to begin implementing some measurements in critical areas. During this step of the measurement process, it is important to be sensitive to the resistance to change. The implementation of metrics causes uneasiness and fear in the ranks.

The most important rule to remember in the design and implementation of metrics is that in all cases, the area that is to be measured must help in the development of the metrics. This will create a sense of ownership over the measurements and will ease the resistance to their implementation. The group should be informed as to the needs of management and should then be empowered to develop the metrics to meet the need. This will result in more relevant data being produced and an increase in quality in that area.

The second important rule to remember in the design and implementation of metrics is that it is absolutely vital that the measures are applied to events and processes, and never individuals. If people get the idea that their performance is being measured, they will be less likely to comply with the metrics process. It must be explicitly stated that the results of the metrics will not be used to measure the productivity or effectiveness of individuals but of the processes used by the individuals to create their products or services.

Keeping these two rules in mind, the next step is to identify the attributes of an effective measure. An effective measure must be able to pass tests of reliability and validity. Reliability defines consistency of a measure, and validity determines the degree to which it actually measures what it was intended to measure. The measure must be meaningful; the data provided by it must have some use to the management and should satisfy a condition of one of the critical metrics set.

Independent Assurance

While management is responsible for complying with regulations and implementing a system of internal controls, they are also responsible for independent assurance that controls are working effectively and efficiently. Independent assurance is provided by either internal or external auditors as discussed in Chapter 3. Management's participation in the audit process is needed to ensure the availability of qualified resources to accomplish the assigned tasks. Management also sets the tone for the organizations by being open to uncovering issues and considering the results of audits as a way of identifying improvements.

Sarbanes–Oxley requires management to perform an assessment of the effectiveness of the internal control structure and procedures for financial reporting. COBIT requires independent assurance at regular intervals that the organization is complying with laws, regulations, contracts, internal processes, and procedures.

Participation in IT Audit Planning

The best way to ensure that audits are both effective and efficient is for management to get involved in the process up front. As discussed in Chapter 4, the audit process begins with the audit planning process. Both user and IT management should participate in the ranking of high-risk areas identified from their risk assessment process as areas for audit consideration. In essence, user and IT management can openly contribute to corporate audit objectives by identifying areas of high risk through their self-evaluation or risk assessment process. Thus, this action or report will allow organization management to provide support to critical areas and use the audit reports to determine where to prioritize activities.

IT management can develop an effective partnership with IT audit by establishing a formal communication process. This will ensure that both IT management and IT audit understand the scope and objectives of an audit and schedule the appropriate resources to complete the audit in a timely manner. An effective engagement model between IT and audit will ensure the organization gets the most value out of the audit. Listed in the following are key questions to ask the audit team:

Preaudit checklist:
1. Who are the members of the audit team, and what are their roles and assignments?
2. What are the credentials and experience of the assigned audit team?
3. What orientation or training can you provide them to be comfortable within the environment?
4. Communicate with your managers and staff in the areas to be audited.
5. If an area was audited before, review the prior report to see the issues raised and the recommendations made. Get an update of corrections or changes made as a result of prior audit work and give your staff and the audit department credit.

Audit checklist:
1. Purpose of the audit?
2. Scope and objectives?
3. Who are the audit staff assigned? (Ask to be notified if any staff are changed.)
4. Timeframe for work to be performed?
5. Use of computer time/access to system/logs/training needed.
6. Access to IT management and staff?
7. Communicate (1) and (2) to all IT staff affected.
8. Set weekly or biweekly meetings with audit manager/audit team to discuss audit progress and issues.
9. Before the audit is finished, request closeout conference from audit group.
10. Request a copy of audit report.

Postaudit checklist:
1. When the audit report is issued, pull your team together and discuss the report; if you follow the preceding steps, there should be no surprises. If there are, there was a communication breakdown somewhere.
2. If you disagree with the report or portions of the report, do so in writing with supporting evidence. Remember, the auditor has supporting evidence for their reports, and this exists in their working papers. For those areas you agree, indicate what corrective actions your team plans to take.
3. Have your team provide a status report to you on a three-month cycle with a copy to go to internal audit. This shows that you value their work.

The purpose of an audit is to give management assurance that controls are working as intended. This is as much a concern for the CIO as it is for the board. An effective partnership between IT and the audit function will ensure that key risk areas are identified and audits are conducted in an efficient manner. A tool that can be used to identify key IT controls in the audit planning process is the COBIT control framework. COBIT provides a control framework that outlines the key processes and controls needed in the organization, in general, and IT specifically.

Control Framework

To help organizations integrate IT with business objectives, the Information Systems Audit and Control Foundation (ISACF) developed a framework that links IT control objectives to business objectives. This study resulted in COBIT. COBIT was built on the COSO model of internal controls and the Software Engineering Institute's Capability Maturity Model (CMM). COBIT provides best practices for the management of IT processes in a manageable and logical structure, meeting the multiple needs of enterprise management by bridging the gaps between business risks, technical issues, control needs, and performance-measurement requirements.

The IT Governance Institute summarized four reasons for the criticality of information and its related technology (COBIT):

- Increasing dependence on information and the system that delivers this information
- Increasing vulnerabilities and a wide spectrum of threats such as cyber threats and information warfare
- Scale and cost of the current and future investments in information and information systems
- Potential for technologies to dramatically change organizations and business practices, create new opportunities, and reduce cost

COBIT provides a framework for governance and control of information technology:

Governance is a structure of relationships and processes to direct and control the enterprise to achieve the enterprise's goals by adding value while balancing risk versus return over IT and its processes.

Controls are the policies, procedures, practices, and organizational structures designed to provide reasonable assurance that business objectives will be achieved and undesired events will be prevented or detected and corrected.

COBIT groups IT processes into four major domains:

1. *Planning and organization.* This domain covers strategies and tactics and concerns the identification of the way IT can best contribute to the achievement of the business objectives.
2. *Acquisition and implementation.* To realize the IT strategy, IT solutions need to be identified, developed, or acquired, as well as implemented and integrated into the business process. In addition, changes in and maintenance of existing systems are covered by this domain to make sure that the life cycle is continued for the systems.
3. *Delivery and support.* This domain is concerned with the actual delivery of required services, which range from traditional operations over security and continuity aspects to training. To deliver services, the necessary support processes must be set up. This domain includes the actual processing of data by application systems, often classified under application controls.

4. *Monitoring*. All IT processes need to be regularly assessed over time for their quality and compliance with control requirements. This domain thus addresses management's oversight of the organization's control process and independent assurance provided by internal and external audit or obtained from alternative sources.

In Chapters 9 through 12, the processes of the COBIT Planning and Organization domain will be discussed and compared to other existing standards.

Conclusion

IT governance establishes a fundamental basis for managing IT to deliver value to the organization. Effective governance aligns IT to the organization and establishes controls to measure meeting this objective. Realizing the value of IT requires a partnership between management and IT. This partnership should include establishing a shared strategy, managing enterprise risk, establishing shared goals, and measuring performance of all parties. Performance measures should be aligned to the objectives of the organization, the underlying data need to be accurate and timely, and reporting needs to be in a format that is easy to understand.

Companies will allocate capital to individual business units based on operational risk. By linking operational risk capital charges to the sources of that risk, individuals with risk-optimizing behavior will be rewarded and those without proper risk practices will be penalized. Establishing effective controls in IT and ensuring regulatory compliance is a joint effort. Well-controlled technology is the result of an organization that considers controls a priority. Organizations need to include controls in system requirements to make this happen.

Internal and external auditors can add tremendous value to an organization by providing independent assurance that controls are working as intended. With the implementation of Sarbanes–Oxley, the knowledge and skills of auditors is a valuable resource to the organization. Auditors understand controls and IT auditors understand IT controls and they can assist the organization in documenting and evaluating internal control structures to comply with Sarbanes–Oxley or other governance models.

Review Questions

1. Why are governance processes needed in the information technology area?
2. What are management's responsibilities with regard to the audit process?
3. What is ERM?
4. Why is ERM becoming more important to organizations?
5. How is ERM expected to grow in importance in the future?

Multiple-Choice Questions

1. IT governance is
   a. The process by which an enterprise's IT is directed and controlled
   b. The evaluation of computers and information processing not as key resources
   c. Management that is only involved in making decisions

    d. User dominance in IT decision making

2. IT governance is controlled through a series of processes and procedures that
    a. Determine how investments are managed
    b. Identify who can make decisions
    c. Determine how results are measured
    d. None of the above

3. For IT to be an effective partner in organizational decision making, the CIO must
    a. Offer proactive solutions to organizational needs
    b. Get agreement on the measures of IT performance
    c. Regularly attend board meetings
    d. None of the above

4. Which of the following is not a main reason for ERM functions being established within organizations?
    a. Increasing software patches
    b. Magnitude of problem
    c. Increasing business risks
    d. Organizational oversight

5. Compliance with laws and regulations is a key business risk because of
    a. The controls outlined in COBIT
    b. The impact on security of an organization
    c. The sheer number of laws and regulations
    d. The automation of financial processes

6. Managing compliance with laws and regulations is challenging because
    a. Sabanes–Oxley requires a compliance program
    b. The number of laws and regulations
    c. There are no tools to help with the process
    d. None of the above

7. Measuring IT performance is dependent on
    a. Delivering successful projects
    b. Keeping operations running
    c. Reducing operating costs
    d. The strategy and objectives of the organization

8. Developing a successful measurement process requires
    a. Alignment between IT and organization objectives
    b. Mature measurement processes
    c. Support from IT and organization management
    d. Automated measurement tools to report accurate metrics

9. A successful measurement process includes all of the following, except
    a. Ownership of the measurement process from the area to be measured
    b. Measure the effective use of resources and alignment with business objectives
    c. Measurement of events and processes rather than individuals
    d. Measurement must be meaningful, reliable, and accurately represent the area measured

10. IT governance requires management action taken at all levels to
    a. Decrease the probability of carelessness
    b. Reduce outside threat and the probability of hostile penetration
    c. Decrease fraud and corruption within the organization
    d. All of the above

Exercises

1. Create an outline of an IT performance measurement plan including the key components.
2. List the governance processes that control the use of IT resources.
3. List and describe IT governance standards.
4. List and describe the four domains in COBIT.

Answers to Multiple-Choice Questions

1—a; 2—d; 3—a; 4—a; 5—c; 6—b; 7—d; 8—c; 9—b; 10—d

Further Reading

1. Anzola, L., IT Governance Regulation—A Latin American perspective, *Inf. Syst. Control J.*, 2, 2005.
2. Bagranoff, N. and L. Hendry, Choosing and using Sarbanes–Oxley software, *Inf. Syst. Control J.*, 2, 2005.
3. Barton, T.L., W.G. Shenkir, and P.L. Walker, *Making Enterprise Risk Management Pay Off*, Financial Times/Prentice Hall, Upper Saddle River, NJ, 2002.
4. Bank for International Settlements and Basel Committee on Banking Supervision, *Consultative Document Operational Risk*, 2001, updated July 2002.
5. Bank for International Settlements and Basel Committee on Banking Supervision, *Sound Practices for the Management and Supervision of Operational Risk*, 2002.
6. Basel Committee on Banking Supervision, Results from the 2008 Loss Data Collection Exercise for Operational Risk, July 2009, http://www.bis.org/publ/bcbs160a.pdf.
7. Basel Committee on Banking Supervision, Sound Practices for the Management and Supervision of Operational Risk, February 2003, http://www.oenb.at/de/img/soundpractices_tcm14-15497.pdf.
8. Basel Committee on Banking Supervision, Sound Practices for the Management and Supervision of Operational Risk, Consultative Document, issued December 2010, http://www.bis.org/publ/bcbs183.pdf.
9. Basel II Mandates a Nest Egg for Banks, *U.S. Banker*, July 1, 2002, p. 48, http://www.accessmy library.com/coms2/summary-0286-25582710-ITM.
10. Bock, J.T., *The Strategic Role of "Economic Capital" in Bank Management*, Midas-Kapiti International, Wimbledon, England, 2000.
11. Burg, W. and T. Singleton, Assessing the value of IT: Understanding and measuring the link between IT and strategy, *Inf. Syst. Control J.*, 3, 2005.
12. Business Banking Board, *RAROC and Operating Risk*, Corporate Executive Board, Washington, DC, 2001.
13. Business Banking Board, *Risk Management Structure*, Corporate Executive Board, Washington, DC, 2001.
14. Carr, N., IT doesn't matter, *Harvard Business Review*, Harvard Business School Publications, Boston, MI, 2003.
15. Dietrich, R., After year one—Automating IT controls for Sarbanes–Oxley compliance, *Inf. Syst. Control J.*, 3, 2005.
16. Hively, K., B.W. Merkley, and J.A. Miccolis, *Enterprise Risk Management: Trends and Emerging Practices*, The Institute of Internal Auditors Foundation, Altamonte Springs, FL, 2001.
17. Ho Chi, J., IT governance regulation—An Asian perspective, *Inf. Syst. Control J.*, 2, 2005.
18. Institute of Internal Auditors, http://www.theiia.org/guidance/standards-and-practices/.
19. Information Systems Audit and Control Association, http://www.isaca.org/Template.cfm?Section=Standards&Template=/TaggedPage/TaggedPageDisplay.cfm&TPLID=29&ContentID=42792.

20. IT Governance Institute, Global Status Report on the Governance of Enterprise IT (Geit)—2011, http://www.isaca.org/Knowledge-Center/Research/Documents/Global-Status-Report-GEIT-10 Jan2011-Research.pdf.
    http://www.prmia.org/pdf/ERM-A_Status_Check_on_Global_Best_Practices.pdf.
21. Jones, W., IT governance regulation—An Australian perspective, *Inf. Syst. Control J.*, 2, 2005.
22. Kendall, K., Streamlining Sarbanes–Oxley compliance, *Internal Auditor*, pp. 39–44, 2007.
23. KPMG, *Leveraging IT To Reduce Costs and Improve Responsiveness*, KPMG International, New York, 2006.
24. Lam, J., Enterprise-wide risk management and the role of the chief risk officer, *ERisk*, March 25, 2000, http://www.erisk.com/Learning/Research/011_lamriskoff.pdf.
25. Lam, J., Top ten requirements for operational risk management, *Risk Management*, November 2001, http://0-proquest.umi.com.opac.library.csupomona.edu.
26. Leung, L., ISACA introduces IT governance certification, *Network World*, 2007, http://www.networkworld.com/newsletters/edu/2007/0910ed1.html.
27. Miccolis, J., Enterprise risk management in the financial services industry: From concept to management process, IRMI, November 2000, accessed August 28, 2002, http://jobfunctions.bnet.com/abstract.aspx?docid=62296.
28. Miccolis, J. and C. Lee, Implementing enterprise risk management: The emerging role of the chief risk officer, January 2001, IRMI, accessed August 28, 2002, http://www.erisk.com/Learning/Research/011_lamriskoff.pdf.
29. National Association of Financial Services Auditors, *Enterprise Risk Management*, Spring 2002, pp. 12–13.
30. Parkinson, M. and N. Baker, IT and enterprise governance, *Inf. Syst. Control J.*, 3, 2005.
31. Professional Risk Managers International Association (PRMIA), Enterprise Risk Management (ERM): A Status Check on Global Best Practices, May 2008.
32. Regulatory Treatment of Operational Risk, Working Paper, 2001, Bank for International Settlements and Basel Committee on Banking Supervision, July 2002, http://www.bis.org/publ/bcbs_wp8.pdf.
33. Smiechewicz, W., Case study: Implementing enterprise risk management, *Institutional Investor Bank Accounting Finance*, 14(4), 21, 2001.
34. Van Grembergen, W. and S. De Haes, Measuring and improving IT governance through the balanced scorecard. *Inf. Syst. Control J.*, 2, 2005.
35. Unknown, *Enterprise Risk Management—Integrated Framework*, Committee of Sponsoring Organizations of the Treadway Commission, September 2004.

Chapter 9

Strategy and Standards

Organizations and IT have undergone significant change at a rapid pace over the past decade. The pace of change is increasing in tempo and at the same time the global economy continues to diminish the autonomy and independent stability of local markets. These changes, coupled with new concepts for managing global enterprise and the dramatic advancement of IT, combine to challenge previously successful business practices as never before. Although predicting the future of global business and the technology it will use in this century is certainly not something that can be done with certainty, we can proactively position ourselves to shape the future rather than be shaped by it. IT has become the critical ingredient in business strategies as both enabler and enhancer of the organization's goals and objectives. Organizations must be positioned to take best advantage of emerging opportunities while also responding to the global requirements of the twenty-first century.

A strategy is an important first step toward meeting the challenging and changing business environment. A strategy is a formal vision to guide in the acquisition, allocation, and management of IT resources to fulfill the organization's objectives. A strategy should be developed, with the involvement of the business users, to address the future direction of technology. This strategy should be part of an overall corporate strategy for IT that would include the future direction of technology in fulfilling the organization's objectives. Supporting the strategy, architectural standards and technology planning ensure that investments in IT lead to efficient maintenance and a secure environment.

IT Processes

Strategy and architecture processes from COBIT are included in the Planning and Organization and Delivery Domain (PO1—Define a Strategic IT Plan; PO2—Define the Information Architecture; and PO3—Determine Technological Direction). All three processes are included in this section to discuss strategic and technical planning for IT (Exhibit 9.1).

PO1 Define a Strategic IT Plan
Control Objectives
1.1 IT value management
1.2 Business–IT alignment
1.3 Assessment of current performance
1.4 IT strategic plan
1.5 IT tactical plans
1.6 IT portfolio management
PO2 Define the Information Architecture
Control Objectives
2.1 Enterprise information architecture model
2.2 Enterprise data dictionary and data syntax
2.3 Data classification scheme
2.4 Integrity management
PO3 Determine Technological Direction
Control Objectives
3.1 Technological direction planning
3.2 Technological infrastructure plan
3.3 Monitoring of future trends and regulations
3.4 Technology standards
3.5 IT architecture board

Exhibit 9.1 Processes for planning and organization.

Strategic Planning

An IT strategic plan is a formal vision to guide in the acquisition, allocation, and management of IT resources to fulfill the organization's objectives. It should be part of an overall corporate strategy for IT and should align to the business strategy it supports. The technology strategy needs to be in lockstep with the business strategy to ensure that resources are not wasted on projects or processes that do not contribute to achieving the organization's overall objectives (see Exhibit 9.2). This alignment should occur at all levels of the planning process to provide continued assurance that the operational plans continue to support the business objectives.

IT governance (discussed in Chapter 8) provides the structure and direction to achieve the alignment of the IT strategy with the business strategy to cascade the strategy and goals down into the IT organization and facilitate the implementation of the IT strategy and goals. Close alignment of the IT strategy with the business strategy is essential to the success of a well-functioning partnership. The business strategy leads the IT strategy and that businesses and IT must participate in strategy development and in its implementation.

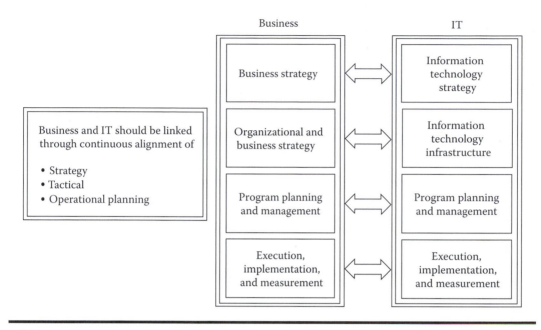

Exhibit 9.2   Linking business and IT.

IT management involves combining technology, people, and processes to provide solutions to organizational problems. The most effective strategy will be determined by the combination of the environment, culture, and technology used by an organization. IT must take the lead in gathering information to incorporate organizational needs with technological feasibility to create an overall strategy.

An IT strategic plan provides a roadmap for operating plans and a framework for evaluating technology investments. The IT strategy supports the business strategy to ensure that technology resources are applied to meeting business objectives while minimizing ongoing support costs. This task sounds fairly simple, but according to a Gartner Group report "95% of enterprises lack a well-defined business strategy." In most cases, the business strategy has to be assumed based on conversation with business executives. The first step in defining an IT strategic plan is to understand the business objectives, whether stated or implied. These objectives guide management in evaluating investments, assessing risk, and implementing controls.

So, why should IT have a strategic plan if the organization has none? The main risk of not having an IT strategic plan is the increased cost of technology. If there is no roadmap, organizations run the risk of investing in technology that increases costs but adds no business value. In a survey conducted by the IT Governance Institute, "alignment of IT investments with business strategy is by far the biggest single issue [organizations] face."

As IT exists to support and enable business, "the ultimate responsibility for IT strategy setting and implementation should rest with business leadership."* However, business leaders need IT management to take the lead in identifying ways IT can support the transformation of an organization to meet its long-term goals. A strong business and IT partnership in the strategic planning process provides the best foundation for success. One way to achieve alignment is to involve business leaders in the development of the IT strategy by establishing an IT Steering Committee.

---

* Williams, P., *IT Alignment: Who Is in Charge?* IT Governance Institute, Rolling Meadows, IL, 2005.

IT Steering Committee

An IT Steering Committee should be composed of decision makers from the various constituencies in the organization to resolve conflicting priorities. Even when business objectives are clearly stated, conflicts will arise with the interpretation of the actions necessary to fulfill those objectives. The IT Steering Committee is responsible for determining the overall IT investment strategy, ensuring that IT investments are aligned with business priorities, IT and business resources are available to enable IT to deliver upon its expectations, and measuring IT performance.

An IT Steering Committee can help ensure integration of the business and IT strategic plan. This group facilitates the integration of business and technology strategies, plans, and operations by employing the principles of joint ownership, teamwork, accountability, and understanding of major projects. This group should be composed of members of senior management and the CIO. The scope of the IT Steering Committee can include the following:

- Review business and technology strategies and plans.
- Prioritize major development projects.
- Develop communication strategies.
- Review development and implementation plans for all major projects.
- Provide business decisions on major design issues for all major projects.
- Monitor status, schedule, and milestones for all major projects.
- Review and approve major change requests for all major projects.
- Review project budgets and return on investments.
- Resolve conflicts between business and technology groups.
- Monitor business benefits during and after implementation of major projects.

Once an IT strategy has been decided, it must be communicated to all levels of management to ensure alignment and reduce conflict.

Communication

Effective communication is critical to coordinate the efforts of internal and external resources to accomplish the organization's goals. Communication should occur at multiple levels:

- Communication within IT through: multiple-level weekly staff/department meetings
- Communication to the entire IT organization through: town hall meetings attended by all employees in the organization
- Communication between IT and organization through: (1) IT management staff attending staff meetings of business partners, (2) the ability to electronically communicate immediately with all customers to ensure consistent and timely communications, and (3) central coordination to ensure a consistent message

After the completion of the strategic planning process, the business and IT goals must be translated into daily action through operational planning.

Operational Planning

Once there is an understanding of the organization's objectives and IT strategy, that strategy needs to be translated into operating plans. Operating plans will define the projects that will be initiated and the service levels expected of IT. Delivery of these plans should be controlled by a series of governance processes as discussed in Chapter 12.

Operational planning translates the IT strategic plan into actionable goals for the coming year. The annual planning process includes setting the top priorities for the IT function overall and for individual IT departments, developing the annual budget (discussed in Chapter 10), scheduling projects, creating resource and capacity plans, and preparing individual performance plans for all IT staff.

Portfolio Management

Portfolio management processes are needed to ensure the effective use of resources and alignment with business objectives (see Exhibit 9.3). This includes processes to initiate projects, design solutions, manage resources, provision services, procure products, and control financial investments. Investments in technology require significant resources in terms of people and funding that need to be directed in support of the organization's objectives.

Portfolio management ensures that investments are made in alignment with organizational objectives. Audit can help by reviewing the prioritization process, ensuring that capital appropriations include reasonable estimates of costs and measurable benefits. They can also verify that there is a process in place to measure and track the actual benefits of IT investments.

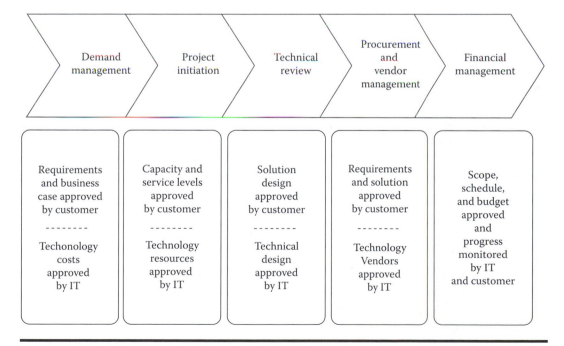

Exhibit 9.3   Governance processes.

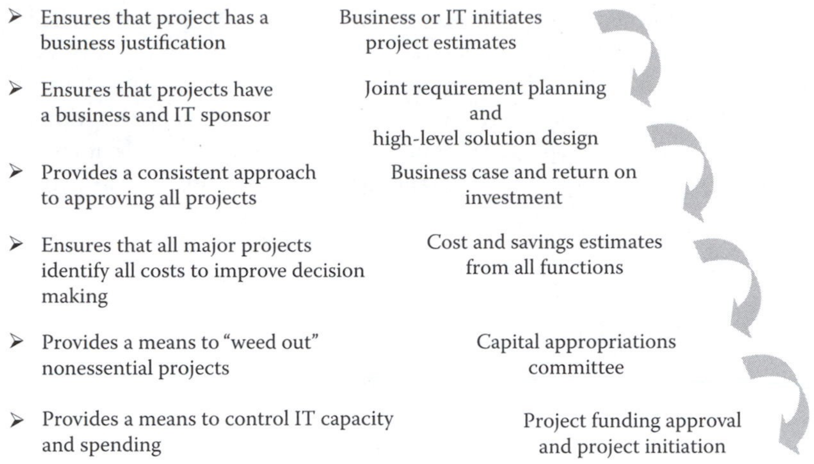

- ➢ Ensures that project has a business justification
- ➢ Ensures that projects have a business and IT sponsor
- ➢ Provides a consistent approach to approving all projects
- ➢ Ensures that all major projects identify all costs to improve decision making
- ➢ Provides a means to "weed out" nonessential projects
- ➢ Provides a means to control IT capacity and spending

Business or IT initiates project estimates

Joint requirement planning and high-level solution design

Business case and return on investment

Cost and savings estimates from all functions

Capital appropriations committee

Project funding approval and project initiation

Exhibit 9.4   Demand management process.

Demand Management

Projects need to be reviewed at the beginning of the project life cycle to make sure they have senior management support and a strong business case (see Exhibit 9.4). Researching technology solutions takes time and consumes resources that could be devoted to providing business value. Managing the project evaluation process requires a governance process that manages IT demand. A demand management process can help ensure that resources are devoted to projects that have a strong business case, which has been approved by the senior management. The demand management process helps ensure that senior management has provided conceptual approval to the project to proceed through the initial requirements definition and conceptual design phases of the development life cycle. All projects should have an appropriate sponsor from senior management before evaluating the costs of implementing a solution to avoid wasted effort on a project that will not get approved.

Demand management processes ensure that a project has business justification, a business and IT sponsor, a consistent approach for approving projects; ensure alignment of application and infrastructure groups; ensure that all project costs are identified to improve decision making; provide a means to "weed out" nonessential projects; and provide a means to control IT capacity and spending.

Project Initiation

Once a project has been approved, it should undergo a project initiation process that determines the total cost and benefit of a project by defining high-level business requirements and a conceptual solution. Building a project estimate takes time and resources. It takes time from business users to develop requirements and a business case. It takes time from software developers to develop a solution and cost estimates. After a project has conceptual approval, the business users and software developers can work together to develop detailed requirements and project estimates that will be used in the final business case and form the basis for the project budget.

Technical Review

The technical solution needs to be evaluated before moving forward to ensure compliance with technology standards. A technical review process helps ensure that the right solution is selected, that it integrates with other components of technology (e.g., network), and that it can be supported with minimal investments in infrastructure. One way to control technology solutions is to implement a technical steering committee with representatives from the various technical disciplines and enterprise architects. A technical steering committee provides a control mechanism for evaluating and approving new technology solutions. A formal product evaluation process assesses

- Technical feasibility
- Alternative technologies
- Architecture
- In-house skill compatibility
- Existing environments/replacements
- Implementation, licensing, and cost considerations
- Research and analyst views
- Vendor company profile and financial viability

Architecture and Standards

The IT strategy provides a vision for the IT organization, and architecture translates vision into infrastructure. The architecture group establishes the standards and blueprint for the organization (see Exhibit 9.5). Business applications must run on underlying technology. Regardless of the platform, the underlying infrastructure drives the total cost of ownership. A lack of standards can result in building applications that use different technology and require redundant infrastructure and maintenance costs. In the Internet space, there are different standards for developing applications. Microsoft has dot-Net, IBM has WebSphere, and Sun has Java. Although these standards can run on the same hardware platform, they cannot be consolidated into a single environment resulting in redundant hardware and infrastructure support. Complexity and redundancy increases cost and increases the risk of outages.

IT spending continues to increase greater than inflation in many industries fueled by increased software development. However, the pressure to keeping infrastructure costs low remains. This creates a challenge for IT as new applications and increased business transactions drive infrastructure costs higher. To meet the organizations expectations, IT must constantly look for ways to reduce the cost of existing and new infrastructure. Many cost-cutting measures can be effective in the short term, but long-term cost saving requires standardizing and simplifying applications and infrastructure. Simplified applications and infrastructure are easier to maintain and change because there are fewer technology products and components. Simplified applications and infrastructures are also more reliable, resulting in improved productivity and reduced cost. There are many other advantages to standardizing and simplifying systems: system reuse, faster implementation, and improved flexibility.

Enterprise Architecture

Web-based solutions have made "new economy" companies (e.g., eBay) more nimble at delivering solutions to the market. Whereas older organizations that began automating in the 1960s are saddled with legacy applications that are costly to maintain and time consuming to change. Many

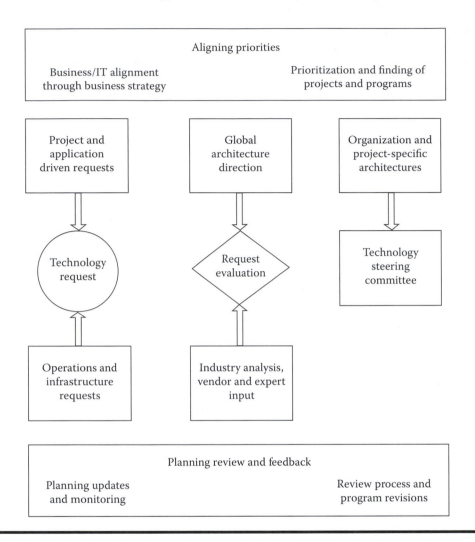

Exhibit 9.5 Strategic IT planning cycle.

organizations have an assortment of legacy applications and new applications connected with a maze of interfaces built over time. With limited resources, it is not feasible to replace all legacy applications at once. What is needed is a "roadmap" to guide in the replacement of legacy applications over time. The solution is to set out the target technology and architecture definition in enterprise architecture.

The enterprise architecture lays out a roadmap between the current and future state of the organizations' infrastructure and application platforms. Enterprise architecture defines the different elements in an enterprise and their interaction. It creates the ability to understand and determine the continual needs of integration, alignment, change, and responsiveness to business, technology, and the marketplace. To be effective, enterprise architecture must work in conjunction with governance, standards, architecture, and standard processes. The enterprise architecture provides a mechanism to communicate the essential elements and functions of the enterprise within the organization.

Benefits to establishing enterprise architecture include

- Reducing time and cost to make decisions and designing solutions to accelerate the delivery of IT responses to business demands
- Providing a common language and terminology for cross-border knowledge sharing within the IT community
- Providing a common reference for IT governance to allow fast and consistent evaluation and decisions on project proposals
- Providing a framework and instruments for discussions between the organization and third parties around solution proposals
- Providing a framework for evaluating third-party software packages to assist in clarifying the integration with existing applications and infrastructure

The Open Group Architecture Framework (TOGAF) provides a tool to aid in the development of enterprise architecture. TOGAF is based on the U.S. Department of Defense Technical Architecture Framework for Information Management (TAFIM).

The enterprise architecture encompasses the business architecture, application architecture, data architecture, and infrastructure architecture to align technology with the organization's objectives.

Business Architecture

Business architecture defines the key business processes and functions of an organization. An understanding of the business processes is the key to developing a technology road map that supports those processes. However, business processes are not static—they change over time. Thus, a flexible modeling approach is needed to provide flexibility and responsiveness to the inevitable and perpetual change in business processes. Examples of key business processes include customer relationship management (CRM), document and content management, and management information.

Application Architecture

Application architecture defines the application framework and common components that can be used across the organization. It ensures alignment with organizational strategy and guides in the purchase, configuration, design, and development of technology.

An overview of the existing application architecture provides a generalized, high-level function map of key applications and supported processes. As with all architectures, it also defines the current state, target, and roadmap to reach the target. There are tools that assist in developing an application architecture using application frameworks. Application frameworks (e.g., services-oriented architecture [SOA]) describe the best practice models and services provided. Examples include process management, business rules engines, portal framework, and security framework.

Common components deliver standard services. This includes a description of existing components, the services they provide, and how they are used. There are usually common services that are needed by multiple applications and it is more efficient to develop these services once and share them with multiple applications. Examples include customer, document composition, and document management.

The complex interaction of technology requires a robust methodology and tools for identifying impact to a stable environment, and the performance of planned technology solutions. Application architecture also considers the scope of technology to be adopted, the options available in vendor/tool selection, alternative protocols, and emerging industry trends.

Information Architecture

All the sources of information (including paper, graphics, video, speech, and knowledge) can be transformed into data useful to customer service, product design, and sales and future planning. Data architecture encompasses the source and destination of information, formal and informal business rules for using that information, its flow through the organization, ownership, and mechanisms for ensuring persistence and security. A subset of this information is data contained in existing and proposed computer applications. Information architecture identifies and models all data elements used to drive an organization's systems, documenting their commonalties, differences, and role in all business transactions. To leverage data across business processes and applications, it must be consistent, accessible, and defined uniformly across the organization and applications.

Infrastructure Architecture

Infrastructure architecture defines the hardware and software infrastructure that supports the applications. The infrastructure architecture guides in the acquisition and implementation of facilities and equipment, disaster recover, capacity planning, office automation, distributed systems, and network and communications. Infrastructure architecture defines the client, server, and network technology supporting application delivery.

Client architecture defines the technology used by the client population to access applications and date. Client technology encompasses a wide variety of devices—personal computers, personal digital devices, Web portals, and so on.

Server architecture defines the operating platforms that support the applications being delivered. Server technology includes mainframe, midrange, and microservers.

Network architecture defines the method(s) for transmitting information between applications and users across an organization and its customers. An organization's ability to transport data between systems and across organizational and physical boundaries is a key success factor in gaining maximum value from existing and new technology. As organizations become increasingly dependent on the exchange of digital information to perform business processes, the structure and engineering of telecommunications and LAN, and WAN architecture is critical to a smoothly functioning organization.

The Architecture Function

The architecture function serves as the owner and manager of the architecture processes and standards. It provides a leadership consulting role in the decision-making process of present and future technology initiatives for strategic business advantage. It builds and strengthens enterprise technology standards and common methodologies, and provides investigation analysis of technology solutions. The architecture function has the following objectives:

■ Define fundamental technology principles for use in selecting standard products, technologies, and best practices.

- Initiate, expand, and refine the technical architecture based on the strategic initiatives.
- Support long-range technology planning in collaboration with decision makers.
- Evaluate technical solutions and monitor emerging global standards.
- Establish technology standards consistent with IT and business objectives.
- Ensure technical planning and designs conform to the organization's technology standards.
- Assist the IT Steering Committee in understanding and mitigating business risk of new and existing technology.

Technology Standards

Technology standards guide industries and organizations in selecting hardware and software and developing new applications. In the United States, the National Institute of Standards and Technology releases publications titled *Federal Information Processing Standards* as guidance to federal agencies and those who do business with the federal government. The worldwide Institute of Electronics and Electrical Engineers (IEEE) has issued standards governing the manufacturing of electrical and electronics products. Hardware and software standards ensure compatibility between applications and ease the burden of technology integration and technical support.

Users may focus on the short-term solutions for getting the job done as quickly as possible, and may ignore the long-term organizational perspective. For example, user departments may invest in an architectural platform that is incompatible with that of the rest of the company. But, when problems occur, users look to the IT organization for support because they do not have the technical expertise. Users want decentralization when it comes to controls over data, but they want centralization when it comes to support. User controlled systems are effective and efficient for solving particular department problems in the short term. However, these implementations may not be appropriate for the organization as a whole.

IT organizations, however, can focus on existing technology and orderly development at the expense of user needs, one of the reasons for the growth in end-user computing. Central IT control can offer advantages to the organization as a whole. IT staff usually have the technical expertise and experience to manage projects using established standards. The challenge is to combine the strengths of these two groups to make better use of the technology to fulfill organizational goals.

> **Example: Importance of Business Strategy in Customer Relationship Management**
>
> In the planning of an organizational support system, the importance of IT standards and strategy comes into play when confronted with the need to better control the relationships with customers. Despite the billions of dollars spent on CRM products and services, as much as 12% of all CRM implementations are complete failures, meaning the systems never even go live. Research conducted by AMR Research of Boston, Massachusetts, found that "only 15 percent of all CRM installations have actually improved business performance in a measurable way." That means that approximately 85% of all CRM users cannot quantify any benefits at all. Since then, CRM project success rates have increased to approximately 50%.[*] While that is a significant improvement, that still leaves 50% of projects failing to deliver. The top three obstacles to success of such systems have been (1) lack of a strategic plan, (2) lack of executive sponsorship, and (3) poor alignment of technology and business processes.

---

[*] http://www.zdnet.com/blog/projectfailures/crm-failure-rates-2001-2009/4967.

Focus on Technology

One of the common myths is that CRM software will fix all of the company's problems, and they need the newest software to fix lagging sales. Analysts and users claim that vendors have hyped CRM's capabilities far beyond what is being delivered, and that because so many customers did not know what they wanted in the first place, many CRM implementations should never have been started. Vendors are hyping their products to all levels of the organization as a solution in all problem areas. In a troubled economy, companies buy the vendors' message and bet on CRM software to turn around their sales. Companies need to understand how to change their business processes and leverage CRM software and best practices to help facilitate this change. The CRM software itself is not going to make a company customer-focused, but proper business process change will. This requires business strategy and IT strategy to coincide.

Resistance to Change

Another common mistake, made by big and small businesses alike, is underestimating the resistance to a new system such as CRM, which is created by organizational habits. New systems fail most often because of cultural barriers, not systems problems. The turf issues that exist within organizations—the invisible but thick walls that exist between parts of the organization and even between different product groups within an organization—really get in the way.

Regardless of any company's current dynamics, the sales force must support a CRM implementation if the system is to succeed. Many large sales organizations, such as Ford Motor, Kodak, Coca-Cola, and others, are justifiably wary, having suffered an ill-conceived attempt at sales force automation in the past. To ease their fears, the strategic plan needs input from the sales team even before a system has been planned. Sales teams will always get behind a solution if it has been introduced in the right manner.

The real problem is that people do not like change, cannot deal with loss of control, like stability, and fear the unknown. If the business and IT management fail to address these issues and adequately communicate these changes to the users, the CRM project will be doomed from the start. The key to changing management is to address the concerns of all levels of employees and gain user acceptance and buy-in. Sales teams typically demonstrate acceptance of a solution that

- Helps organize and streamline their day
- Saves them time
- Improves their response to their customers
- Is easy to use

As long as the sales teams can answer the question of what is in it for them, they will be much more likely to embrace the new CRM solution.

Barriers to User Adoption

The top three obstacles that we have seen that arise with CRM solutions are

1. Poor performance
2. Difficult to navigate and access information
3. Limited value

These key barriers have resulted in lower adoption and utilization levels than management desires to reap the anticipated benefits. In most organizations, CRM has been designed around the sales, reporting the needs of management and not the needs of the end user. As a result, these systems tend to be forced on the sales staff without necessarily addressing their main points or fitting easily into their daily workflow. Project managers need to focus on what functionality and data the users need to be effective.

To determine the needs of the users, they need to identify common frustrations and the best ways to fix them. If the sales representatives do not see value, they simply will not use CRM; therefore, design the CRM solution around their everyday lives. Find out what barriers are coming between the sales representative and the customer. For example, if the sales team member in the field has not been able to access the most up-to-date marketing, product, and pricing information in the field, it is likely that he could not answer customer questions. It makes sense to empower representatives with the information they need to answer questions on the spot, thus maximizing customer interactions. Representatives need the right information that is timely and relevant. It is critical to build an architecture that will flexibly aggregate corporate information.

The system needs to react quickly and not frustrate the users. Monster.com spent $1 million in 1998 on a CRM solution to increase sales force efficiency by providing "immediate" access to information on potential customers. The system was reputed to be so sluggish that field personnel could not download data on their laptops. This forced the company to abandon the solution and build a completely new system from scratch; the company had to spend a million more to get it right. One of the most popular complaints received from various users on a daily basis is the poor performance of the application. This forces the call centers to take more time on calls and frustrate customers who have been on hold for several minutes. Users will scratch down notes on paper instead of in the system and, hopefully, will enter that data into the system later, but at a cost. Others will refuse to use the system at all because it slows them down or does not give them enough value to be worth their time.

This is where standards such as COBIT or COSO can help an organization establish a framework. COSO among other things provides criteria against which control systems can be evaluated. COSO defines internal control as a process, influenced by an entity's board of directors, management, and other personnel that is designed to provide reasonable assurance in the following categories:

- Effectiveness and efficiency of operations
- Reliability of financial reporting
- Compliance with applicable laws and regulations

The report emphasizes that the internal control system is a tool of, but not a substitute for, management and that controls should be built into, rather than built onto, operating activities. According to COSO, the internal control system consists of five interrelated components: (1) control environment, (2) risk assessment, (3) control activities, (4) information and communication, and (5) monitoring.

The "control environment" provides the foundation for the other components. It encompasses factors such as management's philosophy and operating style, human resource policies and practices, the integrity and ethical values of employees, the organizational structure, and the attention and direction of the board of directors. COSO provides guidance for evaluating each of these factors.

"Risk assessment" consists of risk identification and risk analysis. Risk identification includes examining external factors such as technological developments, competition, and economic changes, and internal factors such as personnel quality, the nature of the entity's activities, and the characteristics of information system processing. Risk analysis involves estimating the significance of the risk, assessing the likelihood of the risk occurring, and considering how to manage the risk.

"Control activities" consist of the policies and procedures that ensure employees carry out management directives. Control activities include reviews of the control system, physical controls, segregation of duties, and information system controls. Controls over information systems include general controls and application controls. General controls are those covering access, software, and system development. Application controls are those, which prevent errors from entering the system or detect and correct errors present in the system.

The entity obtains pertinent "information and communicates" it throughout the organization. The information system identifies, captures, and reports financial and operating information that is useful to control the organization's activities. Within the organization, personnel must receive the message that they must understand their roles in the internal control system, take their internal control responsibilities seriously, and, if necessary, report problems to higher levels of management. Outside the entity, individuals and organizations supplying or receiving goods or services must receive the message that the entity will not tolerate improper actions.

"Management's monitoring" of the control system by reviewing the output generated by regular control activities and by conducting special evaluations. Regular control activities include comparing physical assets with recorded data, training seminars, and examinations by internal and external auditors. Special evaluations can be of varying scope and frequency. Deficiencies found during regular control activities are usually reported to the supervisor in charge; deficiencies located during special evaluations are normally communicated to higher levels of the organization.

These are situations that the auditor has to be aware of and report to prevent the organization from making a costly mistake in the IT planning and organization process. The examples cited from the report are common in today's dynamic environment and are among the challenges that organizations face.

Conclusion

Because IT and information security are integral parts of internal controls, we have discussed here and in earlier chapters the Internal Control Integrated Framework publication by COSO, which specifically includes IT controls. Also addressed are the Institute of Internal Auditors' SAC and ISACA COBIT that are both directly related to the frameworks identified by COSO in their reports. These are standards of practice we mentioned earlier to help guide business in the IT strategic planning process. This chapter provides guidance and examples of how critical these components are in setting the direction for what will follow.

Review Questions

1. What is the purpose of developing an IT strategic plan?
2. How can an IT strategic plan be developed without a corresponding business plan?
3. How does architecture fit into the IT strategic plan?

4. What are the advantages of having architectural standards and name one organization that issues standards?
5. In what way does COBIT help in the alignment of business and IT objectives?

Multiple-Choice Questions

1. What is the purpose of developing an IT strategic plan?
   a. Define the IT goals and objectives
   b. Guide the acquisition, allocation, and management of IT resources
   c. Define the technology to be used by the organization for the current year
   d. Provide a process for governing investments in IT
2. The COBIT model is based on the following:
   a. COSO model of internal controls
   b. Capability Maturity Model
   c. Project Management Body of Management
   d. ISO 9000—Quality Management and Quality Assurance Standards
3. The Planning and Organization domain includes all the following except
   a. Project management standards
   b. Architecture planning process
   c. Strategic planning process
   d. Operational readiness process
4. Benefits of establishing enterprise architecture include
   a. Provides a common reference to evaluate project proposals
   b. Accelerates the delivery of IT responses to business demands
   c. Reduces time and cost to make decisions
   d. All the above
5. The architecture function is important because
   a. It develops more efficient applications and systems
   b. Architects are better at writing policies and procedures
   c. It builds and strengthens enterprise technology standards
   d. None of the above
6. One of the obstacles to the success of CRM has been
   a. Project management standards
   b. Lack of strategic plan
   c. Strategic planning process
   d. Architecture planning process
   e. None of the above
7. Portfolio management processes are needed to
   a. Ensure new technology is approved by the appropriate groups
   b. Ensure projects are completed on time, on budget, and with full functionality
   c. Ensure effective and efficient IT operations
   d. Ensure the effective use of resources and alignment with business objectives
8. A technical review process helps ensure that
   a. The project has included all the costs of the technology solution
   b. The right solution is selected that integrates with other technology components
   c. The current infrastructure is sufficient to support the new technology

d. The appropriate level of senior management approvals has been received
9. Architectural standards are needed to
   a. Determine which vendor products to use
   b. Simplify and standardize infrastructure costs
   c. Communicate programming standards to software developers
   d. Speed the implementation process for new technology
10. A technical steering committee provides
   a. A control mechanism for evaluating and approving new technology solutions
   b. A framework for organizing and assessing software development and maintenance
   c. Leadership in advancing the practice of software engineering
   d. Guidance in the acquisition, allocation, and management of IT resources

Exercises

1. Create an outline of an IT strategic plan including the key components.
2. List the processes included in the planning and organization domain.
3. List and discuss four key reasons for the criticality of IS.

Answers to Multiple-Choice Questions

1—b; 2—a; 3—d; 4—d; 5—c; 6—d; 7—d; 8—b; 9—b; 10—a

Further Reading

1. Applegate, L., R. Austin, and D. Soule. *Corporate Information Strategy and Management: Text and Cases*, McGraw-Hill, New York, 2009.
2. Banham, R., CRM rollouts: Mulligans required, *CFO*, August 1, 2002, http://www.cfo.com/article.cfm/3005836
3. Basel Committee on Banking Supervision, Sound Practices for the Management and Supervision of Operational Risk, Bank for International Settlements, accessed July 2, 2002, http://www.bis.org/publ/bcbs86.htm.
4. Blundon, W., How to make CRM work, *Computerworld*, April 11, 2003, http://www.computerworld.com/softwaretopics/crm/story/0,10801,80251,00.html.
5. Bolles, G.A., Can your CRM project be saved? *CIO Insight*, November 2, 2002, http://www.cioinsight.com/article2/0,3959,686268,00.asp.
6. Campbell, B., CRM how to: Close encounters, *Oracle Magazine*, August 2002, http://www.sdlcg.com/sdlsite/Articles/eCoachArticles/CRMHowTo.pdf
7. Close, W., CRM at work: Eight characteristics of CRM winners, *CRM Project*, Vol. 3, from 2002, October 30, http://www.crmproject.com/documents.asp?d_ID=1433.
8. COBIT Framework, *Information Systems Audit and Control Foundation*, Rolling Meadows, IL, 2011.
9. COBIT, 3rd edition, Audit Guidelines, July 2000, http://techtraining.brevard.k12.fl.us/BETC2007/Grachis-Auditguidelines.pdf.
10. Conlon, G., Driving sales, *CRM Magazine*, July 2003, http://www.destinationcrm.com/articles/default.asp?ArticleID=3227.
11. Connell, J., Business goals should come before it needs in a CRM project, *TechRepublic*, September 7, 2001, http://techrepublic.com/article.jhtml?id=r00520010907con02.htm.

12. CRM Magazine, A Slice of the Good Life: Introduction, June 2003, http://dcrm.infotoday.com/articles/default.asp?ArticleID=3150.
13. Federal Financial Institutions Examination Council, *FFIEC IS Examination Handbook*, Vol. 2, 1996, http://www.ncua.gov/ref/ffiec/ffiec_handbook.html, accessed July 2, 2002.
14. Fuchs, G., Aspects of ROI, *DM Review*, June 20, 2003, http://www.ffiec.gov/ffiecinfobase/resources/tsp/ffi-sp-1-int_edp_exam_sched_Dist.pdf.
15. Gomolski, B., U.S. IT spending and staffing survey, 2005, *Gartner Research*, Stamford CT, November 2, 2005.
16. Gray, P. and J. Byun, *Customer Relationship Management*, Claremont Graduate School, Claremont, CA, March 2001.
17. Hass, B., M. Gorsage, and E. Barker, Four CRM strategies for adapting to the changing economy, *CRM Magazine*, November, 2002, http://www.destinationcrm.com/articles/default.asp?ArticleID=2662.
18. IT Governance Institute, *Mapping of TOGAF 8.1 with COBIT 4.0*, IT Governance Institute, Rolling Meadows, IL, 2007.
19. Mac Neela, A. and J. Disbrow, Research note, *Three Steps to Savings in Application Support*, Gartner, Stamford, IL, May 19, 2003.
20. Mack, R. and N. Frey, *Six Building Blocks for Creating Real IT Strategies*, Gartner Group, Stamford, CT, R-17-63607, December 11, 2002.
21. Pearlson, K.E., *Management and Using Information Systems—A Strategic Approach*, Wiley, New York, 2001.
22. Working Council for Chief Information Officers, Budget Watch: IT Spending Trends for 2003, Corporate Executive Board, Washington, DC, 2003.
23. Working Council for Chief Information Officers, Case Studies in Enterprise Architecture Migration, Corporate Executive Board, Washington, DC, 2002.
24. Working Council for Chief Information Officers, IT Standard Setting Bodies, Corporate Executive Board, Washington, DC, May 2001.
25. The Open Group Architecture Framework (TOGAF), The Open Group, www.opengroup.org/architecture.

Chapter 10

Risk Management

This chapter discusses the process of assessing and managing risk in IT environment. Risk management should be part of an organization's thinking, integrated into strategic planning, operational planning, project management, resource allocation, and daily operations. Risk management enables an organization to focus on those areas that can have the highest impact.

Risk assessment occurs at multiple levels of the organization with a focus on different areas. Executive management may focus on business risks, the technology officer may focus on technology risks, the security officer may focus on security risk, and auditors focus on control risks. What are the successful characteristics of a risk assessment process? What are the standards of practice for risk assessment? What are some examples of risk assessment practices used in varied environment? What are some of the approaches to managing risk?

This chapter reviews the processes and techniques used to assess and manage risk. As a result of business failures that seem to occur every decade, risk management has taken on greater importance to organizations. Included in this chapter is information on guidelines for risk management.

IT Processes

The COBIT process (PO9) in the Planning and Organization Domain outlines the risk management processes required to support an effective IT organization. Exhibit 10.1 lists the key control objectives for this section.

What Is Risk Management?

Risk management ensures that losses do not prevent organization management from seeking its goals of conserving assets and realizing the expected value from investments. The functions of risk management include the following:

- Recognizing the exposures to loss by becoming aware of the possibility of each type of loss. This is a basic function that must precede all others
- Estimating the frequency and size of loss by determining its probability from various sources

225

PO9 Assess and Manage Risks
Control Objectives
9.1 IT and business risk management and alignment
9.2 Establishment of risk context
9.3 Event identification
9.4 Risk assessment
9.5 Risk response
9.6 Maintenance and monitoring of a risk action plan

Exhibit 10.1 Planning and organization domain.

- Deciding the best and most economical method of managing the risk of loss, whether it is by assumption, avoidance, self-insurance, reduction of hazards, transfer, commercial insurance, or a combination of these methods
- Administering the programs of risk management, including the tasks of constant reevaluation of the programs and record keeping

These functions should be carried out through the following steps:

- Determining the objectives
- Identifying the risks
- Evaluating the risks
- Considering the alternatives and selecting the risk-treatment device
- Implementing the decision
- Performing an evaluation and review

In following these steps, the organization should consider the odds and should not risk more than the company can afford to lose or risk a lot for a little. These rules point out that risk management is really just a series of cost/benefit decisions.

Determination of Objectives

A set of clearly defined objectives can guide those responsible for developing and administering the risk management program as well as provide a means for evaluating the program's performance. Obviously, each company has objectives specifically suited for its operation; however, some broad objectives can be defined. First, the aggregate cost of risks should be kept below the point at which a company's assets or earnings would be significantly reduced by uninsured losses. The cost of risks is defined as the sum of the following:

- The direct and consequential costs of loss-prevention measures
- Insurance premiums
- The costs of losses sustained (including expenses to curtail the losses)
- Net cost of indemnities from insurers and third parties
- Expenses of relevant management, administration, and finance

Second, the prime goals of a company should not be prejudiced. Third, a company must avoid a loss that it neither insured nor identified. Finally, the life, health, and property of others should be respected. Executive management and the board of directors should be involved in formulating the company's risk management objectives. Above all, management has to recognize that IT is an asset and it should be valued and validated continuously.

IT Risk Identification

This step is critical because unidentified risks are retained by default. As with any business, and IT is no exception, using some of the following identification tools can assure a comprehensive review:

- Audit or inspection by managers, workers, or independent parties of the organization's operational sites or practices.
- Operations or process flowchart of the organization's operations.
- Periodic use of a risk analysis questionnaire where information can be captured about the organization's operations and ongoing activities. If questions are too general, unusual exposures or unique loss areas may be overlooked.
- Financial statement analysis to depict trends in revenue and cost areas, identifying asset exposure analysis.
- Insurance policy checklist—a catalog of various policies or types of insurance that identifies measurable insurable risk.

Using several tools is highly recommended in allowing the analyst or reviewer more coverage of targeted IT areas. The key is to identify those IT areas that can have a substantial impact on business operations and revenue. The use of multiple tools and techniques allows one to view the business from a different perspective, providing a more complete picture of the complexity and interrelationship of various operations and functions. Thus, IT risks can be viewed and assessed by management from different areas.

IT Risk Assessment Tools and Techniques

In view of the increased reliance on IT and automated systems, special emphasis must be placed in the review and analysis of risk in these areas. IT facilities and hardware are often included in the company's overall plant and property review; however, automated systems require a separate analysis, especially when these systems are the sole source of critical information to the organization as in today's e-business movement. There are many risks that affect today's IT environment. Organizations face loss from traditional events, such as natural disaster, accidents, vandalism, and theft, and also from similar events in electronic form. These can be from computer viruses, information or data theft or records or files, electronic sabotage, electronic spamming of e-commerce business, and so on. To assist in the identification and evaluation of these IT-related risks, the following resources for tools and techniques have been identified:

nist.gov. The National Institute of Standards and Technology (NIST) has been a leader in providing tools and techniques to support IT. It has a number of support tools that can be used for risk assessment purposes.

gao.gov. The U.S. Government Accountability Office (GAO) has provided a number of audit, control, and security resources as well as identification of best practices in managing and reviewing IT risk in many areas.

Expected loss approach. A method developed by IBM that assesses the probable loss and the frequency of occurrence for all unacceptable events for each automated system or datafile. Unacceptable events are categorized as
- Accidental disclosure
- Deliberate disclosure
- Accidental modification
- Deliberate modification
- Accidental destruction
- Deliberate destruction

Scoring approach. Identifies and weighs various characteristics of the IT systems. Uses the final score to compare and rank their importance.

IT Risk Evaluation

IT evaluation involves the quantification or ranking of the size and probability of potential loss. The risk can be categorized as follows:

Critical. These exposures would result in bankruptcy.
Important. These are exposures in which possible losses would not lead to bankruptcy but require the business to take out loans to continue operations.
Unimportant. These are exposures that could be accommodated by existing assets or current income without imposing undue financial strain.

Assigning the identified risks to one of these categories gives it a level of significance and helps determine the proper means for treating it.

IT Risk Management

Risks can be managed using one or several of the following techniques:

- Avoidance
- Prevention
- Reduction
- Transfer
- Retention

More than one technique can be applied to a given risk (typically, the case of reduction and transfer or retention). The IT risk management objectives should be used as a guide in choosing a technique. Some of the key questions IT and corporate management need to ask when choosing a technique are as follows:

High severity or catastrophic loss risks:
    Why is the business loss so severe?
    How did the loss evolve?
    What are the shortcomings of the existing control procedures?
Avoidance:
    Is it impossible to avoid?
    Is it impractical to avoid?
    Is it too expensive to avoid?
    Is it too time consuming to avoid?

Prevention:
  Are there any direct countermeasures to prevent the risk from occurring?
  Are they cost effective?
  Do they have beneficial side effects?
  Do they have adverse side effects?
Reduction:
  Are there any direct countermeasures to reduce the risk?
  Are they cost effective?
  Do they reduce the loss occurrence?
  Will other risks be reduced as well?
  Do they have beneficial side effects?
  Do they have adverse side effects?
Transfer:
  By insurance?
  By contractual agreement?
  By other means?
  Are there other benefits?
  Can the risk be best dealt with by a combination of controls?
  Can it be partially reduced and partially transferred?
  What are the benefits of each method?

If consideration is being given to the transfer technique and the use of insurance, in particular, the following items should be taken into account:

Advantage of deductibles. Retaining a portion of the risk such as a higher deductible can greatly reduce the insurance or premium costs.

Tax considerations. The impact of the tax laws on insurance costs and losses may influence the decision. In business, property and liability insurance premiums are a deductible expense, as are uninsured losses. However, contributions by a business to a funded retention program are not deductible.

Selection of the insurer. Factors to consider in selecting an insurer include
  Availability of coverage
  Cost of coverage
  Financial solvency, stability, and profitability of the insurer
  Quantity and quality of insurance services offered, both by the insurer directly and through the agency system it uses

If consideration is being given to retaining the risks, the following major financial aspects must be analyzed in assessing the value of loss retention:

- ■ Cash flow
- ■ Opportunity cost of funds

In general, the financial advantage of loss retention is greater when

- ■ The difference is small between interest rates on liquid accounts and rates of return on capital employed within a business.

- Commercial insurance rates on the risk are relatively high compared with the opportunity cost of funds.
- The firm's perceived needs for liquid loss reserve funds are low such that the firm is willing to accept more risk.

Finally, the records and documents of past losses and choices can be used as a prime information source in the process of choosing the appropriate risk-handling technique. In this manner, the knowledge, experience, and patterns of the past can be used to make better decisions for the future.

Once the appropriate technique has been chosen, it must be implemented. The necessary facts and figures are now available to help negotiate insurance, set up a loss-prevention program, or establish a loss reserve fund. The risk analysis structure has been illustrated earlier. The various implemented plans must be evaluated and reviewed. This is an important process because the variables are changing constantly. Techniques that were appropriate last year may not be so this year, and mistakes do occur. The application of the wrong technique or coverage must be detected early and corrected.

Risk Assessment

Risk assessment is both a tool and a technique that can be used to self-evaluate the level of risk of a given process or function. It is a way of applying objective measurement to a process that is really subjective. The first step is to identify the assets and/or objectives and rate them in terms of their importance to the organization's success.

The process must be thorough and complete; otherwise, the element of risk can be judged to be extremely high. Therefore, management must evaluate the quality of a process, especially in today's world of ever-changing technology with increasing complexity. Credibility and thoroughness of validating and verifying the controls at all levels are extremely important. Managers and auditors should perform risk assessment in their self-evaluation process on an ongoing basis within the IT environment.

Technology Risk Management

An effective technology risk management (TRM) program will be part of an enterprise risk management program. Within IT, there should be a designated risk manager or coordinator, possibly several. This function would fit well with disaster recovery planning and the making of IT policy, as it is another management function of IT. The risk coordinator should be a contact point for user management with questions, and will work with the IT risk manager to roll out TRM as a subset of the enterprise risk management program.

A chief risk officer (CRO) should exist for the entire enterprise at a senior management level. The CRO should report to the CEO, the board of directors, or both. The CRO, in collaboration with the board of directors, should determine risk limits the organization is willing to take on. These risk limits should not be static but should be subject to change—a working document. These risk limits should be published and available to the business units, as each business manager will be held accountable for assessing the line of business' risks, creating a risk action plan, and determining if their risks fall within or outside of the established tolerances.

As part of the strategic planning process each year (or yearly at another time or on a sliding schedule that runs annually by department or on a cycle decided by the business unit and CRO if there is no annual strategic planning process), each business manager should be required to complete a risk assessment of his or her area. Included in that is a risk assessment of the business risks of each application, system, or program that the line of business owns. COBIT or a similar standard should be agreed upon and is to be used as a guideline. This will place all technology risk assessments on similar terms and make them somewhat standardized as to the types of risks identified. These risk assessments should be completed by the line of business with assistance from the TRM coordinator or internal audit. The TRM coordinator can give insight and information to the line of business regarding the specific technical risks faced by the application, system, or program. The business manager would be able to assess these in light of the overall risk facing the line of business. The enterprise technology department should perform the risk assessments of enterprise-wide applications, systems, and programs such as the network or the enterprise-wide e-mail software. The enterprise technology department, headed by the chief technology officer (CTO), would be evaluating, managing, and accepting the risks associated with this type of enterprise-wide technology.

In some ways, the CRO and the officer's staff will serve as facilitators of this process. They will determine if the risk assessments are not adequate, fully considered, or lacking information. They will create tools to assist the line of business in identifying risks and possible controls, deciding which controls to implement, and monitoring and measuring those controls for effectiveness. Appendix V illustrates a sample, partially completed risk assessment for a data center, in a format that could be used for both business and technology risks.

After the risk assessments are filled out and all the risks the particular line of business is facing fully identified, the business manager, with the assistance of the CRO's staff, should review the risks and associated controls. These should be compared to applicable regulatory requirements and board-of-director-approved limits to risk taking. If any risks fall outside of either regulatory or board limits, the CRO and the business management can work together to find solutions to lower the risks to an acceptable level. This could include implementing more controls—for example, requiring two appraisals on high-dollar loans or requiring two management signatures before processing a master file change. It could include purchasing insurance to transfer some of the risk to a third party, such as hazard insurance for the data center if a natural disaster were to strike. Or, it could mean deciding not to offer a particular service, such as opening accounts online due to an unacceptably high risk of fraud. All of these possible solutions result in the risk being lowered, and the goal is to reduce the risk to a level acceptable to both the financial institution's regulatory agencies and its board of directors.

In a yearly cycle, the risk assessments would be reviewed and reconsidered each year. This review should include adding any new risks to the business unit due to new products or services, or perhaps a new technology that has been implemented. The review should also assess whether the ratings for each risk were warranted or may need to be adjusted. The organization may decide to require review of the risk assessments more frequently in the beginning of the implementation until satisfied that all potential risks have been identified and included in the risk management process. The CRO should also implement a scorecard and metrics, such as a maturity model, against which the line of business risk management can be measured. Lines of business with good risk management practices should be rewarded. Financial institutions must ensure that they do not monetarily reward management that does not adequately control their risks, as this could be perceived as discouraging risk management. This could give the wrong message to the rest of the company and make the management feel that ignoring set risk limits and policies is tolerated.

Internal audit will independently evaluate the risk assessments each time they audit a function, area, or application. If the audit feels the risk assessments are not adequate or that all the potential risks have not been identified or adequately controlled, it would be an issue for both the business and the CRO. Periodic audits by external auditors and regulatory bodies are also a necessary part of TRM. Many regulatory bodies have their own TRM experts or examiners who specialize in reviewing the adequacy of TRM at financial institutions. These examiners use Federal Financial Institutions Examination Council (FFIEC) and other related guidance as well as best-practice information to assess the adequacy and effectiveness of each financial institution's TRM program. Exhibit 10.2 shows the basic yearly or cyclical flow of the risk management process. The IT auditor would use this to see if the organization is following the standard in compliance with organizational or regulatory guidance.

An Example of Standards: Technology Risk Management Regulations

TRM for financial institutions is now more than just a buzzword. Regulatory bodies have required an effective TRM program as early as 1996.

Two of the main agencies offering regulatory guidance to financial institutions, which requires a risk management program, are FFIEC and the Basel Committee on Banking Supervision.

FFIEC is a council made up of representatives from the Federal Reserve Board (FRB), Federal Deposit Insurance Corporation (FDIC), Office of the Comptroller of the Currency (OCC), Office of Thrift Supervision (OTS), and National Credit Union Administration (NCUA). This council, with representatives from each bank regulatory body in the United States, was created to address and standardize IT supervision in financial institutions, and it provides guidance on the minimum requirements for IT controls of financial institutions. The handbook also contains audit work programs used by each member agency to test compliance with FFIEC's minimum requirements. Two of the first areas addressed are risk and risk management. According to their handbook, TRM programs at financial institutions should include identification, measurement, control, and monitoring of risk. TRM programs require an informed board, capable management, and appropriate staffing. The Basel Committee on Banking Supervision is a group of representatives from large banks and regulatory bodies from several different countries, primarily North America, Europe, and Japan. Through the Bank of International Settlements, the Basel Committee gathers to publish guidance on various aspects of banking and further the dialogue between the financial industry and the committee on topics such as operational risk management. The Basel Committee's purpose is to create principles that can be widely applied to banks, with the realization that each financial institution is different. Basel recognizes that each financial institution's risk profile will be different, depending on the types of activities and lines of business it takes on. The risk management principles outlined by the Basel Committee are not to be taken as absolute requirements but should be used as a guide and a flexible framework when creating a risk management program. According to the Basel Committee, the following are the basic tenets of an operational risk management program:

- The board of directors must be involved with the approval of the operational risk management plan, which includes technology risk.

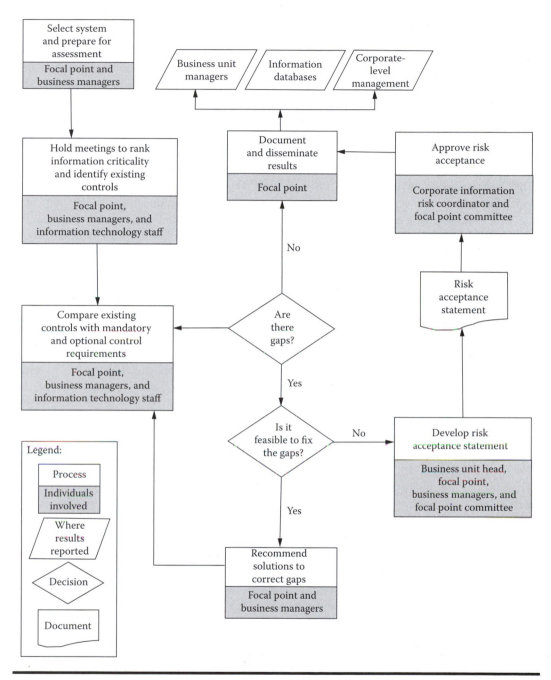

Exhibit 10.2 The risk management process.

- Senior management has the responsibility of implementing the plan and spreading information about the plan throughout the organization.
- Processes must be in place to identify risks, measure them, monitor their occurrence, and control or mitigate their occurrence.

Where Does Technology Risk Management Belong?

Technology risk can occur at two levels. It can be enterprise-wide, for example, as the choice of a new standard operating system. This type of technology risk is normally managed by the enterprise head of technology or CTO. Technology risk can also occur at the business unit level. This is the more common type of technology risk at financial institutions due to the type of IT used and the structure of the bank's IT department. In most cases, the IT department, not the business owner, is the vendor of the system. It is managed by the line of business with IT support and guidance.

There are two general possible structures for a TRM program at a financial institution. Both structures have their own associated pros and cons. The first approach is to have a central risk management department, of which TRM would be a subset. This fits due to the FFIEC statement that all risk management activities should be independent of risk-taking activities. In this scenario, a CRO would have a staff of risk management and TRM professionals. This department would perform all the risk management functions for the entire enterprise.

This structure can add value because risk management professionals, rather than business units, are identifying, measuring, controlling, and monitoring the entire enterprise's risks. In enterprises where the business units have poor communication, this structure has the advantage of allowing a central area to evaluate risks in light of risks of other business units. There may be a specific risk at each business unit level that could be more effectively managed enterprise-wide. For example, if a risk occurs for each of the several different business units but each business unit is independently purchasing insurance to offset that risk, combining the policies into one coverage for the entire enterprise or affected business units may result in cost savings, premium reduction, less administration time, and uniformity of coverage.

The possible drawbacks to this type of structure are that it has the possibility to isolate TRM from business units and place it in an "ivory tower" of the executive suite. This may result in negative situations such as too little involvement from the business units with risk identification, or all the risks may not be fully understood. The business units may feel that the TRM program exists only to satisfy the auditors, while creating more work for them. Additionally, controls put in place by the central risk management area may be seen as unrealistic for the business units to execute.

If each business unit is responsible for its own TRM, the risks may be better understood. Potential controls could be evaluated based on cost and value by the business units which can best determine what controls are feasible for their unit. For example, to mitigate the risk of power outages to normal company computer processing, a central risk management department without adequate technology understanding might determine that having a dual electrical feed (feed from two different power grids) is adequate protection. They may feel that the lower-cost option is acceptable and that it reduces the risk of power outages to an acceptable minimum. However, the data center management might make the decision that installing a generator, although much more costly, would ensure operability in case of a natural disaster, wide-area blackout, or other occurrence. In such a case, the business unit owner (data center manager) is better able to decide how to mitigate risks. The business units often know better what is going on in their area and have the most timely information regarding potential costs of failure or the possibility of adverse events taking place.

In this second scenario, potential issues may also arise. Each business unit becomes responsible for monitoring and controlling its own technology risk and cannot rely on the IT department to do it for them. The business units may downplay their risks to intentionally avoid implementing controls that may be seen as time consuming, unimportant, and a hindrance to normal business operations. Or, the business units may not have enough technology knowledge to adequately assess the risks of their technology.

The OCC's guidance on TRM leads to the conclusion that although technology is created and maintained by the IT department, the technology itself, the use of that technology, and the risks associated with it belong to the business unit and not to the IT department. This attitude mirrors the thoughts of the FFIEC's statement that although financial institutions may have different structures of risk management programs, all risk management should be independent of risk-taking activities. According to Walter Smiechewicz, who has been a CRO at several large financial institutions, risk management must be an enterprise-wide goal headed by the board of directors and exemplified in the CRO or other similar position. In facilitating the risk management program, the CROs will encourage the business units to identify, manage, control, and accept their own risks. This program should increase company-wide communication about risk and add value through reducing risk.

Regulatory and best-practice guidance seem to point toward a blended approach for the structure of a risk management function, with a central risk management figure or department working with the business units to identify, measure, monitor, and control their risk. This blended approach achieves the advantages of a central risk management area heading the risk management effort, coordinating the process, ensuring it complies with regulatory requirements, and reviewing all risks for the duplication of risks or risk transfer. This approach also has the benefit of including business management in the risk management process, making them accountable for the risks of their own area, and working with them to successfully monitor and control those risks.

IT Insurance Risk

The third area of risk assessment related to IT operations is insurance. A clear understanding of insurance and risk management is necessary to review the adequacy of an organization's IT insurance. IT management and data security administrator must be aware of the relationship between risk and insurance to understand the reasons behind insurance choices and the types of insurance that are most applicable to the IT environment. This portfolio provides an overview of the reasons for and the methods of risk analysis, insurance alternatives, and what to look for in IT insurance coverage. As we move toward e-commerce, the need for this review becomes apparent because e-commerce spamming, denial-of-service (DOS) attacks, and so on, can cost lost opportunities. Business must have a way to protect itself and recover its losses.

Problems Addressed

Insurance distributes losses so that a devastating loss to an individual or business is spread equitably among a group of insured members. Insurance neither prevents loss nor reduces its cost; it merely reduces the risk. Risk is the possibility of an adverse deviation from a desired outcome (e.g., the possibility of dying before reaching age 72, a home being destroyed by fire, or an interruption in business operations, and now, an e-commerce site overloaded with invalid transactions or IT business spamming). When not managed, risks may be assumed that should be insured and vice versa. Insurance policies often provide overlapping coverage in some areas and none in other critical ones. Other problems may include lack of control over loss and premium costs, uneconomic insurance arrangements, organizational errors, and failure to adopt loss-prevention techniques.

Insurance Requirements

The following conditions must be met for insurance companies to calculate risk in monetary terms and distribute costs over enough members to cover losses and leave a profit:

- The insured objects must be of sufficient number and quantity to allow a reasonably close calculation of probable loss.
- Losses must be accidental.
- Losses must be capable of being determined and measured.
- All insured objects should not be able to be simultaneously destroyed (i.e., catastrophic hazard should be minimal).

Although there are obvious costs (i.e., premiums) involved in insurance, some economic and social values of insurance that may not be obvious to include are

- The amount of accumulated funds needed to meet possible losses is reduced.
- Cash reserves that insurers accumulate are freed for investment purposes, effecting a better allocation of economic resources and increasing production.
- Because the supply of investment funds is greater than it would be without insurance, capital is available at a lower cost.
- The entrepreneur with adequate insurance coverage is a better credit risk.
- Insurers actively engage in loss-prevention activities.
- Insurance contributes to business and social stability by protecting business firms and their employees.

Insurance is an important means for business to handle risks; it is not, however, the only means. By insurance standards, risks are classified as insurable or uninsurable commercial risks. Risks insurable commercially are as follows:

Property risks. This refers to direct or indirect loss of property
Personal risks. Loss of life or income as a result of
    Premature death
    Physical disability
    Old age
    Unemployment
Legal liability risks. Loss caused by negligent behavior resulting in injury to persons, arising out of
    The use of automobiles
    The occupancy of buildings
    Employment
    The manufacture of products
    Professional misconduct

The following are risks that are not insurable commercially:

Market risks. Factors that may result in loss to property or income, including
    Seasonal or cyclical price changes
    Consumer indifference

Style changes
Competition offered by a better product
Political risks. Loss due to political reasons such as
War or overthrow of the government
Restriction imposed on free trade
Unreasonable or punitive taxation
Restriction on free exchange of currencies
Production risks. Loss related to production such as
Failure of machinery to function economically
Failure to solve technical problems
Exhaustion of raw material resources
Strikes, absenteeism, and labor unrest

How to Determine IT Insurance Coverage

Risk management as discussed earlier acts as a guide during the review of IT insurance coverage. It must be understood how the choice of insurance was arrived at. As mentioned earlier, there are fundamental steps that must be performed:

- The objectives of risk management policy must be in line with the overall goals of the organization.
- The method used to identify the risks associated with IT should provide an accurate and comprehensive list.
- Risk exposures should be properly quantified and categorized.
- The appropriate decision should be made after careful review of the options and alternatives.

After the risk management process has been reviewed, a more detailed investigation of IT-related risks can commence. The following is a list of questions that must be addressed:

Prevention and reduction:
Is there a comprehensive, up-to-date disaster recovery contingency plan?
What efforts have been made to check that the plan is workable?
Are there off-site backups of the appropriate file?
Are the procedures and practices for controlling accidents adequate?
Have practical measures been taken to control the impact of a disaster?
Is physical security adequate to protect property and equipment?
Is software security adequate to protect important or sensitive information?
Are there appropriate balancing and control checks made at key points in the processing?
Are there appropriate control checks on the operations?
Are there appropriate control checks during the development and modification of systems?
Are network firewalls tested weekly and have firewalls been certified on a semiannual basis?
Has e-commerce Website been certified for business commerce by an external organization?
Does the organization have credentials for certification? Does it have liability insurance and limit of losses?
Do contracts for purchases or leases have terms and conditions and remedies that adequately protect the company if there is a problem?

Have contracts been prepared by legal counsel who has expertise in IT and legal issues?

Are facilities, equipment, and network maintained properly?

Transfer:

Are risks handled by insurance according to risk management objectives and risk analysis?

Has the insurer been checked out?

Retention:

Are risks retained according to risk management objectives and risk analysis?

Have deductibles been used judiciously in insurance policies?

Once the methods available to prevent and reduce risk losses have been examined and risks to be insured have been determined, attention can be focused on the insured risks.

In the IT environment, there are special risks that are commonly handled by insurance, including

- Damage to computer equipment
- Cost of storage media
- Cost of acquiring the data stored on the media
- Damage to outsiders
- Business effects of the loss of computer functions

The types of insurance policies that cover these risks include property, liability, business interruption, and fidelity-bonding insurance. The review of the policies especially written for IT-related risks should examine

- Coverage of hardware and equipment (i.e., network, mass storage devices, terminals, printers, and central processing units [CPUs]).
- Coverage of the media and information stored thereon. For example, a disk drive that is destroyed can be replaced at the cost of a new drive. If the drive or mass storage device contains important information, the value of the new replacement drive plus the value of the lost information must be recovered.
- Coverage of the replacement or reconstruction cost and the cost of doing business as usual (i.e., business interruption). This might involve renting time on equivalent equipment from a nearby company or outsourcing to a vendor, paying overtime wages for reconstruction, and detective work. In this area, logging of daily e-commerce business activity resulting in financial transaction is extremely important to identify business interruption or loss due to spamming or information theft.
- Coverage of items such as damage to media from magnets, damage from power failure (blackout) or power cut (brownout), and damage from software failure.

After it has been verified in the policies that the proper items are covered, the dollar values assigned must be checked.

Reduction and Retention of Risks

Risks that are not insurable can be managed in other ways, and just because a risk is insurable does not mean that insurance is the only way to handle it. Risk reduction can be accomplished through loss prevention and control. If the possibility of loss can be prevented, the risk is eliminated; even reducing the chance of the loss from occurring is a significant improvement. If the chance cannot be reduced, at least the severity of the loss can often be controlled. The reduction method is frequently used with insurance to lessen the premiums.

Uninsurable risks can also be reduced by risk retention, which can be voluntary or involuntary depending on the organization's awareness of the risks. The retention method, which is sometimes referred to as self-insurance, should be voluntary and meet the following criteria:

- The risk should be spread physically so that there is a reasonably even distribution of exposure to loss over several locations.
- A study should be made to determine the maximum exposure to loss.
- Consideration should be given to the possibility of unfavorable loss experience and a decision reached as to whether this contingency should be covered by provision for self-insurance reserves.
- A premium charge should be made against operations that are adequate to cover losses and any increase in reserves that appear advisable.

Many companies, however, retain risks without estimating the future losses or reserving funds to pay for these losses. To decide what methods to use, companies must first analyze their risks. Managing the risk of significant losses is essential to protecting the interests of a business. Exhibit 10.3 illustrates the structure of that process.

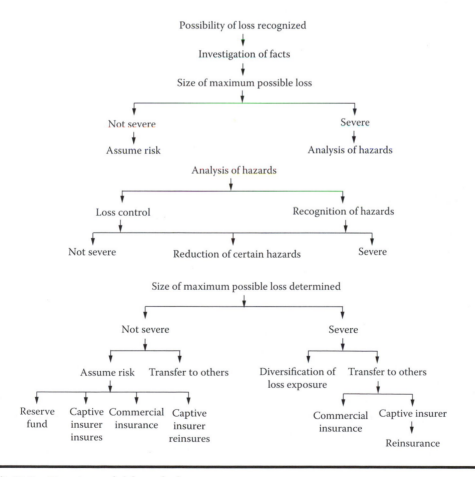

Exhibit 10.3   Structure of risk analysis.

Available Guidance

There are several professional standards documents in place that provide guidance to auditors and managers involved in risk assessment. Standards assist in the development of technology and provide consistent quality measurement if adopted, maintained, and supported by the organization. The following are standards related to assessing risk in IT operations. By no means is this area limited to U.S. issues. Operational review encompasses the global business community. One of the most recent endeavors is the International Standards Organization (ISO) and its effort to develop ISO Guide 73 on risk management terminology. It also has a number of projects under the technical program JTC 1 Committee on IT. ISO/IEC 27005 which provides guidelines for information security risk management. It supports the general concepts specified in ISO/IEC 27001 and is designed to assist the satisfactory implementation of information security based on a risk management approach. Knowledge of the concepts, models, processes, and terminologies described in ISO/IEC 27001 and ISO/IEC 27002 is important for a complete understanding of ISO/IEC 27005:2008. ISO/IEC 27005:2008 is applicable to all types of organizations (e.g., commercial enterprises, government agencies, nonprofit organizations) which intend to manage risks that could compromise the organization's information security. ISO/IEC 27005 revises and supersedes the Management of Information and Communications Technology Security (MICTS) standards ISO/IEC TR 13335-3:1998 plus ISO/IEC TR 13335-4:2000.

U.S. National Institute of Standards and Technology

A major focus of NIST activities in IT is providing measurement criteria to support the development of pivotal, forward-looking technology. NIST standards and guidelines are issued as FIPS for government-wide use. NIST develops FIPS when there are compelling federal government requirements for IT standards related to security and interoperability and there are no acceptable industry standards or solutions. It supports a very fine Website at www.nist.gov and provides very useful information and tools. For example, its Computer Security Resource Center (CSRC) has a package called Automated Security Self-Evaluation Tool (ASSET) and another called Webmetrics, Version 3.0, found in the Information Access Division.

One of the first of several federal documents issued by NIST is FIPS 31, "Guidelines for Automatic Data Processing Physical Security and Risk Management." This standard provided the initial guidance to federal organizations in developing physical security and risk management programs for IS facilities. Then, in March 2006, NIST issued FIPS 200 Minimum Security Requirements for Federal Information and Information Systems. Federal agencies are responsible for "including policies and procedures that ensure compliance with minimally acceptable system configuration requirements, as determined by the agency" within their information security program. Managing system configurations is also a minimum security requirement identified in FIPS 200 and NIST SP 800-537 defines security controls that support this requirement. Then, in August 2011, NIST issued SP 800-128, "Guide for Security Focused Configuration Management of Information Systems?" Configuration management concepts and principles described in this publication provide supporting information for NIST SP 800-53, Recommended Security Controls for Federal Information Systems and Organizations, as amended and in compliance with Risk Management Framework (RMF) that is discussed in NIST SP 800-37, Guide for Applying the Risk Management Framework to Federal Information Systems: A Security Life Cycle Approach, as amended. More specific guidelines on the implementation of the monitor step of the RMF are provided in Draft NIST SP 800-137, Information Security Continuous Monitoring for Federal

Information Systems and Organizations. The purpose of the monitor step in the Risk Management Framework is to continuously monitor the effectiveness of all security controls selected, implemented, and authorized for protecting organizational information and information systems, which includes the configuration management security controls identified in SP 800-53. These documents are a very good starting point for understanding the basis and many approaches one can use in assessing risk in IT today. The current list of FIPS that applies to IT can be found in Appendix III.

Government Accountability Office

The GAO is a nonpartisan agency within the legislative branch of the government. GAO conducts audits, surveys, investigations, and evaluations of federal programs. This may include audits of federal agencies and state, county, and city governments, and extend to private industry, where federal funds are spent. Often, GAO's work is done at the request of congressional committees or members, or to fulfill specifically mandated or basic legislative requirements. GAO's findings and recommendations are published as reports to congressional members or delivered as testimony to congressional committees. GAO has issued numerous reports on computer security, IT vulnerabilities, and risk assessment. Its Website can be found at www.gao.gov. Several of these reports are presented in Appendix III.

The U.S. Federal Government has invested an extraordinary amount of resources in examining risk dating back to the early 1960s. Government Accounting Standards (GAS) and in the 1990s, the Government Accountability Office's Information Management and Technology (IMTEC) reports relate to risk assessment. For example, GAS 4.29, "Safeguarding Controls," is used to help auditors recognize risk factors involving computer processing. IMTEC 8.1.4, "Information Technology: An Audit Guide for Assessing Acquisition Risk," is used in planning and conducting risk assessments of computer hardware and software, telecommunications, and system development acquisitions. In 1999, it issued a very good report titled "Information Security Risk Assessment: Practices of Leading Organizations," GAO/AIMD-00-33. In October 2002, it issued an outstanding document titled "Assessing the Reliability of Computer-Processed Data," supplement to the GAS (Yellow Book)—External Version, GAO–03-273G, October 2002. Then, in 2009, GAO released its *Federal Information Systems Control Audit Manual* (FISCAM). A top-down, risk-based evaluation that considers materiality and significance in determining effective and efficient audit procedures (the auditor determines which IT control techniques are relevant to the audit objectives and which are necessary to achieve the control activities; generally, all control activities are relevant unless the audit scope is limited or the auditor determines that, due to significant IS control weaknesses, it is not necessary to test all relevant IS controls).

The October 2002 report identifies the process of assessing the reliability of computer-processed data and how one might approach it from an audit or management review process. The following is an illustration of the process that IMTEC recommends. Exhibit 10.4 shows an overview. Exhibit 10.5 recommends the key steps one must consider when assessing the reliability of computer-generated information. Exhibit 10.6 shows the depth necessary when assessing the reliability of computer-generated information. These approaches have been incorporated into the 2009 document.

These processes are well reviewed by GAO and certainly provide fine guidance for those wanting to learn the mechanics and details of this process.

American Institute of Certified Public Accountants

SAS are issued by the Auditing Standards Board (ASB) of the AICPA and are recognized as interpretations of the 10 generally accepted auditing standards. As we mentioned in earlier chapters,

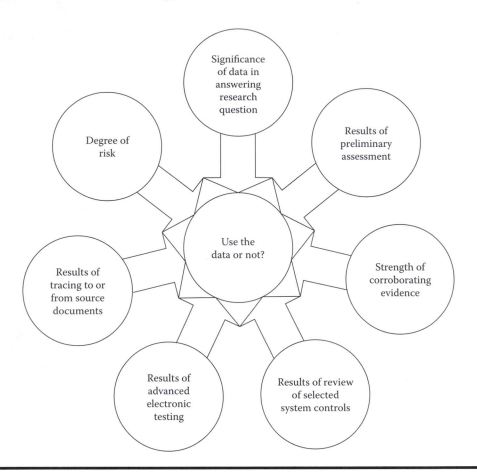

Exhibit 10.4   Factors to consider in making the decision on using the data recommended by GAO. (From Assessing the Reliability of Computer-Processed Data, Supplement to the Government Auditing Standards (Yellow Book)—External Version, GAO–03-273G, October 2002.)

the AICPA has played a major role in the issuance of guidance to the accounting and control profession. An example in applying audit risk and materiality concepts comes with the issuance of SAS 47, "Audit Risk and Materiality in Conducting an Audit," relates to risk assessment. In SAS 47, control risk is defined as the possibility of a misstatement occurring in an account balance or class of transactions that (1) could be material when aggregated with misstatements in other balances or classes and (2) will not be prevented or detected on a timely basis by the system of internal control.

SAS 65 requires that, in all engagements, the auditor develops some understanding of the internal audit function (EDP audit, if available) and determine whether that function is relevant to the assessment of control risk. Thus, if there is an internal audit function, it must be evaluated. The evaluation is not optional. In 1996, AICPA issued SAS 80, which is directly aimed at improving auditing in the EDP environment. This SAS was published in the same year and has made a profound impact on the auditing profession. An excerpt from SAS 80 states: "In entities where significant information is transmitted, processed, maintained, or accessed electronically, the auditor may determine that it is not practical or possible to reduce detection risk to an acceptable level by performing only substantive tests for one or more financial statement assertions. For example,

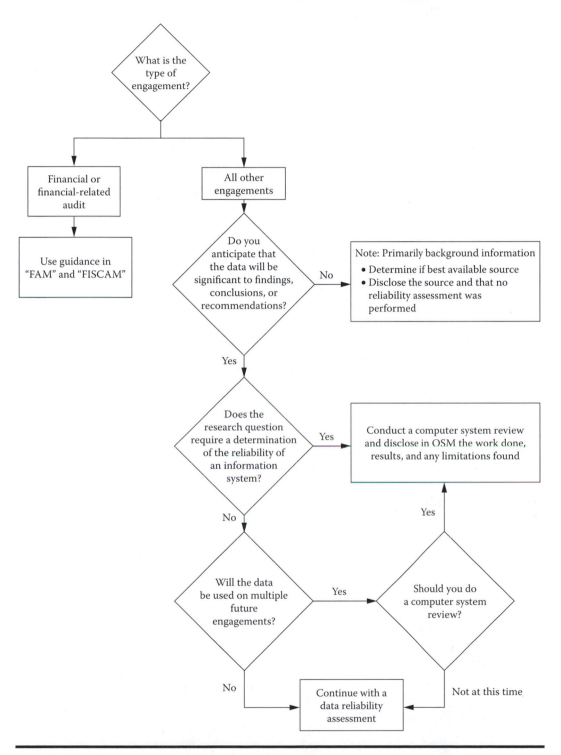

Exhibit 10.5 The decision process to determine whether data reliability assessment is required. (From Assessing the Reliability of Computer-Processed Data, Supplement to the Government Auditing Standards (Yellow Book)—External Version, GAO–03-273G, October 2002.)

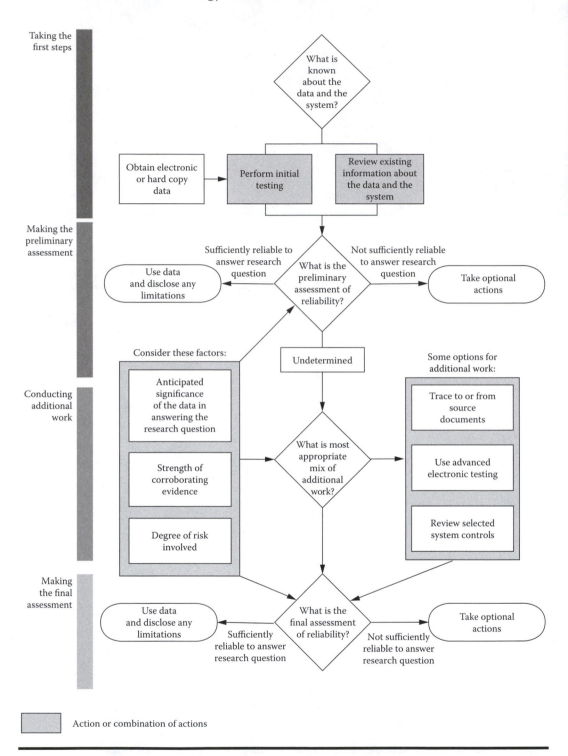

Exhibit 10.6 GAO's recommended data reliability assessment process. (From Assessing the Reliability of Computer-Processed Data, Supplement to the Government Auditing Standards (Yellow Book)—External Version, GAO–03-273G, October 2002.)

the potential for improper initiation or alteration of information to occur and not be detected may be greater if information is produced, maintained, or accessed only in electronic form. In such circumstances, the auditor should perform tests of controls to gather evidential matter to use in assessing control risk, or consider the effect on his or her report." The GAO process illustrated earlier is the federal government guide to implementation of this SAS.

SAS 94 was adopted in 2001. This SAS provides guidance to auditors about the effect of IT on internal control and on the auditor's understanding of internal control and assessment of control risk. SAS 94 amends SAS 55, "Consideration of Internal Control in a Financial Statement Audit." In earlier chapters, we talked about the issuance of SAS 103-111 which examine the Information Technology Considerations in Risk-Based Auditing. Within this set, the issuance of SAS 107 Audit Risk and Materiality in Conducting and Audit is the AICPA's cornerstone of risk-based standards. In their approach for an auditor to fulfill SAS 107 is to fully understand, validate, and verify how information technology contributes to the RMM and whether controls exist to prevent or detect errors or fraud. RMM consists of two components which have been discussed in other chapters: inherent risk (IR) and control risk (CR). The application of detection risk (DR) to the result of IR and CR results in the level of audit risk.

Information Systems Audit and Control Association

The ISACA is a worldwide not-for-profit association of more than 28,000 practitioners dedicated to IT audit, control, and security in over 100 countries. The Information Systems Audit and Control Foundation (ISACAF) is an associated not-for-profit foundation committed to expanding the knowledge base of the profession through a commitment to research. The ISACA standards board has updated and issued several Information System Audit Guidelines (ISAG); these are recognized as system auditing standards.

The ISACA's recent updated guideline titled "Use of Risk Assessment in Audit Planning" specifies the level of audit work required to meet a specific audit objective; it is a subjective decision made by the IT auditor. The risk of reaching an incorrect conclusion based on the audit findings (audit risk) is one aspect of this decision. The other is the risk of errors occurring in the area being audited (error risk). Recommended practices for risk assessment in carrying out financial audits are well documented in auditing standards for financial auditors, but guidance is required on how to apply such techniques to IT audits.

Management also bases its decisions on how much control is appropriate upon assessment of the level of risk exposure it is prepared to accept. For example, the inability to process computer applications for a period of time is an exposure that could result from unexpected and undesirable events (e.g., data center fire). Exposures can be reduced by the implementation of appropriately designed controls. These controls are ordinarily based on the estimation of the occurrence of adverse events and are intended to decrease such probability. For example, a fire alarm does not prevent fires but is intended to reduce the extent of fire damage.

This guideline provides guidance in applying IT auditing standards. The IT auditor should consider it in determining how to achieve implementation of the preceding standards, use professional judgment in its application, and be prepared to justify any departure.

Institute of Internal Auditors

Established in 1941, the Institute of Internal Auditors (IIA) serves more than 85,000 members in internal auditing, governance and internal control, IT audits education, and security in more than

120 countries. The Professional Standards and Responsibilities Committee, the senior technical committee designated by IIA to issue pronouncements on auditing standards, issues SIAS.

The IIA has in place Performance Standard 2110 titled "Risk Management," which specifies that the internal audit activity should assist the organization by identifying and evaluating significant exposures to risk and contributing to the improvement of risk management and control systems. It provides additional guidance in the form of Implementation Standard 2110.A1 (Assurance Engagements) with which the internal audit activity should monitor and evaluate the effectiveness of the organization's risk management system. Implementation Standard 2110.A2 (Assurance Engagements) stipulates that the internal audit activity should evaluate risk exposures relating to the organization's governance, operations, and IS regarding

■ Reliability and integrity of financial and operational information
■ Effectiveness and efficiency of operations
■ Safeguarding of assets
■ Compliance with laws, regulations, and contracts

The last performance standard addresses consulting engagements in Implementation Standard 2110.C1 (Consulting Engagements). The IIA recommends that during consulting engagements, internal auditors should address risk consistent with the engagement's objectives and be alert to the existence of other significant risks.

The IIA has also developed a series of publications that aid in the assessment of internal controls over financial reporting. The "GAIT for IT General Controls Deficiency Assessment" (GAIT) methodology is a top-down and risk-based approach to assessing IT general controls. GAIT 2 provides an approach for evaluating IT general controls deficiencies identified during a financial audit or Sarbanes–Oxley control assessment. GAIT for Business and IT Risk (GAIT-R) is a risk-based audit methodology to align IT audits to business risks.

Committee of Sponsoring Organizations of the Treadway Commission

The COSO was formed in 1985 as an independent, voluntary, private-sector organization dedicated to improving the quality of financial reporting through business ethics, effective internal controls, and corporate governance. COSO consists of representatives from industry, public accounting agencies, investment firms, and the New York Stock Exchange. The first chairman of COSO was James C. Treadway, Jr., executive vice president and general counsel, Paine Webber Inc., and a former commissioner of the U.S. Securities and Exchange Commission; hence the name Treadway Commission. The current chairman is John Flaherty, chairman, retired vice president and general auditor for PepsiCo Inc.

The COSO board assigned PriceWaterhouseCoopers to lead a project to develop a framework for enterprise risk management. The Enterprise Risk Management—Integrated Framework was issued in September 2004. Chapter 8 offers a detailed discussion of integrating enterprise risk assessment into IT governance processes.

Conclusion

Organizations have recognized the benefit of protecting themselves from all types of potential risk exposures. By identifying and mapping risk exposures, an organization can concentrate on mitigating those exposures that can do the most damage. With an understanding of risks, their severity, and their frequency, an organization can turn to solutions, be it retaining, transferring, sharing, or avoiding a particular risk.

Organizations must develop a sound risk management program to be able to determine the adequacy of their IT insurance coverage. The first step in properly developing a program is becoming aware of the limits and advantages of insurance and learning the methods of risk reduction. For the risk management program itself, objectives must be determined; risks must be identified, categorized, and evaluated; and risk-handling techniques must be chosen. Understanding insurance choices and the types of policies available is also important. The development of a comprehensive risk management program requires significant effort from all parties. However, once established, the benefits of managing risk become invaluable.

Review Questions

1. What is risk assessment?
2. What is the purpose of a risk management program?
3. When should managers and auditors perform risk assessment?
4. What affect does insurance have on risk?
5. How should organizations develop a sound risk management program to determine the adequacy of their IT insurance coverage?

Multiple-Choice Questions

1. NIST stands for which of the following?
   a. National Information Security Test
   b. National Institute of Standards and Testing
   c. National Institute of Standards and Technology
   d. National Institute of Security and Technology
2. The GAO conducts audits, surveys, investigations, and evaluations of
   a. Federal agencies
   b. Businesses
   c. State agencies
   d. All of the above
3. Which of the following organizations consists of representatives from industry, public accounting, investment firms, and the New York Stock Exchange?
   a. IIA
   b. COSO
   c. ISACA
   d. AICPA
4. Risk retention (self-insurance) methods should meet all of the following criteria except
   a. Risk should be spread physically to distribute exposure across several locations
   b. Determine whether a self-insurance reserve should be established to cover a possible loss
   c. Develop an internal risk management group to monitor exposures
   d. Determine the maximum exposure to loss
5. Threats to integrity and privacy from inside the organization include
   a. Loss or destruction of assets by malicious acts

 b. Errors from incompetence or carelessness
 c. Deliberate exposure of private or privileged information
 d. All of the above
 6. The cost of risks includes all of the following except
 a. Cost of loss-prevention measures
 b. Cost of security controls
 c. Cost of losses sustained
 d. Insurance premiums
 7. Tools used to identify risks include all of the following except
 a. Risk analysis questionnaire
 b. Flowchart of operations
 c. Audit workflow software
 d. Insurance policy checklist
 8. IT risk evaluation involves
 a. Ranking of the size and probability of potential loss
 b. Evaluation of the level of risk of a given process or function
 c. Ensuring that risk losses do not prevent organization management from meeting its objectives
 d. Retaining a portion of the risk to reduce the insurance or premium costs
 9. The reasons for risk analysis are
 a. Loss or corruption of information and IS assets
 b. Impaired and ineffective management decision making
 c. Disruption to customer service or other critical operations
 d. All of the above
 10. Which of the following statements regarding the effect of insurance on risk is true?
 a. Prevents loss or damage to the organization
 b. Transfers risk of loss or damage to the insurance company
 c. Risks are not managed when insured
 d. None of the above

Exercises

1. Using an Internet browser, research professional standards on risk assessment. List and describe three.
2. Develop an operational risk assessment using the information included in Case 3: Holt Valley Hospital Services, Inc. (Appendix I).
3. Your organization has recently developed criteria for a risk management program. One goal of the program is to determine the adequacy and effectiveness of the company IT insurance coverage. Describe how an effective risk management program can enable a more cost-effective use of IT insurance.

Answers to Multiple-Choice Questions

1—c; 2—d; 3—b; 4—c; 5—d; 6—b; 7—c; 8—a; 9—d; 10—b

Further Reading

1. Berson, A. and G. Anderson, *Sybase and Client/Server Computing, 1996, BITS Technology Risk Transfer Gap Analysis Tool*, BITS, Washington, DC, 2002.
2. Bock, J.T., *The Strategic Role of "Economic Capital" in Bank Management*, Midas-Kapiti International, Wimbledon, England, 2000.
3. Business Banking Board, *RAROC and Operating Risk*, Washington, DC, Corporate Executive Board, 2001.
4. Business Banking Board, *Risk Management Structure*, Washington, DC, Corporate Executive Board, 2001.
5. Crouhy, M., D. Galai, and R. Mark, *Risk Management*, McGraw-Hill, New York, 2001.
6. Elements of a Successful IT Risk Management Program, Gartner, May 2002, http://www.gartner.com/DisplayDocument?id=351500.
7. Ernst & Young, *Integrated Risk Management Practices*, Unpublished PowerPoint slides, 2000.
8. Hoffman, D.G., *Managing Operational Risk*, Wiley, New York, 2002.
9. In Brief: Ferguson urges investing in risk control, *American Banker*, March 5, 2002, www.american-banker.com.
10. Institute of Internal Auditors, http://www.theiia.org/guidance/standards-and-practices/.
11. Information Systems Audit and Control Association, http://www.isaca.org/Template.cfm?Section=Standards&Template=/TaggedPage/TaggedPageDisplay.cfm&TPLID=29&ContentID=42792.
12. IT Governance Institute and the IT Control Practices Committee of ISACA, *IT Control Practice Statement for the COBIT High-Level Control Objective PO-9 Assess Risks*, IT Governance Institute, Rolling Meadows, IL, 2001.
13. Jameson, R. and J. Walsh, The leading contenders, *Risk Magazine*, November 2000, http://www.financewise.com/public/edit/riskm/oprisk/opr-soft00.htm.
14. Lam, J., Top ten requirements for operational risk management, *Risk Management*, November 2001, http://0-proquest.umi.com.opac.library.csupomona.edu.
15. Marks, N., The new age of internal auditing, *The Internal Auditor*, December 2001, http:// 0-proquest.umi.com.opac.library.csupomona.edu.
16. Office of the Comptroller of the Currency, *Results of the 2004 Loss Data Collection Exercise for Operational Risk*, May 12, 2005.
17. Ong, M., Why bother? *Risk Magazine*, November 2000, www.risk.net.
18. Psica, A., Risk watch—Destination ahead, *Internal Auditor*, 2007, pp. 77–80.
19. Singleton, T., What every IT auditor should know about the new risk suite standards, Information Systems Audit and Control Association, *Inf. Syst. Control J.*, 5, 2007.
20. Stoneburner, G., A. Guguen, and A. Feringa, *Risk Management Guide for Information Technology Systems*, National Institute of Standards and Technology, Gaithersburg, MA, Special Publication 800-30, July 2002.
21. The Institute of Internal Auditors, Practice Advisory 2100-3: Internal Audit's Role in the Risk Management Process, March 2001, http://www.theiia.org/ecm/guide-frame.cfm?doc_id=73.
22. United States General Accounting Office, *Information Security Risk Assessment Practices of Leading Organizations*, U.S. GAO, Washington, DC, November 1999, accessed September 2, 2002, http://www.gao.gov/special.pubs/ai00033.pdf.
23. U.S. General Accounting Office, *Assessing the Reliability of Computer-Processed Data [Supplement to the Government Auditing Standards (Yellow Book)—External Version]*, GAO-03-273G, October 2002.
24. U.S. General Accounting Office, *Government Auditing Standards (Yellow Book)—Preliminary Edition*, GAO-03-673G, June 2003.
25. Verschoor, C.C., *Audit Committee Briefing—2001: Facilitating New Audit Committee Responsibilities*, The Institute of Internal Auditors, Altamonte Springs, FL, 2001.
26. Unknown. *Enterprise Risk Management—Integrated Framework*, Committee of Sponsoring Organizations of the Treadway Commission, Washington, DC, September 2004.
27. Unknown, *GAIT for IT General Control Deficiency Assessment*, The Institute of Internal Auditors, Altamonte Springs, FL, 2008.
28. Unknown, *GAIT for Business and IT Risk*, The Institute of Internal Auditors, Altamonte Springs, FL, 2008.

Chapter 11

Process and Quality Management

In Chapter 9, the importance of strategy and standards was discussed. This chapter focuses on the equally important impact of how IT is organized and the process framework needed for IT to be effective. People, process, and technology are the fundamental components of an IT organization. This chapter focuses on the need for effective processes in managing people and technology to deliver quality results. IT processes and quality management provides management with the tools required to deliver high-quality systems and operations. An effective organization model, along with documented processes, facilitates the accomplishment of IT objectives by clearly defining roles and responsibilities. Clearly defined roles and responsibilities help users and IT work together as a team by understanding their interdependencies. IT processes are interconnected and cross organization boundaries. It is important to have processes documented, agreed, and followed to ensure process efficiency and control effectiveness.

There are several frameworks that provide guidance in defining and implementing quality processes in systems development and operations. Quality management processes create an environment where processes deliver the expected results. The Software Engineering Institute (SEI) developed standards for implementing high-quality systems. The ISO developed standards for quality systems and operations. This chapter provides both an approach and experience in attaining ISO 9001 certification. IT auditing plays a key role in this process. It is a reflection of corporate management support, institutional cooperation, and the search for better quality in IT systems and operations.

Organizations establish and communicate policies and procedures for information systems to ensure that organizational goals are met. These policies and procedures should communicate the organization's stand on issues such as systems architecture, testing and validation of requirements and systems, and documentation. These areas are critical to establishing an institutional process for managing applications and infrastructure.

4.1	IT process framework
4.2	IT strategy committee
4.3	IT steering committee
4.4	Organizational placement of the IT function
4.5	IT organizational structure
4.6	Roles and responsibilities
4.7	Responsibility for IT quality assurance
4.8	Responsibility for risk, security, and compliance
4.9	Data and system ownership
4.10	Supervision
4.11	Segregation of duties
4.12	IT staffing
4.13	Key IT personnel
4.14	Contracted staff policies and procedures
4.15	Relationships

Exhibit 11.1　Planning and organization domain.

IT Processes

The COBIT process (PO4) in the Planning and Organization Domain discusses how people and processes support an effective IT organization. Exhibit 11.1 lists the key control objectives for this section.

Organizational Structure

The IT function may be organized to align itself with the corporate strategic business units. This creates business partnerships that better facilitate the use of IT and improve customer service and support. IT may be organized to facilitate the building of a high level of competence in common technical areas such as project management, quality assurance, data processing operations, technical customer services, and distributed systems, which are key to supporting IT in our business operations. These common technical areas provide for consistent quality support to all development and maintenance activities. The question arises as to how to organize IT to best manage today's virtual environment.

There is not one best organizational structure for IT organizations. The structure of the organization will depend on the size and the priorities of the organization. A centralized IT organization makes sense in a standard business environment where the focus is on controlling costs and service levels. A decentralized IT organization makes sense in a highly divergent business environment with the need for local responsiveness. In both models, a steering committee is needed to prioritize projects to ensure that IT resources are directed toward projects that support organizational goals. A formal steering committee decides which projects are completed, in which order. These decisions can be based on a variety of criteria that measure alignment with business objectives and financial metrics such as payback or return on investment. Discussed here are three possible structures and the advantages and disadvantages of each.

Centralized

The mainframe environment was naturally centralized due to the nature of the technology. The information and IT resources were all located with the servers at a data center. Advantages of a centralized model include the ability to leverage scale for pricing concessions and shared services that only add incremental costs. Shared service organizations consolidate responsibility for similar tasks into a single group. This group can leverage resources across an enterprise to reduce costs and provide more consistent service. Shared services groups can be established for procurement, project management, finance, architecture, service desk, quality assurance, application development, and so on. Disadvantages include restrictive standards and typically more bureaucracy in getting service.

Decentralized

The advantage of a decentralized model is that the IT support group is closer to the unit it supports. This model is typically more flexible and responsive to customer needs. Disadvantages include the inability to leverage scale and shared resources resulting in duplicate effort and increased cost. With the proliferation of notebook and pocket PCs and distributed systems, many organizations have developed into a decentralized model. With cost-cutting initiatives, many organizations have consolidated servers into a centralized model. Even in organizations that have centralized/consolidated servers, it may make sense to leave some servers in distributed locations to enhance performance and decrease the cost of telecommunications if remote servers can be centrally managed.

Combination of Centralized and Decentralized

Decentralized models evolved from widely distributed computing environment with many departments creating and maintaining their own applications and databases. The perceived benefits of this distributed environment included flexibility, timely decision support, increased innovation, and better customer service and understanding. Instead, they experienced chaos due to the duplication of effort and reconciliation of the various departments' information. Because of this, organizations have opted for more balanced approach by creating a central database with departmental access to information.

The International Center for Information Technology takes a more liberal approach to distributed computing. They do not mind duplicated effort as long as the business units perform and achieve their results. They believe that it is better to have five people with the same ideas than not having the resources for anyone to have those ideas. Their focus is on innovation instead of control.

In most organizations, some degree of coordination would help minimize the amount of duplicated effort and confusion regarding the proliferation of data. Now that end users have PCs and the knowledge to create their own applications, they will not go back to a central host and limited autonomy. Rather than totally distributed or centralized IT management, a combination of the two makes more sense for most large organizations.

Shared Services

Shared services organizations consolidate responsibility for similar tasks into a single group. This group can leverage resources across an enterprise to reduce costs and provide more consistent service. Shared services groups can be established for procurement, project management, finance, architecture, service desk, quality assurance, application development, and so on. Quality assurance, such as security, should be an independent function reporting to the CIO to avoid conflict of interest with the local development teams.

Coordinating Management

One means of managing the widely distributed information resources within a company is to designate a coordinator to maintain and communicate what information business units are creating and using. The focus in this position would be on information as opposed to technology, which is the focus of the information systems organizations. Another means of coordinating end-user computing is to establish a forum for exchanging ideas and applications with other departments. This can be achieved by using a company-wide bulletin board; e-mail for individual contributors to post notices of applications; or inquiries for information much like the Internet functions across company boundaries. These solutions can also be used in conjunction with one another to foster the sharing of information within an organization.

Roles and Responsibilities

Regardless of the organizational structure, the organization, department management, and users have specific control responsibilities. The organization must establish uniform policies, procedures, and standards that govern information systems. Department managers are responsible for ensuring data integrity and compliance with established organizational standards. Individuals are responsible for maintaining control over access to computing resources (SAC 35-40).

IT Management Responsibilities

IT management is responsible for creating overall guidelines and standards for information systems. Guidelines are needed to provide users with the information necessary to implement systems that meet organizational goals. Standards are needed to ensure compatibility and portability of systems and user knowledge across an organization. To ensure consistent and effective implementations of technology, IT management should be responsible for the following areas:

- Information systems strategy
- Standards
- Emerging technology
- User support
- Purchasing/contracts

User Management Responsibilities

Standards and guidelines are useless if they are not followed. Therefore, the successful implementation of technology rests with the end user. User management must communicate and enforce the organization's standards. The users are ultimately responsible for implementing standards because they are closest to the data and control how that data is used. User departments should be responsible for managing the use of computer systems in the following areas:

- Access controls
- Training
- Security
- Backup and recovery
- Inventory of hardware/software
- Data integrity

There is no one structure that can be applied in all situations. The role of IT and users will vary depending on the structure and culture of an organization. This role will change as the business and technology environments change. IT and users must work together and recognize the value of each other's contribution to the overall success of an organization.

Separation of Duties

Separation of duties is important in any system for security control. It is no less important in an end-user environment. Separation of duties provides a system of checks and balances to prevent unauthorized access and changes to programs and data. The following are the areas that need to be separated:

- Operations from data entry
- Origination from approval
- Creation from testing
- Procedures from data

Resource Management

The two key IT resources are people and technology. In today's global workplace, teams are more often geographically dispersed. Resource management is the process used to effectively manage people by creating an environment for the training and development of skills and knowledge that lets individuals perform their software management and technical roles capably. The purpose is to match the right people with the right skills for the right roles. Resource management ensures IT has the right resources at the right time and the tools to fulfill their job responsibilities. With remote workers, it is becoming more common for the supervisor and staff not to be in the same location. This requires new approaches to managing a remote workforce. The following processes support this goal:

- Formal authorization process for hiring contractors or internal personnel
- Monthly reporting of staffing levels by organization or project
- Formal recruitment process for obtaining experienced and entry-level technical candidates
- Career development program for technical and management career paths
- Formal process for skills inventory identification through use of a skills database
- Equipment and facilities allocation process to ensure people have the tools needed to do their job
- Process for selecting individual and group training programs to best fit the overall IT strategy
- Performance management process that rewards individuals for exceptional performance and encourages improvement in all

PO8 Manage Quality
Control Objectives
8.1   Quality management system
8.2   IT standards and quality practices
8.3   Development and acquisition standards
8.4   Customer focus
8.5   Continuous improvement
8.6   Quality measurement, monitoring, and review

Exhibit 11.2   Planning and organization domain.

Managing Quality

The COBIT process (PO8) in the Planning and Organization Domain covers the quality management process and Exhibit 11.2 lists the control objectives.

COBIT recognizes quality management as a process that impacts the effectiveness, efficiency, integrity, and availability of information systems and involves IT resources that include people, applications, technology, and facilities. It describes the controls over the IT process of managing quality that satisfies the business requirement. It takes into consideration the following:

- Establishment of a quality culture
- Quality plans
- Quality assurance responsibilities
- Quality control practices
- System development life cycle methodology
- Program and system testing and documentation
- Quality assurance reviews and reporting
- Training and involvement of end user and quality assurance personnel
- Development of a quality assurance knowledge base
- Benchmarking against industry norms

The goal of quality assurance is to provide management with appropriate visibility into the processes being used to manage projects and products. To accomplish this objective requires regular reviews and audits of the software products and activities to verify that they comply with the applicable procedures and standards. Standards and procedures need to be established for valid quality assurance measurement processes in every project and operation. Quality assurance begins with the definition of a new project or product. Project activities and work products throughout the project life cycle need to comply with established plans, standards, and procedures. These processes must be documented and controlled (see Exhibit 11.3).

Quality Management Standards

In support of quality management is extensive research into the processes that drive maturity. CMM is at the foundation of COBIT and other process models that identify "best practices" in

Goals
Quality assurance activities are planned and documented.
Adherence of project activities and products to applicable standards, procedures, and requirements is verified objectively.
All impacted groups are aware of and cooperative with quality assurance activities.
Noncompliance issues are addressed with senior management.

Commitments
The SQA functions are in place on all software projects.
The SQA group has a reporting channel to senior management that is independent of all project-related groups.
Senior management periodically reviews SQA activities and results.

Abilities
The SQA group exists and is active.
Adequate resources and funding are provided.
SQA personnel are adequately trained.
Project team members understand and support the SQA function within their project.

Activities
An SQA plan is prepared according to a documented procedure.
The SQA plan is reviewed by all impacted groups.
The SQA plan is managed and controlled (i.e., change control).
SQA activities are performed according to the SQA plan that covers responsibilities and authority, resource requirements, schedule and funding, role in establishing software development plans, standards and procedures, evaluations to be performed, audits and reviews to be conducted, project standards and procedures to be used in audits, and procedures for documenting and reviewing findings.
The SQA function participates in the preparation and reviews of the project development plan, standards, and procedures.
The SQA function reviews the software engineering activities to verify compliance.
The SQA function audits designated software work products to verify compliance with standards, procedures, and contractual obligations, and identifies documents, and tracks deviations and corrections.
The SQA function periodically reviews its findings with the customer SQA function and IT senior management.

Measurements
Measurements are devised and utilized to determine the cost, schedule, and effectiveness of SQA activities.

Exhibit 11.3   Auditing quality assurance.

controlling the delivery of IT services. The two key standards that govern the system development process are CMM for software (SEI) and 9000 Quality Management and Quality Assurance Standards (ISO).

Capability Maturity Model Integration

The Capability Maturity Model Integration (CMMI®) provides a framework for organizing and assessing the maturity level of IT processes for software development and maintenance of products and services. Software process maturity is the extent to which a specific process is explicitly defined, managed, measured, and controlled, and is effective. Maturity implies a potential for growth in capability and indicates both the richness of an organization's software process and the consistency with which it is applied in projects throughout the organization. CMM was developed by the SEI, a research and development center established in December 1984 by the U.S. Department of Defense and operated as an extension of Carnegie Mellon University in Pittsburgh. CMM provides a model for assessing the level of process maturity within an organization. With CMM, maturity is defined in one of five levels (see Exhibit 11.4).

The specific practices to be executed in each key process area evolve as the organization achieves higher levels of process maturity. The U.S. Department of Defense established the SEI to advance the practice of software development with the goal of having quality systems produced on schedule and within budget—a critical need for the U.S. defense industry. SEI's mission was to provide leadership in advancing the practice of software engineering so as to improve the overall quality of defense systems. And although CMM was initially created for defense industry use, the model was found to be applicable to companies in the private sector that also depended on software development. The SEI combined two other source models with software maturity levels—the Electronic Industries Alliance Interim Standard and the Integrated Product Development Capability Maturity Model—into a single improvement framework, the CMMI, for use by organizations pursuing enterprise-wide process improvement. The CMM model defines two representations (staged and continuous)

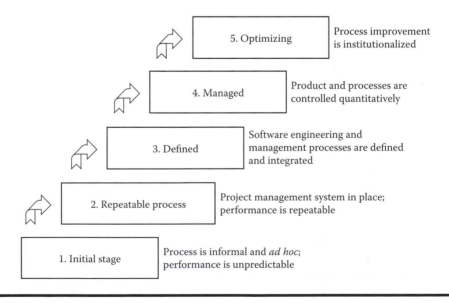

5. Optimizing	Process improvement is institutionalized
4. Managed	Product and processes are controlled quantitatively
3. Defined	Software engineering and management processes are defined and integrated
2. Repeatable process	Project management system in place; performance is repeatable
1. Initial stage	Process is informal and *ad hoc*; performance is unpredictable

Exhibit 11.4   CMM maturity levels.

and four models (systems engineering, software engineering, integrated product and process development, and supplier sourcing).

Software Engineering Institute

The SEI developed the CMM in 1993. The purpose of SEI is to put a program in place so that the good ideas about what can be done to improve an organization could be heard and acted upon. The CMM specifies which areas need to be addressed first by identifying six key process areas to help provide a road map to go from level one (the lowest level on the scale) to level two. These areas include

- Requirements management
- Software configuration management
- Project planning
- Project tracking and oversight
- Subcontract management
- Software quality assurance (SQA)

Each key process area (KPA) was assigned a champion and the champions meet once a month. Companies and organizations establish quality improvement teams, which spawn working groups. The working groups form a framework for the software engineering process group to address the tasks associated with the action plan that came out of the SEI assessment findings. Since 1993, the SEI replaced CMM with the CMMI Model Foundation (CMF), including CMMI for Development v1.2 (2006) and the CMMI for Acquisition v1.2 (2007) to aid organizations in implementing process improvement programs.

How Maturity Correlates to Quality

Identifying the relationship between maturity and quality involves looking at facts. Significant data supports maturity that brings numerous benefits such as

- Increased predictability
- Reduced defects
- Reduced rework
- Increased delivery on schedule
- Reduced risk of exceeding cost/budget
- Increased metrics and measurement
- Increased process improvement

Ultimately, maturity enables a company to achieve quality by eliminating steps that introduce error or by introducing steps to eliminate error. Although many studies can be cited, one of the most comprehensive in the area of software development is from the Boeing Corporation. They maintained detailed statistics on their software development from 1991 to 1999 while conducting 175 maturity assessments. A summary of benefits they identified is shown in Exhibit 11.5.

The SEI of Carnegie Mellon conducts periodic surveys on the performance results for organizations implementing CMMI. Exhibit 11.6 provides a summary of the performance improvements realized from implementing CMMI-based process improvements.

Benefits	Level 1–2 (%)	Level 2–3 (%)	Level 3–4 (%)
Reduce defects	12	40	85
Reduce time	10	38	63
Reduce cost	8	35	75
Schedule variances	145	24	25

Other benefits include

1. Focused investments make significant benefits possible. Investments are focused on those areas that can be expected to deliver the best possible results.

2. Strong correlation between practice and performance: Studies have shown that the adoption of best practices correlates strongly with the achievement of highest levels of performance.

Exhibit 11.5 Boeing Corporation's maturity assessments.

Category Improvements	Median Improvement
Cost	34%
Schedule	50%
Productivity	61%
Quality	48%
Customer satisfaction	14%
Return on investment	4.0:1

Exhibit 11.6 Performance results of CMMI-based process improvements. (Reproduced from Gibson, D., D. Goldenson, and K. Kost, Performance Results of CMMI-Based Process Improvement, Carnegie Mellon University, 2006. With permission.)

International Standards Organization 9000 Series

The ISO 9000 series of standards is a set of documents dealing with quality systems that can be used for external quality assurance purposes. They specify quality system requirements for use where a contract between two parties requires the demonstration of a supplier's capability to design and supply a product (see Exhibits 11.7 and 11.8). The standard ISO 9001, Model for Quality Assurance in Design/Development, Production, Installation, and Servicing, is for use when conformance to specified requirements is to be assured by the supplier during several stages. In the ISO 9000 series, it is the standard that is pertinent to software development and maintenance.

The specific ISO standard that provides for assessing software development processes is the Software Process Improvement and Capability Determination (ISO 15504). The objective is to

ISO 9001 Clause	Description
1. Management responsibility	ISO 9001 requires that the quality policy be defined, documented, understood, implemented, and maintained; that responsibilities and authorities for all personnel specifying, achieving, and monitoring quality be defined; and that in-house verification resources be defined, trained, and funded. A designated manager ensures that the quality program is implemented and maintained.
2. Quality system	ISO 9001 requires that a documented quality system, including procedures and instructions, be established.
3. Contract review	ISO 9001 requires that contracts be reviewed to determine whether the requirements are adequately defined, agree with the bid, and can be implemented.
4. Design control	ISO 9001 requires that procedures to control and verify the design be established. This includes planning design activities, identifying inputs and outputs, verifying the design, and controlling design changes.
5. Document control	ISO 9001 requires that the distribution and modification of documents be controlled.
6. Purchasing	ISO 9001 requires that purchased products conform to their specified requirements. This includes the assessment of potential subcontractors and verification of purchased products.
7. Purchaser-supplied product	ISO 9001 requires that any purchaser-supplied material be verified and maintained.
8. Product identification and traceability	ISO 9001 requires that the product be identified and traceable during all stages of production, delivery, and installation.
9. Process control	ISO 9001 requires that production processes be defined and planned. This includes carrying out production under controlled conditions, according to documented instructions. Special processes that cannot be fully verified after the fact are continuously monitored and controlled.
10. Inspection and testing	ISO 9001 requires that incoming materials be inspected or verified before use and that process inspection and testing be performed. Final inspection and testing are performed before the release of finished product. Records of inspection and testing are kept.
11. Inspection, measuring, and test equipment	ISO 9001 requires that equipment used to demonstrate conformance be controlled, calibrated, and maintained. When test hardware or software is used, it is checked before use and rechecked at prescribed intervals.

Exhibit 11.7   Clauses in ISO 9001.

ISO 9001 Clause	Description
12. Inspection and test status	ISO 9001 requires that the status of inspections and tests be maintained for items as they progress through various processing steps.
13. Control of nonconforming product	ISO 9001 requires that nonconforming product be controlled to prevent inadvertent use or installation.
14. Corrective action	ISO 9001 requires that the causes of nonconforming product be identified. Potential causes of nonconforming product are eliminated; procedures are changed resulting from corrective action.
15. Handling, storage, packaging, and delivery	ISO 9001 requires that procedures for handling, storage, packaging, and delivery be established and maintained.
16. Quality records	ISO 9001 requires that quality records be collected, maintained, and dispositioned.
17. Internal quality audits	ISO 9001 requires that audits be planned and performed. The results of audits are communicated to management, and any deficiencies found are corrected.
18. Training	ISO 9001 requires that training needs be identified and that training be provided, as selected tasks may require qualified personnel. Records of training are maintained.
19. Servicing	ISO 9001 requires that servicing activities be performed as specified.
20. Statistical techniques	ISO 9001 states that, where appropriate, adequate statistical techniques are identified and used to verify the acceptability of process capability and product characteristics.

Exhibit 11.7   (Continued) Clauses in ISO 9001.

assist the software industry in making significant gains in productivity and quality, while reducing the risk associated with large software projects and purchases. The standard International Organization for Standardization (ISO)/International Electrotechnical Commission (IEC) TR 15504 provides a comprehensive reference framework for the assessment of software processes. The model is designed as a baseline to perform process capability determination in an organization. It was developed under the auspices of the ISO with the intention to harmonize the key concepts contained in the SEI's CMM, BOOTSTRAP, ISO 12207, and TickIT. This framework can be used by organizations involved in planning, managing, monitoring, controlling, and improving the acquisition, supply, development, operation, evolution, and support of software.

ISO Accreditation

ISO accreditation is accomplished after being certified by what is known as a notified body. Accreditation itself is the act whereby the National Accreditation Council for Certification Bodies

Where Errors Are Introduced	Requirements Gathering and Analysis/ Architectural Design (1X)	Coding/ Unit Test (5X)	Integration and Component/ RAISE System Test (10X)	Early Customer Feedback/ Beta Test Programs (15X)	Post-Product Release (30X)	Total Percent
Requirements Gathering and Analysis/ Architectural Design	3.5	10.5	35	6	15	70
Coding/Unit Test		6	9	2	3	20
Integration and Component/ RAISE System Test			6.5	1	2.5	10
Total	3.5	16.5	50.5	9	20.5	100
Note: X is a normalized unit of cost and can be expressed in terms of person-hours, dollars, etc.						

Exhibit 11.8   Overall product quality defects found. (RAISE: reliability, availability, installability, serviceability, and ease of use.) (From National Institute of Standards and Technology, *The Economic Impacts of Inadequate Infrastructure for Software Testing—Final Report,* **prepared by RTI for NIST, May 2002. With permission.)**

(NACCB) approves an organization to operate an assessment and registration or certification scheme approved by NACCB. This organization or notified body conducts an audit to certify adherence to the appropriate standard. If the company passes the audit criteria, it then registers with the notified body as ISO 9000 compliant and may use the ISO seal to advertise compliance.

National Standards Authority of Ireland (NSAI) and British Standards Institute (BSI) are examples of notified bodies for a registration effort. ISO 9001, also known as EN29001, Q91, and BS5750 Part 1, is the model for quality assurance in design/development, production, installation, and servicing. ISO 9001 is the specific quality system that applies to companies such as UNISYS, Hewlett-Packard, and INTEL because they design, manufacture, and service products that are produced here.

The most important benefit from the registration is access to markets such as the European Community (EC), which require compliance. A second benefit is competitive advantage over another supplier who cannot establish ISO 9001 compliance.

Getting Started: ISO 9001

In general, if an ISO initiative would result in a business objective that is part of a business plan, it should be pursued. Thus, a company may decide to seek ISO 9001 certification as a necessary action to remain competitive within the product area in the emerging worldwide marketplace. The first step is to hire or appoint someone to lead the effort. That person's job would be to lead the effort, determine what direction to take, select an appropriate auditing body for determining compliance and awarding registration, develop training materials for an internal auditing staff, and oversee implementation of general ISO 9001 quality initiatives. One of the primary objectives and roles of this person is to select the notified body from which to obtain certification and which would then come on site to conduct periodic conformance audits. Other responsibilities of this person are to roll out an internal auditor-training program and help establish individual quality manuals and processes that would then be used as a basis to quality for certification.

ISO 9001 is the most comprehensive standard. It states specific requirements for the following kinds of work: design, development, production, installation, and servicing. It is process oriented and not product or people oriented.

Any company wishing to sell software products or services in Europe was required to register by November 1992. Countries such as Canada, Australia, Japan, Mexico, and the U.S. Department of Defense have adopted it. ISO has come to represent good business practices.

Registration gives formal recognition that the processes used to produce, deliver, and support products meet an acceptable level of standard of control and effectiveness. Initial registration depends on passing an audit by a qualified organization such as NSAI. Continued registration depends on passing continued audits. The registration is site specific.

More about NSAI

NSAI, a division of EOLAS and also the national standards body of Ireland, was established in 1946 and currently operates under the Industrial Research and Standards Act (1961) as well as the Science and Technology Act (1987) of Ireland and is actually a body of the Irish government. Although the main office is located in Dublin, there is a branch office for North America that is located in Merrimack, New Hampshire. An additional office has been opened in Fremont, California.

NSAI has a reciprocal agreement with all the EC countries (Belgium, Denmark, France, Germany, Greece, Ireland, Italy, Luxembourg, Netherlands, Portugal, Spain, and the United Kingdom) and the European Free Trade Association (EFTA)—Austria, Finland, Iceland, Norway, Sweden, and Switzerland—that recognize its certificates without payment of additional registration fees, and also has a separate bilateral agreement with the Canadian General Standards Board (CGSB). Each of the 12 European Economic Community (EEC) nations has a recognized governing body. FORFAS, a division of the government of Ireland and parent of NSAI, is that body for Ireland.

> Industrial Development Agency (IDA), Ireland is the subdivision of FORFAS, which is responsible for attracting business into Ireland.
> FORBAIRT is the subdivision of FORFAS, which is chartered to develop Irish industrial infrastructure, investments, and so on.

Standards development is to go to the EEC for input to directives. Every 6 months, each nation meets to provide the political framework for problem solving.

Certification is provided in five groups, for example, product certification in the food industry, pharmaceuticals, and chemicals. The rest look after other industrial segments of the country. There are 300+ such companies in Ireland from Dublin to the south. The overall goal is to result in a consistent product.

Principal Themes of an ISO 9000 Review

ISO 9000 standards set the requirements for a quality system. Its principal themes focus on five areas: documentation, practices, records, audits, and corrective action. Documentation says what we do. Practices provide examples of what we say we do. Records are evidence of what we have done. Audits check what we do. Corrective action corrects discrepancies that are found.

The IT auditor, or any internal auditor, has the experience to perform such a review or assist in training corporate staff to perform their own self-evaluation to ISO compliance standards and processes.

For an ISO 9001 review, there are 20 items specifically reviewed. Appendix V is an example of an Audit Analysis Worksheet to summarize the comprehensive review. Each of the major areas is identified and the outcome of the review indicates whether the area passed, was not covered, and the number of corrective action requests (CARs). Included in Appendix V is an example of a CAR form recently used by a software company in its ISO 9001 review.

An example of summary ISO 9001 review findings is described in Appendix V for a software vendor located at a New York City site and a summary of its lessons learned are detailed in the following.

The staff associated with the New York City review and the ISO certification efforts were asked for their comments. Following is a summary of their comments:

- Expect to be challenged. You will not get complete buy-in because people are being asked to go beyond the scope of what they believe they were hired to do. It is important that employees have a forum to vent their frustrations. Such comments can be a good indicator of the attitude and commitment employees are making and how well they understand why the company has chosen specific approaches to meeting its business needs.
- It was very poor planning to have another group within our facility to have its own ISO certification in the same plant with the rest of us. It increases costs and duplicates services.
- It is much harder to achieve and maintain certification for a site, which does not have a single site manager. If we could change the world, we would have all organizations in New York City report up to one manager who is located here.
- We did too much work when we first started. We had people with backgrounds in product quality assurance running the program and they made it a major effort. Perhaps if we had known, we would not have had these same people calling the shots. Instead, we might have quickly gone to the streamlined internal auditing system.
- A site-wide document control system and team ... common numbering and formats would have helped. More document templates would have helped. Developing our own online document control system has been a tragedy of errors. Do not do it.

In terms of the description, experience, and examples given earlier regarding ISO certification, the IT auditor can contribute to the training and development of internal staff in performing the audit process.

There are a number of questions the organization must ask itself before performing this function. It is an intensive effort and process that must be followed and performed to the letter. There must be a commitment to training, learning, and education if it is to succeed. Organization management must support the process. IT auditing plays a key role in this process. It is a reflection of corporate management support, institutional cooperation, and the search for better quality in information systems (IT) operations. Sample documents and work steps are provided in Appendix V.

IT Process Framework

A process framework is needed to ensure that all critical processes are defined, reviewed, validated, and maintained. Defining processes and procedures is an ongoing effort as technology and organizations change. A process is a series of events or phases that take place over time and usually has an identifiable purpose or result. Some processes include multiple conditions and results.

Policies and Procedures

Organizations establish and communicate policies and procedures for information systems to ensure that organizational goals are met. These policies and procedures should communicate the organization's stand on issues such as systems architecture, testing and validation of requirements and systems, and documentation. These areas are critical to establishing an institutional process for managing applications and infrastructure. Policies and procedures require management's support to be enforced. Users must also be sold on standard policies and procedures by communicating the advantages such as better help desk support and training.

Policies are a set of specific statements of guiding actions or intent that provide a basis for consistent decision making. They are characterized by widespread application, infrequent change, and statements that describe what IT is required to do (but not necessarily how). They enforce principles and influence both present and future decision making to be in line with the objectives and strategic plans. A principle is the reason why we do something; a policy is what we must do as a consequence. This document includes only group policies that apply to all parts of the business, and not those with local scope.

Processes describe the steps taken to implement principles and provide services. They may relate to one or more policies or standards. Often a process is required as a way of carrying out our business, unrelated to specific policies or standards. They establish a particular way of doing something. Processes are characterized by narrow application; frequent changes; and statements that describe how, when, and sometimes who in detail.

Standards are the current set of decisions about preferred or mandatory solutions. They represent a snapshot at a point in time and need to be regularly maintained. Sometimes they are similar to principles as they describe what has to be done to support a particular need. Sometimes they appear as lists (e.g., of acceptable software). They are more specific in scope than the processes and policies that they complement.

A number of professional societies have issued guidelines to assist managers in this area. Organizations such as the AITP, Society for Information Management (SIM), IFAC, IIA, and ISACA are examples of professional societies that recognize the need for general guidance. Examples of these can be found in Appendixes II and III.

Comparing Processes and Procedures

A procedure describes steps that a person is directed to perform, whereas a process describes events or phases about which the reader needs to be aware. Processes and procedures have quite different purposes. Readers respond differently to the imperative language of a procedure and the descriptive language of a process.

Language and Definition: The following table compares process and procedure.

Comparing	Process...	And Procedure
Description	Processes are what happens in the world or what happens inside our own bodies.	Procedures are steps that the reader follows to achieve some objective.
Language used	We usually talk about process in the third person. First, it does this, then that happens, etc.	We usually talk about procedures in the second person: first you do this, then you do that, etc.; or as in a command: First, open cover; then pull the switch, etc.

Questions: Another way of distinguishing process from procedure is to look at the kinds of questions you would ask to find out about them. The following table compares the questions the writer might ask to find out more about process and procedure.

Comparing	Process...	And Procedure
Questions to ask	*If* you ask a person to describe what happens in particular systems or what changes take place...	*If* you ask someone how to solve a problem, produce a product, or perform an action...
	Then their answers describe a process.	*Then* their answers describe a procedure.
Examples of questions	How does the payroll system operate?	How do you clear a bank draft?
	What happens when you use the RUN command?	How do you find the reciprocal of a number?
	How does the machine behave when the WT-409 circuit is out?	How do you replace the WT-409 circuit?

Auditing Policies and Procedures

When conducting an audit of an external client or in-house management, one must consider the policies and procedures of management. Management dictates how the organization will be divided into subgroups that control small portions of a company. To accurately assess the scope of the audit environment, the IT auditor should first verify the existence of a policies and procedures manual. This step becomes very important in most audits because, if a finding is made, it helps the auditor establish where to place the cause and how to rectify the problem.

Policies and procedures are only as good as the management structure, which formed them and enforces the action taken. The IT auditor should examine the corporate structure of the policies and procedures set by management. The auditor should then verify that the policies and procedures follow audit standards set by ISACA. ISACA has some very good examples of proper IT environment procedures that are easy to adopt for almost any organization.*

A good rule of thumb to keep in mind is that the client's management developed the policies and procedures with the hopes of meeting their company's desired goals more efficiently with the maximum amount of control and profit.

Each function in the organization, including internal audit and IT, needs complete, well-documented polices and procedures to describe the scope of the function of its activities and the interrelationships with other departments. As policies and procedures are developed and organized into a standards manual, they should be tied directly to the goals and objectives of the organization.†

Even today, many companies are lacking in written policies and procedures; therefore, it is hard for the auditor to compare them to compliance standards. This is where the auditor can aid them in developing a new set of procedures that would be written and given to each employee who worked in that IT area. Thus, the auditor can provide value-added recommendations and help the organization to establish new policies and procedures for the upcoming year. By doing so, this helps the auditor gauge compliance with known standards that are acceptable in the IT audit profession. IT auditors will use this gauge the following year to test personnel compliance to the administration's new directives.

Conclusion

The search for quality is a goal we strive for as audit professionals. This chapter provides both an approach and experiences in attaining ISO 9001 certification. IT auditing plays a key role in this process. It is a reflection of corporate management support, institutional cooperation, and the search for better quality in information systems (IT) operations. Sample documents and work steps are provided in Appendix V.

The goal of quality assurance is to provide management with appropriate visibility into the processes being used to manage projects and products. To accomplish this objective requires regular reviews and audits of the software products and activities to verify that they comply with the applicable procedures and standards. Standards and procedures need to be established for valid quality assurance measurement processes in every project and operation. Quality assurance begins with the definition of a new project or product. Project activities and work products throughout the project life cycle need to comply with established plans, standards, and procedures. IT processes are interconnected and cross organization boundaries. It is important to have processes documented, agreed, and followed to ensure process efficiency and control effectiveness.

---

* Anonymous, Price Waterhouse LLP, National, Information Systems Resource Management (ISRM), New York, 1996.

† The Institute of Internal Auditors Research Foundation, Systems Auditability and Control (SAC), Module 2, Audit and Control Environment, 1991, Altamonte Springs, FL, pp. 2–4.

Review Questions

1. What are the key properties in a quality system?
2. List the control objectives related to process and quality and explain four of them.
3. What is ISO 9000? What is the ISO?
4. How does maturity correlate to quality?
5. What is an ISO 9001 review?
6. What are some of the major quality programs?
7. What are the five areas of focus in the ISO 9000 principals?
8. What were some of the lessons learned from an ISO 9000 review?

Multiple-Choice Questions

1. Advantages of a centralized organization model include all of the following except
   a. Ability to leverage scale for pricing concessions
   b. Flexibility and responsiveness to customer needs
   c. Shared services only add incremental costs to increased volumes
   d. Centrally located server environment
2. To ensure consistent and effective implementations of technology, IT management should be responsible for
   a. Information systems strategy
   b. Standards
   c. User support
   d. All of the above
3. Resource management ensures
   a. IT has the right resources at the right time
   b. Appropriate organizational structure is selected
   c. Quality assurance processes are followed
   d. None of the above
4. Quality Management Standards include
   a. National Strategy for Securing Cyberspace
   b. ISO 9000
   c. ISACA
   d. All of the above
5. Which of the following is not true about ISO 9001 certification?
   a. Accreditation is accomplished after being certified by a notified body.
   b. All organizations can establish ISO 9001 compliance.
   c. The most important benefit from the registration is access to markets such as the EC that require compliance.
   d. The NACCB approves an organization to operate an assessment and registration or certification scheme.
6. All of the following are CMM key processes except
   a. Requirements management
   b. Subcontract management
   c. Asset classification and control
   d. Software configuration management

7. A process framework is needed to
   a. Ensure noncompliance issues are addressed with senior management
   b. Ensure all critical processes are defined, reviewed, validated, and maintained
   c. Describe the steps that a person is directed to perform
   d. None of the above
8. Which of the following is not true about well-documented policies and procedures?
   a. Describe the function of activities
   b. Define interrelationships with other departments
   c. Ensure quality systems are implemented
   d. Should tie directly to goals and objectives of the organization
9. Objectives of a quality assurance audit include all of the following except
   a. Satisfies performance guidelines
   b. Adherence of project activities to standards and procedures
   c. All impacted groups cooperate with quality assurance activities
   d. Quality assurance activities are planned and documented
10. The purpose of a procedure is to
    a. Describe steps that a person is directed to perform
    b. Describe steps to achieve some objective
    c. Describe how to produce a product
    d. All of the above

Exercises

1. You are asked to perform an ISO 9001 review on your corporation's software development activity, which accounts for 30% of the corporation profits. The president is concerned because revenue in this area is down and returns due to software errors were up by 39% from last year.
2. List three professional organizations and standards that provide guidance on quality assurance.
3. Using the Internet, identify three examples of failures caused by inadequate quality assurance.

Answers to Multiple-Choice Questions

1—b; 2—d; 3—a; 4—b; 5—b; 6—c; 7—b; 8—c; 9—a; 10—d

Further Reading

1. Carnegie Mellon University, *The Capability Maturity Model Integration*, SEI, Pittsburgh, PA, December 2001, http://www.sei.cmu.edu/pub/documents/02.reports/pdf/02tr001.pdf.
2. Carnegie Mellon University, *CMMI for Development, Version 1.2*, Pittsburgh, PA, August 2006.
3. Coyle, D.M., *Company Improves IT Services and Support by Standardizing Processes*, Gartner Group, Stamford, CT, February 2006.
4. Curtis, D. and C. Haight, *Gartner Poll Suggests IT Management Processes Aren't Maturing*, Gartner Research G00126294, April 4, 2005.

5. Gibson, D., D. Goldenson, and K. Kost, *Performance Results of CMMI-Based Process Improvement*, Carnegie Mellon University, Pittsburgh, PA, August 2006.
6. Iyengar, P., *Wipro: Best Practices in CMM-Based Software Delivery*, Gartner Research, Stamford, CT, Case Studies, CS-19-6994, May 27, 2003.
7. Mallette, D., IT performance improvement with COBIT and the SEI CMM. Information Systems Audit and Control Association, *Inf. Syst. Control J.*, 3, 2005.
8. Morello, D., *IT Skills and Competencies on the Risk through 2003*, Gartner Research COM-15-6441, Stamford, CT, April 18, 2002.
9. Murphy, T., *Key Issues for Software Quality and Testing, 2007*, Gartner Research G00145611, Stamford, CT, February 15, 2007.
10. National Institute of Standards and Technology (NIST), *The Economic Impacts of Inadequate Infrastructure for Software Testing*, Survey conducted by Research Triangle Institute (RTI), RTI Project Number 7007.01, May 1, 2002.
11. Reingold, S., Refining IT processes using COBIT, Information Systems Audit and Control Association, *Inf. Syst. Control J.*, 3, 2005.
12. *The Economic Impacts of Inadequate Infrastructure for Software Testing—Final Report*, prepared by RTI for NIST, May 2002.
13. Working Council for Chief Information Officers, Software Quality Assurance Metrics, Corporate Executive Board 2001, Catalog No.: 1-766GM, May 2001.
14. Working Council for Chief Information Officers, IT Organizational Structures, Corporate Executive Board, Catalog No.: 1-23615, December 2000.
15. Working Council for Chief Information Officers, IT Organizational Structures at Multinational Companies, Corporate Executive Board, Catalog No.: 1-O8QAW, April 2002.
16. Working Council for Chief Information Officers, Quality Assurance Organizational Structures and Automation Tools, Corporate Executive Board, Catalog No.: 1-PKH00, May 2002.

Chapter 12

Financial Management

As more business processes have been converted to IT applications and the Internet infrastructure has grown, IT spending as a percentage of total spend has continued to increase in many industries. In addition, increased regulatory requirements are driving demand and related IT costs higher. However, pressure remains on keeping operating budgets flat. Therefore, it is critical for IT to have a solid financial framework to meet these conflicting demands. In an environment where there is an unlimited demand for technology and limited resources available, the IT spend has to be controlled and managed. At the same time, it is important to protect against underinvestment in technology.

The organization is responsible for determining the appropriate level of investment in technology as part of the overall business plan and profit-and-loss goals. IT cannot plan or budget in a vacuum, but rather takes direction from the organization it supports to determine what and how much to budget. The drivers of cost for IT include the number of employees, customers, locations, and the type and scope of applications. An organization may decide it wants to move from a call center support desk to a Web-based application for customer self-service. This new application will drive the amount budgeted by the IT organization for the initial development costs and the ongoing support costs.

IT spending is controlled by implementing a solid financial framework that defines decision-making rules, prioritizing IT investments, ensuring that benefits are realized from IT investments, managing to an operating budget, and understanding and managing IT costs.

IT Processes

Financial processes from COBIT are included in both the Planning and Organization and Delivery (PO5 manage the IT investment) and Support Domains (DS6 identify and allocate costs). Both processes are included in this section for a complete discussion of IT financial management (Exhibits 12.1 and 12.2).

Financial Management Framework

A solid financial framework establishes the rights and responsibilities of business and IT management in making financial decisions. Investments in IT as well as normal operations require

PO5 Manage the IT Investment
Control Objectives
5.1   Financial management framework
5.2   Prioritization within IT budget
5.3   IT budgeting process
5.4   Cost management
5.5   Benefit management

Exhibit 12.1   Planning and organization domain.

DS6 Identify and Allocate Costs
Control Objectives
6.1   Definition of service
6.2   IT accounting
6.3   Cost modeling and charging
6.4   Cost model maintenance

Exhibit 12.2   Delivery and support domain.

decisions on significant financial transactions on a regular basis. These transactions can commit an organization to a technology, capacity, payment stream, and so on. Financial decisions should be part of the project approval and procurement process along with other important disciplines (e.g., architecture) to ensure future value from today's decisions. For example, it may make sense to purchase storage media in bulk as the unit price is lower and demand is constantly increasing. However, the technology may be changing in the near term making the purchase obsolete. The architecture group is an important decision maker in this case as they are the keepers of the technology roadmap. A formal committee of the various IT disciplines that approves projects and major purchases helps ensure alignment with organizational objectives.

An IT Investment Committee composed of representatives from the business functions and the various IT disciplines is a good control mechanism for ensuring that decisions on IT investments (technology and business projects) comply with organizational priorities and technology standards. To be effective, the IT Investment Committee must have authority to make decisions on behalf of the board and senior management. Although overall funding decisions are made during the financial planning process, the IT Investment Committee would approve individual capital purchases and projects. The investment approval process is discussed in more detail in the following text.

Investment Approval Process

The cost of developing new applications or implementing new technology is costly and consumes significant resources. Before approving a new technology investment, it is important to make sure the application fits within the enterprise architecture and aligns to business objectives. An investment approval process helps ensure that efforts are aligned with organizational objectives and enterprise architecture, and the business case is realistic.

The cost of developing an application is just the beginning. Add to that the cost of the infrastructure required to support applications, cost of changing applications, and the overhead associated with running a professional IT organization and you get the true cost of implementing a new application. The costs of a service include personnel costs, third-party services costs, software and hardware costs, and other costs (e.g., facilities).

While estimating the cost of a new technology, it is important to include all the costs to build and maintain the technology to avoid surprises in the future and ensure that the right decision is made based on a realistic cost/benefit. Of course, not all decisions will be based on cost/benefit but there should be a solid reason for investing in technology (e.g., competitive, regulatory). An investment approval request should include six major components:

1. Business need
2. Financial return and contingencies
3. Alternatives considered
4. Business issues and assumptions
5. Legal, legislative, environment, and safety issues
6. Resources required and proposed technology

An investment approval request should have sufficient information for the business sponsor(s) and IT functions to review and approve the new project/purchase and ensure compliance with standards.

Project Pricing

Project cost estimates should include the total development costs and infrastructure costs to allow management to understand the impact on the operating budget and make an informed decision. Project pricing provides user groups with the total cost implications of a project, but also causes significant conflict. If the project includes all overhead associated with a new investment (e.g., architecture, security, infrastructure), it makes the project costs appear overstated. Typically, an external provider will not include these costs in estimates although an organization will incur these costs. Rightly or wrongly, IT may appear to be too costly. Properly communicating the project-pricing model is the key to helping user groups understand the true cost of any new application and the impact of making shortsighted decisions. For example, an organization wanted to Web-enable its policy processing applications. The estimates from IT seemed too high; therefore, they went with an external service provider. Unfortunately, the external service provider did not include the cost to integrate the new functionality with the existing applications, the infrastructure required to deliver the application to the end user, and the cost to maintain the application going forward. The organization ended up paying more than the original IT estimate as the application had to be retrofitted to work with existing applications, and had to pay for additional staff to support a new technology platform and increased security infrastructure required for doing business over the Internet. This situation could have been avoided with effective communication between IT and the user groups.

The opposite situation can occur when IT selects expensive technology standards that inhibit business units from investing in new projects. A "one size fits all" approach will rarely result in customer satisfaction. IT should be making decisions on standards that align to the organization strategy and the cost/benefit of each technology decision. A fully redundant server with mirrored storage and full disaster recovery is probably overkill for a single department productivity tool. IT can improve its partnership with user groups by being actively engaged in the business planning process and selecting technologies that support business objectives. To support business objectives, IT can provide multiple options for new applications depending on the business requirements.

Realizing the Benefits from IT Investments

Projects are usually done to add business value by growing revenue or reducing expenses. It is important to verify that the benefits expected are delivered. Project benefits should be stated in measurable terms during the project approval phase to provide a means for validating the benefits received. Each project should have an owner with accountability for delivering the benefits.* A formal process that requires project owners to show realization of benefits creates an organizational culture of accountability.

Financial Planning

Financial planning and controlling processes are key processes in managing the investment in IT. An effective relationship between IT and management requires transparent financial planning and reporting. Management needs to understand demand quality, quantity, and pricing to make informed decisions about the appropriate level of IT spending.

Financial planning in IT begins with an understanding of the annual business plans, including business volume growth projections and new technology investments. There are many approaches to financial planning and budgeting. Presented in the following are two possible approaches to developing a financial plan using top-down targets and bottom-up budgeting. A top-down approach involves setting spending targets based on an organization's overall financial plans and then building a detailed budget for each service to fit within the overall targets set by the organization.

If an organization follows a bottom-up financial planning approach, IT will have a spending target amount of either a percentage of revenue or a fixed amount. Under this model, the organization will need to make trade-offs between increased demand and existing operating costs to fit within the target amounts. With a bottom-up approach, the organization will need to determine demand for the IT unit to estimate the budget required to fulfill those demands. Even with the top-down approach, a detailed bottom-up budget needs to be developed to guide spending at the department (e.g., operations) and cost element level (e.g., labor). In either case, the IT unit will need to determine the cost of services for the operating budget and estimate the cost of development projects for the capital budget.

As IT planning is usually a subset of the overall organization planning, it is difficult to determine the appropriate IT budget without careful integration with organizational planning. Organizations usually need to know the cost of IT before finalizing their plans and IT needs to understand the organization's plans before finalizing its budget. To that end, the IT budget can be split into two planning streams—service and project planning (see Exhibit 12.3).

---

* Williams, P., Optimising returns from IT-related business investments. *Inf. Syst. Control J.*, 5, 2005.

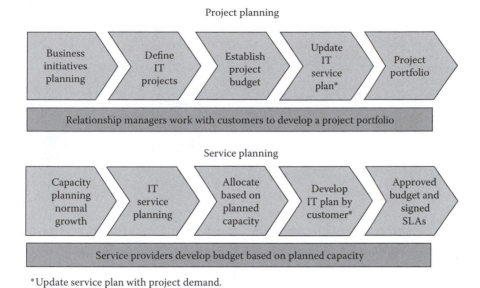

Exhibit 12.3   Illustration of two-tiered planning model.

Operating Budget

The first step in developing the operational budget is to determine estimated growth based on normal historical trends and additional/reduced demand from business plans. Organizational demand can then be factored into staffing plans for application development that can be factored into infrastructure capacity plans that can then be translated into a budget for labor, hardware, software, and so on.

Service planning involves developing a budget for each of the services based on the expected demand, cost increases, and savings for each service. Project planning involves working with user groups to ensure alignment with business strategic planning. Changes in demand from the current year forecast are factored into the application development budget.

Once the budget is completed, it needs to be reviewed and approved by the organization responsible for funding. Funding of the IT budget can be achieved by gaining approval for a stand-alone cost-center budget, allocating costs to business units based on a business metric or developing a chargeback process based on usage (see chargeback discussion).

With the complexity of the IT budget, it is important to explain not only the cost of services and projects, but also the change year over year. Exhibit 12.4 is an illustration of a possible variance explanation in the form of a waterfall diagram. This provides more transparency into the reasons behind a change in the IT budget.

Capital Budget

The capital budget defines the cash needs and the expense impact over a period of time. Organizations that comply with International Accounting Standards (IAS) or GAAP capitalize developed software, packaged software, and infrastructure and amortize the expense over a period of time. International Financial Reporting Standards (IFRS) 38 and Statement of Position 98-1 provide

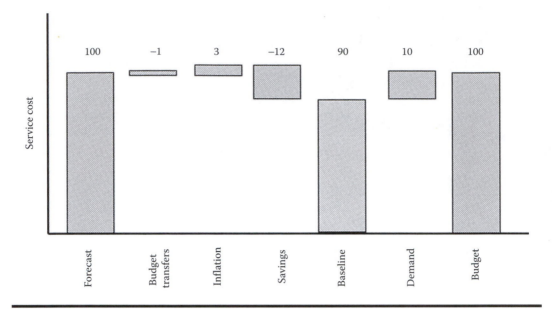

Exhibit 12.4   Illustration of variance explanation.

guidance for capitalizing internally developed software (intangible assets). The capital budget should include both software development and infrastructure projects (e.g., technology refresh).

Track against Budget

Throughout the year, it is important to track actual to planned results. There are two possible variances—volume and rate. Volume variances are caused by an increase or decrease in demand. Rate variances are caused by an increase or decrease in costs. It is important to understand both components of any variance, as demand variances are attributable to user activity, whereas IT management causes rate variances.

Identify and Allocate Costs

The method of pricing IT services is a controversial topic as it creates conflict between the user and IT. Conflict arises when the total cost of IT has not been transparent in the past or when comparing services to independent parties. An IT chargeback model should be simple to administer and should fairly represent the cost of service and provide business units with predictable costs over time. Business units want to have control over their costs; therefore, it is important for them to understand the charging model and how their behavior influences the charges they receive.

Costing of IT services is not an exact science and the method of cost allocation can shift costs between business units. There is no single approach that can be identified as the best possible method, and the cost of implementing various chargeback models has to be considered against the benefit. Theoretically, charging for services drives user behavior, as users have to pay for what they consume. The assumption is that if it is free, users will not be careful with the use of the resource.

This would result in increased demand and IT costs. There are several advantages of implementing IT service pricing:

- It holds individuals accountable for the IT resources they consume
- Provides visibility into the cost of IT resources
- Encourages organizations to understand their IT costs as part of an overall profit-and-loss responsibility

According to a study of 19 U.S.-based companies conducted by IDC's Industry Insights, "most companies allocate IT infrastructure cost ...".* Charging for services allows the customer to see the total cost of a particular service that they may not have been aware of and do not understand. For example, the cost to deliver a desktop to a user includes the cost of the hardware itself, maintenance, software licensing, software imaging, testing, configuration and distribution, software support, help desk, desktop support, network cabling, network equipment, data circuits, server hardware, server software, backup hardware, shared file storage hardware, monitoring software, server support, facilities, and management overhead. This fully loaded cost can create the misperception that IT costs are high compared to an individual buying a personal computer (PC) at the local technology superstore and plugging it into the Internet. Users do not realize that there is a tremendous amount of infrastructure required when you consider enterprise-wide applications, networking, security, and so on. This can cause users to make bad decisions as they may purchase services outside the IT-controlled environment without realizing the additional costs to integrate new technology into an existing operating environment.

Prerequisites for implementing a chargeback model involve decisions from senior management establishing guidelines that the organization must follow. Underlying decisions must be made on a sourcing policy, cost recovery policy, and accountability for IT charges. A sourcing policy defines where IT services are to be purchased. In a centralized, shared-services model, the business units are required to purchase from the central IT group. This approach allows IT to standardize technology solutions and leverage size/scale for procurement. There may be situations where the central IT group cannot provide a requested service. In this case, there needs to be a process in place to source solutions through a third party (see Chapter 15). Sourcing IT services with third parties can complicate the internal chargeback model. In many cases, the pricing model of the third party will differ from the internal pricing model of IT. In addition, there may be subsets of the service that are retained by the internal IT organization that need to be added to the externally provided service to create a single service. The challenge is to create a chargeback model that allocates both internal and external service costs while maintaining the transparency into the underlying pricing of the services.

A cost recovery policy guides the development of the chargeback model. An organization must decide whether the model recovers all costs, charges a "profit" for shared investments, modifies pricing to encourage adoption of new technology, the allocation of fixed costs, how to handle exit costs, and so on. This policy establishes the foundation for developing a chargeback model and helps communicate the underlying assumptions to business units. Accountability for IT charges is a key component of the pricing model as it determines the roles and responsibilities for managing IT costs. Defined properly, it can reduce the conflicts that arise from implementing chargeback. One possible approach is to have the business units accountable for consumption and IT accountable for unit costs.

* Pucciarelli, J.C., *IT Chargeback—Resource Limitations Gate Process Effectiveness*, IDC's Industry Insights, Insight #ITMS5057, December 2006.

Developing a Pricing Model

There are many approaches to developing a pricing model. The method chosen really depends on the IT strategy. A chargeback model for a centralized IT strategy with shared services will differ from a decentralized IT organization with business unit-specific services. Listed in the following are possible alternatives defined by the Gartner Group.

No chargeback. In this model, the IT budget is a separate function approved as part of the organization's planning process. To be effective, the organization must have a centralized prioritization and approval process to control IT spending. This is a low-cost alternative, which also provides a centralized approach to funding for the good of the enterprise. Disadvantages include no accountability for demand and users do not necessarily understand the cost of the IT resources they are consuming.

Non-IT-based chargeback. In this model, IT costs are allocated to business units based on a non-IT allocation metric (e.g., percentage of revenue). Again, this is a simple, low-cost approach to allocating IT costs but does require a centralized prioritization and approval process to effectively manage IT costs. The disadvantages with this approach are that cost allocations do not necessarily correlate to the cost of the service and consumption/demand cannot be allocated to the business unit using the service.

IT-based chargeback. This approach uses IT measurements to allocate costs to user groups. This model does align consumption with costs; however, IT measurements (e.g., operating system instances) are difficult and costly to implement. In addition, IT measurements can be difficult for users to understand and relate to business activities.

Direct chargeback. This approach allocates specific costs for an entire service to a business unit. Unfortunately, this approach is not conducive to shared environments that can reduce costs for an organization.

Fee-based chargeback. This approach charges are based on the level of service or a negotiated fixed fee for a specified level of demand/service. This model can work well with a homogenous service such as a charge per PC. This model gets more complicated when users have nonstandard services, hardware, or software. A tiered rate can be offered to address levels of service (e.g., desktop, laptop, executive), but this increases the complexity of usage tracking and splitting costs between multiple services.

Business-based chargeback. This model allocates costs based on a business transaction. Business transactions could include number of business transactions and customer accounts. Although this approach is easy to understand from a business perspective, it is difficult to correlate IT costs with business transactions as there are usually many types of business transactions making this approach extremely complex and costly.

Profit-oriented pricing. This model charges a fee for service similar to an external service provider. This model may provide short-term benefits as IT must compete with external providers, but in the long term may result in suboptimal decision making, as organizations may not invest internally to ensure long-term effectiveness. Depending on the organization and tax rules, profit can be added to standard pricing to fund internal IT projects. It is difficult for IT to compete with business projects for infrastructure projects, as the business case for IT projects are usually less attractive and the requirement to do the project usually involves long-term flexibility, security, and cost control rather than revenue growth.

Chargeback can be a very emotional and political issue as it impacts the expenses of a business unit or government organization. Effectively implementing and managing a pricing model requires support from senior management (CEO/CFO) and constant communication with the impacted groups to ensure buy-in. The Gartner Group recommends that organizations

- Be open and transparent about the charges for IT.
- Balance the four issues of ability to pay, transfer pricing regulations, strategic goals, and profit-and-loss responsibility.
- When chargeback issues arrive, determine the root cause of the problem. Do not assume the chargeback model is flawed just because stakeholders complain. The cause of the conflict is usually not the chargeback model, but rather a distrust of IT, perceived fairness, cost/value, strategy, or a political issue.
- Standardize the IT environment. Standardized platforms help an organization develop consistent models for usage and chargeback across the globe.
- Ensure that IT has the financial expertise needed to manage global chargeback. Managing a global chargeback model requires expertise in IT services, technology, contracts, and financial expertise in accounting, tax, and financial management.

With the increase in the size and complexity of IT services, an IT finance position has developed in many IT organizations. The IT finance professional has an understanding of technology and finance to control the IT budget, implement a pricing model, and act as a liaison between IT and the finance community. Developing a pricing model requires knowledge of cost accounting, contracts, IT services, tax, and regulatory requirements.

An important consideration when developing a pricing model are the regulatory requirements for transfer pricing. Transfer pricing is the term used for billing service across tax jurisdictions. This is an important issue as global organizations centralize services in support of multiple countries and in the United States for charging services between states. The Internal Revenue Service (IRS) has issued guidance for allocating income or deductions between related entities. In addition, individual states and regulatory agencies may have additional requirements. Generally, the expectation is that transactions are treated as arm's length and are not intended to avoid taxes.

Transfer Pricing

A professional pricing model is required for global organizations that charge for IT services across country boundaries. The OECD provides guidance in its "Transfer Pricing Guidelines for Multinational Enterprises and Tax Administrations" (Guidelines) and Section 482 of the Internal Revenue Code (IRC) of the United States. The guidelines were established to ensure that countries receive their fair share of income tax revenue and to prevent double taxation. The key principle for pricing IT services is the model used to allocate costs must be "arm's length." In other words, the prices charged must be comparable to what independent service providers would charge in the same circumstances.

Determining Charging Method

The allocation of cost between the service recipients must follow the arm's-length principle and reflect the expected benefit at the level of the service recipient.

Direct-Charge Method

The OECD Guidelines permit the determination of intragroup services through the direct-charge method and through various indirect-charge methods. The direct-charge method should be used when specific services are rendered and such services are provided to both related and independent parties, the latter on a regular, as opposed to an occasional or marginal, basis.

Indirect-Charge Method

Because the facts to support a direct charge arise relatively infrequently, the most common method for charging intragroup services is the indirect-charge method. This method is specifically acceptable in situations where the proportional value of the service rendered to various entities can only be approximated or estimated and when the separate recording and analysis of the relevant service activities for each beneficiary would involve a disproportionately heavy burden in relation to the activities themselves.

Allocations under Indirect-Charge Method

Paragraph 7.23 states: "Any indirect-charge method should be sensitive to the commercial features of the individual case (e.g., the allocation key makes sense under the circumstances) . . . ." Paragraph 7.25 states: "The allocation might be based on turnover, or staff employed, or some other basis. Whether the allocation method is appropriate may depend on the nature and usage of the service. For example, the usage or provision of payroll services may be more related to the number of staff than to turnover . . . ."

Determining Arm's-Length Price

To satisfy the arm's-length principle, the price for the direct- or indirect-charge method should be consistent with what comparable independent enterprises would have been accepted. To achieve this, the transaction should be considered from both the perspective of the service provider and the service recipient. Relevant considerations include the value of the service to the recipient and how much a comparable independent enterprise would pay for the service in comparable circumstances, as well as the costs to the service provider.

These sections outline the basis of transfer pricing methods: comparable uncontrolled price (CUP) method, resale price method, cost plus method, contribution analysis profit split, residual analysis profit split, and transactional net margin method. These methods apply to both goods and services. The first three methods are referred to as transactional methods and are preferred to other methods.

Paragraph 7.37, however, states: "Charging all relevant costs rather than an arm's-length price may provide a satisfactory result for multi-national enterprises (MNEs) and tax administrations. This concession is unlikely to be made by tax administrations where the provision of a service is a principal activity of the associated enterprise . . . ."

Cost Contribution Arrangements

Paragraph 8.3 states: "[a] CCA is a framework agreed among business enterprises to share the costs . . . ." This means that there is no markup on the shared costs. Paragraph 8.7 states: "CCAs could exist for any joint funding or sharing of costs and risks, for developing or acquiring property or for obtaining services. For example, business enterprises may decide to pool resources for acquiring centralized management services . . . ."

Because under the guidelines, a cost contribution arrangements (CCA), with its no markup approach, can exist for services, and is specifically cited for centralized services, any tax administration that bases its cross-border transfer pricing analysis under OECD principles should accept as arm's-length pricing a no markup on costs method for intragroup services charged either under a direct-charge method or under a reasonably applied indirect-charge basis.

Structure of U.S. Guidance

IRC Section 482 and Treasury Regulations (Treas. Reg.) thereunder give the IRS broad authority to allocate income or deductions between related entities if the IRS determines that such allocation "is necessary in order to prevent evasion of taxes or clearly to reflect the income" of such related entities. Treas. Reg. Sec. 1.482-1(b) states: "In determining the true taxable income of a controlled taxpayer, the standard to be applied in every case is that of a taxpayer dealing at arm's length with an uncontrolled taxpayer."

Pricing of Services

The regulations under Section 482 provide separate rules for the pricing of services and goods. The pricing of services is primarily controlled by Treas. Reg. Section 1.482-2(b).

Benefit Test

Under Treas. Reg. Sec. 1.482-2(b)(2)(i), an arm's-length charge must be levied for services performed by a controlled group member for the benefit of another member of the controlled group (the "benefit test"). The arm's-length charge must be made not only for services performed by one member of a controlled group for the exclusive benefit of another member of the group, but also for services undertaken for the joint benefit of more than one member of the group. However, "no allocations shall be made if the probable benefits to the other members were so indirect or remote that unrelated parties would not have charged for such services."

Nonallocable services would include services, such as shareholder services, that provide only a remote benefit to the subsidiary. Also, under Treas. Reg. Sec. 1.482-2(b)(2)(ii), "allocations will generally not be made if the service is merely duplicative of a service that the related party has independently performed or is performing for itself."

Integral Services and Nonintegral Services

Determining the arm's-length price depends on whether the services are integral or nonintegral services. Four independent factors determine if the service provided is an integral part of a member's business activity; only one factor must be satisfied for a service to be treated as integral under the regulations.

1. The renderer or the recipient of the services is engaged in the trade or business of rendering or providing similar services to unrelated parties.
2. The renderer provides services to one or more controlled group members as one of its principal activities. It is presumed that if the cost of services provided to related parties

during the taxable year does not exceed 25% of the renderer's total costs for the taxable year, the renderer does not provide services to related parties as one of its principal activities.
3. The renderer is peculiarly capable of rendering the services and such services are a principal element in the operations of the recipient.
4. The recipient has received the benefit of a "substantial" level of services from one or more controlled group members during its taxable year. Generally, if the costs of the renderer that are directly or indirectly related to the provision of services are less than an amount equal to 25% of the total costs or deductions of the recipient for the taxable year, a "substantial" level of services are not considered to have been received. No consolidated return rule applies for purposes of this 25% test.

If none of these factors is present, a service is a nonintegral service.

Determining the Pricing for Integral Services

Under Treas. Reg. Sec. 1.482-2(b)(7), "[a]n arm's length charge shall not be deemed equal to costs or deductions with respect to services which are an integral part of the business activity of [the renderer or the recipient]." Unfortunately, the regulations then do not state how this price should be computed.

It is understood, however, that the pricing should then be referred to the pricing of tangible property discussed in Treas. Reg. Sec. 1.482-3. Methods discussed under this section are the CUP method, the resale price method, the cost plus method, the comparable profits method, the profit split method, and unspecified methods. The method selected should satisfy the best method rule of Treas. Reg. Sec. 1.482-1(c). The best method is that method which, when applied to the controlled transaction, yields the most reliable measure of an arm's-length result under all of the facts and circumstances of the transaction.

Determining the Pricing for Nonintegral Services

If the service provided is not an integral part of the renderer's or receiver's business activity, under Treas. Reg. Sec. 1.482-2(b)(3), "the arm's-length charge shall be deemed equal to the costs or deductions incurred with respect to such services by the member or members rendering such services unless the taxpayer establishes a more appropriate charge."

Treas. Reg. Sec. 1.482-2(b)(4) discusses the "costs or deductions to be taken into account." Subparagraph (i) states that all direct and indirect costs or deductions should be reasonably taken into account. Subparagraph (ii) states that such items "include, but are not limited to, costs or deductions for compensation, bonuses, and travel expenses attributable to employees directly engaged in performing such services, for material and supplies directly consumed in rendering such services, and for other costs such as the cost of overseas cables in connection with such services."

Subparagraph (iii) states that "[indirect costs or deductions generally include costs or deductions with respect to utilities, occupancy, supervisory and clerical compensation, and other overhead burden ... [and] also generally include an appropriate share of the costs or deductions relating to supporting departments and other applicable general and administrative expenses to the extent reasonably allocable to a particular service or activity." Treas. Reg. Sec. 1.482-2(b)(6)(ii) provides a bit more guidance on apportionments from supporting departments.

Treas. Reg. Sec. 1.482-2(b)(6) discusses the allocation and apportionment of such costs or deductions. The general rule under subparagraph (i) is that a method used by a taxpayer that is "reasonable and in keeping with sound accounting practice" will "not be disturbed." Subparagraph

(ii) lists some of the possible bases and factors to be considered for allocation and apportionment are "total expenses, asset size, sales, manufacturing expenses, payroll, space utilized and time spent."

Documentation Requirements

Many jurisdictions have established documentation requirements for intercompany transactions. As with all transfer-pricing regulations, such requirements are based on local legislation and vary by country, state, and industry. At a minimum, documentation of the pricing model should include a definition of the services provided, benefits received, and costing of the service. In addition, each jurisdiction should have a formal service-level agreement (SLA) that defines the service provided and charging methodology (see Chapter 18 for more information on SLAs). Finally, there should be a formal invoicing process between entities in line with the services and charges defined in the SLA.

Implementing a Pricing Model

Whether starting from scratch or changing an existing pricing model, there are several steps to successfully implement a new pricing model. Following is a list of key tasks required to implement a pricing model:

- Gain an understanding of the underlying costs structure. IT costs are typically broken down into cost centers aligned to the management structure. These cost centers will have to be converted into service costs once the services have been defined.
- Document the current pricing model, including services, allocation measurements, and service recipients. The current state will need to be compared to the new model to determine the change/impact to service recipients.
- Interview service providers and service recipients to gain an understanding of the issues with the current cost allocation model and the perceived value of the services provided by IT.
- Define new services based on research, benchmarking information, and the overall strategy of the organization. As mentioned earlier, there are several models that can be used.
- Define service descriptions and process for allocating the underlying people, hardware, software, facilities, and so on to each of the services.
- Prepare a model of the new pricing model with a comparison to the old pricing model. This information will be needed to determine the impact of the change and to gain approval/agreement for the new model.
- Gather the IT measurements available at the level of granularity required to allocate the costs. Verify that the information is accurate and can be produced on a monthly basis. Also, document the process for gathering and reporting the information to ensure auditability and consistency.
- Develop a proposal for the new pricing model to gain approval from the CIO, CEO, and CFO. Senior management support is crucial for implementing a change, as there will be disagreement from the individual service recipients.
- Develop SLAs that document the pricing model, payment terms, service description, service levels, and allocation measures. This document forms the basis for charging services to the service recipient and tax documentation and should be reviewed and approved by legal, finance, and tax.
- Communicate new pricing model, services, and impact on service recipients. A formal presentation showing the change, reason for the change, and approval from senior management is helpful in gaining buy-in from each of the service recipients.

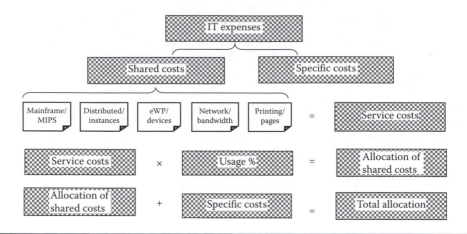

Exhibit 12.5   Illustration of an IT pricing model.

Discussed in the following is an example of a costing model developed by creating service cost pools of direct and indirect expenses (Exhibit 12.5).

In this model, costs are split between shared and specific. Costs specific to a customer are charged directly to the customer receiving the benefit of the service or product. Shared IT service costs are determined by adding all related costs (labor, hardware, software) into a "cost pool" divided by the total number of units supported (e.g., mainframe usage, processors, PCs). Costs are then allocated based on percentage of use. This approach eliminates the variance between planned unit costs and actual unit costs; however, it can shift fixed costs between user groups if demand/consumption changes out of proportion (e.g., one group increases and another decreases demand/consumption).

A slightly different approach would be to determine the unit cost (e.g., cost per printed page) and charge for the number of units times the cost per unit. Any unit/cost variance would be apportioned back to the various customers at the end of the year based on the actual unit cost times the actual units. This situation also has its challenges as unit cost and usage variances need to be clearly explained and actual costs and usage are not known until after the year-end.

While both approaches are relatively straightforward, it can become quite complicated if the services or customers are too granular. The higher the number of services and customers, the costlier it can be to develop and maintain cost accounting and usage metrics. In the end, no model is going to be perfect so the benefit has to outweigh the cost of the pricing model.

Maintaining a Pricing Model

Services evolve over time, new services are added, and user groups are added and deleted. The cost model needs to be changed periodically to accommodate this change. However, the change process needs to be properly controlled, as modifications will change the allocation of costs between services and user groups. From a tax and user perspective, simplicity and consistency are more important than tweaking a pricing model. Again, the benefit of change has to outweigh the cost of the change in terms of both the cost of making the change and the effort to communicate the change to the impacted groups.

Measuring Consumption

Whatever model is selected for IT chargeback, there will be some level of allocation or usage measurement. In a consumption allocation model, measuring consumption is a key component of appropriately charging for IT services. For example, IT costs may be based on the number of PCs in an organization. This sounds fairly simple; however, tracking and attributing each individual PC with a specific function is no easy task. It requires a solid asset management process to track individual devices, users, and the charging function from the time a device is deployed until it is disposed. In addition, users typically have additional hardware and peripheral devices that will also need to be allocated. Even multinational organizations that specialize in this service find it difficult to track individual devices and components within a dynamic organization. A prerequisite for implementing a pricing model based on IT consumption is an effective IT asset management process.

IT Asset Management

IT asset management is the process of tracking hardware and software assets. IT asset management is important for several reasons. At the most basic level, an inventory is required to support the value of assets on the balance sheet. For leased assets, it is important to track the location of assets to return assets at the end of the lease term. Tracking installed software is important for ensuring compliance with license agreements. An accurate inventory of hardware and software is also a fundamental prerequisite for effective change control and configuration management. It is also a prerequisite for developing a pricing model based on the consumption of IT services. A pricing model that charges for the consumption of IT resources is useless if the consumption measurements are not accurate and readily available for reporting and validation.

Surprisingly, many organizations are not even aware of the number of devices they own. Unisys Corporation's desktop services regularly have customers with reported numbers that are 50% off the actual number of devices that they own. This is a concern not only for auditors, but for accountants as well, because organizations are understating their assets.

Companies have typically kept track of hardware assets and depreciated them. However, software may have been expensed and the number of licenses may not have been tracked. Without this information, it is virtually impossible to determine the number of licenses owned to audit license compliance. Complicating software tracking is the ability of managers to purchase inexpensive shrink-wrapped software packages and write them off on corporate expense accounts. According to Personal Computer Asset Management Institute, this practice accounts for as much as 30% of software purchases. This has made it virtually impossible to centrally track the number of software licenses.

Adding to the complexity of tracking company software is that license contracts are not uniform. Some licenses provide for a single user on multiple workstations, others are for one workstation only. Network licenses may only require licensing for concurrent users, whereas others may offer site licensing. In addition, some license agreements may have vague terms, such as shareware software, that require clarification to avoid licensing violations. Organizations should centralize software licensing to take advantage of pricing and contract term negotiations. License terms should then be communicated to the users so that they understand the proper use of the software product.

Benefits of IT Asset Management

Effective asset management provides the following benefits:

- More accurate cost assignments for computer assets
- Better purchase and deployment decisions
- Optimal management of computer life cycles
- Better use of warranty and service contracts
- Improved planning for future acquisitions
- Greater security of existing assets
- More accurate and timely fulfillment of users' needs

IT asset management is part of the process required to link procurement, finance, contracts, inventory, service management, and compliance with the information necessary to answer the following questions:

- When do we need to renew leases?
- Do I have tax liabilities in inventory?
- What do I have in inventory that can be redeployed?
- Is the broken item covered by maintenance?
- Did we take advantage of contracted discounts?
- Is what we received what was ordered?
- What cost center gets charged for this item?
- Is there budget available for additional licenses?
- Am I compliant with software contracts?

IT asset management is important because it provides the underlying information needed to support the following processes:

- Purchasing
- Technology planning and deployment
- Asset identification
- Physical management
- Support strategies
- Inventory management
- Electronic distribution
- Version tracking
- Usage monitoring
- Refresh/retirement
- Provisioning
- Contracting
- License compliance
- Contract maintenance
- Supplier management
- SLA
- Procurement
- Budgeting

- Cost control
- Chargeback
- Help desk support
- Configuration management

IT asset management tools can track several types of assets. Tracking hardware devices is important for financial records and maintenance. Tracking operating systems and patches is important for maintenance and security. Internally developed software can be tracked to support configuration management and quality assurance. Purchased software can be tracked for configuration management, quality assurance, and compliance.

Tools

There are a number of asset management tools that ease the chore of managing hardware and software. The prerequisite for the use of these tools is to have all devices connected to the network. Software is available that will inventory the hardware and software connected to the network, and some of these tools can be used to distribute software to end users. Software licensing can be controlled with the use of metering software that limits and tracks the number of licenses in use at any given time. Another benefit of some of these tools is the ability to provide remote support and diagnose problems on remote terminals.

Because PC components are small and transferable, it is very simple to swap out or remove components. There are tools that can be installed on the network that scan workstations to examine components and produce inventory reports. Integrated tools offer hardware component detection, software application detection, as well as communications tools to assist in monitoring problems.

IT asset management tools also provide value in the financial management of IT. Used properly, asset management tools can help control the demand for IT services by limiting users to standard hardware/software and having the tools to enforce compliance. Asset management tools provide information on the number of software licenses owned versus used. In some cases, organizations overpurchase licenses because they are unable to confirm the number of licenses in use and reuse existing licenses. This information can help reduce the cost of new licenses and maintenance.

Understanding and Managing Costs

Demand for IT services is increasing as organizations continue automating business processes, transmit more information across the network, and increase the number and complexity of transactions. Increasing costs of compliance and security is driving IT costs higher. Organizations are required to store more data, track and report on more information, and better secure data to comply with an increasing number of regulations (e.g., Sarbanes–Oxley Act, Privacy Act). This puts increased pressure on the IT group to look for ways to reduce operating costs to offset increased demand.

IT is faced with another conflicting requirement. How to keep costs low while remaining flexible enough to shed fixed costs when demand is reduced either from the business cycle or outsourcing to a third party. For example, business process outsourcing may strip out selected services and consumption units to be provided by a third party. This creates challenges for IT to be able to shed fixed costs associated with these services/demand to avoid impacting other units. Outsourcing and hardware and software acquisition processes are discussed in more detail in Chapter 15. Capacity planning and volume purchases are standard ways to keep hardware and software costs under control. However, it is difficult to shed the cost of hardware and software assets once they are purchased.

Optimizing IT costs is an ongoing activity for any organization. There are many ways to improve efficiency and technology to reduce costs. At the same time, IT organizations need to protect against shortsighted cost cutting and underinvestment that result in increased costs over the long term. For example, hanging on to obsolete hardware can be more costly than refreshing technology as maintenance costs will be increased and the risk of service breakdowns will be higher. The cost of lost productivity from the users of an application can be many times greater than an investment in a reasonable technology refresh program. In addition, IT resources can be used more effectively with newer technology that is easier to manage and fails less frequently than obsolete equipment.

Refreshing Technology

Refreshing technology provides an organization with additional opportunities to reduce costs in a variety of ways. Hardware continues to improve in performance and decrease in cost. A technology refresh can replace multiple platforms with new technology that is less costly to maintain and has higher performance and security. Standard hardware platforms can also reduce the cost of operations, utilities, facilities, and software by taking advantage of new pricing models. New server platforms (mainframe and midrange) allow workload partitioning that can reduce the size of processors that serve as the basis for many software contracts. New storage media allows more data storage on smaller devices, reducing the space and power required. New networking technology allows data and voice to be shared across the same network, reducing hardware, software, and support costs.

Standardizing Technology

One of the key methods for getting the most value out of IT investments is a solid enterprise architecture and standard technology. Continuing to add new applications on new platforms while keeping existing legacy applications on obsolete platforms prevents an organization from realizing cost savings. Developing a roadmap of legacy application replacement in conjunction with new application development will result in long-term savings as old platforms are decommissioned and new applications become standardized. Standardized technology enables the leveraging of existing components, staff, and skills to develop and maintain systems. Standardized platforms are also important in developing a pricing model that is easy to understand and manage.

Consolidating Infrastructure

Consolidating infrastructure to a central location or platform can reduce costs by leveraging existing resources to support higher infrastructure capacity. Fewer resources and less overhead may be needed when reducing from multiple locations to a single location. Shared infrastructure can reduce the cost of existing and new applications where operating platforms are already in place (e.g., security services, technology refresh, remote monitoring, and disaster recovery). However, there are risks to consider with consolidating infrastructure to a single location or platform. Disaster recovery is an important consideration before consolidating to a single location or platform. Performance and security also need to be considered when moving distributed servers to a central location as information is now being transmitted across a wide area network. In some cases, telecommunication costs can offset the savings realized from consolidation. In addition, system failures in a consolidated environment can be more pervasive than a distributed environment.

Managing Demand and Service Levels

Users are demanding higher levels of service and flexibility. However, this demand comes with a price. The higher the level of service and the complexity of service offerings, the higher the cost. To keep costs low requires a standard service offering with the right level of service. To deliver 100% availability 24 × 7 service is going to require significant redundancy to provide service when the inevitable component fails. This level of service may be required in certain situations, but it is something to think about when defining service levels. Another process that needs to be considered is demand management. Left to their own devices, users may consume more than the company is willing to spend. Demand management policies define who gets what and when. Keeping users confined to a preset standard helps keep costs from running out of control. In any case, the performance and consumption levels need to align to the organization's business and IT strategy as well as annual operating plans.

Standardizing Governance and Processes

Standardized governance and processes make it easier to do business with IT for the customer, suppliers, and IT personnel. Governance and processes need to be aligned to the business and IT strategy to support the organization in achieving its goals. Standardized governance enables lower costs and higher satisfaction as customers and suppliers are managed consistently. Standardized processes make shared services possible as people in different locations follow the same processes in delivering services. However, decision making and processes need to be efficient so as to not create bureaucratic overhead. Simplified processes help keep organizational costs lower as they are easier to understand and follow for all involved parties. Quality improvement initiatives can also reduce costs in the long term by reducing the number of issues and rework.

Conclusion

A solid financial framework establishes the rights and responsibilities of business and IT management in making financial decisions. IT costs typically represent a major portion of an organization's operating costs. Left unmanaged, IT costs can increase in excess of the value delivered. Service and project pricing model can help ensure that the cost of IT investments and services are transparent and well understood. Aligning spending to an organization's strategic and operating plans ensures that spending is in alignment with the organization's goals.

A solid financial framework is key to understanding and managing IT costs. IT costs are managed by implementing governance and budgets that are aligned to the organizational strategy and operating plans. Financial planning and controlling processes are key processes in managing the investment in IT. An effective relationship between IT and management requires transparent financial planning and reporting. The management needs to understand demand quality, quantity, and pricing to make informed decisions about the appropriate level of IT spending. With pressure on IT to reduce costs, it is important to make sure cost cuts are not made that deliver short-term savings but increase costs in the future.

Business units want to have control over their costs; therefore, it is important for them to understand the pricing model and how their behavior influences the charges they receive. The IT pricing model can consume a lot of time and energy as various groups argue over the details. An IT pricing model should be simple to administer and should fairly represent the cost of service and provide business units with predictable costs over time. Theoretically, an effective pricing model should drive user behavior to realize the optimal value for the services consumed. However, additional controls may be needed to manage demand and manage IT costs for long-term benefit.

Review Questions

1. What makes it challenging to manage IT costs?
2. What are the critical components of financial management?
3. What are some of the advantages to implementing an IT pricing model?
4. What information is required for an investment approval request?
5. What processes are supported by information provided by IT asset management?

Multiple-Choice Questions

1. IT asset management delivers the following benefit(s):
   a. More accurate cost assignments for computer assets
   b. Improved planning for future acquisitions
   c. Better purchase and deployment decisions
   d. Better use of warranty and service contracts
   e. All of the above
2. Project capital budget requests should include
   a. The business benefits of the proposed solution
   b. The financial impact on the operating budget
   c. The total development costs and infrastructure costs
   d. The project staffing and schedule
   e. All of the above
3. An investment approval request should include all of the following except
   a. Business issues and assumptions
   b. Financial return and contingencies
   c. SLAs
   d. Resources required and proposed technology
   e. None of the above
4. Project benefits should be stated in measurable terms
   a. To audit the investment approval request
   b. To determine the financial impact on the operating budget
   c. To provide a means for validating the benefits
   d. To determine the resources required for the project
   e. None of the above
5. Approaches to developing a pricing model include
   a. IT-based consumption model
   b. Business-based consumption model
   c. Fee-based chargeback
   d. Profit-oriented chargeback model
   e. All of the above
6. Developing a pricing model requires knowledge of

a. Security requirements
b. Tax and regulatory requirements
c. Third-party charging models
d. Project pricing model
e. All of the above
7. Steps to successfully implement a new pricing model include all of the following except
   a. Gain an understanding of the underlying costs structure
   b. Benchmark existing services to the industry
   c. Compare the new to the old pricing model
   d. Develop SLAs
   e. Gather IT measurements
8. Project cost estimate should include
   a. Alignment to enterprise architecture standards
   b. Financial return and contingencies
   c. The total development and infrastructure costs
   d. The business benefits of the proposed solution
   e. All of the above
9. Financial planning in IT begins with an understanding of
   a. Business volume growth projections
   b. Enterprise architecture standards
   c. IT organizational model
   d. Regulatory compliance requirements
   e. None of the above
10. Managing demand and service levels
    a. Is a prerequisite to implementing a pricing model
    b. Ensures performance meets expectations
    c. Aligns demand with service offerings
    d. Keeps costs from running out of control
    e. None of the above

Exercises

1. List and discuss four ways IT asset information can be used.
2. List and discuss the advantages and disadvantages of chargeback.
3. List and discuss possible ways to optimize IT costs.

Answers to Multiple-Choice Questions

1—e; 2—e; 3—c; 4—c; 5—e; 6—b; 7—b; 8—c; 9—a; 10—d

Further Reading

1. Bell, M., *Using IT to Reduce Overhead Costs*, Gartner Research, Gartner Group, April 8, 2003.
2. Creswich, B.P., *Developing Successful Organizational IT Strategies: IT Chargeback as a Component of Effective IT Financial Management*, Project Performance Corporation, McLean, VA, 2004.

3. Denne, M.J., Chargeback demonstrates IT value in the enterprise, *CIO Magazine*, Stamford, CT, January 1, 2007, http://www.cio.com/article/27821/Chargeback_Demonstrates_IT_Value_in_the_enterprise.

4. Duncan, G.A. and D.T. Cousineau, *Creating and Operating an Effective and Equitable Shared Services Chargeback Framework*, Accenture, New York, 2004.

5. Goldstein, P.J., *Chargeback and Information Technology Funding*, Vol. 2005, Issue 23, ECAR, Center for Applied Research, Washington, DC, November 8, 2005.

6. Gomolski, B., *Managing the Finances of the IS Internal Service Company*, Research Note, Gartner Group, March 18, 2003.

7. Gomolski, B. and S. Mingay, *Best Practices for Global Chargeback*, Gartner Research ID Number: G00144150, Gartner Group, November 14, 2006.

8. Gomolski, B., *U.S. IT Spending and Staffing Survey*, Gartner Research, November 2, 2005.

9. Guldentops, E., What is in our IT portfolios? *Inf. Syst. Control J.*, 5, 2007.

10. IRS, Internal Revenue Code, Internal Revenue Code Section 482: Allocation of income and deductions among taxpayers, US Internal Revenue Service, Washington, DC.

11. Kirwin, B., *TCO Must Be Measured and Managed to be Controlled*, Research Note, Gartner Group, April 7, 2003.

12. OECD, *Transfer Pricing Guidelines for Multinational Enterprises and Tax Adminstrations*, OECD Publishing, Paris, France, June 18, 2001.

13. Sayana, A.S., Auditing realization of benefits from IT, *Inf. Syst. Control J.*, 3, 2005.

14. Working Council for Chief Financial Officers, *Improving the Yield on Information Technology*, Research Brief, 2003.

15. Working Council for Chief Information Officers, *Budget Watch: IT Spending Trends for 2003*, Corporate Executive Board, 2003.

16. Working Council for Chief Financial Officers, *The Digital Productivity Imperative. Best-in-Class IT-Enabled Business Cost-Savings Practices*, Corporate Executive Board, 2001.

17. Working Council for Chief Financial Officers, *Improving the Yield on Information Technology*, Research Brief, Corporate Executive Board, 2003.

18. Working Council for Chief Financial Officers, *The IT Cost-Savings Diagnostic*, Corporate Executive Board, May 2001.

19. Working Council for Chief Financial Officers, *Strategies for Securing Buy-In and Employing Chargebacks for Infrastructure Standardization*, Corporate Executive Board, 2002.

20. Young, C., *Running IS Like a Business: Introducing the ISCo Model*, Strategic Analysis Report, Gartner Group, January 16, 2003.

21. Young, C., *Mainstream IT Service Delivery Strategies Are Misaligned*, Research G00139881, Gartner Group, June 20, 2006.

IT ACQUISITION AND IMPLEMENTATION

Chapters 13 through 17

The third part of this text examines IT acquisition and implementation. This section discusses risks and controls in terms of the life cycle of application systems. Specifically, it includes acquiring new systems, implementing new systems, maintaining applications, and change management.

This area emphasizes the importance of identifying issues during the development process as they are more costly to correct after the system becomes operational. Ideally, auditor involvement provides the most significant value during the acquisition and implementation phase. IT and general auditors as well as other IT security professionals give risk and control expertise to these project teams. The auditor can ensure that risks are evaluated up front and controls are integrated within the system as opposed to after the fact. However, many companies marginalize their auditors to scheduled programmed audits that negate the ability of the auditor to be a partner in the process. Conversely, involving auditors in the acquisition and implementation can infer to others that the auditor's independence is compromised. The auditor and audit management must manage this perception through the use of objective audit tools and their professionalism.

Once applications are purchased and implemented, they must be maintained. Application maintenance can introduce risk to a once stable and secure system. Additionally, maintaining applications involves costs to the organization and should be effectively managed. Auditors often review maintenance procedures and change control procedures to ensure that the application is meeting its stated objectives and performing as intended by management.

For an auditor, member of the management team, or significant user of a company's application systems, it is beneficial to understand the goals of the system and the associated risks that could impede those expectations. Consequently, risks can be managed through controls, which will ensure the success and security of the application.

In this section, the Manage Projects process of the COBIT planning and organization domain (Exhibit III.1) will be discussed in more detail and compared to other existing standards.

PO10 Manage Projects
Control Objectives
10.1   Program management framework
10.2   Project management framework
10.3   Project management approach
10.4   Stakeholder commitment
10.5   Project scope statement
10.6   Project phase Initiation
10.7   Integrated project plan
10.8   Project resources
10.9   Project risk management
10.10   Project quality plan
10.11   Project change control
10.12   Project planning of assurance methods
10.13   Project performance measurement, reporting, and monitoring
10.14   Project closure

Exhibit III.1   Processes for planning and organization.

Planning and organization. This domain covers strategies and tactics, and concerns the identification of the way IT can best contribute to the achievement of the business objectives.

In this section, the seven processes of the COBIT acquire and implement domain (Exhibit III.2) will be discussed in more detail and compared to other existing standards.

AI1 Identify Automated Solutions
Control Objectives
1.1   Definition and maintenance of business functional and technical requirements
1.2   Risk analysis report
1.3   Feasibility study and formulation of alternative courses of action
1.4   Requirements and feasibility decision and approval
AI2 Acquire and Maintain Application Software
Control Objectives
2.1   High-level design
2.2   Detailed design

Exhibit III.2   Processes to acquire and implement.

2.3	Application control and auditability
2.4	Application security and availability
2.5	Configuration and implementation of acquired application software
2.6	Major upgrades to existing systems
2.7	Development of application software
2.8	Software quality assurance
2.9	Applications requirements management
2.10	Application software maintenance

AI3 Acquire and Maintain Technology Infrastructure

Control Objectives

3.1	Technological infrastructure acquisition plan
3.2	Infrastructure resource protection and availability
3.3	Infrastructure maintenance
3.4	Feasibility test environment

AI4 Enable Operation and Use

Control Objectives

4.1	Planning for operational solutions
4.2	Knowledge transfer to business management
4.3	Knowledge transfer to end users
4.4	Knowledge transfer to operations and support staff

AI5 Procure IT Resources

Control Objectives

5.1	Procurement control
5.2	Supplier contract management
5.3	Supplier selection
5.4	Software acquisition
5.5	Acquisition of development resources
5.6	Acquisition of infrastructure, facilities, and related services

AI6 Manage Changes

Control Objectives

6.1	Change standards and procedures
6.2	Impact assessment, prioritization, and authorization
6.3	Emergency changes

Exhibit III.2   (Continued) Processes to acquire and implement.

6.4	Change status tracking and reporting
6.5	Change closure and documentation

AI7 Install and Accredit Solutions and Changes
Control Objectives

7.1	Training
7.2	Test plan
7.3	Implementation plan
7.4	Production test environment
7.5	System and data conversion
7.6	Testing of changes
7.7	Final acceptance test
7.8	Promotion to production
7.9	Software release
7.10	System distribution
7.11	Recording and tracking of changes
7.12	Postimplementation review

Exhibit III.2   (Continued) Processes to acquire and implement.

Acquisition and implementation. To realize the IT strategy, IT solutions need to be identified, developed, or acquired, as well as implemented and integrated into the business process. In addition to these processes, this domain makes sure that the life cycle is continued in order for the systems to cover changes in and maintenance of existing systems.

Chapter 13 discusses project management processes needed to ensure that projects are well controlled from inception through implementation. Systems development failures and project management failures continue to appear in reports and studies. Managing technology in today's dynamic times is not an easy process. Effectively controlling projects requires a disciplined approach to project initiation, execution, implementation, and postimplementation.

Chapter 14 reviews the phases of the system development and implementation processes. Implementing a system consists of configuring the system, testing functionality, converting data, training users, and preparing for production support. The purpose of the system implementation process is to verify that the solution meets its intended purpose. An auditor's role in system implementations is to ensure that risks are identified and proper controls are considered during the implementation process. Auditors are encouraged to participate in system implementations so that they can provide security and control expertise. Additionally, identifying risks or recommending controls after a system is implemented is more costly and may limit the organization's ability to implement the most effective controls.

Chapter 15 provides an overview of software, infrastructure, and resource acquisition processes as well as the associated risks and controls. Organizations acquire software, infrastructure, and resources to support their business needs in automating in an effective and efficient manner. This chapter provides an overview of the acquisition and vendor management processes. It also discusses suggestions for an auditor in performing a review of the acquisition and vendor management processes.

Chapter 16 provides an overview of risks and controls associated with application systems and their associated maintenance. Applications represent a significant investment for organizations as well as being critical for conducting business. Computer-based applications provide automated functions, which effectively support the business process. Applications also introduce risks to organizations in the form of increased costs, loss of data integrity, weaknesses in confidentiality, lack of availability, or poor performance. Owing to the significant investment that companies make in applications systems as well as the significant investment of funds, the auditor's role is critical in reviewing the risk, effectiveness, and efficiencies associated with application systems.

Chapter 17 discusses the change management process. Systems and applications are changed frequently throughout their useful life. Maintaining applications and systems is a costly endeavor, may introduce problems, becomes inconsistent with business or IT strategies, degrades performance, and can monopolize the resources of an organization.

Chapter 13

IT Project Management

IT project management refers to the processes and techniques used in the beginning-to-end development of software or other systems. Project management is one of the key controls that ensures delivery of projects on time, on budget, and with full functionality. The purpose of project management is to identify, establish, coordinate, and monitor activities, tasks, and resources for a project to produce the product or services meeting the requirements. Effectively controlling projects requires a disciplined approach to project initiation, execution, implementation, and postimplementation. This includes having the right people involved, following standard project management processes, and using a set of project management tools for effective execution. COBIT recognizes project management as a process that impacts both the effectiveness and the efficiency of information systems and involves IT resources that include people, applications, technology, and operational facilities. It describes the controls over the IT process of managing projects that satisfy the organizational business requirement. It considers the following:

- Business management sponsorship of project
- Program management
- Project management capabilities
- User involvement
- Task breakdown, milestone definition, and phase approvals
- Allocation of responsibilities
- Rigorous tracking of milestones and deliverables
- Cost and manpower budgets, and balancing internal and external resources
- Quality assurance plans and methods
- Program and project risk assessments
- Transition from development to operations (COBIT)

The COBIT process (PO10) in the Planning and Organization Domain discusses how project management processes support an effective IT organization. Exhibit 13.1 lists the key control objectives for this section.

PO10 Manage Projects
Control Objectives
10.1   Program management framework
10.2   Project management framework
10.3   Project management approach
10.4   Stakeholder commitment
10.5   Project scope statement
10.6   Project phase initiation
10.7   Integrated project plan
10.8   Project resources
10.9   Project risk management
10.10   Project quality plan
10.11   Project change control
10.12   Project planning of assurance methods
10.13   Project performance measurement, reporting, and monitoring
10.14   Project closure

Exhibit 13.1   Planning and organization domain.

IT Processes

Program Management

Program management is the process required to coordinate multiple, related projects. Today's applications have increasing complexity with requirements from multiple groups and the integration of functionality with multiple applications (e.g., ERP). Most new applications also require action from various functions within IT (software development, network engineering, security, production support, etc.). Program management brings all the pieces of a major program together and includes the following components:

- Defining program management framework
- Creating a program management office (PMO)
- Setting staffing requirements, processes, and metrics
- Establishing consistent project management practices
- Implementing technology for managing projects

According to the Gartner Group, organizations that establish enterprise standards for project management, including a project office with suitable governance, will experience half the major project cost overruns and delays and cancellations of those that fail to do so.[*]

---

[*] Light, M. and M. Halpern, *Understanding Product vs. Project Portfolio Management*, Gartner Research, G00130796, Gartner Group, Stamford, CT, May 2, 2006.

Program Management
Keeper of "the vision"
Source of "leadership"
Master communicator
Deliverable and process focused
Leadership discipline focused on delivering results
Focused on the process to create a deliverable or subdeliverable (domain of methodology, process improvement)
Project Management
Focused on a deliverable or set of deliverables
Planning and control based on output and deliverables, milestones and schedule, resource consumption, quality attributes, and risk management
Work management

Exhibit 13.2   Program management versus project management.

Program Management versus Project Management

The business and technology environments drive the demand for multiple complex programs and the need for enterprise-wide program coordination (see Exhibit 13.2). Because no development project is completed by just one function, program management is required to ensure success.

Project Management

The project management process involves two basic elements:

- A project management life cycle (PMLC) that can be applied generically—but often tailored to fit the project size—to any project. This chapter focuses on project management processes.
- A development life cycle that addresses the specific needs of the application or other deliverable being considered. There can be many of these in use. A mainframe application may follow one type of system development life cycle (e.g., waterfall approach), and Web-based application may follow another type (e.g., iterative). This topic is discussed in more detail here.

Project management has often been described as part art and part science. The part art side of it involves the human element, the experience project managers bring to the project, the support they can muster from their management, and, a critical point, how project managers relate to the client and the client's willingness to provide the right level of support to make the project succeed. Many times, the relationship between the project manager and the client has not been built as a partnered approach. This can lead to loss of productivity by the project team and should be captured as a project risk as soon as recognized. The second part of the equation, the part science side, is somewhat easier to deal with. The project manager should put in place the right project governance and a PMLC, and integrate these two elements with the appropriate system development life cycle. The IT industry analysts have made general and specific recommendations on why projects are successful. Although not foolproof, the recommendations in the following are a good place to start. Other IT industry organizations have built their own body of knowledge to document acceptable practices.

The Gartner Group identifies what it calls "Project Management's 10 Best Practices":

1. All projects (other than IT infrastructure projects) must be owned by business units.
2. All projects must be launched in an orderly and rational fashion—that is, ideas must go through appropriate due diligence before they become projects.
3. A consistent and stable system must be established to manage cross-project priorities.
4. Project success criteria are defined early and monitored throughout the project development cycle.
5. The roles and responsibilities of sponsorship are well understood and taken seriously.
6. The rules and responsibilities for the management of projects are clearly defined and understood by all.
7. The process for assigning individuals to projects is rational, and assignments are reasonably stable.
8. Projects are expected to have comprehensive plans, realistic estimates, and viable schedules.
9. Project status is systematically, forthrightly, and consistently reported.
10. Projects are not considered complete until functionality is fully operational and benefits are realized.

Strategic and tactical initiatives are dependent on effective, efficient, timely, and quality project initiation, planning, execution, management, and completion.

Project Management Body of Knowledge

The primary standards organization for project management is the Project Management Institute (PMI). The PMI developed project management standards published as the Project Management Body of Knowledge (PMBOK). This document represents the sum total of all knowledge within the project management profession.

Project Management Framework

A project management framework or a PMLC provides guidelines to project managers on the processes that must be followed to ensure successful project implementation. The PMLC is different from the SDLC. The PMLC provides a structure around the SDLC being used to ensure that the project has the proper controls to succeed. It is focused on the project scope, schedule, and budget, and the SDLC is focused on the analysis, construction, and testing. As an additional clarification, the SDLC deals with developing an application, and the PMLC applies to developing software, upgrading infrastructure, or moving an office. The PMLC begins where the project initiation process ends (i.e., after project approval). It provides an organized structure around every project and guidance for both new and experienced project managers as well as a reference point for auditors, executives, and business sponsors. The PMLC assists the project manager with project controls by ensuring that the proper mechanics and infrastructure are in place. It also provides a standard for the PMO or auditors to assess projects and the project managers' compliance with the defined project management processes. The PMLC does reference the defined SDLC to ensure that the project team is following the company standard. One final point about the difference between the PMLC and the SDLC is that there may be multiple SDLCs in use at an organization, but there should be only one PMLC.

Establishing and complying with the PMLC and the SDLC will provide the environment required for the project's success, but does not guarantee success. The project manager and the project team have the ultimate accountability for the success or failure of the project.

Project Management

Effective project management ensures that the project tasks are adequately defined, resources are available and used efficiently, quality is maintained, and the project is completed on time and within budget. Auditors can assist by reviewing the project plan to ensure that tasks and deliverables are defined in sufficient detail, resource requirements are defined, time estimates are reasonable, resources are available at the right time, and project progress is regularly reported.

Depending on the organization, project planning may be formal or informal. In either case, basic project management techniques should be used to ensure that the project is well planned and effectively monitored. There are many tools available to assist the project manager in preparing a project plan. Project management tools allow the user to define tasks and dependencies, and track progress. A project plan should include interim milestones and regular review of project deliverables. Exhibit 13.3 lists examples of project deliverables.

Resource Management

There are many individual functions that are required to deliver a successful project. The business has to define the requirements, the application developers have to deliver the code, the quality assurance group and testers have to validate the code, and the infrastructure groups have to support the application. People with various skill sets may be assigned to a project team. Project assignments may be full or part time. Team members may be transferred or matrixed to the project team. The challenge for the project manager is making sure that

- Appropriate governance is in place.
- The right resources (money, people, facilities, etc.) are available at the right time.

Project Phase	Deliverable
Planning	Project plan
Analysis	User requirements
Design	Program specifications
Testing	Test objectives
Implementation	System documentation

Exhibit 13.3 Project deliverables.

- The project has a work breakdown structure that is sufficiently detailed to carry out the project.
- The project tasks are prioritized to prevent interference with other projects' due dates.
- The deliverables are produced in a timely fashion and are the right quality.
- Management (all levels) is being communicated with and sufficiently involved.
- The end user is involved and takes delivery of the agreed-to project results.

The program manager helps ensure that all groups are connected throughout the process.

Project Planning

The objective of project planning is to be able to predict the project duration, resources required, and cost. The project manager should establish reasonable plans by estimating the work to be performed, establish commitments, and define the plan (see Exhibit 13.4).

Goals	
1.	Estimates are documented
2.	Activities and commitments are planned and documented
3.	Impacted groups and individuals agree to their commitments
4.	Commitments
5.	Project manager is designated
6.	Project manager negotiates commitments and develops plan
7.	Policy and plan for managing planning activities are documented and followed
8.	Allocated requirements used as basis for planning
9.	Involvement of other entities is negotiated and documented
10.	Plans and estimates are reviewed by impacted groups following a documented plan
11.	Plans are reviewed by senior management
12.	Plans are managed and controlled following documented procedures and processes
13.	Changes are incorporated in a controlled and documented manner
14.	Both "version" and "change" control are utilized following a documented process
Abilities	
1.	A documented and approved statement of work exists
2.	Statement of work includes scope, technical goals and objectives, standards, assigning responsibilities, goals, costs and schedule constraints, dependencies, resource constraints, and other constraints and goals
3.	Statement of work is reviewed by all involved parties

Exhibit 13.4   Project planning.

4.	Plan development responsibilities are assigned and documented
5.	Adequate resources and funding are provided
6.	Tools required for planning are provided
7.	Responsible parties are trained in estimating and planning functions
8.	Results documented
Activities	
1.	Software engineering group participates in the project proposal activity
2.	Software project planning begins concurrently with overall project planning
3.	Software project planning group participates in overall project planning throughout the project life cycle
4.	All commitments, internal and external, are reviewed by senior management
5.	The project life cycle is identified and defined with predefined stages of manageable size
6.	Development and planning activities follow a documented process and procedure
7.	The project plan is documented
8.	The project plan includes purpose, scope, goals, and objectives
9.	The project plan identifies procedures, methods, and standards for developing and maintaining the plan
10.	The work products, size estimates, effort and cost estimates, use of computer resources, schedules, milestones, reviews, and risks are identified and described in the plan
11.	Facilities and support tools are identified
12.	Estimates for size, effort, cost, required computer resources, schedule, risks, and engineering facilities and support tools are developed using documented procedures
13.	Software planning data are recorded, managed, and controlled
Measurements	
1.	Measurements are devised and utilized to monitor management of all planning activities
Verification	
1.	Management activities reviewed periodically with senior management
2.	Management activities reviewed periodically with project management
3.	Quality assurance audits management of planning activities and reports the results

Exhibit 13.4   (Continued) Project planning.

Project Tracking and Oversight

An oversight and tracking process helps ensure that a project lives up to its commitments. As with anything, the best laid plans can fail due to poor execution. Controls need to be put in place to identify projects that are running astray. Oversight and tracking during all phases of the development process helps ensure that standard processes are followed and control is maintained. Oversight and tracking continues after the project is implemented to ensure that the business benefit promised when the project was approved is realized and the ongoing costs stay in line with the original estimates. The objective of project tracking and oversight is to provide adequate visibility into actual progress so that the management can take effective actions when the project's performance deviates significantly from the plans. These requirements must be documented and controlled (see Exhibit 13.5).

Goals	
1.	Actual results and performance are tracked against the plans
2.	Corrective actions are taken and managed to closure when actual results and performance deviate significantly from the plans
3.	All changes to commitments are agreed to by affected groups or parties
Commitments	
1.	Project manager is designated to be responsible for the project's activities and results
2.	Project follows a documented organizational policy for managing software projects that includes a documented software development plan
3.	Project manager is informed of project status and issues
4.	Corrective action is taken as necessary
5.	Affected groups are involved and agree with all changes to commitments
6.	Senior management reviews all changes to commitments
Abilities	
1.	Software development plan is documented and approved
2.	Project manager explicitly assigns responsibilities for work products and activities
3.	Adequate resources and funding are provided for tracking and oversight activities
4.	Managers are trained
5.	First-line managers understand the technical aspects of the project
Activities	
1.	A documented development plan is used for tracking project activities and communicating status

Exhibit 13.5 Project tracking and oversight.

2.	Revisions to the plan are made using documented procedures
3.	Commitments and changes to commitments, either to individuals or to groups, are reviewed with senior management
4.	Changes to commitments are communicated to all affected individuals and groups according to a documented procedure
5.	The sizes of work products or changes to work products are tracked and corrective action taken when necessary
6.	The effort and cost of the project are tracked and corrective action taken when necessary
7.	Critical computer resources are tracked and corrective action taken when necessary
8.	Project schedule is tracked and corrective action taken when necessary
9.	Technical activities are tracked and corrective action taken when necessary
10.	Risks are tracked and corrective action taken when necessary
11.	Actual measurement and replanning data are recorded
12.	Periodic internal reviews to track technical progress, plans, performance, and issues against the plan are conducted
13	Formal reviews are conducted at selected project milestones according to a documented procedure
Measurements	
1.	Measurements are devised and utilized to monitor management of all tracking and oversight activities
Verification	
1.	Management activities are reviewed periodically with senior management
2.	Management activities are reviewed periodically with project management
3.	Quality assurance audits management of planning activities and reports the results

Exhibit 13.5   (Continued) Project tracking and oversight.

Project Management Tools

Effective project management requires the use of a set of tools that enables plan development and tracking. There are many tools on the market for both stand-alone and enterprise-wide project management. There are several functions that can be automated and integrated by selecting an enterprise-level project management tool:

- Project task planning and tracking
- Resource and time tracking

- Labor hour tracking
- Time capture and billing
- Time reporting
- Project budgeting
- Project communication
- Project documentation

Enterprise-level project management tools allow for tracking multiple people working on multiple projects and aid in identifying cross-project dependencies and issues. They also integrate tasks, resources, and costs into a single repository.

If the management has decided to use time and measurement tools (e.g., project manager, critical path method [CPM], program [or project] evaluation and review technique [PERT], Gantt charts), then the auditor must ensure that these tools are used according to the management's specifications. The use of one of these tools during the SDLC can help the auditor and managers with the time management for the entire project. The auditor can use these charts to help get recommendations through and show the management how much time is needed to implement recommended controls at early and late stages of systems development.

Additional project management tools are task sheets used to allocate time (actual versus forecasted), assign personnel, and log the completion date and cost. In this way, the auditor and management can obtain a more detailed account of the time and money spent on a project and can track what is being worked on and what is finished. Future projects benefit most from these sheets because management can base future SDLC estimates on a history of times and costs (see Exhibit 13.6).

The auditor may often find it easier to enforce controls than standards (e.g., time sheets, CPM, PERT). Unfortunately, standard costs are more difficult to show than control costs. With a control cost, an exposure can be discovered and fixed, but the necessity for a standard is often overlooked because project phases are often completed without the standard.

Project Name: Customer:								Start Date __/__/__
Systems Manager Assigned:								
Lead Analyst Assigned:								End Date __/__/__
		Work Days		Completion Date		Cost		Risk
Design Tasks	*Priority*	*(Est)*	*(Act)*	*(Est)*	*(Act)*	*(Est)*	*(Act)*	*(H/M/L)*
Describe the business or system problem								
Describe the existing environment								
Describe the possible solutions								

Exhibit 13.6 Systems design task list.

Recommend a proposed solution									
Prepare a data flow diagram of the proposed solution									
Determine the educational requirements of users of the system									
Estimate the staff needed to meet the educational requirements									
Define the legal considerations									
Estimate the staff needed to resolve the legal issues									
Define the security and audit requirements									
Prepare a general design and feasibility report									
Estimate the cost and time frame for the next sequential project phases									
Prepare an implementation strategy for the proposed solution									
Prepare a presentation to management on the proposed solution									
Give the presentation to management									
Obtain management approval to proceed to the next phase									
Totals:									
Footnotes:									
Supervisor and review date: ___ /___ /___									

Exhibit 13.6   (Continued) Systems design task list.

Auditor's Role in the Project Management Process

The auditor's role in project management depends on the organization's culture, maturity of the information systems function, and philosophy of the auditing department. The objective of a project management audit is to provide an early identification of those issues that may hinder an on-time, within-budget implementation of an application that is controlled, documented, and able to be operated by an adequately trained user community. Auditing project management requires specific knowledge about the PMLC and development process. Understanding these allows the auditor to identify key areas that would benefit from independent verification. The scope of a project management audit can include an evaluation of the administrative controls over the project (e.g., feasibility results, staffing, budgeting, assignment of responsibilities, project plans, and status reports) or an evaluation of specific deliverables to validate that the project is following established standards. By becoming involved at strategic points, the auditor can ensure a project that is well controlled. If the auditor feels that their knowledge, skills and abilities are not current with the technologies being applied, he or she should request preliminary training on the technology prior to being assigned. Attending training sessions concurrent with the auditee can help gain an understanding of the tools and techniques available to them. The following list highlights some of the key tasks the auditor may perform during a project's development:

- Gain the support and cooperation of the users and IT professionals
- Check project management tools for proper usage
- Perform project reviews at the end of each phase
- Assess readiness for implementation
- Present findings to management
- Maintain independence to remain objective

These tasks can help provide early warning of project management issues. To determine the level of involvement, the auditor should first complete a risk assessment of the project development process and determine the amount of time to be allocated to a particular project. Next, the auditor should develop an audit plan that includes a schedule for the specific review points tied to the project schedule. Finally, the auditor needs to communicate the scope of involvement and any findings to the project manager, users, and IT management. A summary of this entire process is shown in Exhibit 13.7. During the early phases, auditors do not determine how controls will be implemented, but they should establish the review points. This helps IT personnel to better understand audit objectives.

Planning	*Development*	*Implementation and Operation*
Conception of Plan	**Project Coordination**	**System Testing**
Project reasonableness	Initial control recommendations	Test logic of program
Adequate communications	Project budgeting	User involvement
Auditor becomes partner	Time schedules	All eventualities
		Control test process

Exhibit 13.7 **Summary of auditor involvement in systems development phases.**

Project Organization	General Design	Installation
Project team structure	Functional specification relates to business goals	Effects on user
Define responsibilities	User approval of basic system	Resolving user problems
Understand the user	Use of structured programming techniques and best practices	Solidifying procedures
	Specification includes recommended controls	User training
	Insertion of embedded audit routines	
Preliminary Requirements	**Detailed Design**	**Documentation**
Gathering user information	Design relates to functional specification	Allows system operation
Group sessions	Completed documentation	Ease of update
System concept documentation		Complete description of system
		Hierarchical format
Feasibility Study	**Programming**	**System Conversion**
Formal management documentation	Structured programs	Parallel operation of old system
System justifications	Analysis of code	Retention of data
Terminate or proceed	Inclusion of controls	Control data integrity
Cost/Benefit Analysis	**Hardware and Software**	**Postimplementation**
Economic feasibility	Selection process	Solve original business problem
Management approvals	Proper approvals	Perform control analysis
	Adaptability of system	Ensure continued operation
		Maintenance
		Control of changes
		Testing system integrity

Exhibit 13.7   (Continued) Summary of auditor involvement in systems development phases.

Audit Risk Assessment

Depending on the organization, auditors may not have enough time to be involved in all phases of every project. Project involvement will depend on the assessment of process and project risks (see Exhibit 13.8).

The level of risk may be a function of the size of the project, scope of organizational change, complexity of the system being developed, the number of people involved, and the importance of

Process Risks
Lack of strategic direction
Lack of project management standards
Lack of a formal project management process
Negative organizational climate
Project Risks
Resource unavailability and budget
Project complexity and magnitude
Inexperienced staff
Lack of end-user involvement
Lack of management commitment

Exhibit 13.8   Project risk assessment.

the project to the organization. The scope of the audit involvement will depend on the maturity of project management in the organization. Audit involvement may be minimal if the IT group has a well-established PMLC and project office that performs regular oversight and tracking activities. In this case, the auditor may focus more on project-specific risks rather than on project management risks. For less mature organizations, the auditors may take on the role of oversight and tracking for the project.

Audit Plan

The audit plan will detail the objectives and the steps to fulfill the audit objectives. As in any audit, a project management audit will begin with a preliminary analysis of the control environment by reviewing existing standards and procedures. During the audit, these standards and procedures should be assessed for completeness and operational efficiency. The preliminary survey should identify the organization's strategy and the responsibilities for managing and controlling development.

Project Management Process Review

A project management process review would assess the adequacy of the control environment for managing projects. The review points listed represent checkpoints in the project management process. Auditors can use these checkpoints to determine both the status of the project's internal control system and the status of the development project itself. These reviews eliminate the necessity of devoting large amounts of audit resources to the development effort. As long as the development process is well controlled, the need for audit involvement is minimized.

Project Management

Auditors may assist the project manager in identifying project risks and evaluating plans to mitigate and manage risks (e.g., training, devoted resources, management support, and end-user commitment). Auditing can provide management with an independent review of project deliverables (e.g., project charter, task list, schedule, and budget). Auditing may also review the project task list and budget to verify that all project tasks are defined and all milestones have a deliverable.

During the planning phase, the auditor can facilitate communication between functions and raise issues that may impact the quality or timeliness of the project. In a development project, resources from various departments need to come together to implement an automated process that may affect multiple-user functions. Because of various audit projects, auditors develop an overall knowledge of the organization and establish relationships in multiple departments. These relationships are helpful in a development project for making sure the information is flowing between the development team and other functionaries. Consider the following groups:

- Primary users
- Secondary users
- Vendors and consultants
- Programmers and analysts
- Database administrators
- Testing teams
- Computer operations
- Interfacing systems
- Implementation team
- Production support (i.e., maintenance programmers)

Verify that adequate resources are assigned responsibility for tasks and have the time to complete assignments. This includes development, computer operations, user functions, and support functions (e.g., help desk).

Communication

The first area to communicate is the auditor's role in the systems development project. It is very important to make sure that the management and development teams' expectations of the auditor's role are understood and communicated to all participants. To influence the systems development effort, the auditor must develop an open line of communication with both management and users. If a good relationship between these groups does not exist, information might be withheld from the auditor. This type of situation could prevent the auditor from doing the best job possible. In addition, the auditor must develop a good working relationship with the manager, the analysts, and the programmers. Although the auditor should cultivate good working relationships with all groups that have design responsibilities, he or she must remain independent.

Control Recommendations

Throughout the development project, the auditor will be making control recommendations. Depending on the organization's culture, these recommendations may need to be handled informally by reviewing designs with the project team or formally by presenting recommendations to the steering committee. In either case, the auditor must always consider the value of the control recommendation versus the cost of implementing the control. Also, recommendations should be specific, identifying the problem and not the symptom. This allows the proper controls to be implemented and tested.

Recommendations are often rejected because of a time and cost factor. Managers may sometimes feel that implementing an auditor's recommendations will put them behind schedule. The auditor must convince the management that if the recommendations are not implemented, more time and money will be spent in the long run (see Exhibit 13.6). Informing the management of the cost of implementing a control now rather than shutting down the system later to repair it or leaving possible exposures open will help convince management of the need to spend time and money now.

Example of Project Management Checkpoints and Tools in a Telecom Project

It is very hard to avoid new technology implementation in telecommunications projects. Often, the telecommunications manager has to avoid using new, cutting-edge technology for its own sake. The temptation to test new products almost always exists for telecommunications project managers. The success of a design is not measured by how many brand new products it involves; it is measured by how well it works and how well it meets a business need. A good network project manager has the ability to weigh the temptation to use cutting-edge technology against the desire for a solution that is mature, time proven, and stable. It is extremely important that all members of a project realize that the benefits of using a brand new technology may be outweighed by the risk associated with using an unproven product.

A telecommunications project manager should also consider organizational objectives when implementing a telecommunications project. A project's development should not occur in a vacuum, separated from the organizational directives and goals. It is also important for a project manager to convey to his or her team the impact the project will have on the current infrastructure and how its project supports corporate objectives. While supporting corporate objectives, it is equally important that a project manager ensures that his or her project does not become excessively expensive. Respect for project and departmental budgets are definitely a must in telecommunications project management. Often, the greatest technical design in the world is useless if it costs too much money to implement. Managers must consider that as design progresses, for most projects the costs of hardware and software are not the only project-related costs. The costs of tangible equipment or applications are easily calculated. The tougher costs to identify are less tangible and include those associated with training, installation, configuration, and ongoing administration of the design product. Effective telecommunications project management requires identifying the fixed costs and the hidden costs up front, defining a total cost of ownership figure, and then aligning those figures with a design and a given budget.

Combating User Resistance to Telecommunications Project Implementation: Involve the User

In many telecommunications project implementations, a great deal of emphasis is placed on the technical aspects of the implementation and interfaces, and often the entity most affected

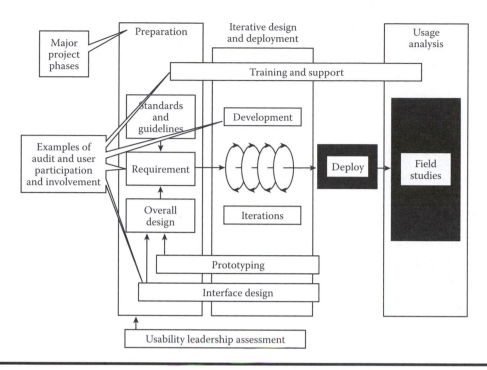

Exhibit 13.9   Methodology for integrating users in the design and deployment phase.

by the project, the end user, is ignored. Essentially, consideration of the end users' needs should be a high priority in the project implementation process. If a telecommunications project manager neglects the consideration of user preferences and inclusion in the project design and execution processes, they run a high risk of user resistance. Often, if end users are not informed or knowledgeable about a project, they can become withdrawn and uncooperative. Exhibit 13.9 graphically describes a good method to combat the user's propensity for rejecting a telecommunications project. Exhibit 13.8 shows that in the three major phases of a project—preparation, iterative design and development, and usage analysis—the user has been integrated. Everything from the user interface to project requirements and training requires input and involvement from the end user. Although all end-user interaction with a project team may not be perfect, certainly including users in the project implementation process can create a more seamless interaction.

Project Management Tools: Project Management Software

A significant element to a successful telecommunications project is the integration of powerful project management software tools. Project management software allows project managers to produce plans and forecasts in graphical, easy-to-read formats. They also help keep the entire project team on task. The complexity of today's projects virtually requires the use of high-powered tools such as Microsoft Project and Open Plan.

One of the project management tools is Microsoft's Project. In the Microsoft Project Website, Microsoft states that this product is a powerful, flexible tool designed to help a project manager manage a full range of projects. The project manager can schedule and closely track all tasks and use Microsoft Project Central, the Web-based companion to Microsoft Project, to exchange project information with the project team and senior management. Some of the benefits and features of Microsoft Project include

- *Personal Gantt chart.* Renders Gantt views such as those in Microsoft Project to outline each team member's own tasks across multiple projects.
- *Task delegation.* Once assigned by the project manager, tasks may be delegated from team leaders to team members or from peer to peer. The delegation feature can also be disabled if desired.
- *View nonworking time.* Team members can report nonworking time to the project manager, such as vacation or sick leave, and also report work time that cannot be devoted to the project.
- *Database performance.* Gets improved performance and access to data with changes to the Microsoft Project database.
- *Network diagram.* Customizes network diagrams with new filtering and layout options, increased formatting features, and enhanced box styles (formerly, the PERT chart).

Microsoft Project is especially useful if an organization currently uses Microsoft Office because Project integrates very well with the Office suite. PowerPoint presentations and Word documents encompassing project charts can be designed and distributed throughout an organization with ease. Essentially, the telecommunications project manager's tasks are streamlined with the use of Microsoft Project.

Another powerful project management tool is Open Plan, a software package designed by Welcom. Open Plan is an enterprise project management system that substantially improves an organization's ability to complete multiple projects on time and on budget. With multiproject analysis, critical path planning, and resource management, Open Plan offers the power and flexibility to serve the differing needs of businesses, resources, and project managers. Welcom also offers a product suite that is designed to be a totally integrated solution for enterprise project environments. The Welcom suite includes Cobra, a cost and earned value management tool, and WelcomHome, a Web-based project collaboration tool. Features of Open Plan and the Welcom suite include*

- Integration with other existing enterprise applications
- Secure multiuser access to data
- Multiproject analysis
- Risk management tools
- Cost analysis applications

The methods for project planning and implementation vary among different organizations. Each telecommunications project manager and team member develops and follows some type of schema for project management. For example, at Chevron Texaco, they implement projects based on Chevron Texaco Project Development and Execution Process (CPDEP, pronounced "chip dip"). The details of this process are somewhat proprietary and privileged; therefore, they cannot be disclosed. However, the methodology of CPDEP is very detailed and seeks to eliminate error and

---

* http://www.welcom.com

project failure by outlining, during each phase of project implementation, what is required and by whom.

A good planning and project management case example is the Stanford University Information Technology Services department. The Network Transport Service project was a major component of a large infrastructure redesign that Stanford conducted, beginning in 1996. The project documentation is very thorough. The scope of the project includes history of Stanford University's network (SUNet) and the problems that were associated with it. An especially attractive element of the project plan is that it outlines what elements would make the project successful, including management commitment, organizational change, and staff training. The goals of the Network Transport Service project include

- Ensuring that the SUNet planning and design process is accountable to the requirements of all areas of campus
- Improving the security, reliability, and functionality of the basic data transport infrastructure at Stanford
- Providing methods to evaluate whether the operational requirements established for the transport system are being met

Finally, the project documentation is complete with a Gantt chart that displays due dates for each element of the project, which spanned over 2 years.

Telecommunications project management requires a great deal of consideration to reach success. The design and budgeting elements must coincide well with business objectives and user needs. The costs and relevance of a project must also be thoroughly considered. Furthermore, a telecommunications project manager may look toward the future study and implementation of technology such as voice-over-IP (VoIP). VoIP can significantly reduce telecommunications costs because it allows organizations to use networking equipment to route data packets as well as voice packets, eliminating the need for separate PBX phone systems. Also, Microsoft's .NET technology may also be a practical future implementation for project managers. The .NET allows organizations to not only securely communicate over long distances but interorganizational transactions to occur automatically via a computer. The telecommunications project manager now has immense options when designing project implementation. In the present business environment, and with the current telecommunications technology available, the telecommunications manager most assuredly should take into account both the organizational and global implications of his or her project.

Conclusion

Developing new applications and/or systems can be a costly and time-consuming endeavor. A well-controlled environment with an overall strategy, standards, policies, and procedures helps ensure the success of IT projects. There are many processes that need to be well controlled to ensure the overall success of a project. There are many opportunities for auditor involvement in the development process, in general, and project management, specifically. Auditors need to develop the skills and relationships to work with the development team to ensure that controls are built into the system. Auditors can assist organizations by reviewing the project management environment—including tools, evaluating standards for project management, monitoring project progress, and evaluating phases in the project.

Review Questions

1. What are the main components of a project plan?
2. What is the intent of the planning phase?
3. When auditors do not have enough time to be involved in every phase of the development project, how do they minimize the project's risk?
4. What are the key causes of system implementation failure?
5. What skills must auditors have to provide a quality audit on a systems development project?

Multiple-Choice Questions

1. The PMLC
   a. Provides a structure for defining requirements and developing applications
   b. Is focused on project scope, schedule, and budget
   c. Is focused on the analysis, construction, and testing of applications
   d. Provides a structure for evaluating IT investments
2. Effective project management ensures that
   a. Processes are explicitly defined, managed, measured, controlled, and effective
   b. Applications are designed, developed, and implemented
   c. Project tasks are defined, and resources are available and completed on time and within budget
   d. The project has included all the costs of the technology solution
3. During the planning phase, the auditor can
   a. Review project deliverables to identify control weaknesses
   b. Review project management processes for appropriateness
   c. Facilitate communication between the project team and senior management
   d. Facilitate communication between functions and raise issues
4. A project management process review would
   a. Assess the adequacy of the control environment for managing projects
   b. Ensure the right solution is selected that integrates with other technology components
   c. Ensure clearly defined requirements in the request for proposal
   d. Ensure projects are completed on time, on budget, and with full functionality
5. Project management tools allow the user to
   a. Track metrics for measuring third-party vendors
   b. Help determine which vendor products to use
   c. Provide a process for governing investments in IT
   d. Define tasks, dependencies, and track progress
6. Key tasks during a project management review are
   a. Check project management tools for proper usage
   b. Assess readiness for implementation
   c. Maintain independence to remain objective
   d. All of the above
7. Which of the following is not a process risk?
   a. Processes are explicitly defined, managed, measured, controlled, and effective
   b. Lack of strategic direction
   c. Lack of project management standards
   d. Negative organizational climate

8. Which of the following is not a project risk?
   a. Review of project deliverables to identify control weaknesses
   b. Inexperienced staff
   c. Lack of management commitment
   d. Project complexity and magnitude
9. One of the biggest obstacles in implementation is
   a. The adequacy of the control environment for managing projects
   b. User resistance
   c. Clearly defined requirements in the request for proposal
   d. Ensuring projects are staffed
10. Project management tools could be
    a. Microsoft Project
    b. Open Plan
    c. CPM or PERT
    d. All of the above

Exercises

1. List and describe key tasks that should be included in a project plan. Consider phases in the development process as well as support tasks that are needed for implementation and maintenance.
2. List and describe the best practices in project management.
3. List and describe possible review areas that auditors may be involved in during the project life cycle.
4. List and describe controls over the project management process.
5. Develop an audit program for auditing the project management process.

Answers to Multiple-Choice Questions

1—b; 2—c; 3—d; 4—a; 5—d; 6—d; 7—a; 8—a; 9—b; 10—d

Further Reading

1. Brown, C.V. and H. Topi, Eds. *IS Management Handbook*, CRC Press, Boca Raton, FL, 2000.
2. Doerscher, T., *2008 PMO 2.0 Survey Report. The Continued Evolution of the Project, Program and Portfolio Management Office (PMO)*, Planview, Inc., 2009.
3. Gomolski, B. and M. Smith, *Program and Portfolio Management: Getting to the Next Level*, Gartner Research, G00155601, Gartner Group, Stamford, CT, November 27, 2006.
4. Light, M. and T. Berg, *The Project Office: Teams, Processes and Tools*, Strategic Analysis Report, Gartner Group, Stamford, CT, August 2000.
5. Singleton, T., What every IT auditor should know about project risk management, Information Systems Audit and Control Association, *JournalOnline*, 2006.
6. Smith, M., *Express IT Project Value in Business Terms Using Gartner's Total Value of Opportunity Methodology*, Gartner Research, G00131216, Gartner Group, Stamford, CT, January 11, 2006.

Chapter 14

Software Development and Implementation

Organizations are constantly building, replacing, and maintaining information systems. There are many different approaches to systems development, but the most successful systems follow a well-defined development methodology. The success of a systems development project is dependent on the success of key processes: project management, analysis, design, testing, and implementation. Because development efforts can be costly, organizations have recognized the need to build well-controlled quality systems. IT processes information that is integral to the financial stability and profitability of organizations. Therefore, these systems must be built with adequate internal controls to ensure the completeness and accuracy of transaction processing.

IT Processes

The COBIT processes (AI1, AI2, AI3, AI4, and AI7) in the Acquire and Implement Domain discuss how software acquisition, development, and implementation processes support an effective IT organization. Exhibit 14.1 lists the control objectives for this section.

Approaches to Software Development

There are various approaches to software development: traditional development, purchasing and modifying a packaged system, prototyping and rapid application development (RAD), and less formal end-user development (EUD). Although each approach is unique, they all have similar steps that must be completed. For example, each approach will have to define user requirements, design programs to fulfill those requirements, verify that programs work as intended, and implement the system. Auditors need to understand the different approaches, the risks associated with a particular approach, and help ensure that all the necessary components are included in the development process.

AI1 Identify Automated Solutions	
Control Objectives	
1.1	Definition and maintenance of business functional and technical requirements
1.2	Risk analysis report
1.3	Feasibility study and formulation of alternative courses of action
1.4	Requirements and feasibility decision and approval
AI2 Acquire and Maintain Application Software	
Control Objectives	
2.1	High-level design
2.2	Detailed design
2.3	Application control and auditability
2.4	Application security and availability
2.5	Configuration and implementation of acquired application software
2.6	Major upgrades to existing systems
2.7	Development of application software
2.8	Software quality assurance
2.9	Applications requirements management
2.10	Application software maintenance
AI3 Acquire and Maintain Technology Infrastructure	
Control Objectives	
3.1	Technological infrastructure acquisition plan
3.2	Infrastructure resource protection and availability
3.3	Infrastructure maintenance
3.4	Feasibility test environment
AI4 Enable Operation and Use	
Control Objectives	
4.1	Planning for operational solutions
4.2	Knowledge transfer to business management
4.3	Knowledge transfer to end users
4.4	Knowledge transfer to operations and support staff

Exhibit 14.1   Processes to acquire and implement.

Software Development Process

A formal systems development process provides an environment that is conducive to successful systems development. This includes (1) an IT strategy that guides developers in building systems that are consistent with the organization's technical and operational goals; (2) standards that guide in the selection of hardware, software, and developing new systems; (3) policies and procedures that support the organization's goals and objectives; and (4) project management that ensures projects are completed on time, within budget, and with expected functionality. Auditors can assist organizations by reviewing the systems development process to ensure that developed systems comply with the organization's strategy and standards.

Prototypes and Rapid Application Development

In general, prototyping includes the transformation of the user's basic requirements into a working model, the revision and enhancement of the model, and the decision to accept the model as the final simulation of the actual system to be built. The model should show how the design would work in real life and provide insight into why the design is successful. The prototype can facilitate interaction between the users, system analysts, and the auditor. These techniques can be applied to production report development, a specific application module, or the entire support system. The advantages of prototyping include the following:

- Models can be viewed and analyzed before commitment of large funding for systems.
- User approval and final satisfaction is enhanced because of increased participation in the design of the project.
- The cost of modifying systems is reduced because users and designers can foresee problems earlier and are able to respond to the users' rapidly changing business environment.
- A rudimentary prototype can be redesigned and enhanced many times before the final form is accepted.
- Many systems are designed "from scratch" and no current system exists to serve as a guide.

Because prototypes appear to be complete when presented to the users, programmers may not be given adequate time to complete the system and implement the prototype as the final product. Often the user will attempt to use the prototype instead of the full delivery system. The user must understand that the prototype is not a completed system. Risks associated with prototyping and RAD include

- Incomplete system design
- Inefficient processing performance
- Inadequate application controls
- Inadequate documentation
- Ineffective implementations

End-User Development

End-user developed applications are created, operated, and maintained outside of the IT organization. There are many factors that have led the end user to build their own systems. First, and probably foremost, is the shift in technology toward personal computers (PCs) and fourth-generation programming languages. This shift has been due, in part, to the declining hardware and software costs that have enabled individuals to own computers. Because of this, individuals have become more computer literate. At the same time, users are frustrated with the length of time that it takes for traditional systems development efforts to be completed. Fourth-generation programming languages have provided users with the tools to create their own applications. Examples of EUD include the following:

- *Mainframe-based query tools* that enable the end user to develop and maintain reports. This includes fourth-generation languages such as EZ-TRIEVE and SAS or programmer-developed report generation applications using query languages.
- *Vendor packages* that automate a generic business process. This includes accounting packages for generating financial statements and legal packages for case management.
- *End-user developed applications* using PC-based tools, databases, or spreadsheets to fulfill a department or individual information processing need.

Because PCs seem relatively simple and are perceived as personal productivity tools, their effect on an organization has largely been ignored. In many organizations, end-user developed applications have limited or no formal procedures. End users may not have the background knowledge to develop applications with adequate controls or maintainability. This becomes an issue when organizations rely on user-developed systems for day-to-day operations and important decision making. Coupled with this is the fact that end-user systems are becoming more complex and are distributed across platforms and organizational boundaries. Risks associated with end-user computing include

- Weak security
- Limited backup
- Inefficient use of resources
- Inadequate training
- Inadequate support
- Incompatible systems
- Redundant systems
- Inconsistent reporting across departments
- Reliance on inaccurate information
- Ineffective implementations

Traditional Information Software Development

The traditional approach to systems development is a sequential process with defined phases beginning with the identification of a need and ending with implementation of the system. The traditional approach uses a structured SDLC that provides a framework for planning and developing applications or systems. Although there are many variations of the traditional SDLC, they all have the following common phases in one form or another:

Feasibility. Identify a need and decide whether to make, buy, or do nothing.
Analysis. Define what is required of the new system.

Design. Define how to build the new system to satisfy the requirements.

Construction. Build the new system using the design information.

Testing. Verify that the completed system meets the user's needs.

Implementation. Deliver the completed system to the end users.

Maintenance. Modify the system to correct problems as found or meet changing needs.

Although the traditional development process provides structure and organization to systems development, it is not without risks. The traditional approach can be a long development process that is costly due to the amount of resources and length of time required. The business environment may change between the time the requirements are defined and when the system is implemented. The users may have a long delay before they see how the system will look and feel. To compensate for these challenges, a project can be broken down into smaller subprojects where modules are designed, coded, and tested. The challenge in this approach is to bring all the modules together at the end of the project to test and implement the fully functional system.

Software Development Phases

The systems development process can be broken down into four phases:

1. Planning
2. Development
3. Implementation
4. Maintenance

The planning phase sets the stage for the success of the development effort. If not done properly, the budget and schedule may not be sufficient, the problem may not be adequately defined, the final project may not solve the business problem, and the right people may not be involved. The planning phase of systems development includes the following activities:

Needs analysis. A study to determine whether a new system should be developed

Current system review. A study of the current system to identify existing processes and procedures that will continue in the new system

Conceptual design. Preparation of the proposed system flow and other information illustrating how the new system will operate

Equipment requirements. Hardware configuration needed to process and use the new systems (e.g., processing speed, storage space, and transmission media)

Cost/benefit analysis. Detailed financial analysis of the cost to develop and operate the new system, the savings or additional expense, and the return on investment

Project team formation. Identify people from programming, user departments, and support departments to develop and implement the new system

Project plan. An overall project plan with defined tasks and deliverables to monitor actual results and ensure successful progress

Auditing can be involved in the planning process to develop an understanding of the proposed system, make sure time is built into the schedule to adequately define controls, and verify that all the right people are involved.

There is a definite correlation between a well-managed systems development process and a successful system. The use of a proven systems development methodology increases the probability that the system's internal controls will be effective and reliable. As discussed under the traditional development approach, systems development includes the following phases:

Analysis. Define what is required of the new system.
Design. Define how to build the new system to satisfy the requirements.
Construction. Build the new system using the design information.
Testing. Verify that the completed system meets the needs and functions of the users without fault.
Implementation. Deliver the completed system to the end users; obtain satisfactory feedback.
Maintenance. Modify the system as needed to correct problems or meet changing needs.

Auditing can review the development process to ensure that the software is designed with user requirements documented, that management approves the design, and that the application is tested before implementation. An additional focus is ensuring that the end user is able to use the system based on a combination of skills and supporting documentation.

Analysis

In the analysis phase, the users and systems analysts define the system requirements in terms that can be measured. These same measurable terms will be the basis for the functional testing that will occur later in the development process. The functionality of the existing system is matched with the new functionality and the requirements are defined and validated with the user so that they can become the basis for the design phase. A good checkpoint for IT auditors is to ensure that in the analysis, defining security requirements is included. Identify and document security requirements early in the development life cycle and make sure that subsequent development artifacts are evaluated for compliance with those requirements. When security requirements are not defined, the security of the resulting system cannot be effectively evaluated and the cost to retrofit into the system later in its life cycle can be extremely costly.

Design

In the design phase, the systems analyst defines all system interfaces, reporting, and screen layouts, and specific program logic. At this time, controls should also be defined for input points and processing. Screen layouts, controls, and reports should be reviewed and approved by the user before moving on to the next phase. Programmers will use the detailed specifications from the design phase for the construction phase.

Construction

The construction phase is complete once the programmer completes the program construction and validates the construction through individual unit testing. The program is tested for both syntax and logic flow. All logic paths are exercised to ensure error routines work and the program terminates processing normally.

Testing

During the testing phase, the system is tested to verify that it works as intended and meets design specifications. An overall testing strategy should be developed to define the individual test events, roles and responsibilities, test environment, problem reporting and tracking, and test deliverables. Although each project may define different test events, in general, test events include unit testing, integration testing, technical testing, functional testing, and acceptance testing (see Exhibit 14.2).

Each test event should have a plan that defines the test-scope resources (people and environment) and test objectives with expected results. It should provide test case documentation and a test results report. It is often desirable to have the end user participate in the functional testing.

Within this area, the quality of testing within each application and at the integration stage is extremely important. The four fundamental tests mentioned earlier should be applied and documented. At minimum, the thoroughness of the level of testing should be completed and reviewed by the development team and quality assurance staff.

Also, US-Cert, in its March 2011 list, advocates the use of model threats. Use threat modeling to anticipate the threats to which the software will be subjected. Threat modeling involves identifying key assets, decomposing the application, identifying and categorizing the threats to each asset or component, rating the threats based on a risk ranking, and then developing threat mitigation strategies that are implemented in designs, code, and test cases.

Test Event	Objectives
Unit testing	Unit testing verifies that stand-alone programs match specifications. Test cases should exercise every line of code.
Integration testing	Integration testing verifies that all software and hardware components work together. Data are passed from one program to the next. All programs and subroutines should be tested during this phase. Test cases should cover all components (e.g., hardware and software).
Functional testing	Functional testing verifies that the application meets user requirements. Test cases should cover screens, navigation, function keys, online help, processing, and output (reports, files, and screens).
Technical testing	Technical testing verifies that the application works in the production environment. Test cases should include error processing and recovery, performance, storage requirements, hardware compatibility, and security (e.g., screens, data, and programs).
Acceptance testing	Acceptance testing verifies that acceptance criteria defined during the project definition stage are tested. Test cases should include system usability, management reports, performance measurements, documentation and procedures, training (e.g., users, help desk, production support, and operations), and system readiness (operations/systems sign-off).

Exhibit 14.2   Testing events.

System Documentation

System documentation helps maintenance programmers to understand the system, correct problems, and make enhancements. Documentation builds at each phase in the development process. The initial justification defines the application functionality, which is converted into program specifications for creating test cases and is used for implementation training. Documentation can be created as flowcharts, graphs, tables, or text for organization and ease of reading. Documentation may include

- Source of the data
- Data attributes
- Input screens
- Data validations
- Data selection criteria
- Security procedures
- Description of calculations
- Program design
- Interfaces to other applications
- Control procedures
- Error handling
- Operating instructions
- Archive, purge, and retrieval
- Backup, storage, and recovery

Implementation

The final step to implementing the system includes conversion, documentation, training, and support. To ensure smooth implementation, it is important that users and technical support people receive adequate training. To facilitate this training, both system and user documentation need to define the functionality of the system. Components of implementation include

Strategy. Covers who, what, when, where, and how of the implementation process
Conversion. Defines the procedures for correcting and converting data to the new application
Documentation. Includes both user and system support procedures
Training. Includes end users, computer operators, and maintenance programmers
Support. Includes help desk and problem reporting

Strategy

An implementation strategy should be documented to guide the implementation team and users in the implementation process. The strategy should cover resources required, roles and responsibilities, the means of communication between the implementation team and users, the methods of training, and a schedule of the various events.

Conversion

Unless a process is new, existing information will need to be converted into the new system. Conversion is the process where this information is either entered manually or transferred programmatically from the old system to the new system. In either case, the existence of procedures should verify the conversion of all records and the accuracy of data entered into the new system.

Documentation

Documentation consists of descriptions of procedures, instructions to personnel, flowcharts, data flow diagrams, display or report layouts, and other materials that can describe an overall system. System documentation should provide maintenance programmers with enough information to understand how the system works to decrease the learning cycle and speed up analysis of program changes. User documentation should include both automated and manual workflow for initial training and ongoing reference. In both cases, documentation should be updated as the system is modified.

Training

Training is an important aspect of any project implementation. According to a Gartner Group study, the cost of not training will far exceed the investment organizations will make to train both end users and IS professionals in new technologies. One reason for this paradox is that users who are forced to learn on their own take as much as six times longer to become productive with the software product. The Gartner Group study also showed that an effective training program reduces support costs by three to six times because users make fewer mistakes and have fewer questions.

Support

Along with training, ongoing user support is another important component needed to ensure a successful implementation. The previously mentioned Gartner Group study found that the need for support is inelastic, and the gap between "needed-" and "formal" support will be filled by "underground support." This underground support, which is informal support by peers or department-purchased outsourcing, accounts for as much as 30% of user computing costs.

System Implementation Process

The purpose of the system implementation process is to verify that the solution meets its intended purpose. Implementing a system consists of configuring the system, testing functionality, converting data, training users, and preparing for production support. It is another key IT audit review point because implementation is often where critical controls may be overwritten or deactivated to bring the system up and operational to meet organizational needs and requirements. Good planning and requirement definitions, management support, end-user involvement and support, and management of the configuration are the elements that contribute to successful implementation. Search any of the U.S. Government Accountability Office (GAO) reports as shown in Appendix II, news magazines such as *InfoWorld*, *Computer World*, and *Network World*, Auerbach Publications, and other sources where you can read about those system implementations that are successful and those that fail, and the lessons to be learned.

The implementation phase not only includes implementing the system itself but also guarantees that it meets its purpose, it works, and that the necessary process and procedures are in place for production. To ensure a well-controlled system implementation, the following controls should be included in the system implementation process:

- Implementation approach
- System testing

- User processes and procedures
- Management reports and controls
- Problem management/reporting
- User acceptance testing
- Help desk and production support training and readiness
- Data conversion and data correction processes
- Operational procedures and readiness
- Security

A well-controlled implementation phase minimizes production issues such as system bugs, performance issues, misunderstood expectations, and misaligned staffing.

Implementation Approach

An implementation approach should be documented to guide the implementation team and users in the implementation process. The strategy should cover the implementation schedule, the resources required, roles and responsibilities of the implementation team, the means of communication between the implementation team and users, decision processes, issue management procedures, and a training plan for the implementation team and end users.

System Testing

Testing is by far the most critical part of any system implementation. However, it is also the first to get short-changed when go-live dates get challenged. The primary purpose of testing is to validate that the system works as expected and identify bugs at an early stage because bugs discovered later are costly to fix. The testing plan should address the effects on online help functions and user manuals, as well as installation and operational guidelines.

An overall testing strategy should be developed to define the individual test events, roles and responsibilities, test environment, problem reporting and tracking, and test deliverables. The testing process should be based on existing testing methodologies established by the organization. An effective testing process allows for documentation that will prevent duplicate testing efforts.

A testing plan should be made in accordance with the organization's standards and should include test scenarios, the role of the test participants, acceptance criteria, and testing logistics. All types of users should perform testing and they should not be developers. The testing plan should also identify responsibility for documentation, review, and approval of tests and test results. End users and system owners should sign off that appropriate testing was performed with expected results for all requirements. Senior management sign-off is required when programs are promoted to production with known errors.

Although each application may define different test events, in general, test events include unit testing, integration testing, technical testing, functional testing, and acceptance testing (see Exhibit 14.2).

The test scenarios, associated data, and the expected results should be documented for every condition and option. Test data should include data that is representative of relevant business scenarios, which could be real or generated test data. Regardless of the type of test data chosen, it should represent the quality and volume of data that is expected. However, controls over the production data used for testing should be evaluated to ensure that the test data are not misused or compromised.

Performance and load testing defines and tests the performance expectations in advance. It ensures that the application is scalable (functionally and technically). It also ensures that applications can be implemented without disruption to the business. The entire infrastructure should be represented in performance and load testing to ensure capacity and throughput at all levels: central processing, input and output media, networks, and so on. The test environment should reflect the live environment as much as possible.

User Processes and Procedures

User reference materials and procedures should be included as part of the development and maintenance of associated applications. They should be reviewed and approved as part of acceptance testing. User reference materials should be designed for all levels of user expertise and should instruct them on the use of the application. The documentation should be kept current as changes are made to the dependent systems.

Management Reports and Controls

The development of management reports and their associated controls needs to be included within the scope of the system implementation. The reports generated should be aligned with business requirements. The reports should be relevant to ensure effectiveness and efficiency of the report development effort.

In general, report specifications should include its recipients, usage, required details, and frequency, as well as the method of generation and delivery. The format of the report needs to be defined so that the report is clear, concise, and understandable. Each report should be validated to ensure that it is accurate and complete. The control measures for each report should be evaluated to ensure that the appropriate controls are implemented so that availability, integrity, and confidentiality are assured.

Problem Management/Reporting

No matter how well a system is tested, there will always be problems discovered after implementation. There needs to be a way for the users to report system problems to the programmers, and in turn for the programmers to communicate to the users when the problem has been fixed. It ensures that problems are resolved and the causes are investigated to prevent their reoccurrence.

A problem management system should consist of audit trails for problems and their solutions, timely resolution, prioritization, escalation procedures, incident reports, accessibility to configuration, information coordination with change management, and a definition of any dependencies on outside services.

The problem management process should ensure that all unexpected events (errors, problems, etc.) are recorded, analyzed, and resolved in a timely manner. Incident reports should be established in the case of significant problems.

Escalation procedures ensure that problems are resolved in the most timely and efficient way possible. Escalation procedures include prioritizing problems based on the impact severity as well as the activation of a business continuity plan when necessary.

Problems should be traceable from the incident to the source cause (e.g., new software release and emergency change). The problem management process should be closely associated with change management.

User Acceptance Testing

User acceptance testing is a key to a successful system implementation. It ensures that the application fulfills the agreed-upon functional expectations of the users, meets established usability criteria, and satisfies performance guidelines before being implemented into production. Acceptance testing minimizes the risks that the new application will cause business interruptions or be disjointed with business processes. Acceptance testing should include all components of the system (facilities, application software, procedures, etc.).

Acceptance Team

The process owner should establish the acceptance team. The team is responsible for developing and implementing the acceptance process. The acceptance team should be composed of representatives from various functions including developers, IT operations, technical support, capacity planning, the help desk, and database administration.

Agreed-Upon Requirements

Requirements for acceptance testing need to be identified, prioritized, and agreed upon. Indirectly, the acceptance requirements become the criteria for making go/no-go decisions for determining if the system satisfies the critical requirements before being implemented.

Acceptance criteria should be specific with detailed measures. Acceptance plans should include inspections, functional tests, and workload trials. Ideally, users should use actual samples of their work in designing and executing acceptance tests.

Management Approval

Acceptance plans and test results need to be approved by the affected functional department as well as the IT department.

To avoid surprises, users should be involved in system testing throughout the development processes. This minimizes the risk of key functionality being excluded or having it not work.

Help Desk and Production Support Training and Readiness

Help desk and production support processes ensure that any problems experienced by the user are appropriately resolved in a timely manner. A help desk function should provide first-line support to end users. It should provide the ability for customers to ask questions and receive effective answers. Help requests should be monitored to ensure that all problems are resolved in a timely manner. Trend analysis should be conducted to identify patterns in problems or solutions. Problems should be analyzed to identify root causes. Procedures need to be in place for escalating problems based on inadequate response or level of impact. Questions that cannot be resolved immediately should be escalated to higher levels of management or expertise.

All problems should be recorded with the help desk to allow for their complete analysis and resolution. Problems should be monitored to ensure that they are resolved in a timely manner. The help desk function should work closely with the problem management function.

Organizations with established help desks will need to staff and train help desk personnel to handle the new application. Good training will minimize the volume of calls to the help desk and thereby keep support costs down. Help desks can be managed efficiently with the use of problem management software, automated telephone systems, expert systems, e-mail, voice-mail, and fax.

Training is an important aspect of any project implementation. According to a Gartner Group study, the cost of not training will far exceed the investment organizations will make to train both end users and IS professionals in new technologies. One reason for this paradox is that users who are forced to learn on their own take as much as six times longer to become productive with the software product. The Gartner Group study also showed that an effective training program reduces support costs by three to six times because users make fewer mistakes and have fewer questions.

Ongoing user support is another important component needed to ensure a successful implementation. The previously mentioned Gartner Group study found that the need for support is inelastic, and the gap between needed- and formal support will be filled by "underground support." This underground support, which is informal support by peers or department-purchased outsourcing, accounts for as much as 30% of user-computing costs. Ongoing support materials can include quick reference guides, access to answers to commonly asked questions, or the ability to call a subject matter expert.

Data Conversion and Data Correction Processes

Unless a process is new, existing information will need to be converted to the new system. Conversion is the process whereby this information is either entered manually or transferred programmatically from the old to the new system. In either case, the existence of procedures should verify the conversion of all records and the accuracy of data entered into the new system.

A data conversion plan defines how the data are collected and verified for conversion. Before conversion, the data should be "cleaned" to remove any inconsistencies that introduce errors during the conversion or when the data are placed in the new application.

Tests to be performed include comparing the original and converted files and checking the compatibility of the converted data with the new system, and ensuring transactions affecting both converted and not-yet unconverted data. This will keep the data current during the period between initial conversion and final implementation. A detailed verification of the processing with the converted data in the new system should be performed to confirm successful implementation. The system owners are responsible for ensuring that data are successfully converted.

The data conversion process often gets intermingled with data cleanup. Data cleanup is a process that companies embark upon to ensure that the most accurate and complete data get transferred into the new system. A common example is company names in a vendor file. A company can be input into a vendor file multiple times in multiple ways. For example, "ABC Manufacturing" can be "ABC mfg," "abc Mfg.," and so on. Many of these data cleanup changes can be dealt with systematically because many errors happen consistently.

Ideally, the data cleanup effort should happen before planning for data conversion. This allows the conversion programmers to focus on converting the data as opposed to coding for data differences. However, in reality, the exemptions from data conversion become issues for the data cleanup team to deal with. Data conversion and data cleanup teams should work closely with one another to ensure that the most accurate and complete data are converted. Management should sign off on test results for converted data as well as approve changes identified by the data cleanup team.

Operational Procedures and Readiness

System documentation ensures maintainability of the system and its components and minimizes the likelihood of errors. Documentation should be based on a defined standard and consist of descriptions of procedures, instructions to personnel, flowcharts, data flow diagrams, display or report layouts, and other materials that describe the system. System documentation should provide maintenance programmers with enough information to understand how the system works to ensure effective and efficient analysis of program changes and troubleshooting. Documentation should be updated as the system is modified.

The processing logic should be documented in a manner that is understandable, using pseudocode, flowcharts, and so on, while containing sufficient detail to allow programmers to accurately support the application. The software must also include documentation within the code, with descriptive comments embedded in the body of the source code. These comments should include cross-references to design documentation and requirements documents. The documentation should describe the sequence of programs and the steps to be taken in case of a processing failure.

System documentation helps maintenance programmers understand the system to correct problems and make enhancements. Documentation builds at each phase in the development process. The initial justification defines the application functionality that is converted into program specifications and used to create test cases. Test cases are used for implementation training and exercises. Documentation can be created as flowcharts, graphs, tables, or text for organization and ease of reading. Documentation may include

- Source of the data
- Data attributes
- Input screens
- Data validations
- Data selection criteria
- Security procedures
- Description of calculations
- Program design
- Interfaces to other applications
- Control procedures
- Error handling
- Operating instructions
- Archive, purge, and retrieval
- Backup, storage, and recovery

IT Disaster/Continuity Plans

This is another key review point for both management and the IT auditor and security personnel. As part of the system implementation, requirements for its recovery in the event of a disaster or other disruption should be accounted for. IT continuity plans should be reviewed to ensure that the company plans incorporate the resources necessary to recover the new application. Significant upgrades to existing applications may also require modification to disaster recovery requirements in areas such as processor requirements, disk storage, or operating system versions. Recovery procedures related to the new application should be tested as soon as possible after it is put into production.

In the rush to implement a system, documentation and procedures can be the first to "slide." However, the price is paid when decisions to address problems become reactionary. Formalizing documentation and procedures is the difference between delivering a technology versus delivering a service. This plan should be in place at the point of implementation and carried through into operations.

Security

When new systems are developed, appropriate security access controls need to be developed. Additionally, existing security processes, procedures, and controls may need to be reviewed. The goal of application security is to safeguard information against unapproved disclosure or modification, and damage or loss.

Logical access controls are used to ensure that access to systems, data, and programs is limited to appropriate users and IT support personnel. Application security should consider privacy and confidentiality requirements, authorization and authentication processes, business access requirements, user training, and monitoring.

In one case, a packaged enterprise resource planning (ERP) software implementation caused a company to revisit its authentication process and standards, security management process, and information access practices. Authentication was previously provided by each application. As a consequence of implementing a package, the company decided to consolidate authentication from many systems into one system using Lightweight Directory Access Protocol (LDAP). Based on that decision, the process for approving access needed to be consolidated to ensure consistency in policies and practices. Finally, information access practices needed to be revisited due to the combination of various types of data and users into one system. Data that were once specific to only one group in their individual application were now contributed to and needed by multiple departments.

Also, one must keep in mind that development efforts generate code. Organizations must understand that this is where security and control of any system starts. In March 2011, US-Cert issued its top 10 Secure Coding Practices. These practices should be adhered to as one starts, designs, develops, tests, implements, and maintains their system:

1. *Validate input.* Validate input from all untrusted data sources. Proper input validation can eliminate the vast majority of software vulnerabilities. Be suspicious of most external data sources, including command line arguments, network interfaces, environmental variables, and user-controlled files.
2. *Heed compiler warnings.* Compile code using the highest warning level available for your compiler and eliminate warnings by modifying the code [C MSC00-A, C++ MSC00-A]. Use static and dynamic analysis tools to detect and eliminate additional security flaws.
3. *Architect and design for security policies.* Create a software architecture and design your software to implement and enforce security policies. For example, if your system requires different privileges at different times, consider dividing the system into distinct intercommunicating subsystems, each with an appropriate privilege set.
4. *Keep it simple. Keep the design as simple and small as possible.* Complex designs increase the likelihood that errors will be made in their implementation, configuration, and use. Additionally, the effort required to achieve an appropriate level of assurance increases dramatically as security mechanisms become more complex.

5. *Default deny.* Base access decisions on permission rather than exclusion. This means that, by default, access is denied and the protection scheme identifies conditions under which access is permitted.

6. *Adhere to the principle of least privilege.* Every process should execute with the least set of privileges necessary to complete the job. Any elevated permission should be held for a minimum time. This approach reduces the opportunities an attacker has to execute arbitrary code with elevated privileges.

7. *Sanitize data sent to other systems.* Sanitize all data passed to complex subsystems [C STR02-A] such as command shells, relational databases, and commercial off-the-shelf (COTS) components. Attackers may be able to invoke unused functionality in these components through the use of SQL, command, or other injection attacks. This is not necessarily an input validation problem because the complex subsystem being invoked does not understand the context in which the call is made. Because the calling process understands the context, it is responsible for sanitizing the data before invoking the subsystem.

8. *Practice defense in depth.* Manage risk with multiple defensive strategies, so that if one layer of defense turns out to be inadequate, another layer of defense can prevent a security flaw from becoming an exploitable vulnerability and/or limit the consequences of a successful exploit. For example, combining secure programming techniques with secure runtime environments should reduce the likelihood that vulnerabilities remaining in the code at deployment time can be exploited in the operational environment.

9. *Use effective quality assurance techniques.* Good quality assurance techniques can be effective in identifying and eliminating vulnerabilities. Fuzz testing, penetration testing, and source code audits should all be incorporated as part of an effective quality assurance program. Independent security reviews can lead to more secure systems. External reviewers bring an independent perspective, for example, in identifying and correcting invalid assumptions.

10. *Adopt a secure coding standard.* Develop and/or apply a secure coding standard for your target development language and platform.

Auditor's Role in the Development Process

Auditor involvement may vary from project to project and auditors may not be involved in every systems development project. Each systems development project will need to be risk assessed to determine the level of audit's involvement. The type of review will also vary depending on the risks of a particular project. Auditors may only be involved in key areas or the entire development project. In any case, auditors need to understand the development process and application controls to add value and ensure adequate controls are built into the system. Auditors can take on two different roles in a systems development project: control consultant or independent reviewer. As a control consultant, the auditor becomes a member of the development team and works with analysts and programmers to design application controls. In this role, the auditor is no longer independent of the development team. As an independent reviewer, the auditor should have no design responsibilities and not report to the project team, but can provide recommendations to be acted on or not by the project manager.

Software development audits are performed to evaluate the administrative controls over the authorization, development, and implementation of new applications and review the design of the controls/audit trails of the proposed system.

The scope of a systems development audit can include an evaluation of the software development life cycle or an evaluation of the quality of the deliverables from each systems development and implementation phase (e.g., an evaluation of the controls design and audit trails, systems test plan and results, user training, and systems and program documentation).

Recommendations from systems development audits might include improvements in user requirements, application controls, or the need to document test plans and expected test results.

Developing new systems can be a costly and time-consuming endeavor. A well-controlled environment with an overall strategy, standards, policies, and procedures helps ensure the success of development efforts. There are many processes that need to be well controlled to ensure the overall success of an application: analysis, design, testing, and implementation. Because of the cost to implement controls after a system has already gone into production, controls should be defined before a system is built.

There are many opportunities for auditor involvement in the development process. Auditors need to develop the skills and relationships to work with the development team to ensure that controls are built into the system. Auditors can assist organizations by reviewing the systems development environment, evaluating standards for systems development, and evaluating phases in the systems development process. Auditors can assist management by reviewing critical systems for input, processing, and output and verifying that the new system provides an adequate audit trail. The auditor's role in a systems development project depends on the organization's culture, maturity of the IS function, and philosophy of the auditing department.

Auditing systems development requires specific knowledge about the development process and application controls. Understanding the development process allows the auditor to identify key areas that would benefit from independent verification. Understanding application controls allows the auditor to evaluate and recommend controls to ensure complete and accurate transaction processing.

By becoming involved at strategic points, the auditor can ensure that a system is well controlled and auditable. The following list highlights some of the key tasks the auditor may perform during a system's development:

- Review user requirements
- Review manual and application controls
- Check all technical specifications for compliance with company standards
- Perform design walk-throughs at the end of each development phase
- Submit written recommendations for approval after each walk-through
- Ensure implementation of recommendations before beginning the next phase
- Review test plans
- Present findings to management
- Maintain independence to remain objective

These tasks can help minimize control weaknesses and problems before the system becomes operational rather than after it is in use.

To determine the level of involvement, the auditor should first complete a risk assessment of the systems development process and determine the amount of time to allocate to a particular development project. Next, the auditor should develop an audit plan that includes a schedule for the specific review points tied to the development schedule. Finally, the auditor needs to communicate the scope of involvement and any findings to development, users, and management.

Risk Assessment

Depending on the organization, auditors may not have enough time to be involved in all phases of every development project. Involvement will depend on the risk assessment of the process risks and the system risks.

Process risks:

- Lack of strategic direction
- Lack of development standards
- Lack of a formal systems development process
- Negative organizational climate

Application risks:

- Application complexity and magnitude
- Inexperienced staff
- Lack of end-user involvement
- Lack of management commitment

The level of risk may be a function of the need for timely information, complexity of the application, and the degree of reliance for important decisions, the length of time the application will be used, and the number of people who will use it.

The scope defines which aspects of a particular application are covered by the audit. Depending on the risk, the scope may include requirements, design and testing deliverable reviews, application controls, operational controls, security, problem management, change controls, or postimplementation review.

Audit Plan

The audit plan will detail the objectives and the steps to fulfill the audit objectives. As in any audit, a systems development audit will begin with a preliminary analysis of the control environment by reviewing existing standards and procedures. During the audit, these standards and procedures should be assessed for completeness and operational efficiency. The preliminary survey should identify the organization's strategy and the responsibilities for managing and controlling applications. The auditor can provide reasonable assurance that the following tasks are performed with regard to the systems development:

- Compliance with standards and procedures
- Efficient and economical operation
- Conform systems to legal requirements
- Include the controls necessary to protect against loss or serious error
- Provide the controls and audit trails needed for management, auditor, and operational review
- Document the system: provide an understanding of the system that is required for appropriate maintenance and auditing

Software Development Controls Review

A software development controls review would assess the adequacy of the control environment for developing effective systems. The following areas would be covered:

- Development standards
- Testing strategy
- Implementation and training
- Problem management
- Change management

The review points listed represent checkpoints in the systems development process. Auditors can use these checkpoints to determine both the status of the application control system and the status of the development project itself. These reviews eliminate the necessity of devoting large amounts of audit resources to the development effort. As long as the development process is well controlled, the need for audit involvement is minimized.

Software Development Life Cycle

For any kind of a partnership involving auditors, users, and IS management, it is important that the organization establish a formal procedure for the development of a system. Without a formal SDLC, complete with defined phases of development and specified points for review and evaluation, the auditor's job is much more difficult and recommendations are not as readily accepted.

- Auditor influence is significantly increased when there are formal procedures and required guidelines identifying each phase and project deliverable in the SDLC and the extent of auditor involvement.
- Auditors will be able to review all relevant areas and phases of the SDLC, identify any missing areas for the development team, and report independently to management on the adherence to planned objectives and procedures.
- Auditors can identify selected parts of the system and become involved in the technical aspects based on their skills and abilities.
- Auditors can provide an evaluation of the methods and techniques applied in the systems development process, as defined earlier.

Analysis

The project team should expend considerable effort toward the analysis of the business problem and what the system is to produce without initially attempting to develop the design of the system. The auditor should observe that the primary responsibility is not to develop a product but to satisfy the user. Often, the user does not understand what is truly needed. Only by understanding the user's business, its problems, goals, constraints, weaknesses, and strengths can the project team deliver the product the user needs. Auditors can participate by reviewing requirements, and verifying user understanding and sign-off.

Design

The auditor may review the design work to make sure that the user's requirements are met. The system's design may also be reviewed for any possible exposures or forgotten controls and for adherence to company standards (company standards should be documented as part of the SDLC methodology and defined before the beginning of the project). If an exposure is found, the auditor should recommend the appropriate controls or procedures.

A technique that brings users and project team members together for an intensive workshop in which they create a system proposal into a detail design is called Joint Application Design (JAD). Usually a trained JAD facilitator, having some claim to neutrality, takes the group through formatted discussions of the system. The auditor may be an active participant in this process. The result of the JAD session is a user view of the system for further development. This is an excellent setting for the discussion of the advantages and cost effectiveness of controls. In addition, analysis time is compressed, discrepancies resolved, specification errors reduced, and communications greatly enhanced. Auditors can review deliverables and recommend application controls. Application controls are discussed in more detail in Chapter 16.

Construction

The auditor may review the new system's programs to verify compliance with programming standards. These standards help ensure that all the code has a similar structure, tracking dependencies and making maintenance easier. The auditor may review a sample of programs to verify that the standards are being followed and that the programs conform to systems design. In addition, programs may be checked for possible control exposures and for the placement of proper controls per design. If it is determined that controls are needed, the auditor should make recommendations, following the same criteria that were used during the design phase. During this phase, however, cost and time factors must be carefully considered because the cost of changing programs to include controls increases as the project progresses.

Testing

The auditor may be called on to assure management that both developers and users have thoroughly tested the system to ensure that it

- Possesses the built-in controls necessary to provide reasonable assurance of proper operation
- Provides the capability to track events through the systems and thus supports audit review of the system in operation
- Meets the needs of the user and management

If the level of testing does not meet standards, the auditor must notify the development team or management who will then take corrective action.

Documentation

The auditor may review system, user, or operating documentation for completeness and accuracy. The maintenance programmers and users should easily understand the documentation. For instance, diagrams of information flow and samples of possible input documents/screens and output reports enhance understanding of the system.

Implementation

The auditor may review the implementation strategy, communication and training material, documentation, conversion procedures, and production readiness. Production readiness may include evaluating the readiness of the system in relation to the results of testing, the readiness of production support programmers, computer operations, and users in terms of training, and the readiness of the help desk with trained staff and a problem-tracking process.

Postimplementation

Once the system is in production, the auditor may survey users to evaluate the effectiveness of the application from a workflow perspective, review error detection and correction procedures to confirm they are working as intended, or perform tests of data to confirm completeness of transaction processing and audit trail.

Change Control

Changes to a system in production come from two sources: problems not detected during testing and change in user requirements. A change control review would evaluate whether problems are reported, tracked, prioritized, and resolved, and whether changes are authorized, tested, documented, and communicated. The following areas would be covered:

- Authorization
- Testing (system and user acceptance)
- Documentation
- Communication

Application Controls

When reviewing the systems development phases, the auditor examines application and manual control points. The user department is responsible for specifying the needed controls and the systems analysts and programmers are responsible for implementing these controls. Although the responsibility for the auditability and controls in the new system lies with the user departments, systems analysis, and programmers, these groups may not have the expertise to design adequate controls into the new system. The auditor should interact with each of these groups during the development process to ensure the adequacy of audit and control provisions. The completion of each of the phases usually corresponds to the key points for auditor involvement.

Communication

The first area to communicate is the auditor's role in the systems development project. It is very important to make sure that the management and development teams' expectations of the auditor's role are understood and communicated to all participants. To influence the systems development effort, the auditor must develop an open line of communication with both management and users. If a good relationship between these groups does not exist, information might be withheld from the auditor. This type of situation could prevent the auditor from doing the best job possible. In addition, the auditor must develop a good working relationship with analysts and programmers. Although the auditor should cultivate good working relationships with all the groups that have design responsibilities, the auditor must remain independent.

Recommendations

Throughout the development project, the auditor will be making control recommendations. Depending on the organization's culture, these recommendations may need to be handled informally by reviewing designs with the project team or formally by presenting recommendations to the steering committee. In either case, the auditor must always consider the value of the control recommendation versus the cost of implementing the control. Also, recommendations should be specific, identifying the problem and not the symptom. This allows the proper controls to be implemented and tested.

Recommendations are often rejected because of a time and cost factor. Managers may sometimes feel that implementing an auditor's recommendations will put them behind schedule. The auditor must convince the management that if the recommendations are not implemented, more time and money will be spent in the long run. Informing management of the cost of implementing a control now, rather than shutting down the system later to repair it or leaving possible exposures open, will help convince the management of the need to spend time and money now.

Audit Report

Depending on the audit scope and the length of the project, interim reports may be needed at the completion of major phases in the development process. Key reporting points include

Planning. Adequacy of the project plan and cost/benefit analysis
Design. Adequacy of the controls and auditability of the design
Testing. Adequacy of the test strategy and completeness of the test objectives
Implementation. Readiness of the system and user components for production
Postimplementation. Effectiveness and efficiency of the live system and whether the initial system criteria were met

If the auditor becomes part of the development team, the team manager would become the auditor's management, and the auditor's reports and recommendations might be modified before being sent to higher management. To remain objective, the auditor should issue reports independent of the project team.

In a publication issued by the U.S. NIST, they state that various SDLC methodologies have been developed to guide the processes involved, and some methods work better than others for specific types of projects. Regardless of the type of the life cycle used by an organization, information security must be integrated into the SDLC to ensure appropriate protection for the information that the system is intended to transmit, process, and store. Security is most useful and cost effective when such integration begins with a systems development or integration project initiation, and is continued throughout the SDLC through system disposal. A number of federal laws and directives require integrating security into the SDLC, including the Federal Information Security Management Act (FISMA) and OMB Circular A-130, Appendix III.

U.S. Federal agencies are advised by NIST in its 2006 guidance *SP 800-100 Information Security: A Handbook for Federal Managers* to implement security integration into the SDLC and their advice is not intended to prescribe any particular model or methodology. Each phase of the SDLC includes a minimum set of information security-related activities required to effectively incorporate security into a system. An organization can either use a generic SDLC as described in this section or develop a tailored SDLC that meets its specific needs. NIST *Special Publication (SP) 800-64 Rev. 1, Security Considerations in the Information System Development Life Cycle* presents a framework for incorporating security into all phases of the SDLC to ensure the selection, acquisition, and use of appropriate and cost-effective security controls.

Conclusion

Developing new systems can be a costly and time-consuming endeavor. A well-controlled environment with an overall strategy, standards, policies, and procedures helps ensure the success of development efforts. There are many processes that need to be followed to ensure the overall success of a project and system: project management, analysis, design, testing, and implementation. Because of the cost to implement controls after a system has already gone into production, controls should be defined before a system is built.

The purpose of the system implementation process is to verify that the solution meets its intended purpose. Implementing a system consists of configuring the system, testing functionality, converting data, training users, and preparing for production support. A number of questions have to be asked before implementation to ensure that a successful and secure transition takes place minimizing any vulnerabilities.

There are many opportunities for auditor involvement in the development process. Auditors need to develop the skills and relationships to work with the development team to ensure that controls are built into the system. Auditors can assist organizations by reviewing the systems development environment, evaluating standards for systems development, monitoring project progress, and evaluating phases in the systems development process. Auditors can assist management by reviewing critical systems for input, processing, output, and verifying that the new system provides an adequate audit trail.

An auditor's role in system implementations is to ensure that risks are identified and proper controls are considered during the implementation process. In some organizations, auditors are members of the implementation team and participate like any other member. In some cases, auditors review documentation at key stages of the implementations. If organizations do not have the resources to include auditors during the implementations, auditors then do postimplementation reviews to test for implemented controls after implementation. In these cases, there is no assurance that the controls implemented were completed or all the risks accounted for. Consequently, identifying risks or recommending controls after a system is implemented is more costly and may limit the organization's ability to implement the most effective controls.

Review Questions

1. What are the primary benefits of systems development standards?
2. What technique is used to bring users and project team members together to create a detail design?
3. Name and describe 10 controls for the system implementation process.

4. What is the purpose of a testing plan? What should be included in a testing plan?
5. Describe the purpose of test data. Compare and contrast the difference between real or generated test data.
6. Describe the purpose of developing user processes and procedures as part of the system implementation. What type of procedures should be included?
7. Why is a help desk and production support critical to system implementations? Discuss its interrelationship with the problem management and reporting system.
8. What risks are associated with data conversion? What controls should be considered in a data conversion process?
9. Name and describe items that should be included as part of operation procedures and documentation.
10. Why is it necessary for maintenance programmers to have good documentation?
11. Why should continuity plans be addressed during an implementation as opposed to after?
12. Describe the benefit of having an IT auditor as part of the system implementation team.

Multiple-Choice Questions

1. A well-controlled implementation minimizes the following risks except
   a. Staff turnover
   b. System bugs
   c. Misaligned staff
   d. Performance issues
2. Which of the following is not a test event?
   a. Functional testing
   b. Negative testing
   c. Unit testing
   d. Acceptance testing
3. The risks associated with prototypes and RAD are
   a. Incomplete system design
   b. Inefficient processing performance
   c. Inadequate documentation
   d. All of the above
4. The following are examples of EUD except
   a. Mainframe-based query tools
   b. Vendor packages that automate a generic business process
   c. Operating systems
   d. End-user developed applications
5. Which of the following is a risk associated with end-user computing?
   a. Weak security
   b. Inadequate support
   c. Inadequate training
   d. All of the above
6. Testing which verifies that the application can be implemented without interruption to business and that there is enough capacity is
   a. Unit testing
   b. Functional testing

   c. Technical testing
   d. Performance and load testing
7. End-user acceptance testing ensures that the system
   a. Fulfills the agreed-upon functional expectations
   b. Meets established usability
   c. Satisfies performance guidelines
   d. Meets state regulations
   e. a, b, and c
8. Conversion is defined as the process of
   a. Cleaning data in the legacy system
   b. Testing data
   c. Transferring data from the legacy system to the new system
   d. Testing data during an implementation
9. What is not considered a form of documentation in a system implementation?
   a. The sequence of programs and steps to be taken in case of processing failure
   b. Code with comments embedded
   c. IS strategy
   d. Pseudocode and flowcharts
10. Key tasks an auditor might perform during systems development are
   a. Reviewing user requirements
   b. Checking all technical specification for compliance with organizational standards
   c. Reviewing test plans
   d. All of the above

Exercises

1. Describe possible approaches to a systems development effort and the advantages and disadvantages of each approach.
2. Describe the general phases of an SDLC and what activities are completed in each phase.
3. Describe the different test events and what aspects of the system are covered during each event.
4. List and describe 10 possible review areas that auditors may be involved in during the development process.

Answers to Multiple-Choice Questions

1—a; 2—b; 3—d; 4—c; 5—d; 6—d; 7—e; 8—c; 9—c; 10—d

Further Reading

1. Hettigei, N., The auditor's role in IT development projects, Information Systems Audit and Control Association, *Inf. Syst. Con. J.*, 4, 2005.
2. Information Systems Audit and Control Foundation, *IT Control Practice Statement: AI-2 Acquiring and Maintaining Application Software*, Information Systems Audit and Control Foundation, February 2002.

3. Information Systems Audit and Control Foundation, *COBIT Audit Guidelines*, Information Systems Audit and Control Foundation, July 2000.

4. Markus, M.L. and C. Tanis, The enterprise systems experience—From adoption to success, In: *Framing the Domains of IT Research: Glimpsing the Future through the Past*, R.W. Zmud, Ed., Pinnaflex Educational Resources, Inc., Cincinnati, OH, 2000.

5. Schiesser, R., *Guaranteeing Production Readiness Prior to Deployment*, Prentice Hall PTR, New York, http://www.informit.com/isapi/product_id·%7B0CF23CBC-CDCC-4B50-A00E-17CBE595 AA31%7D/content/index.asp, verified on August 1, 2003.

6. The Capability Maturity Model Integration, Software Engineering Institute, Carnegie Mellon University, Pittsburgh, PA, December 2001, http://www.sei.cmu.edu/pub/documents/02.reports/pdf/02tr001.pdf.

7. Working Council for Chief Information Officers, Software Quality Assurance Metrics, Corporate Executive Board 2001, Catalog No.: 1-766GM, May 2001.

8. US-CERT, *Top 10 Coding Practices*, Software Engineering Institute, Carnegie Mellon University, https://www.securecoding.cert.org/confluence/display/seccode/Top+10+Secure+Coding+Practices, March 2011.

Chapter 15

IT Sourcing

An organization's reason for acquiring software is to effectively and efficiently support one or more business processes. Before acquiring software, the requirements of these processes should have already been identified. Once the business objectives have been defined for the solution being sought, the process for acquiring software can begin. Both the IT auditor and management need to be aware of the importance of this area and the critical control processes that need to be in place to support and protect the organization.

A critical success factor to purchasing services or products from third parties is a sourcing strategy and supplier management processes. The supplier management process helps ensure that the expected value is delivered from the contract and supplier. The negotiated contract clearly defined service-level agreements (SLAs), performance measures, pricing terms, and escalation processes to effectively manage a third-party supplier. It is also important to have an effective relationship with the supplier and fair contract terms that enable both parties to be successful.

IT Processes

The Control Objectives for Information and Related Technology (COBIT) process (AI5) in the Acquire and Implement Domain discusses how procurement processes support an effective IT organization. Exhibit 15.1 lists the control objectives for this section.

Sourcing Strategy

A sourcing strategy establishes the roadmap for services, hardware, and software contracts. It is important to have a sourcing strategy to avoid conflicting contracts. The sourcing strategy should align to the organization's overall strategy and IT strategy. Alignment of business process outsourcing and IT outsourcing are also critical to avoid conflicting contract terms. For example, conflicts can arise when IT is outsourcing services (horizontal) to a third party and an organization wants to slice off a business segment, location, or process across an IT service (vertical). Contracts can have minimum commitment levels established at the time of the initial contract, and significant volume

AI5 Procure IT Resources
Control Objectives
5.1   Procurement control
5.2   Supplier contract management
5.3   Supplier selection
5.4   Software acquisition
5.5   Acquisition of development resources
5.6   Acquisition of infrastructure, facilities, and related services

Exhibit 15.1   Processes to acquire and implement.

changes can trigger contract renegotiation. Contract renegotiation can be costly in terms of the time required to renegotiate and price/term changes of the contract from reduced volumes. Organizations typically have more negotiating strength with increased volumes.

Another key point to define in the sourcing strategy is will the organization have a single supplier or multiple supplier strategy. Both approaches have advantages and disadvantages that should be considered before engaging in an outsourcing arrangement. A single supplier is easier to govern and should offer better volume discounts. However, having at least two suppliers allows increases competition, and minimizing the risk of a dependency on a single supplier.

Once a sourcing strategy is defined, it is time to develop an understanding of the current state of services and costs to form a baseline for comparison against sourcing arrangements. It is important to look at the total cost of the outsourcing option. This includes the vendor's cost of knowledge acquisition, your cost of time to train the vendors people, communications overhead of offshore connectivity, any new infrastructure required, the ongoing costs of that infrastructure, the overlap with existing staff if downsizing, and any offers made to downsized staff in addition to raw cost of the resources provided.

The key to getting value is to establish a win-win partnership with your vendors. Any contract that does not have a profit for the vendor is doomed to failure. Once the partnership is established, both sides should be looking for additional win-win opportunities and a symbiotic relationship. On the flip side, if the relationship is failing and the win-win is not possible due to inefficiency with the vendor then there must be an exit strategy from the relationship that will allow value to continue with a new vendor with minimized transition costs.

Software Acquisition Process

There has been much written in this area. The software acquisition process should include the identification and analysis of alternative solutions that are each compared with the established business requirements. In general, the acquisition process consists of the following:

■ Defining the information and system requirements
■ Identifying various alternatives
■ Performing a feasibility analysis

- Conducting a risk analysis
- Defining ergonomic requirements
- Carrying out the selection process
- Procuring the selected software
- Completing final acceptance

Defining the Information and System Requirements

One of the greater challenges in procuring or developing any information system is to define its requirements. System requirements describe the needs or objectives of the system. They define the problem to be solved, business and system goals, system processes to be accomplished, and the deliverables and expectations for the system. It includes defining the information being given to the system to process, the information to be processed within the system, and the information expected out of the system. Each should be clearly defined so that later gaps in requirements and expectations are avoided.

Information and system requirements can be captured by interviews, deriving requirements from existing systems, identifying characteristics from related system, and discovering them from a prototype or pilot system. Generally, gathering requirements is accomplished by

- Interviewing the management to understand their expectations for the system as well as to understand the business context within the industry and the company itself
- Interviewing those expected to use the information produced by the system as well as those expected to produce the information input into the system
- Reviewing related paper and electronic forms and reports
- Observing related business processes
- Meeting with IT management and support staff regarding their expectations and constraints for implementing and supporting the system
- Researching other companies in a related industry, of similar company size, and with a similar technical environment to identify best practices and lessons learned

Prototypes and Rapid Application Development

In general, prototyping information systems design includes the transformation of the user's basic requirements into a working model, the revision and enhancement of the model, and the decision to accept the model as the final simulation of the actual system to be built. The model should show how the design would work in real life and provide insight into why the design is successful. The prototype can facilitate interaction between the users, system analysts, and the auditor. These techniques can be applied to production report development, a specific application module, or the entire support system. Advantages of prototyping include the following:

- Models can be viewed and analyzed before commitment of large funding for systems.
- User approval and final satisfaction are enhanced because of increased participation in the design of the project.
- The cost of modifying systems is reduced because users and designers can foresee problems earlier and are able to respond to the user's rapidly changing business environment.

■ A rudimentary prototype can be redesigned and enhanced many times before the final form is accepted.
■ The prototype serves as a guide because many systems are designed "from scratch" and no current system exists to serve as a guide.

Requirements Document

A requirements document is intended to record the requirements and expectations of the system. Although system requirements documents vary in design, each, in general, provides the following information:

The intended users of the system. The users of the system include those who actually interact with it as well as those who use the information that it produces.

The scope and objectives for the system. The scope should be "holistic," incorporating both the technical environment as well as a business perspective.

A statement of the *problem* needing to be solved by the system.

The system goals and objectives. Be sure to include goals and objectives from a technical as well as a business perspective.

Feasibility analysis. Feasibility analysis defines the constraints or limitations for the system from a technical as well as a business perspective. Feasibility should be assessed in the following categories: economic, technical, operational, schedule, legal or contractual, and political. Feasibility can include those things that are tangible, intangible, one-time, or recurring.

Other assumptions made regarding the system such as compliance with existing business practices.

Expected system functions to be provided such as authorizing payments and providing account status.

System attributes such as ease of use, fault tolerance, response time, and integration with existing platforms.

The context or environment in which the system is expected to operate. This includes a description of the system that is expected to fit or interface within the environment (industry context, company culture, technical environment, etc.).

Identifying Various Alternatives

Many options exist in procuring software solutions, which include any combination of the following: purchasing an off-the-shelf product, contracting for development, developing the system in-house, or outsourcing a system from another organization.

Off-the-Shelf Solutions

Purchasing commercially available products requires that the organization's business adapt to the functionality of the system. This business adaptation process requires that the organization could also customize the software product and subsequently maintain those customizations within the processes that have been modified and changed. The advantages of using off-the-shelf products are shorter implementation time, use of proven technology, availability of technical expertise from outside the company, availability of maintenance and support, and easier-to-define costs. The disadvantages include incompatibility between packaged system capabilities and the company's requirements, long-term reliance on a supplier for maintenance and support, specific hardware or software requirements, and limitations on the use or customization of the software.

Purchased Package

Suppliers develop packaged systems for wide distribution that satisfy a generic business problem. For example, a payroll system is somewhat generic for most organizations. Often, a purchased package can satisfy the business needs for much less than developing a system internally. If various packages are available, organizations will develop a request for proposal that defines the system requirements and asks for the supplier's solution to those requirements. Organizations then weigh how well each package meets the business requirements and whether a purchased application makes sense. When selecting a supplier package, organizations should consider the following:

- Stability of the supplier company
- Volatility of system upgrades
- Existing customer base
- Supplier's ability to provide support
- Required hardware or software in support of the supplier application
- Required modifications of the base software

Although packaged applications may appear to be less costly to implement than building a new system internally, there are risks to consider before selecting this option. A packaged application may not meet the majority of the business needs, resulting in extensive modification or changes to business processes. Also, any future releases of this software may require extensive programming to retrofit all of the company-specific code. Because packaged systems are generic by their nature, the organization may need to modify its business operations to match the supplier's method of processing. Changes in business operations may be costly due to training and the new processes may not fit into the organization's culture or other processes.

Contracted Development

Contracted development requires that the organization procure personnel to develop a new system or customize an existing system to the company's specifications. Contracting for systems development can provide increased control over costs and implementation schedules, legal and financial leverage over the contractor, additional technical expertise, and the ability to adhere to company policies, processes, and standards. Disadvantages associated with contracting for development include higher labor costs when compared to in-house staff, turnover of contract staff, business viability of the contracted company, exclusion of maintenance in development costs, and a lack of organizational understanding by the contractor.

Outsourcing a System from Another Organization

Many companies choose to outsource system functionality from another organization. Outsourcing allows the company to cost-effectively remain focused on their core competencies and quickly respond to business needs as well as take advantage of the expertise of another organization. Outsourcing provides increased control over costs without the need to acquire or maintain hardware, software, and related staff. However, outsourcing systems increases reliance on the outsourcer, limits the company to what is provided by the outsourcer, and decreases the ability of the company to acquire related experience and expertise.

Performing a Feasibility Analysis

A feasibility analysis defines the constraints or limitations for each alternative from a technical as well as a business perspective. Feasibility analysis includes the following categories: economic, technical, operational, schedule, legal or contractual, and political. Feasibility can include those matters that are tangible, intangible, one-time, or recurring.

Economic feasibility analysis provides a cost–benefit justification. The expenses of a system include procurement, start-up, project-specific issues, and impact to operations. It includes one-time and recurring costs. Sample of costs include consultants, start-up infrastructure, support staff, application software, maintenance contracts, training, communications, data conversion, and leases. Benefits include cost reduction or avoidance, error reduction, increased speed, improved management decisions, improved response to business needs, timely information, improved organizational flexibility, better efficiency, and better resource utilization.

Technical feasibility analyzes the technical practicality of the proposed system. It evaluates the consistency of the proposed system with the company's technical strategy, infrastructure, and resources. It answers the question of whether the organization has the resources to install and support the solution. Technical feasibility evaluates whether the company has the necessary hardware, software, and network resources to support the application as well as whether it provides reliability and capacity for growth. It also assesses the technical expertise requirements and compares it with those provided by the organization.

Operational feasibility examines how well the proposed system solves business problems or provides opportunities to the business. It also evaluates the extent of organizational changes required to accommodate the system. These changes can include personnel, business processes, and products or services offered.

Legal and contractual feasibility reviews any related legal or contractual obligations associated with the proposed system. Legal constraints include federal or state law as well as industry-related regulations. In addition to any new contract obligations introduced by the new system, existing contracts are also reviewed to ensure that there are no preexisting commitments that regulate the installation or use of the proposed system. Legal counsel should be involved in this process and is one of the critical points for IT auditors to review. Note that the underlying theme is protection of the company and the establishment of the remedy process should the contractor fail to perform or deliver as promised. Organizations looking for assistance in this area should refer to their legal counsel or an organization such as the Computer Law Association whose members specialize in this area.

Political feasibility evaluates how the internal organization will accept the new system. This includes an assessment of the desirability of the system within the organization as well as its fit with the organization's corporate culture.

Conducting a Risk Analysis

A risk analysis reviews the security of the proposed system. It includes an analysis of security threats and potential vulnerabilities and impacts, as well as the feasibility of other controls that can be used to reduce the identified risks. Controls include systematic or automated methods as well as audit trails. Risks, as discussed in other chapters of this book, affect control objectives in the areas of confidentiality and privacy of information, integrity and accuracy of the data, timeliness of the information for decision making, ability to access the system, as well as staff organization and knowledge required to support the system.

Defining Ergonomic Requirements

The goal of ergonomics is to provide a work environment that is safe and efficient for the employee. In the context of a computer system, ergonomics includes the design of the computer workstation and human interface components such as the monitor, keyboard, or mouse. Repetitive motion injuries and eyestrain are two of the most common ergonomic considerations in computer-related systems. A company's risk management or occupational safety department may provide guidelines for ergonomic requirements.

Carrying out the Selection Process

The selection process includes identifying the best match between the available alternatives and the identified requirements. The selection process consists of soliciting proposals from interested providers, evaluating the proposals in terms of the identified requirements, and selecting the best available alternative. The selection process should be structured to ensure that the process would be completed diligently and in a timely manner. If done correctly, the selection process promotes buy-in for the selected solution.

Request for Information

A request for information (RFI) seeks information from suppliers for a specific purpose. However, neither the company nor the suppliers are obligated by the response to the RFI. The RFI serves as a tool for determining the alternatives or associated alternatives for meeting the organization's needs. An RFI often asks suppliers to respond to questions that will assist the organization in obtaining additional relevant information. Information from the RFI may then be used to prepare a request for proposal (RFP).

Request for Bid

A request for bid (RFB) is used to purchase specific goods or services. RFBs are used in cases where multiple suppliers are capable of meeting all of the technical and functional specifications or only one supplier can meet them. In either case, the selection process is solely determined based on cost and schedule requirements. In these cases, contract terms and conditions are more likely to be nonnegotiable or fixed.

Request for Proposal

An RFP is a document that specifies the minimally acceptable requirements (functional, technical, and contractual) as well as the evaluation criteria used in the selection process. An RFP offers flexibility to respondents to further define or explore the requested requirements. RFPs may lead to a purchase or continued negotiation.

Potential suppliers are supplied with copies of the RFP and are requested to submit proposals by a specified date. After a supplier has submitted a proposal, the response cannot be changed. The RFP should be communicated to as many prospective bidders as possible. It should contain the selection criteria that will be used. The criteria should be written with enough detail that it prevents any misunderstanding or misinterpretation. Any specific criterion that will influence the selection must appear in the RFP. The RFP should also describe the members of the selection committee. Any calculations that are required in the submittal should also be included, such as equipment, software, communications, utilities, site preparation, system conversion, file conversion, training, and continued operation of the system.

All questions from bidders should be answered in writing and made available to all bidders. Verbal answers to questions should be avoided. All questions should be received with enough time before the deadline so that answers can be incorporated in the proposal. Public meetings such as "bidder conferences" are used as a means to receive and respond to questions from all prospective bidders. The basic components of an RFP are

- Background information about the company, business problem, and the computing environment. It may also include results of any needs assessment performed.
- Schedule of important dates such as when the supplier's RFP response is due, when the decision is expected, when the actual purchase is expected, and when implementation is expected.
- Contact names and sources for answering questions for the RFP.
- Instructions for formatting the response to the RFP. Some RFPs include an explicit description of what the supplier should and should not include in their response.
- Specific requirements being sought.
- Technical requirements for the system, such as specifications for an operating system or a network environment.
- List of documents required as attachments, such as sample reports and standard contract language.
- Additional requirements for the selection process, such as supplier presentations, supplier demonstrations, or on-site installation and testing.

The entire process listed in the preceding text must be followed to the letter before the next step can be performed. If it is not followed as the company has specified, a "bid protest" could be filed by one of the potential suppliers. Again, this is another audit/management/legal counsel review point before the evaluation process can begin.

Evaluating Proposals

A selection committee of one or more key stakeholders evaluates submitted proposals using a list of objective selection criteria. A list of the objective selection criteria is used as a means for identifying the best match between the product's features and functionality and the identified requirements. The basis for the selection criteria is the user and system requirements. Features and functionality are normally the most significant factors in the decision-making process.

Selection criteria may also include evaluating the consistency of the proposal with the company's business and IT strategy, the breadth of the supplier's products and services, supplier's relevant experience, supplier's customer support, scalability of the solution, supplier viability, total cost of ownership, integration and growth capabilities, and reliability. Supplier viability is one of the most critical factors identified by companies in the selection process.

Participants in the selection process often include representatives from key stakeholders such as management and anticipated users as well as the IT department. The selection committee should consist of representatives that are impartial to any one provider or solution, have knowledge of best practices, and knowledge of the market. However, the participants should not have any conflict of interest and should sign a statement before they serve on the selection committee, indicating that they do not. If they do, someone must replace them who meets the qualifications warranted and does not have a conflict of interest.

Procurement and Supplier Management

Once a technical solution has been selected, the procurement process helps ensure that the right terms and conditions are negotiated. One of the integral processes in any project is the procurement of services, hardware, and software. In most cases, organizations consider whether to make or buy systems. In either case, the procurement of external services is usually required. Depending on the extent of the service, a formal RFP or other requirements document needs to be prepared to request competitive bids. The requirements should include service levels with contract penalties and tracking metrics/success criteria (see Exhibit 15.2).

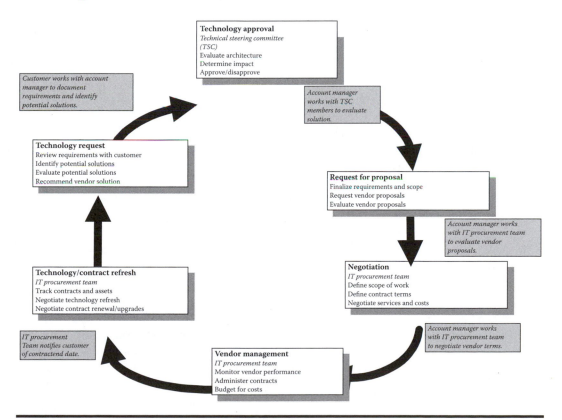

Exhibit 15.2   Procurement and supplier management.

Procuring the Selected Software

The procurement process sounds simple but is actually the most complicated of all the acquisition steps. It requires that the purchase price and conditions be stipulated and agreed upon. These agreements take the form of contracts.

When procuring software, IT managers complain about unpredictable license fees, pressured sales methods, poor technical support, and unclear pricing for ongoing maintenance fees.

Software Contracts and Licenses Agreements are used to document agreements for development, marketing, distribution, licensing, maintenance, or any combination. Contracts can specify a fixed price or a price based on time and materials. Contracts based on time and materials state that the fees charged are directly attributable to actual expenses of time (hourly) or materials. These contracts place more financial risk on the buyer if the initial definition of pricing, the scope or desired requirements are unclear or poorly defined.

Contract terms and conditions normally include the following:

- A functional definition of the work to be performed
- Specifications for input or output designs, such as interfaces, screens, or reports
- Detailed description of the necessary hardware
- Description of the software systems or tools required for development or implementation
- Terms or limitations with the use of any related trademark rights or copyrights
- Requirements for the conversion or transfer of data
- System performance or capacity such as speed, throughput, or storage
- Testing procedures used to identify problems and the results expected to define acceptance. Information and system requirements serve as the basis for defining the acceptance tests
- Supplier staffing and specified qualifications
- Contact and relationship protocols between the buyer and the supplier
- Expected schedules for development, implementation, and delivery
- Methods for providing progress reports, such as meetings or reports
- Definition of deliverables, which includes a clear description of each item to be delivered or provided by the supplier, when it is to be delivered, and any consequences for missed deliverables
- Explicit criteria for defining acceptance of each deliverable as well as for final acceptance
- Requirements and expectations for installation
- Documentation expected to be provided to the supplier or by the supplier as well as any intellectual property rights needed to maintain or customize the documentation
- Training expected to be provided as part of the product or service
- Any applicable warranties or maintenance, including provisions for future versions currently in development
- Any requirements for indemnity or recovery for losses, such as insurances or bonding requirements
- A statement of future support that is to be provided as well as anticipated costs
- Clear definition of ownership or licensing of relevant copyrights and patents
- Terms and conditions related to confidentiality or trade secrets for either party
- Terms or limitations related to staff changing employers from one party to another (e.g., raiding staff)
- Description of payment terms
- Process for accepting changes to contract definition, such as changes in terms, scope, or deliverables

Other Considerations for Software Contracts and Licenses

Software contracts should also address the following:

- Flexibility and choice for upgrades and updates. Some contracts specify required upgrades to receive updates or maintenance.
- SLAs for defining expectations for support and maintenance.
- Annual maintenance costs. Should be fixed at the time of purchase and should not vary.
- Provisions for protecting the company against unforeseen problems such as software interoperability.
- Intellectual property rights for modifications. Customer may not be granted the rights for modifications.
- Terms and conditions for termination options such as what transfer process will take place when the license ends, length of the transition period, and the impacts from the termination.
- Assignment clauses requiring consent. Assignment clauses allow the supplier to segregate the customer's payments from that of the service provider. Under an assignment clause, the supplier can transfer the customer's financial obligations to another firm or ongoing service components to a third party. With the payment and service separated, the supplier's motivation to perform to the terms of the contract may be reduced.
- Verification of any export or import restrictions by customers. Specifically, the export of the specified technology should be allowed by U.S. legal restrictions and the import allowed by the foreign government. The license should specify responsibility for any costs or duties.
- Regulatory approvals that may be required. Some governments, such as Japan, require that they approve the license. If the approval is not sought, the license can be considered void. The license should specify which party is responsible for obtaining the approval.
- Review of competition or antitrust laws to ensure compliance with any related legal requirements.
- Consideration of currency exchange rates. Exchange rates should be agreed in the contract to minimize the risk of fluctuating currency rates.
- In the case of outsourcing, specification in the contract for the financial and legal interests in the company's software now being supported by the outsourcer. For example, in some cases, the software license may transfer to the outsourcer, which will require relicensing its own software if the company later chooses to discontinue outsourcing. The other option is to allow the outsourcer to use the software with the company retaining responsibility for all license agreements.

Completing Final Acceptance

An acceptance plan should be agreed upon and defined in the contract. This plan defines the terms and condition for acceptance. Normally, final payment is withheld until all acceptance tests have been completed and the software and equipment meet all specifications in the contract.

Technology acquisition is dependent on other key processes and must integrate to operate effectively. For example, acquired devices must integrate with existing infrastructure architecture and project dependencies tied to the delivery of components. In addition, the life cycle of acquired devices does not end with the acquisition process. Assets must be installed, secured, tracked, maintained, and disposed of properly.

IT Contract Issues

The increased use of computers has forced organizations to enter into more contracts for computer hardware, software, and services. Poorly informed and counseled computer buyers, however, are at a disadvantage relative to the suppliers. The suppliers have familiarity with the products and contract terms. The rising costs associated with upgrading equipment and keeping pace with the state of the art, the acquisition of services from suppliers to design, develop, and maintain equipment and continue IT operations have generated more concern among top management. Management has recognized that its traditional posture of accepting supplier contracts without negotiation is a poor business practice. Negotiating computer-related acquisitions is being taken very seriously by management and raised to a higher priority as we have become much more dependent on information systems to support strategic and day-to-day operations. IT auditors can assist their organization in preparing for negotiating computer hardware, software, and services contracts. Within the Big Four environment, management advisory services (MAS) can help their clients contract for computer hardware, software, and services.

IT users want systems that perform as intended; resorting to litigation in response to dissatisfaction with products or services is admitting that the selection or acquisition process has failed. IT users need the protection of having systems that meet their needs, not lawsuits. Some examples are companies such as Catamore Enterprises, a 30-year-old business, which hired a major computer firm to automate its production control system. The system failed to match incoming orders with inventory records. The computer company, IBM, disclaimed responsibility for the software because the contract did not include it. The court awarded the business over $11 million in damages and it settled with IBM out of court for an undisclosed amount. In another case, Triangle Underwriters, a 40-year-old insurance business, filed for bankruptcy three years after converting to a new computer system that never worked to meet their needs.

IT auditors can help their companies avoid similar predicaments, especially those lacking in-house computer contracting expertise in areas such as first-time purchases, contract services for computer maintenance, custom applications, and multiple supplier procurements. Many times, the evidence gathered by auditors can help or assist the organization in specifying both performance standards and remedies for nonperformance.

Borthick and Massingale identify three areas where IT auditors and the Big Four MAS consultants can be very helpful in their review of IT-related contracts. These areas are

- Review of supplier contract terms that limit supplier liability
- Review of contract objectives and performance measurements to ensure objectives have been met
- Review and inclusion in future contracts of contract clauses for protecting customer interests

In many instances, the auditor will review the contract if the scope of the audit encompasses activities or actions they are to audit. This is done in the gathering of background or detailed information phase of an audit. Several types of standard supplier contract clauses to look for are listed in Exhibit 15.3.

In the development or review of any IT contract, the objectives of the contracting process should focus on preparing or examining the acceptance criteria. There are three key goals to achieve while contracting for computer goods and services. The first is the preparation of explicit criteria that can be used for acceptance, and the criteria will clearly allow the customer to see that their requirements have been either met or exceeded. Next is the process of negotiating the contract

Standard Supplier Contract Clause	Effect on Customer Assumption of Risk
Integration into writing	Pre-contract promises are negated by supplier
Defect-free media warranty	Only the physical media, not the software on the media, is warranted
Warranty disclaimer	Not expressed or implied warranties
Abbreviated time for filing suit	Too short a period to confirm failure
Limitation of remedies	Remedy limited by supplier to price of goods, excludes ancillary damages incurred
Shrink-wrap contract	Buyer bound without signature

Exhibit 15.3 Types of standard supplier contract clauses.

and the inclusion of clauses that assure supplier compliance. Finally, the process of monitoring contract compliance is the responsibility of the entire organization if they wish to protect their rights and leverage. For an IT auditor, this is an area that often is to be identified as a major control weakness, and as a result of the audit process, problems and contract issues are identified, which many times require immediate management and organizational attention.

In reviewing the procurement and contract negotiation process, the IT auditor can look for the following tasks to be accomplished:

- The contract accurately reflects the organization's requirements, and appropriate levels within the organization have verified them.
- The requirements have been translated into measurable acceptance criteria that can be monitored and verified.
- That the RFP contains the needs and requirements has been ensured.
- The process for evaluating the contractor bids includes thorough evaluation of how they will meet requirements.
- The negotiation process has been reviewed.
- The legal counsel or contracting officer was present at all meetings, and documentation of proceedings was recorded.
- Changes or agreements were reached in refining contract terms and were verified with management.
- The contract has been executed and monitored to assure customer's rights.
- Acceptance tests are performed on all products or services provided and tests are documented and reviewed by management.
- Acceptance tests are documented, evaluated, and the results are reviewed and signed off by customers at affected levels including management.
- Your organization exercises its right to accept or decline the contract, and documentation from above supports its decision.

In contracting for IT services, it is very important that the requirements be stated in terms of business needs. For example, a savings and loan supporting customer transactions with online terminals might require 98% uptime to avoid customer dissatisfaction. Another important

Clause	Functional Performance	Installation on Time within Budget	Maintainability over Useful Life
Warranty against latent defects			X
Guarantee of reliability and exercise of "due professional care"			X
Operation of system "as a whole" required for acceptance		X	
Continuation and access rights			X
Incremental payments to maintain supplier incentive		X	
Performance warranty to guarantee sustained functional performance	X		
Warranty again limiting routines			X
Right to make backups			X
Right to unrestrained use			X
Customer-determined acceptance to permit rejection of unworkable products	X		

Exhibit 15.4   Sample clauses providing protection.

provision to include is identifying the need for maintainability over the useful life of the systems or services provided. The integration of wording to this effect into the contract during the negotiation process can provide some assurance of protecting the customers' rights. Exhibit 15.4 lists some sample clauses that can provide this level of protection.

These types of clauses used in the contract, especially IT-related contracts, can be effective instruments for providing a minimum level of assurance. As you are aware, these are clauses that suppliers do not like to see in contracts, and they will try to eliminate them from the contract language during negotiation. This is where corporate legal counsel with IT experience and past audit evidence and research can assist in getting them into the contract. One company was awarded over $3 million because they had included such clauses into their contract for systems development effort that did not meet their requirements and lacked "due professional care." Many professional organizations have established standards of practice for their profession and membership in the form of a code of ethics and define due professional care (see Appendix III).

Strategic Sourcing and Supplier Management

A sourcing policy defines where IT services are to be purchased. In a centralized, shared-services model, the business units are required to purchase from the central IT group. This approach allows IT to standardize technology solutions and leverage size/scale for procurement. There may be situations where the central IT group cannot provide a requested service. In this case, there needs to be a process in place to source solutions through a third party. Although third-party services/ solutions may be used, it is important that IT manage the procurement and relationship to ensure compliance with internal standards.

The supplier management process begins once a contract is signed and helps ensure that suppliers live up to their commitments. This should include SLAs with measurable criteria and mechanisms to monitor actual performance to goal on a regular basis. Spending with third-party suppliers on hardware, software, and services consumes 45–60% of an average IT budget.* This not only increases the risk of reliance on third parties for service delivery, but also provides an opportunity to drive costs down by negotiating purchases, contracts, and services. Using external resources provides flexibility and scalability by leveraging the expertise and staff of third-party suppliers for temporary staffing needs for development projects. There is also an opportunity to drive development costs down by outsourcing programming to offshore suppliers with mature development processes and inexpensive labor rates. There are a variety of sourcing models from internal delivery to full outsourcing. All models require internal processes to manage service levels, costs, and risk. Key criteria to making a decision to insource or outsource include strategy, competency, and risk.†

Audit Involvement

The IT auditor can play an important role in IT contract planning, formulation, and monitoring. The IT auditor provides management with information when they conduct their independent reviews, examining the various sources of information that can be of value to management and the organization. Contract nonperformance often end up in the court. The cost in time and resources can be great as mentioned earlier.

Auditing Software Acquisitions

A purchased software solution should effectively and efficiently satisfy user requirements. It is also a situation where IT audit may be called upon to provide an external evaluation of the processes and procedures in place and whether the acquisition was in compliance with institutional processes and operating procedures. IT can also be a place where these procedures are lacking and the IT auditor can offer help and suggestions for improvement.

The most common risks associated with acquiring software are that the selected solution does not satisfy the intended purpose or is not technically feasible. The consequences of a poor software purchase are increased costs, missed deadlines, or neglected requirements. To offset these risks, the IT auditor should evaluate the following controls:

■ Alignment with the company's business and IT strategy
■ Definition of the information requirements
■ Feasibility studies (cost, benefits, etc.)
■ Identification of functionality, operational acceptance, and maintenance requirements
■ Conformity with existing information and system architectures

---

* Working Council for Chief Information Officers, Strategic Supplier Management and Outsourcing, Corporate Executive Board, 2003, p. iv.
† Da Rold, C. and T. Berg, *Sourcing Strategies: Relationship Models and Case Studies*, Gartner R-18-9925, Gartner, Inc., Stamford, CT, February 7, 2003.

- Adherence to security and control requirements
- Knowledge of available solutions
- Understanding of the related acquisition and implementation methodologies
- Involvement and buy-in from the user
- Supplier requirements and viability

Alignment with the Company's Business and IT Strategy

Any system development project, whether the system is developed by the organization or purchased elsewhere, should support the organization's business and IT strategy. The business requirements associated with the solution being sought should link to goals and objectives identified in the company's business and IT strategy. For further information about IT alignment with the business, see Chapter 9.

Definition of the Information Requirements

System and information requirements should be evaluated to determine if they are current and complete. Owing to the fast pace of business, requirements can change quickly. Consequently, requirements that are gathered too far in advance of the actual purchase may not capture any changes in business requirements or newly available technical features.

The biggest challenge with defining system requirements is getting them to be complete. The requirements for a system can never be 100% complete. Conversely, revising requirements throughout the system acquisition process can result in change in scope, expectations, cost, and consequently, success.

Prototypes

Because prototypes appear to be complete when presented to the users, expectations, requirements, and feasibility may be misaligned. If users are shown a prototype, they may view the prototype as a final product and not understand the "back end" work that needs to be done to make it a complete system. Often, the user will want to use the prototype instead of the full delivery system. However, a prototype is a method of validating the requirements—not a workable system. In this case, programmers may not be given enough time to complete the system and are expected to implement the prototype as the final product. The user must understand the need to develop and test a fully functioning production system. Risks associated with prototyping and other rapid application development (RAD) approaches include

- Incomplete system design
- Inefficient processing performance
- Inadequate application controls
- Inadequate documentation
- Ineffective implementations

Feasibility Studies (Cost, Benefits, etc.)

Feasibility studies should be reviewed to ensure that the selected solution not only meets the requirements but also is compared and contrasted with the feasibility of the other solutions.

Related controls and risks are illustrated in the following using economic and technical feasibility as examples.

Economic feasibility should be reviewed and approved by an involved and knowledgeable sponsor before the final decision to ensure that the "make versus buy" question is effectively evaluated. Management should formally sign off on the cost–benefit analysis. In one circumstance, a government agency purchased a software solution without traceable documentation of the alternatives reviewed and the related cost–benefits associated with each. Consequently, regulators scrutinized the competency of senior management and the fairness of the selection process.

There are multiple examples of companies that prepare misleading cost–benefit studies that are based on immeasurable benefits and incomplete costs. Benefits are often presented in terms of functions that are not measured in the current environment. Consequently, it is difficult to prove benefit in the new environment. Indirect or in-kind costs are often excluded from cost estimates. Examples include staff costs associated with reassigning staff from their regular duties to the implementation project. These costs can include fees for temporary staff, loss of revenue associated with reduced service due to reduced staff, or changes in employee compensation resulting from increased job responsibilities or expected skills.

Technical feasibility should be reviewed and approved by an involved and knowledgeable sponsor before the final decision to ensure the organization's ability to implement and support the selected solution. In one example, a company's chief financial officer (CFO) purchased a financial enterprise resource planning (ERP) package without consulting the company's technology division in advance. The technology division was placed in the position of scrambling to incorporate the package into the existing architecture following the purchase. Consequently, changes were required to the design of the technical infrastructure resulting in unplanned hardware and software purchases.

Identification of Functionality, Operational, Acceptance, and Maintenance Requirements

Requirements need to extend beyond end-user expectations. They should include the internal functionality of the system with consideration for operational and maintenance requirements. Examples of functionality that can be missed include printing requirements or the business-specific algorithms for calculations. In one example, a company unexpectedly had to change its check printing process due to the implementation of a software package. Because the checks were now completely laser printed, the printed check had to include the account information in optical characters as well as the associated bar code. The banking information on the new check had to be reviewed and approved by the bank. Additionally, the font size had to be adjusted appropriately for the post office to systematically sort the mail. Finally, the checks were jamming in the mail sorter at the post office. Because the check was now a self-enclosed mailer without a separate envelope, the paper used to print and mail the check became stressed from being passed through the folding machine, postage meter, and the mail sorter. The company subsequently purchased a different folding machine and implemented other alternatives to apply the postage.

Acceptance criteria should be specific with detailed measures. Acceptance plans should include inspections, functional tests, and workload trials. Without acceptance guidelines, the selected solution may not comply with user requirements, performance expectations, or the terms of the contract. There are many cases where inadequate acceptance guidelines have resulted in business interruptions from inadequate system performance or nonworking functions.

Conformity with Existing Information and System Architectures

This control is directly correlated with the evaluation of technical feasibility and the business's information elements. As mentioned in the Requirement Document section, conformity with the existing system architecture is critical. In addition, the feasibility analysis defines the constraints or limitations for the system. Feasibility should be assessed in the following categories: economic, technical, operational, schedule, legal or contractual, and political. Feasibility can include those things that are tangible, intangible, one-time, or recurring.

In one case, a company selected a software package that did not accommodate the company's method for recording the commission for its sales agents in the general ledger. Consequently, the company chose to modify the software's structure for the chart-of-accounts structure, which resulted in changes and maintenance to the basic data structure of the product as well as all the associated code and screens.

Adherence to Security and Control Requirements

A complete understanding of the company's security and control requirements is needed to ensure that the selected solution is appropriate. Company security policies and applicable regulations need to be reviewed during the selection process to ensure that security and control requirements are considered in the selection process. The company security officer should be involved in defining the security and control requirements as well as participate in the selection process.

System acquisitions and implementations become more difficult when these requirements are not well understood or documented. The results will be missed security functionality or poorly implemented security. In instances where the security policy or requirements are not well documented, it would be wise to have them documented and approved by senior management before the selection process to ensure that security and control requirements are met.

In situations where there are gaps in security between requirements and the evaluated solutions, cost and benefits of controls should be evaluated to ensure that the costs do not exceed the benefits. This provides an opportunity for risks and controls to be revised and updated to reflect changes in business and technology. The security officer and management should participate in and approve any changes to security requirements or selected controls.

Knowledge of Available Solutions

Often, system development and acquisition efforts become more focused on a specific solution due to the knowledge or experience of the participants. By focusing on a specific end result, other alternatives are not considered. By not considering other alternatives, the selected solution may increase cost, scope, or the timeline for the project because they did not meet basic requirements such as incompatibility with the current company infrastructure or business practices. Specifically, it takes additional time and resources to integrate the selected solution into company technical infrastructure or business practices.

Understanding of the Related Acquisition and Implementation Methodologies

Acquisition methods of an organization can be very specific or general based on a variety of factors such as government regulations. As an example, government acquisition guidelines require that equal opportunity be provided to all potential providers. Consequently, there are specific requirement for advertising RFPs, evaluating bidders, as well as awarding contracts. If these guidelines are not followed, agreements may not be considered valid.

Selected implementation methods may be inadequately understood, and this may introduce risk to the deadlines, scope, and costs of the project. As an example, a company selected an implementation partner to assist it in converting its legacy billing system into a state-of-the-art system using object-oriented technologies. The company's experience and culture was based on traditional mainframe technologies and the traditional waterfall system development methodologies. The staff was ill equipped to understand and participate in the RAD approaches employed by the selected implementation partners. The company actually experienced failed contracts with several implementation partners and there were subsequent lawsuits filed by the company and implementation partners.

Involvement and Buy-In from the User

User involvement and buy-in is critical. Without user involvement, requirements will be missed and they will not support new systems. There is an increased awareness of the criticality of user support and buy-in. As a means for increasing user support, many projects are now including communication and business change management as part of their project plans.

Change management, in this context, includes people, organizations, and culture. A culture that shares values and is open to change contributes to success. To facilitate the change process, users should be involved in the design and implementation of the business process and the system. Training and professional development supports this as well.

System-implementation success relies on effective communication. Expectations need to be communicated. Communication, education, and expectations need to be managed throughout the organization. Input from users should also be managed to ensure that requirements, comments, and approvals are obtained. Communication includes the formal promotion of the project team as well as the project progress to the organization. Employees should also know the scope, objectives, activities and updates, and the expectation for change in advance.

Supplier Requirements and Viability

The acquisition process should ensure that the selected supplier meets the supplier requirements of the organization as outlined in the proposal. As mentioned previously, these requirements include:

- Stability of the supplier company
- Volatility of system upgrades
- Existing customer base
- Supplier's ability to provide support
- Required software in support of the supplier application
- Required modifications of the base software

To determine the viability of the supplier, the following elements should also be evaluated:

- Financial condition
- Risk of acquisition
- Likelihood of exiting the market
- Reputation for responsiveness during problems

Audit Involvement

While participating in a software acquisition process or reviewing it after the fact, the auditor should evaluate processes and evidence related to the following:

■ Alignment with the company's business and IT strategy
■ Definition of the information requirements
■ Feasibility studies (cost, benefits, etc.)
■ Identification of functionality, operational, acceptance, and maintenance requirements
■ Conformity with existing information and system architectures
■ Adherence to security and control requirements
■ Knowledge of available solutions
■ Understanding of the related acquisition and implementation methodologies
■ Involvement and buy-in from the user
■ Supplier requirements and viability

Other Resources for Help and Assistance

In this area, there is quite a bit of published literature and studies available to help organizations. The U.S. Government Accountability Office (GAO) has published a number of reports on software acquisition problems within the federal government. Using the training and resources of Carnegie Mellon's Software Engineering Institute (SEI), GAO IT auditors have helped organizations and individuals to improve their software engineering management practices. Carnegie Mellon's SEI has developed very good information about software engineering management, SEI projects, sourcing, and software engineering. Some of the products they have developed have been applied in commercial environments. Some of their products listed in the following focus on increased efficiency and quality in software acquisition or development:

■ Organizations using good product-line practices can exploit commonalities across software systems to reduce costs and increase quality in software product lines.
■ Small organizations, especially small manufacturing enterprises (SMEs), are using techniques from the technology insertion demonstration and evaluation (TIDE) program to improve and expand their businesses by acquiring and adopting commercially available IT.
■ The commercial off-the-shelf (COTS)-Based Systems Initiative provides techniques for assembling and evolving software-intensive systems based on commercially available software components.
■ Software engineers trained in the Personal Software Process (PSP) routinely produce work on schedule with reduced development time and significantly reduced numbers of defects in delivered code.
■ PSP-trained engineers work together using the Team Software Process (TSP). The TSP was developed to help integrated engineering teams more effectively develop software-intensive products. This process method addresses many of the current problems of developing software-intensive products and shows teams and their management explicitly how to address them.
■ An "open systems" approach can help you efficiently acquire and maintain high-quality systems that are technically up to date.

Other organizations such as National Institute of Standards and Technology (NIST), Association of Computing Machinery (ACM), Association of Information Technology Professionals (AITP), and others have materials that may be of help as identified in Appendices II and III.

Conclusion

Software acquisitions are often thought to be faster, easier, and cheaper for companies to meet their business needs. Although acquiring software can be very successful, it can also miss the mark. Purchased software can miss user requirements, exceed implementation goals or implementation costs, as well as introduce delays in business or project schedules. This chapter discussed the following basic steps in the software acquisition process:

- Defining the information and system requirements
- Identifying various alternatives
- Performing a feasibility analysis
- Conducting a risk analysis
- Defining ergonomic requirements
- Carrying out the selection process
- Procuring the selected software
- Completing final acceptance

Once a contract has been completed, the supplier management process helps ensure that the expected value is received. It is critical that the negotiated contract clearly defined SLAs, performance measures, pricing terms, and escalation processes to effectively manage a third-party supplier. It is also important to have an effective relationship with the supplier and fair contract terms that enable both parties to be successful.

IT auditors can provide an important service by being involved in the acquisition process to highlight risks before the contract is signed. Understanding the software acquisition process, critical contract terms, and supplier management processes will enable the auditor to be a valuable member of the acquisition team.

Review Questions

1. Name and describe the eight basic steps of a software acquisition process.
2. Name and describe the methods that can be used in gathering information and system requirements.
3. What are the advantages and disadvantages of prototyping?
4. Name and describe the components of a requirements document.
5. Compare and contrast the various options that exist for acquiring software.
6. While purchasing a software solutions provided by a vendor, what should be considered?
7. What are the advantages and disadvantages for contract development?
8. What are the advantages and disadvantages for outsourcing a system from another organization?
9. Name and describe the various categories of feasibility analysis.

10. When a customer during the negotiation process is able to get the vendor to accept a clause such as "Guarantee of reliability and exercise of due professional care," what does that mean?
11. What are the steps in negotiating a contract? What should the auditor look for?
12. What are the potential ramifications of poorly written IT contracts? What is the auditor's role? How can auditors or MAS staff assist?
13. What are the basic components of an RFP?
14. What are the basic steps and components needed to evaluate submitted proposals?
15. In a contract for software or programming services, name and describe the terms and conditions that should be included.
16. In evaluating a software acquisition process, name and describe the areas that the auditor should include in his or her review.
17. What criteria should be evaluated to determine the viability of the proposed supplier?

Multiple-Choice Questions

1. One of the basic steps in the software acquisition process is
   a. Identifying a single alternative
   b. Defining the information and system requirements
   c. Performing user and site surveys
   d. Replacing existing hardware platforms
2. What is the most important step in the software acquisition process?
   a. Defining information requirements
   b. Identifying alternatives
   c. Performing the feasibility analysis
   d. Conducting risk analysis
3. As a means of increasing user support, many projects are now including as part of their project plans
   a. Infrastructure diagrams
   b. Outsourcing
   c. Communication and business change management
   d. Sales and marketing
4. Gathering information and system requirements can be accomplished by all of the following except:
   a. Interviewing those expected to use the information produced by the system as well as those expected to produce the information input into the system
   b. Interviewing the software supplier to find the best-selling software in the market
   c. Developing a prototype of the proposed system
   d. Researching other companies
5. A document that specifies the minimal acceptable requirements as well as the evaluation criteria for a solution is called a
   a. Request for bid
   b. Request for information
   c. Request for proposal
   d. Request for quote
6. Participants in the selection process may not include representatives from
   a. Management

    b. Anticipated users

    c. IT department

    d. Supplier

7. Contract terms and conditions normally do not include the following:

    a. An organizational chart of the customer's IT department

    b. A functional definition of the work to be performed

    c. Supplier staffing and specified qualifications

    d. Methods of providing progress reports

8. What is not an advantage of purchasing off-the-shelf solutions?

    a. Shorter implementation time

    b. The ability to use the company's existing IT infrastructure

    c. Use of proven technology

    d. Easier to define costs

9. When selecting a supplier package, organizations should consider all of the following except:

    a. Stability of the supplier company

    b. Supplier's ability to provide support

    c. Required modifications to the base software

    d. Sales and marketing literature

10. Effective supplier management is based on

    a. SLAs with contract penalties

    b. Clearly defined requirements in the RFP

    c. Measurable service levels and regular monitoring

    d. Strong negotiation skills of the procurement team

Exercises

Scenario: You work in your company's payroll department and are asked to acquire software that will automate the process for employees to submit their timesheets to the payroll department. Timesheets are the means by which hourly employees submit their time. Time sheets are approved by managers and then processed by the payroll department for payment. Using the new system, employees will input their time weekly into a computer system. Once employees complete their time sheets, managers will be able to view and approve them when they log into the system. Using the preceding scenario described, answer the following:

1. What methods would you use and why to gather the requirements for the system?

2. Document the information and system requirements using the outline of the requirements documented provided in the chapter.

3. Describe two or three alternatives solutions that should be considered.

4. Using the categories provided in the text and one of the alternatives that you described in Exercise 2, perform a feasibility analysis.

5. Perform a risk analysis for the proposed system.

6. Who would you recommend to be on the acceptance testing team?

7. In the acceptance plan, what tests would you recommend to ensure that information requirements are met?

8. In the acceptance plan, what tests would you recommend to ensure that the system performance requirements are met?

9. In the acceptance plan, what tests would you recommend to ensure that the system requirements are met?
10. How can a resource such as NIST or Carnegie Mellon's SEI be helpful in the software acquisition process?

Answers to Multiple-Choice Questions

1—b; 2—a; 3—c; 4—b; 5—c; 6—d; 7—a; 8—b; 9—d; 10—c

Further Reading

1. Applegate, L.M., F.W. McFarlan, and R.D. Austin, *Corporate Information Strategy and Management: Text and Cases*, 6th Edition, McGraw-Hill Irwin, New York, 2002.
2. Ambrose, C., *A Sourcing Executive Can Help Optimize Sourcing and Vendor Relationships*, Gartner Research, Gartner, Inc., Stamford, CT, April 24, 2006.
3. Bachelor, B., Implementation imperative, *Information Week*, April 28, 2003.
4. Bakalov, R. and F. Nanji, Offshore application development done right, *Inf. Sys. Control J.*, 5, 2007.
5. Bartels, A., *Global IT Spending and Investment Forecast, 2006 to 2007*, Forrester Research, Inc., Cambridge MA, November 21, 2006.
6. Benvenuto, N. and D. Brand, Outsourcing—A risk management perspective, *Inf. Sys. Control J.*, 5, 2007.
7. Bostick, J., The soul searching that comes with sole-sourcing, *Inf. Sys. Control J.*, 5, 2007.
8. Burgunder, L., *Legal Aspects of Managing Technology*, 3rd Edition, Thomson Corporation–South-Western, Mason, OH, 2004.
9. Corporate Executive Board, *Case Studies of Software Purchasing Decisions*, Working Council for Chief Information Officers, February 2003.
10. Corporate Executive Board, *Negotiating Global Licensing Agreements*, Working Council for Chief Information Officers, June 2001.
11. Davison, D., *Assessing the Supplier's Viability*, ZDNet, January 24, 2002. http://techupdate.zdnet.com/techupdate/stories/main/0,14179,2841191-2,00.html, accessed on January 8, 2003.
12. Ferrara, G., J. Aresty, M. Reder, R. Bird, J. Darrow, J. Klosek, and S. Lichtenstein. *CyberLaw: Text and Cases*, 3rd Edition. South-Western, Independence, KY, 2011.
13. Hefley, W. and E. Loesche, *The eSCM-CL v1.1: Model Overview*, The eSourcing Capability Model for Client Organizations (eSCM-CL) v1.1. Carnegie Mellon University, Pittsberg, PA, 2006.
14. Information Systems Audit and Control Foundation, *COBIT Audit Guidelines*, Information Systems Audit and Control Foundation, July 2000.
15. Intelligence and National Security Alliance, Report: Cyber Intelligence: Setting the landscape for an emerging discipline Sept. 2011.
16. IT Governance Institute, *Governance of Outsourcing*, IT Governance Domain Practices and Competencies, 2005.
17. Kroemer, K., *Ergonomics: Definition of Ergonomics*, National Safety Council, http://www.nsc.org/issues/ergo/define.htm, accessed on July 28, 2003.
18. Kyte, A., *Vendor Management Is a Critical Business Discipline*, Gartner Research, Gartner, Inc., February 24, 2005.
19. Landis, K., Deloitte Consulting Study, *Calling a Change in the Outsourcing Market*, New York, NY, http://www.deloitte.com/dtt/cda/doc/content/us_outsourcing_callingachange.pdf, 19 April 2005.
20. Markus, M.L. and C. Tanis, The enterprise systems experience—From adoption to success. In *Framing the Domains of IT Research: Glimpsing the Future through the Past*, R.W. Zmud, Ed., Pinnaflex Educational Resources, Inc., Cincinnati, OH, 2000.

21. McKinney, C., Capability maturity models and outsourcing: A case for sourcing risk management, *Inf. Sys. Control J.*, 5, 2007.
22. Minevich, M. and R. Frank-Jurgen, *Global Outsourcing Report 2005*, Going Global Ventures Inc., New York, 2005.
23. Nah, L.K., Critical factors for successful implementation of enterprise systems, *Bus. Proc. Manage. J.*, 7(3), 285–296, 2001.
24. National Consortium for Justice Information and Statistics, *Court Technology Model Request for Proposals*, SEARCH, http://www.search.org/services/ta/three.asp, accessed on July 25, 2003.
25. Pereira, B., A customer-centric software contract, *Network Magazine*, September 2002.

Chapter 16

Application Controls and Maintenance

Computer-based applications provide automated functions, which effectively support the business process. Applications also introduce risks to organizations in the form of increased costs, loss of data integrity, weaknesses in confidentiality, lack of availability, or poor performance. Assuming that these risks were addressed during the development thru implementation phases, when the application needs to be changed, these risks may be reintroduced. Once an application is implemented, programs may be periodically modified to correct program errors or implement system enhancements. Maintenance of applications need to be in-line with business or IT strategies; otherwise, it may cause performance issues and inefficient use of resources.

IT Processes

The COBIT process (AI2) in the Acquire and Implement Domain discusses how application controls support an effective IT organization. Exhibit 16.1 lists the control objectives for this section.

Application Risks

The risks in a computer-based system include both the risks that would be present in any manual processing system and those that are unique to an automated environment. In a manual system, errors are made individually, but in computer systems, errors are made in quantity because automated systems apply rules (good and bad) consistently. Additionally, automated systems can contain errors that can trigger errors in an unrelated part of the system and so on. This cascading effect can occur between applications when they become more integrated, which magnifies the potential risks.

In a manual system, data is voluminous and stored in many places. Conversely, in automated systems, the data is concentrated and is in a format that can be easily accessed. The concentration

AI2 Acquire and Maintain Application Software
Control Objectives
2.1   High-level design
2.2   Detailed design
2.3   Application control and auditability
2.4   Application security and availability
2.5   Configuration and implementation of acquired application software
2.6   Major upgrades to existing systems
2.7   Development of application software
2.8   Software quality assurance
2.9   Applications requirements management
2.10   Application software maintenance

Exhibit 16.1   Processes to acquire and implement.

of data can also increase the risks by placing greater reliance on a single piece of data or on a single computer file or database table. If the data entered is erroneous, the more the applications that rely on that piece of data, the greater the impact of the error. Further, the more applications that use the concentrated data, the greater the impact when that data becomes unavailable because of problems with either the hardware or software used for processing it.

IS professionals need to consider the levels of risk associated within an application to establish appropriate controls. Risks associated with automated applications include:

- Weak security
- Unauthorized access to data
- Unauthorized remote access
- Inaccurate information
- Erroneous or falsified data input
- Misuse by authorized end users
- Incomplete processing
- Duplicate transactions
- Untimely processing
- Communications system failure
- Inadequate training
- Inadequate support

Weak Security

IS security should be a concern of IT, users, and management. However, security, for many companies, is not a top priority. Past reports indicate that organizations were found to be more concerned with budgets and staff shortages than security. Even after the September 11 tragedy, when resources are tight, it is difficult to sell management on spending money for the intangible benefits of security efforts. Respondents to such surveys still continue to identify obstacles to reducing security risks as lack of human resources, funds, management awareness, and tools and solutions. However, the surveys did discover that organizations have increased their security staff. Advanced technology and increased end-user access to critical information has fueled the increase in security risks. According to an Infosecurity News survey, the primary concern regarding security involves a lack of end-user awareness.

Unauthorized Access or Changes to Data or Programs

Applications should be built with various levels of authorization for transaction submission and approval. Once an application goes into production, programmers should no longer have access to programs and data. If programmers are provided access, the access should be a "read-only" access for the purpose of understanding issues reported by the user.

User's access should be limited to the "need-to-know" basis. This means that the information made available to a user, whether it is a read-only access or the ability to modify data, should be in accordance with his job functions. For example, a payroll clerk needs access to the payroll systems, but not to the billings system.

Unauthorized Remote Access

More and more users are demanding remote access to a company's computer resources. The easiest method to provide security is to eliminate modem access completely. With weak access controls, a modem allows access to an organization's resources to virtually anyone. To protect against unauthorized access, remote dial-up access could have a callback feature that identifies the user with a specific location. A more complicated solution is to have key cards with encrypted IDs installed on the remote terminal and a front-end server on the host. At a minimum, user IDs and passwords should be encrypted when transmitted over public lines. In addition, confidential data that is transmitted over public lines should be encrypted. The security solution depends on the sensitivity of the data being transmitted.

Inaccurate Information

Accurate information is an issue whether the end user is accessing a database on the mainframe or a departmental database on a PC. End users may be asked to generate reports without their fully understanding the underlying information or they may not be sufficiently trained in the reporting application to ask the appropriate questions. Additional complications occur when end users download information from the mainframe for analysis and reporting. Departmental databases may have redundant information with different timeframes. The result is waste of time in reconciling two databases to determine which data is accurate. Another major area of concern is that management may fail to use information properly. The reasons for such neglect include:

- Failure to identify significant information
- Failure to interpret the meaning and value of the acquired information
- Failure to communicate critical information to the responsible manager or chief decision maker timely

Erroneous or Falsified Data Input

Erroneous data input is when inaccurate data is inputted in the system unintentionally due to human error. Preventative measures include building in application controls, such as check digits and double entry. Falsified data input is when inaccurate data is inputted to the system intentionally to defraud the organization or its stakeholders. Preventative measures include safeguarding access to programs and data thru user authentication and authorization mechanism.

Misuse by Authorized End Users

Systems are designed for use by end users, but they can also be misused by them. When an authorized user misuses its authority, it is often difficult to proof it.

Incomplete Processing

Incomplete processing occurs when transactions or files are not processed due to an error. It may occur in batch processing when a file is not present, or during online processing, when a transaction trigger fails to kick off a transaction.

Duplicate Transaction Processing

Duplicate transaction processing includes processing transactions more than once. It can occur during batch processing if files are run multiple times, or during online processing when a transaction trigger kicks off a transaction more than once. It may also occur when a job abends, but some of the records that have been processed are not reset.

Untimely Processing

This includes delayed processing due to production problems or missing a time cutoff. For example, financial processes must occur at month-end closing to ensure that the detailed transactions processed in one system match the transaction posting to the general ledger. In addition, when an online system post transactions to a batch system, there is usually a cutoff time where processing ends on day one and begins for day two.

Communications System Failure

Information that is routed from one location to another over communication lines is vulnerable to accidental failures and intentional interception and modification by unauthorized parties.

Inadequate Testing

As previously discussed, independent testing is important to identify design flaws that may have been overlooked by the developer of a system. Often, the individual who creates the design will be the only one testing the program, and therefore, he or she is only confirming that the system performs exactly as they designed it to be. The end user should develop acceptance criteria that can be used to confirm that end-user requirements are met and that the system in fact performs as expected. This acceptance-testing criterion must be measurable.

Inadequate Training

Organizations may decide not to invest in training by looking only at the up-front costs. According to one study by the Gartner Group and a study by the U.S. National Institute of Standards and Technology, the cost of not training will far exceed the investment organizations will make to train both end users and IT professionals in new technologies. One reason for this paradox is that end users who are forced to learn on their own take as much as six times longer to become productive with the software application. Self-training is also inefficient from the standpoint that end users tend to ask their colleagues for help, which results in the loss of more than one individual's time, and they may also be learning inappropriate or inefficient techniques. Both studies also show that an effective training program reduces support costs by a factor of three to six because end users make fewer mistakes and have fewer questions.

Inadequate Support

The increasing complexity of technical environments and more sophisticated technical tools has fueled the increased demand for end-user support. Because traditional IT departments do not have the staffing or advanced technical knowledge to help end-user departments, end users have turned to "underground support" (i.e., support by peers or department-purchased outsourcing) to fill the gap. The previously mentioned studies found that the need for support is inelastic, and the gap between needed and formal support is filled by underground support. This underground support accounts for as much as 30% of end-user computing (EUC) costs. End users need "focal points" that are local for assistance. A focal point is a functional support person. Many times, the functional support person is an accomplished end user. However, without a central support organization, there may be limited coordination between end-user departments, which ensures that procedures are consistent and applications are compatible.

Insufficient Documentation

End users typically focus on solving a business need and may not recognize the importance of documentation. Any program that is used by multiple users or has long-term benefits must be documented, particularly if the original developer is no longer available. Documentation also assists the developer in solving problems or making changes to the application in the future, in addition to facilitating testing and familiarizing new users to the system.

End-User Computing Application Risks

End-user computing (EUC) generally involves the use of department-developed spreadsheets and databases, which are frequently used as tools in performing daily work. These spreadsheets are essentially an extension of the IT environment and output generated from them may be used in making business decisions and may have an impact on the company's financial statements. As a result, the use of EUC has extended the scope of audits outside the central IS environment. The level of risk and the required level of controls depend on the criticality of the application. Three key questions should be asked to determine the importance of an application:

- Does the application yield information that impacts the direction or goals of the company?
- Is the data within the application considered to be sensitive or important to the company?
- Does the application access other critical or sensitive applications located on other computers?

If the answer is yes to any of these questions, the validity, integrity, and accuracy of the data from these applications must be protected and ensured. For example, an application that consolidates data from several departments that will later be an input into the financial reporting system is a prime target for an audit.

In addition to determining which applications should be audited, each EUC group must be evaluated to determine the audit approach required for that specific environment. The following four basic end-user environments require different audit approaches: stand-alone microcomputers, local area networks (LANs), wide area networks (WANs), corporate client/server, and a departmental mainframe or microcomputer server. In addition to various audit approaches, the inherent risks in each of these environments must be evaluated and the appropriate matching controls must be tested. Stand-alone PCs, LANs, and client/servers are probably the most complex environments because of the variety of ways in which they can be configured, and each requires a different auditing approach.

The IT auditor must be aware of additional threats or risks common to microcomputers configured within a LAN environment. For example, there is the possibility of unauthorized users monitoring, duplicating, modifying, or altering the message or process that may be flowing across the network. Threats of these types emphasize the need for developing an audit approach that considers the additional controls required in an LAN environment.

The WAN environment is a centralized area designed to provide users access to computerized tools with assistance and guidance from knowledgeable IT personnel. Although this information center is controlled, users can still develop their own applications that will require appropriate attention by IT auditors to ensure that proper controls are in place.

The client/server environment is one of considerable growth and evolution, especially in the area of Internet, intranet, and extranet support. Development and application controls must be assessed and validated. Another environment is the departmental server, which is the least common and probably the most difficult to audit. In this case, the computer is used for a special purpose. Its users are typically more technically sophisticated, and they frequently ignore corporate internal controls.

Sometimes, risks in EUC are not readily identified because of lack of awareness and the absence of adequate resources. Because PCs (notebook, laptop, and mobile computing) seem relatively simple and are perceived as personal productivity tools, their effect on an organization has largely been ignored. In many organizations, EUC has limited or no formal procedures. The control or review of reports produced by EUC is either limited or nonexistent. The associated risk is that management may be relying on end-user-developed reports and information to the same degree as those developed under traditional centralized IT controls. The management should consider the levels of risk associated with end-user applications and establish appropriate levels of control. The risks associated with EUC include:

- Inefficient use of resources
- Incompatible systems
- Redundant systems
- Ineffective implementations
- Absence of separation of duties
- Unauthorized access to data or programs
- Copyright violations
- The destruction of information by computer viruses
- Lack of back-up and recovery options

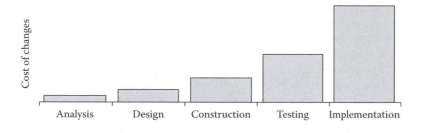

Exhibit 16.2   Cost comparison of changing a program.

Inefficient Use of Resources

End-user development may at first appear to be relatively inexpensive compared to traditional IT development. However, a number of hidden costs are associated with EUC that organizations should consider. In addition to operation costs, costs may increase due to lack of training and technical support. Lack of end-user training and their inexperience may also result in the purchase of inappropriate hardware and the implementation of software solutions that are incompatible with the organization's systems architecture. End users may also increase organizational costs by creating inefficient or redundant applications. The cost of change to an existing or new application in the latter stages can be expensive, as shown in Exhibit 16.2.

Incompatible Systems

End-user-designed applications that are developed in isolation may not be compatible with existing or future organizational IT architectures. Traditional IT systems development verifies compatibility with existing hardware and related software applications. The absence of hardware and software standards can result in the inability to share data with other applications in the organization.

Redundant Systems

In addition to developing incompatible systems, end users may be developing redundant applications or databases because of the lack of communication between departments. Because of this lack of communication, end-user departments may create a new database or application that another department may have already created. A more efficient implementation process has end-user departments coordinating their systems application development projects with IT and meeting with other end-user departments to discuss their proposed projects.

Ineffective Implementations

End users typically use fourth-generation languages, such as database or Internet Web development tools to develop applications. In these cases, the end user is usually self-taught. However, they lack formal training in structured applications development, do not realize the importance of documentation, and omit necessary control measures that are required for effective implementations. In addition, there is no "segregation of duties." Because of insufficient analysis, documentation and testing, end-user developed systems may not meet management's expectations.

Absence of Segregation of Duties

Traditional systems application development is separated by function, and tested and completed by trained experts in each area. In many end-user development projects, one individual is responsible for all phases, such as analyzing, designing, constructing, testing, and implementing the development life cycle. There are inherent risks in having the same person creating and testing a program because he or she may overlook his or her own errors. He or she will ensure the system works just as they designed it to. It is more likely that an independent review will catch errors made by the end-user developer, and such a review helps to ensure the integrity of the newly designed system.

Incomplete System Analysis

End-user departments eliminate many of the steps established by central IT departments. For example, the analysis phase of development may be incomplete and not all facets of a problem may be appropriately identified. In addition, with incomplete specifications, the completed system may not solve the business problem. End users must define their objectives for a particular application before they decide to purchase existing software, have IT develop the application, or use their limited expertise to develop the application. Incomplete specifications will ensure system deficiencies.

Unauthorized Access to Data or Programs

Access controls provide the first line of defense against unauthorized users who gain entrance to a system's programs and data. The use of access controls, such as user IDs and passwords, are typically weak in user-controlled systems. In some cases, user IDs and passwords may not be required, shared or easily guessed. This oversight can subject applications to accidental or deliberate changes or deletions that threaten the reliability of any information generated. Programs require additional protection to prevent any unexpected changes. To prevent any accidental changes, the user should be limited to execute only.

Copyright Violations

Organizations are responsible for controlling the computing environment to prevent software piracy and copyright violations. However, most organizations do not specifically address software piracy in training, in policy and procedures, or in the application of general internal controls. Since software programs can easily be copied or installed on multiple computers, many organizations are in violation of copyright laws and are not even aware of the potential risks.

The Copyright Act of 1976 makes it illegal to copy computer programs, except for backup or archival purposes. Any business or individual convicted of illegally copying software is liable for both compensatory and statutory damages of up to $100,000 for each illegal copy of software found on the premises. Software piracy is also a federal crime that carries penalties of up to five years in jail. The Software Publishers Association (SPA) was established in 1984 to promote, protect, and inform the software industry regarding copyright issues. The original purpose was to provide its two dozen software publisher members representation with policy makers. The membership later grew to more than 500 software and information companies. In 1999 it was merged with the (IIA) to form the Software & Information Industry Association (SIIA). Today, SIIA continues to represent its members in lawsuit against software piracy and other illegal use of software.

An organization faces a number of additional risks when they tolerate software piracy. Copied software may be unreliable and carry viruses. Litigation involving copyright violations is highly publicized, and the organization is at risk of losing potential goodwill. The Los Angeles Unified School District was one of the largest school systems targeted by the Washington-based Business Software Alliance. It spent $5 million a year to replace the unlicensed software. Furthermore, tolerating software piracy encourages deterioration in business ethics that can seep into other areas of the organization.

Organizations should inform end users of the copyright laws and the potential consequences that result from violations of those laws. To prevent installation of unauthorized software, organizations may restrict user's ability to install software by disabling administrative access to their PC. Additionally, when users are given access to a personal or desktop computer, they should sign an acknowledgment that lists the installed software, the individual's responsibilities, and any disciplinary action for violations. Written procedures should clearly define user's responsibility for maintaining a software inventory, auditing compliance, and removing unlicensed software.

Destruction of Information by Computer Viruses

Most end users are knowledgeable about virus attacks, but the effect of a virus remains only a threat until they actually experience a loss. By 2011, the number of malware attacks numbered more than 200 million. According to McAfee's report, the cost to organizations of downtime due to virus attacks was $6.3 million per day, and a Fox News report estimated that $86 billion is lost worldwide annually.

A virus is the common term used to describe self-reproducing programs (SRP), worms, moles, holes, Trojan horses, and time bombs. In today's environment, the threat is great because of the unlimited number of sources from which a virus can be introduced. For example, viruses can be copied from a disk or downloaded from an infected Web page.

A virus is a piece of program code that contains self-reproducing logic, which piggybacks onto other programs and cannot survive by itself. A worm is an independent program code that replicates itself and eats away at data, uses up memory, and slows down processing. A mole enters a system through a software application and enables the user to break the normal processing and exits the program to the operating system without logging off the user, which gives the creator access to the entire system. A hole is a weakness built into a program or system that allows programmers to enter through a "backdoor," bypassing any security controls. A Trojan horse is a piece of code inside a program that causes damage by destroying data or obtaining information. A time bomb is a code that is activated by a certain event such as a date or command.

The boot sector of a disk is the most susceptible to virus infection because it is accessed every time that the computer is turned on, providing easy replication of the virus. When a virus is activated, it copies code to the hard drive, and it can spread to additional floppies by executing a common application such as a word processor or mail program. The floppies that contain the virus will continue to infect other computers and spread the virus throughout an organization.

Viruses can also spread among computers connected within a network (local, Internet, etc.). They can spread when infected files or programs are downloaded from a public computer bulletin board through attachments to e-mails through codes hidden within hyperlinks, and so on. Viruses can cause a variety of problems such as

- Destroy or alter data
- Destroy hardware

- Display unwanted messages
- Cause keyboards to lock (i.e., become inactive)
- Slow down a network by performing many tasks that are really just a continuous loop with no end or resolution
- Produce spam
- Launch denial-of-service attacks

A virus can consume processing power and disk space by replicating itself multiple times. The risk to organizations is the time involved in removing the virus, rebuilding the affected systems, and reconstructing the data. The cost to remove viruses periodically exceeds $1.5 billion, in addition to the costs in lost data and downtime, which translates into a total of $5–$10 billion worldwide. In addition, organizations should be concerned about sending virus-infected programs to other organizations. Viruses cause significant financial damage, and recipients may file lawsuits against the instituting organization.

Lack of Back-Up and Recovery Options

End-user developed applications are often stored in one's personal PC and not backed-up. In case of disaster or virus attack, these applications may not be recoverable since back-up of the application and/or data may not exist. It may not be possible for the end user to recreate the application within a reasonable period of time. In this situation, controls would be the first that get overlooked.

Electronic Data Interchange Application Risks

Auditors, management, developers, and security consultants need to be aware of the business risks associated with Electronic Data Interchange (EDI) as they provide a framework for placing appropriate security and control mechanisms within an EDI application or in an EDI environment. Risks include the following:

Loss of business continuity/going-concern problem. Inadvertent or deliberate corruption of EDI-related applications could affect every EDI transaction entered into by an organization, impacting customer satisfaction, supplier relations, and possibly business continuity eventually.

Interdependence. There is increased dependence on the systems of trading partners, which is beyond the control of the company.

Loss of confidentiality of sensitive information. Sensitive information may be accidentally or deliberately divulged on the network or in the mailbox storage system to unauthorized parties, including competitors.

Increased exposure to fraud. Access to computer systems may provide an increased opportunity to change the computer records of both a single organization and that of its trading partners by staff of the trading parties or by third-party network staff. This could include the introduction of unauthorized transactions by user organization or third-party personnel.

Manipulation of payment. A situation where amounts charged by or paid to suppliers are not reviewed before transmission. Therefore, there is a risk that payments could be made for goods not received, payment amounts could be excessive, or duplicate payment could occur.

Loss of transactions. Transactions could be lost as a result of processing disruptions at third-party network sites or en route to the recipient organization, which could cause losses to the organization and inaccurate financial reporting.

Errors in information and communication systems. Errors in the processing and communications systems, such as incorrect message repair, can result in the transmission of incorrect trading information or inaccurate reporting to management.

Loss of audit trail. EDI eliminates the need for hard copy. There will be less paper for the auditors to check. The EDI user may not provide adequate or appropriate audit evidence, either on hard copy or on magnetic media. The third-party vendor may not hold audit trails for a significant length of time, or audit trails could be lost when messages are passed across multiple networks.

Concentration of control. There will be increased reliance on computer controls where they replace manual controls, and they may not be sufficiently timely. The use of EDI with its greater reliance on computer systems concentrates control in the hands of fewer staff, increases reliance on key people, and increases risk.

Application failure. Application or EDI component failures could have a significant negative impact on partner organizations within the respective business cycles, especially for Just-In-Time inventory management, production, and payment systems. In addition, there is a possibility of error propagation across other systems due to integration with other business applications.

Potential legal liability. A situation where liability is not clearly defined in trading partner agreements, legal liability may arise due to errors outside the control of an organization or by its own employees. There is still considerable uncertainty about the legal status of EDI documents or the inability to enforce contracts in unforeseen circumstances.

Overcharging by third-party service providers. Third-party suppliers may accidentally or deliberately overcharge an organization that is using their services.

Manipulation of organization. The information available to the proprietors of third-party networks may enable them or competitors to take unfair advantage of an organization.

Not achieving anticipated cost savings. Happens where the anticipated cost savings from the investment in EDI are not realized for some reason by an organization.

The Institute of Chartered Accountants in England and Wales (ICAEW) Working Party on EDI (1992) classifies EDI risks into general, internal, and external categories. General risks are those inherent in using EDI and that occur throughout the trading cycle. Internal risks are those within the territory and control of the organization using EDI. External risks are those under the control of another party, such as other trading parties, value-added network (VAN) providers, or network management services organizations. These categories can be further subdivided into existing and new risks.

Implications of Risks in an Electronic Data Interchange System

Implications arising from the aforementioned potential risks include:

■ Potential loss of transaction audit trail, thereby making it difficult or impossible to reconcile, reconstruct, and review records. This could possibly be a breach of legislation and result in prosecution and fines.

■ Increased exposure to ransom, blackmail, or fraud through potential disruption of services or increased opportunities to alter computer records in an organization and its trading partners' IS.

- Disruption of cash flows when payment transactions are generated in error or diverted or manipulated.
- Loss of profitability occurring through increased interest charges or orders going to a competitor due to lack of receipt of EDI messages.
- Damage to reputation through loss of major customers, especially if EDI problems are widely publicized.

Financial collapse (the repudiation of EDI orders after manufacture and delivery of a product) where, for example, errors occur in order quantities for high-value products, for instance, 500 instead of 50, therefore when the goods are manufactured and delivered, the recipient refuses to accept responsibility for sending the inaccurate order. This could cripple smaller manufacturing firms. This is a new implication and risk arising from the implementation of EDI.

Application Controls

Application controls ensure the accuracy and completeness of a transaction through the use of screen edits, processing checks against valid values, balancing totals between jobs, reasonableness checks against expected volumes or values, reconciliation between systems, and controlled distribution of output. To minimize application risks, various functional and operational requirements need to be included as part of a company's control structure, such as

- Application controls and security requirements
- Functional (quality assurance) and (user) acceptance testing
- Documentation requirements
- Application software life cycle
- System development methodology
- User–machine interface
- Package customization or configuration

Application controls can be described as the manual or automated techniques used to control input, processing, and output of information in an application. As discussed in the previous section, the purpose of application controls is to ensure the complete processing and integrity of data. Application controls can be broken down into three main categories: input, processing, and output controls.

Input Controls

Input controls are meant to minimize risks associated with data input into the system. Defining input requirements ensures that the method of capturing the data is appropriate for the type of data being input and how it is subsequently used. Performance problems and accuracy issues can be introduced with inappropriate methods for capturing data.

Input requirements should specify all valid sources for data as well as the method for validating the data. Input controls prevent invalid transactions from being entered and prevent invalid data within valid transactions. These controls ensure that any errors identified are captured and effectively resolved.

Input controls ensure the authenticity, accuracy, completeness, and timeliness of data entered into an application. Authenticity is ensured by limiting access at the screen and field level, and requiring secondary approvals of transactions above a defined threshold. Accuracy is ensured by edit checks that validate data entered before accepting the transaction for processing. Completeness is ensured through error-handling procedures that provide logging, reporting, and correction of errors. Timeliness is ensured through monitoring transaction flow, logging, and reporting exceptions.

User Interface

The "user interface" is the means by which the user interacts with the system. In most cases, this is the screen, mouse, and keyboard. An effective interface for the users will help reduce desk costs and improve accuracy and efficiency. Additionally, a user interface should provide a means for the user to obtain context-sensitive help.

Interfaces

Interfaces can be considered a means of providing input into a system. Controls over interfaces should be carefully reviewed because of the volume of transactions and the automated methods used for interfaces. An inventory of all interfaces should be compiled and reviewed for systems. The interface definitions include the source, format, structure, content, and support requirements. In the instance of one company, a general ledger application had over 80 interfaces providing input of journal entries from the company subsidiary units. In this situation, the company chose to develop interface standards to minimize the number of interface formats as well as the effort in coding interfaces, which in turn reduced risk. The company designed five different interface formats that the 80 interfaces needed to adapt. Consequently, the auditors needed to only audit five interface mechanisms as opposed to 80 different interfaces.

Authenticity

Authenticity ensures that only authorized users have access to entering transactions. During the development process, business users should define the authorized users of the application and the security levels for data access. This information can be used when designing input screens to limit screens or fields to particular user groups. Controls can also be designed to enforce separation of duties. For example, a user may be able to enter a transaction, but a supervisor may need to approve the transaction before it is submitted for processing.

All authentication needs to be considered when automated applications interface to other applications. Often, scheduled batch jobs operate under the authority with specified access privileges to the database. Risks associated with these access accounts as well as the access privileges need to be reviewed. Generic accounts should not be used. The batch jobs should be given minimal privileges and system-level accounts should not be used.

Accuracy

Accuracy ensures that the information entered into an application is consistent and complies with procedures. This is accomplished by designing input screens with edits and validations that check the data being entered against predefined rules or values.

The accuracy of transactions processed can be ensured by having all transactions entered into the application go through data validation checks, whether coming from an online screen, an interface from another application, or generated by the system. Programs that automatically generate transactions (e.g., time triggered) should have built-in edits that validate transaction accuracy similar to transactions entered by a user. It is also important to track transaction volume and frequency against expected trends to ensure that transactions are triggered properly. Missing and duplicate checks should also be programmed in case an error occurs in the triggering logic.

Edit and validation routines are generally unique to the application system being used, although some general-purpose routines may be incorporated. These routines may include checking the validity of codes, recording length, range, sequence, number of fields in a record, reasonability of values, authorization and approval codes, check digits, transactions, amounts, calculations, missing and extra data, and signs.

Edit and validation routines are placed in a system to aid in ensuring the completeness and accuracy of data. Therefore, overriding edit routines should not be taken lightly. In most systems, the user is not provided this capability. Overriding edit routines is allowed only to privileged user IDs belonging to user department managers or supervisors, and from a master terminal. Overrides should be automatically logged by the application so that these actions can be analyzed for appropriateness and correctness.

Processing Controls

Processing controls ensure the accuracy, completeness, and timeliness of data processing during either batch or online processing. These controls help ensure that the data is accurately processed through the application and that no data is added, lost, or altered during processing.

Jobs scheduled within an application should be reviewed to ensure that the changes being made are appropriate and do not introduce risk. As an example, in an enterprise resource planning (ERP) application, a Structure Query Language (SQL) program can be written to modify data directly against the database, avoiding the controls within the application and operating against the database with system administrator privileges. However, from the screen, this program can look like a report if the underlying code is not evaluated.

Completeness

Completeness can be ensured in batch processing by balancing transactions going in with transactions going out of a predecessor. Balancing steps should occur in major processing points. The following control points are examples of major processing points:

- *Input points.* Programs that accept transactions from input processing (e.g., user interface)
- *Major processing modules.* Programs that modify the data (e.g., performs calculation)
- *Branching points.* Programs that split or merge data (e.g., a program that merge data from two or more different input sources into one file; the file is then used as data feed for the financial reporting system)
- *Output points.* Result of data processing (e.g., financial or operational reports, printed checks, output data file)

Designed properly, balancing totals for transaction count and amount can detect missing or duplicate transactions (see Exhibit 16.3).

In addition to balancing between jobs within an application, balancing should also occur between applications that share common data. This can be achieved by creating a reconciliation

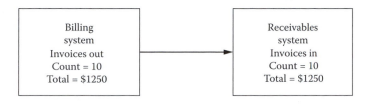

Exhibit 16.3   Batch balancing totals.

report that lists data from both systems and reports on any differences for a user group (e.g., accounting) to review and follow upon any exceptions (see Exhibit 16.4).

Balancing totals should include a transaction count and totals for all amount fields for each type of transaction, and cross-foot totals for detail fields to total fields. In Exhibit 16.5, for example, the total quantity and price for parts A, B, and C should equal the total order amount.

In files where there are no meaningful totals, hash totals can be created that add all of the figures in a column to verify that the same total is accepted by the next process. For example, totaling part numbers does not mean anything, but this total can be used to verify that all the correct part numbers were received. Transaction flows should be balanced on a daily basis and cumulatively to monthly jobs before the register closes. Balancing totals should also consider both error transactions leaving and entering the processing flow. In Exhibit 16.6, for example, 10 total

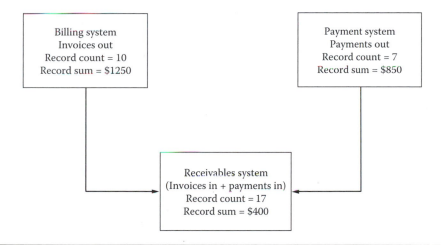

Exhibit 16.4   Cross-application balancing totals.

Order	Quantity	Part Number	Unit Price	Total
Part A	100	1288543	$1.20	$120.00
Part B	80	0982374	$0.60	$48.00
Part C	200	5436682	$0.45	$90.00
Total	380	7707599		$258.00

Exhibit 16.5   Sample balancing totals.

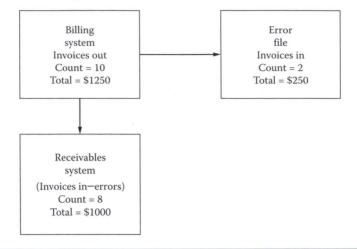

Exhibit 16.6 Balancing totals with error transactions.

transactions entered minus 2 transactions written to an error file should equal 8 transactions written out to the next job step.

Error Correction

Logging error activity, reporting open errors, and recording error correction as part of the transaction's audit trial can ensure transaction completeness. As part of ensuring accuracy, programs should be built with logic to detect and correct errors. Error handling procedures should include:

- Approval of error correction and resubmission
- Defined responsibility for suspense files
- Reports of unresolved errors
- Aging and prioritization of unresolved errors

Output Controls

Output controls ensure the integrity of output and the correct and timely distribution of the output produced. To be useful, information must be accurate and received in time to benefit decision making. Output controls include procedures to verify if the data is complete, accurate, and properly recorded; procedures for report distribution and retention; and procedures to correct output errors. If outputs are produced centrally, then conventional controls, such as a security officer and distribution logs may be appropriate. If output is distributed over a data communication network, control emphasis shifts to access controls for individual workstations. To maintain confidentiality, access to reports should be based on a "need-to-know" basis.

Output Reconciliation

Output should be verified against an independent source to verify completeness and accuracy. For example, transaction totals posted to the general ledger should be reconciled against the detailed balance due in the accounts receivable system. As mentioned earlier, data that is common to two or more applications should be reconciled to verify consistency. Often, applications are developed over time using the same information for different purposes. For example, an inventory system may use purchasing information to know when to reorder, an accounting system for financial statements, and a billing system for invoices.

Output Distribution

Distribution of output should be clearly defined and physical and logical access should be limited to authorized personnel. The need for output should be regularly reviewed as reports may be requested at the time an application is developed, but may no longer be useful. Also, the same information may be used for more than one system with different views, organization, and use. For example, the marketing department may use sales information to pay commission and monitor sales quotas, whereas the accounting department uses the same information for financial statements. These two systems should be reconciled to make sure that the amount reported for paying sales staff is the same as the amount reported on the financial statements.

Record Retention

Because storage space (computer and physical) is expensive, retention periods and storage requirements should be defined for programs, data, and reports. Critical information should be stored securely (e.g., encrypted) and its destruction should be permanent and conducted in such a way as to prevent unauthorized viewing. Organizations should consider any law and regulations that may govern the duration of retention periods.

Functional (Quality Assurance) and (User) Acceptance Testing

Functional testing and acceptance testing are keys to application controls. They ensure that the application fulfills the agreed-upon functional expectations of the users, meets established usability criteria, and satisfies performance guidelines before being implemented into production. Acceptance testing minimizes the risk that the new application may cause business interruptions or be disjointed with business processes. It should include all components of the system (facilities, application software, procedures, etc.).

Acceptance criteria should be specific with detailed measures. Acceptance plans should include inspections, functional tests, and workload trials. Users should be involved in system testing throughout the development processes. This minimizes the risk of key functionality being excluded or not working. Ideally, users should use actual samples of their work in designing and executing acceptance tests.

Management Approval

Functional and acceptance plans and the respective test results need to be approved by the affected functional department as well as the IT department.

Web-Based Application, Risks, and Controls

Use of Web applications has become key strategic for direction for many companies. Some simply use it for marketing purposes, but most are using it to replace traditional client–server applications. Web-based applications use Web 2.0 technology, such as Asynchronous Java Script Technology and XML (AJAX), FlashTM, and HTML 5.

Advantages of using Web-based applications include eliminating the need for "thick" client-side applications and the management and associated maintenance costs. "Thick clients" are full-featured computers connected to a network. Thick clients are functional whether they are connected to a network or not. While a thick client is fully functional without a network connection, it is only a "client" when it is connected to a server. The server may provide the thick client with programs and files that are not stored on the local machine's hard drive. It is not uncommon for workplaces to provide thick clients to their employees. This enables them to access files on a local server or use the computers offline.

A "thin" client functions like a regular computer, but it does not have hard drive and no software is installed. It runs programs and accesses data from a server. For example, students in a classroom could all run the same program from a server, each using his own thin client machine. Because the server provides the software to each computer on the network, it is not necessary for each computer to have a hard drive. Thin clients also make it easier to manage computer networks since software issues need to be managed only on the server instead of on each machine.

Other characteristics of Web applications include the use of a Web browser on the client side that is usually platform independent, and requires less computing power. Some benefits include reduced time to market, increased user satisfaction, and reduced expenses related to maintenance and supports. The top 10 most critical Web application security risks are shown in Exhibit 16.7.

Application controls described in the previous section applies to Web-based applications. In addition to understanding generic application controls, IT auditors should learn new technologies, such as Web services and service-oriented architecture (SOA) as some application controls are built-in within the Web 2.0 technology. For example, a Web-based application written in Java uses

Application Security Risks	Description of Risks
Injection	Injection flaws, such as SQL, OS, and LDAP injection, occur when untrusted data is sent to an interpreter as part of a command or query. The attacker's hostile data can trick the interpreter into executing unintended commands or accessing unauthorized data.
Cross Site Scripting (XSS)	XSS flaws occur whenever an application takes untrusted data and sends it to a Web browser without proper validation and escaping. XSS allows attackers to execute scripts in the victim's browser which can hijack user sessions, deface Websites, or redirect the user to malicious sites.
Broken Authentication and Session Management	Application functions related to authentication and session management are often not implemented correctly, allowing attackers to compromise passwords, keys, session tokens, or exploit other implementation flaws to assume other users' identities.

Exhibit 16.7   OWASP top 10 application security risks. (Adapted from OWASP, The Ten Most Critical Web Application Security Risks. 2010. www.owasp.org/index.php/Top_10_2010.)

Insecure Direct Object References	A direct object reference occurs when a developer exposes a reference to an internal implementation object, such as a file, directory, or database key. Without an access control check or other protection, attackers can manipulate these references to access unauthorized data.
Cross Site Request Forgery (CSRF)	A CSRF attack forces a logged-on victim's browser to send a forged HTTP request, including the victim's session cookie and any other automatically included authentication information, to a vulnerable Web application. This allows the attacker to force the victim's browser to generate requests the vulnerable application thinks are legitimate requests from the victim.
Security Misconfiguration	Good security requires having a secure configuration defined and deployed for the application, frameworks, application server, Web server, database server, and platform. All these settings should be defined, implemented, and maintained as many are not shipped with secure defaults. This includes keeping all software up to date, including all code libraries used by the application.
Insecure Cryptographic Storage	Many Web applications do not properly protect sensitive data, such as credit cards, SSNs, and authentication credentials, with appropriate encryption or hashing. Attackers may steal or modify such weakly protected data to conduct identity theft, credit card fraud, or other crimes.
Failure to Restrict URL Access	Many Web applications check URL access rights before rendering protected links and buttons. However, applications need to perform similar access control checks each time these pages are accessed, or attackers will be able to forge URLs to access these hidden pages anyway.
Insufficient Transport Layer Protection	Applications frequently fail to authenticate, encrypt, and protect the confidentiality and integrity of sensitive network traffic. When they do, they sometimes support weak algorithms, use expired or invalid certificates, or do not use them correctly.
Unvalidated Redirects and Forwards	Web applications frequently redirect and forward users to other pages and Websites, and use untrusted data to determine the destination pages. Without proper validation, attackers can redirect victims to phishing or malware sites, or use forwards to access unauthorized pages.

Exhibit 16.7   (Continued) OWASP top 10 application security risks. (Adapted from OWASP, The Ten Most Critical Web Application Security Risks. 2010. www.owasp.org/index.php/ Top_10_2010.)

Java Messaging Service (JMS). To ensure accuracy or data transmitted, the messages in XML format retains data structure in transit; data transmitted in the body of an XML message is read-only, therefore, it is not subject to manipulation; and using the persistent delivery method, the technology guarantees that messages are delivered once-and-only once.

Documentation Requirements

Documentation ensures maintainability of the system and its components and minimizes the likelihood of errors. Documentation should be based on a defined standard and consist of descriptions of procedures, instructions to personnel, flowcharts, data flow diagrams, display or report layouts, and other materials that describe the system. System documentation should provide maintenance programmers with enough information to understand how the system works to ensure effective and efficient analysis of program changes and troubleshooting. Documentation should be updated as the system is modified.

The processing logic should be documented in a manner that understands using pseudocode, flowcharts, and so on, while containing sufficient detail to allow programmers to accurately support the application. The software must also include documentation within the code, with descriptive comments embedded within the body of the source code. These comments should include cross-references to design documentation and requirements documents. The documentation should describe the sequence of programs and the steps to be taken in case of a processing failure.

Additional documentation includes a recovery plan for the application, service-level agreements with user departments, training plans, inventory of system components, interfaces, development tools, and third-party components.

Application Software Life Cycle

The software life cycle encompasses the development, acquisition, implementation, and maintenance of software. Further related information regarding each of these various phases is incorporated within various chapters in this book. The software life cycle is described in Chapter 14, the acquisition process is discussed in Chapter 15, and this chapter covers application maintenance.

Application Maintenance

Organizations often feel that once an application is put into production, all the work is done. However, applications require maintenance and changes over time, and changes provide an opportunity for risk.

Application Maintenance: Defined

Software maintenance is an important phase in the systems development life cycle. Maintenance can be separated into the following three categories:

1. *Corrective maintenance.* Emergency program fixes and routine debugging
2. *Adaptive maintenance.* Accommodations of change
3. *Perfective maintenance.* User enhancements, improved documentation, and recoding for efficiency

Corrective Maintenance

Corrective maintenance involves resolving software errors, commonly known as "bugs." The purpose of corrective maintenance is to correct existing functionality to make it work as opposed to providing new functionality. This type of maintenance can occur at any time during software use and usually is a result of inadequate software testing. Corrective maintenance can be required to accommodate a new type of data that was inadvertently excluded or modify code related to an assumption of a specific type of data element or relationship.

As an example of the latter, it was assumed in a report that each employee's employment application had an employee requisition (request to hire) associated with it in the system. However, when users did not see a complete listing of their entire employee applications listed, they discovered that not every employee application had an associated hiring request. In this case, the requirement for each application to be associated with a hiring request was a new system feature provided in the latest software release. As a result, employee applications entered into the system previous to the installation of the new release did not have hiring requests associated with them.

Adaptive Maintenance

Adaptive maintenance results from regulatory and other environmental changes. The purpose of adaptive maintenance is to adapt to some change in business conditions as opposed to providing new functionality. An example of adaptive maintenance is modifications to accommodate changes in tax law. Annually, federal and state laws change, which requires changes to financial systems and their associated reports.

A past example of this type of issue was the Year 2000 (Y2K) problem. Many software programs were written to handle dates up to 1999 and were rewritten at significant costs to handle dates beginning January 1, 2000. Although these changes cost organizations many millions of dollars in maintenance effort, the goal of these changes is not to provide users with new capabilities, but simply to allow users to continue using programs the way they are using them today. Some people argue that fixing code to accommodate Y2K was actually corrective maintenance, as software should have been designed to accommodate years beyond 1999. However, due to the expense and limitations of storage, older systems used two digits to represent the year as a means to minimize the cost and limits of storage.

Perfective Maintenance

Perfective maintenance includes incorporation of new user needs not met by the current system. The goal of perfective maintenance is to adapt software to support new requirements. Perfective maintenance can be relatively simple, such as modifying the layout of an input screen or adding new columns to a report. Complex changes can involve sophisticated new functionality. In one example, a university wanted to provide its students with the ability to pay for their fees online. A requirement for such a system involves a number of complexities including the ability to receive, process, and confirm payment. These requirements include additional requirements such as the ability to secure the information and protect the student and institution by maintaining the integrity of the data and information. Along with this, additional requirements are necessary to protect the process in its ability to recover and continue processing, as well as the ability to validate, verify, and audit each transaction.

Measuring Risk for Application Maintenance

The following metrics should be reviewed to evaluate the effectiveness and efficiency of the application maintenance process:

■ The ratio of actual maintenance cost per application versus the average of all applications
■ Requested average time to deliver change requests
■ The number of change requests for the application that were related to bugs, critical errors, and new functional specifications
■ The number of production problems per application and per respective maintenance changes
■ The number of divergence from standard procedures, such as undocumented applications, unapproved design, and testing reductions
■ The number of modules returned to development due to errors discovered in acceptance testing
■ Time elapsed to analyze and fix problems
■ Percent of application software effectively documented for maintenance

Audit Involvement

Application systems audits are performed to evaluate the controls and documentation over existing computerized applications. The scope of these audits could include an evaluation of the control procedures, data integrity, user training, segregation of duties, records retention, recoverability, access controls, and systems or user documentation. The major accountabilities included in these audits are software management, data access and recoverability, file control and balancing practices, and staffing/training.

The objectives of application systems audits are to identify risks to the integrity and recoverability of the data, the software that has been developed to process the data, the efficient and timely processing of the data, or the timely recognition of incomplete or inaccurate data.

Recommendations from application system audits might include the need for an additional file control procedure, more timely backup practices, increased data access restrictions, or additional user instructions.

Conclusion

Applications represent a significant investment for organizations as well as being critical for conducting business. Additionally, applications are a point of risk to organizations. Specifically, applications introduce the following risk:

■ Weak security
■ Unauthorized access to data
■ Unauthorized remote access
■ Inaccurate information
■ Erroneous or falsified data input
■ Misuse by authorized end users
■ Incomplete processing
■ Duplicate transactions

- Untimely processing
- Communications system failure
- Inadequate training
- Inadequate support

Owing to these risks, controls need to be employed to reduce the risk as well as to ensure that the application continues to meet the business needs in an effective and efficient manner. The following is a list of components in a control structure for applications:

- Definition of the application's control and security requirements
- Definition and use of functional testing and acceptance plans
- Development of system documentation
- A documented application software life cycle
- A documented system development methodology
- A well-designed user–machine interface

Applications require maintenance to correct errors, adapt the application to a new requirement, or perfect the application through additional functionality to meet a business need.

Maintenance also introduces risk. An auditor assigned to evaluate the risk, effectiveness, and efficiency of application maintenance associated with application should review various metrics. The metrics look at actual performance and issues related to the application when compared to the established thresholds. Additionally, maintenance issues need to be traced back to their source causes.

Review Questions

1. List and explain five application risks.
2. How can applications become incompatible systems?
3. What are the key questions an IT auditor can ask to help determine which end-user applications have top priority in an organization?
4. What are the four basic end-user environments?
5. In preparation for the audit of an end-user-developed application, what are the important questions the auditor can ask about the data that can help in assessing application risk?
6. In end-user developed applications, list three reasons why new applications may fail.
7. Why are copyright violations an area of application risk with end-user-developed applications?
8. Name and describe three potential risks associated with viruses.
9. Name and describe three potential risks areas associated with EDI applications.
10. Name and describe five application controls.

Multiple-Choice Questions

1. The following are examples of application risks except
   a. Inaccurate data
   b. Incomplete data
   c. Repeated data
   d. Duplicate data

2. Within a convenient store register system used to total orders and receive payment from customers, which of the following has the highest risk?
   a. Duplicate transactions
   b. Communications failure
   c. Unauthorized remote access
   d. Misuse by authorized users
3. The following are examples of application controls except
   a. Testing the data-entry screen
   b. User ergonomic requirements
   c. Documentation of backup procedures
   d. A list of valid sources of input data
4. A company allows data from their sales tracking system to be extracted to spreadsheets by all users. Which of the following is the highest risk associated with this practice:
   a. Copyright violations
   b. Inefficient user of resources
   c. Unauthorized access to data
   d. Incompatible systems
5. Which one of the following is an example of a risk associated with EUC?
   a. Employees make copies of software to work at home
   b. Employees enter time into company time sheet system
   c. Employees can view all sales data within the company's sales tracking system
   d. Employee can modify his time sheet data after he has entered it into the time sheet system
6. The following are examples of misuse of resources associated with EUC except
   a. Employees can purchase their own computer equipment for their work
   b. Employees can purchase their own software to be used at work
   c. Employees can purchase their own computer training
   d. Employees create their own end-user procedure manuals
7. A department employee creates and maintains a spreadsheet for the employees in that department to enter the hours they worked. The spreadsheets are subsequently used to load the employees' working time into the system. Which of the following is the highest risk associated with the specific use of the spreadsheet?
   a. The time sheet does not accurately compute the total time worked
   b. Employees may see the time worked by their fellow employees
   c. Employees do not enter their time correctly
   d. The spreadsheets are not signed by the employee
8. Viruses pose all of the following risks except
   a. Loss of data
   b. Loss of paper documents
   c. Loss of hardware
   d. Loss of performance
9. Interfaces are another form of
   a. Output
   b. Report
   c. Input
   d. Processing

10. Which form of documentation would be the most critical to an applications programmer?
    a. Procedures
    b. Flowcharts
    c. Report layout
    d. Processing logic

Exercises

1. List and describe the five most prominent application risks associated with a spreadsheet system used to maintain a company's budget. The company uses the spreadsheet to solicit the budget from each of its departments. The budget department subsequently compiles the individual spreadsheets into a master sheet, reviews and revises the budget based on its constraints, and then uses it to load the budget values into the company's finance system where the department can then view its finalized budget.

2. A catalog company allows orders to be placed directly through their Web site. Additionally, customers can also call directly to their customer service line. Describe the three most prominent risks that could contribute to unauthorized access to a customer's order information. Identify the controls.

3. A payroll department has a time sheet application where employees enter their hours worked. Describe the three most prominent risks and respective controls.

4. A company allows data from their sales tracking system to be extracted to spreadsheets by all users. Name and describe three risks associated with this practice.

5. Each department has its own technical support person who creates and maintains applications for his or her assigned department. Name three risks associated with this practice. What three controls would you recommend to help minimize those risks?

6. Research and summarize a recent virus outbreak. Include costs and impacts (depth and breadth).

7. A company has a centralized accounting system. Each individual department currently compiles its accounting paper transactions from its local accounting system. To eliminate the paper and increase efficiency, the company wants to implement an interface from the department accounting systems to the centralized accounting system. Name and describe the three most critical controls that you would recommend.

8. For the application controls described in the chapter, classify them as preventative, detective, or corrective.

9. Using the scenario described in Exercise 7, list and describe the three most critical documents that should be provided.

10. For each type of application maintenance, describe an example using the scenario described in Exercise 7.

Answers to Multiple-Choice Questions

1—c; 2—d; 3—b; 4—c; 5—a; 6—c; 7—a; 8—b; 9—c; 10—d

Further Reading

1. Baker, S., S. Waterman, and G. Ivanov, In the Crossfire: Critical Infrastructure in the Age of Cyber War. 2010.
2. Computer Security Institute, 2003 CSI/FBI Computer Crime and Security Survey, 2003, http://www.gocsi.com/press/20030528.jhtml. Verified on 8/8/03.
3. Executive Office of the President, Memorandum for Agency Chief Information Officers and Senior Procurement Executives, July 21, 2006. http://www.whitehouse.gov/omb/procurement/pbsa/pba_2006_memo.pdf.
4. GAO, Report to the Chairman and Ranking Minority Member, Subcommittee on Readiness and Management Support, Committee on Armed Services, U.S. Senate, "Greater Use of Best Practices Can Reduce Risks in Acquiring Defense Health Care System", September 2002, GAO-02-345. http://www.gao.gov/new.items/d02345.pdf.
5. ISACA. *COBIT and Application Controls: A Management Guide*. 2009.
6. ISACA. Web Application Security: Business and Risk Considerations. 2011.
7. OWASP. OWASP Top 10 - 2010: Top 10 Most Critical Web Application Security Risks. www.owasp.org/index.php/Top_10_2010. 2010.
8. White, J., Important, but often dismissed: Internal control in a Microsoft access database, *Inf. Sys. Audit Control Assoc.*, JournalOnline, 2006.

Chapter 17

Change Management

Change management is the overall process that ensures effective changes in an IT environment. The purpose of change management is to minimize the likelihood of disruption and unapproved changes as well as errors. A change management process is one that consists of analysis, implementation, and review of all changes. From an IT perspective, change management is thought of in terms of changes made to the existing IT systems. However, changes affecting the organization are also a factor. In many cases, it is the organizational changes that introduce changes to the IT systems.

This chapter provides an introduction to change management, in terms of both IT and organizational change. IT change management is one of the single most important controls to ensure the integrity, availability, reliability, security, confidentiality, and accuracy of an organization or IT system supporting the organization. Organizational change also deserves consideration, due to its potential impact to the organization and the increased relationships with changes in the IT environment. Organizational change is impacted by limitations introduced by the technology and the organization's culture. Research debates whether the technology is a product of the culture or whether the organization's practices are dictated by technology. Regardless, it is safe to say that they are interdependent. Consequently, we have expanded change management to include those related to the organization.

IT Processes

The COBIT process (AI6) in the Acquire and Implement Domain and (DS9) in the Delivery and Support Domain discusses how change and configuration management processes support an effective IT organization. Exhibit 17.1 lists the control objectives for this section.

Change Management

The most important area of control in any information-processing environment is changes to existing systems. Given the complexity of hardware, software, and application relationships in the operating environment, each change must be properly defined, planned, coordinated, tested, and implemented.

AI6 Manage Changes
Control Objectives
6.1   Change standards and procedures
6.2   Impact assessment, prioritization, and authorization
6.3   Emergency changes
6.4   Change status tracking and reporting
6.5   Change closure and documentation
DS9 Manage the Configuration
Control Objectives
9.1   Configuration repository and baseline
9.2   Identification and maintenance of configuration items (CIs)
9.3   Configuration integrity review

Exhibit 17.1   Processes to acquire and implement.

Effective change management reduces the risk of disruption of IT services. Once a change has been proposed, it must be evaluated for risk and impact. If a proposed change introduces significant risk to the operating environment, all parties affected must be notified, the appropriate level of management must approve the implementation schedule, and back out plans must be developed to remove the change from the system if necessary. The proposed change must first be reviewed by change management personnel to identify potential conflicts with other systems. The change management process should be reviewed periodically to evaluate its effectiveness. A well-defined, structured, and well-implemented change management system benefits the IT organization by

- Reducing system disruptions that can lead to business losses
- Minimizing the number of back outs caused by ineffective change implementation
- Providing consistent change implementation that permits management to allocate staff and system time efficiently and meet scheduled implementation dates
- Providing accurate and timely documentation to minimize the impact to change-related problems

The implementation of a sound change management process simplifies systems maintenance tasks.

Importance of Change Control

The U.S. Government Accountability Office (GAO) in their *Federal Information System Control Audit Manual* makes change control a specific checkpoint in their review process. Application software is designed to support a specific function, such as, payroll or loan processing. Typically, several applications may operate under one instance of operating system software. Controls over operating system software are discussed in later chapters. Establishing controls over the modification of application software programs helps to ensure that only authorized programs and authorized modifications are implemented. Instituting policies, procedures, and techniques that help make sure all programs and program modifications are properly authorized, tested, and approved and that access to accomplish this and distribution of programs are carefully controlled. Without proper controls, there is a risk that security features could be inadvertently or deliberately omitted or "turned off" or that processing irregularities or malicious code could be introduced. For example:

- A knowledgeable programmer could surreptitiously modify program code to provide a means of bypassing controls to gain access to sensitive data.
- The wrong version of a program could be implemented, thereby perpetuating outdated or erroneous processing that is assumed to have been updated.
- A virus could be introduced, inadvertently or on purpose, that disrupts processing.

The primary focus of this section is on controlling the changes that are made to software systems in operation, as operational systems produce the financial statements and a majority of program changes are made to maintain operational systems. However, the same risks and mitigating controls apply to changes associated with systems under development, once both user management and the project development team have formally approved their baseline requirements.

Organizations need to implement good change controls and configuration management. Configuration management is the process that is used to monitor the installation of and updates to system hardware, operating system software, and firmware to ensure that hardware and software function as expected and that a historical record of application changes is maintained.

Change Control

An IT change control system ensures that there is segregation of duties between who initiates the change, who approves the change, and who implements the change so that unauthorized changes cannot be implemented into a production environment. Each change made to any component of an IT infrastructure or system within should be

- Identified
- Categorized
- Prioritized
- Assessed for impact
- Authorized

Changes can be introduced to fix a bug or add new functionality. Changes can also be introduced from new software releases and the distribution of new software. Additionally, changes can result from configuration management and business process redesign. Large enterprises employ automated tools to help ensure effective change management.

Change Management System

A change management system consists of the following processes:

- Process for requesting changes
- Assessment of impact by the change
- Control process over changes

- Process for emergency changes
- Revisions to documentation and procedures
- Authorization of maintenance changes
- Policy for new software releases
- Process for distributing software

Change management should be documented in the form of an organizational policy. Exhibit 17.2 is an example of such a policy suggested.

XX Agency
INTERIM POLICY DOCUMENT
XX Agency Configuration Management

1. **Purpose.** This Interim Policy Document (IPD) establishes XX Agency procedures for maintaining a standard configuration of the XX Agency network and at the client desktop.

2. **Objective.** The objective is to comply with the XX Agency guidelines and "standard push" to maintain a proper level-of-standard configuration on XX Agency network and client desktop.

3. **Reference**

    A. Computer Security Act of 1987 (PL 100-235).

    B. OMB Circular A-130, Appendix III, Security of Federal Automated Information Resources.

4. **Policy.** It is XX Agency policy to protect information and corporate assets. One way of facilitating this requirement is to formally manage and control hardware and software configuration.

5. **Responsibilities**

    A. The Council of Management Officials (CIMO) is responsible for

        1. Ensuring coordination among program area offices on IRM issues (including the network) and activities

    B. Client Work Group (CWG) is responsible for

        1. Maintaining desktop design, development, and maintenance.

        2. Developing procedures for software change control and synchronized software distribution.

        3. Evaluating, recommending, and coordinating the implementation of desktop solutions consistent with XX Agency strategic and technical plans.

        4. Providing updates to XX Agency desktop software; resolving Tier 1 and Tier 2 issues and problems among XX Agency offices.

    C. The Security Working Group (SWG) is responsible for

        1. Approving or coordinating on documents prepared by the Bureau Chief Information Systems Security Manager for the purpose of maintaining network security and for Director, XX Agency signature.

Exhibit 17.2   Draft agency configuration management policy.

D. Bureau Information Technology Security Manager (BITSM) is responsible for

1. Ensuring that IT resources are adequately safeguarded throughout the Bureau

2. Developing and implementing an overall network security plan for XX Agency systems

3. Issuing guidelines and procedures for the Bureau

4. Providing oversight for XX Agency network security

5. Maintaining current inventory of sensitive systems and a schedule for testing system contingency plans

Scope

Involved Persons: Every worker at the XX Agency—no matter what their status (employee, contractor, consultant, temporary, etc.)—must comply with the information security policies found in this and related information security documents.

Involved Systems: This policy applies to all computer and network systems owned by or administered by the XX Agency. Similarly, this policy applies to all platforms (operating systems), all computer sizes (personal computers through mainframes), and all application systems (whether developed in-house or purchased from third parties). The policy covers only information handled via computers or networks.

Procedures

With the exception of emergency situations, all changes to XX Agency computer networks must be (1) documented in a work order request and (2) approved in advance by the authorized XX Agency officials. All emergency changes to XX Agency networks must only be made by persons who are authorized by the respective XX Agency officials. This process prevents unexpected changes from inadvertently leading to denial of service, unauthorized disclosure of information, and other problems. This process applies not only to workers as defined in the Scope section of this policy but also to vendor personnel.

XX Agency has formally established a consistent, cross-organizational configuration management process for the architecture and its components. Configuration management involves identifying the configuration of a network system at given points in time, systematically controlling changes to the configuration, and maintaining the integrity and traceability of the configuration throughout the life cycle. The items placed under configuration management include the software and hardware products that comprise the network, as well as items required to create or maintain these products. Proper configuration management enables an organization to answer the following questions:

What is the process for making changes to the network and its components?

Who made a change to the network and its components?

What changes were made to the network and its components?

When were the changes made?

Why were the changes made?

Who authorized the changes?

Exhibit 17.2   (Continued) Draft agency configuration management policy.

The following sections present the configuration change control activities for the XX Agency network:

At a high-level, the XX Agency change control process consists of the following basic steps:

- Identifying and classifying a change to the network
- Evaluating what components in the current network configuration need to be changed
- Testing or modeling the impact of the change upon the current network
- Implementing the change if it is approved

Misuse: XX Agency management reserves the right to revoke the system privileges of any user at any time. Workers who deliberately violate this and other information security policy statements will be subject to disciplinary action up to and including termination.

Exhibit 17.2   (Continued) Draft agency configuration management policy.

Change Request Process

A change request process ensures that only authorized changes are made. It requires that a record is kept of all changes to the system, appropriate resources are allocated, and changes are prioritized. Changes should be prioritized in terms of benefit, urgency, and effort required, as well as possible impact on existing operations. The process should also manage coordination between changes to account for any interdependencies that may exist. Change management procedures should be documented and require

- A record of change requests to be kept for each application and system.
- A definition of the authority and responsibility of the IT department, as well as the user.
- Approval by management after all the related information is reviewed.
- A schedule for changes as well as allow for changes outside of the schedule. This allows changes made outside of the schedule to receive specific management approval.
- A notification process included in the procedures so that requesters are kept informed regarding the status of their requests.

Impact Assessment

Each change requires an impact assessment to ensure that potential negative consequences of a change are identified and planned for. Changes can introduce risk to the availability, integrity, confidentiality, and performance of a system. Each change request needs to include supporting evidence of the impact assessment. The impact analysis should include specific measures compared with prescribed limits. This enables the extent of the impact to be evaluated. Changes should also be reviewed to determine the effect on compliance with existing policy, procedures, and processes.

Controls over Changes

The control over changes is enabled via the processes and automated tools that are needed to ensure the integration of change requests, software changes, and software distribution. These controls would ensure that not just authorized changes were made but also the detection of unauthorized changes, reduction of the errors due to system changes, and an increase in the reliability of changes.

Controls over the change control process include an independent verification of the success or failure of implemented changes. Another control is the update to the infrastructure or system configuration. By formally updating the configuration record, it allows for the detection of unauthorized changes that are not in the record.

Emergency Change Process

Emergency changes are changes that are required outside of the prescribed schedule. Normally, emergency changes are required to fix errors in functionality that adversely effect system performance or business processes. Emergency changes may also be required to fix discovered imminent vulnerabilities to availability, integrity, or confidentiality. Conversely, emergency changes should not compromise the integrity, availability, reliability, security, confidentiality, or accuracy of the system. Because of the consequences that can occur with emergency changes, they should only be implemented in declared emergencies.

Emergency change procedures should not only describe the process for implementing emergency changes but should also include description of what constitutes an emergency change. The definitive parameters and characteristics of an emergency change need to be clearly described. Emergency changes should be documented like regular changes but the documentation may not occur until after the change is made due to the nature of the emergency. Emergency changes do require formal authorization by those responsible for the system as well as by management before implementation. In some cases, backups before and after the change are retained for later review.

Emergency changes, by their nature, pose increased risk as they bypass some of the formal analyses and processes of the traditional change control process. As a result, audits of change control procedures should pay particular attention to emergency changes.

Revisions to Documentation and Procedures

In most cases, changes to production environments will require that existing documentation and procedures be updated to reflect the nature of the change. Current documentation ensures the maintainability of the system by any assigned staff member and minimizes reliance on individual staff.

Change control procedures should include a task for updating documentation, operational procedures, help desk resources, and training materials. Changes to business processes should also be considered. Documentation, procedures, and business processes should actually receive the same consideration and testing as other components impacted by the change.

Authorized Maintenance

Maintenance updates are also considered changes and should be accounted for in the change control procedures. Maintenance tasks should be described to the level of detail necessary to ensure appropriate controls. Maintenance actions should be logged and the log reviewed to ensure appropriateness. Access controls should be used to limit the actions of personnel performing the maintenance to only the access required. An example of a routine maintenance task is defragmenting a hard disk to remove fragmented files or lost clusters.

Software Release Policy

Like any change, new software releases require management approval to ensure that the change is authorized, tested, and documented before the new software release is applied to the production environment. The following controls need to be applied specifically to new software releases:

- Appropriate backups of the system's data and programs should be made before the change.
- Version control should be accounted for in the process. Version control is the manner in which the set of files associated with a version is tracked. It also defines the coordination between the developers working on various aspects of the system. There are automated systems that contain databases to store the various versions of files.
- Software releases should only be considered received from the prescribed central repository.
- A formal handover process is also required so that authorized personnel are involved in the process, the implemented software is unchanged from what was tested, and software media is prepared by the appropriate function based on the formal build instructions.

Software Distribution Process

The purpose of a software distribution process is to ensure that all copies of the software are distributed in accordance with their license agreements. A software distribution process minimizes the risk of multiple versions of the software being installed at the same time. Multiple versions of a software package increase support costs as users and support staff need to be trained and skilled in the features, functionality, and issues with each version.

A software distribution process should also account for a verification of the software's integrity, as well as verification for compliance with software license agreements. License agreements normally grant permission to use the specified software based on limitations, number of users, location, type of use, and so on. Software licenses can be for unlimited use by a specifically named person, for concurrent use by an unlimited number of simultaneous users, a site license for unlimited use on one site, or an enterprise license for unlimited use by the enterprise.

Violating software agreements has legal ramifications for companies, including costs for installed copies not licensed, damages and legal fees, and loss of corporate reputation. News stories about software piracy mainly focus on court cases related to someone's setting up a Web site distributing software illegally. However, the unprinted stories are those settled out of court with companies. The SIIA is an organization composed of companies of the software and information industry. One of their objectives is to protect the intellectual property of their members. SIIA is instrumental in influencing laws to protect intellectual property and taking action to combat software piracy. SIIA's Corporate Anti-Piracy Program identifies, investigates, and resolves software piracy cases on behalf of its members. Software distributions practices should include the following controls:

- Distribution is made in a timely manner only to those authorized.
- A means is in place for ensuring verification of integrity, and this is incorporated into the installation.

■ A formal record exists of who has received software and where it has been implemented. This record should also match with the number of purchased licenses.

Change Management Tools

Keeping track of all the components and versions in most systems is a daunting task, especially in environments with multiple applications on multiple platforms. That complexity makes this process an ideal candidate for automation. There are many products in this area that track the inventory of objects and offer workflow for submitting, approving, and tracking changes. Some examples of change and configuration management software products in this category are listed as follows:

KONFIG® Configuration Management (KONFIG CM) by Auto-trol Technology Corporation is a comprehensive Web -based information, configuration, and data management solution that includes the core components of fully integrated configuration management, data/ document management, product data management, workflow, and change management. KONFIG CM is designed to be an enterprise solution.

HP Change and Configuration Center by HP, Inc. is a complete software suite that provides discovery, change modeling, scheduling, and approval. A complete life cycle solution can help reduce an application's total cost of ownership.

TurnOver™ Change Management by SoftLanding Systems, Inc. is an AS400 and iSeries change management package. TurnOver gives a software management strategy and a strong, flexible foundation. Much more than just source and object management, it organizes and automates an entire development cycle from change request to risk-free installation.

IBM Tivoli® Configuration Manager by IBM Corporation helps gain control over software and hardware installations, deploys complex mission-critical applications to multiple locations from a central point, and automatically scans for and collects configuration information from diverse computer systems for rapid, centralized application deployment and management.

MKS Integrity for Application Lifecycle Management by MKS, Inc. helps regain control of source code and increase developer productivity by increasing the understanding of software systems. It graphically tracks the progress of software projects throughout their life cycles and identifies potential defects earlier in the development life cycle, saving time, and expense.

Another organization that has generated information and research about change control and tools, techniques, and metrics is US-CERT Software Assurance community. For example, their research of content changes includes nine new entries, mostly related to integration, authentication, and business logic, and updates to 236 entries, especially mitigations, names, descriptions, demonstrative examples, and relationships. There were no deprecations or schema changes. International in scope and free for public use, Common Weakness Enumeration (CWE) (version 1.1.2, March 30, 2011) provides a unified, measurable set of software weaknesses that is enabling more effective discussion, description, selection, and use of software security tools and services that can find these weaknesses in source code and operational systems. CWE also provides a better understanding and management of software weaknesses related to architecture and design. CWE and other security-related enumerations are accessible via Making Security Measurable, which publishes collaboration efforts aimed at improving the measurability of security through enumerating baseline security data, providing standardized languages as means for accurately communicating the information, and encouraging the sharing of the information with users by developing repositories. The other listed activities and initiatives have similar concepts or compatible approaches. Together all of these efforts are helping to make security more measurable by defining the concepts that need to be measured, providing for high-fidelity communications about the measurements, and providing for sharing of the measurements and the definitions of what to measure.

To assist in enhancing security throughout the software development life cycle, and to support the needs of developers, testers, and educators, the Common Attack Pattern Enumeration and Classification (CAPEC) is another of these efforts sponsored by DHS NCSD as part of the Software Assurance strategic initiative. The objective of this effort is to provide a publicly available catalog of attack patterns along with a comprehensive schema and classification taxonomy. Linked with CWE, this CAPEC site contains the initial set of content and will continue to evolve with public participation and contributions to form a standard mechanism for identifying, collecting, refining, and sharing attack patterns among the software community.

Change Management Procedures

Change management procedures ensure that all members of an organization are following the same process for initiating, approving, and implementing changes to systems and applications. The following are possible areas to consider in developing a change management procedure.

Objectives

In the following is a list of possible objectives to consider for change management procedures:

- Document the reason for change
- Identify who is requesting the change
- Formalize who will make the change
- Define how the change will be made
- Document back out procedures should the need arise
- Assess the risk of failure and impact of the change
- Aid in communicating with those affected by the change
- Identify disaster recovery considerations
- Identify conflicts between multiple changes
- Enhance management's awareness of all of the above

Scope

The scope for these procedures can include the following:

- Hardware (UNIX, NT, Client, Sun)
- System software (UNIX, NT, Oracle, Client)
- Database instances
- Application software
- Third-party tools
- Telecommunications (circuits)
- Firewalls
- Network (local area network, wide area network, routers, servers, software delivery, etc.)
- Facilities environment (uninterruptible power supply, electrical, etc.)

Change Management Boards or Committees

These are common entities to deal with coordinating the communication of changes within an organization. Following are possible sources for members of a change management board:

- Application development/support teams (finance, human resources, etc.) who can provide leads
- Data center operations
- Networks/telecommunications
- Help desk
- Key user representatives

The individuals on the change board should be selected based on their in-depth perspective and broad knowledge of the areas they represent as well as their awareness for other functional areas involved. The goal is to ensure that the decisions made are objective as these changes have the potential of affecting the organization. Change committees meet daily or weekly. The following types of changes are often considered during daily change review meetings:

- Emergency releases, fixes, and so on. These are normally related to circumstances in which the production is down.
- Database clones, restores, links, or new instances.
- "Fast-tracked" requests that cannot wait for the normally scheduled dates for updates. Fast-tracked requests can be associated with new functionality to meet a business need by a published deadline.
- Oracle account maintenance.
- Upgrades to development tools.

The following topics are often covered during weekly meetings:

- Migrations of new releases
- Upgrades to production or development tools
- Environment setup for migrations
- Environment setup for tools
- Third-party upgrades
- Configuration changes
- Hardware changes

Criteria for Approving Changes

Approval can be based on the following criteria:

State of the production environment. Before determining if a change should be approved, the change board should evaluate the performance and availability of each system in the production environment during the previous week. In general, if the production environment has performed well and has been available to the users, the change board is more likely to approve changes that provide new functionality or changes that might have a higher risk of failure. Conversely, if the state of the production environment during the previous week has been poor, the change board is more likely to approve only those changes designed to correct problems.

Change level. As part of the approval process, the change level is examined along with the detailed information and instructions attached to the change request. The attachments should detail the associated risk and impact of the change. Particularly important are the subjective comments provided by the change author indicating the reasons for the assigned change level. The change level can be based on six factors: risk, impact, communication requirements, install time, documentation requirements, and education or training requirements.

Cumulative effect of all proposed changes. The change board is one place where all of the changes requested for the week come together. The change board has the ability to examine several changes, each of which may appear to carry a reasonable risk if taken independently, but when all changes proposed for a particular week are considered as a group, the composite effect may result in too much change activity—hence, risk. When the change board reaches this conclusion, its responsibility is to prioritize the various changes, approve the most significant ones, and recommend that the others be rescheduled.

Resource availability. The change board evaluates the availability of people, time, and system resources when considering the scheduling and approval of changes.

Criticality. There are issues that may affect the impact of the change as viewed by the requester. For example, the change author may feel that the impact is relatively low because his change affects a small percentage of the user community. However, the change board may view the criticality to be high because that small percentage of users is a critical client or user. An example might be the finance department during a year-end close process.

Postimplementation

Following a change, the following items need to be evaluated:

■ Were the change procedures followed?
■ Did the change adequately meet its objectives?
■ Were the implementation and back out procedures adequate? (Any problems encountered can be addressed during future planning.)
■ The status is updated and identified as to be complete, not complete, in progress, failed, or cancelled.

Changes can be introduced to fix a bug or add new functionality. Changes can also be introduced from new software releases and the distribution of new software. Additionally, changes can result from configuration management and business process redesign. Large enterprises employ automated tools to help ensure effective change management.

There are three types of changes: routine, nonroutine, and emergency. Routine changes typically have minimal impact on daily operations. They can be implemented or backed out quickly and easily. Nonroutine changes potentially have a greater impact on operations. They frequently affect many users and typically have lengthy, complex implementation and back out procedures. An emergency change is any change, major or minor, that must be made quickly, without following standard change control procedures. Management must approve such changes before they are undertaken or implemented. Exhibit 17.3 is a typical flowchart for nonemergency changes. Exhibit 17.4 documents emergency change procedures.

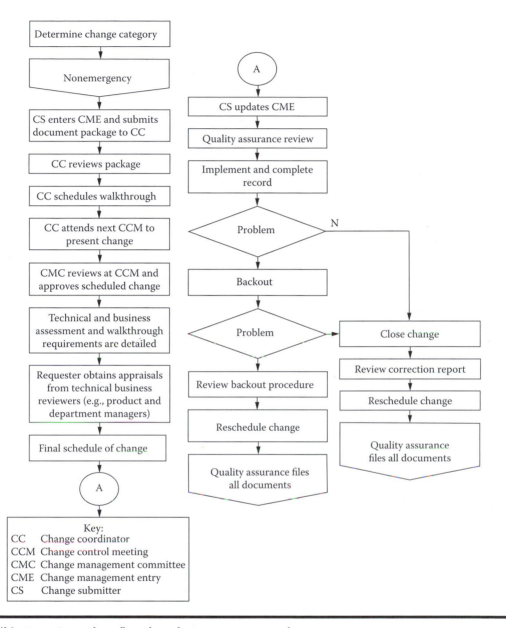

Exhibit 17.3 Procedure flowchart for nonemergency changes.

Points of Change Origination and Initiation

The change control process should identify the people or groups who initiate changes. Vendors, computer operations staff, application or system programmers, or users request most changes. In addition, the process should ensure that all requests are submitted on a standard change request form that contains the following information:

■ Date of request
■ Name of requester

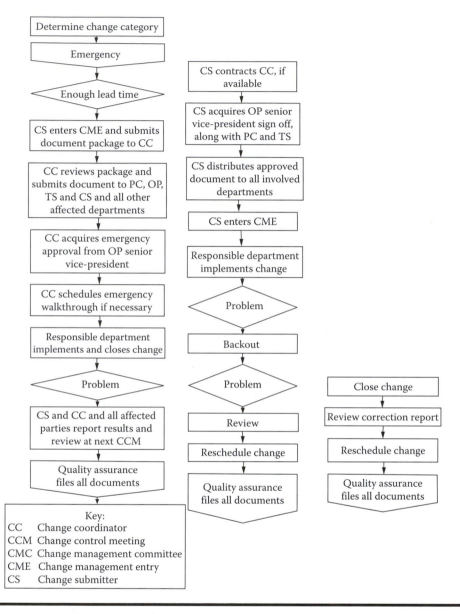

Exhibit 17.4   Procedure flowchart for emergency changes.

- Description of the change
- Reason for the change
- Approvals of the request
- Areas that may be affected by the change

The urgency of each request should be determined and all requested changes should be filed by priority and date. The process must also provide the means for implementing emergency changes in response to an operational problem. Control points for emergency change processing should be established to record, document, and obtain subsequent approval for changes. Emergency changes should be cross-referenced to operations problem reports to help verify the proper recording and handling of the changes.

Each change request should be numbered sequentially and recorded in a change log at a central control point. Most organizations use online tools to facilitate this process. The change request is entered online and, based on the areas affected, electronically routed to those areas for approval. The responsible area's approval is also recorded online. Any and all discussions regarding that change are documented online. Once the change has been scheduled, the online system will notify users of the upcoming change; it will provide a confirmation once the change has occurred. Storing this information online allows management to perform a subsequent review of all changes for a variety of reasons. One may be the routine occurrence of the same type of emergency, indicating that the changes are fixing the symptom and not the underlying problem. Also, management could analyze what amounts of their resources are devoted to the routine, nonroutine, and emergency changes. If one application is requiring a significant amount of resources for changes, this may be an indicator that the application is reaching the point where replacing it may be more cost effective.

Approval Points

Approval points should be scheduled throughout the change control process. All key people and departments affected by a change should be notified of its implementation schedule. Those who may require notification include

- Users of the system
- Vendors
- Application programmers
- IT management
- Operations personnel
- Data control personnel
- Network management
- Auditors
- Third-party service providers

An important part of the approval process often overlooked is testing. Ideally, testing would occur in a mirror of the production system. System changes need to be tested to ensure that they do not negatively impact the applications. Application changes can be grouped into system or functionality changes. System changes typically do not Impact the end user and usually improve the speed of processing transactions. The programming support group, instead of the end users, typically tests these changes. Functionality changes are obvious to the end user and should be tested and approved by them. Functionality changes should be verified in a test environment. The test environment is a mirror of the production environment, which includes the data, programs, or objects. The data files should be expanded to include unusual or nonroutine transactions to ensure that all transaction types are used in the testing.

Approval levels should be predetermined as to who can approve what changes. Part of the change control process should ensure that the appropriate approval level is obtained before any changes are moved into production.

Changes to Documentation

As a system ages, the task of keeping track of changes and their impact on the operating system, operations environment, and application programs becomes increasingly difficult. The organization should maintain a record of all the changes made to the system. Without such a record, it is impossible to determine how proposed changes will affect the system. Not only should the change be documented with the change request but also in the programmer's documentation. Programmer documentation is absolutely necessary for future maintenance.

It is also important to know when and why changes were requested but not implemented. With personnel changes, you may be revisiting an issue already deemed to be undeserving of time but it must be revisited to ensure integrity. The opposite can also be true where a previously undeserving issue could have merit due to the changing business environment.

Review Points

The change control process must be carefully coordinated if changes to the system are to be successfully implemented. The following steps should be included in the change review process:

- Pending changes are reviewed with key personnel in operations, application programming, network and data control, and auditing.
- Written change notification is sent to all interested parties, informing them of the nature of the change, scheduling of the change, purpose of the change, individual responsible for implementing the change, and systems affected by the change.
- Sufficient response time is provided for interested parties to examine proposed changes. The change notification should indicate the response deadline and the individual to contact for additional information.
- Periodic (e.g., weekly) change control meetings should be held to discuss changes with key personnel.
- Reports are filed on implemented changes to record postimplementation results and successes as well as problems.

Appendix V, Exhibit A5.1 provides a generalized audit program for use in most IT environments. Depending on the size and complexity of the organization, the program may need to be revised or expanded to obtain adequate audit coverage of the system maintenance function. Exhibit 17.5 illustrates program maintenance activities and controls and provides examples of errors.

Configuration Management

Configuration management is controlling the physical inventory and relationships among components that form a set of "baseline" objects that are subject to change. This includes the configuration management of applications, system software, hardware, and networks. The National Institute of Standards and Technology defined the process of software configuration management (SCM) in its Publication 500-223, "A Frame Work for the Development and Assurance of High Integrity Software." The major objectives of the SCM process are to track the different versions of the software and ensure that each version of the software contains the exact software outputs generated and approved for that version. It must be established before software development starts

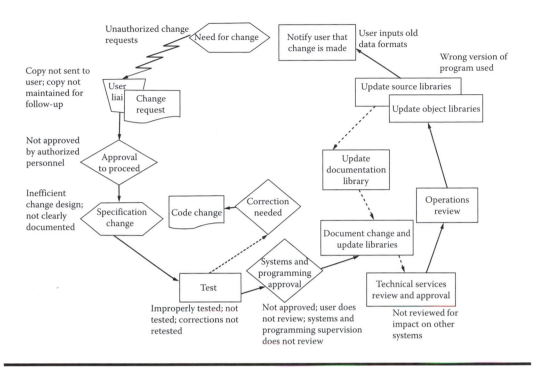

Exhibit 17.5   Program maintenance activities and examples of potential errors.

and continue throughout the software life cycle. SCM is responsible for ensuring that any changes to software during the development processes are made in a controlled and complete manner.

The SCM process produces a software configuration management plan (SCMP). When the software is integrated with system components, system configuration management begins. However, any changes to the software necessitates that SCM be invoked. Exhibit 17.6 lists the activities of the SCM process.

Organizational Change Management

Organizational change relates to the organization's ability and methods for adopting, managing, and adapting to change. Factors for evaluating change vary based on the scope of the change (i.e., changes to work habits as opposed to changes to the organization itself). Regardless of how IT is managed, it is still enacted by organizations to realize their expected monetary results. Consequently, an IT project can actually be considered a product of the organization's culture.

There are many studies to support the assertion that many IT projects fail due to the inability of the organization to adapt to the change necessary to take advantage of IT. Organizations find it difficult to change their practices and structures, especially if the application is perceived to be in conflict with the company's culture.

Organizational Culture Defined

According to Robert Kling and Roberta Lamb, organizational culture is composed of structures for incentives, politics, support for interorganizational relationships, and social repercussions.

Generate a Software Configuration Management Plan
Software Configuration Identification
Identify CIs, that is, select the most significant and critical functions that will require constant attention and control throughout software development.
Assign a unique identifier/number to each CI.
Establish baselines for the following CIs, that is, documents that have been formally reviewed and agreed upon, (1) which serve as the basis for further development and (2) which can be changed only through formal change control procedures.
Functional baseline (the completion and acceptance of the system requirements specification): prerequisite for the development of the software requirements specification (SRS) for each CI.
Allocated baseline (the review and acceptance of the SRSs): the prerequisite of the development of the software design description (SDD) for all components making up a CI.
Developmental configuration (developer-controlled "rolling" baseline): all of the documents and code accepted and committed for configuration control up to the establishment of the product baseline.
Product baseline (established with the successful conclusion of a configuration audit): prerequisite to the operation and maintenance of the software.
Problem Reporting, Tracking, and Corrective Action
Document when a software development activity does not comply with its plan, output deficiency, or anomalous behavior and give the corrective action taken.
Change Control
Document, evaluate, resolve, and approve changes to the software.
Change Review
Assess problems and changes, implement approved changes, and provide feedback to processes affected by changes.
Traceability Analysis
Trace forward and backward through the current software outputs to establish the scope of impacted software.
Configuration Control
Delegate authority for controlling changes to software; determine method for processing change requests.
Configuration Status Accounting
Keep records detailing the state of the software product's development, for example, record changes made to the software, status of documents, changes in process, change history, and release status, etc.
Configuration Audits and Reviews

Exhibit 17.6   Activities of the SCM process.

Audit CIs before release of product baseline or updated version of product baseline; review to determine progress and quality of product.   *Functional configuration audit.* Prove that a CI's actual performance agrees with its software requirements stated in the SRS   *Physical configuration audit.* Ensure that the documentation to be delivered with the software represents the content of the software product.
Archive, Retrieval, and Release
Archive software outputs (with backups) so that it cannot be changed without authorization and it will not deteriorate data to ensure it can be retrieved if necessary; describe software being released to ensure it is authorized.

Exhibit 17.6   (Continued) Activities of the SCM process.

Incentives offered by the organization can impact the success of the organization in adapting to change because users do not necessarily see the "natural" advantages of adopting the change. As a point of caution, incentives should not conflict with other rewards or incentives or the culture. For example, if employees are told that they will be offered training to learn a new state-of-the-art system, but they will risk losing their bonus due to their increase in nonbillable time, the employee will see the training as a punishment as opposed to being considered an incentive.

Company politics can have significant effects on the success of a new IT system or change in the organization. Most models of organizational change exclude recognition for the importance of political influences over organizational change. For example, a new IT system can shift the power of information. In one case, it provided the corporate office direct online access to the live sales activity in each sales office. Prior to the new system, the field offices were able to determine how and when to present their sales figures to the corporate office. In some cases, the sales office would modify actual sales data with sales that were not yet realized. This enabled the sales offices to present their "best" sales figures. With direct access to the sales information, the corporate office was empowered to see the data when and how they wanted, allowing them insight into the volatility of the sales for a given office. Because it transferred control over the information to the corporate offices, the system was perceived to transfer decision power to the corporate office away from the sales offices. Subsequent power struggles ensued between the sales offices and the corporate office.

Organizational and technical support is critical for the effective use of IT. A supporting infrastructure includes organizational practices, key support staff, and access to technical and organizational skill sets. In this model, individual and organizational learning are considered a subset of the IT system. Many major IT system implementations are now including business process review sessions within their implementation scope. This enables the organization to review their business process in terms of the change that will be introduced into the system. This fit-gap analysis identifies gaps in functionality, which is integral to business processes. Subsequent plans can be made to accommodate for these gaps in redesigned business process, changes in business services, or modifications to the system itself.

Interorganizational relationships and social networks are supported and impacted through the use of IT. The influence of relationships and social networks are believed to explain why some technologies are supported and others are not. Looking at online communities and electronic market places—is it the influence of technology on relationships and networks that created online communities and electronic market places or vice versa?

An example of a successful online community is eBay. eBay defines itself as an online community. Its community is composed of individual buyers and sellers as well as large and small companies. Member relationships are supported with discussion boards. The sense of community is used to ensure that eBay guidelines are followed with a "neighborhood watch" philosophy. The eBay community has also joined together to support social causes such as fundraising for victims of September 11, 2001.

Managing Organizational Change

Culture and structure change should be managed through the life cycle. It includes people, organization, and culture. A culture that shares values and is open to change contributes to success. To facilitate the change process, users should be involved in the design and implementation of the business process and the ERP system. A communications plan and training and professional development plans also support this.

The business processes associated with a software implementation need to be aligned. In adapting packaged software packages, organizations face the question of whether to adapt the organization to the software or vice versa. To minimize maintenance of the software, the company should consider changing the business process to fit the software and the software should be modified as little as possible. Reducing customization reduces errors and improves the ability to utilize newer releases.

Organizational change relies on effective communication. Expectations need to be communicated. Communication, education, and expectations need to be managed throughout the organization. Input from users should also be managed to ensure that requirements, comments, and approval are obtained. Communication includes the formal promotion of the implemented change as well as the organization's progress with adopting the change. Employees should also know the scope, objectives, activities, and updates and the expectation for change in advance.

Training and professional development plans should be incorporated into any effort to introduce change into an organization. Employees need to be trained in the new processes and procedures. Additionally, the team assigned to implement the change requires special training in the process and procedures. Training in adapting to change is also beneficial to all employees.

Some organizations adopt formal change management programs as a means of assisting employees to adapt to major changes. *Who Moved My Cheese*, by Spencer Johnson, MD, and Kenneth Blanchard, is a popular book being adopted by major organizations to introduce the concept of changes and why change is important to the organization, as well as how change is beneficial for the employee. Cheese is used as a metaphor for the things that people want out of their lives. There are four characters in the book. Each character represents different approaches to adapting to change. The characteristics of each mouse are observed as they embark on a journey through a maze in search of the cheese that has been moved.

Audit Involvement

A change control review would determine whether system changes are authorized, tested, documented, communicated, and controlled. The following areas would be covered:

- Authorization
- Testing (unit, system, and user acceptance)

- Documentation
- Communication
- Controls

Defined broadly, change management is any process that has an impact on the production-processing environment. This includes changes to hardware, application software, and networks. With respect to the application change management review, change management is defined as any modification to programs that may impact production processing, including mainframe and client/server changes. Production processing includes system availability/reliability and integrity. Many organizations have migrated from a mainframe-dominated environment to a heterogeneous environment with mainframe, client/server, and minicomputers. These systems require very different procedures, tools, and skill sets to manage change.

As organizations have evolved to this new architecture, the control environment over the change process (especially within the client/server environment) may not have kept pace with this level of change, thereby increasing the risk that production could be adversely impacted. Insufficient change control processes have the following risks:

- System outages due to error, omissions, or malicious intent
- Data loss or errors due to error, omissions, or malicious intent
- Unauthorized changes
- Fraud/abuse of company systems and/or data
- Repeated errors
- Reruns of system or application processes

The objectives of a change management review are to ensure that changes made to production systems and applications do not adversely affect system, application, or data availability or integrity. To that end, auditors need to verify that all changes made to the production systems and applications are appropriately authorized and documented. A critical success factor for change management is the culture of the organization. Does management understand the critical role of change management and does it recognize the impact change management has on the success of the organization? Are change management policies, procedures, and processes in place over client/server, mainframe, and desktop environments? Are controls in place to ensure that changes made to not adversely impact system stability or data integrity? The audit should include the following steps in a review of the change control process:

- Obtain copies of policies/procedures related to change management.
- Interview application support staff to determine formal, informal, and emergency procedures used to implement changes to production systems and applications.
- Obtain copies of change control request form and logs.
- Select a sample of changes from the changes logged. Determine compliance with policies, procedures, and best practices.
- Obtain copies of help desk call logs to determine adverse impacts from changes.
- Review system availability reports.
- Review system change logs. Select sample to trace back to change control request logs.
- Determine if new software, and changes to existing software are properly authorized, in writing, by the appropriate manager.
- Determine that all new software and software changes are properly tested, using test files and directories, before they are moved into production.

- Determine that all test results are reviewed by someone other than the originator.
- Determine that program and file names are properly controlled to avoid duplicate names.
- Determine that all supporting documentation is updated before an application is placed into production.
- Determine that production applications are stored in a directory protected from unauthorized changes.
- Determine the means of tracking production application changes. Is there a check-out/check-in system to prevent unauthorized changes?
- Determine that original programs are secured off-site. These can be used to compare with the current production version to detect changes and for disaster recovery.

The auditor obtains the necessary background information, determines the key controls, performs limited substantive testing to assess the reliability and effectiveness of the process controls, and evaluates the process.

The auditor must take the time to become thoroughly familiar with the change control process. He or she should develop a flowchart of the process in which points of origination and initiation, approval points, changes to documentation, and review points are all identified.

The auditor should develop flowcharts documenting the procedures for emergency and nonemergency changes.

Conclusion

Change management is one of the single most important controls to ensure the integrity, availability, reliability, security, confidentiality, and accuracy of an organization or IT system supporting the organization. Many IT change control systems are not only documented but also automated. These automated systems enable the systematic implementation and control of the change control process. Additionally, automated change control systems also enable an auditor to perform an effective and efficient review through the evaluation of rule sets, access lists, and log files.

As mentioned, in the United States, organizations such as US-CERT and DHS are strong advocates of better configuration management and change control practices. As a strategic initiative of the DHS National Cyber Security Division, the key objective of the Software Assurance Program is to shift the security paradigm from patch management to software assurance. This shift is designed to encourage software developers to raise overall software quality and security from the start, rather than relying on applying patches to systems after vulnerabilities are discovered. It starts with secure software engineering to "build security in." The IT auditor can play a critical role in this process.

Recognizing that software security integrated with change control and configuration management must be addressed in a systematic way throughout the software development life cycle, the Software Assurance Program encourages all software developers, from the public sector and private industry, to raise the standard on software quality and security. Together, government, industry, and academia will raise expectations for product assurance with requisite levels of integrity and security, by promoting security methodologies and tools as a normal part of business.

Organizational change also deserves consideration by the IT auditor due to its potential impact on the organization and the increased relationships with changes in the IT environment.

Organizational change is impacted by limitations introduced by the technology and the organization's culture. An organization's culture is composed of its structures for incentives, politics, and relationships with other organizations and the community.

Review Questions

1. Identify and describe the five goals of an IT change management system.
2. Name and describe the eight controls of a change management system.
3. Describe the risks associated with maintenance.
4. Name and describe the four controls associated with the software release process.
5. Name and describe three risks associated with the software distribution process.
6. Describe the responsibilities of a change management board.
7. Name and describe five criteria for approving changes.
8. Name and describe the components of organizational culture.
9. Name and describe the components of an organizational change management plan.

Multiple-Choice Questions

1. In classifying the importance of each of the goals for change management, which one is the most important?
   a. Identification
   b. Categorization
   c. Prioritization
   d. Authorization
2. In the change request process, the following information should be obtained except
   a. User contact and responsibility
   b. List of future changes
   c. IT contact and responsibility
   d. Management approval
3. In an emergency change control process, which of the following is the highest risk?
   a. Unauthorized changes are made
   b. Emergency change introduces performance problems
   c. Changes are approved after they are implemented
   d. Lack of analysis
4. In the following list of criteria for approving changes, select the one that is most important:
   a. Criticality
   b. State of the production environment
   c. Resource availability
   d. Effect of all proposed changes
5. Following a change, the condition of which of the following should be evaluated?
   a. Requester
   b. Change objectives
   c. Technical support
   d. Staffing

6. The following are components of organizational culture that affect the success of IT except
   a. Incentives
   b. Company politics
   c. Interorganizational relationships
   d. Government politics

7. Managing organizational change would include all of the following except
   a. Marketing plans
   b. Training and professional development plans
   c. User involvement in design
   d. Communication plans

8. Business process review sessions review
   a. Requests for system changes
   b. Requests for business process changes
   c. Changes introduced by the new system
   d. Training requests

9. An IT system that now allows the corporate office to view data from their individual sales offices introduces the most change to
   a. Social relationships
   b. Technical support
   c. Interorganizational relationships
   d. Company politics

10. In auditing an automated change control system, an auditor would review all of the following except
    a. License agreements
    b. Rules
    c. Access lists
    d. Log files

Exercises

1. Discuss the impact if all changes are not identified.
2. Develop a high-level flowchart for an emergency change process. On the flowchart, label the control points. If there are residual risks, make note of those as well.
3. Discuss why revising documentation is an important part of change management.
4. Discuss the importance of why system maintenance activities need to be approved.
5. Discuss the importance of violating software agreements for a publicly traded company?
6. Research a news story related to software license agreements. What controls would prevent or minimize an outbreak within a company?
7. A company would like to include facilities management in the change management board. Describe the benefits associated with including facilities management in the change management board.
8. Describe the interdependencies between IT change management and organizational change management.
9. From your experience, describe a situation where IT affected the distribution of power within the organization.

10. A university currently provides the ability to register for classes via a telephone registration system. However, the university is in the process of modifying its student registration system so that it allows registration via the Web . The university is evaluating whether it should discontinue the phone service or continue it once the online service is available. Perform a fit-gap analysis of this scenario considering organizational/social changes as well as IT changes.

Answers to Multiple-Choice Questions

1—d; 2—b; 3—a; 4—b; 5—b; 6—d; 7—a; 8—c; 9—d; 10—a

Further Reading

1. Bartol, N. Practical Measurement Framework for Software Assurance and Information Security, Version 1.0, Booz Allen Hamilton, October 2008, http://www.gao.gov/products/GAO-09-232G.
2. Common Weakness Enumeration (Version 1.1.2), http:// http://cwe.mitre.org/, March 30, 2011.
3. Corporate Executive Board, *Change Management Models*, Working Council for Chief Information Officers, January 2003.
4. Ebay, Ebay Community, http://www.ebay.com/aboutebay98/community/, verified on August 8, 2003.
5. Gallegos, F., *Auditing Global Information Infrastructure and National Information Infrastructure*, EDP Auditing Series, #75-10-55, Auerbach Publishers, Boca Raton, FL, 2000, pp. 1–16.
6. Gallegos, F. and J. Yin, *Auditing in a Client Server Environment*, EDP Auditing Series, #74-10-25, Auerbach Publishers, Boca Raton, FL, 2000, pp. 1–20.
7. Gallegos, F. and J. Yin, *Auditing Oracle*, EDP Auditing Series, #74-15-37, Auerbach Publishers, Boca Raton, FL, 2000, pp. 1–12.
8. Gallegos, F. and A. Carlin, *Auditing Systems Maintenance—A How to Approach*, EDP Auditing Series, #74-30-25, Auerbach Publishers, Boca Raton, FL, 2000, pp. 1–12.
9. Gallegos, F. and A. Carlin, *Key Review Points for Auditing Systems Development*, EDP Auditing Series, #74-30-37, Auerbach Publishers, Boca Raton, FL, 2000, pp. 1–24.
10. Information Systems Audit and Control Foundation, *IT Control Practice Statement: AI6 Manage Changes*, Information Systems Audit and Control Foundation, February 2002.
11. Information Systems Audit and Control Foundation, *COBIT Audit Guidelines*, Information Systems Audit and Control Foundation, February 2002.
12. Johnson, S. and K. Blanchard, *Who Moved My Cheese*, Putnam Publishing, New York, 1998.
13. Kling, R. and R. Lamb, IT and organizational change in digital economies: A sociotechnical approach, In *Understanding the Digital Economy: Data Tools and Research*, Brynjolfrson, E. and B. Kahin, Eds., MIT Press, Cambridge, MA, 2000, pp. 295–324.
14. Melançon, D., Beyond checklists: A socratic approach to building a sustainable change auditing practices, Information Systems Audit and Control Association, *Journal Online*, 2006.
15. Oseni, E. Change management in process change, Information Systems Audit and Control Association, *JournalOnline*, 2007.
16. Software & Information Industry Association (SIIA), About SIIA, http://www.siia.net/membership/overview.asp.
17. U.S. General Accounting Office, *Federal Information System Controls Audit Manual: Vol. 1, Financial Statement Audits*, AIMD-12.19.6, June 2001.
18. U.S. General Accounting Office, *Federal Information Systems Controls Audit Manual* GAO-09-232G, February 2009, http://www.gao.gov/products/GAO-09-232G.
19. U.S. CERT Software Assurance Community, https://buildsecurityin.us-cert.gov/swa/measwg.html, September 2011.

IT DELIVERY AND SUPPORT

COBIT Operational Controls

The COBIT address operational controls in the processes and control objectives for the delivery and support domain, as shown in Exhibit IV.1.

Comparing COBIT and General Controls for Operational Auditing

Exhibit IV.2 provides a cross-reference between traditional general controls used in operational information systems auditing and operational controls from COBIT. This section includes sample descriptions of three audits that general and operational COBIT controls can be applied to in the case of problem management, data center reviews, and call center reviews.

Chapters 18 through 22

The fourth part of this text examines IT general controls and managing service delivery. Computer applications operate within this environment and are very dependent on the general controls that protect IT systems. Service management provides a framework for delivering quality IT services to the organization.

Chapter 18 discusses the service management processes that control service delivery and measurement of IT performance. This chapter discusses the ongoing process designed to understand the services required by the organization, design services, identify processes to engage services, price service, develop and negotiate SLA, define SLA metrics, measure and report on services, manage service issues, and maintain/update services.

Chapter 19 discusses how training, service desk, and incident/problem management are underlying processes needed to ensure the effective use of technology and customer satisfaction. Effective training helps users make the best use of their applications and reduces calls to the service desk. The service desk responds to user questions and problems that may occur with hardware,

DS1 Define and Manage Service Levels
Control Objectives
1.1   Service-level management framework
1.2   Definition of services
1.3   Service-level agreements
1.4   Operating-level agreements
1.5   Monitoring and reporting of service-level achievements
1.6   Review of service-level achievements
DS2 Manage Third-Party Services
Control Objectives
2.1   Identification of all supplier relationships
2.2   Supplier relationship management
2.3   Supplier risk management
2.4   Supplier performance management
DS3 Manage Performance and Capacity
Control Objectives
3.1   Performance and capacity planning
3.2   Current capacity and performance
3.3   Future capacity and performance
3.4   IT resources availability
3.5   Monitoring and reporting
DS4 Ensure Continuous Service
Control Objectives
4.1   IT continuity framework
4.2   IT continuity plans
4.3   Critical IT resources
4.4   Maintenance of the IT continuity plan
4.5   Testing of the IT continuity plan
4.6   IT continuity plan training
4.7   Distribution of the IT continuity plan
4.8   IT services recovery and resumption
4.9   Off-site backup storage
4.10   Post resumption plan

Exhibit IV.1   Processes for the delivery and support.

DS5 Ensure Systems Security
Control Objectives
5.1   Management of IT security
5.2   IT security plan
5.3   Identity management
5.4   User account management
5.5   Security testing, surveillance, and monitoring
5.6   Security incident definition
5.7   Protection of security technology
5.8   Cryptographic key management
5.9   Malicious software prevention, detection, and correction
5.10 Network security
5.11 Exchange of sensitive data
DS6 Identify and Allocate Costs
Control Objectives
6.1   Definition of services
6.2   IT accounting
6.3   Cost modeling and charging
6.4   Cost model maintenance
DS7 Educate and Train Users
Control Objectives
7.1   Identification of education and training needs
7.2   Delivery of training and education
7.3   Evaluation of training received
DS8 Manage Service Desk and Incidents
Control Objectives
8.1   Service desk
8.2   Registration of customer queries
8.3   Incident escalation
8.4   Incident closure
8.5   Trend analysis

Exhibit IV.1   (Continued) Processes for the delivery and support.

DS9 Manage the Configuration
Control Objectives
9.1 Configuration repository and baseline
9.2 Identification and maintenance of configuration items
9.3 Configuration integrity review
DS10 Manage Problems
Control Objectives
10.1 Identification and classification of problems
10.2 Problem tracking and resolution
10.3 Problem closure
10.4 Integration of change, configuration, and problem management
DS11 Manage Data
Control Objectives
11.1 Business requirements for data management
11.2 Storage and retention arrangements
11.3 Media library management system
11.4 Disposal
11.5 Backup and restoration
11.6 Security requirements for data management
DS12 Manage the Physical Environment
Control Objectives
12.1 Site selection and layout
12.2 Physical security measures
12.3 Physical access
12.4 Protection against environmental factors
12.5 Physical facilities management
DS13 Manage Operations
Control Objectives
13.1 Operations procedures and instructions
13.2 Job scheduling
13.3 IT infrastructure monitoring
13.4 Sensitive documents and output devices
13.5 Preventive maintenance for hardware

Exhibit IV.1   (Continued) Processes for the delivery and support.

General Control	COBIT Control
Organizational policy and organizational controls	Manage third-party services Manage operations
Data files and program controls	Manage performance and capacity Ensure systems security Identify and allocate costs Manage data
Backup/restart and disaster recovery controls	Ensure continuous service
Environmental controls	Manage the configuration Manage the facility
Physical security access controls	Ensure systems security

Exhibit IV.2   General controls versus COBIT controls.

systems, and applications. The incident and problem management processes ensure that service is restored and problems resolved.

Chapter 20 provides on overview of security and continuity planning processes needed to prevent, detect, and respond to threats. Information security processes prevent and reduce the impact of incidents. Continuity planning processes help the organization recover from partial or total service outages. Fundamental to managing IT is a security policy that defines the guidelines and practices for configuring and managing security in the organization.

Chapter 21 discusses systems maintenance, reviewing operating systems, open systems standards, and database management systems controls. Operating systems software must be kept up-to-date and stable to support applications systems. Database management systems must be secure and well controlled as they contain the organization's data.

Chapter 22 discusses IT audit methods and techniques used in the review of operations. The focus of this chapter is the key control points in operation of which the IT auditors must be cognizant in conducting their review. Several different operations environments will be addressed, such as general controls over operating systems, production, data communication, and end-user computing.

Chapter 18

Service Management

IT is measured both by the services it delivers and by the cost of those services. IT organizations need to have defined services, service levels, and measurements to track performance. This area is one of constant change as new technologies and business methods evolve. Therefore, the identification, collection, and application of metrics may change constantly. These changes have to be reflected against the baseline to help management understand the impact on control structure and architecture. As discussed in Chapter 9, IT is responsible for delivering services in support of the organization's objectives. This chapter discusses how to define services that meet organizational objectives and how to measure performance of IT services.

IT Processes

The COBIT processes (DS1 and DS2) in the Delivery and Support Domain discuss how service and supplier management processes support an effective IT organization. Exhibit 18.1 lists the control objectives for this chapter.

Information Technology Infrastructure Library

Both COBIT and Information Technology Infrastructure Library (ITIL) cover similar processes for service management. The IT Governance Institute prepared a mapping of COBIT to ITIL and other standards—available to members on www.isaca.org. ITIL was published by the Central Computer and Telecommunications Agency (CCTA), now called British Office of Government Commerce (OGC). It was developed beginning in the late 1980s with the input of many organizations, including the U.S. Navy and Proctor & Gamble. By collecting the best practices from top companies, CCTA established a best practice framework called ITIL. According to a

DS1 Define and Manage Service Levels
Control Objectives
1.1   Service-level management framework
1.2   Definition of services
1.3   Service-level agreements
1.4   Operating-level agreements
1.5   Monitoring and reporting of service level achievements
1.6   Review of service level achievements
DS2 Manage Third-Party Services
Control Objectives
2.1   Identification of all supplier relationships
2.2   Supplier relationship management
2.3   Supplier risk management
2.4   Supplier performance management

Exhibit 18.1   Processes for the delivery and support.

survey conducted by the Gartner Group, most organizations preferred ITIL as the standard for service delivery processes. Currently, the ITIL collection consists of eight books and is referred to as the only consistent and comprehensive best practices for IT service management to deliver high-quality IT services:

1. Service support
2. Service delivery
3. Planning to implement service management
4. Infrastructure management
5. Application management
6. Security management
7. Software asset management
8. Business perspectives

Service management is an ongoing process designed to understand the services required by the organization, design services, identify processes to engage services, price service, develop and negotiate SLAs, define SLA metrics, measure and report on services, manage service issues, and maintain/update services.

Depending on the organization's requirements, SLAs will be formal or informal. In organizations where IT costs are not allocated, service levels may be set for the organization as a whole. In cases where services are provided across tax jurisdictions (states or countries), a formal document will be required and should be reviewed by the organization's legal and tax representative.

In any case, the setting of service expectations is a major checkpoint to developing an effective partnership between IT and the organization. Exhibit 18.2 shows the cyclical nature of service management.

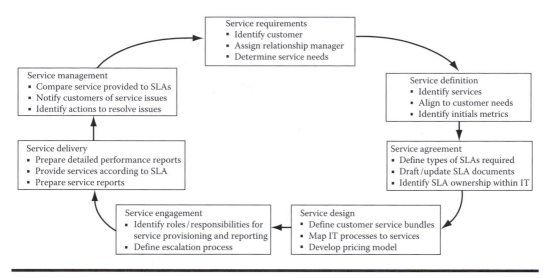

Exhibit 18.2   Service management process.

Implementing IT Service Management

According to the Gartner Group, implementing a service management process can increase overhead costs, as new skills and tools will be required to implement and manage a service management process. Benefit has to be derived from mature processes that help manage demand and operate efficiently. Implementing a service management function does not necessarily require hiring new staff. Organizations can look at existing individuals and functions that are currently providing service management roles. These individuals and functions can form the basis for a service management team. Next, review existing service management processes to gain an understanding of the current state. Compare the current state to a service management framework (e.g., ITIL) to determine gaps in existing processes. Develop the remaining processes, as needed, to form the service management framework. Finally, identify existing tools and technology that can be leveraged to capture and report on service measurements.

Review Services and Requirements

The Gartner Group also believes that identifying the customer is the first step in developing a service management process. Obviously, you cannot have an SLA with individual end users, and one SLA with the CEO would not result in customer satisfaction from the entire organization. In addition, the process of creating, reporting, and managing SLAs can take time to implement and result in increased cost to the organization. The right number will depend on the organization, but it is important to maintain a reasonable number of customers and services. Once the customers have been identified, the organization needs to designate individuals responsible for managing the relationship with the customer. A relationship manager meets first with the customer to gain an understanding of the business objectives and the IT services that are important to realizing those objectives. This information can then be used to align the customer needs with the services offered by IT. A relationship manager is the key contact for negotiating the SLA with the customer, ongoing reporting against performance measures, and a central contact point for issue escalation and resolution.

Define IT Services

Defining services requires the organization to consider what services are important from a customer perspective. Most user organizations care about the applications it uses. For example, the finance function is dependent on the availability of the accounting systems. Finance users are not really interested in platform availability, although this may be an important aspect of delivering the accounting application. The accounting application only works if all components involved in delivering the application work. The client hardware and software, the networking components, the server hardware and software, and the database must all function to deliver the accounting application to the end user. From a customer perspective, the measurement of end-to-end availability of the accounting application is important. From an IT perspective, each of the individual platforms must be available to deliver the service expected from the customer. The processes that go into delivering platform availability include all aspects of IT.

Delivering high-quality IT services is dependent on the delivery of high-quality applications and all of the processes that go into managing IT operations: capacity management, change control, security, disaster recovery, vendor management, and so on. Another complicating factor in measuring and delivering IT services is the dependencies on third-party providers of services, networks, hardware, and software. With all this complexity, delivering high-quality IT services is very challenging.

An organization with a large volume of applications makes the task of measuring service even more difficult. It is probably not cost effective to measure every application in an organization; therefore, it makes more sense to measure selected key applications. These and other factors have to be negotiated with the identified customers, keeping in mind that trade-offs will need to be made on the value delivered compared to the cost.

Service-Level Agreements

An SLA is a formal agreement between a customer requiring services and the organization that is responsible for providing those services:

- *Service.* A set of deliverables that passes between a service provider and a service consumer
- *Level.* The measurement of services promised, services delivered, and the delta between the two
- *Agreement.* Contract between two entities—the one providing the service and the recipient

SLAs should include a definition of the services, the expected quality level, how service will be measured, the planned capacity, the cost of the service, the roles and responsibilities of the parties, and a recourse process for nonperformance. For an internal service agreement, performance can be tied to compensation (e.g., bonuses). External agreements may involve payment of a penalty or compensation for poor performance.

It is important to engage the customer in the service-level definition process to help gain agreement and buy-in. Organization management will make trade-offs between service quality and cost. These decisions must be communicated across the organization to set expectations at all levels. Otherwise, customer satisfaction results may reflect unreasonable expectations versus agreed IT service levels.

Types of Service-Level Agreements

SLAs can be made between IT and its customers, operations and application groups, and between suppliers and IT. A customer service-level agreement (CSLA) encompasses all of the subservices being provided both internally and externally to deliver the services needed by the customer as defined earlier. An operating-level agreement (OLA) between operations and application groups defines the underlying operating services required to deliver projects and applications to the customer under the CSLA. Supplier SLAs define the services required by operations, applications, or end users to deliver in accordance with the CSLA.

Customer Service–Level Agreement

A CSLA is a formal agreement between IT and a user organization. It encompasses all of the subservices being provided both internally and externally to deliver the services needed by the customer. The customer is a user group defined as the first step in the process and is usually an organization function that is the primary user of a key application (e.g., finance, HR). It is better to have the primary owner for each key application to gain agreement on service levels and pricing. The primary-user organization can include the IT services and cost in services to its customers. Although it is possible to split the cost of a shared application into separate user groups, it is not possible to provide varying levels of service for the same application. Examples of customer services include

- Client services (desktop, laptop, personal digital assistant hardware, software, and support)
- Storage services (direct access storage devices, storage area network, tape, etc.)
- Networking services (telecom, data, Internet, etc.)
- ERP services (accounting, human resources, procurement, etc.)
- Business processing services (manufacturing, policy processing, etc.)

Service levels that are provided to all user groups (e.g., personal computers) may have to be agreed at the organization level. It is possible to offer different hardware (e.g., laptop, desktop), software, and support (e.g., basic, premium) options to end users; however, this can be more costly. Standardizing hardware, software, and support allows an organization to leverage scale in negotiation and gain processing efficiencies. These are decisions that are best made at the organization level.

Operating-Level Agreement

OLAs, whether formal or informal define the underlying services required by application development and maintenance groups to deliver the end-to-end application services to customers. A formal agreement helps set expectations between the application and operations groups on the quality of service; roles and responsibilities; expected capacity; and in some cases, service cost. Examples of operating services include

- Mainframe application hosting services
- Distributed application hosting services
- Web application hosting services
- Storage services (DASD, SAN, tape, etc.)
- Networking services (telecom, data, Internet, etc.)

Storage and network services may be provided directly to the customer without bundling with other services. They may also be shown on the OLA to have all underlying operating services in one agreement for accountability purposes.

Supplier Service–Level Agreements

A portion or all of a service may be provided by a third party through outsourcing, cosourcing, or selective sourcing. It is important to align the SLAs from third parties to customer SLAs to prevent a misunderstanding or misinterpretation of the agreement. For example, it would be virtually impossible to be successful if the supplier's SLA promises 95% availability and the customer's SLA promises 99%. To successfully manage services provided by a third party, IT must have a solid understanding of the services it provides, the services expected from the third party, and how the internal and external services work together. Examples of third-party services include

- Service desk, desktop support, etc.
- Application development or maintenance
- Application hosting
- Intrusion detection

To be successful, organizations must have processes in place to consistently monitor fulfillment of service levels from all key suppliers. As third-party services and spending represent a significant portion of IT services and costs, it is worth the investment in managing third-party service delivery.

Service Design and Pricing

Chargeback and cost allocation models were discussed in Chapter 12. Discussed in this chapter is how underlying subservices and costs are aggregated into customer services. Service design can be quite complicated, depending on the breakdown of the organization and the components needed to support an application.

Once the services are defined, the internal functions and processes have to be mapped to each of the services. At the lowest level, IT organizations typically separate costs into cost centers aligned to individual managers. These cost centers will need to be aligned to services entirely or as a percentage based on an allocation of the time spent or some other appropriate measurement. For example, an operations group may spend 20% of its time supporting the client environment, 20% supporting the mainframe environment, 30% supporting the distributed environment, and 30% supporting the network environment. For example, developing the pricing for mainframe application hosting will require the aggregation of all the costs that go into supporting the mainframe environment. Mainframe application hosting may include engineering, backup, archive, recovery, disaster recovery, performance monitoring, capacity management, and provisioning.

Behind customer services are one or more IT functions or processes required to deliver those services. For example, designing an ERP service requires adding the ERP application maintenance costs plus the underlying infrastructure service costs plus the overhead costs. Exhibit 18.3 illustrates how costs can be aggregated to create a customer service.

Further complicating service design is providing varying levels of service based on availability requirements. The more options, the more complex the service model, and the more complicated the pricing model and resulting measurement process. Organization and IT management must understand the cost/benefit before implementing a complicated service/pricing model. The author recommends keeping the service structure as simple as possible for the initial implementation. More complexity can be added once the service management processes (e.g., measurement) are mature.

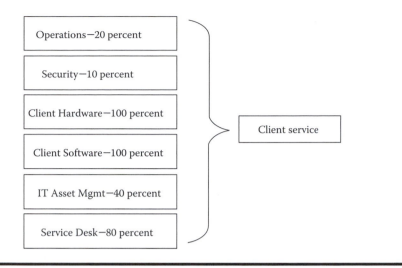

Exhibit 18.3   Illustration of service design.

There are some services that will most likely be required for all customers depending on the organization's service strategy. Required services may include minimum levels of disaster recovery, security, risk management, and project management. Making these services mandatory reduces some of the conflict in pricing projects and services as they are required by the organization and built into the service and pricing model. It is important to explicitly state the mandatory services that are included in the service or pricing model to improve transparency into IT services.

Processes to Engage Services

An important aspect of service management is how services are delivered to the user organization. Provisioning service is the first point of contact with users and the point of capture for usage information. For delivering end-user services (e.g., client, telecom), the first point of contact sets the stage for delivering customer satisfaction. Procurement, asset management, and service desk are processes that are dependent on service provisioning to function properly. Procurement processes for end-user services should be agreed with the user organizations to ensure that only approved hardware, software, and system access are provided to end users. The procurement process can be the trigger for creating user and asset information used by security, finance, asset management, operations, service management, and the service desk to identify users and client configurations.

For application development and maintenance, the entry point into IT is entry into the systems development life cycle, and mature processes in this area can make or break the relationship with the customer. Demand management, requirements definition, and change control were discussed in previous chapters. Again, these processes should be agreed between IT and organization management to ensure alignment on the rules of engagement. These processes are even more critical in an outsourced environment where service requests need to be approved before incurring charges. There are automated solutions for entering, approving, and tracking application requirements and service requests that were discussed in earlier chapters.

Roles and Responsibilities

Service management is the responsibility of every function in IT and the customer. The customer is responsible for understanding the services it needs and working effectively with IT to deliver value to the organization through its investments in IT. IT is responsible for having the processes in place to define, measure, and deliver the required services to the customer.

As there are so many groups (internal and external) involved in delivering IT service, it is important to have a focal point for the customer, suppliers, and service management processes. Depending on the size of the organizations, these roles may be filled by a single person or a team. The team can be centralized or distributed, but it is important that the roles and responsibilities are clearly defined and all individuals operate under similar processes. Consistent processes help the customer, supplier, and IT operate efficiently by avoiding miscommunication and errors.

Relationship Management

Relationship managers develop and maintain a close relationship with key personnel in the user organization. They are responsible for negotiating SLAs, monitoring performance, reporting on results, and resolving escalated issues. Relationship managers ensure that IT services are aligned with current and future needs of customers and end users and acts as an advocate for IT with the customer and the customer with IT. They work with the customer to determine consumption and implement processes to control demand and help the customer identify appropriate actions to maximize benefits and minimize costs of IT services. Relationship managers may coordinate development activity and be a member of the user groups planning and steering committee to influence the strategic direction of IT investments to maximize future benefits.

Service Management

Service managers develop and maintain the IT service catalog. They are responsible for developing service definitions, processes, SLA templates, service measurement, monitoring, and reporting tools. Service managers may also be involved in understanding and reporting on service issues from all areas. They may produce regular service reports from information provided from the underlying service providers (internal and external) by the service and customer. Reporting should be based on actual customer impact and show "end-to-end" delivery and must highlight key business applications. Reporting should be transparent, meaningful, and readable. This information is also important to IT management in identifying trends that need to be addressed or communicated with the customer.

Financial Management

Financial managers develop and maintain IT pricing model and charging process. They are responsible for charging IT services in alignment with the SLAs. They may also be involved in paying for third-party services in alignment with contracts and supplier SLAs. As the cost of IT services can directly impact satisfaction, it is important to include financial managers in the service management, supplier management, and relationship management processes. Both IT and organization managers need to understand the underlying cost of IT services (internal and external) so they can make informed decisions about service quality, capacity, and changes. Financial management is discussed in detail in Chapter 12.

Supplier Management

Solid contract and service management processes are key to managing third-party service delivery. Designated individuals may be tasked with managing the relationship with the supplier and monitoring performance. Sizable contracts may require a team to ensure value is realized as expected. Supplier management requires constant effort, as issues will arise on services, billing, contract terms, and performance. Supplier communication works both ways; organizations need to let suppliers know about changes in the organizations to be able to respond effectively. Suppliers are really part of the service delivery team. Suppliers need to be made aware of the implementation of new products, processes, procedures, and technology to be prepared and positioned to support the change. Supplier management is also discussed in Chapter 15.

Service Delivery

Service delivery is the day-to-day execution of service delivery processes (problem management, change control, security administration, service provisioning, etc.) Service delivery is the responsibility of all functions in IT to deliver the committed quality of service and constantly look for ways to reduce the long-term cost of services delivered. Service delivery processes ensure restoration of normal service operation as quickly as possible, minimize the adverse impact on business operations, and ensure that the agreed levels of service quality and availability are maintained. There must be processes in place to communicate and escalate issues that impact services and customers, identify the root cause of issues, and recommend process improvements to minimize future issues. Where services are provided by third parties, internal service delivery personnel must work with suppliers to resolve the problem and restore service. They also ensure provision of key services according to service levels and handle requests from customers for additional services.

Change Management

Change management is the responsibility of everyone in the organization. Changes occur in systems, applications, environments, and processes. Individuals responsible for change management

- Assess the risks and potential conflicts of all IT and organization-related changes, aimed at protecting service availability and quality
- Review all changes from infrastructure, applications, and third parties to ensure they are tested and back out plans are appropriate
- Maximize both system availability and the volume of managed change
- Protect organization from change and change from the organization
- Manage individual and cumulative risk of changes
- Ensure changes are performed safely without conflicts

Both planned and unplanned changes create the greatest risk to service availability. As such, this area should receive a high degree of focus from the service management group. It is an important area to measure. Chapter 17 provides more detailed information on change management.

Problem Management

Problem management processes ensure that problems are reported, analyzed, and resolved to enable the delivery of agreed services. Problem resolution includes escalating unresolved issues, reporting trends and initiating service improvement programs, reviewing the root cause of the problem, follow-up on the resolution of problems, and communicating resolution with the appropriate parties. Escalation processes also need to be aligned to disaster recovery and business resumption plans where problems impact the overall service availability for an extended period.

Service Desk

The service desk is the initial and possibly single point of contact for end users for IT-related incidents and queries. The primary purpose of the service desk is to help the user. Service desk personnel must ensure that all hardware or software problems that arise are fully documented and escalated based on the priorities established by procedures. This area is discussed in more detail in Chapter 19.

Security Administration

User access is an important aspect of ensuring customer satisfaction. It is important to have people and processes in place to effectively manage and maintain end-user application profiles. Individuals need to be able to access the systems and applications needed to fulfill their responsibilities. Issues in this area can be very frustrating to users resulting in lower customer satisfaction and reduced operating efficiency.

Customer Roles and Responsibilities

To effectively provide the services described earlier, there are a number of areas where the customer is required to provide support to IT. Customer responsibilities are as follows:

- Clearly define requirements for services and applications. Develop test plans that validate applications meet requirements and work as intended.
- Advise IT as soon as possible of significant changes in demand, changes in business processes, planned physical moves, change in support requirements, etc.
- Follow processes for provisioning services, support, and problem reporting.
- Report issues (this includes incidences of slow performance and significant degradation in application response times).
- Follow the published escalation process for any incidents requiring escalation or for service complaints.
- Participate in IT satisfaction surveys to help IT assess where to improve.
- Maintain effective business continuity plans and escalate IT risks to the appropriate IT contact.
- Adhere to the defined IT standards and procedures.
- Adhere to IT security policies, rules, and guidelines.
- Communicate the expected service levels and IT processes within the customer's organization.

Communication

Communication is important for all organizational activities and is integral for successful service management. IT is a complex area that is difficult to understand and communicate in easy-to-understand terms. Effective communication helps establish trust and rapport between IT and the organization. Conversely, there are many stated and unstated expectations of IT from all levels of an organization. It can be challenging for IT to understand and virtually impossible to meet these expectations. As discussed earlier, it is critical for IT to have alignment to the organization's strategy and objectives. Finally, suppliers are important members of the service delivery team and need to be included in discussions that impact the services they provide.

Service Delivery and Monitoring

Service management creates a framework for defining and reporting on services, but service delivery is the responsibility of the application and operations groups. Success is dependent on the maturity of the people, process, and technology of the organization. Measuring service performance is a way to track how well an organization is delivering service and identify problem areas.

Service Measurement

Areas that are measured get the focus and tend to improve as a result. Focusing only on customer service may lead to an improvement in one area at the sacrifice of others (e.g., cost and security). That is why it is important to measure the right things. According to the Gartner Group, it is also important to have different internal and external measures. Internal measures keep the IT group focused on what they need to do to achieve service levels. External (customer) measures should be focused on things the customer cares about.

Because internal IT functions and processes impact customer services in different ways, it is important to align the internal measures to the external customer services. The internal IT measurements need to be designed to hold individual groups accountable for delivering their portion of the service.

It is also important to coordinate measuring IT services with IT process improvement and governance metrics. Measuring too many processes for too many purposes can create measurement overload. Leveraging the same information for multiple purposes is far more efficient. A little up-front planning on what to measure and the use of the measurements will go a long way toward implementing an effective measurement process. Once the measurements have been decided, the source of the information needs to be identified. The source must be reliable and consistent to ensure the measurement can be delivered. The rules around measurement must also be decided and agreed by all parties. Having a measurement that is not trusted is counterproductive.

What to Measure

What to measure will depend on the services provided and the agreed quality level. It is important to keep any measurement program simple as the cost to deliver more detailed measurements may far outweigh the benefit. However, measurement must be granular enough to help identify the root cause of problems and hold individuals accountable for their share of the service. Consideration also needs to be given to the level of maturity in the IT organization. It may be necessary to start with simple measurements that get expanded as the IT organization matures. The underlying data must be available for more complicated metrics and the acquisition of the right data needs to be planned for in advance.

Application services typically include maintaining existing applications, making changes and enhancements to existing applications, and building new applications (i.e., projects). As discussed earlier, customers care about the availability of their key applications. To determine availability, all components of an application must be measured to determine end-to-end availability.

Infrastructure services include building and maintaining operating platforms. Availability can be measured at the operating platform (e.g., mainframe, UNIX, Windows) or the environment level (e.g., online, application, database). Infrastructure metrics will depend on the services provided.

Determining the required availability percentage will depend on the organization's objectives, function of the application, tolerance for risk, and cost/benefit of higher availability. With the complexity of today's applications and technology, increasing availability from 99% to 100% would be costly and maybe even impossible.

Measuring project success includes delivering to the agreed-upon scope, schedule, budget, and quality. Measuring change could include the average cost per change, time to deliver, and quality. Measuring quality could include issue/problem quantity, severity, backlog, and time to resolve. The challenge with quality metrics is that there are many factors that go into a quality system that may not be within the control of the IT group. Quality problems can arise from a failure on the part of the user group to define requirements, validate acceptance, and train users on how to effectively use the system. It is important to track the underlying cause of issues/problems to be able to identify the root cause and attribute only those problems associated with IT against the SLA.

An important measure for both application and infrastructure services is the number of changes. A high quantity of changes can indicate a failure on the part of user groups to properly define requirements, a failure on the part of the applications group to understand requirements or implement high-quality code, a failure of the operations group to carefully manage change to the infrastructure, or an overall problem with the change control process.

How to Measure

As important as what to measure is how to measure. Whatever method is selected, it should be measured consistently and clearly communicated to the user organizations. Although no measure is going to be perfect, the following are some possible approaches to measuring processor usage:

Peak consumption. This method measures the highest level of consumption. As hardware/ software must be purchased to support peak capacity, it more closely aligns costs to consumption. However, the organization needs to decide how to measure and charge for peak versus off-peak consumption.

Capacity allocated. This method measures the processors or capacity allocated to user groups or applications. The challenge comes with measuring shared environments and the capacity allocated to system functions. If system capacity is excluded, only production capacity is measured and allocated. However, what happens during the month when the accounting systems need additional capacity for month-end processing?

Average consumption. This method measures either average capacity or consumption over a period of time. This approach seems to overcome some of the limitations with the other two methods. However, it does not encourage workload optimization to minimize peak workload.

End-to-end availability is based on component outages as well as reported problems/outages during the core hours of services. End-to-end availability can be measured by dividing the application downtime by the available connect time. However, this does not take into account the number of users impacted. An outage in the early morning may have much less impact than an outage at peak usage during the day. A more meaningful measure from a customer perspective would be the number of users impacted multiplied by the amount of time the system is unavailable. Multiplied by the average cost per user can give an approximate financial impact of an outage.

This information can be used when determining the cost/benefit of increasing service levels or considering process improvements.

A common tool used to reflect many of these are graphs, charts, or tables. It is very important that if such data are analyzed and shown, the information about the time period and source of data be clearly provided. Also, any anomalies or assumptions should be communicated clearly, especially if the data are forecasted or projected. Without the proper communication, such tools can easily distort the results and be counterproductive to the organization.

Service Management Tools

There are many tools available to assist organizations in implementing service management processes (defining, monitoring, reporting). Tools are needed to capture performance, and usage metrics from the various platforms and tools consolidate and report on all of this information. Automation is required to deliver an efficient measurement and reporting process. Many of the performance management tools used by systems programmers, operations, and network administrators can also be used to measure service delivery. Exhibit 18.4 provides a sample of tools that can be used to measure service delivery.

Supplier	Features
BMC Software	Integrated service management portfolio for service desk, incident, problem, change, asset, and service-level management
Computer Associates	Service catalog, metric analysis, service accounting, service desk, and asset management
Compuware	SLA reporting, metrics, monitoring
Digital Fuel Technologies	Manages the entire life cycle of an SLA, service performance, compliance with SLAs, and exposure to financial credits
HP	IT service, asset, identity, and access management
IBM	Asset management, service management, process management, service delivery, and support
Indicative Software	Network, systems, and service management software
InfoVista	Analytics and reporting for networks, servers, and IP telephone
Lucent	Integrated network management tools, performance management, reporting, and monitoring
Managed Objects	SLA, monitoring, and reporting
NetScout	Network and application performance management, network troubleshooting, and capacity planning
ProactiveNet	Performance data, service statistics, and problem identification

Exhibit 18.4   Service management tools.

Customer Satisfaction Surveys

Customer satisfaction surveys are an important tool used to measure the quality of the services provided by IT. There may be multiple customer satisfaction surveys for different services. Senior management may be asked questions on the value of IT, and end users may be asked questions on satisfaction with the service desk and application availability.

Senior management satisfaction should be measured separately as there will be different objectives and questions. Senior management will be more focused on the value delivered by IT. This may include project delivery, IT understanding of business needs, application delivery and support, cost effectiveness, service quality, and overall satisfaction.

Client satisfaction surveys may include the time to provision client requests, time for the service desk to answer a call, satisfaction with issue resolution, and system response time. Using customer satisfaction surveys to measure system response time in addition to using technical measures helps to determine if there is an expectation gap. This information can then be used in discussions with the organization management to either increase the expected service level or improve communication to the user population.

Along with reporting survey results, a follow-up process is needed to respond to issues raised in the survey. This is an important communication tool and can also help boost customer satisfaction. Customer satisfaction is partly a result of expectations and just active listening can boost results. That is another reason why customer satisfaction may have more to do with communication and the IT/organization relationship than with actual service issues.

Benchmarking

Two factors impact the cost of IT—demand and cost effectiveness. Demand can be confirmed with the usage measurements discussed earlier. Cost effectiveness can be confirmed by comparing against historical unit cost or benchmarking against similar organizations. The biggest challenge with benchmarking is finding an organization that is similar in type, size, and structure with similar business needs. This is particularly difficult as every organization is different. One organization may be an early adopter of technology, whereas similar organizations may be late adopters. These differences may impact the service and cost comparison in a benchmarking exercise.

Benchmarking services attempt to align costs and services by using standard definitions of service and cost elements. This makes benchmarking a time-consuming and costly task as financial information and service structures must be restated to align to the benchmark. Even with the restatement of services and costs, benchmarking will have limited value as there may be valid reasons for cost difference from the benchmark. For example, an organization may have lower automation and a higher unit cost offset by efficient manual operations. The opposite could be true, high automation with low unit cost combined with inefficient manual operations. The bottom line is no one data point can provide conclusive information on the efficiency or effectiveness of IT services.

Another issue that reduces the value of benchmarking information is that the results will not be the same services that user organizations are familiar with. This makes it difficult to confirm and communicate that the unit cost charged to individual user functions compares favorably to the benchmark. The advantage of using external benchmark information is the independent source of comparison data. The information provided to the benchmark provider must be auditable to ensure the credibility of the results. Having internal audit validate the submission may also be a good way to validate the results.

Benchmarking can be a useful tool in evaluating the design, quality, and cost of IT services. However, because of limitations, benchmarking should be considered as an input into evaluating the underlying cost of IT services rather than the end result.

Ongoing Service Management

Customer services and the underlying service design will evolve over time as IT, technology, and the organization's environment change. For example, the evolution from pagers to cell phones to PDAs has very different technology, service, and cost profiles. Changes to the service design should be carefully considered due to the cost of adding new services and impact on existing customers when changing the price of existing services. Consistency may be more valuable to the organization than trying to provide a more precise service model.

Service Management of Third Parties

Outsourcing is the transfer of service delivery to a third party. Off-shoring is the transfer of service delivery to a third party outside the client's country. Both have been common practice in the manufacturing industry for decades. IT outsourcing and off-shoring have become a common business practice for organizations around the globe. There are many benefits and risks to IT outsourcing and off-shoring.

Although organizations can increase productivity and reduce costs using internal resources, there are additional benefits to outsourcing or using offshore suppliers. Outsourcing can provide increased flexibility by leveraging the resources of a third party to ramp-up or ramp-down resources for a variable workload. In some organizations, it is very difficult to reduce the labor force due to legislation or union agreements. Outsourcing allows an organization to transfer this responsibility to a third party. A global supplier can transfer resources to other engagements eliminating the need for labor force reductions and providing individuals with better career opportunities.

Off-shoring can increase productivity if sequential work or services can be provided 24 × 7 with resources in different time zones. Help desk support is a good example of a service that can be outsourced to a third party in multiple time zones to provide customers with around the clock service.

Outsourcing to a mature service provider can enable an organization to leverage the technology and processes of the third party. For example, a large desktop support supplier will already have mature processes and technology for deployment, support, security, and refresh that can be implemented in the target organization.

There are also many risks with outsourcing, including reliance on a third party, reduced flexibility, and increased costs. Outsourcing risks include

- Lack of executive buy-in and full support for the project
- Reduced employee morale, productivity, and service levels
- Inflexible and unfavorable contract terms with the supplier
- Poorly managed internal and external communication
- Failure to realize savings on retained costs
- Weak governance and service management processes
- Lack of control over key knowledge resources
- Geopolitical risk

Outsourcing and off-shoring may require significant changes to the way people work. Managers will have to start managing deliverables rather than people. This change may require a paradigm shift as well as a process shift for many managers. Organizations need to be prepared for an off-shoring program by having the processes in place to ensure success. Service management is a critical process to have in place before outsourcing services to a third party. The following decisions and processes need to be considered:

- A clear definition of the work to be outsourced and be performed offshore.
- How work will be initiated, transferred, and received from the third party.
- Educate staff on working with people remotely, with a different culture, different language, and probably a different time zone.
- Are there data privacy issues that need to be considered? In some countries (e.g., Germany), some data cannot be taken out of the country or viewed by people outside the country. Work-arounds may be needed to accommodate these requirements.

One of the challenges the sourcing project team has to manage is scope creep. It is very important to clearly define the scope of work that will be outsourced to the supplier and the work to be retained by the organization. Clearly defined roles and responsibilities, processes, and SLAs are also key to ensure a successful outsourcing engagement. A mature organization will be in a better position to manage the work being performed by an outsourcer.

Key to the up-front planning is to develop a statement of work for the transition project that defines the deliverables. Examples of deliverables include documentation, the future SLA, and people with knowledge. Acceptance criteria for each of these are essential and must be documented in advance. Every effort should be made to make the transition fixed price or even totally at vendor expense, and the team should not move to the steady-state outsourced mode until the agreed acceptance criteria are passed.

Effective governance over the process helps ensure that the benefits are realized and the risks are mitigated. Although service delivery is transferred—accountability remains with the client organization. SLAs and benchmarking existing performance are absolutely critical if the outsourcing is to be service based rather than just staff augmentation. The ultimate intention is to "commoditize" the service and be in a position to expect service against an agreed level and move to another provider with total continuity of service if the service is not adequate. This is difficult in practice when the service relies upon large amounts of organization-specific knowledge and it is essential to make sure that as much of this is stored in digital form and belongs to the organization or is kept within the organization so that it can be transferred to a new vendor if required.

Supplier management includes processes to manage third-party suppliers and integrate with the process to deliver IT services to users. Supplier SLAs specifically state expectations between the service provider and receiver. This includes measurable criteria that can be monitored on a regular basis. Measurement should include service response time, quality level, operating efficiency, pricing, escalation process, and penalties for noncompliance. Services need to be actively managed to ensure the organization receives the greatest value.

Evolution of Standards

IT operations have undergone much change and evolution since the first business computers were introduced in the early 1950s. When looking for the application of standards, many professional, government, and industry organizations have worked hard in pursuit of issuing guidance and standards that can help an organization create a baseline for measurement of its operations and evaluation of its performance. Each organization can review the collection of guidance, and select those best suited for the type of business they represent and services they provide.

Management must make this decision. They must understand that as the business or services provided change, the standards and guidance may require change as well. The IT auditor can add great value in providing the objective feedback needed on their compliance with the standards they have selected. The IT auditor can provide follow-up reviews to see if their changes or adjustments have helped or hindered. Or maybe it is time for management to strategically seek more appropriate standards/guidance that can help be more efficient, effective, and economic in what and how they do their work and how their services are provided.

Conclusion

Service management is a process to define services, service quality, and measure and track performance. To be effective, service management is dependent on all areas of IT. Service management is dependent on well-functioning processes in asset management, financial management, service delivery, service desk, problem management, change management, and relationship management. In addition, the customer has the responsibility for ensuring the successful delivery of IT services by communicating, defining requirements, and complying with processes. Auditing can play an important role by providing an objective review of service management processes. Service expectations can be a very contentious area for an organization due to the trade-offs between service quality and cost.

Review Questions

1. What is the purpose of measuring service levels?
2. What are the types and purpose of service level agreements?
3. Why is communication integral for successful service management?
4. What are the steps required for implementing service management?
5. What are the components of a service level agreement?

Multiple-Choice Questions

1. Formal service-level agreements are required when
   a. Services are provided across tax jurisdictions
   b. Charging for IT services
   c. Applications share the same processor
   d. None of the above
2. Service-level agreements should include
   a. Definition of services
   b. Service quality
   c. Roles and responsibilities
   d. All of the above

3. Customer service–level agreements
   a. Define services from the customer's perspective
   b. Describe operating platform availability
   c. List key applications
   d. All of the above
4. Operating-level agreements are used to
   a. Measure platform availability
   b. Set expectations between application and operations groups
   c. Define application development and maintenance services
   d. All of the above
5. Supplier service–level agreements
   a. Define services and quality
   b. Help manage third-party services
   c. Align to customer service-level agreements
   d. All of the above
6. Service design and pricing requires
   a. Allocation of overhead to all services
   b. Inclusion of disaster recovery
   c. Aggregation of the underlying process costs
   d. All of the above
7. Service provisioning processes are needed to
   a. Create user information for security
   b. Create asset information for inventory
   c. Create usage information for finance
   d. All of the above
8. A relationship manager's role is to
   a. Develop and maintain a close relationship with the customer
   b. Ensure that IT services are aligned with customer needs
   c. Influence the strategic direction of IT investments to maximize future benefits
   d. All of the above
9. Service measurement should be
   a. Coordinated with IT process improvement and governance metrics
   b. Frequent and detailed
   c. Based on peak usage
   d. None of the above
10. The customer is responsible for
    a. Reporting issues
    b. Following procedures
    c. Defining requirements
    d. All of the above

Exercises

1. Using the Internet, research performance measurement tools.
2. Develop requirements for a service management tool set.

3. Compare the functionality of three of the service management suites and determine which processes are covered by each of the tool set.

Answers to Multiple-Choice Questions

1—a; 2—d; 3—a; 4—b; 5—d; 6—c; 7—d; 8—d; 9—a; 10—d

Further Reading

1. Hefley, W. and E. Loesche, *The eSCM-CL v1.1: Model Overview. The eSourcing Capability Model for Client Organizations (eSCM-CL) v1.1*, Carnegie Mellon University, Pittsburgh, PA, 2006.
2. Morello, D., *Service Management Roles and Competencies: What's Hot, What's Missing, What's Next*, Gartner Research Number: G00139336, Gartner, Inc., Stamford, CT, June 26, 2006.
3. O'Neill, P. and E. Hubbert, *The Forrester Wave: Business Service Management, Q1 2007*, Forrester Research, Inc., Cambridge, MA, March 28, 2007.
4. Sayana, S., Auditing IT service delivery, *Inf. Sys. Control J.*, 5, 2005, Information Systems Audit and Control Association.
5. Working Council for Chief Information Officers, *Evaluating Application Development and Performance*, Corporate Executive Board, 2001.
6. Young, C., *Choose the Right IT Service Management Model*, Gartner Research Number: G00129216, Gartner, Inc., Stamford, CT, August 2, 2005.
7. Young, C., *Mainstream IT Service Delivery Strategies Are Misaligned*, Gartner Research Number: G00139881, Gartner, Inc., Stamford, CT, June 20, 2006.
8. Young, C., *Mature Your IT Service Portfolio*, Gartner Research Number: G00142206, Gartner, Inc., Stamford, CT, August 25, 2006.
9. Young, C., *A Framework for Designing IT Service and Process Metrics*, Gartner Research Publication: G00143161, Gartner Inc., Stamford, CT, September 18, 2006.
10. Young, C. and S. Mingay, *The Six Myths of IT Service Management*, Gartner Research Number G00141173, Gartner, Inc., Stamford, CT, June 14, 2006.

Chapter 19

Service Desk and Problem Management

A service desk is the primary contact most users have with IT. As such, a well-functioning service desk is a key component in delivering high customer satisfaction. To get the best value from a service desk, users must be trained to use technology effectively. In this way, the service desk is able to deal with real issues instead of providing ad hoc training to users who are unfamiliar with technology. Training also increases user satisfaction as they become more comfortable with using applications and more productive as a result.

It can be incredibly difficult to diagnose problems in today's complex environment. Consider the example of a user accessing a Web site on the Internet. All of the following components have to function properly for a transaction to complete successfully: data entry, client environment, hardware, operating system, applications, add-on software, cabling, network, host security access, server environment, hardware, operating systems, applications, databases, and add-on software. Considering that each of these components is also highly complex, problems are inevitable. Effectively managing IT service delivery requires managing the cost of the service desk, focusing on the highest-priority problems, and making sure processes are in place to minimize the impact of incidents and problems.

As problems are inevitable, it is important to resolve problems quickly and effectively to maintain high levels of customer satisfaction. An effective problem management process is very critical to delivering the problem to the individual with the ability to resolve the problem and communicating resolution back to the end user. Problem management processes also provide reporting of statistics that aid in identifying trends, problem areas, prioritizing issues, and monitoring compliance with SLAs.

IT Processes

The COBIT processes (DS7, DS8, and DS10) in the Delivery and Support Domain discuss how user training, service desk, and problem management support an effective IT organization. Exhibit 19.1 lists the control objectives for this chapter.

DS7 Educate and Train Users
Control Objectives
7.1 Identification of education and training needs
7.2 Delivery of training and education
7.3 Evaluation of training received
DS8 Manage Service Desk and Incidents
Control Objectives
8.1 Service desk
8.2 Registration of customer queries
8.3 Incident escalation
8.4 Incident closure
8.5 Trend analysis
DS10 Manage Problems
Control Objectives
10.1 Identification and classification of problems
10.2 Problem tracking and resolution
10.3 Problem closure
10.4 Integration of change, configuration, and problem management

Exhibit 19.1 Processes for the delivery and support.

Training

Training is an important aspect of using IT effectively. According to a Gartner Group study, the cost of not training will far exceed the investment organizations will make to train both end users and IT professionals in new technologies. One reason for this paradox is that users who are forced to learn on their own take as much as five times longer to become productive with the software product. Self-training is also inefficient from the standpoint that end users tend to ask their colleagues for help, which results in the loss of more than one individual's time, and they may also be learning inappropriate or inefficient techniques.

The demand for training will continue to rise as environments and applications become more complex. How well organizations respond to the need for training will determine their success with information systems. Traditional training methods may not be appropriate for the changing environment. Today, there are so many areas of specialization for programmers and end users that a traditional approach to training is no longer feasible. With the increased number of users and applications, creative solutions are needed to meet training needs. An economical approach could involve using existing resources to train users. Tutorials that are included in almost every shrink-wrapped package today are excellent sources of training that are often ignored. Organizations should assess the existing user knowledge and use experts within the organization to train other employees. Using the tutorial as an introduction and training with a resident expert to reinforce the tutorial will not only reduce costs, but also ensure more consistent training.

The Gartner Group study also showed that an effective training program reduces support costs by three to six times because users make fewer mistakes and have fewer questions. The increasing complexity of technical environments and more sophisticated personal computer (PC) tools has fueled the increased demand for end-user support. Because traditional IT departments do not have the staffing or the PC knowledge to help end-user departments, end users have turned to "underground support" (i.e., support by peers or department-purchased outsourcing) to fill the gap. The previously mentioned studies found that the need for support is inelastic, and the gap between needed and formal support is filled by underground support. This underground support accounts for as much as 30% of end-user computing costs. End users need "focal points" as "local" as possible for assistance. A focal point is a functional support person. Many times, the functional support person is an accomplished end user. However, without a central support organization, there may be limited coordination between end-user departments to ensure that procedures are consistent and applications are compatible. An integrated service desk can have a single phone number as telephony software can route calls around the world based on defined rules.

Service Desk

Functionally, a service desk offers technical support to the user community. Organizationally, the service desk may act as a separate department or a support component of the information systems department. It can be centralized or decentralized, but should be integrated with common tools and processes. It may be outsourced partially or in total to an organization with locations around the world. Service desks can handle problem calls; log and route service requests; create work orders; dispatch and coordinate desk-side support; install, move, add, change (IMAC) support; document status and progress; update asset records; provide ownership to resolution; close problem tickets when resolved; and prepare standard monthly reports.

The objective of the service desk is to respond to questions or problems that may occur with hardware, systems, and applications. The service desk is responsible for tracking problems from reporting through resolution. The service desk acts as a central point to prioritize, route, and report on issues and problems. The service desk is also a key source of information needed by other IT processes. Change management can use reported problems to identify application and system changes needed to improve service quality. Asset management can use service requests to track the movement of assets. And, service management can use problem trends to identify organizations in need of more training.

Depending on the organization, users, and applications, there may be multiple service support groups with specialized knowledge. It would be virtually impossible to be an expert on the hundreds of possible types of hardware, systems, and applications. Organizations may select a tiered service desk to delineate service based on the type of problem. The primary service desk takes the initial call, diagnoses and resolves common problems, and routes more complex or specialized issues to the service desk with the appropriate expertise. Examples of the specialized service support groups include

- Customer service support for Web -based applications
- End-user support for client hardware, systems, and applications
- User support for ERP and proprietary applications

- Internal technical support for hardware, systems, telecom, and networking issues
- Supplier technical support of proprietary hardware, systems, and tools
- Internal competency center with specialized knowledge for function-specific applications

Support Structures

The structure of end-user support will depend on the organizational environment and the sophistication of the users. Central support may be appropriate in organizations with a low level of user computer knowledge and standard hardware and software. Dedicated consulting groups within IT would be helpful where users have some basic computer skills, but need specialized support on proprietary applications and advanced technology. Departmental support groups are useful when knowledgeable users are dedicated to a particular department for supporting standard applications.

Decentralized support can be helpful by keeping support close to the end user with detailed understanding of the applications used by that group and the issues they encounter. A decentralized service desk can have several specialized groups dedicated to various hardware and software platforms. The challenge with this model is that users can become confused about which service desk to call for a particular problem. The separate groups can be integrated with the use of common processes and software for problem resolution and tracking. A consolidated service desk function can make support requests easier for the user and allow central problem resolution tracking to identify trends.

Another option for support involves outsourcing the service desk function. In a survey conducted by *Computer Economics* in 2007, about a third of the organizations surveyed outsourced the help desk. Shrink-wrapped software products are typically not specific to an organization and organizations can take advantage of general product support. They can also provide support on customer applications, with additional training and cost. This approach may be appealing because it is usually not economically feasible for organizations to provide support on all of the applications their users want. More organizations are considering outsourcing as an option for providing economical support to their users.

Outsourcing

Service desks are very critical to keeping customers satisfied, especially in today's virtual environment. The extent to which these functions are performed depends on the business objectives and the philosophy of the organization. Service desks today are structured to handle telephone inquiries, inbound and outbound e-mail, online chat, and even Internet telephony. This function can be handled internally or outsourced to third-party service providers. Some of the benefits that have been reported by organizations using outsourcing are trouble-free maintenance, quicker implementation time, productive use of systems, and lower training costs. However, some companies have reported less-than-satisfactory support from third-party service providers and do not like the thought of sharing or shipping out their customer data beyond their firewall protection. Successful outsourcing of the service desk is dependent on the maturity of the organization's processes and effective knowledge transfer.

The decision to outsource the service desk cannot be based on cost alone, although the cost of building a service desk is highest in the mind of management. Costs not only include the physical space—a separate office where agents can work 24 hours a day/seven days a week—but also buying the hardware and software mentioned earlier. Hardware includes interactive voice response systems which route the call to the correct agent and servers for running the software required.

Software includes license fees for the help desk, e-mail management, customer relationship management, and workforce management applications. Support agents can be internal or outsourced from external support resources. Depending on the type of service desk established and the number of agents and the type of support services desired, costs have been estimated to approximately $40,000 per agent (licenses, hardware, and training) to high-end packages that cost hundreds of thousands of dollars to license and deploy.

Knowledge Management

The knowledge and abilities of service desk personnel can make a tremendous difference in employee and customer satisfaction. A weak service desk will quickly show up in poor customer satisfaction survey results. To ensure customer satisfaction, organizations need to provide service desk personnel with the appropriate training and tools to be successful. As mentioned earlier, it is not possible for one individual to be an expert on all hardware, systems, and applications. In addition, training all service desk personnel on all possible problems is not practical either. To address these issues, organizations have developed knowledge management tools and processes that share information and expertise.

Knowledge management includes developing detailed knowledge of the hardware, systems, and applications in an organization. It involves documenting how-to-use, problems and fixes for packaged and developed applications, and making that information accessible to users and service support personnel. There are many tools on the market that aid in developing and maintaining a knowledge base. A knowledge base is a collection of problems and solutions in a database that can be accessed by others to share the knowledge. This tool is used frequently for online self-help support and service desks for problem resolution.

Reporting

Service desk reporting should include both measurement of its performance and measurement of IT performance overall. Metrics that measure the efficiency and effectiveness of the service desk include the number and types of calls, time to answer calls or inquiries, the ability to provide quality answers, the number of calls resolved, and the number of problems reopened. Service desk metrics can be acquired from telephony reporting tools, customer surveys, selective monitoring of calls, and the problem management reporting tool.

The service desk provides a single data source to report and track problems from inception through closure. Problem reporting is important for tracking performance against agreed service levels, identifying trends in service quality, and prioritizing problem areas for process improvement efforts. Service desk reporting can include the quantity of problems reported, severity, time to resolve, aging, and other categorization that helps isolate problem areas. Problem management software can be part of an overall service management suite integrated with asset management, contract management, change control, and human resources.

Tools

Service desks can be managed efficiently with the use of problem management software, automated telephone systems, expert systems, e-mail, voicemail, and fax. Service desk tools can also be integrated with network performance, availability, security, and human resources information.

Service desks can be configured as self-hosting, multi- or single-tenant host, or Web based. In a single-tenant system, individual customers own their own servers, databases, and applications. Service desks can be staffed internally or they can be outsourced. In an outsourced situation, the contract should hold the third-party service provider accountable to appropriately run, manage, and maintain the system. In a multitenant environment, the application gives the customers a generic template-driven product provided by the service provider. Thus, you are running on the external service provider resources. In a Web -based service desk/customer relationship management product, user agents must access the server (and customer data) via a Web browser and the Internet, not a stand-alone, PC resident application in a client/server environment.

Web-based service desk support systems are slower in providing screen updates of customer information than a client/server-based system. This can often result in delays, which are frustrating to the customer and agent. However, this environment is much easier to maintain. All software updates occur at the server level, with users concerned only about browser enhancements. Such browser-based systems reduce the training time of support agents. According to several studies, service desks experience high agent turnover rates, 60%–70% annually.

For example, the company AntiClue has developed and is currently marketing software project management tools that focus on IT problem management. These tools were developed in the IT healthcare industry. Their approach focuses on the goal of problem management activities to ascertain the root causes of incidents and to minimize their impact on the business operations of a company. This is done through the following processes:

- *Problem control.* The purpose of problem control is to identify problems within an IT environment and to record information about those problems. Problem control identifies the configuration items at the root of a problem and provides the service desk with information on workarounds.
- *Error control.* The purpose of error control is to keep track of known errors and to determine the resource effort needed to resolve the known error. Error control monitors and removes known errors when it is feasible and worthwhile.
- *Proactive problem management.* The purpose of proactive problem management is to find potential problems and errors in an IT infrastructure before they cause incidents. Stopping incidents before they occur provides improved service to users.

The primary measure of the success of the problem management process is how many problems are identified and removed from an IT infrastructure. Therefore, the primary output from this IT service management process renders problems that are resolved and closed. The work of problem management produces the following outcomes:

- *Records of known errors and available workarounds.* These records are kept in the configuration management database (CMDB), and they provide information to the service desk and other ITSM processes.
- *Requests for change (RFCs).* RFCs describe changes needed to remove a known error. Problem management does not approve or perform the change. RFCs are sent to another ITSM process, change management.
- *Changed records in the CMDB.* Information about a known error and any affected change incident (CIs) is forwarded to the configuration management process, the IT service management process that maintains the CMDB.

When the problem management process is used to identify the root causes of problems, it is far more likely that they will be diagnosed correctly and fixed properly. As a result, problems are permanently eliminated. Again, support tools like this can help IT managers as well as auditors isolate issues.

Incident and Problem Management

Incident and problem management processes are intended to handle problems that are raised through the service desk as well as responses to major incidents and problems, restoration of IT services, and resolution of the root cause of any issue. Other subprocesses involved include incident and problem escalation as well as root cause analysis.

Incident Management

The objective of incident management is to restore operations as soon as possible, whereas the objective of problem management is to minimize the adverse impact of incidents and problems on the organization caused by errors within the IT infrastructure and prevent reoccurrence of incidents related to these errors. The ITIL definition of an incident is "an incident is any event which is not part of the standard operation of a service and which causes, or may cause, an interruption to, or a reduction in, the quality of that service." The aim of incident management is to restore service to the customer as quickly as possible, often through a workaround, rather than through the determination of a permanent resolution.

Problem Management

Problem management is a process that is used to report, log, correct, track, and resolve problems within the hardware, software, network, telecommunications, and computing environment of an organization. Problems can be anything from a customer being unable to print a report to a line connecting the computer to the controller going down (dropping). Problem management provides the framework to open, transfer, escalate, close, and report problems. It establishes procedures and standards for handling customer problems. The ITIL definition of a problem is "a problem is a condition often identified as a result of multiple incidents that exhibit common symptoms." Problems can also be identified from a single significant incident, indicative of a single error, for which the cause is unknown, but for which the impact is significant. Problem management differs from incident management in that its main goal is the detection of the underlying causes of an incident and their subsequent resolution and prevention.

Roles and Responsibilities

Clearly defined roles and responsibilities are critical in problem management to make sure problems are reported, routed to individuals with the ability to resolve the problem, and resolution or workaround communicated to the end user.

> *Gatekeeper.* This role coordinates the consolidated reporting, tracking of service interruptions, problem notification and escalations, and problem coordination and facilitation.

Reporter. This role is responsible for documenting service interruptions, trending analysis, problem resolution, root cause analysis, and proactive problem avoidance.

Change management. This role is responsible for documenting and facilitating a structured change management process, including tracking, scheduling change meetings, and reporting problems caused as a result of change.

Site coordinator. This role is responsible for problem coordination at key service locations, quickly reporting problems, analysis, escalating high-impact problems, resolution, and communicating with the site.

Crisis coordinator. This role is responsible for coordinating the identification and resolution of high-impact problems.

Procedures

Effective problem management procedures are vital to the long-term control over the performance of an IT organization. At most installations, these procedures have been developed piecemeal, as the need for recognizing and resolving specific problems in the organization has arisen. In the early stages of growth, this approach works well, but as the organization grows, this piecemeal approach limits its ability to identify and solve problems effectively.

Problem management procedures should include audit trails for problems and their solutions, timely resolution, prioritization, escalation procedures, incident reports, accessibility to configuration, information coordination with change management, and a definition of any dependencies on outside services.

The problem management procedures should ensure that all unexpected events (errors, problems, etc.) are recorded, analyzed, and resolved in a timely manner. Incident reports should be established in the case of significant problems.

Escalation procedures ensure that problems are resolved in the most timely and efficient way possible. Escalation procedures include prioritizing problems based on the impact severity as well as the activation of a business continuity plan when necessary.

Problems should be traceable from the incident to the source cause (e.g., new software release and emergency change). The problem management process should be closely associated with change management.

Problem Severity

In today's complex environment combined with a high volume of transactions, it is inevitable that problems will occur. The cost of resolving problems must be weighed against the benefit. Thus, a system is needed to identify the severity of problems to ensure that the problems with the greatest impact are resolved first. Impact definitions will depend on the organization, but, in general, the following areas are to be considered:

- Number of users impacted (as a percentage of total users)
- Critical nature of the application (e.g., online banking)
- Regulatory/compliance issues
- Length of outage
- Dependency on system (no workaround)

Problem Escalation

The service desk will not be able to resolve all problems. Some problems will need to be escalated due to the severity or complexity of the issue. A problem escalation process is needed to ensure that high-impact issues are routed to the appropriate groups for resolution and communicated to impacted groups.

Root Cause Analysis

For critical and major problems, a full problem review should be undertaken to ensure that the root cause has been understood and appropriate mitigating actions taken. The results of such a review should be communicated to key organization contacts.

Service Improvement Programs

Processes should be implemented to identify those areas of the organization that are most impacted by IT problems (beyond those affected by specific severity issues that are resolved in isolation). Specific service improvement programs should be investigated and jointly developed, with priorities agreed among the IT, relationship manager, and key organization contacts.

Tools

Problem management is a service delivery process that focuses on proactive outage prevention and standardized diagnostic and postrecovery processes. An efficient problem management process flow includes infrastructure and application reporting, communication, tracking, root cause analysis, proactive trending analysis, with an ultimate goal of problem avoidance. To accomplish this requires a common set of tools integrated with asset management, change management, and the service desk.

Problem Reporting

A problem reporting process identifies and collects problems for both the technical and application system environments. It monitors the resolution of these problems, in terms of initial- and long-term response, and reports on the impact the problem has had on the user community. During the process

- A problem is identified and reported by a user
- The report is recorded in a problem database
- Technical personnel are consulted if a problem requires immediate attention, in which case an emergency resolution may be applied
- The problem is assigned to the technical group that is responsible for its long-term resolution
- The cause of the problem is determined, and its full impact is evaluated
- The problem is resolved, and documentation is restored in the problem database

Although individual problems are managed based on severity, daily summary reports are needed for IT organizations to identify issues that impact operational availability. Problems should be collected and combined into a single daily report and reviewed by a team of representatives from all areas of IT (e.g., operations, security). During a daily service meeting, problems are reviewed for root cause, permanent resolution, customer impact, and proactive outage prevention. Follow-up action responses are assigned to the manager who supports the platform or application.

Daily problem reporting can be aggregated and summarized on a weekly or monthly basis for management reporting. Reporting should include the number of incidents, problems, resolution, and trends for key systems and applications.

Availability reporting is based on outages and incidents reported in the daily report. Such reports include information such as the outage or incident's length, duration, and impact to users. The availability report is used for measuring performance against agreed SLAs. This information can be used to communicate service availability and incidents to both business and IT senior management.

Because it is basically reactive—wait for a problem to develop and then fix it—the IT organization creates a perception of poor performance in its user community. At some point in its growth, it is best to develop procedures that allow anticipation of problems. Having a reliable problem management system will allow the organization to anticipate, report, track, and solve problems in a timely and effective manner.

Case Example: Acme Computing Services Business

Problem management is the process of effectively managing problems that have an impact on the delivery of system service from problem identification to resolution. At ACS, problem management includes resolving problems, recognizing recurring problems, problem addressing procedures, and containing or reducing the number and impact of problems that occur. Various types of records can be created in ACS's problem management. When a call is received and the caller is helped immediately, an incident record is created. The information from the call and any procedures that the help desk consultant performed are placed in the incident record and it is closed; no follow-up is necessary.

When a customer has a problem that will take some time to solve, a problem record is created. The information is placed in the problem record and the record is kept open until the problem is resolved. A problem record can receive various status classifications (e.g., monitored, opened, transferred, completed, and closed), and all problem records are assigned a priority code (0 = catastrophe, 1 = critical, 2 = intermediate, 3 = minor, 4 = small impact, 5 = no impact).

Purpose

Problem management establishes procedures and standards to handle customer problems that are under the responsibility of ACS. These include the detection, reporting, and correction of problems that have an impact on service and processes. In this way, ACS is better able to meet SLAs and have procedures for analyzing and resolving problems and preventing their recurrence.

Scope

Problem management begins with the recognition of a problem and ends when a problem has been resolved to the customer's satisfaction. It involves all systems and applications. Within these environments, problem management includes but is not limited to

- Local and remote hardware and software problems
- Incomplete or unavailable functions and applications

- Local and remote facility (environmental) problems
- Operational problems
- Local and remote network problems
- Process problems

Objectives

The objectives of problem management at ACS are to reduce failures to an acceptable level at an acceptable cost, help ensure that SLAs are achieved, and effectively use personnel resources. The primary objectives of problem management are to

- Ensure that all problems are reported and recorded correctly
- Ensure that all problems are assigned appropriate priority
- Recognize and escalate recurring problems
- Ensure all outstanding problems are managed to resolution
- Identify and escalate to management problems that are not resolved within stated criteria
- Review closed problems and validate their resolutions
- Provide management with an overview of the problems having an impact on the delivery of applications or system service
- Advise management on methods to prevent problem recurrence

Key Success Factors

The success of problem management at ACS is measured against indications that include but are not limited to

Problem reassignment. When the help desk receives a problem that the help desk consultant cannot solve, the problem is reassigned to one of the support groups for resolution. The support group that is assigned the problem can reassign it to another group or resolve the problem and assign it back to the help desk for closure. Reports can be generated that detail how many times a problem has been assigned to other groups.

Problem duplication. Problem management keeps track of all problems, date of occurrence, and their resolution. In this way, if the same problem appears several days or months later, it has already been documented. The old problem record can be checked for any special activities that may help solve the current problem. The old problem records are also used to report on how well the equipment is working. If a piece of equipment has the same problem repeatedly over a period of time, this could indicate a major problem with the equipment.

Problem escalation. At times, problems take longer to resolve than the customer, help desk consultant, or support group consultant would like. Each problem is assigned a priority when it is first opened. Each priority has an allotted time within which the problem must be resolved. If the problem is not resolved within this allotted time, it is escalated to the next-higher management level.

Conclusion

The objective of the service desk is to respond to questions or problems that may occur with hardware, systems, and applications. The service desk acts as a central point to prioritize, route, and report on issues and problems. Asset, change, and service management processes are all dependent on the information gathered by the service desk.

Training end users to effectively use applications is important for user productivity and a cost-effective service desk. There are many possible approaches to training end users, including online, instructor led, and train the trainer. The selected approach will depend on the skill level of users and complexity of applications. Whatever approach is selected, the cost of not training will exceed the cost of training by three to six times.

Incident and problem management processes are needed to handle problems that are raised through the service desk as well as respond to major incidents and problems, restore IT services, and resolve the root cause of any issue. Effective incident and problem management processes address inevitable problems and are important for maintaining high customer satisfaction.

Review Questions

1. What is the relationship between training and the service desk?
2. What is the service desk? What does it do?
3. What are problem management procedures?
4. Explain why a problem management system is important.
5. What is problem management? What does it do?

Multiple-Choice Questions

1. Providing end users with training is important because users
   a. Make fewer calls to the help desk
   b. Will use applications more effectively
   c. Make few mistakes and have fewer questions
   d. All of the above
2. Responsibilities of the service desk include all of the following except
   a. Log and route service requests
   b. Handle problem calls
   c. Provide desk-side support
   d. Prepare standard monthly reports
3. Information gathered by the service desk can be used by the following process:
   a. Asset management
   b. Change management
   c. Service management
   d. All of the above
4. Specialized service support groups provide
   a. Resolution of more complex issues
   b. Primary diagnosis and resolution of common problems
   c. Support for more knowledgeable users
   d. None of the above
5. Advantages of outsourcing the service desk include
   a. Quicker implementation time
   b. Lower customer satisfaction

    c. More comprehensive training
    d. None of the above
6. Knowledge management includes
    a. Documenting how-to-use applications
    b. Sharing information on problems and fixes
    c. Making information available to users
    d. All of the above
7. The objective of incident management is to
    a. Minimize the adverse impact of incidents and problems
    b. Restore operations as soon as possible
    c. Develop a workaround
    d. Resolve problems
8. Problem severity is an important aspect of problem management needed to
    a. Prioritize problem resolution
    b. Determine the cost/benefit of resolving individual problems
    c. Identify regulatory compliance issues
    d. All of the above
9. Problem management tools should be part of a common toolset integrated with
    a. Asset management
    b. Change management
    c. Service desk
    d. All of the above
10. A problem reporting process is needed to
    a. Measure against SLAs
    b. Identify the root cause of problems
    c. Follow up on action responses
    d. All of the above

Exercises

1. You have been asked to write an audit program to review the problem management function for a software vendor that provides technical support over the Internet. Prepare a scope, an objective, and a list of 10 audit steps to be performed.
2. Discuss possible approaches to training end users.
3. Develop a problem management audit program for ACS.

Answers to Multiple-Choice Questions

1—d; 2—c; 3—d; 4—a; 5—a; 6—d; 7—b; 8—d; 9—d; 10—a

Further Reading

1. Dorfman, P., *ITIL3: Executive Validation for KM*, KMWorld, February 5, 2008, http://www.kmworld.com/Articles/News/News-Analysis/ITIL-3-executive-validation-for-KM-40807.aspx.

2. Elyse, R., *ITL Problem Management*, Anti-Clue, June 2007, http://www.anticlue.net/archives/000839.htm.
3. Fiering, L., *Best Practices in PC Life Cycle Services*, ID Number: G00138551, Gartner, Inc., Stamford, CT, March 16, 2006.
4. Fiering, L. and B. Kirwin, *Untrained Users Cost More to Support Than Trained Users*, ID Number: G00138330, Gartner, Inc., Stamford, CT, March 14, 2006.
5. Information Systems Audit and Control Foundation, Aligning COBIT, ITIL, and ISO 17799 for Business Benefit, 2005.
6. Levinson, M., ABC: An introduction to knowledge management (KM), *CIO Magazine*, CXO Media Inc., 2008, http://www.cio.com/article/40343.
7. The Information Technology Infrastructure Library (ITIL) Directory of Software & Services for ITIL and ITSM, http://www.itil-itsm-world.com/.
8. Unknown, The prevalence of IT outsourcing, *Computer Economics*, August 2007, http://www.computereconomics.com/article.cfm?id = 1265.

Chapter 20

Security and Service Continuity

As we have entered the decade of 2010, as a world dependent on global economy, we have seen just how fragile and vulnerable we really are. Our world has seen fairly severe natural environmental disasters such as earthquakes, tsunamis, hurricanes, tornados, volcanic eruptions, flood, and fires, all of which covered by the press worldwide, that have led to loss of life and created economic chaos and severe business interruptions and consequences. Whether natural or unnatural (cyber attacks, disruption of service, fraud, terrorism, market collapse, etc.), such events cost organizations.

Therefore, security and continuity planning are fundamental controls needed to prevent, detect, and respond to threats. According to the U.S. Federal Government's recently published FIPS 200, "The minimum security requirements cover seventeen security-related areas with regard to protecting the confidentiality, integrity, and availability of federal information systems and the information processed, stored, and transmitted by those systems." The security-related areas include (1) access control; (2) awareness and training; (3) audit and accountability; (4) certification, accreditation, and security assessments; (5) configuration management; (6) contingency planning; (7) identification and authentication; (8) incident response; (9) maintenance; (10) media protection; (11) physical and environmental protection; (12) planning; (13) personnel security; (14) risk assessment; (15) systems and services acquisition; (16) system and communications protection; and (17) system and information integrity. The 17 areas represent a broad-based, balanced information security program that addresses the management, operational, and technical aspects of protecting federal information and information systems. Through the selection and application of homogeneous and appropriate controls, security is a chance to meet the objectives of the organization. Each organization will have unique threats and responses depending on the organization's objectives and tolerance for risk.

Security standards and guidelines provide a framework for implementing comprehensive security processes. The ISO provides generic security standards under ISO 27002. The NIST has several FIPS on security and privacy. The COBIT includes the basic controls required for information security. And there are several resources available on the Internet to help organizations develop an information security policy.

A security policy defines the guidelines and practices for configuring and managing security in the organization. An information security policy defines the security practices that align to the strategic objectives of the organization. Information is a valuable and strategic resource to most organizations today. Along with defining what information is critical, determining who has access to that information is crucial to managing this important resource.

Managing user authentication is a fundamental control in securing information. Information is one of the most critical resources in organizations today. Whether it is customer information, financial information, or proprietary business information, it needs to be protected from internal and external threats. According to the 2010/2011 Computer Crime and Security Survey done by the CSI, malware infection continued to be the most commonly seen attack, followed by phishing which is showing an upward trend.

IT Processes

The COBIT processes (DS4 and DS5) in the Delivery and Support Domain discuss how security and continuity processes support an effective IT organization. Exhibit 20.1 lists the control objectives for this section.

Information Systems Security

Information and information systems are critical assets in most organizations today. Without reliable and properly secured information and information systems, organizations would quickly go out of business. Likewise, the preservation and enhancement of an organization's reputation is directly linked to the way in which both information and information systems are managed. Maintaining an adequate level of security is one of the several important aspects of both information management and information systems management. The purpose of information security is to help ensure that the organization's strategic business objectives are met. The three fundamental objectives for information are confidentiality, integrity, and availability. Each of these has associated risks that would prevent achieving these objectives.

- *Confidentiality* is the protection of information from unauthorized access. This is important in maintaining our company image and complying with privacy laws. Possible risks associated with confidentiality include
  - Security breaches allow unauthorized access or disclosure of sensitive or valuable company data, such as policyholder information or corporate strategic plans, to competitors or public.
- *Integrity* is the correctness and completeness of information. This is important in maintaining the quality of information for decision making. Possible risks associated with information integrity include
  - Security breaches allow unauthorized access to information systems, resulting in corrupted information
  - Security breaches allow unauthorized access to information systems, resulting in fraud or misuse of company information or systems
- *Availability* is maintaining information systems in support of business processes. This is important in maintaining operational efficiency and effectiveness. Possible risks associated with availability include

DS4 Ensure Continuous Service
Control Objectives
4.1   IT continuity framework
4.2   IT continuity plans
4.3   Critical IT resources
4.4   Maintenance of the IT continuity plan
4.5   Testing of the IT continuity plan
4.6   IT continuity plan training
4.7   Distribution of the IT continuity plan
4.8   IT services recovery and resumption
4.9   Off-site backup storage
4.10   Postresumption review
DS5 Ensure Systems Security
Control Objectives
5.1   Management of IT security
5.2   IT security plan
5.3   Identity management
5.4   User account management
5.5   Security testing, surveillance, and monitoring
5.6   Security incident definition
5.7   Protection of security technology
5.8   Cryptographic key management
5.9   Malicious software prevention, detection, and correction
5.10   Network security
5.11   Exchange of sensitive data

Exhibit 20.1   Processes for the delivery and support.

- Significant disruption or failure of information systems, including loss of our ability to process business
- Crash of systems due to a variety of sources, such as catastrophes, viruses, or sabotage

Security Threats and Risks

Expanding computer use has resulted in serious abuses of data communications systems. Computer hackers and sometimes employees use an organization's data communications system to tamper with the organization's data, destroying information, introducing fraudulent records, and stealing assets with the touch of a few keys. First occurrences of this vulnerability appeared in 1981.

A grand jury in Pennsylvania charged nine students (aged 17–22 years) with using computers and private telephone services to make illegal long-distance calls and have merchandise delivered to three mail drops in the Philadelphia area without getting billed. Over a 6-month period, the group was responsible for $212,000 in theft of services and $100,000 in stolen merchandise.

Three decades later, the methods have become more sophisticated and the vulnerabilities continue to exist. For example, on November 8, 2008, a series of theft occurred across the globe nearly simultaneously. Over 2100 money machines in at least 280 cities on three continents, in countries such as the United States, Canada, Italy, Hong Kong, Japan, Estonia, Russia, and Ukraine were compromised. Within 12 hours, the thieves—lead by four hackers—stole a total of more than $9 million in cash. The only reason the theft ceased was because the ATMs were out of money. This was one of the most sophisticated and organized computer fraud attacks ever conducted.

According to 2010 Internet Crime Report published by Internet Crime Complaint Center (IC3), a partnership between the FBI and the NW3C, nondelivery of payment or merchandise, scams impersonating the FBI, and identity theft were the top three most common complaints made. The most common techniques used to commit cybercrimes is shown on Exhibit 20.2.

Type	Description
Spamming	Sending unsolicited commercial e-mail advertising for products, services, and Websites. Spam can also be used as a delivery mechanism for malware and other cyber threats.
Phishing	A high-tech scam that frequently uses spam or pop-up messages to deceive people into disclosing their credit card numbers, bank account information, Social Security numbers, passwords, or other sensitive information. Internet scammers use e-mail bait to "phish" for passwords and financial data from the sea of Internet users.
Spoofing	Creating a fraudulent Website to mimic an actual, well-known Website run by another party. E-mail spoofing occurs when the sender address and other parts of an e-mail header are altered to appear as though the e-mail originated from a different source. Spoofing hides the origin of an e-mail message.
Pharming	A method used by phishers to deceive users into believing that they are communicating with a legitimate Website. Pharming uses a variety of technical methods to redirect a user to a fraudulent or spoofed Website when the user types in a legitimate Web address. For example, one pharming technique is to redirect users—without their knowledge—to a different Website from the one they intended to access. Also, software vulnerabilities may be exploited or malware employed to redirect the user to a fraudulent Website when the user types in a legitimate address.
Denial-of-service attack	An attack in which one user takes up so much of a shared resource that none of the resource is left for other users. Denial-of-service attacks compromise the availability of the resource.

Exhibit 20.2 Techniques used to commit cybercrimes. (Adapted from United States General Accounting Office, *CYBERCRIME—Public and Private Entities Face Challenges in Addressing Cyber Threats*, GAO-07-705, June 22, 2007.)

Distributed denial-of-service	A variant of the denial-of-service attack that uses a coordinated attack from a distributed system of computers rather than from a single source. It often makes use of worms to spread to multiple computers that can then attack the target.
Viruses	A program that "infects" computer files, usually executable programs, by inserting a copy of itself into the file. These copies are usually executed when the infected file is loaded into memory, allowing the virus to infect other files. A virus requires human involvement (usually unwitting) to propagate.
Trojan horse	A computer program that conceals harmful code. It usually masquerades as a useful program that a user would wish to execute.
Worm	An independent computer program that reproduces by copying itself from one system to another across a network. Unlike computer viruses, worms do not require human involvement to propagate.
Malware	Malicious software designed to carry out annoying or harmful actions. Malware often masquerades as useful programs or is embedded into useful programs so that users are induced into activating them. Malware can include viruses, worms, and spyware.
Spyware	Malware installed without the user's knowledge to surreptitiously track and/or transmit data to an unauthorized third party.
Botnet	A network of remotely controlled systems used to coordinate attacks and distribute malware, spam, and phishing scams. Bots (short for "robots") are programs that are covertly installed on a targeted system allowing an unauthorized user to remotely control the compromised computer for a variety of malicious purposes.

Exhibit 20.2 (Continued) Techniques used to commit cybercrimes. (Adapted from United States General Accounting Office, *CYBERCRIME—Public and Private Entities Face Challenges in Addressing Cyber Threats***, GAO-07-705, June 22, 2007.)**

To help prevent potentially devastating impact to systems and operations and the critical infrastructures, President Bush issued a 2003 national strategy and related policy directives aimed at improving cybersecurity nationwide, including both government systems and those cyber-critical infrastructures owned and operated by the private sector. Because the threats have persisted and grown, a commission—commonly referred to as the Commission on Cybersecurity for the 44th Presidency and chaired by two congressmen and industry officials—was established in August 2007 to examine the adequacy of the strategy and identify areas for improvement. At about the same time, the Bush administration began to implement a series of initiatives aimed primarily at improving cybersecurity within the federal government. The key strategy improvements can be seen in Exhibit 20.3.

Progress has not been as quick as it is anticipated. The U.S. General Accounting Office (GAO) testified before the Subcommittee on Oversight and Investigations, Committee on Energy and Commerce, House of Representative in July 2011 that although actions have been taken, there is a continued need to address the challenges in the cybersecurity area, including enhancing cyber

- Develop a national strategy that clearly articulates strategic objectives, goals, and priorities.
- Establish White House responsibility and accountability for leading and overseeing national cybersecurity policy.
- Establish a governance structure for strategy implementation.
- Publicize and raise awareness about the seriousness of the cybersecurity problem.
- Create an accountable, operational cybersecurity organization.
- Focus more actions on prioritizing assets, assessing vulnerabilities, and reducing vulnerabilities than on developing additional plans.
- Bolster public/private partnerships through an improved value proposition and use of incentives.
- Focus greater attention on addressing the global aspects of cyberspace.
- Improve law enforcement efforts to address malicious activities in cyberspace.
- Place greater emphasis on cybersecurity research and development, including consideration of how to better coordinate government and private sector efforts.
- Increase the cadre of cybersecurity professionals.
- Make the federal government a model for cybersecurity, including using its acquisition function to enhance cybersecurity aspects of products and services.

Exhibit 20.3 The key strategy improvements identified by cybersecurity experts. (Adapted from United States General Accounting Office, *National Cybersecurity Strategy: Key Improvements Are Needed to Strengthen the Nation's Posture*, GAO-09-432T, March 10, 2009.)

analysis and warning capabilities and strengthening the public–private partnerships for securing cyber-critical infrastructure. The ongoing challenges include

- Poor computer security program planning and management continue to be fundamental problems. Of the 24 recommendations in the President's May 2009 cyber policy review report, 2 have been fully implemented, and 22 have been partially implemented. The draft of cybersecurity guidelines still lack critical elements, such as the risk of attacks that use both cyber and physical means.
- Break-ins and damage of various levels of significance have been acknowledged, including sophisticated computer attack, known as Stuxnet.
- Serious weaknesses in data communications and network controls place critical federal operations and assets at risk. In March 2011, according to the Deputy Secretary of Defense, a cyber attack on a defense company's network captured 24,000 files containing Defense Department information. He added that nations typically launch such attacks, but there is a growing risk of terrorist groups and rogue states developing similar capabilities.

Also, the GAO recently noted some very interesting trends reported by both the FBI and the Carnegie Mellon's CERT. The FBI identified multiple sources of threats to our nation's critical infrastructures, including foreign nation states engaged in information warfare, domestic criminals and hackers, and disgruntled employees working within an organization, as shown in Exhibit 20.4. The CERT Center has also been reporting increasing activity in vulnerabilities.

Along with these increasing threats, the number of computer security vulnerabilities reported to the National Vulnerability Database has reached over 47,500 vulnerabilities by August 2011. The rate is about 12 vulnerabilities per day. According to the GAO report, the director of the CERT Center stated that as much as 80% of actual security incidents go unreported in most cases because the organization (1) was unable to recognize that its systems had been penetrated

Threat	Description
Criminal groups	There is an increased use of cyber intrusions by criminal groups that attack systems for monetary gain.
Foreign nation states	Foreign intelligence services use cyber tools as part of their information gathering and espionage activities. Also, several nations are aggressively working to develop information warfare doctrine, programs, and capabilities. Such capabilities enable a single entity to have a significant and serious impact by disrupting the supply, communications, and economic infrastructures that support military power—impacts that, according to the director of the Central Intelligence Agency, can affect the daily lives of Americans across the country.
Hackers	Hackers sometimes crack into networks for the thrill of the challenge or for bragging rights in the hacker community. While remote cracking once required a fair amount of skill or computer knowledge, hackers can now download attack scripts and protocols from the Internet and launch them against victim sites. Thus, attack tools have become more sophisticated and easier to use.
Hacktivists	Hacktivism refers to politically motivated attacks on publicly accessible Web pages or e-mail servers. These groups and individuals overload e-mail servers and hack into Websites to send a political message.
Disgruntle insiders	The disgruntled insider, working from within an organization, is a principal source of computer crimes. Insiders may not need a great deal of knowledge about computer intrusions because their knowledge of a victim system often allows them to gain unrestricted access to cause damage to the system or to steal system data. The insider threat also includes contractor personnel.
Terrorists	Terrorists seek to destroy, incapacitate, or exploit critical infrastructures to threaten national security, cause mass casualties, weaken the U.S. economy, and damage public morale and confidence. However, terrorist adversaries of the United States are less developed in their computer network capabilities than other adversaries. Terrorists likely pose a limited cyber threat. The Central Intelligence Agency believes terrorists will stay focused on traditional attack methods, but it anticipates growing cyber threats as a more technically competent generation enters the ranks.

Exhibit 20.4   Sources of cyber threats to critical infrastructure observed by the FBI. (Adapted from United States General Accounting Office, *Information Security: TVA Needs to Address Weaknesses in Control Systems and Networks*, GAO-08-526, May 21, 2008.)

because there was no indication of penetration or attack or (2) was reluctant to report the incidents.

As both governments and businesses worldwide place increasing reliance on interconnected systems and electronic data, a corresponding rise is occurring of risks in fraud, inappropriate disclosure of sensitive data, and disruption of critical operations and services. The same factors that benefit business and government operations also make it possible for individuals and organizations to inexpensively interfere with, or eavesdrop on, these operations from remote locations for purposes of fraud or sabotage, or other mischievous or malicious purposes.

Security Standards

Security standards and guidelines provide a framework for implementing comprehensive security processes and controls. The ISO provides generic security standards under ISO 27002. The NIST has several FIPS on security and privacy (Appendix III). COBIT includes the basic controls required for information security (Exhibit 20.1). And, there are several resources available on the Internet to help organizations develop an information security policy.

International Organization for Standardization and ISO 27002

The ISO is the world's largest developer and publisher of international standards. It is a network of the national standards institutes of 162 countries with a Central Secretariat in Geneva, Switzerland. The ISO 27000 series of standards have been specifically reserved by ISO for information security matter. According to their Website, ISO 27002 "established guidelines and general principles for initiating, implementing, maintaining, and improving information security management within an organization." The standard is also intended to provide a guide for the development of "organizational security standards and effective security management practices and to help build confidence in inter-organizational activities."

The ISO 27002 standard is the rename of the ISO 17799 standard, and is a code of practice for information security. It outlines hundreds of potential controls and control mechanisms in 12 major sections (Exhibit 20.5). The basis of the standard was originally a document published by the UK government, which became a standard "proper" in 1995, when it was republished by BSI as BS7799. In 2000, it was again republished, this time by ISO, as ISO 17799. A new version of this appeared in 2005, along with a new publication, ISO 27001. These two documents are intended to be used together, with one complementing the other.

The ISO 27000 Toolkit is the major support resource for the ISO 27001 and ISO 27002 standards. It contains a number of items specifically engineered to assist with implementation and audit. These include

- A copy of ISO 27001 itself
- A copy of ISO 27002 itself
- A full business impact assessment (BIA) questionnaire
- A certification guide/roadmap
- A network audit checklist
- A complete set of ISO 27002 aligned information security policies
- A disaster recovery kit, including checklist and questionnaire
- A management presentation to frame the context of the standards
- A substantial glossary of IS and IT terms and phrases

1. Risk assessment

2. Security policy

3. Organization of information security

4. Asset management

5. Human resources security

6. Physical and environmental security

7. Communications and operations management

8. Access control

9. Information systems acquisition, development, and maintenance

10. Information security incident management

11. Business continuity management

12. Compliance

Exhibit 20.5   Major sections covered by the ISO 27002 standard.

An enterprise that is ISO 27002-certified could win business over competitors who are not certified. If a potential customer is choosing between two different services, and security is a concern, they will usually go with the certified choice. In addition, a certified enterprise will realize

- Improved enterprise security
- More effective security planning and management
- More secure partnerships and e-commerce
- Enhanced customer confidence
- More accurate and reliable security audits
- Reduced liability

National Institute of Standards and Technology

The major focus of NIST activities in IT is developing tests, measurements, proofs of concept, reference data, and other technical tools to support the development of pivotal, forward-looking technology. Under Section 5131 of the Information Technology Reform Act of 1996 and the Computer Security Act of 1987, Public Law 104-106, and the FISMA of 2002, NIST develops standards, guidelines, and associated methods and techniques for federal computer systems. These standards and guidelines are issued by NIST as FIPS for use government-wide. NIST develops FIPS when there are compelling federal government requirements, such as security and interoperability and there are no acceptable industry standards or solutions.

There are several standards and guidelines developed by the NIST (see Appendix III). The NIST publishes Special Publication 800-series reports on Information Technology Laboratory (ITL) research, guidelines, and outreach efforts in information system security. ITL bulletins provide an in-depth discussion of significant information systems topics. The guide to NIST Information Security Documents (http://csrc.nist.gov/publications/CSD_DocsGuide.pdf) provides a summary of all the resources available from the NIST. The NIST also developed *An*

Management Controls
Computer security policy
Computer security risk management
Security and planning in the computer system life cycle
Assurance
Operational Controls
Personnel/user issues
Preparing for contingencies and disasters
Computer security incident handling
Awareness, training, and education
Security considerations in computer support and operations
Physical and environmental security
Technical Controls
Identification and authentication
Logical access control
Audit trails
Cryptography

Exhibit 20.6   Controls covered by the NIST handbook.

Introduction to Computer Security—the NIST handbook that provides an overview of computer security controls that an organization would include in an overall security program. Exhibit 20.6 lists the controls covered by the handbook.

Information Security Controls

As the online threats keep rising, businesses need to address the security issue seriously and quickly find ways to cope with it. To effectively fight these potential threats, they need to carefully design and develop a good security plan and then fully implement and enforce it. They need to consider and value its effectiveness in the long run when investing in security rather than the instant savings from the security investments.

Return on Investments (ROI) in Security

Although investing in security can bring businesses many benefits in that it helps protect their valuable information assets and prevent other devastating consequences, many companies have not spent enough on security expenditures. According to many chief security officers, it is very hard to prove the value of the investments in security unless a catastrophe has occurred. A thorough understanding of the benefits brought by the investments in security will be a strong motivation in encouraging businesses to devote adequate money in security expenditure.

Security Architecture

Systems should be designed with security to integrate with the existing security architecture. The security architecture is not a set of products. Security architecture is a model that specifies what services, such as authentication, authorization, auditing, and intrusion detection, need to be addressed by technologies. It provides a model to which applications can be compared to answer questions such as "How are users authenticated?" In addition, security architecture helps developers recognize that the same security services are needed by many different applications and that applications should be designed to the same security model.

Information Security Policy

An information security policy describes ways to prevent and respond to a variety of threats to information and information systems including unauthorized access, disclosure, duplication, modification, appropriation, destruction, loss, misuse, and denial of use. The information security policy is intended to guide management, users, and system designers in making decisions about information security. It provides high-level statements of information security goals, objectives, beliefs, ethics, controls, and responsibilities.

The most important factor to implement a security policy in an organization is to do an assessment of security needs. This is achieved by first understanding the organization's business needs and second by establishing security goals. There are some common questions that have to be answered:

- What information is critical to the business?
- Who creates that critical information?
- Who uses that information?
- What would happen if the critical data were stolen, corrupted, or lost?
- How long can the company operate without access to the critical data?

Information security crosses multiple areas. Systems and disaster recovery plans must be built with security in mind. The information security policy must be coordinated with systems development, change control, disaster recovery, compliance, and human resource policies to ensure consistency. An information security policy should state Web and e-mail usage ethics and discuss access limitations, confidentiality policy, and any other security issue. Good policies give employees exact instruction as to how events are handled and recovery escalated if necessary. The policy should be available and be distributed to all users.

Roles and Responsibilities

To be effective, information security must be a team effort involving the participation and support of every user who deals with information and information systems. An information security department typically has the primary responsibility for establishing guidelines, direction, and authority over information security activities. However, all groups have a role in protecting the organization's information.

Information Owner Responsibilities

Information owners are the department managers, senior management, or their designees within the organization who bear the responsibility for the acquisition, development, and maintenance of production applications that process information. Production applications are computer programs that regularly provide reports in support of decision making and other organization activities. All production application system information must have a designated owner. For each type of information, owners designate the relevant sensitivity classification, designate the appropriate level of criticality, define which users will be granted access, as well as approve requests for various ways in which the information will be used.

Information Custodian Responsibilities

Custodians are in physical or logical possession of either organization information or information that has been entrusted to the organization. Whereas IT staff members clearly are custodians, local system administrators are also custodians. Whenever information is maintained only on a personal computer, the user is necessarily also the custodian. Each type of application system information must have one or more designated custodians. Custodians are responsible for safeguarding the information, including implementing access control systems to prevent inappropriate disclosure and making backups so that critical information will not be lost. Custodians are also required to implement, operate, and maintain the security measures defined by information owners.

User Responsibilities

Users are responsible for familiarizing themselves with and complying with all policies, procedures, and standards dealing with information security. Questions about the appropriate handling of a specific type of information should be directed to either the custodian or the owner of the involved information. As information systems become increasingly distributed (through mobile computing, desktop computing, etc.), users are increasingly placed in a position where they must handle information security matters that they did not handle in days gone past. These new distributed systems force users to play security roles that they had not played previously.

Third-Party Responsibilities

Access to information from third parties needs to be formally controlled. With the use of contractors and outsourcing, third parties will have the need to access the organization's information. There must be a process in place to grant the required access while complying with rules and regulations. This process should include a nondisclosure agreement signed by the third party that defines responsibility for use of that information. A similar process should be in place when individuals in the organization have access to third-party information.

Information Classification Designations

Organizations need to establish an information classification system that categorizes information into groupings. Information groupings help determine how information is to be protected. In the private sector, there may be legal or regulatory reasons to classify information into public, internal, or confidential. In the government sector, there may also be national security reasons to classify information into various categories (e.g., top secret).

If information is sensitive, from the time it is created until the time it is destroyed or declassified, it must be labeled (marked) with an appropriate information classification designation. Such markings must appear on all manifestations of the information (hard copies, floppy disks, CD-ROMs, etc.). The vast majority of information falls into the Internal Use Only category. For this reason, it is not necessary to apply a label to Internal Use Only information. Information without a label is therefore by default classified as Internal Use Only.

Access to information in the possession of, or under the control of, the organization must be provided based on the need to know. In other words, information must be disclosed only to people who have a legitimate need for the information. At the same time, users must not withhold access to information when the owner of the information in question instructs that it be shared. To implement the need-to-know concept, organizations should adopt an access request and owner approval process. Users must not attempt to access sensitive information unless granted access rights by the relevant owner.

Organization information, an information that has been entrusted to the organization, must be protected in a manner commensurate with its sensitivity and criticality. Security measures must be employed regardless of the media on which information is stored (paper, overhead transparency, computer bits, etc.), the systems that process it (personal computers, firewalls, voice mail systems, etc.), or the methods by which it is moved (electronic mail, face-to-face conversation, etc.). Information must also be consistently protected no matter what its stage is in the life cycle from origination to destruction.

Vulnerability Management

Vulnerabilities are "weakness or exposures in IT assets or processes that may lead to a business risk or security risk."* As of August 2011, the National Vulnerability Database had documented over 47,000 vulnerabilities and was adding 9 new vulnerabilities a day. Furthermore, approximately 42% of vulnerabilities have a "high severity." A vulnerability management process is needed to combat this risk. This includes the identification, evaluation, and remediation of vulnerabilities. Prerequisites for responding to vulnerabilities includes asset management processes (see Chapter 12) to determine the software installed on organization hardware and change management processes (see Chapter 17) to manage the testing of patches. Patches should be reviewed and tested before implementation to verify that the system continues to work as intended and that no new vulnerabilities are introduced. With these processes in place, the security group can identify the vulnerabilities that apply to the organization. Once identified, the vulnerabilities need to be prioritized and implemented based on the risk of the particular issue.

Threat Management

Threat management includes virus protection, spam control, intrusion detection, and security event management. Virus protection software should be loaded on all workstations and the servers to regularly scan the system for new infections. Sooner or later a virus will find its way into a system. Even some of the largest software vendors have sent out products with viruses by mistake.

---

* Romanosky, S., G. Kim, and B. Kravchenko, *Global Technology Audit Guide (GTAG) 6: Managing and Auditing IT Vulnerabilities*, Institute of Internal Auditors, Altamonte Springs, FL, 2006.

Policies regarding virus protection should be implemented to prevent, detect, and correct viruses. Virus software must be continuously updated with virus definitions as new viruses are introduced daily. User awareness training is another important process for making users aware of the danger to the system of infected software that is downloaded from any source.

Trust Management

Trust management includes encryption and access controls. To ensure cryptography is applied in conformance with sound disciplines, there has to be a formal policy on the use of cryptography that applies across the organization. A formal policy should be supported by comprehensive standards/guidelines (e.g., for selection of algorithms, cryptographic key management) and take into account cross-border restrictions. Many encryption routines require that the user provide a seed or a key as input. Users must protect these security parameters from unauthorized disclosure, just as they would protect passwords from unauthorized disclosure. Rules for choosing strong seeds or keys should likewise follow the rules for choosing strong passwords.

Encryption technologies electronically store information in an encoded form that can only be decoded by an authorized individual who has the appropriate decryption technology and authorization to decrypt. Encryption provides a number of important security components to protect electronic information:

Identification. Who are you?
Authentication. Can you prove who you are?
Authorization. What can you do?
Auditing. What did you do?
Integrity. Is it tamperproof?
Privacy. Who can see it?
Nonrepudiation. Can I prove that you said what you said?

When information is encoded, it is first translated into a numerical form and then encrypted using a mathematical algorithm. The algorithm requires a number or message, called a key, to encode or decode the information. The algorithm cannot decode the encrypted information without a decode key.

Identity Management

Identity management is the process used to determine who has access to what in an organization. It is also one of the most difficult areas to manage due to the number of functions that must work together to implement proper controls. Identity management must be a collaborative effort between information security, applications development, operations, human resources, contracts/ procurement, and business groups to implement. There are many reasons for implementing an identity management solution: regulatory compliance, risk management, and expense reduction.

Automating identity management into a single application that manages access to systems speeds the development of applications and reduces operating costs. Organizations have developed systems and applications over time with stand-alone user identity programs. With the number of applications and systems increasing, users have a difficult time remembering the number of user IDs and passwords. This causes users to create easy-to-guess passwords, write down passwords, not change them, or change a single digit.

Implementing identity management can result in savings for the help desk with reduced call volume and operations from fewer password changes, and users will have increased productivity from reduced log-on time and password resets. Implementing common process for administering access rights provides a consistent level and security and accountability across applications. Automating identity management can enable implementation of security access rights based on business roles and improve the turnaround time for adding, changing, and removing access. Additional benefits include

- Reduced manual processes and potential for human error
- Improved management reporting of user access rights
- Ability to enforce segregation of duties according to business rules
- Automatically revoked access rights of inactive employees
- Audit trail of requests and approvals

Integrating all these systems with a common identity management program can be costly and time consuming. The Gartner Group recommends implementing identity management over time by first proving success with a single function or application.

Security Monitoring

Computer systems handling sensitive, valuable, or critical information must securely log all significant computer security relevant events. Examples of computer security relevant events include password-guessing attempts, attempts to use privileges that have not been authorized, modifications to production application software, and modifications to system software. Logs of computer security relevant events must provide sufficient data to support comprehensive audits of the effectiveness of and compliance with security measures. All commands issued by computer system operators must be traceable to specific individuals through the use of comprehensive logs. Logs containing computer security relevant events must be retained per established archiving procedures. During this period, such logs must be secured such that they cannot be modified, and such that they can be read only by authorized persons. These logs are important for error correction, forensic auditing, security breach recovery, and related efforts. To assure that users are held accountable for their actions on computer systems, one or more records tracing security relevant activities to specific users must be securely maintained for a reasonable period of time. Computerized records reflecting the access privileges of each user of multiuser systems and networks must be securely maintained for a reasonable period of time.

Incident Management

To deal with security incidents that affect the installation in a disciplined manner, security incidents (e.g., malfunctions, loss of power or communications services, overloads, mistakes by users or personnel running the installation, access violations) have to be dealt with in accordance with a formal process. The process has to apply to all forms of security incident. Incidents have to be

- Identified and recorded
- Reported to a focal point
- Prioritized for action
- Analyzed and acted upon

Each incident has to be dealt with by a person equipped to understand the full implications of the incident as well as the consequences for the enterprise and initiate appropriate action. Significant incidents, and the pattern of incidents over time, have to be reported to and reviewed by the person in charge of the installation and user representatives, so that appropriate action can be initiated and properly documented. Incidents have to be reported to management.

Contingency and Disaster Recovery Planning

The contingency plan or disaster recovery plan is an important tool to business. It is a survival tool to help a business recover in the wake of an event that disrupts normal business operations. Provided management and staff support the plan, updated frequently and maintained and tested, it offers the chance for the business to survive. Contingency and disaster recovery planning requires significant resources to develop. Should a disaster occur, the payoff is to recover without significant business or operations downtime and loss.

Disasters can occur to businesses of any size and, frequently, those that are unprepared do not survive to continue. On August 14, 2003, an enormous power failure blacked out population centers from New York City to Cleveland, Detroit, and Toronto, crippling transportation networks and trapping tens of thousands of people in subways, elevators, and trains. Computers became useless to those who did not have battery power. On September 11, 2001, after the New York Twin Towers disaster, 37% of the businesses that had offices there did not survive. In the Los Angeles earthquake of 1994, which occurred in the San Fernando Valley, 75% of the area's small businesses did not survive. Of the medium-sized businesses, 50% did not survive. Toyota and Honda automakers suffered a 99.4% and 88.3% drop in first-quarter profit respectively after the 2011 massive tsunami and earthquake in Japan. Part of the reasons for this decline is because of lower production due to the restricted supply of parts after the quake. Small- and medium-sized business would not have been able to stand this type of loss. The impact of incidents like these were felt not only by the business, but also by the supplier and the customers who relied on that business for its products and sales.

Disaster recovery planning has taken on greater importance as organizations focus on the control requirements associated with Sarbanes–Oxley. Enterprise risk management (Chapter 9) also identifies critical information that organizations depend on and places priority on this asset to keep the information available and secure to the authorized users. Disaster recovery and resumption planning are complex undertakings in today's distributed environment. Most companies rely on personal computers and distributed servers to conduct day-to-day operations, and they would be hard-pressed to do anything without them. Therefore, it is very important to include plans for distributed hardware, software, and data recovery in a disaster recovery plan. The first step in disaster recovery planning is identifying who is responsible for distributed disaster recovery. Is recovery of all technology the sole responsibility of IT or the business units? The answer is it depends on who has control over the hardware, software, and data. "Many (organizations) are pulling servers back into the data center to better manage and protect information." In most cases, IT and users must work together to identify critical information and resources that will need to be recovered in the event of a disaster.

Disaster recovery plans should address both partial and total destruction of computing resources. Distributed systems and microcomputer systems should be included. Critical functions that are performed on these platforms should be identified and procedures established for restoring operation. Microcomputers are an important tool for daily work processing, and the recovery of these tools should not be overlooked. Information on the basic microcomputer configuration, including hardware and software, should be maintained for ease of recreating the processing environment. In addition, a backup of critical datafiles should be kept off-site along with operating and recovery procedures.

Control planning must be based on the assumption that any computer system is subject to several different types of failures. In particular, procedures must exist and must be tested for recovery from failures or losses of equipment, programs, or datafiles.

In the case of equipment failures, each installation might have a contractual agreement covering the use of an alternate site with a comparable computer configuration, if one is available. In most cases, such agreements will be reciprocal, with two or more computer users agreeing to come to one another's aid in the event of a catastrophe.

Backup and restart capabilities for both programs and datafiles require specific retention cycles and the storage of backup copies or programs and files at remote, protected locations. Copies of system documentation, standards, and procedure manuals should also be protected through remote, off-site storage.

Risk Assessment/Priorities

The first step in assessing risk and priorities involves identifying the organization's assets and the replacement value of those assets. This includes hardware, software, facilities, personnel, administrative, and data. The next step is to identify specific risks that would result in temporary or permanent loss of assets (e.g., fire, flood, sabotage, viruses). Next, assess the impact of these losses (e.g., modification, destruction, denial of service). Finally, compare the value of the asset with the frequency of loss to cost justify the disaster recovery solution.

Planning/Testing/Maintenance

Once the risk exposures have been identified, a disaster recovery plan can be assembled that details a plan for hardware, software, data, and personnel. The plan should identify various levels of recovery, from an isolated event to a widespread disaster. The timeliness of recovery will depend on the loss exposure for the particular application. When the plan is completed, it should be tested to identify problems in the plan. Testing should be conducted on a periodic basis to validate assumptions and update the plan based on the changing environment. It also provides the opportunity to practice the recovery procedures and identify missing elements that need to be added.

Disaster Recovery Planning Steps

Each contingency and disaster recovery plan should have major steps or processes. The following steps should be considered as important to a disaster recovery plan:

1. Steps put in writing
2. Hot/cold site selected
3. Full and incremental system backups made on a daily or weekly basis
4. Data backed up
5. Tests and drills scheduled
6. Data and system backups stored off-site
7. Disaster recovery chairperson and committee appointed
8. Emergency telephone numbers listed
9. Critical applications identified
10. Operating system, utilities, and application files backed up
11. Insurance coverage in place

12. Communication plan made
13. Up-to-date system and operation documentation confirmed
14. Employee relocation plan made for alternate work site
15. Food and water stocked
16. Key personnel positions backed up
17. Cardiopulmonary resuscitation (CPR)/first aid education in place
18. Care planned for families in an emergency
19. List made of hardware and software
20. Mission statement drawn up for disaster recovery plan
21. Manual procedures in place as a backup to automated procedures
22. Contractual arrangements signed with cleanup crew to remove debris

Written Disaster Recovery Plan

As stated earlier, a disaster recovery plan is a plan set up to enable an organization and its computer installation to quickly restore operations and resume business in the event of a disaster. Additionally, as the resources in an installation usually are in a constant state of flux—new applications are being developed, existing systems are being modified, personnel are turning over, and new hardware is being acquired—the plan must be updated on a regular basis. The objective of maintaining the plan in a continued state of readiness is to reduce the likelihood of incorrect decisions being made during the recovery process and decrease the level of stress that may be placed on the disaster recovery team members during this process.

Once the plan is developed, members of the organization should be familiar with the plan. If an emergency occurs, it is easy for staff members to execute their roles in the plan. Exercising the plan confirms that efforts are not duplicated and all the necessary steps are taken. It is important to have a written disaster recovery plan with detailed steps as individuals unfamiliar with the process may need to perform the disaster recovery process in a real emergency.

Mission Statement for Disaster Recovery Plan

A mission statement and objectives should be developed for the disaster recovery plan. These objectives should be realistic, achievable, and economically feasible. These objectives provide direction in preparing the plan and in continually reevaluating its usefulness.

Disaster Recovery Plan Tests and Drill

Disaster simulation drills or tests are used to test the staffing, management, and decision making of both the technical and procedural aspects of an organization's disaster recovery plan. The test reduces the opportunity for miscommunication when the plan is implemented during a real disaster. It also offers the management an opportunity to spot weaknesses and improve procedures.

Unfortunately, organizations are often unwilling to carry out a test because of the disruption that occurs to daily operations and the fear that a real disaster may arise as a result of the test procedures. Therefore, a phased approach to testing would be helpful in building up to a full test. In the following is a suggested phased approach:

1. Begin testing by using desk checks, inspections, and walk-through.
2. Next, a disaster can be simulated at a convenient time (during a slow period in the day).
3. Personnel also might be given prior notice of the test so that they are prepared.
4. Finally, simulate a disaster without warning.

Unless a disaster recovery plan is tested, it seldom remains usable. A practice test of a plan could very well be the difference between the success and the failure of the plan. The process is parallel to the old adage about the three things it takes for a retail business to be successful: location, location, and location. What is needed for a company's disaster recovery plan to allow it to continue to stay in business is testing, testing, and more testing.

The audit of contingency and disaster recovery planning is an important check. The major elements and areas, such a plan, should be validated against recent publications on the subject. In turn, this approach can be used as a checklist to help both the auditor and the management assess their plans.

Conclusion

Current and future business activities are based on information. Information and the associated IT systems and networks are of vital significance to the organization activity. Information availability, integrity, and confidentiality are essential to maintain competitive edge, cash flow, profitability, legal compliance, and respected organization image. An information security policy is intended to guide the organization in making decisions about information security. An information security policy provides high-level statements of information security goals, objectives, beliefs, ethics, controls, and responsibilities. Standards and procedures that define specific implementation of the policies are documented separately.

The organization, management, and staff and the IT audit, control, and security professionals must work together to establish, maintain, and monitor the organization's security policy. Important elements, such as a policy, include end-user awareness; business contingency (such as the World Trade Center Disaster) and continuity plan; security audits; security practices; training of management and staff; use of tools, techniques, and encryption; and the formation of an incident response team. The only consistent way to establish security in environments with intranets, extranets, and Websites that transport corporate data over public and private networks is to make security a top priority and move to implement the best practices for all phases of the security policy life cycle.

Under the topic of disaster recovery planning, we have presented several crucial steps that disaster recovery planning authors have written about in detail. The repetition of the same steps by several different authors proves the importance of the subject. These can be used as audit steps to check the validity and reliability of the contingency and the disaster recovery plan. These steps are crucial in determining where companies are regarding their disaster recovery planning. Based on this information, auditors are able to determine the current condition of a company and provide the recommendations for each of the disaster recovery step findings.

Review Questions

1. What are the planning and control areas when establishing security management?
2. What cyber threats are critical to infrastructure as observed by the FBI?
3. What is the purpose of a security policy?

4. What steps are considered as important to a disaster recovery plan?
5. Why does a disaster recovery plan need to be tested?

Multiple-Choice Questions

1. ISO 17799 covers
   a. Security policy
   b. Security organization
   c. Asset classification and control
   d. All of the above
2. An information security policy provides all of the following except
   a. Guide to decision making about information security
   b. High-level statements of security objectives
   c. Instructions for implementing security attributes
   d. Ways to prevent and respond to threats
3. According to the CERT, what percent of actual security incidents goes unreported?
   a. 20%
   b. 40%
   c. 60%
   d. 80%
4. Information security requires participation and support from which one of the following groups?
   a. Local system administrators
   b. Department managers
   c. Contractors
   d. All of the above
5. Vulnerability management includes which one of the following process?
   a. Inventory of physical assets
   b. Change management
   c. Virus protection software
   d. None of the above
6. Implementing identity management can result in all of the following benefits except
   a. Reduced help desk call volume
   b. Consistent security and accountability
   c. Improved password selection
   d. Improved turnaround time for adding users
7. Encryption technologies electronically store information in an encoded form that can only be decoded by an authorized individual who has the appropriate decryption technology and a
   a. Private key
   b. Public key
   c. Authorization to decrypt
   d. Ability to decrypt
8. To be effective, which one of the following groups must support a contingency and disaster recovery plan to offer a business the best chance to survive?
   a. Auditors and management
   b. Technical personnel and management

    c. Management and staff
    d. Auditors and security officers
9. To be usable, a disaster recovery plan must be
    a. Written
    b. Approved
    c. Tested
    d. Enforced
10. Which of the following would not be included in a company-wide policy on end-user computing (EUC)?
    a. Wireless encryption standards
    b. Appropriate documentation
    c. Segregation of duties
    d. Backup procedures

Exercises

1. List five professional organizations that provide guidance or written studies on contingency planning and disaster recovery planning.
2. Using Web browsers, review two reports issued by the GAO or the NIST on the subject of information security: http://www.gao.gov and http://www.nist.gov.
3. Read Case 6 from Appendix I on Wedco Electronics, and answer the questions.
4. You have been asked to audit your company security plan as it applies to acceptable employee use of the Internet and e-mail. Write a preliminary audit plan, include scope, objectives, and audit steps.
5. A previous audit of your company recommended a disaster recovery plan. In performing your follow-up review, you find that although a plan is in place, it has not been tested. Write your audit finding regarding the weakness of an untested disaster recovery plan.

Answers to Multiple-Choice Questions

1—d; 2—c; 3—d; 4—d; 5—b; 6—c; 7—c; 8—c; 9—c; 10—a

Further Reading

1. Bresz, F., T. Renshaw, J. Rozek, and T. White, *Global Technology Audit Guide (GTAG) 9: Identity and Access Management*, Institute of Internal Auditors, Altamonte Springs, FL, 2007.
2. Cam-Winget, N., T. Moore, D. Stanley, and J. Walker, *IEEE 802.11i Overview*, Presentation at NIST 802.11 Wireless LAN Security Workshop, December 4, 2002.
3. Computer Security Institute/FBI, *Computer Security Institute/Federal Bureau of Investigation Computer Crime and Security Survey Results*, Computer Security Institute, Manhasset, NY, 2003.
4. Director of National Intelligence, Statement for the Record on the Worldwide Threat Assessment of the U.S. Intelligence Community, statement before the Senate Select Committee on Intelligence, February 16, 2011.
5. Gallegos, F., *Security and Control over Intranets and Extranets: Part 2*, #75-10-36, Auerbach Publishers, Boca Raton, FL, 2002, pp. 1–20.

6. Harrison, R., The 10 most important things an IT person must understand about security across the enterprise, Information Systems Audit and Control Association, *Journal (ISACA)*, 2005. Available at: http://www.isaca.org/Journal/Past-Issues/2005/Volume-3/Pages/JOnline-The-10-Most-Important-Things-an-IT-Person-Must-Understand-About-Security-Across-the-Enterprise1.aspx

7. Hunter, J.M.D., *An Information Security Handbook*, Springer, New York, 2001.

8. McCarthy, L., *IT Security: Risking the Corporation*, Prentice Hall PTR/Sun Microsystems Press, Englewood Cliffs, NJ, 2003.

9. Musaji, Y., A holistic definition of IT security—Part 1, Information Systems Audit and Control Association, *Journal (ISACA)*, 2006. Available at: http://www.isaca.org/Journal/Past-Issues/2006/Volume-3/Pages/A-Holistic-Definition-of-IT-Security-Part-11.aspx

10. Musaji, Y., A holistic definition of IT security—Part 2, Information Systems Audit and Control Association, *Journal (ISACA)*, 2006. Available at: http://www.isaca.org/Journal/Past-Issues/2006/Volume-4/Pages/A-Holistic-Definition-of-IT-Security-Part-21.aspx

11. National Vulnerability Database, DHS National Cyber Security Division/US-CERT, http://nvd.nist.gov.

12. O'Bryan, S., Critical elements of information security program success, Information Systems Audit and Control Association, *Journal (ISACA)*, 2006. Available at: http://www.isaca.org/Journal/Past-Issues/2006/Volume-3/Pages/Critical-Elements-of-Information-Security-Program-Success1.aspx

13. Pang, L., A manager's guide to identity management and federated identity, Information Systems Audit and Control Association, *Inf. Syst. Control J.*, 4, 2005. Available at: http://www.isaca.org/Journal/Past-Issues/2005/Volume-4/Documents/jpdf0504-A-Managers-Guide.pdf

14. Pescatore, J., *Wireless Networks: Can Security Catch Up with Business*, Presentation at NIST 802.11 Wireless LAN Security Workshop, December 2002.

15. Pironti, J., Key elements of information security program success, Information Systems Audit and Control Association, *Inf. Syst. Control J.*, 1, 2005. Available at: http://www.isaca.org/Journal/Past-Issues/2005/Volume-1/Documents/jpdf051-Key-Elements-of-an-is-program.pdf

16. Pironti, J., Key elements of a threat and vulnerability management program, Information Systems Audit and Control Association, *Journal (ISACA)*, 2006. Available at: http://www.isaca.org/Journal/Past-Issues/2006/Volume-3/Pages/Key-Elements-of-a-Threat-and-Vulnerability-Management-Program1.aspx

17. Richardson, R., *CSI Computer Crime and Security Survey*, Computer Security Institute, Manhasset, NY, 2007.

18. Ross, S., Contents and context, Information Systems Audit and Control Association, *Journal (ISACA)*, 2006. Available at: http://www.isaca.org/Journal/Past-Issues/2006/Volume-1/Pages/Contents-and-Context1.aspx

19. Saddat, M., *Network Security Principles and Practices*, Cisco Press, Indianapolis, IN, 2002, pp. 5–12.

20. Sarva, S., Cost-effective implementation of identity management, Information Systems Audit and Control Association, *Inf. Syst. Control J.*, 1, 2005. Available at: http://www.isaca.org/Journal/Past-Issues/2005/Volume-1/Documents/jpdf051-Cost-effective-Implementation-of-IM.pdf

21. Ungerman, M., Creating and enforcing an effective information security policy, Information Systems Audit and Control Association, *Journal (ISACA)*, 2005. Available at: http://www.isaca.org/Journal/Past-Issues/2005/Volume-6/Pages/JOnline-Creating-and-Enforcing-an-Effective-Information-Security-Policy1.aspx

22. United States General Accounting Office, *Critical Infrastructure Protection*, GAO-03-233, February 2003.

23. United States General Accounting Office, *Information Security: Progress Made, but Challenges Remain to Protect Federal Systems and the Nation's Critical Infrastructures*, GAO-03-564T, April 8, 2003.

24. United States General Accounting Office, *Critical Infrastructure Protection: Efforts of the Financial Services Sector to Address Cyber Threats*, GAO-03-173, January 30, 2003.

25. United States General Accounting Office, *Information Security: Computer Controls over Key Treasury Internet Payment System*, GAO-03-837, July 30, 2003.

26. United States General Accounting Office, *Information Security: Further Efforts Needed to Fully Implement Statutory Requirements in DOD*, GAO-03-1037T, July 24, 2003.

27. United States General Accounting Office, *Information Security: Continued Efforts Needed to Fully Implement Statutory Requirements*, GAO-03-852T, June 24, 2003.
28. United States General Accounting Office, *FDIC Information Security: Progress Made but Existing Weaknesses Place Data at Risk*, GAO-03-630, June 18, 2003.
29. United States General Accounting Office, *Information Security: Progress Made, but Weaknesses at the Internal Revenue Service Continue to Pose Risks*, GAO-03-44, May 30, 2003.
30. United States General Accounting Office, *Homeland Security: Information Sharing Responsibilities, Challenges, and Key Management Issues*, GAO-03-715T, May 8, 2003.
31. United States General Accounting Office, *Electricity Grid Modernization: Progress Being Made on Cybersecurity Guidelines, but Key Challenges Remain to Be Addressed*, GAO-11-117, January 12, 2011.
32. United States General Accounting Office, *Information Security: TVA Needs to Address Weaknesses in Control Systems and Networks*, GAO-08-526, May 21, 2008.
33. United States General Accounting Office, *National Cybersecurity Strategy: Key Improvements Are Needed to Strengthen the Nation's Posture*, GAO-09-432T, March 10, 2009.
34. United States General Accounting Office, *CYBERCRIME—Public and Private Entities Face Challenges in Addressing Cyber Threats*, GAO-07-705, June 22, 2007.
35. Unknown, *2007 CSI Computer Crime and Security Survey*, Computer Security Institute, Manhasset, NY, 2007.
36. Unknown, *The NIST Handbook—An Introduction to Computer Security*, Special Publication 800-12, US Department of Commerce.
37. Unknown, *Guide to NIST Information Security Documents*, National Institute of Standards and Technology, March 2007.
38. Wagner, R., R. Witty, J. Enck, and G. Kreisman, *The Do's and Don'ts of Identity and Access Management*, Gartner, Inc., Stamford, CT, April 4, 2006.
39. Wang, G., Strategies and influence for information security, Information Systems Audit and Control Association, *Journal (ISACA)*, 2005. Available at: http://www.isaca.org/Journal/Past-Issues/2005/Volume-1/Pages/JOnline-Strategies-and-Influence-for-Information-Security.aspx
40. Wheatman, V. and P. Proctor, *Eight Steps Needed to Define Reasonable Security*, Gartner Research G0012783, Stamford, CT, June 1, 2005.
41. Huffman, L. and J. Hamilton, Employee revenge, Tech TV, November 5, 2002, May 2, 2003, http://www.techtv.com/cybercrime/viceonline/story/0,23008,3386967,00.html.
42. Unknown, The National Strategy to Secure Cyberspace, May 2003, http://www.whitehouse.gov/pcipb/cyberspace_strategy.pdf.

Chapter 21

System Management

The operating system and system utilities form the foundation for the computing environment. As such, control failures at the system level can impact the entire organization. This chapter focuses on the controls needed to ensure the effective functioning of the underlying systems. System software and utilities are important tools to the IT personnel responsible for maintaining the software and important tools that IT auditors can use provided that they have been properly trained in their use. System software is computer software designed to operate the computer hardware and to provide a platform for running application software.

Utility software should be compared and contrasted with application software, which allows users to do things like creating text documents, playing games or music or exploring the Web. Rather than providing these kinds of user/output-oriented functionality, utility software usually focuses on how the computer infrastructure (including the computer hardware, operating system, application software and data storage) operates. Therefore, utilities are often rather technical and targeted at people with an advanced level of computer knowledge.

Database management software (DBMS) and database management system (DBMS) should be carefully controlled to ensure information is accurate, reliable, and protected from unauthorized access. In the crash or failure of a DBMS, all or a portion of the data can become unusable. For an IT manager, this can be a nightmare. Appropriate procedures must be followed to restore, validate, and return the system to normal. In a client/server environment with distributed databases or where data warehousing, data mining, and Web-based databases are used, additional procedures are needed. Users and IT professionals must do their part to ensure the security, integrity, and validity of information and DBMS transactions. This section provides a checklist of major areas of concern to the IT manager and staff regarding DBMS recovery.

During an audit of the operating system and other system software, it is important that the auditor constructs an audit program that will enhance the evaluation of the operating system and system utilities. This chapter identifies the key control areas of operating systems and provides the auditor with a sample audit program as shown in Appendix V.

DS3 Manage Performance and Capacity
Control Objectives
3.1   Performance and capacity planning
3.2   Current capacity and performance
3.3   Future capacity and performance
3.4   IT resources availability
3.5   Monitoring and reporting
DS11 Manage Data
Control Objectives
11.1   Business requirements for data management
11.2   Storage and retention arrangements
11.3   Media library management system
11.4   Disposal
11.5   Backup and restoration
11.6   Security requirements for data management

Exhibit 21.1   Processes for the delivery and support.

IT Processes

The Control Objectives for Information and Related Technology (COBIT) processes (DS3 and DS11) in the Delivery and Support Domain discuss how systems and data management processes support an effective IT organization. Exhibit 21.1 lists the control objectives for this section.

Systems Software

Systems software is a highly specialized set of computer software programs. It is an efficient set of integrated software programs written in machine language designed to communicate with the hardware. Systems software performs a specialized function that supports computer operations. It provides the operating routines that make the computer workable at a level for computer programs at the application level. Systems software includes any program or system that helps interconnect or control the elements of input, output, processing, data, and application programs. Typically, this software is provided by outside vendors and is discussed in the following sections.

Systems software controls application programs, tape and disk computer files, and other resources require greater security. For example, program library systems usually control all application programs, including the functions for accessing files, updating information, and converting from source-to-object code. Most of these packages contain an audit trail feature that records all changes made to application programs, including identification of the programmers making the changes. When properly implemented, this software promotes better security and backup of application programs.

Types and Uses of System Software

Most organizations rely on the operating system to

- Manage computer resources with minimal operator intervention
- Help programmers and operators control the operation and allocation of peripheral devices and other computer resources
- Minimize the differences between a given manufacturer's line of computers, thus facilitating the transfer of application programs

To ensure that the computer and networks that support applications are running effectively requires support personnel to be equipped with the necessary know-how, skills, time, operating procedures, and supervision. The use of powerful access privileges and system utilities must be rigorously controlled. All access to the application and supporting computers/networks has to be logged (including access by system administrators, operators, development or audit staff). Logs have to be unalterable and arrangements must be made to enable processing to continue when logs become full. Libraries and directories have to be checked periodically for signs of unauthorized access or changes and reported accordingly.

System Software

System software protects the integrity of files during processing and checks the accuracy and validity of new files generated by processing. Several individual processes accomplish this validation. First, the system software compares the name of the file specified by an application program with a field containing a label code at the head of the data file to be processed. The two designations must match before processing can take place. At the same time, the file integrity is verified during processing. One of the components of file labels in most computer systems is a count of the blocks of records contained in the file. Virtually, all files have machine-sensible labels at the end, or trailer labels, that contain control totals compared with current totals developed by the computer in the course of processing. When the computer writes a new file, it routinely counts the number of blocks used and writes the new trailer label accordingly. The computer also adds the date, generation, and iteration number in the header record to specify the version of the file created. The verification of file version is crucial to reliable processing.

Memory protection governs the allocation of computer memory and storage to application programs. If a user specifies execution of a given program, system software determines that there is enough capacity in the main memory to hold this program during execution. Most computer systems currently in use are capable of storing and processing data under multiple user programs on a concurrent basis. System software must also allocate and monitor the use of computer memory capabilities. Systems software first verifies that there is enough room for the program and prevents the loss of program content through overflow of available memory space. By building control tables to indicate memory allocation, system software provides assurance that data and instructions generated by user programs do not obliterate existing memory content.

System Utility Software

The use of system utility software varies greatly among organizations. The most commonly used utilities are copy and sort programs. Regardless of type, system utilities should be properly implemented to ensure:

- Utilities are properly controlled
- Control features within the utilities are properly used
- Utilities can be used to bypass control features of other systems or software packages

Program Library Systems

Library protection monitors a computer's files automatically to keep track of the application programs stored at any given moment. Further, when a user calls for the execution of an application program, system software requires that the user identifies the program, including the proper version of the program to be executed. System software then verifies a match between the user's identification and the program actually on file at that time.

Program library systems, when properly implemented and operated, add another level of control over an organization's application programs. Because software packages are vulnerable to misuse and inadvertent error, they should be implemented to ensure

- Adequate manual procedures support and enhance the reliability of the program library system
- Control features of the program library system are fully used and cannot be overridden or bypassed
- The program library system consistently and accurately controls application programs

File Management Systems

File management systems perform similar functions for security and backup of tape and disk files. These software packages help reduce manual library functions and, in many cases, eliminate the need for external file labels. The audit trail feature is usually standard and shows when and by whom a particular file was created and used.

File maintenance systems are similar to program library systems except that they help control automated data files instead of application programs. If implemented and operated properly, file maintenance systems increase the level of control. These tools should be implemented to ensure

- Adequate manual procedures support and enhance the reliability of the file maintenance system
- Control features of the file maintenance systems are fully used and cannot be overridden or bypassed
- The file maintenance system consistently and accurately controls automated data files

Security Software

Security software packages are one of the methods of automating access controls. They control the access to the computer system by identifying individuals who try to gain access to various system resources and verifying access legitimacy. Typically, these packages control terminals (e.g., hardwired or remote access); remote job entry stations; individual tape, disk, or mass storage datasets; individual application programs; and other systems software (e.g., operating systems and DBMSs). These packages usually provide an audit trail of all accesses, including authorized and unauthorized attempts.

For applications using online dial-up terminals, data communications software usually provides an interface among messages to and from terminals, the operating system, data files, and, if present, the DBMS. In addition, this system software typically

- Controls access to and from terminal devices
- Polls and receives messages from computer terminals or other computers
- Addresses messages and sends them back to terminals or other computers
- Edits input and output messages
- Handles errors
- Reroutes messages when a particular terminal or communications line is inoperative
- Performs online formatting on visual display terminals

Security software also provides an extra level of protection. To ensure that reliance on this software does not create a false sense of security, the security control features should be used and not bypassed or overridden.

Data Communications Systems

Data communications concern the transmission of digital messages to devices external to the message source. Data communication systems are a collection of "external" devices that are generally thought of as being independently powered circuitry that exists beyond the chassis of a computer or other digital message source. As a rule, the maximum permissible transmission rate of a message is directly proportional to signal power and inversely proportional to channel noise. It is the aim of any communications system to provide the highest possible transmission rate at the lowest possible power and with the least possible noise.

Information sent through a communications channel has a source from which the information originates, and a destination to which the information is delivered. Although information originates from a single source, there may be more than one destination across the communications system depending on how many receiver stations are linked to the channel and how much energy the transmitted signal possesses. In a digital communications channel, the information is represented by individual data bits, which may be encapsulated into multi-bit message units. A byte, which consists of eight bits, is an example of a message unit that may be conveyed through a digital communications channel. A collection of bytes may itself be grouped into a frame or other higher-level message unit. Such multiple levels of encapsulation facilitate the handling of messages in a complex data communications network or system.

Database Management System

When data throughout an organization has been combined into a single database to eliminate redundancy and improve access, a DBMS is used to update the database, retrieve data from it, and provide controls over its use. The DBMS enables several users to share data and allows many different application programs to access the single database. The DBMS provides the interface between the application program's logical view of the database and the computer system's physical storage of the database.

For applications in the database environment, a DBMS can control and maintain the organization's database. An effectively managed DBMS ensures

- Consistently maintained accurate and reliable data
- Security over different data elements restricts access to authorized users only
- Proper backup of the database structure and data elements

Controlling Access to Systems Software

To maintain separation of duties, management must keep the responsibility for controlling and maintaining systems software separate from the responsibility for applications; that is, a distinction should be made between systems and applications programmers.

The job of systems programmers is to ensure that the systems software continues to function accurately and reliably. Systems programmers usually have access to all systems software. This concentration of functions, however, causes a control problem because the systems programmer can control the entire operation of the organization's computers. As a result, activities of systems programmers must be controlled to reduce the programmers' ability to perform unauthorized or damaging acts that could impair the accuracy and reliability of the systems. A primary control is strong supervision. Adequate supervisory procedures should be established, although supervisors may lack the technical proficiency needed to ensure detailed scrutiny. In addition, security background investigations should be conducted periodically.

In a database environment, the database administrator usually has complete access to and control over the DBMS. This administrator is usually responsible for preserving the integrity of the database, maintaining data definitions, and preventing unauthorized use of or change to the database. Database administrators, such as systems programmers, should be carefully supervised and double checks with database users should be performed. For example, a database administrator may initiate DBMS changes that a systems programmer implements. The database administrator, however, should be the only person with complete access to the entire database and the only one who changes access levels for other database users.

Controlling Changes to System Software

Control procedures over changes to system software must be established and followed. Such controls help maintain software integrity and prevent unauthorized or inaccurate software changes. Although most changes are initiated as maintenance changes described by the software vendor, the organization should control system software changes by

- Establishing formal change procedures and forms that require supervisory authorization before implementation
- Ensuring that all changes are thoroughly tested
- Removing critical files and application programs from the computer area while the system programmer is making the change

Systems Maintenance

Systems maintenance can be defined simply as changes made to systems or applications software to maintain an effective, efficient, operational, and up-to-date system. These changes are generally requested by system users or provided by vendors or programmers. The changes are made to meet users' requirements or correct minor system errors before they become major problems. Maintenance can be applied to several areas within the IT facility, including

- Systems hardware
- Systems software
- Database software
- Applications software
- Environmental areas
- Network software
- Network hardware

This section of the chapter addresses maintenance for systems, applications, and network software. (Because systems and network software maintenance is generally performed by the systems programming group, no distinction is made between the two types of software in this chapter; both are classified as systems software.) The major difference between systems and applications software maintenance is that changes to systems software can affect an organization's entire data processing capability, whereas changes to application system or program within the facility have more limited effects.

As a result, systems software changes present a higher level of risk than applications software changes. Systems software is especially vulnerable because it supports and interacts with database systems. An erroneous change or faulty link to a database system or its supporting systems software can corrupt information throughout an organization. Therefore, maintenance changes affecting such systems should be closely reviewed.

The primary process involved in effective systems maintenance is the change of control process, or how IT personnel manage change. Adequate controls must be in place to minimize, detect, and correct accidental errors and omissions and malicious or fraudulent changes to software systems. The following sections describe change management within IT organizations and detail the steps needed to audit systems maintenance.

Database Technology

A database is a collection of data stored in an electronic format that can be used by many applications. A DBMS is the software that organizes the data for use by other applications. A few examples of useful databases include financial information databases, credit reporting systems, demographic databases, bibliographic databases, and industrial databases.

A DBMS helps to input, maintain, and extract information from a database. Using a DBMS can help an organization manage the complexity of information by providing central management of storage, access, utilization, and security. The central management reduces data redundancy and confusion by defining the information structure and components. Access, availability, and flexibility of information systems can be attained by using DBMSs. There are four basic types of database structures: hierarchical, network, relational, and object-oriented.

Hierarchical Data Model

The hierarchical data model employs the traditional method of database storage. It is composed of parent–child data relationships. A parent can have more than one child, but a child can only have one parent. Exhibit 21.2 provides an illustration of a hierarchical database structure.

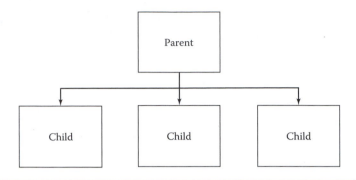

Exhibit 21.2   Hierarchical database structure.

The hierarchical data model processes data efficiently and is appropriate for stable applications with large volumes of data. It is not, however, flexible and the relationships must be defined in advance and cannot be easily changed.

Network Data Model

The network data model is similar to the hierarchical model with the added feature of multiple pointers to data. The pointers enable many-to-many relationships that can limit redundancy and speed up processing.

Relational Data Model

Relational databases are stored in tables and relate to one another based on key fields such as Social Security Number or Part Number. The relational data model is designed for flexibility and *ad-hoc* requests. It is easier to design and maintain a relational model; however, it has relatively slow processing efficiency, limiting its use in high-volume transaction applications. Relational database models have increased over the last 10 years and are the most common model used for databases (Exhibit 21.3).

Object-Oriented Model

Traditional database models are insufficient to handle drawings, images, photographs, video, and voice. An object-oriented database stores data and procedures as objects that can be retrieved, copied, and shared. Object-oriented models promise programmer efficiency by only having to define an object once. Once the object is defined, it can be used and modified by other programs.

Order Table				
Order Number	*Part Number*	*Quantity*	*Description*	*Total Price*
1234	G33S	2	Widget	20.00
1235	G38N	1	Whatsit	15.00

Exhibit 21.3   Relational database structure.

Changes to programs do not require the data objects to be redefined. Object-oriented programming is more common in Web application development and has been integrated into many existing program languages. Object-oriented technology has been slow to catch on and many users are not convinced that it will offer greater efficiency than a relational model. Relational vendors are beginning to offer object-oriented features in their products to offer both technologies to users.

Combining Technologies

Each of the database models offers a unique set of advantages and disadvantages. Users of information have invested heavily in their database structures, and the cost would be prohibitive to switch entire systems to every new technology that is developed. However, users want to be able to access more than just text. Many businesses use visual data such as, graphs, maps, blueprints, and pictures in the normal course of business. The current trend is to utilize all database models to store information and develop query software that can access all information. This approach helps organizations keep costs down by not having to rewrite legacy applications and converting databases, while still enabling the use of Web-based applications on the front end.

Distributed Databases

Databases can be separated and stored on computers at various locations connected by telecommunications lines. Distributed systems store data in several locations that can be accessed whenever needed.

There are three basic distributed database models:

1. *Simple distribution*: Using a PC to access information on a host (mainframe)
2. *Complex distribution*: Databases are located throughout the enterprise
3. *True distribution*: Copies of data are kept at different locations

Distributed databases are intended to enable decentralization of information systems. It enables disconnected access and improved local performance; however, this may be offset by the increase in the complexity of managing data, security, and the need to replicate information between locations.

Database Management Systems Recovery

Many organizations such as banks and airlines have online computer systems that must function at all times. With the Internet, online commerce worldwide has become a reality. In most online applications, there are many application programs that access databases concurrently. Therefore, the databases must be correct and up to date at all times.

Yet technology is imperfect and computer systems and their supporting communications infrastructures are subject to many types of failure. When a system fails, recovery procedures must be in place to restore, validate, and return the system to normal. Information is an essential tool used by all levels of management in planning and organizing, directing, and controlling an organization. Therefore, the security, availability, and integrity of information are of utmost importance.

Technological advances have significantly influenced the way an organization's information is collected, processed, and distributed. DBMSs have evolved from some of these technological advances and are of primary concern to IT managers who are responsible for securing an organization's data while facilitating the efficient dissemination of information. Although DBMSs can organize, process, and generate information designed to meet user needs, the integrity and security of this information are also essential to protect users.

Recovery Process

The DBMS recovery process is designed to restore database operations to their pre-failure status. Users and IT professionals play a critical role in restoring the DBMS to operation; that is, after the system has been successfully restored, the entire staff—IT and corporate—must participate to ensure the security, integrity, and validity of the information and its transaction properties.

Transaction Properties

The transaction is the fundamental activity of a DBMS and an area of concern for the reviewer. Transactions maintain consistency constraints or controls determined for an application. This consistency must be maintained at all times, even during a transaction failure. Concurrent processing must also be protected against adverse effects during a transaction failure.

A transaction is a command, message stream, or input display that explicitly or implicitly calls for a processing action (e.g., updating a file). Transaction processing is a sequential process that does not overlap or parallel a single application. It is started with a "Begin Transaction" and ended with an "End Transaction" identifier. The following typical transaction properties must be reviewed in assessing recovery controls:

Atomicity. During a transaction, either all or none of its operations are performed on the database; atomicity ensures the preclusion of partially completed transactions.

Permanence. If a transaction completes the "End Transaction" function, the results of its operation will never subsequently be lost.

Serialization of transactions. If more than one transaction is executed concurrently, the transactions affect the database as if they were executed in serial order. This ensures that concurrently executing jobs do not use inconsistent data from partially completed transactions.

Prevention of cascading aborts. An incomplete transaction cannot reveal results to other transactions, thereby limiting the effect of a transaction error throughout the entire system.

Consistency. A transaction that reaches its usual end commits its results to memory, thereby preserving the consistency of the database contents.

Transactions are more effective when written in enterprise resource planning systems (ERPS) such as SAP, PeopleSoft, Baan, and J. D. Edwards or in DBMS languages such as Sybase, Oracle, Access, Visual Basic, MAGIC, SQL, and ASP than in legacy software such as COBOL or BASIC. They are well suited to structured programming and can help make systems development a routine process by modularizing the actions being performed in code and simplifying the treatment of failures and concurrency. These transaction properties have specific control functions, which, from a review standpoint, should be organized and verified for DBMS operational validity and reliability.

Causes of Database Management Systems Failure

There are many causes of DBMS failure. When a DBMS fails, it falls into an incorrect state and will probably contain erroneous data. Typical causes of DBMS failures include errors in the application program, an error by the terminal user, an operator error, loss of data validity and consistency, a hardware error, media failures, a network transmission error, an error introduced by the environment, and errors caused by mischief or catastrophe.

Typically, the four major types of failure that result from a major hardware or software malfunction are transaction, system, communications, and media. A natural disaster, computer crime, or user, designer, developer, or operator error may cause these failures.

1. *Transaction failure.* Transaction failures occur when the transaction is not processed and the processing steps are rolled back to a specific point in the processing cycle. In a distributed database environment, a single logical database may be spread across several physical databases. Transaction failure can occur when some, but not all, physical databases are updated at the same time.
2. *System failure.* Bugs, errors, or anomalies in the database, operating system, or hardware can cause system failure. In each case, the transaction processing is terminated without control of the application. Data in the memory is lost; however, disk storage remains stable. The system must recover in the amount of time it takes to complete all interrupted transactions. At one transaction per second, the system should recover in a few seconds. System failures may occur as often as several times a week.
3. *Communications failure.* With transactional systems now linked globally, the importance of the successful transfer of information to the DBMS is critical in maintaining the concurrency, reliability, and relevance of financial information. A formidable example is a stock exchange and monitoring of business trading activity internationally. Transactional activities not recorded or "lost" could mean substantial losses to investors. The ability to recover is critical in this environment.
4. *Media failure.* Disk crashes or controller failures can occur because of disk-write bugs in the operating system release, hardware errors in the channel or controller, head crashes, or media degradation. These failures are rare but costly.

By identifying the type of DBMS failure, an organization can define the state of activity to return to after recovery. To design the database recovery procedures, the potential failures must be identified and the reliability of the hardware and software must be determined. The following is a summary of four such recovery actions:

1. *Transaction undo.* A transaction that aborts itself or must be aborted by the system during routine execution.
2. *Global redo.* When recovering from a system failure, the effects of all incomplete transactions must be rolled back. This means the ability of the system to contact all linked DBMSs to retransmit missing, incomplete, or lost information across communication networks.
3. *Partial undo.* While a system is recovering from failure, the results of completed transactions may not yet be reflected in the database because execution has been terminated in an uncontrolled manner. Therefore, they must be repeated, if necessary, by the recovery component.

4. *Global undo.* If the database is totally destroyed, a copy of the entire database must be reloaded from a backup source. A supplemental copy of the transaction is necessary to roll up the state of the database to the present. This means the ability of the system to contact all linked DBMSs (i.e., client/server) to retransmit missing, incomplete, or lost information across communication networks.

Database Users

The four primary classes of database users are database administrators, applications and systems programmers, Web designers and developers, and end users—and each has a unique view of the data. The DBMS must be flexible enough to present data appropriately to each class of user and maintain the proper controls to inhibit abuse of the system, especially during recovery, when controls may not be fully operational.

Database Administrator

The database administrator is responsible for ensuring that the database retains its integrity, and is accountable if the database becomes compromised, no matter what circumstances arise. This individual has the ultimate power over the schema that the organization has implemented. The database administrator must approve any modifications or additions to this schema. Permission to use subschemas (i.e., logical views) is given to end users and programmers only after their intentions are fully known and are consistent with organizational goals.

Because the database administrator has immediate and unrestricted access to almost every piece of valuable organizational information, an incompetent employee in this position can expose the organization to enormous risk, especially during DBMS recovery. Therefore, an organization should have controls in place to ensure the appointment of a qualified database administrator.

The database administrator must ensure that appropriate procedures are followed during DBMS recovery. The database administrator should also validate and verify the system once it has been recovered before allowing user access so that if controls are not functioning or if accessing problems continue, users will not be affected.

Applications and Systems Programmers

After recovery, programmers must access the database to manipulate and report on data according to some predetermined specification or access whether data loss has occurred. Each application should have a unique subschema to work with. After recovery, the database administrator validates the subschema organization to ensure that it is operating properly and allowing the application to receive only the data necessary to perform its tasks.

Systems programmers must be controlled in a slightly different manner than applications programmers. They must have the freedom to perform their tasks but be constrained from altering production programs or system utility programs in a fraudulent manner.

Web Designers and Developers

This new breed of database integrators uses the Internet as their work desk and the world as their product show place. They are involved in the design and development of applications to support communication and marketing of their company's products. The Internet has become the staging ground for electronic commerce. Products such as intranets and extranets are enhancing organization communication. Because of information's exposure to a worldwide audience, care in the quality, integrity, and validity as well as the professionalism of the information presented are critical.

End Users

End users are defined as all organizational members not included in the previous categories that need to interact with the database through DBMS utilities or application programs. Data elements of the database generally originate from end users. As mentioned earlier in a data-warehousing application, they are often the ones who recognize data inaccuracies, inconsistencies, and duplication.

Each data element should be assigned to an end user. The end user is then responsible for defining the element's access and security rules. Every other user who wishes to use this data element must confer with the responsible end user. If access is granted, the database administrator must implement any restrictions placed on the request through the DBMS.

For example, Website diagnostic tools are available that can detect and report errors and discrepancies such as broken links of an intranet or Internet Website, missing images, suspect pages, and suspect graphics or applets. Such software even allows the user to access the files containing errors and fix or correct problems with information.

Assigning ownership of specific data elements to end users discourages the corruption of data elements, thereby enhancing database integrity. Reviewers should ensure that this process exists and is appropriately reinstituted after the recovery process has been completed and the database administrator has provided operational approval.

After recovery, the database administrator should ensure that all forms of security practices and procedures are reinstated. These processes are a part of database security.

With data-warehousing applications, summary tables are the most powerful performance improvement technique. Summary tables are typically the most frequently used data assembled into tables. Recovery and rebuilding the summary tables is crucial. Data quality must be preserved by running the source data through cleansing tools continuously to ensure accuracy of the warehouse. Personnel responsible for entry and maintenance should be provided with incentives to ensure quality.

Capacity Management

Capacity management includes the processes to cost-effectively match IT resources to organization demand. The high-level ITIL activities include

- Application sizing
- Workload management
- Demand management
- Modeling
- Capacity planning
- Resource management
- Performance management

Capacity management should begin during the development process to ensure that applications are programmed to run efficiently on the operating platform. Once an application is deployed, it is more difficult and costly to make changes that improve performance. The total cost of an application includes the cost of the operating environment that it runs on and should not be ignored during project justification and maintenance. This includes the cost of hardware and systems software licenses that may be based on the quantity of computing cycles used (e.g., processor size/units). The capacity management team should be involved from the beginning of the development process to consult on the processing needs of applications and optimizing code to minimize resource consumption.

Managing capacity is a balancing act of having sufficient capacity to meet demand while at the same time minimizing unused capacity to keep costs down. The capacity planning team needs to work with user management and the application development and maintenance teams to forecast demand for the various platforms. This information is critical in the procurement process as well as purchasing in volume will be more cost effective than buying incremental processing capacity as needed.

Capacity management resources include processors, storage, bandwidth, and so on and prioritized based on service level agreements. Applications may be prioritized based on business needs. For example, customer-facing applications may have a higher priority than back-office applications. The processing speed of Web-based, customer applications may be much higher than back-office applications. Prioritizing applications is helpful when decisions need to be made when allocating resources.

Server Virtualization

Server virtualization is made possible by the masking of server resources, including the number and identity of individual physical servers, processors, and operating systems, from server users. The server administrator uses a software application to divide one physical server into multiple isolated virtual environments. The virtual environments are sometimes called virtual private servers, but they are also known as guests, instances, containers or emulations. From the standpoint of the IT Auditor, this is an area for concern as there are various ways of creating the virtual environment. In this process, the organization must ensure that the method selected for virtualization is controlled, monitored and documented as there are three popular approaches to server virtualization: the virtual machine model, the paravirtual machine (PVM) model, and virtualization at the operating system (OS) layer.

Virtual machines are based on the host/guest paradigm. Each guest runs on a virtual imitation of the hardware layer. This approach allows the guest operating system to run without modifications. It also allows the administrator to create guests that use different operating systems. The guest has no knowledge of the host's operating system because it is not aware that it is not running on real hardware. It does, however, require real computing resources from the host—so it uses a hypervisor to coordinate instructions to the CPU.

The PVM model is also based on the host/guest paradigm—and it uses a virtual machine monitor too. In the PVM model, however, The VMM actually modifies the guest operating system's code. This modification is called porting. Porting supports the VMM so it can utilize privileged systems calls sparingly. Like virtual machines, PVMs are capable of running multiple operating systems. Xen and UML both use the PVM model.

Virtualization at the OS level works a little differently. It is not based on the host/guest paradigm. In the OS level model, the host runs a single OS kernel as its core and exports operating system functionality to each of the guests. Guests must use the same operating system as the host, although different distributions of the same system are allowed. This distributed architecture eliminates system calls between layers, which reduces CPU usage overhead. It also requires that each partition remain strictly isolated from its neighbors so that a failure or security breach in one partition is not able to affect any of the other partitions. In this model, common binaries and libraries on the same physical machine can be shared, allowing an OS level virtual server to host thousands of guests at the same time. Virtuozzo and Solaris Zones both use OS-level virtualization.

The decision to select server virtualization can be viewed as part of an overall virtualization trend in enterprise IT that includes storage virtualization, network virtualization, and workload management. A decision like this must be supported within the organization and an understanding of controls need in place to ensure configuration management and support. This trend is one component in the development of autonomic computing, in which the server environment will be able to manage itself based on perceived activity. If properly implemented, managed and monitored, server virtualization can be used to eliminate server sprawl, to make more efficient use of server resources, to improve server availability, to assist in disaster recovery, testing and development, and to centralize server administration.

Conclusion

Systems software forms the basis for hardware to communicate with applications. As such, systems software is an important resource that must be effectively managed and controlled. Systems software includes any program or system that helps interconnect or control the elements of input, output, processing, data, and application programs. Organizations rely on systems software in varying degrees to control information-processing functions. To maintain separation of duties, different IT professionals should be responsible for managing systems and applications.

The auditor should first identify the types and uses of systems software that affect the system under review and then determine the organization's level of reliance on that software. Through a comprehensive review of this area, the IT auditor can evaluate the organization's change management process to determine whether software fixes and changes compromise the system's integrity.

Databases are an integral component of business processes and IT solutions. Business worldwide is highly dependent on information collection and dissemination, recording of the business transaction, and reporting of the profitability. Protecting and maintaining databases is the responsibility of business and IT professionals. The ability to recover from database failures is a critical component in maintaining the integrity of an organization's information.

Review Questions

1. Define systems maintenance; what does it involve and encompass?
2. What are the types of system changes an IT auditor should be aware of? Diagram the processes of those three types of changes. What are the control points?
3. What is an operating system? Why are audits of this area viewed as complex?
4. What is the reliance placed in system software working? And when operating systems do not work properly, what are the consequences in business terms?

5. Why is security software necessary in operating systems?
6. Define the term DBMS recovery.
7. What is a DBMS transaction?

Multiple-Choice Questions

1. Which of the following is not true about systems maintenance?
   a. Maintenance is noticed when it is done right.
   b. Maintenance carries one of the highest risks of exposure.
   c. The maintenance group is responsible for making changes requested by the user.
   d. All systems require some maintenance.
2. The primary focus of a systems maintenance audit is
   a. Systems software
   b. Network software
   c. Network hardware
   d. How IT personnel manage change
3. Which of the following information would an auditor not look for on a standard change request form?
   a. Date of request
   b. Description of the change
   c. Approvals of the request
   d. Auditor initiation of the request
4. Which of the following is not a system software category?
   a. Operating systems
   b. Documentation systems
   c. Data communication systems
   d. File maintenance systems
5. Most organizations rely on the operating system to
   a. Maximize the difference between a given manufacturer's line of computers, thus facilitating the transfer of application programs
   b. Prevent programmers and operators from controlling the operation and allocation of peripheral devices and other computer resources
   c. Manage computer resources with minimum operator intervention
   d. Limit copy and sort programs
6. An auditor should determine whether file maintenance systems perform all of the following except
   a. Whether the file maintenance system consistently and accurately controls automated data files
   b. Whether the program library system consistently and accurately controls application programs
   c. Whether control features of the file maintenance systems are fully used and cannot be overridden or bypassed
   d. Whether manual procedures support and enhance the reliability of the file maintenance systems
7. The first step in the DBMS recovery process is
   a. Taking corrective action

   b. Determining the source and extent of the damage
   c. Suspending normal processing
   d. Identifying that the database is an erroneous, damaged, or in a crashed state
8. Database users include
   a. Database administrators
   b. Applications programs
   c. End users
   d. All of the above
9. The database administrator is responsible for
   a. Defining the information and system requirements
   b. Ensuring that the database retains its integrity
   c. Developing a prototype of the proposed system
   d. None of the above
10. To design the database recovery procedures, the database administrator must identify
   a. Required modifications to the base software
   b. Potential failures
   c. Infrastructure diagrams
   d. None of the above

Exercises

1. List five professional organizations that have provided studies or research on DBMS recovery or data-warehousing control concerns.
2. Read Appendix I, Case 7: Amazon Industries. Answer the questions.
3. Add on to Case 7, above, the following: The system programmer has disappeared, he leaves no forwarding address, and his phone is disconnected. You are asked to perform an audit of the operating system. How would you approach it?

Answers to Multiple-Choice Questions

1—a; 2—d; 3—d; 4—b; 5—c; 6—b; 7—b; 8—d; 9—b; 10—b

Further Reading

1. Ford, W. and M.S. Baum, *Secure Electronic Commerce: Building the Infrastructure for Digital Signatures and Encryption, 2/E*, 2nd Edition, Prentice Hall PTR, Upper Saddle River, NJ, 2001.
2. Gallegos, F., *Auditing Global Information Infrastructure and National Information Infrastructure*, EDP Auditing Series, #75-10-55, Auerbach Publishers, Boca Raton, FL, January 2000, pp. 1–16.
3. Gallegos, F., *Reviewing Focus Database Applications*, EDP Auditing Series, #74-10-23, Auerbach Publishers, Boca Raton, FL, January 2001, pp. 1–24.
4. Gallegos, F. and A. Carlin, *Auditing Systems Maintenance—A How to Approach*, EDP Auditing Series, #74-30-25, Auerbach Publishers, Boca Raton, FL, October 2000, pp. 1–12.
5. Gallegos, F. and A. Carlin, *Key Review Points for Auditing Systems Development*, EDP Auditing Series, #74-30-37, Auerbach Publishers, Boca Raton, FL, October 2000, pp. 1–24.

6. Gallegos, F. and D. Manson, *Auditing DBMS Recovery Procedures*, #75-20-45, Auerbach Publishers, Boca Raton, FL, September 2002, pp. 1–20.
7. Gallegos, F. and J. Yin, *Auditing in a Client Server Environment*, EDP Auditing Series, #74-10-25, Auerbach Publishers, Boca Raton, FL, August 2000, pp. 1–20.
8. Gallegos, F. and J. Yin, *Auditing Oracle*, EDP Auditing Series, #74-15-37, Auerbach Publishers, Boca Raton, FL, August 2000, pp. 1–12.
9. Hoesing, M. and V. Raval, Auditing Linux, Information Systems Audit and Control Association, *Inform. Syst. Control J.*, 4, 2005.

Chapter 22

Operations Management

Within an IT installation, operational controls are in place to implement organizational policy and organization controls. Operations controls focus on protecting data files and programs as well as assuring the security of the computer installation itself. Computer installation controls can be classified as physical security and access controls, environmental controls, software and data security controls, and administrative security controls. Data communications are an integral part of today's organizations, yet many auditors are not trained sufficiently in analyzing and assessing data communications controls. This chapter presents an overview of operational processes and provides guidelines for reviewing key control areas.

End-user access to systems is another key area requiring mature operational processes. The knowledge worker's application of technology to help business solve problems has been one of the major forces of change in business today. User dominance will prevail. Auditors, as knowledge workers and users, can assist departments in identifying sensitive or critical personal computer (PC) applications that require special attention. In organizations where controls are inadequate or nonexistent, auditors can play a key role in developing these controls for End-user computing (EUC) groups. Once controls are in place, auditors can review them for adequacy and effectiveness. Auditing an EUC group can encompass the entire spectrum of information systems (IS) reviews from systems development to disaster recovery. This section covers steps performed in auditing EUC groups.

IT Processes

The Control Objectives for Information and Related Technology (COBIT) processes (DS12 and DS13) in the Delivery and Support Domain discuss how operations and physical environment controls support an effective IT organization. Exhibit 22.1 lists the key control objectives for this section.

DS12 Manage the Physical Environment
Control Objectives
12.1 Site selection and layout
12.2 Physical security measures
12.3 Physical access
12.4 Protection against environmental factors
12.5 Physical facilities management
DS13 Manage Operations
Control Objectives
13.1 Operations procedures and instructions
13.2 Job scheduling
13.3 IT infrastructure monitoring
13.4 Sensitive documents and output devices
13.5 Preventive maintenance for hardware

Exhibit 22.1 Processes for the delivery and support.

Operational Maturity

Much attention has been focused on software quality assurance and the maturity of the systems development life cycle. Just as important is the maturity of the underlying infrastructure and the day-to-day management of operations. The Information Technology Infrastructure Library (ITIL) provides a process structure for the operation and maintenance of existing systems that can be used as a standard for determining and developing mature operational processes. An effective operations group is critical as it is responsible for executing many of the processes discussed in earlier chapters (e.g., asset management, security administration, business continuity). The IT Governance Institute, the U.K.'s Office of Government Commerce, and the IT Service Management Forum developed a summary of best practices and guidance on implementation in a publication *Aligning COBIT, ITL, and ISO 17799 for Business Benefit.*

Operating Policy and Procedures

Every computer installation should have specific standards and procedure manuals covering operations. Although most operations have some type of standards and manuals covering them, having policies and procedures in place is much easier than actively enforcing policies and procedures. The weakness with many operations policy and procedures manuals is their lack of use.

In other cases, problems arise because procedure manuals have been prepared on the basis of the capabilities of highly experienced, competent operators. These people may feel they do not have to refer to the documentation. Often, they regard their specialized knowledge as a kind of job security. Having these people available can become a rationale for not supplying more detail.

However, apart from the inherently poor practice that this attitude represents, situations may arise when these operators are not available for consultation. New hires may have to be trained during peak operational periods. For example, systems may have to be restarted by less-experienced personnel in the event of a major disaster that injures or incapacitates key operations personnel. In this situation, systems analysts who are unfamiliar with the systems may need to use the manuals to gain an overview. Manuals generally fall short of guiding people in such situations.

Managers should regard operating standards and procedures manuals as highly important controls. Accordingly, these controls should be tested periodically. This can be done through observing execution to determine if the standards and procedures described in the manuals actually are being followed in the day-to-day operation of the computer center.

An important element of any set of standards or manuals should be the requirement that operators maintain logs on which any unusual events or failures are recorded, according to time and in detail. These logs can be used to identify unfavorable trends, detect unauthorized access, and provide a data source for determining the root cause of system failures.

Data Files and Program Controls

Each computer installation should have a data library and procedures that control access to programs, data files, and documentation. An important data library control centers on assurance that all file media are clearly and accurately labeled. That is, external labels should be affixed to or marked upon the data media themselves. On tape cartridges and disk packs, pressure-sensitive labels usually are affixed to identify both the volume and the file content. Procedures should be in place to assure that all labels are current and that all information they contain is accurate.

Library procedures should assure that only authorized persons receive files, programs, or documents, and that these persons acknowledge their responsibility at the time of each issuance. Each time a file is removed for processing, controls over data files should assure that a new file would be generated and returned to the library. If appropriate to the backup system in place, both the issued and the new files should be returned together, with the prior version serving as backup.

Control is enhanced by the practice of maintaining an inventory of file media within the data library. That is, an inventory record should exist for each tape cartridge or disk pack. The record should note any utilization or activity. After a given number of users, the file medium or device is cleaned and recertified. Further, if any troubles are encountered in reading or writing to the device, maintenance steps are taken and noted.

Ideally, a full-time person independent of computer operations will be assigned as the data librarian. In smaller installations, however, such assignment might not be economically feasible. When an installation cannot afford a full-time librarian, this custodial duty should be segregated from operations. That is, for adequacy of control, the function of a librarian should be assigned as a specific responsibility to someone who does not have access to the system.

Physical Security and Access Controls

The objective of physical security and access controls is to prevent or deter theft, damage, and unauthorized access, and control movement of servers, network-related equipment, and attached devices. Some physical controls also prevent unauthorized access to data and software.

General physical controls that can be used to protect office equipment and networks include personnel badges, which help employees identify authorized personnel, and alarms and guards, which deter theft of network equipment. In addition, placement of the network equipment and office design will further secure the network. For example, network equipment should be placed in areas where the office traffic is light. If possible, the servers, printers, and other equipment should be placed behind locked office doors. Data center operations managers may want to use combination locks to prevent the duplication of keys; another alternative is to use a locking device that operates on magnetic strips or plastic cards—a convenient device when employees regularly carry picture identification (ID) badges.

Network equipment should be attached to heavy immovable office equipment, permanent office fixtures, special enclosures, or special microcomputer workstations. The attachment can be achieved with lockdown devices, which consist of a base attached to permanent fixtures and a second interlocking base attached to the microcomputer equipment. The bases lock together, and a key, combination, or extreme force is required to remove the equipment. All network equipment should be locked down to prevent unauthorized movement, installation, or attachment.

Many microcomputers and other equipment attached to the network may contain expensive hardware and security-sensitive devices. The removal of these devices not only incurs replacement costs but also could cause software to fail and may be a means of circumventing security or allowing for unauthorized disclosure of company-sensitive information such as customer lists, trade secrets, payroll data, or proprietary software. Internal equipment can be protected by lockdown devices, as previously discussed, and special locks that replace one or more screws and secure the top of the equipment. These special locks are called central processing unit (CPU) locks because they prevent access to the CPU area.

Cabling enables the various users and peripheral equipment to communicate. Cabling is also a source of exposure to accidental or intentional damage or loss. Damage and loss can occur from the weather or by cutting, detaching, or attaching to and from equipment and other incidents. In many networks, if the cable is severed or damaged, the entire system will be impaired.

Cabling should not be accessible to either the environment or individuals. The communications manager may want to route and enclose cabling in an electrical conduit. If possible and if the exposure warrants the cost, cabling can also be encased in concrete tubing. When the cable is encased, unauthorized access through attachment is lessened. In addition, unauthorized movement of the cabling will not occur easily, and this situation will enable the network manager to more efficiently monitor and control the network and access to it.

To alleviate potential downtime, cable may be laid in pairs. In this arrangement, if one set is damaged, the alternate set can be readily attached. The second pair is usually protected in the same manner as the original but is not encased in the same tubing, thus preventing the same type of accident from damaging both cables.

Notebook microcomputers should also receive the same care and attention as cited earlier. These are even more vulnerable in that they can be taken and used off-site by employees and then brought back into the office and attached to the network. Off-site vulnerability to theft and sabotage such as viruses or theft of programs and data is reduced when protected in a secure off-site storage location.

Environmental Controls

All network equipment operates under daily office conditions (e.g., humidity, temperature, and electrical flow). However, a specific office environment may not be suited to a microcomputer because of geographical location, industrial facilities, or employee habits. A primary problem is the sensitivity of microcomputer equipment to dust, water, food, and other contaminants. Water and other substances can not only damage the keyboard, CPU, disk drive, and diskettes but also may cause electrocution or a fire. To prevent such occurrences, the operations manager should adhere to a policy of prohibiting food, liquids, and the like at or near the servers and network equipment.

Although most offices are air-conditioned and temperatures and humidity are usually controlled, these conditions must nonetheless be evaluated by the operations manager. If for any reason the environment is not controlled, the operations manager should take periodic readings of the temperature and humidity. If the temperature or humidity is excessively high or low, the server equipment and the network should be shut down to prevent loss of equipment, software, and data. When server or network equipment is transported, either within the building or especially outdoors to a new location, the equipment should be left idle at its new location for a short time to allow it to adjust to the new environmental conditions.

Airborne contaminants can enter the equipment and damage the circuitry. Hard disks are susceptible to damage by dust, pollen, air sprays, and gas fumes. Excessive dust between the read/write head and the disk platter can damage the platter or head or cause damage to the data or programs. If there is excessive smoke or dust, the servers should be moved to another location. Static electricity is another air contaminant. Using antistatic carpeting can reduce static electricity as well as pads placed around the server area, antistatic chair and keyboard pads, and special sprays that can be applied to the bottoms of shoes. Machines can also be used to control static electricity in an entire room or building.

Major causes of damage to servers or network equipment are power surges, blackouts, and brownouts. Power surges, or spikes, are sudden fluctuations in voltage or frequency in the electrical supply that originates in the public utility. They are more frequent when the data center is located near an electrical generating plant or power substation. The sudden surge or drop in power supply can damage the electronic boards and chips as well as cause a loss of data or software. If power supply problems occur frequently, special electrical cords and devices can be attached to prevent damage. These devices are commonly referred to as power surge protectors.

Blackouts are caused by a total loss of electrical power and can last seconds, hours, or days. Brownouts occur when the electrical supply is diminished to below-normal levels for several hours or days. Although brownouts and blackouts occur infrequently, they are disruptive to continuing operations. If servers are essential and the organization's normal backup power is limited to necessary functions, special uninterruptible power supply (UPS) equipment can be purchased specifically for the server or network equipment. UPS equipment can be either battery packs or gas-powered generators. Battery packs are typically used for short-term tasks only (e.g., completing a job in progress or supporting operations during a transition to generator power). Gas-powered generators provide long-term power, and conceivably, could be used indefinitely.

To prevent loss of or damage to equipment, services, or facilities, safeguards to power supply and physical access to machine rooms and other critical areas have to be restricted to authorized personnel. Specialized equipment has to be installed to

- Restrict access to authorized personnel using badges and password controls
- Avoid transient surges and outages in power supplies
- Provide alternative sources of power in the event of extended power failures

To reduce the risk of services being disrupted by loss of power or deterioration of ambient conditions, critical computer equipment and facilities have to be protected from transient surges and outages in power supplies and extended power failure by

- Installing devices that stabilize power supplies
- Providing backup generators
- Protecting power cables

To reduce the risk of services being disrupted, equipment and facilities have to be protected against loss or damage. Access to the information-processing environment has to be restricted to authorized personnel. Easily portable equipment and data storage devices (tapes, diskettes) have to be physically secured. Security perimeters (something that builds a barrier, for example, a wall and a card-controlled entry gate) have to be used to protect areas that contain information-processing facilities. The following guidelines and controls have to be considered:

- The security perimeter has to be clearly defined and physically sound.
- The perimeter may not be compromised by positioning ancillary office equipment (e.g., photocopiers, fax machines, etc.) within the perimeter.
- Physical barriers extending from floor to ceiling have to be incorporated.
- Within the perimeter, IT facilities that are managed by third parties have to be housed in separate areas to those that are under the business unit's direct control.
- A secure area has to be physically locked when vacated.
- A secure area has to be periodically checked for intruders or other hazards.
- Authorization has to be obtained before maintenance personnel or suppliers are allowed access to secure areas.
- Maintenance personnel or suppliers have to be allowed only restricted access to secure areas; access has to be monitored.
- Between areas with different security requirements within the perimeter, additional barriers have to be incorporated.

An isolated holding area should be used for deliveries to and loading from computer rooms supporting critical business activities. All computer and network equipment should be physically secured with antitheft devices if located in an open office environment. Servers and network equipment should be placed in locked cabinets, locked closets, or locked computer rooms.

Output Controls

In today's automated environment, most output is posted online or printed and processed by machines. It is important to have completeness and accuracy controls from the time the output is processed until it is posted online or delivered. In addition, security, confidentiality, and privacy need to be maintained from the time the output is created until delivered to the appropriate party. Whether output of information processing is displayed on an online or paper form, traditional output controls are needed to ensure the accuracy and completeness of the information. Output controls include balancing and completeness checks to confirm the number of pages processed are created for online or paper printing. This can be accomplished by creating a page total before and after posting or printing the output for comparison. Accuracy can be confirmed by selecting key data fields for comparison before and after output processing. The output controls should also be able to detect where information is missing. It would be difficult to determine the problem from just page count when thousands of pages are printed and there is no way to determine where the failure occurred. In addition, a process needs to be in place to recreate all or a subset of documents where output errors are discovered. Additional controls are needed for sensitive information or checks as the original documents may need to be destroyed and this needs to be carefully controlled to verify the destruction of the sensitive data or checks.

Data Communications Controls

Several data communications controls for protecting and recovering data have been developed and applied successfully. These controls, which are primarily transmission oriented, depend on human interaction and regular reviews to ensure that they are functionally sound. In addition, data entry, computer processing, data storage, and output controls all play interdependent roles in the protection and recovery of information. If one of these controls is not functioning properly or an unauthorized intervention overrides complementary control processes, the data communications system becomes vulnerable.

These controls can be oriented toward prevention, detection, or correction of errors and abuse. Preventive controls ensure that events proceed as intended. Detective controls signal an alert or terminate a function and stop further processing when the system is violated or an error occurs. Corrective controls may perform an alert or terminate a function, but they also restore or repair part of the system to its proper state.

Errors in data communications usually occur because of the distances involved, speeds of transmission, or equipment malfunctions. To address these data communications controls, managers should ask the following key questions:

1. Is a unique hardwired ID code, requiring no human intervention for its use, incorporated into each workstation device (PC, laptop, personal digital assistant [PDA], etc.)?
2. Is this ID code checked and validated by the computer to ensure that no unauthorized workstations are used?
3. Does the communications system avoid the general switchboard to reduce the data transmission error rate and the chance of wiretapping?
4. Are there appropriate controls for voice grade lines to reduce data transmission errors and maintain the integrity of data transmitted?
5. Are data communications lines conditioned for improved accuracy and physical security?
6. Does the system have an automatic store-and-forward capability to maintain control over messages queued for an inoperative or a busy communications device?
7. If leased lines fail, is there an automatic switch over to backup lines?
8. Is a message intercept function used to receive messages directed to inoperable or unauthorized workstations?
9. Does the system use parity checks to detect errors in data transmission?
10. Are validity checks used to compare character signals transmitted with the set of valid characters?
11. Does the system use echo checking to verify each character so that erroneous data is detected?
12. Are forward errors correcting techniques and sophisticated redundancy codes used for detecting and reporting data communications errors?

13. Are techniques available for detecting erroneous retransmissions of data?
14. Are modems equipped with loop back switches for fault isolation?
15. Is there validity checking of hardwired terminal ID codes and transmitted data characters?
16. Are there specially conditioned transmission lines to reduce noise, fading, and amplitude and frequency distortion?
17. Is parity checking done of both individual characters and blocks of characters?
18. Is echo checking done, comparing characters entered with characters received?
19. Are we using wireless technology within our infrastructure? If so, did we implement security to keep our traffic from being intercepted and analyzed?

Other hardware controls that can be incorporated into the data communications system include encryption of sensitive data to reduce the effectiveness of wiretapping and automatic storing of data at intermediary points when lines or other devices are inoperative. These controls are designed to ensure that only valid data is entered, transmitted, and received and that no data is lost, accessed, or tampered with during entry or transmission.

Data Center Reviews

Data center and computer operations reviews are performed to evaluate the administrative controls over data center resources and data processing personnel (computer operations, systems analysis, and programming personnel). The scope of the review could include an evaluation of the planning, staffing, policies/procedures, assignment of responsibilities, budgets, management reports, records, and performance measures in the following major areas of accountability: hardware management, software management, resource protection and recovery, access controls, operations management, and network/communications management. A data center/computer operations audit may focus on any one of these accountabilities, or may include all of them depending on the size of the data center, operations staff, and time budget. For example, for a large data center with multiple computers and an extensive number of users, the data center review may focus only on access controls and security administration. For a small data center, the audit might include all of the accountabilities.

The objectives of data center audits are to identify audit risks in the operating environment and the controls in place and functioning to reasonably mitigate those audit risks in accordance with the intentions of the company's management. For each control objective, the auditor must evaluate control mechanisms and determine whether the objective has been achieved. Pre-audit preparation is required for effective data center reviews. These include meeting with IS management to determine possible areas of concern. At this meeting, the following information should be obtained:

- Current IT organization chart
- Current job descriptions for IT data center employees
- List of application software supported and the hardware they reside
- IT policy and procedures manual
- Systems planning documentation and fiscal budget
- Disaster recovery plan

Audit personnel should review the preceding information and become familiar with the way the data center provides user services. In addition, auditors should become familiar with basic terminology and resource definition methodology used in support of the operations environment. Engagement personnel should review the audit program and become familiar with the areas assigned for the completion of an audit task. The following is an example of typical audit program steps performed during a data center review.

Software and Data Security Controls

Data and software security and access controls are the key controls over today's network-oriented business systems. These are considered operational controls in the sense that these controls function day in and day out to meet the needs of business. The administration of the network is similar to the administration and management of any information processing facility. In the information processing manager's scenario, the main objective is to prevent, detect, and correct unauthorized access to the network's hardware, software, and data, and ensure the network's sound operation and the security of the corporate intellectual property and information.

Daily management of such an operation is required due to the reliance on the information provided that supports decision making and operations. Daily management ensures that security controls are maintained, although changes occur in the software, applications, and personnel. Daily management can be classified into various categories, which are discussed in the following sections and areas for IT auditor review and evaluation.

Physical and Environmental Controls Management

All such controls in active use must be tested periodically. Such testing includes the evaluation of the effectiveness of current controls and the implementation of additional controls as determined to be necessary. The results of the testing of physical and environmental controls should be reported to the senior management.

Data Access Management

The data center operations manager, the network administrator, or the corporate IT security manager, whoever assigned this responsibility, must perform it in a very responsible manner. This person must accurately maintain user IDs and passwords and associated file and data access schemes, as well as receive computer-generated reports of attempted unauthorized accesses. Reports on data access and traffic analysis should be reviewed. Such reports will allow the administrator to manage network growth and help foresee future security needs.

Policy and Procedures Documentation

The objectives here are to provide standards for preparing documentation and ensuring the maintenance of documentation. The IT operations manager must set documentation standards so that when employees change jobs, become ill, or leave the organization, replacement personnel can adequately perform the task of that employee. The IT operations manager must periodically test the documentation for clarity, completeness, appropriateness, and accuracy.

Data and Software Backup Management

Backup media must be labeled, controlled, and stored in an appropriate manner. The IT manager must maintain control logs of all backups as well as provide documentation on how to recover files, data, directories, and disks.

Other Management Controls

The internal audit department, external auditors, contingency or disaster recovery planning, personnel background checks, and user training are included in this category. The IT auditor can aid in establishing proper testing requirements and in reviewing, testing, and recommending the proper controls to establish the necessary safeguards. Contingency planning and disaster recovery are essential for the proper maintenance of the network and supporting systems. The contingency plan establishes the steps to recover from the destruction of hardware, software, and data.

Operational controls include items such as periodic personnel background checks on all employees who have access to key organizational information directly or through support functions. The background check should involve a review of credit history, financial health, personal problems, and other areas that may identify potential risks. This information can establish potential integrity breaches before they occur.

User training should be established for all network functions. End users should be trained in microcomputer/workstation use, general computer knowledge, security, policies and procedures, consequences of noncompliance, and general network use. In addition, users should undergo more specific training for the different software on the network as required. Such user training can prevent many problems from occurring.

End-User Computing

End-user computing (EUC) groups are growing rapidly in pervasiveness and importance. The knowledge worker's application of technology to help business solve problems has been one of the major forces of change in business today. User dominance will prevail. Auditors, as knowledge workers and users, can assist departments in identifying sensitive or critical PC applications that require special attention. In organizations where controls are inadequate or nonexistent, auditors can play a key role in developing these controls for EUC groups. Once controls are in place, auditors can review them for adequacy and effectiveness. Auditing an EUC group can encompass the entire spectrum of IS reviews from systems development to disaster recovery. This section covers steps performed in auditing EUC groups.

Auditing End-User Computing

Once it is determined that an audit of an EUC group is required, the IT auditor needs management's agreement as to the audit objectives, audit method, and audit scope. The audit objectives may cover specific applications, end-user support, financial issues, or provide for strategic information to be reported to the management. Depending on the control environment and audit objectives, the audit method will be either formal or informal. Defining the EUC group for a particular environment will determine the audit scope of the audit.

Preliminary Audit Planning

PC applications have grown from individuals creating personal productivity tools into critical applications that are used by the entire organization. The management may not fully realize the importance of EUC groups to the organization to dedicate the necessary resources for a complete and thorough applications audit. However, it is essential to have the management's support to overcome any obstacles put forth by the EUC groups. End users tend to think of their PCs as personal property, and they may be resentful of an intrusion by auditors. However, the end user's cooperation can be gained, in part, by explaining the criteria that the audit will measure. In addition, management support can be gained by providing them with a risk analysis that identifies the exposures of EUC.

Defining the Audit Methodology

The method used to conduct the audit depends on the environment being reviewed and the agreed-upon audit objectives. An inventory of end-user applications can be used to gain a general understanding of the EUC group. The auditor should discuss this inventory with management to determine what type of audit should be performed. For example, a more formal audit can be used if a specific application is being evaluated for reliance on financial information, whereas a statistical audit that collects sample data from transactions or supporting logs can confirm end-user practices. Auditors could also perform a quick, informal assessment by interviewing the IT staff about their impressions of the EUC group.

Defining the Scope and Content of the Audit

The scope limits the coverage of the audit to a particular department, function, or application. The content defines what aspects of a particular area are covered. Depending on the audit objective, the content covers general controls, application controls, hardware and software acquisition, systems development controls, change controls problem management, or disaster recovery.

Audit Plan

The audit plan details the objectives and the steps to fulfill those objectives. Like any audit, an audit of an EUC group begins with a preliminary survey or analysis of the control environment by reviewing existing policies and procedures. During the audit, these policies and procedures should be assessed for completeness and operational efficiency. The preliminary survey or analysis should identify the organization's position and strategy for the EUC group and the responsibilities for managing and controlling it. The following are the kinds of steps performed to gather the necessary evidence on which to base audit findings, conclusions, and recommendations.

Evidence gathering. A review of any documentation that the end-users group uses

Inquiry. Conducting interviews with end users and any IT support technicians

Observation. A walk-through to become familiar with department procedures and assess physical controls

Inventory. A physical examination of any inventoried goods or products on hand in the EUC group

Confirmation. A review of the end users' satisfaction surveys that were handed out and completed during the preliminary audit planning stages

Analytical procedures. A review of data gathered from statistical or financial information contained in spreadsheets or other data files

Mechanical accuracy. A review of the information contained in any databases used by the EUC group through testing procedures

After the evidence is gathered, the auditor should assess control strengths and weaknesses, considering the interrelationships between compensating and overlapping controls. These controls should be tested for compliance and to ensure that they are applied in accordance with management's policies and procedures. For example, management policy states that end users should change their passwords periodically to protect information resources. To test for compliance, the auditor identifies the controls that force password changes. Substantive tests determine the adequacy of these controls to prevent fraudulent activity. For example, software piracy puts the company at risk for fines and the potential loss of goodwill. Reviewing the directories on the LAN and PC drives for unlicensed software would assess the effectiveness of controls to ensure that only property-licensed software is installed.

Reviewing End-User Computing Group's Procedures and Objectives

IT should have policies or guidelines that cover EUC. These should be designed to protect company data. IT should also have standards to ensure that end users are not using hardware or software that is not supported by them. There should be an EUC policy that encompasses and is applicable to all EUC groups. If only departmental policies exist, each policy should be similar to ensure continuity between departmental policies. A companywide policy should cover:

- Assignment of ownership of data
- User accountability
- Backup procedures
- Physical access controls to PCs
- Appropriate documentation of all EUC groups' applications and adequate documentation changes and modifications
- Segregation of duties

Evaluating End-User Computing Group's Effectiveness by Reviewing Their Documentation

Because many end users are developing their own applications, often there is little or no documentation apart from the end user's own notes. Another audit concern is that several end users may be developing the same type of application independently of each other, which is an inefficient use of computer resources. For example, if an end user in accounting is developing an application that is already in use in payroll, there should be some type of documentation or reference for end users to consult to prevent duplication of effort.

Another problem posed by inadequate documentation is illustrated by this example. An end user has developed several applications that have become crucial to the operation of the company. This individual has left the company without leaving any documentation on those applications, and other end users must use this application and make modifications to it. This potential exists for multiple problems because of the lack of end-user documentation.

End users must assume responsibility for the maintenance of documentation for their application and ensure that it is complete, current, and accurate. The IT auditor can perform an effective management advisory role by highlighting and emphasizing the importance of EUC documentation.

Audit Testing

The auditor must address many considerations that cover the nature, timing, and extent of testing. The auditor must devise an auditing testing plan and a testing methodology to determine whether the previously identified controls are effective. The auditor also tests whether the end-user applications are producing valid and accurate information. For microcomputers, several manual and automated methods are available to test for erroneous data. An initial step is to browse the directories of the PCs in which the end-user-developed application resides. Any irregularities in files should be investigated. Depending on the nature of the audit, computer-assisted techniques could also be used to audit the application. The auditor should also conduct several tests with both valid and invalid data to test the ability and extent of error detection, correction, and prevention within the application. In addition, the auditor should look for controls such as input balancing and record or hash totals to ensure that the end user reconciles any differences between input and output. The intensity and extent of the testing should be related to the sensitivity and importance of the application. The auditor should be wary of too much testing and limit his or her tests to controls that cover all the key risk exposures and possible error types. The key audit concern is that the testing should reveal any type of exposure of sensitive data and that the information produced by the application is valid, intact, and correct.

Audit Report

The audit report should inform management about the results of the review of the EUC group. It can also suggest support for resources to enhance end-user controls. In addition, the audit report should recommend policies and procedures that could strengthen end-user controls. Finally, the audit report should convince end users and management of the need for controlling EUC by identifying the importance of the information and assets stored on the PCs and LANs and by pointing out the risks to those assets.

The auditor's report should also inform management of the types of controls that are needed to increase efficiency and decrease risk and exposure. These recommended controls should be defined in a cost versus benefit manner and should be expressed in terms that management will understand: How much it will cost the company if these types of controls are not in place? or how much the company can save if such types of controls are in place? After these recommendations have been made, approved, and implemented, the auditor should reevaluate the controls to ensure that they have been implemented and are effective.

Conclusion

We have provided an overview of operational controls and their importance. Operational controls form an underlying foundation for the availability and security of the entire system. We have provided some approaches and techniques that IT auditors can use to evaluate the effectiveness of general controls. These general controls are extremely important in protecting the applications and support systems. Any breakdown in their effectiveness can have a catastrophic impact to the applications and systems.

Such controls are costly because many of them involve human interaction. But they are necessary in giving the user, management, and the customer assurances that they are protected, and assurances that they can rely on the information provided to make sound business decisions. Operational controls are the first line of protection.

Data communications is a critical part of an organization's business systems. In this chapter, some steps and suggestions to help the auditor begin to understand this area are presented; however, the rapid technological advances occurring in this field as well as the growth of data communications systems require that the auditor be familiar with new technological areas such as wireless technology and the emerging standards being applied in business as discussed in Chapter 23.

Finally, the importance of EUC groups has grown considerably as a reaction to the strictly controlled IT environment. Unfortunately, EUC groups, to their detriment, have neglected most of the controls that were developed by IT. As end users create and maintain critical information, organizations must institute controls to ensure complete and accurate information. A balance should be achieved between control and flexibility to encourage innovation in a stable environment.

The role of IT and end users continues to change as technology changes. The role of the auditor will also continue to evolve in response to these changes. IT auditors must be aware of the changing environments to respond with viable suggestions for controlling information and resources. The changing environment provides many opportunities for IT auditors' involvement in identifying risks and educating users and management on the need for effective controls. All areas are within the purview of IT, and they are all important for the IT auditor and the business manager.

Review Questions

1. What are operational controls? What purpose do they serve?
2. Why are policies, procedures, and standards viewed as examples of operational controls?
3. Provide two examples of data files and program controls.
4. What are environmental controls? List and explain three examples.
5. What problems can power surges cause to computer systems?
6. In conducting a data center review, list information that an IT audit should request or obtain at the preaudit meeting? Why is this information important in auditing operational controls?
7. What might be the components of a data center audit program?
8. List and explain three areas of daily management that IT auditors need to review.
9. What are other management control areas IT auditors may need to review with regard to testing operational controls?
10. What are the three reasons that errors in data communications usually occur?

Multiple-Choice Questions

1. Operating standards and procedures can be validated by
   a. Reviewing operating manuals
   b. Observing operation of the data center

    c. Interviewing operations management

    d. Testing a sample of transactions

2. Copies of system documentation, standards, and procedure manuals should be protected through

    a. Local backup

    b. Off-site storage

    c. Anti-virus software

    d. Firewalls

3. Which of the following is not a major cause of damage to network equipment?

    a. Flooding

    b. Power surges

    c. Blackouts

    d. Brownouts

4. An important data library control centers on assurance that

    a. Tapes are stored at an off-sight location

    b. All file media are clearly and accurately labeled

    c. Data files are copied to a backup location

    d. Transaction logs of access to data files are maintained

5. The objective of physical security and access controls is

    a. Consistent security and accountability

    b. Determining the source and extent of the damage

    c. To prevent or deter theft, damage, and unauthorized access

    d. To prevent and respond to threats

6. In a data center audit program, the administration of IT activities includes all of the following except

    a. Reviewing the organization chart

    b. Determining if written policies by IS administration personnel exist

    c. Determining if short-range planning is maintained by IS management

    d. Assessing the accuracy of inventory procurement

7. Data communications software typically performs all of the following except

    a. Receives messages from computer terminals or other computers

    b. Edits input and output programs

    c. Handles errors

    d. Blocks messages when a particular terminal or communications line is inoperative

8. The results of testing of physical and environmental controls should be reported to

    a. Supervisors

    b. Auditors

    c. Senior management

    d. Outside agencies

9. Operational controls are costly because many of them involve

    a. Human interaction

    b. Technology

    c. Auditors

    d. Software

10. Which of the following would not be included in a company-wide policy on EUC?

    a. Wireless encryption standards

    b. Appropriate documentation

    c. Segregation of duties

    d. Backup procedures

Exercises

1. You are an internal auditor assigned to perform an operations audit of a data center. On reviewing the operations policy and procedures manuals, you find that the manuals appear to be fairly complete and up to date. Describe three audit tests you would perform to test whether the manuals are actually used and followed.

2. Describe five required capabilities for effective auditor use of tape management software.

3. Your organization is considering signing a contract with a company to provide off-site storage. You have been asked to review the contract to see if backup and recovery needs have been addressed. List five areas that you would look for in the contract related to backup and recovery needs.

Answers to Multiple-Choice Questions

1—b; 2—b; 3—a; 4—b; 5—c; 6—c; 7—d; 8—d; 9—a; 10—a

Further Reading

1. Govekar, M., D. Scott, R. J. Colville, D. Curtis, W. Cappelli, P. Adams, K. Brittain et al., *Hype Cycle for IT Operations Management, 2006*, Gartner Research G00141081, Stamford, CT, July 7, 2006.

2. Information Systems Audit and Control Foundation, *COBIT Control Objectives*, Information Systems Audit and Control Foundation, July 2007.

3. Information Systems Audit and Control Foundation, *Aligning COBIT, ITIL, and ISO 17799 for Business Benefit*, 2005.

4. Paquet, R., *The Best Approach to Improving IT Management Processes*, Gartner Research TU-17-3745, Stamford, CT, September 5, 2002.

5. The IIA, *The GAIT Methodology: A Risk-Based Approach to Assessing the Scope of IT General Controls*, The Institute of Internal Auditors, Altamonte Springs, FL, August 2007.

ADVANCED TOPICS   V

Chapters 23 through 26

The fifth part of this text goes beyond the COBIT processes to examine advanced topics in IT. The virtual environment leveraging the Internet and E-commerce are now the norm for organizations and government institutions. The risks in this area have not diminished markedly in the past decade, but controls are maturing.

Computer applications operate within this environment and are very dependent on the general controls that protect the applications. It is the operations environment that is an integral component and helps control user devices and sophisticated network applications. The domain can encompass worldwide activities supported by wide area network architectures.

Chapter 23 discusses the virtual environment where organizations operate today. The virtual environment is composed of a complex configuration of clients, servers, and networks to function. The design of such systems is complex and management can be very difficult. As the name implies, the virtual organization is critically dependent on the timely flow of accurate information throughout the organization. This chapter discusses the organization's dependency on networking and the controls over various types of networks including the Internet and intranets. Cloud computing and mobile computing topics are introduced.

Chapter 24 provides a discussion of the security risks in a virtual environment and inherent controls necessary to mitigate these risks. Internet security has had significant impacts on businesses worldwide. The emergence of new and more dangerous types of attacks from cyber criminals continues to pose big challenges for businesses and security professionals.

Chapter 25 discusses the risks associated with doing business on the Internet and controls that help mitigate these risks. The complex nature of E-commerce systems means that they are always at risk if they do not monitor internal and external security trends continuously. This chapter also discusses the risks associated with the use of Java to integrate with an organization's existing systems and networks. Security risks related to cloud and mobile computing implementation and mitigating factors are discussed.

Chapter 26 discusses the benefits and risks associated with implementing enterprise resource planning (ERP) solutions. ERP systems have replaced individual applications for back-office functions in most large organizations. In ERP systems, people and passwords can be the weakest link. Both must be managed effectively to ensure the protection of ERP systems. Thus, systems security features can only be effective when reinforced with policies and procedures that prevent the compromise of security.

ADVANCED TOPIC

Chapter 23

Virtual Environment

Historically, organizations have perceived several advantages in centralizing computer operations. A major advantage relates to economies of scale. It was widely accepted that a large computer was more cost effective than a small computer. Advances in processor technology and vendor pricing policies, however, have made this belief obsolete. It is now possible for a microcomputer to connect "seamlessly" through a LAN to a host file server, midrange, or mainframe computer, which, in turn, may be connected to other remote computers.

As technology advances, it has become increasingly important to be able to access data anytime, anywhere. In recent years, Web applications and cloud computing have been gaining popularity and a major selling point used by many IT vendors. Gartner estimates that over the course of the next 5 years, enterprises will spend $112 billion cumulatively on software as a service (SaaS), platform as a service (PaaS), and infrastructure as a service (IaaS), combined. The most cited advantages of using cloud computing includes quick set up, lower cost, increased storage, improved flexibility, enhanced mobility, and device independence. Although these may be true benefits, organizations should consider the risks associated with using Web applications and cloud technology. Some risks may be acceptable to some organizations, and some data may not be suitable to be shared in the cloud. For example, Sony's Playstation Network was hacked in early 2011, resulting in ongoing intermittent downtime for paying subscribers. Amazon was forced to apologize for an extended outage to customers of its computing and database services in April 2011. Therefore, organizations should thoroughly assess the risks, especially security of data, and ensure adequate controls are in place before signing up for a cloud service.

Virtual Environment

To be successful in the twenty-first century, organizations need to have some presence on the Internet. Nearly all sales begin with a search on the Internet; it could be as simple as finding a certain type of store in an area, the phone number, or the address or direction to the store. Some organizations are completely "virtual" and only do business online. Products are not displayed in a physical store; instead they are completely dependent on photos posted on the Website. Others will incorporate tools that allow customers to zoom in and out, as well as to rotate the product to

527

get a 360° view. The design of such systems may be complex, and management of it may be very difficult.

The virtual organization is critically dependent on the timely flow of accurate information throughout the organization. A good way to view how stringent the network requirements are is to analyze them in terms of the quality of telecommunications service. Most telecommunication experts believe that the network must be able to reach anyone anywhere in the world and be capable of supporting the sharing of a wide range of information, from simple voice, data, and text messages to cooperative transactions requiring the information updating of a variety of databases. The CEO and CIO want to meet or exceed their business objectives and attain maximum profitability through an extremely high degree of availability, fast response time, extreme reliability, and a very high level of security.

To achieve this objective, the IT infrastructure and applications that the business uses need to be of high quality, rich in information content, and come packaged with a variety of useful services, to meet the changing business conditions and competition. Flexible manufacturing and improvement programs such as JIT, "lean manufacturing," and TQM will enable low-cost production. Flexible manufacturing will permit products to be produced economically in arbitrary lot sizes through modularization of the production process.

The unpredictability of customer needs and the shortness of product life cycles will cause the mix of production capabilities and underlying resources required by the virtual organization to change constantly. The virtual organization must be capable of assembling its capabilities and resources quickly, thereby bringing a product to the market swiftly. To achieve a high degree of organizational flexibility and value chain coordination necessary for quick market response, excellent product quality, and low cost, the virtual organization will employ a network, team-oriented, distributed decision-making organizational approach rather than a more traditional hierarchical, vertically integrated, command-and-control approach.

The virtual organization will possess a dynamic network organization, synthesizing the best available design, production, supply, and distribution capabilities and resources from enterprises around the world and link them and the virtual organization's customers together. Its multienterprise nature will enable the virtual organization to respond to a competitive opportunity quickly and with the requisite scale, while, at the same time, enabling the individual network participant's cost and risk to be reduced. The network will be dynamic because participant identities and relationships will change as the capabilities and resources require change. The global scope of the network will enable virtual organizations to capitalize on worldwide market opportunities. Work will be performed by multidisciplinary and multienterprise teams, which will function concurrently and, to reduce production time, be granted significant decision-making authority. Team members will be able to work collaboratively, regardless of location and time zone. Openness, cooperativeness, and trust will characterize the relationships among the organizations in the network and their personnel.

Aside from reach, range, and service responsiveness, the network must be highly interconnected so that people, organizations, and machines can communicate at any time, regardless of location. Also, the network must be very flexible because the organization is constantly changing. Finally, the network must be cost effective because low cost is one of the ingredients in the mass-customization strategy. In addition, a control structure must be designed, developed, and implemented that provides assurances of integrity, reliability, and validity.

So, how can this be accomplished? The ability to reach anyone anywhere in the world requires global area networks. Clearly, the Internet and global carrier services, such as ATT and Verizon, will be crucial. Also, because the intended receiver need not be in the office or even at home, wireless networks will play a part. This will be true on-premise, such as with the use of wireless PBXs, LANs, and VoIP, with the use of cellular networks and global satellite networks, such as Iridium and Personal Communications. To support the sharing of a wide range of voice, data, and video information, bandwidth-on-demand will be required all the way to the desktop as well as the mobile terminal. Also, various collaborative service platforms such as Microsoft SharePoint will be necessary. Finally, perfect service will have to be designed into the network. Speed can be achieved through broadband networking: locally via fast ethernet, gigabit, and ATM LANs, and over a wide area via SMDS, ATM, and multiprotocol label switching (MPLS) services.

Cloud Computing

The latest trend toward virtualization is moving data and services to the "cloud." By using cloud computing technology, which is based on the distributed computing concept, users now can stay in sync—at all time—using a PC and mobile devices as well as share data—photos, movies, contacts, e-mail, documents—with friends, family, and coworkers instantaneously. The NIST and the Cloud Security Alliance (CSA) defined cloud computing as a "model for enabling convenient, on-demand network access to a shared pool of configurable computing resources (e.g., networks, servers, storage, applications, services) that can be provisioned and released with minimal management effort or service provider interactions." Examples of these applications are Google Apps, Facebook, YouTube, Flickr, and Wikipedia. The characteristics of cloud computing are shown in Exhibit 23.1.

Before an organization considers adopting cloud computing, the first thing they should do is determine the exact problems the company is trying to solve, and the business goals they want to achieve. Second, they need to identify which area of the organization holds the greatest potential for optimization using cloud computing. It is also important to know which applications make the most sense to deploy into the cloud as there are various options and opportunities.

Because of the potential security exposures and the early stages of the technology, the assessment process is very complex and encompasses many factors, none of which can be overlooked if a company wants to ensure successful cloud implementation. The CSA, a member-driven organization, chartered with promoting the use of best practices for providing security assurance within cloud computing, published Security Guidance for Critical Areas of Focus in Cloud Computing version 3.0 in November 2011. The major sections and domains are shown in Exhibit 23.2. Additionally, ISACA published IT Control Objectives for Cloud Computing: Controls and Assurance in the Cloud, which can be used by auditors in their risk assessment process.

Deployment Models

Understanding of the key aspects of cloud computing and its core architectures is vital to pursuing the right cloud computing solution. Each company chooses a deployment model and a cloud delivery service based on their specific business, operational, and technical requirements. Currently, there are four deployment models:

1. *Public cloud.* A public cloud is a Web service that is made available to the general public or a large industry group. Only nonsensitive information, such as marketing material and general product information, may be stored in a public could. Sensitive information, such as customer data and proprietary information, should not be stored in a public cloud. The Web service is owned by an organization that sells cloud services. The term "public" does not mean it is free, although it can be. Examples of public and free cloud services include Internet

Characteristics	Definition
On-demand self-service	The cloud provider should have the ability to automatically provision computing capabilities, such as server and network storage, as needed without requiring human interaction with each service's provider.
Broad network access	According to NIST, the cloud network should be accessible anywhere, by almost any device (e.g., smart phone, laptop, mobile devices, PDA).
Resource pooling	The provider's computing resources are pooled to serve multiple customers using a multitenant model, with different physical and virtual resources dynamically assigned and reassigned according to demand. There is a sense of location independence. The customer generally has no control or knowledge over the exact location of the provided resources. However, he/she may be able to specify location at a higher level of abstraction (e.g., country, region, or data center). Examples of resources include storage, processing, memory, network bandwidth, and virtual machines.
Rapid elasticity	Capabilities can be rapidly and elastically provisioned, in many cases automatically, to scale out quickly and rapidly released to scale in quickly. To the customer, the capabilities available for provisioning often appear to be unlimited and can be purchased in any quantity at any time.
Measured service	Cloud systems automatically control and optimize resource use by leveraging a metering capability (e.g., storage, processing, bandwidth, and active user accounts). Resource usage can be monitored, controlled, and reported, providing transparency for both the provider and customer of the utilized service.

Exhibit 23.1 Cloud computing characteristics. (Adapted from ISACA, Cloud Computing: Business Benefits with Security, Governance and Assurance Perspectives, 2009.)

mail, such as Google mail and Hotmail. Examples of public but not free cloud services include Amazon Elastic Compute Cloud (EC2), IBM's Blue Cloud, Sun Cloud, Google AppEngine, and Windows Azure Services Platform. The term "public" does not mean that the data are publicly visible. Public cloud vendors typically provide an access control mechanism for their users, such as user ID and password.

2. *Private cloud.* A private cloud is a system or collection of systems that provide hosted access to systems and applications, where the resources are dedicated to one organization. The system(s) may be hosted on-premises or off-premises by a third-party provider. With a private cloud, the subscriber get many of the benefits of public cloud computing—including self-service, scalability, and elasticity—with the additional control and customization available from dedicated resources. An example of private cloud is VMWare or Citrix.

3. *Community cloud.* A community cloud is a cloud infrastructure that is shared by several organizations and supports a specific community, such as healthcare, that has shared

Section I. Cloud Architecture   Domain 1: Cloud Computing Architectural Framework

Section II. Governing in the Cloud
  Domain 2: Governance and Enterprise Risk Management
  Domain 3: Legal Issues: Contracts and Electronic Discovery
  Domain 4: Compliance and Audit Management
  Domain 5: Information Management and Data Security
  Domain 6: Interoperability and Portability

Section III. Operating in the Cloud
  Domain 7: Traditional Security, Business Continuity, and Disaster Recovery
  Domain 8: Data Center Operations
  Domain 9: Incident Response
  Domain 10: Application Security
  Domain 11: Encryption and Key Management
  Domain 12: Identity, Entitlement, and Access Management
  Domain 13: Virtualization
  Domain 14: Security as a Service

Exhibit 23.2   Security Guidance for Critical Areas of Focus in Cloud Computing (Adapted from Cloud Security Alliance. Security Guidance for Critical Areas of Focus in Cloud Computing V3.0. November 2011. https://cloudsecurityalliance.org/research/security-guidance/.)

concerns around mission, policy, and compliance considerations. The cloud may be managed by the organizations or a third party and may exist on- or off-premise. An example of a community cloud is IBM's Federal Community Cloud for Government Organizations. This cloud service is specifically designed to help federal government organizations respond to technology requirements more quickly.

4. *Hybrid cloud.* A hybrid cloud is composed of two or more clouds (private, community, or public) that remain unique entities, but are bound together by standardized or proprietary technology that enables data and application portability (e.g., cloud bursting for load balancing between clouds). In this model, users typically outsource non-business-critical information and processing to the public cloud, while keeping business-critical services and data in their control.

Service Delivery Models

The three service delivery models and their characteristics are

1. *Software as a Service (SaaS).* SaaS is a software delivery model provided by a vendor through an online service. The software is running on a provider's cloud infrastructure and a user can access it via Web browser. The vendor makes the required software available to a business

based on subscription and the user is charged based on the product usage. A major advantage of this approach is that the user does not have to install or maintain the application. The user also does not need to maintain a data center or manage the infrastructure where the application is hosted. This is a major cost savings on hardware, software, and maintenance cost for most organizations. Example of Saas providers are Google Apps, Salesforce.com, eFax, and Zoho.

2. *Platform as a Service (PaaS).* PaaS enables organizations to develop applications more quickly and efficiently in a cloud environment using programming languages and tools supported by the provider. The provider is responsible for maintenance and control of the underlying cloud infrastructure, including network, servers, and operating systems. With PaaS, organizations can build PaaS environments on demand with no capital expenditures. Examples of PaaS providers are Google code, Windows Azure Platform, and CodeRun.

3. *Infrastructure as a Service (IaaS).* With IaaS, a company outsources the equipment used to support IT operations, including storage, hardware, servers and networking components. The service provider owns the equipment and is responsible for housing, running and maintaining it. Essentially, IaaS puts IT operations into the hands of a third party and the client typically pays on a per-use basis. This service enables fast deployment of applications and improves the agility of IT services by instantly adding computing processing power and storage capacity when needed. Examples of IaaS providers are HP, Unisys, and Amazon Web services.

Exhibit 23.3 shows a graphical view of cloud computing deployment and service delivery models. Note that community cloud is not depicted on the diagram as it is not as widely used as the other service delivery models.

Key Benefits of Cloud Computing

Some key benefits of cloud computing are

Reduced costs and capital expenditures. Since the applications are running in the vendor's location/infrastructure, there is no need to build a data center, purchase hardware and the operating systems, or hire IT staff to manage these systems. Additionally, since the services are shared with other organizations, the costs of the services are "shared," which means lower cost overall for the individual company.

Increased scalability and flexibility. Since cloud services are paid on per-usage basis, a company may instantaneously increase its computing power, such as server time and network storage when needed.

Quick-time-to-market. One of the major selling points of cloud computing is that the infrastructure and applications are already available and can be launched quickly. Setup time is greatly reduced.

Configurable. Applications can be configured to fit specific business needs. This includes the ability to make the application mimic the look and feel of the business, such as the ability to include business logo, color scheme, and a particular font.

Allow organizations to focus on core business. Organizations can redirect their focus on business core competencies rather than spend their efforts and resources on IT operations/maintenance.

The risks associated with cloud computing will be discussed in Chapter 25.

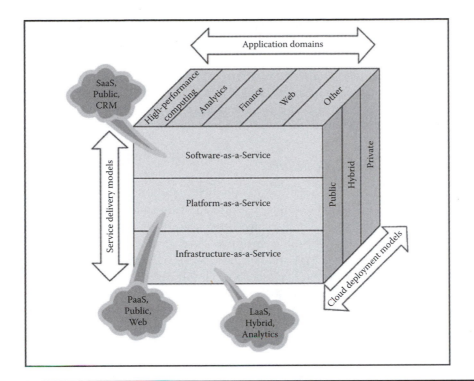

Exhibit 23.3   Cloud computing deployment and service delivery models. (Adapted from Cloud Computing Service Delivery and Development Model, © Cloud Security Alliance, https://clodsecurityalliance.org. With permission.)

Mobile Computing

Mobile computing is the ability to remain connected and access enterprise data while being mobile or away from the office. Nowadays, it is easy to find people browsing the Internet on their phones or iPad at every street corner, while waiting at a bus stop, checkout stand, or at the park. According to Gartner, mobile and Internet adoption will continue to rapidly rise through 2014, and by then, over 3 billion of the world's adult population will transact electronically via mobile or Internet technology.

The most commonly used devices for mobile computing are

- Smartphones with personal-computer-like functionalities, such as iPhone, Droid, and Blackberry
- Laptops, notebooks, and netbooks
- iPad and tablet PCs (by HP, Acer, Motorola, etc.)
- Portable Universal Serial Bus (USB) devices for storage (such as thumb drives and MP3/4 devices) and connectivity (such as Wi-Fi, Bluetooth, and modem cards)
- Digital cameras

The use of mobile devices has definitely increased convenience and productivity in the workforce. Other benefits realized by the individuals using the device and the enterprises include

Improved customer service. Field representative can easily access enterprise data through the Internet at the customer's business location, complete an online transaction, or walk the customer through a process.

Improved turnaround time for problem resolution. Mobile computing may also help reduce the response time to customer questions, which in turn increase customer satisfaction.

Enhanced employee retention rate. The use of mobile device provides employee the opportunity to work remotely which helps with work–life balance.

Areas of Control and Risk Issues

The competitive success of the virtual organization will depend heavily on information and its timely, reliable, and secure communication. Backups and redundancy will increase the network's availability. The use of firewalls and encrypted communication can increase security. Increased interconnectivity can be achieved by using broadly accepted standards. Designs should be modular and open architectures such as TCP/IP and Integrated Services Digital Network (ISDN) should be employed. Finally, flexibility can be achieved by using software-driven solutions, such as virtual LANs and common carrier or Internet VPNs in which intranet, extranet, or other network reconfigurations are easily made through the software rather than the hardware. Similarly, public networks, which can be reconfigured easily, are preferable to harder-to-reconfigure private networks.

Currently, some of these building blocks are not entirely capable of meeting the virtual organization's stringent requirements. In a recent survey of network managers in Fortune 1000 firms, over 75% reported that they would not send sensitive traffic over the Internet because of lack of faith in its security. In addition to security problems, response time is suffering from congestion on the Internet and it is likely to get worse. This is especially true in the Cloud Computing environment. According to CSA, the top seven threats to cloud computing are (1) Abuse and Nefarious Use of Cloud Computing; (2) Insecure Interfaces and APIs; (3) Malicious Insiders; (4) Shared Technology Issues; (5) Data Loss or Leakage; (6) Account or Service Hijacking; (7) Unknown Risk Profile. More of these security considerations will be discussed in Chapter 25.

Although greater reliability is available through wired rather than wireless solutions, wireless networking is a network connection of choice for individual users and organizations. Wireless technology is the ability of computing devices to communicate on a network without the need of a physical connection to that network. Wireless popularity means that organizations can no longer choose not to deploy wireless LANs (WLANs). However, with a wireless network, the network signal is transmitted through the air, thus posing a greater risk of abuse. Organizations should control the application of wireless technology through the use of sanctioned WLANs and user authentication, and take steps to prevent employees creating WLANs using unauthorized access points.

Mobile devices have made work and life more convenient for individuals and organization. These benefits are not without risks. Mobile devices have been, and continue to be, a source of various types of security incidents, such as device loss, malware, and external breaches. If sensitive company data are stored in those devices and taken by unauthorized person thru physical or logical means, the company may face significant legal consequences due to privacy law violation and noncompliance to regulatory requirements. The consequences may include civil and criminal lawsuits. Therefore, it is essential for organizations to apply proper risk management and security controls to maximize the benefits while minimizing the risks associated with such devices. Examples of mobile computing vulnerabilities, threat, and risks can be seen in Exhibit 23.4 and strategies to address those risks can be found in Exhibit 23.5.

Vulnerability	Threat	Risk
Information travels across wireless networks, which are often less secure than wired networks	Malicious outsiders can do harm to the enterprise	Information interception resulting in a breach of sensitive data, enterprise reputation, adherence to regulation, legal action
Mobility provides users with the opportunity to leave enterprise boundaries and thereby eliminates many security controls	Mobile devices cross boundaries and network perimeters, carrying malware, and can bring this malware into the enterprise network	Malware propagation, which may result in data leakage, data corruption and unavailability of necessary data
Bluetooth technology is very convenient for many users to have hands-free conversations; however, it is often left on and then is discoverable	Hackers can discover the device and launch an attack	Device corruption, lost data, call interception, possible exposure of sensitive information
Unencrypted information is stored on the device	In the event that a malicious outsider intercepts data in transit or steals a device, or if the employee loses the device, the data are readable and usable	Exposure of sensitive data, resulting in damage to the enterprise, customers, or employees
Lost data may affect employee productivity	Mobile devices may be lost or stolen due to their portability. Data on these devices are not always backed up	Workers dependent on mobile devices unable to work in the event of broken, lost, or stolen devices and data that are not backed up
The device has no authentication requirements applied	In the event that the device is lost or stolen, outsiders can access the device and all of its data	Data exposure, resulting in damage to the enterprise and liability and regulation issues
The enterprise is not managing the device	If no mobile device strategy exists, employees may choose to bring in their own, unsecured devices. While these devices may not connect to the virtual private network (VPN), they may interact with e-mail or store sensitive documents	Data leakage, malware propagation, unknown data loss in the case of device loss or theft

Exhibit 23.4 Mobile device vulnerability, threat, and risk. (Adapted from ISACA, Securing Mobile Devices, 2010.)

The device allows for installation of unsigned third-party applications	Applications may carry malware that propagates trojan horses or viruses; the applications may also transform the device into a gateway for malicious outsiders to enter the enterprise network	Malware propagation, data leakage, intrusion on enterprise network

Exhibit 23.4 (Continued) Mobile device vulnerability, threat, and risk. (Adapted from ISACA, Securing Mobile Devices, 2010.)

Even if technology permits, there is a question whether or not security requirements can be satisfied due to the complexity of the management problem. In addition to the ordinary network management headaches, such as user demands for higher levels of security, shrinking budgets, and inadequate training, network managers in virtual organizations will continue to face new challenges. First is the mission-critical nature of the network to the firm. It is the lifeblood of the firm.

Risk	Strategy
A lost or stolen mobile device	Implement a central management console for device remote control, that is, location tracking, data wipe-out, password/PIN change, or strong user authentication. Ensure that mobile devices are encrypted so information is unusable in the event of loss or theft
Providing support to various devices	Turn to cross-platform centrally managed mobile device managers
Controlling data flow on multiple devices	Secure the systems that are accessed with authorization, encryption, and privileges control
Preventing data from being synchronized onto mobile devices in an unauthorized way	Monitor and restrict data transfers to handheld or removable storage devices and media from a single, centralized console
Keeping up with the usage of the latest and greatest devices	Create keen user awareness on information assets, risks, and value to the enterprise
Promoting accountability, responsibility, and transparency with device usage	Track the way devices are used, and provide regular feedback to management
Demonstrating regulatory compliance	Implement a central management console to manage all stages of asset management, from installation to retirement

Exhibit 23.5 Strategy to address mobile computing risks.

Second is the fact that these requirements are very stringent. Complexity is a major problem now for network managers and it will get worse as the industry becomes more deregulated, competition intensifies, and technology offers more choices. It is especially difficult in the virtual organization because the network is a multienterprise one. It is not only that but also one that is continually changing.

IT Operations Issues in Network Installation

IT operations issues focus on the planning, implementation, and operation of networks. The following list provides a quick reference identifying the installation issues most relevant to the subject:

Wiring and cabling. Many articles and case studies have shown that approximately 80% of network problems are due to improperly installed or poor-quality cabling. When quality is sacrificed for cost, operations may be detrimentally affected once the network is put into service, resulting in retrofit costs.

Throughput or traffic. This is an area in which effective planning and visits to organizations that have implemented a similar network can pay off. Major decisions include specifying the type of file servers needed to support the desired application and determining connectivity with other networks and peripherals. An assessment of the organizations' current and planned applications is an important input to this process.

Layout. To facilitate enhancements and the ability to adapt to organizational change, layout should be part of the planning process. This can save the organization's money in the long run and help identify control concerns.

Measuring performance. Tools that help monitor performance and analyze change can be very valuable to the network manager. In addition, network analysis products can assist in diagnosing data bottlenecks as well as system and control failures.

Because a network represents a substantial investment in microcomputer equipment, network equipment, network-operating software, shared software, individual user software, data, personnel, administration, and training, the network or the information contained in the network files may represent an organization's major assets. Therefore, an organization must evaluate the major controls to be used in the network architecture.

LANs have become commonplace in most medium and large organizations and their capabilities extend to the smaller enterprises. Now, WANs and WLANs have become the next communications frontier. However, WANs and WLANs are much more complicated than LANs. In most WAN environments, the more devices an individual has to manage, the more time consuming is the process of monitoring those devices. Complexity also increases very rapidly because each new device on the network invariably has to interface with many existing devices.

WLAN protocols are a moving target for organizations today. Standard 802.11b was a fixture for several years and considered as a wireless standard. Within recent years, change has been considerable within the wireless industry as services for wireless has considerably increased and many protocols have been created. As discussed later in Chapter 24, Institute of Electrical and Electronics Engineers (IEEE) 802.11n is an improved security measure. Organizations considering WLANs must consider trade-offs between frequency, modulation, and data rate in addition to security and compatibility issues. A list of the most common wireless network standards is shown in Exhibit 23.6.

Protocol	Author	Frequency	Modulation	Data Rate	Comments
802.11	IEEE	900 MHz ISM	FHSS	300 kbps	Original standard of the series (obsolescent)
802.11a	IEEE	5 GHz UNII	OFDM	Up to 54 Mbps	Standard not backward compatible with 802.11
802.11b	IEEE	2.4 GHz ISM, 900 MHz legacy	DSSS FHSS legacy	1–11 Mbps	Extended throughput to up to 11 Mbit/s using the same 2.4 GHz band
802.11e	IEEE	5 GHz UNII	OFDM	Up to 54 Mbps	Adds quality of service (QoS) capability to 802.11h
802.11g	IEEE	2.4 GHz ISM	DSSS FHSS	Up to 54 Mbps	Intended to maintain backward compatibility with 802.11b
802.11h	IEEE	5 GHz UNII	OFDM	Up to 54 Mbps	Adds transmit power control dynamic frequency selection to 802.11a to counter European Union (EU) area interference issues
802.11i	IEEE	5 GHz UNII	OFDM	54 Mbps or beyond	Intended to specifically include security and authentication
802.11j (5UP—2003)	IEEE, ETSI	5 GHz UNII	OFDM, GMSK	54 Mbps or beyond	Effort to converge 802.11 and HiperLAN standards to permit interoperation in the 5 GHz band designed specifically for the Japanese market
802.11n	IEEE	2.4 GHz ISM and 5 GHz UNII	OFDM	Up to 600 Mbps	Intended to increase data throughput speed and potentially range,

Exhibit 23.6   Most common WLAN standards.

					backward compatible with existing IEEE WLAN legacy solutions (802.11a/b/g), fully compatible with 802.11i (data protection), 802.11r (secure interaccess point roaming), and 802.11w (management frame protection)
HiperLAN	ETSI	5.15–5.30 GHz or 17.1–17.3 GHz	GMSK	23.529 Mbps	European Community-backed standard HiperLAN and IEEE 802.11 are roughly equivalent
HiperLAN/2	ETSI	5.15–5.30 GHz or 17.1–17.3 GHz	GMSK	54 Mbps	European Community-developed standard equivalent to IEEE 802.11a

Exhibit 23.6   (Continued) Most common WLAN standards.

To get a further understanding of WANs, it is useful to explore the differences between WANs and LANs. LANs are defined as communications networks in which all components are located within several miles of each other and communicate using high transmission speeds, generally 10 bps or higher. They are typically used to support interconnection within a building or campus environment.

WANs connect system users who are geographically dispersed and connected by means of public telecommunications facilities. WANs provide system users with access to computers for fast interchange of information. Major components of WANs include CPUs, ranging from microcomputers to mainframes, intelligent terminals, modems, and communications controllers. WANs cover distances of about 30 miles and often connect a group of campuses.

WANs are usually static in nature. Changes to them require rerouting telephone lines and installing modems. LANs, however, can be quickly reconfigured; communications lines are set up and rerouted more easily and gateways to host computers can be quickly added.

Types of WANs

There are two basic types of WANs: centralized and distributed. Centralized WANs consist of a mainframe or minicomputer that serves remotely distributed dumb terminals. Network managers lease communications channels from a common long-distance carrier and tie together terminals and the central computer using a star (or other) topology. (WAN topologies are described in more detail later in this chapter.) Communications are fairly straightforward; the smart computer polls the dumb terminals to find out if they have anything to transmit, and then it controls data transmission so that there are no collisions.

Distributed networks provide an environment that allows independent computers to have equal levels of control in the communications architecture. Distributed networks have grown as smart computers have increased throughout organizations. Today's packet WAN technologies are capable of supporting worldwide transmission at rates that are less than LAN transmission rates (LAN transmission rates of 100 MB and higher over relatively short distances).

A VPN is a private data network that utilizes public communication infrastructures, such as the Internet, while ensuring privacy through the use of tunneling protocols and security procedures. VPNs essentially eliminate the costs of a real private network, where organizations can own or lease their own private lines. Most organizations now use VPN to provide secure remote access to company data for their mobile workforce.

There are two main categories of VPNs that utilize the Internet as their public telecommunications infrastructure. VPNs that operate at the network layer (layer 3) of the Open System Interconnection (OSI) Network Architecture Model are called Internet Protocol Security (IPS) VPNs. VPNs that function at the application levels (layers 4–7 of OSI) are called Secure Sockets Layer (SSL) VPNs.

Elements of WANs

WANs differ according to their access methods, connective hardware and software, communications protocols, types of network services, and network topologies. These differences affect network installation, growth, and operating costs. In addition, WANs depend on the network management system for efficient and reliable operation. The following sections describe these elements.

Access Methods

Connections to remote networks may be accomplished over public data networks or private lines provided by long-distance and interexchange telephone carriers. The Internet requires the use of 32-bit addresses, which are administered by the network information center. Locally administered private networks should encourage the use of addresses that are compatible with Internet addresses to facilitate connection to the Internet.

Connective Devices

Information is transmitted over WANs in packets. In addition to user data, these packets contain information necessary for network management and protocols that permit local and remote devices on the network to recognize one another. For example, each packet contains address information, which is necessary to ensure the correct routing of the packet. Bridges and routers are the primary connective devices used to handle these transmissions.

Bridges

A bridge is a hardware and software device used to connect networks using various media and signaling systems. Bridges operate at the Data Link Layer of the OSI Model. Bridges read and filter data packets and frames, passing traffic only if the address is on the same segment of the network cable as the originating station. Frames contain information that is necessary for reassembling the messages contained in packets after they reach their destination. There are two types of frames: control frames for link management and information frames for the transfer of information.

Routers

A router is a sophisticated hardware and software device that connects LANs and WANs. It serves packets or frames containing certain protocols and it routes packets using network layer protocols. Multiprotocol routers can operate in heterogeneous environments by simultaneously using multiple protocols.

Protocols

WAN protocols are designed to provide connections for many devices within a wide area. Their purpose is to support a peer network of terminals, microcomputers, and hosts. A number of WAN protocols are available, including TCP/IP. The TCP/IP provides the primary communications procedures for the Internet. IBM's Systems Network Architecture (SNA) is designed to provide communications compatibility among microcomputers, minicomputers, and mainframes. For example, it can be used to connect IBM token-ring LANs to a host environment (see Exhibit 23.7).

Network Services

Frame relay and ATM are technologies used to support network traffic. Their method of operation is described in the following sections. There are a number of vendors of frame relay and ATM products.

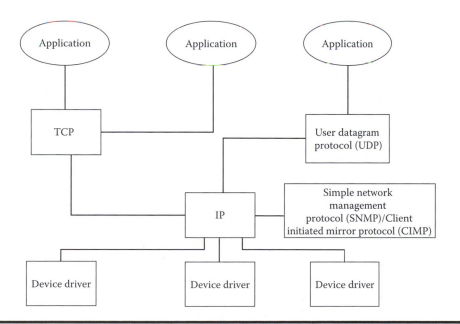

Exhibit 23.7   A schematic diagram of different types of layers involving TCP/IP.

Frame Relay Network Services

Frame relay is an extremely flexible and cost-effective technology that supports variable network traffic. Service bandwidth is scalable from 56 kbps to 45 Mbps, and it offers a variable-length frame size from 262 bytes to 8 kB.

Frame relay allows users to gain the advantages of high-speed circuits without having to run dedicated links between all the endpoints on a private network. The other major advantage of frame relay is its minimal packet overhead.

ATM Network Services

ATM refers to a high-bandwidth, low-delay switching, and multiplexing technology. ATM network services provide a foundation for high-speed digital transmission, LAN connectivity, imaging, and multimedia applications. ATM is based on cell switching technology that is equally effective at transmitting voice, video, and data at high speeds.

ATM is better suited than packet switching to real-time communications (e.g., video) because it uses standard length cells with small headers containing packet and address information. ATM supports transmission speeds of up to 622 Mbps. It supports services requiring both circuit-mode information transfer capabilities (characterized by a constant bit rate) and packet-mode capabilities (characterized by a variable bit rate).

Network Management Systems

Every major business wants to have the most efficient and economical operation of the corporate network. For a business to achieve this, it must effectively manage the computer and communications resources over the WAN. Because most businesses buy their networking products from more than one vendor, network management systems must be able to support a wide variety of equipment on the same network. This diversity makes the task of management and troubleshooting more challenging. (Network management software is discussed later in Chapter 24.)

Network Topologies

Although the star topology is the most popular WAN topology, a number of other network topologies are available and depicted in Exhibit 23.8. Each of the topologies has consequences with respect to reliability and availability.

Star Topology

The star topology is highly reliable; loss of one node results only in the loss of a single line. Loss of that line prevents communication between the hub and the affected node, but all other nodes continue to operate normally.

This topology is more limited with regard to ensuring availability. The network can only support the level of traffic that can be handled by the hub. In some cases, the hub is only able to handle one request at a time, which can cause serious delays during peak workloads.

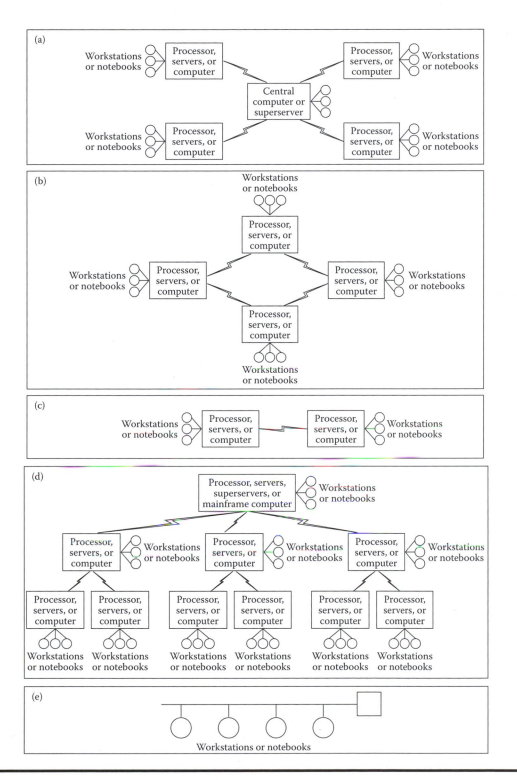

Exhibit 23.8   Network topologies. (a) Star network, (b) fully connected mesh network, (c) point-to-point network, (d) hierarchical or tree network, and (e) bus network.

Ring Topology

The ring topology uses link segments to connect adjacent nodes; each node is actively involved in the transmission of tokens to and from other nodes. The loss of a link causes operation of the entire network to cease. Therefore, this topology is not considered very reliable.

The ring topology is less effective than the mesh topology at ensuring availability of network services, but it is more effective than the star topology. Its effectiveness is limited because each node on the ring waits to receive the token before transmitting data.

Bus Topology

The bus topology is also not considered reliable. If the link fails, the entire segment connected to that link also fails. However, if the node fails, the rest of the network will continue to operate.

The availability of network resources using this topology depends on the access control protocol used, the length of the bus, and the transmission load. Under a light load, availability is virtually assured, but as the load increases, so also does the chance of collisions among transmissions. The chance of collisions also increases with greater bus length.

Mesh Topology

This kind of topology is highly reliable because it provides a diverse set of transmission routes. If one segment of the line fails, the rest of the line is not affected. Because of its multiple transmission paths, mesh topology also provides a high level of availability.

Hybrid Topology

The hybrid topology is highly reliable; the failure of one node does not affect the operation of other nodes. It also provides a high degree of availability because it provides a large number of connections to users.

Tools for Network Monitoring

A number of automated tools can assist the security specialist in identifying risks to network security. These include

- Protocol analyzers
- Network monitors
- Network management software
- General statistical tools
- Hybrid tools

The following sections describe each of these types of tools.

Protocol Analyzers

Protocol analyzers can be used to observe data packets as they travel across a network, measure rates of line use, and simulate traffic to gauge changes in the network configuration. They are designed to capture and decode data packets, breaking traffic down according to the Seven-Layer OSI Reference Model; the device is physically connected to the network segments being monitored. Wandell and Goltermann's DA-30C is an example of a protocol analyzer. As described in the following section, a WAN protocol analyzer is a specialized type of protocol analyzer.

WAN Protocol Analyzers

High-speed WAN protocol analyzers can be used to help network and security specialists plan and maintain multiple LANs linked to WAN services. With their unparalleled packet-filtering capabilities, these instruments are able to monitor the overall network activity, view organizational data traffic patterns, simulate new circuits, and pinpoint problems. WAN analyzers allow the user to track exactly how much of a leased line is being used for a particular protocol. These analyzers can also capture and store data samples and filter out specific data packets for scrutiny. WAN analyzers are being developed with capabilities to provide fault management filters and rule-based judgments, performance trend analysis, and reports that identify problems and assign responsibility for their diagnosis and tracking.

For efficient monitoring and diagnosis, it is vital that the analyzer be able to filter out specific packets from the overall data stream. This requires that the analyzer keep pace with system line speeds so that it does not overlook packets that may be critical to the network. In practice, most high-speed WAN protocol analyzers do not really filter data at the full rate of a T1 line, and the filtering and decoding processes further slow down the analyzer's operation.

Because of this most vendors of protocol analyzers specify a frame rate for their products indicating the number of packets or frames per second that the analyzer can process. The vendors also specify the size of frames for which rates are given. Most analyzers come with simulation programs that allow network managers to gauge the possible effects of specific types of data traffic on WAN circuits. With this software, sample packets are actually launched onto the network so that the analyzer can measure the effects of adding different types of protocol loads. (Running simulation applications may require shutting down network traffic.) Because most analyzers already have sophisticated packet-filtering and time-stamping capabilities, it is relatively easy to add statistical software for data sampling and analysis. Such statistical packages can generally be run without interfering with network traffic.

Network Monitors

Network monitors track and statistically analyze traffic on network segments. As with protocol analyzers, the device is physically connected to the segments being monitored. Sample products include Bay Mountain's IT Appliance and DPS Telecom's Network Alarm Management System.

Network Management Software

Network management software and workstations are designed to monitor and report on the conditions of network elements such as bridges, routers, and hubs, typically displaying information using multicolored icons on a map. These products typically use the SNMP. A number of products are available, including Hewlett-Packard's HP-OpenView, Sun Microsystems' SunNet Manager, IBM's NetView/6000, and Compuware Corporation's Application Expert 2.1. Their products offer reliable network security and data integrity services.

General Statistical Tools

These tools are designed primarily to provide statistical information about network performance. They typically track CPU and memory levels of use, free disk space, and network 1/0. Among the available products is HP's PerfView.

Hybrids

It should be noted that many products are actually hybrids that offer elements of two or more of the proceeding categories of monitoring tools. For example, many network management stations include the statistical analysis capabilities of network monitors; some network monitors provide basic protocol analysis capabilities. Among hybrid products that combine traffic monitoring, protocol analysis, and network mapping are the InfraTool Network Discovery 4.0, Peregrine Systems, Spectrum 6.0 from Aprisma Management Technologies, and OpenView NetWork Node Manager Release B.06.10 from HP.

Internet, Intranet, and Extranet

The Internet was started in the 1960s by the U.S. Defense Department's Advanced Research Projects Agency to link the department with its suppliers. Today, the Internet is a worldwide collection of millions of computers tied together by means of high-speed communication lines to form an apparently single network. The Internet provides an electronic forum in which people can share information and ideas, exchange electronic mail (e-mail) and data, use remote computers, and access public-domain information and software.

Corporate customers now represent the fastest-growing segment of the overall Internet user population. They use the Internet for many reasons, including file transfers, e-mail, system maintenance, and interactive sessions. For example, one chemical company uses the Internet to disseminate the results of its research; the company prefers using Internet because it is available 24 hours a day, every day. An oil company uses the Internet to transmit maps and land surveys to remote locations for oil and gas exploration; the Internet is able to reach nearly all countries. Users can connect to the Internet in several ways: dialing into a personal account on an Internet-connected computer, connecting through a commercial gateway, or subscribing to a commercial service.

Intranet Definition and Components

There is a close relationship between the Internet and the intranet because intranets incorporate the protocols, processes, and standards found in the Internet. Intranets are more than a hybrid of network and Internet technologies; they improve on the capabilities of both. The Internet is an immense network that connects innumerable smaller networks and their individual resources, the heart of which is the TCP/IP. In its simplest form, an intranet can be defined as Internet services and sharing provided within an organization.

An intranet is an internal company network that uses the Internet standards of Hypertext Markup Language (HTML), eXtensible Markup Language (XML), HTTP, and the TCP/IP communication protocol along with a graphical Web browser to support business applications and provide departmental, interdepartmental, and company-wide communication solutions. An intranet uses a Web server that is connected only to a company's LAN. Intranets can also use news and mail servers to create private newsgroups for the company's intranet and to send and receive e-mail among the company's users.

The term "intranet" was introduced in late 1995. They were previously called "enterprise Internets." Although the former name better describes its functionality, the term "intranet" is used more frequently because of its closeness with the Internet. An exact definition of the Internet and intranet is difficult, as Internet experts have not agreed on what exactly it is. For intranet, it is difficult because many kinds of intranets exist with different purposes.

The four main components of an intranet are

1. *TCP/IP.* This is the primary protocol of an intranet. On a TCP/IP intranet, information travels in discrete units called IP packets. TCP/IP software makes each computer attached to the network a sibling to the others; in essence, it hides the routers and underlying network architectures and makes everything seem like one big network.
2. *Information services.* These are any software application that enables data manipulation (receive, store, and send) over an intranet. Examples of information services are e-mail, newsgroups, remote log-in, File Transfer Protocol (FTP), database search engines, electronic commerce (e-commerce), intranet systems management, security, gateways, and firewalls.
3. *Clients.* They are the applications needed to access the IS. The most common intranet client is the Web browser.
4. *Authoring tools.* These are applications that create, edit, alter, or manipulate the data handled by an information service's server.

Intranet Benefits and Obstacles

There are many advantages of an intranet, including easy access and immediate delivery, cross-platform, reduced distribution costs, scalability, and increased internal communication, among others.

Easy access and immediate delivery. The intranet is available to anyone connected to the company's network *whether* at the local site or remotely via direct dial-up or the Internet. In general, intranets are available 24 hours a day, 7 days a week. Authorized personnel can update it anytime and the information becomes available instantaneously throughout the entire organization.

Cross-platform. Employees can use the tools of their choice on any major platform (PC, Mac, and UNIX) to create and manage information. This is one of the greatest benefits of intranets in which the exchange of information across multiple platforms is crucial.

Reduced distribution costs. The traditional mechanisms of corporate communication, memos, printed documents, flyers, booklets, and so on are no longer necessary with an intranet. All these printed material can be published electronically on the company's intranet, saving printing costs and time. Typically, all this printing, duplicating, and distributing costs $25–$100 per employee per year. In a company such as HP, with more than 105K employees, this represents a huge saving. Also, it can be used to deliver software upgrades (www.pathfinder.com/fortune/specials/intranets).

Scalability. Intranets can grow as necessary according to the company's needs. Starting small could be a good strategy due to the rapidly emerging intranet technologies and price changes within very little timeframe. Later, based on the company's needs, the system can grow easily.

Increased internal communication. Communication in a worldwide company can sometimes be problematic; time differences and the expense of long-distance communication can impede collaboration between branches. Intranets help employees from all over to communicate easily using e-mail, sending documents electronically, creating online forums or training sessions, and videoconferencing.

Despite all the benefits that intranets provide, there are some problems or obstacles to overcome. They include controls, inertia, performance, and costs.

Controls. These are needed when developing an intranet and include content proliferation, security, and conformity.

Inertia. This refers to the following areas: training users, integrating legacy applications and documents, and overcoming the fear of new technology.

Performance. Depending on the company's network structure the adoption of the new technology can impact the network performance, which may degrade. This is mainly due to the network's bandwidth. Also, company managers worry about employee productivity because employees will spend time surfing the Net, causing their work activities to suffer.

Costs. Intranets are not free. Funds are needed to buy software and hardware. Although intranets create costs, they also save money by conserving paper and ink, as well as reducing transportation costs.

Intranet Trends

The media, especially the Internet and network-focused publications, and general and business news, has played a major role in disseminating and making intranets popular. The intranet phenomenon is not artificial. Below are some compelling reasons that move intranet implementation in organizations.

- Internet technology can be transferred fairly easily to intranets, and most organizations already have experience with the Internet.
- The tools used on intranets by users are similar to those used on the Internet. Therefore, the learning curve is not too high.
- There is rapid development of new tools such as scheduling tools, workflow, database-query applications, and so on. Also, Web fronts can usually interface with old legacy systems giving old applications a longer life span.

The cost and complexity of building intranets is, usually, significantly less than other in-house development efforts. One of the more compelling reasons to deploy intranets is to reduce costs. An early example of how organizations are saving money on intranets is taken from the history of HP. HP created and deployed a corporate intranet called InfoNet. The initial goal of InfoNet was to make general information such as personnel policy manuals available to its 105K+ employees on the company's internal TCP/IP network. Owing to the success of publishing its personnel policies electronically, HP's management decided to provide all major forms electronically to reduce distribution costs, printing costs, and e-mail traffic to personnel. Another example is found at Cisco Systems. Its intranet is called the Cisco Connection Online, and it has saved the company $90 million a year through lowered operating costs, improved productivity, and better information flow. Managers like to see numbers come into play when the benefits of having an intranet include saving them a lot of money. For example, E-PeopleServe estimates that moving human resources information to a company's intranet can save it approximately 40%. Moreover, eliminating the paper for reports on travel and expenses can save a company as much as 93% in processing and administration.

Development of internal knowledge assets, external information sources, and content engineering in the following areas:

Retrieval of product and market information

Retrieval of best practices and lessons learned

Retrieval of employee and organizational information

Manuals

Procedures

Job opportunities

Personnel announcements

Department or employee Web page

Design, development, review, implementation, and revision or updating of project or organizational documentation

Retrieval of information from organizational databases

Statistics (overall and by areas)

Graphics

Trends and forecasts

Status of goods, services, and suppliers/vendors

Time management support

For scheduling meetings and conferences

Attending events

Meeting due dates and reporting dates

Exhibit 23.9 Functional uses of intranets by corporations.

The statistics show that the growth in intranets is steady, and magazines such as the *Intranet Journal* indicate that the evolution and development of intranet with organizations has evolved into actuaries of internal knowledge assets, external information resources, and content engineering management. Several studies have shown that intranet adoption has gone beyond leading-edge organizations and now is penetrating traditional organizations.

Another interesting aspect of intranets is how they are being used. There are many ways in which organizations are using intranets today (see Exhibit 23.9). Exhibit 23.9 provides some functional examples of how they are deployed in corporate setups in today's environment. Additionally, organizations now post audio and video files on the intranets to enhance communication and inspire corporate employees in novel ways. For example, organizations are using the intranet to broadcast their CEO's quarterly briefing to employees.

Conclusion

Although there is little doubt that organizations small and large in the twenty-first century will be competing in a turbulent environment, the virtual organization, with its mass-customization strategy, dynamic global network organization, and team-oriented collaborative approach to work seems particularly well suited for the task. This chapter has identified the requirements, design, and management of IT operations network as high-risk areas that are critical to the success of the organization. Examples are the need for stringent network requirements; very flexible networks; heavy reliance on the Internet, intranet, and extranet; collaborative services/platforms; broadband networks and open network architectures; compatible partner networks; and network management approaches consistent with the organizations' overall management philosophies.

The CEO and CIO must continually ask the hard questions. Should we sign up for a cloud service? What service delivery models fit our business goals? Should we expand our mobile computing capability? Doing so would provide an answer to the important question of how virtual organizations respond to factors such as growth, competition, security, and new technology when making their telecommunications network design and management decisions. Perhaps through funded research with universities and the sampling of larger, more broadly based samples of virtual organizations, the impact on network decisions of factors such as company size, age, industry, and location can be investigated more thoroughly.

For businesses worldwide, the benefits of intranets have greatly exceeded the problems predicted. In addition to all the benefits mentioned in this chapter, there is a significant value to organizations, especially those geographically dispersed, in bringing people together regularly and at a low cost to solve problems, train, or do many other business and personal tasks.

The rapid growth of intranets is imminent; surveys and research made by a number of different firms have corroborated this. In fact, these estimates do not include all the applications packages, programming tools, and other items that go along with this technology.

The harnessing of Internet technologies within a corporate environment is the most important development to emerge in the computer industry in the 1990s. The power of the intranet will transparently deliver the immense information resources of an organization to each individual's desktop with minimal cost, time, and effort.

However, both the organization and audit have a joint responsibility if security is a priority. The more absolute the security requirement is for a given system, the less it will be connected to any network, let alone the Internet. But the price to pay for absolute security is minimal access for legitimate users. Many experts agree that there is no perfect answer on where to draw the line.

The IT auditor has a very important role in assuring management that general controls are being followed in all aspects. IT operations controls help ensure that programmed procedures are consistently and correctly applied to the transmission, processing, and storage of data. Computer operations and network software advances have provided improvements in data center management. Vendors who used to compete with one another in marketing their products are now working together to provide a common routing protocol. This protocol will give customers the ability to implement an open computing environment using components from multiple vendors. Customers will no longer have to rely on a single vendor to meet their networking requirements, which will provide them greater flexibility and efficiency and help reduce network-operating costs.

Review Questions

1. What is a virtual organization?
2. Why are IT operations, especially networks, important to virtual organizations?
3. What are some of the key areas of control and risk issues associated with IT operations, especially in the virtual environment?
4. What are some of the control concerns associated with wireless technology?

5. List and describe the different network topologies. As an IT auditor, why is it important to understand these aspects of IT operations?
6. What are network-monitoring tools? What do they do?
7. What is the Internet? What is an intranet? What is an extranet?
8. What are cloud service delivery models? What are cloud deployment models? Which one is the best?
9. According to Cloud Security Alliance, what are the top seven threads to cloud computing?
10. Name three mobile computing risks and potential strategies to address those risks.

Multiple-Choice Questions

1. Which of the following is not a virtual organization business objective?
   a. Availability
   b. Response
   c. Downtime
   d. Security
2. Virtual organization products, where IT provides consumer feedback, will be rich in
   a. Bells and whistles
   b. Features
   c. Bugs
   d. Information content
3. IT operations issues in network installation include all of the following except
   a. Wiring and cabling
   b. Customer service
   c. Throughput or traffic
   d. Measuring performance
4. Which of the following WLAN standards is not backward compatible?
   a. 802.11a
   b. 802.11b
   c. 802.11g
   d. 802.11
5. Which wireless standard is not compatible with Bluetooth?
   a. 802.11a only
   b. 802.11b only
   c. 802.11g only
   d. All of the above
   e. None of the above
6. VPNs are
   a. Mainframes or minicomputers that serve remotely distributed dumb terminals
   b. An environment that allows independent computers to have equal levels of control in the communications architecture
   c. A private data network that utilizes public communication infrastructures such as the Internet while ensuring privacy through the use of tunneling protocols and security procedures
   d. Capable of supporting worldwide transmission at rates that are less than LAN transmission rates

7. Which of the following is not a tool for network monitoring?
    a. Connective devices
    b. Protocol analyzer
    c. General statistical tools
    d. Network management software
8. Which of the following is not a main component of an intranet?
    a. Peer-to-peer software
    b. TCP/IP
    c. Information services
    d. Authoring tools
9. The most vulnerable network area for CIOs and CEOs to review is the structure of
    a. Telecommunications equipment standards
    b. Firewall policies
    c. Network management within IT operations
    d. Wireless standards
10. Corporate customers use the Internet for all of the following except
    a. File transfers
    b. Illegal software downloads
    c. Electronic mail
    d. Interactive sessions

Exercises

1. The National Institute of Standards and Technology, a federal government agency, provides information that can assist IT managers and users on current IT topics. The Association of Computing Machinery is another IT organization that provides information to the IT community in general. Visit the Websites of both these organizations and identify five reports or information that can be beneficial to an IT manager.
2. From an auditor's perspective, which network topology do you believe would be the easiest to audit? Why? Which network topology would be the most difficult to audit? Why?
3. Why would audit weaknesses potentially be more serious when an organization uses a WAN than a LAN?
4. Why are virtual organizations difficult to audit in terms of assessing responsibility and liability for control weaknesses?
5. If your company is considering adopting cloud computing, what steps would you take in the preliminary assessment process? What security considerations should your company consider?

Answers to Multiple-Choice Questions

1—c; 2—c; 3—b; 4—a; 5—e; 6—c; 7—a; 8—a; 9—c; 10—b

Further Reading

1. Appavoo, J., V. Uhlig, and A. Waterland, Project Kittyhawk: Building a Global-Scale Computer, ACM Sigops Operating System Review, January 2008.

2. Appavoo, J. et al., Kittyhawk: Enabling cooperation and competition in a global shared computational system, *IBM Journal of Research and Development*, August 2009.

3. Appavoo, J. et al., Providing a Cloud Network Infrastructure on a Supercomputer, Science Cloud 2010: 1st Workshop on Scientific Cloud Computing, Chicago, IL, June 21, 2010.

4. Author unknown, 802.11b Wireless LAN security FAQ from Internet security systems, October 2002, http:// documents.iss.net/whitepapers/wireless_LAN_security.pdf.

5. Author unknown, Industry Embraces 802.1x WLAN Standard and EAP-TTLS Security Protocol, from Funk Software, May 6, 2002, http://www.funk.com/News&Events/8021x_partner.asp.

6. Author unknown, The Wireless LAN ROI/Cost–benefit study, from RF Smart, June 2003, http://www.rfsmart.com/downloads/R_WP_ROI.PDF.

7. Author unknown, Wireless LANs: Growing, but slowing down, from mobileinfo.com, August 2002, http://www.mobileinfo.com/News_2002/Issue32/WLAN_growth.htm.

8. Carr, N., *The Big Switch: Rewiring the World, from Edison to Google*, W. W. Norton & Company, New York, 2008.

9. Cloud Security Alliance, *Top Threats to Cloud Computing V1.0*, March 2010.

10. Cloud Security Alliance, *Security Guidance for Critical Areas of Focus in Cloud Computing V2.1*, December 2009.

11. ENISA, http://www.enisa.europa.eu/publications.

12. ENISA, *Cloud Computing Information Assurance Framework*, 2009.

13. Foster, I. and C. Kesseller, *The Grid2: Blueprint for a New Computing Infrastructure*, 2003.

14. Gallegos, F., *Security and Control over Intranets and Extranets: Part 1*, #75-10-35, EDP Auditing, Auerbach Publishers, Boca Raton, FL, 2002, pp. 1–12.

15. Gallegos, F., *Security and Control over Intranets and Extranets: Part 2*, #75-10-36, EDP Auditing, Auerbach Publishers, Boca Raton, FL, 2002, pp. 1–20.

16. Gallegos, F., *Wireless LANs: Technology and Security Issues*, Enterprise Operations Management, #46-40-65, Auerbach Publishers, Boca Raton, FL, 2001, pp. 1–16.

17. Gallegos, F. and S.R. Powell, *Securing Local Area Networks, Information Management: Strategy, Systems and Technologies Series*, #1-06-25, Auerbach Publishers, Boca Raton, FL, 2001, pp. 1–20.

18. Gartner Inc., *Gartner Highlights Key Predictions for IT Organizations and Users in 2010 and Beyond*, January 13, 2010.

19. Gartner Inc., Gartner Says Worldwide Cloud Services Market to Surpass $68 Billion in 2010, press release, June 22, 2010, http://www.gartner.com/it/page.jsp?id=1389313.

20. ISACA, *IT Control Objectives for Cloud Computing: Controls and Assurance in the Cloud*, 2011.

21. ISACA, *Cloud Computing Management Audit/Assurance Program*, 2010.

22. ISACA, *Cloud Computing: Business Benefits with Security, Governance and Assurance Perspective*, 2009.

23. ISACA, Mobile Computing Security Audit/Assurance Program, 2010.

24. Jansen, W. and T. Grance, NIST: Guidelines on Security and Privacy in Public Cloud Computing, Draft Special Publication 800-144, January 2011.

25. Kabara, J., P. Krishnamurthy and D. Tipper, Information Assurance in Wireless Networks, University of Pittsburgh (electronic journal; cited September 4, 2001), http://www.cert.org/research/isw/isw2001/papers/Kabara-31-08.pdf.

26. Kennard, L., Cordless and Cable-Free: The Risks and Rewards of Going Wireless, Novell Connection (electronic journal; cited July 2001, pp. 6–21), http://www. ncmag.com/2001_07/wireless71/.

27. Lannerstrom, S., Wireless Enterprise PC Security, Smart Trust (electronic white paper; cited September 12, 2002), http://www.smarttrust.com/whitepapers/.

28. McCollum, T., Wireless Security, *Internal Auditor Magazine* (electronic magazine; cited October 2002), http://www.theiia.org/ecm/magazine.cfm?doc_id=3951.

29. Saita, A., The Wild Wireless West, Information Security (electronic magazine; cited January 2002), http://www.infosecuritymag.com/2002/jan/cover_case_study.shtml.

30. Stanley, R.A., *Wireless LAN Risks and Vulnerabilities*, ISACF, 2, 57–61, 2002.

Chapter 24

Virtual Infrastructure Security and Risks

The development of Internet technology has originated a surge of new application solutions to improve business practices in organizations and government. For organizations, this technology has allowed companies to be more competitive and profitable from a global perspective and has changed the way people do business. For government, the Internet serves as a way of providing better services and information to the public. In Chapter 23, we examined some of the infrastructure used to support Internet technology. In this chapter, we take one step further in examining security and privacy issues from an infrastructure point of view.

Maintaining security and privacy requires corporate planning, training, implementing controls properly, monitoring the effectiveness of controls, and taking necessary corrective action. Owing to the nature of e-commerce, the Web applications that were created utilized electronic interfaces that often replaced human relationships. As these interfaces become standard to customers and business partners, the challenge for companies is that they need to provide the same level of trust and confidence from their e-commerce site compared to businesses that run without them. The security technology that underlies these e-commerce applications is crucial in building this trust, enabling clients to deal with the company with confidence and security. Security is the most important factor for e-commerce businesses because it is the bind for strengthening the relationships and tying the company more closely to its customers and partners. As business success depends largely on the close ties with clients, the security technology needed for e-commerce differs from the tools that are often used to secure corporate networks.

Information Flows in the Current Marketplace

For today's consumer, understanding the complex transfers of personal information that occur offline and online is a daunting task. Indeed, these information flows take place in almost every conceivable consumer interaction. For example, a consumer goes to work and provides sensitive information to her employer, such as her Social Security number, to verify her employment eligibility, and bank account number, so that she can get paid. After work, she uses an application on her smartphone to locate the closest ATM so that she can withdraw cash. She then visits her local grocery store and signs up for a loyalty card to get discounts on future purchases. Upon returning home, the consumer logs onto her computer and begins browsing the Web and updates her social networking profile. Later, her 12-year old grabs her smartphone and plays games on a mobile app.

All of these activities clearly benefit the consumer— she gets paid, enjoys free and immediate access to information, locates places of interest, obtains discounts on purchases, stays connected with friends, and can entertain herself and her family. Her life is made easier in myriad ways because of information flows. There are other implications, however, that may be less obvious. Her grocery store purchase history, Web activities, and even her location information may be collected and then sold to data brokers and other companies she does not know exist. These companies could use her information to market other products and services to her or to make decisions about her eligibility for credit, employment, or insurance. And the companies with whom she and her family interact may not maintain reasonable safeguards to protect the data they have collected.

Some consumers have no idea that this type of information collection and sharing is taking place. Others may be troubled by the collection and sharing described above. Still others may be aware of this collection and use of their personal information but view it as a worthwhile trade-off for innovative products and services, convenience, and personalization. And some consumers—some teens for example—may be aware of the sharing that takes place, but may not appreciate the risks it poses.

Interconnected Systems and E-Commerce

An area of great attention under this topic and mentioned in earlier chapters is the Internet. After organizations used the Internet to do business externally, they realized the great potential in using it internally as well. That is how the conception of the intranet or corporate intranet began to change the way people work. Intranet technology allows employees to accomplish tasks more effectively by sharing the company's information easily. Some of these tasks are online search, distribution of documents and policies, electronic mail (e-mail), and help desk, among others.

Network managers thought that because intranets are not open to the public, they are just networks within a corporation and so there were no security concerns. However, several recent surveys have shown that 9 out of 10 break-ins come from inside the organization. In essence, intranets are prime targets for disgruntled employees, hackers, and competitors. Internal networks are now taking on all the properties of the public networks that frighten us—openness, complexity, and flatness. Another factor is that user-controlled intranets can leave security to the clueless. Now, with communication links moving to wireless technologies, network vulnerabilities have expanded to another level. Certainly, the international community has not stood still and has taken action.

Therefore, the purpose of this chapter is twofold. The first objective is to address the most common security issues that organizations and e-governments encounter today, a new and dynamic area for IT auditors. The second is to enumerate recommendations to improve security, which IT auditors need to look for as they assess and evaluate controls within these environments (Exhibit 24.1).

	Priority 1	*Priority 2*	*Priority 3*	*Priority 4*	*Priority 5*
	National Cyberspace Security Response System	National Cyberspace Security Threat and Vulnerability Reduction System	National Cyberspace Security Awareness and Training Program	Securing Government's Cyberspace	National Security and International Cyberspace Security Corporation
Home user/ small business		X	X		
Large enterprises	X	X	X	X	X
Critical sectors/ infrastructures	X	X	X	X	X
National issues and vulnerabilities	X	X	X	X	
Global					X

Exhibit 24.1   Roles and responsibilities in securing cyberspace. (From U.S. Government, author unknown, *Cyberspace Threats and Vulnerabilities*, http://www.whitehouse.gov/pcipb/case_for_action.pdf)

Battleground: The Internet

The CERT Coordination Center (CERT/CC) is located at the SEI, a federally funded research and development center at Carnegie Mellon University in Pittsburgh, Pennsylvania. For IS auditors and IT security personnel, it has been an excellent resource. Following the Internet Worm incident which brought 10% of Internet systems to a halt in November 1988, the Defense Advanced Research Projects Agency (DARPA) charged the SEI with setting up a center to coordinate communication among experts during security emergencies and to help prevent future incidents. Since then, the CERT/CC has helped to establish other response teams while maintaining leadership in analyzing vulnerabilities and threats.

Since 2001, the CERT Insider Thread Outreach and Training team has been collecting information about malicious insider activity within U.S. organizations. In each of the incidents they have collected, the insider was found guilty in a U.S. court of law. In 10 years, CERT has collected approximately 700 cases of insider activity that resulted in the disruption of an organization's critical IT services; the use of IT to commit fraud against an organization; the use of IT in the theft of intellectual property or national security espionage; as well as other cases where an insider used IT in a way that should have been a concern to an organization. These data provide the foundation for all of CERT insider threat research, CERT insider threat lab, insider threat assessments, workshops, exercises, and the models developed to describe how the crimes tend to evolve over time.

Responding to critical cyber events requires technical knowledge and skills, decision-making abilities, and effective coordination. The best way to prepare IT staff is to have them practice under realistic conditions; however, it can be difficult and expensive to create and administer these types of training scenarios. Therefore, CERT created Exercise Network (XNET) to help organizations solve this problem. The XNET allows organizations to create customized, realistic, interactive simulations on an isolated network. Through a Web-based interface, participants across multiple locations can work together to analyze and respond to the latest threats. Instructors can easily monitor, control, and evaluate participants' activities to identify problem areas. XNET has been used in multiple cyber defense exercises conducted by the U.S. government and will be featured in the upcoming International Cyber Defense Workshop. The use of practices developed by the CERT/CC has resulted in improved resistance to attacks on networked computers and, thus, improved protection for the information stored on or transmitted by those computers.

The 2011 CyberSecurity Watch Survey, conducted by CSO magazine in cooperation with the U.S. Secret Service, the Software Engineering Institute CERT Program at Carnegie Mellon University, and Deloitte, suggests that the annual monetary losses from cybersecurity events have dropped from $395,000 in 2010 to $123,000 per organization in 2011. However, they believe these numbers are a result of organizations associating incidents to different domains, such as privacy and fraud rather than traditional cybersecurity. The survey also uncovered that more attacks (58%) are caused by outsiders (those without authorized access to network systems and data) versus 21% of attacks caused by insiders (employees or contractors with authorized access) and 21% from an unknown source; however, 33% view the insider attacks to be more costly, compared to 51% in 2010. Insider attacks are becoming more sophisticated, with a growing number of insiders (22%) using root kits or hacker tools compared to 9% in 2010, as these tools are increasingly automated and readily available.

Based on the U.S. General Accounting Office (GAO) recommendations, the Federal Computer Incident Response Capability (FedCIRC), which is the CERT/CC incident response team, was established in 1996. FedCIRC is a joint effort of the NIST, the CERT/CC, and the Computer Incident Advisory Capability (CIAC). The FedCIRC provides incident response and other security-related services to federal civilian agencies.

Tools

In the early days of the Internet, personal computers (PCs) were scarce. Access to the Internet was limited primarily to university students with Unix to Unix CoPy (UUCP) accounts. Today, the sheer size of the Internet makes it vulnerable to attacks from anywhere in the world. Tools used by IT designers, developers, and system maintainers are also tools of the hackers. And as mentioned in earlier chapters, they are also tools of the IT auditors, security, and control professionals.

Scanners

Scanners comprise a major category of attacking tools used by crackers. Scanners are mainly TCP scanners that probe weaknesses by launching attacks against the targeted host's TCP/IP ports. The response from the targeted host is recorded. Valuable information, such as probing results for anonymous user log-in, is recorded. Some scanners are merely operating system utilities. For instance, "fingers" are UNIX utilities that scan for users who are currently logged on. Most scanners currently run on UNIX operating systems. However, movement to port scanners to

Windows operating systems has become increasingly popular as Windows gained popularity as an Internet server. Creating scanners is relatively easy. Anyone with an extensive knowledge of TCP/IP routines and any UNIX shell languages, such as C, C++, or Perl, can create a scanner.

Scanners are important to Internet security because they reveal weaknesses in the network. System administrators can use scanners to help strengthen security. These tools are often found in the public domain. Scanners provide the following capabilities:

- Finding a machine or network
- Finding the type of services that is being run on the host
- Testing those services for holes

Still one of the most controversial scanners is the Security Administrator's Tool for Analyzing Networks (SATAN). The authors of SATAN, Dan Farmer and Wietse Venema, are both security experts who have created other security tools. SATAN primarily runs on UNIX. It ports poorly to Linux platform. SATAN scans remote hosts for most known holes, including

- Internet File Transfer Protocol Server (FTPD) vulnerabilities and writable FTP directories
- Network File System (NFS) vulnerabilities
- Network Information Service (NIS) vulnerabilities
- Remote shell (RSH) vulnerabilities
- Sendmail
- X-server vulnerabilities

Password Crackers

Password crackers are tools that use brute-force tactics to guess user passwords. For the security administrators, these tools check for weak passwords that are easy to crack. Programs can be run as parallel processes to speed up the cracking. Since a cracking program utilizes large quantities of system resources, a cracker running distributed cracking processes is easily detected. Password crackers are very simple in concept. The program uses a word in a predefined wordlist or dictionary and submits the list through the encryption process. This process repeats itself until a match is found. If the output matches the encrypted password, the password is cracked. Another technique of password cracking takes the entire list and submits it through the password encryption process. Using the encrypted wordlist, each password is matched against the wordlist. If a match is found, the password is found. This second technique is much faster because the wordlist is encrypted once. The success level of the password depends on the completeness of the wordlist. The Computer Operations, Audit, and Security Technology (COAST) project at Purdue University has one of the most comprehensive dictionary listings. At the Purdue COAST site, password listings are available in English, German, Italian, Swedish, Chinese, Japanese, and so on. Wordlists are also available by categories such as sports, cartoons, and places.

For crackers to make full use of the password crack program, the user listing must be obtained. In the UNIX environment, the fingers and rusers should be disabled to stop the outside world to obtain a password listing. Holes that leak user listings should be fixed. For instance, Kerberos 4 has a bug that allows the capture of user names. It turns out that on receiving a malformed User Datagram Protocol (UDP) packet, the Kerberos 4 server returns a packet containing an error string and the principle from some unsanitized data structures. A perfect example is the UDP packet containing a null. Because not as much data are handed in as it is expecting, the pointer to the reused structure references the unpurged principle information. These unsanitized data contain the name of the last user to request a Transaction Group Type (TGT) and the Kerberos realm name. Needless to say, this is all the information you need to then request a TGT for that user and dictionary to attack the response.

Organizations can help themselves from crackers by implementing security policy appropriate for the type of data being secured. An example of an electronic authentication guideline can be found in the NIST special publication 800-63. The guideline defines technical requirements for four levels of assurance in the areas of identity proofing, registration, tokens, authentication protocols, and related assertions.

Trojan Horse

As the name implies, Trojan horse is an unauthorized computer program within possibly an authorized computer program, which performs a function or series of functions unknown to the user. Internet Request for Comment 1244 defines Trojan horse as

> One of the ruses used by attackers to gain access to a system is by the insertion of a so-called Trojan horse program. A Trojan horse program can be a program that does something useful, or merely something interesting. It always does something unexpected, like steal passwords or copy files without your knowledge. Imagine a Trojan login program that prompts for username and password in the usual way, but also writes that information to a special file that the attacker can come back and read at will. Imagine a Trojan editor program that, despite the file permissions you have given your files, makes copies of everything in your directory space without you knowing about it (Holdbrook, P. and J. Reynolds).*

One hacker suggested a Trojan horse attack to gain passwords. The attacker sends garbage to a remote terminal while a user is logged on to the point that the user logs off. While the person remains logged off, the attacker runs a script to simulate the log-in screen. When the user attempts to log-in again, the script records the password and sends it to the attacker. The script then displays an error message before deleting itself.

Insiders who devise elaborate nondestructive programs to collect intelligence write the most dangerous Trojan horse–type computer programs. The discovery of such programs is mostly accidental. The infamous security tool, SATAN, fell victim to the attack. A programmer gained physical access to the computer that housed a Linux version of SATAN. The programmer modified the main ( ) function and altered an fping file so that when users ran SATAN, a special entry would be placed in the password file. The attacker hoped to compromise the servers that ran this utility. Owing to poor programming, the Trojan version could not handle systems that used password shadow files. Only two known servers were compromised.

A technique known as object reconciliation protects the system against Trojans. Objects within the system are compared against an earlier recorded time stamp (i.e., from system backup). If the time stamp changes, possible attacks may be staged. Another method is examining the file size. However, both techniques are extremely unreliable. Since time stamps can be easily changed, reconciliation is not a good technique. Comparing file size does not always work. The really devious programmers may carefully consider the date, time stamp, and file size to minimize discovery.

---

* Holdbrook, P. and J. Reynolds. *Site Security Handbook Request for Comment 1244.* July 1991. http://www.ietf.org/rfc/rfc1244.txt

One technique that works against file modification is digital fingerprinting. Algorithms, such as MD5, generate a digital signature of a file. MD5 belongs to a family of one-way hash functions called message digest algorithms. The algorithm produces a 128-bit fingerprint of the file. According to RFC 1321, producing the same key using different files is "infeasible."

Sniffers

Sniffers are devices that grab information traveling along a network. By placing network interfaces (i.e., ethernet adapter) into a promiscuous mode, a sniffer captures the network traffic. Normally, network devices listen only to their own traffic (nonpromiscuous) while ignoring others. When placed in the promiscuous mode, network devices listen to all traffics on the network. Information, such as IP datagrams, can be captured in this manner. A sniffer is nothing more than a hardware or software that hears all packets sent across the wire. Information captured is then stored and archived for later viewing. Virtually any machine in a network can be used as a sniffer.

For crackers, the strategic placement of sniffers is important. One of the best points to place a sniffer is anywhere adjacent to a computer that receives many passwords. Connections to other networks (i.e., Internet) are especially of interest because capturing authentication procedures between two networks allows the cracker to expand his or her activity.

Sniffers represent a high level of risk. The simple existence of an unauthorized sniffer in the network is a telltale sign that the network is already compromised. As early as February 1994, CHIPS advisory notices from Naval Computer and Telecommunications Area Master Station, LANT Advisory, issued this warning:

> An unidentified person installed a network sniffer on numerous hosts and backbone elements collecting over 100,000 valid user names and passwords via the Internet and Milnet. Any computer host allowing FTP, Telnet, or remote login to the system should be considered at risk.*

To defeat a sniffer attack, encryption is one of the best tools. By providing link encryption, information disclosed is minimized. Good network topology also helps. A network should be designed to trust other networks only if there is a reason. The design of the network should center on the trust relationships among the staff, not what the hardware needs.

Destructive Devices

There are two major types of destructive devices: harassment and data destruction. These tools are often readily available off the Internet. This availability means that anyone with a devious intent can launch an attack without much technical knowledge. Both large and small networks under the attack can come to a halt when enduring an e-mail attack. In general, these devices can be grouped into three major categories:

1. E-mail bombs and worms
2. Denial-of-service (DoS) tools
3. Viruses

---

* CHIPS advisory notices from Naval Computer and Telecommunications Area Master Station, LANT Advisory, February 1994.

E-Mail Bombs and Worms

The concept of the e-mail bomb is based on anonymous e-mail writing via port 25 on the Internet. Anyone running Windows can open a Telnet session from the DOS command prompt while logging on to any Internet service. Once logged on to port 25, any anonymous e-mail can be composed with falsified addresses (e-Hack or KwAnTAM_PoZeEtroN's Hacking Pages). The e-mail bomber simply automates the process.

The most famous e-mail bomber is Up Yours 3.0©. This application is freely distributed among hacking pages. The Up Yours mail-bombing program is extremely efficient with a friendly user interface. The features of the program include being able to specify times of day to start and stop as well as the number of messages with which it will hammer the victim. A variation of the e-mail bombing is list linking. List servers are e-mail servers on the Internet that distribute mail messages collected from various sources, usually for special interest groups. The attacker forges subscription to the list server using the victim's e-mail address. Tools, such as Kaboom, are a variation of the e-mail bomber that automates this process.

The most common way that the worm achieves this is by infecting the system's e-mail program and sending itself to everyone in the host system's e-mail address book. In August 2003, the Blaster worm penetrated a number of Windows support systems worldwide and created havoc among end users infested with strains of the virus. The MS Blaster worm is a piece of malicious software that unscrupulous persons place on other people's computers to gain unauthorized access to that computer. If a computer is infected, it can be used as part of a distributed DoS attack against a Website by flooding the site with requests for pages from that computer and others across the Internet. The worm exploits vulnerability in some versions of Microsoft's Windows operating system, including Windows NT, Windows 2000, and Windows XP. (It does not affect Win 95, 97, ME, or MacOS.)

Another example of a particularly effective worm was the Sircam worm, which infected many Windows systems. The Sircam worm had its own Simple Mail Transfer Protocol (SMTP) engine and would attach itself to a random document from the infected system and e-mail that document and itself to other systems. The Sircam worm also had a one-in-twenty chance of deleting files and folders in the C: drive of any system that was dated October 16 that were using the D/M/Y date format.

Denial-of-Service Attacks

The U.S. Air Force's CERT group defines DoS as "action(s), which prevent any part of AIS (Automated Information Service) from functioning in accordance with its intended purpose." This technique does not involve an intruder gaining access to the network. The DoS attack exploits holes in the protocol or operating system. The attacker simply invokes remote procedures that render a portion or the entire target inoperable.

Besides the current MS Blaster worm mentioned earlier, which can be used to launch DoS attacks, another famous case of DoS attacks occurred in February 2000 and affected many major companies. This DoS incident targeted many popular Websites such as Yahoo Inc., eBay Inc., Amazon.com Inc., CNN.com, Buy.com Inc., and e-Trade and resulted in huge damages for these companies. The total loss of money caused by the attack was estimated in excess of $1 billion. This figure was calculated based on the estimated revenue losses at the affected Websites ($100 million), market capitalization losses on the days of the attack ($1 billion), and the amount needed to be spent on security upgrades after the incident ($100–$200 million). The assaults were categorized as distributed DoS (DDoS) type in which the hackers used multiple compromised computer systems to launch their attacks. During the incident, the companies experienced slowdowns in services ranging from two hours and forty-five minutes to five hours. Besides money losses, these companies also suffered other consequences such as loss of consumer confidence, damaged public images, and loss of business opportunities.

Another example of DDoS is Operation Payback, coordinated by internet activists called themselves "Anonymous." Operation Payback started as retaliation to DDoS attacks on torrent sites; piracy proponents then decided to launch DDoS attacks on piracy opponents. The initial reaction snowballed into a wave of attacks on major pro-copyright and antipiracy organizations, law firms, and individuals. Following the U.S. diplomatic cables leak in December 2010, the organizers commenced DDoS attacks on Websites of banks who had stopped working with or giving donations to WikiLeaks. Organizations targeted include Amazon, PayPal, Bank of America, PostFinance, MasterCard, and Visa.

Viruses

Computer viruses are programs or scripts that can create files, move files, erase files, consume computer's memory, and cause computer not to function correctly. Some viruses can duplicate themselves, attach themselves to programs, and travel across networks. Opening an infected e-mail attachment is the most common way to get a virus. Some viruses inflict damages as soon as their code is executed; other viruses lie dormant until circumstances cause their code to be executed by the computer. Some viruses are benign or playful in intent and effect ("Happy Birthday, Ludwig!") and some can be quite harmful, erasing data or causing your hard disk to require reformatting. A virus that replicates itself by resending itself as an e-mail attachment or as part of a network message is known as a worm.

Viruses have become a major concern for many businesses because virus attacks result in a variety of devastating consequences for them. They can destroy valuable confidential information, cause productivity loss and operation disruptions, and bring about huge financial losses. Examples of virus/worm attacks include the following:

- The "Slammer" sent 55 million meaningless database server requests around the world. This attack knocked out Internet service, emergency 911 dispatchers, and business services around the globe. The worm took advantage of a buffer overflow and is estimated to have caused more than $1 billion in damages.
- The "SoBig.F" virus was the fastest spreading virus at that time. It brought down commuter and air traffic and shut down systems at many major companies. The sixth version of the SoBig virus was embedded in e-mail messages, which when opened would scan for other e-mail addresses to forward the message. Estimated damages worldwide were $14.62 billion.
- The Blaster worm exploited a vulnerability in versions of Microsoft Windows. The worm also attacked the Windows update Web page, preventing users from downloading the patch needed to secure Windows against the worm. The worm infected approximately 48,000 computers and caused $1.2 million in damages.

This area is a huge topic in itself and much has been written about it in a number of publications.

Exploiting the TCP/IP Holes

Like IP spoofing, DoS attacks exploit vulnerabilities in the TCP/IP. The UDP DoS attacks can be staged by anyone who is on the network. No authentication is necessary. The UDP DoS from one host can cause poor performance. If the attack is staged from a different host, both networks will experience heavy congestion. The attacker often exploits chargen and filter services. CERT made the following recommendations to avoid such attacks:

- Disable unnecessary UDP server. Chargen and filter are usually not used. Disable these two services. Use firewall instead.
- Use proxy gateway when using UDP. If UDP server must be used, proxy mechanism can protect the system from DoS attacks.
- Ensure the system is not subjected to IP spoofing. The UDP often follows after the initial break-in.

In 1996, a New York-based ISP called Public Access Networks Corporation (Panix.com) came under attack from the unknown. The method used is known as syn_flooder. The syn_flooder attack is a DoS technique that exploits the Three-Way Handshake Protocol in TCP/IP, as shown in Exhibit 24.2.

In three-way handshaking, the requesting machine sends a packet requesting connections. The target machine responds with an acknowledgment. The requesting machine then returns its own, as shown in Exhibit 24.3.

In the syn_flooder attack, the attacker sends a series of connection requests but fails to acknowledge the target's response. The target never receives an acknowledgment and waits for the answer. Eventually, the target's port becomes useless because the target is waiting for the response. The Panix.com attack in New York rendered the ISP out of service for more than a week.

The syn_flooder attack creates a high number of half-open connections. Because each connection opened must be processed, the system awaits the acknowledgment from the attacking machine. This is an inherent problem in the design of the TCP/IP suite. However, acceptable remedies are not available. Any system that is connected to a TCP/IP-based network (Internet or intranet) and offers TCP-based services is vulnerable to the syn_flood attack. The attack does not distinguish between

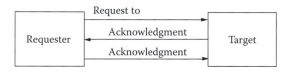

Exhibit 24.2 Three-part handshake.

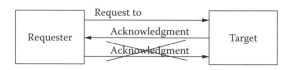

Exhibit 24.3 The sync_flooder attack.

operating systems, software version levels, or hardware platforms; all systems are vulnerable. CERT recommends packet filtering to protect the network against the syn_flood attack.

IP Spoofing

IP spoofing was made famous by Kevin Mitnick's 1996 Christmas break-in of UC San Diego. The technique is also known as the sequence number attacks. This technique was discovered in 1984 and not addressed until 1996. The IP spoofing attack exploits the three-way handshaking. As mentioned earlier, three-way handshaking requires both the requester and the server to acknowledge. On receiving the request, the host acknowledges by using a sequence number; the requester receives the information and sends back the acknowledgment with the sequence number. The sequence number is generated based on random sequence routine (see Exhibit 24.4).

The assumption here is that if the receiver sends a response back, the response is from a valid address. However, a flaw in the randomized algorithm and the restriction of the protocol allows the attacker to guess the sequence number. The attacker penetrates the system by guessing the sequence number of a valid node during the authentication process known as the three-way handshaking. If the guess is successful and no other authentication takes place, the attacker succeeds in the attack (see Exhibit 24.5).

Kerberos can address problems, such as IP spoofing. Authentication is performed using ticket-granting services. The node requesting the service must establish a session with the Kerberos server. The Kerberos server then sends an encrypted session key to the requesting node and a key to the ticket-granting server. The ticket-granting server then sends an encrypted copy of the session keys with a user ID. If the requesting node can decrypt the key with the password, then authentication is successful. Kerberos must authenticate each node requesting the service. In this situation, attackers cannot spoof the system by guessing authentication.

On July 21, 2003, EarthLink, FBI, and FTC made a joint presentation, which was televised by CSPAN, on the subject of Internet identity theft. They presented information on the Phisher site case they were currently prosecuting. The basics of the process are highlighted in the following:

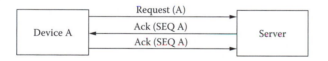

Exhibit 24.4   Sequence numbering in three-way handshaking.

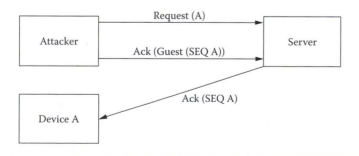

Exhibit 24.5   IP spoofing technique.

- Thief sends e-mail to customer claiming to be a legitimate company that has lost the customer's personal information
- Customer reads e-mail and goes to the fake Website
- Customer enters credit card or other personal information on the Website
- Thief steals personal information
- The individual had attempted to impersonate (spoof) Earthlink to gain information for identity fraud purposes

LAN Security Issues: Wired versus Wireless

Both the wired LAN and WLAN are subject to substantial security risks and issues. These include

- Threats to the physical security of the network
- Unauthorized access and eavesdropping
- Attacks from within the network's (authorized) user community

A WLAN has all of the properties of a wired LAN, and thus security measures taken to ensure the integrity and security of data in the wired-LAN environment are also applicable to WLANs as well. The only difference between a wired LAN and a WLAN is at the physical layer and super high frequency (SHF); all other network services and vulnerabilities remain. WLANs in fact include an additional set of unique security elements that are not available in the wired world, leading to the proposition that WLANs are actually more secure than their wired counterparts—an opinion that is shared by many industry analysts and experts.

Physical Security: Site Control and Management

Given the obvious reliance of wired LANs on a wired physical plant, anyone gaining access to that wire can damage the network or compromise the integrity and security of information on it; therefore, physical access to network wires needs to be protected. However, the vast amount of wire inherent in most LANs provides many points for unauthorized access.

User Authentication

One of the great concerns of LAN technology relating to user authentication is access. Remote access products that allow traveling sales and marketing people to connect to their e-mail, remote offices connected via dial-up lines, intranets, and extranets that connect vendors and customers to a network can all leave the network vulnerable to hackers, viruses, and other intruders. Firewall products offering packet filtering, proxy servers, and user-to-session filtering add additional protection, but hackers seem to get smarter all the time.

Eavesdropping Countermeasures

The most difficult threat to detect is someone just looking at and likely copying raw data on the LAN. Inexpensive and readily available programs let anyone with physical access to the network to read, capture, and display any type of packet data on the Net, especially when the network administrator does not have some kind of "packet sniffer" or LAN-traffic analyzer for troubleshooting the network. Additionally, even wired LANs have an unintended wireless component.

Many types of LAN cabling, particularly the unshielded twisted pair, radiate significant energy. This leads to the possibility that anyone can sit in the parking lot outside a building and actually intercept wired ethernet data packets without detection. Data encryption is the only line of defense against this kind of threat. Unfortunately, a sense of complacency among network managers has resulted in the limited use of in-building encryption, often with unforeseen and unknown results.

Why WLANs Are More Secure

As can be seen from the above discussion, data security considerations impact the entire network architecture and also apply equally to WLANs. In addition to this, the various standards in place and the many professionals across the world working on improving the IEEE standards give hope to improved security measures being developed now. The very different physical layer of WLANs actually increases the overall network security as discussed below.

Spread-Spectrum Technology

Most WLANs use spread-spectrum radio transmission techniques. Spread-spectrum technology was first introduced about 80 years ago by the military for improving both message integrity and security. Spread-spectrum systems are designed to be resistant to noise, interference, jamming, and unauthorized detection. Spread-spectrum transmitters send their signals out over a broad range of frequencies at very low power, in contrast to narrowband radios that concentrate all of their power into a single frequency. There are two common ways to implement spread-spectrum transmission: they are direct sequence (DS) and frequency hopping (FH). Then, we should know the basics in the DS and FH transmission module, which makes it extremely difficult for an eavesdropper to obtain the data being transmitted in the air. In the case of DS, an eavesdropper must know the chipping code. Someone trying to intercept an FH transmission must know the hopping pattern. In both cases, the specific frequency band and modulation techniques in use must also be known. Radio systems also use a form of data scrambling for purely technical reasons, which is to assist in managing the timing and decoding of radio signals. An unintended receiver would also need to know this scrambling pattern. In addition to the secure features embedded in DS and FH techniques, they also allow the use of encryption. Indeed, many WLAN products include encryption features as a standard or optional component. The IEEE 802.11 standard, for example, includes a security technique known as wired equivalent privacy (WEP), which is based on the use of 64-bit keys and the popular RC4 encryption algorithm. Other emerging developments, such as the possibility of including better encryption capability and key management techniques, are being developed under new IEEE initiatives.

Station Authentication

Most WLAN products have the ability, as an authentication management function, to specifically authorize or exclude individual wireless station. Thus, an individual wireless user can be either included in the network or locked out. More importantly, users need to know a wide variety of information, including radio domains, channels (specific frequencies or hopping patterns), sub-channels, security IDs, and passwords. Other information, such as in-building roaming, also needs to be known. Combining all of the above-mentioned aspects, the network administrators can make unauthorized network access extremely difficult for hackers even when they possess the specific wireless equipment being used at a given site.

Physical Security

Compared to the wired LANs, which have a significant amount of wire being exposed to the outsiders, the WLANs eliminate the possible mass physical contact points. Although WLANs usually involve the use of a wired backbone network for access-point interconnection, the amount of wire is quite small, and extra steps can be taken to safeguard its physical integrity without inordinate cost. Moreover, because the access points used in WLANs function as bridges, individual wireless users are isolated from the majority of LAN traffic, again limiting user access to raw network packets.

Network Management Control Issues

Perhaps the most vulnerable area for organizations to review is the structure of network management within IT operations. In August 2003, the northeast area of the United States up through Canada experienced a massive electrical outage that hampered many IT facilities. Cell stations used for transfer of wireless communications had no power. Also, a 22-hour outage of a major AT&T frame relay is a reason enough for executives to ask if it could happen to them and the potential losses incurred as a result of one procedural error and two software routines not working as planned. Where were the network management controls in place to quickly identify and resolve the problem?

The question is that after the network has been designed and implemented, will it be manageable in terms of the ability to respond and recover from any possible interruption of quality service? Challenging as network management is for today's enterprises, it could be even more challenging for virtual organizations. First, network expectations will be higher, involving both wired and wireless topologies. Although telecommunications networks can be a source of competitive advantage to many firms in the twenty-first century, they will be mission-critical to virtual organizations. Next, network management will be a complex problem in virtual organizations. As stated earlier, network managers face a variety of interconnectivity, integration, policy setting, control and coordination, and security issues in their enterprise networks. Network managers in virtual organizations will face the same problems, but in a more challenging multienterprise network context. Lastly, the network management environment in virtual organizations will be much more dynamic than it is in today's companies. Because the virtual corporation's business requirements and organizational structure will be changing constantly, the telecommunications network that supports them will be in a continual state of flux.

In some respects, however, managing telecommunications networks in virtual organizations could be less challenging. Network management systems are improving and a really effective integrated system could be available. In addition, telecommunications are likely to have greater senior management support in virtual organizations than in many conventional organizations because the virtual organizations depend so critically on telecommunications for their success. Also, given the heavy emphasis that virtual organizations place on the need for compatibility and complementary capabilities among venture partners, venture partners are likely to have compatible networks and complementary telecommunications capabilities. Venturing with partners whose telecommunications platforms, policies, and organizations are compatible would reduce the interconnectivity problem immensely. Similarly, an organization possessing experience in designing and managing telecommunications networks would fit well in a partnership with organizations lacking such capabilities. The final reason that the network management job could be less challenging in virtual organizations is that the structure of the telecommunications organization and the caliber of its personnel will be ideally suited for the dynamic and complex environment of telecommunications.

Development of a national information infrastructure policy and assurances that it addresses the global information infrastructure are ways in which the CEO and CIO can strategically plan for the coming of the virtual enterprise. The organizational philosophy of the virtual corporation, the telecommunications organization, will be lean, close to the users, and opportunistic, making it exceedingly adaptable to change. Knowledgeable, trained, empowered, team-oriented personnel, enabling it to respond quickly and surely to problems as they arise, will staff this function.

Recommendation to IT Auditors, Security, and IT Professionals

Hacking is simple: hackers exploit security holes. The security administrator should look for these holes in four major areas:

1. *Physical security holes.* Giving unauthorized persons physical access to the system causes potential problems. Flaws in hardware may give way to the break-in.
2. *Software security holes.* These are flaws in operating systems and protocols (i.e., TCP/IP) that allow the breach of security.
3. *Incompatible systems.* These occur when systems are not compatible, causing inferior setup of security configuration.
4. *Lack of security.* Absence of security and weak security policies allow hackers to break into the system. One hacker noted that default passwords in hardware, such as routers, are often not changed.

Security administrators should constantly check for these types of flaws. The following are some recommendations:

- Regularly check for security advisories, such as CERT advisories, NIST Special Publications, and vendor advisories.
- Review security policies on a regular basis.
- Report security breaks to authorities and organizations, such as CERT. This helps other security administrators to prevent the same type of attack.
- Conduct security audit on a regular basis. This will uncover security weaknesses.
- Check for hacking sites to gain a better understanding on hacking methods.
- Think like a hacker. Look for security holes. Apply methods such as password crackers and tools, such as SATAN, to uncover security holes.

Hackers are here to stay. Regardless of how they see themselves in the society, hackers are a threat to the information asset. With the fast-changing world of IT, security administration should be an active process. As security holes are fixed, new ones are being implemented. In a very unusual way, hackers help the development of security measures. However, good tools are only good when the administrator uses them.

Intranet/Extranet Security

The responsibility for network security and intranet/extranet security is a task of the network administrator, and has to do with ensuring not only that authorized persons use the network but also that they use it in authorized ways. Intranet security includes making the network hardware, software, and data available whenever the authorized users need it.

Based on the current trends explained in the previous sections, most major organizations are already providing Internet access from each employee's PC or workstation. Most of the Internet access is gained from the corporate LAN, which raises some security concerns. But with employees being on the move, the uses of their mobile devices now provide communication linkage with the corporate office. This can be wired or wireless in communication form. The major concern is that the Internet was developed for interoperability and communication, not for impenetrability. Therefore, connecting the corporate intranet to the outside world will bring a whole new set of potential problems. Organizations must define clearly the security policies to protect their information. However, before establishing policies, it is important to understand the risks or problems that can attack a company's intranet or network. Internal problems are the most common. This is when a disgruntled employee breaks the network to get confidential information from the company.

The security policy that a corporation puts into place depends on the degree of security desired on its network system. This degree may range from full restriction to complete public access. This should be a top priority in any organization. Management will be extremely concerned about how security is implemented and administered. There are four major areas in need of protection. The first is the corporate information traveling over intranets and should have the greatest protection. The next area is the extranet applications, which connect corporate users with their suppliers or vendors. This information has to cross two security areas. The third area is the Website. Here, information traveling to and from the corporate center needs to pass four security areas and has to meet the access requirements of each area. The last area is the mode of access, wired or wireless. Each has special considerations and levels of protection, which needs to be implemented, tested, maintained, and monitored.

Technology Tactics Used to Protect Networks

Firewalls. These are protective software and hardware that block unwanted users and activities from the intranet. The firewall sits between the private local network and the Internet, and all the traffic from one to the other must flow through the firewall. There are several firewall categories, which are application gateways, packet-filtering systems, and circuit-level gateways. Firewalls are not only most often found in the form of stand-alone hardware devices, but can also be entirely built into a piece of software that is loaded on the gateway server in a company's network. It also allows user authentication and traffic information log and report generation. A firewall can be used as the main mechanism of a company's security policy or plan. However, there are some shortcomings in using firewalls. The cost and performance trade-offs protecting Internet firewalls may not be practical for high-traffic intranets because many firewalls impose severe performance penalties. On a network infrastructure, a traffic cop versus a roadblock approach is needed. Try to allow the traffic to flow, but be in a monitoring and execution position to shut it down if something bad happens.

Proxy servers (PS). PS is a program that handles traffic to external host systems on behalf of client software running on the protected network; this means that users of the intranet can access the Internet through the firewall. PS hide the true address of the client workstation.

Encryption. This is the process of encoding information in a special way so that it is secure from unauthorized access; the reverse process is called decryption. Encryption allows the communication to be secure over an unsecured communication channel. Secure Web servers use public key encryption techniques for different purposes such as user authentication, encryption, and digital certificates. To set up a secure server, first a digital certificate must be obtained. This depends on the server the company is using; for example, Microsoft and Netscape servers use VeriSign as the certifying authority. Once the certificate and the encryption keys are obtained, the SSL can be used to add security to the intranet as well as secure HTTP to make sure that all the company's documents and forms are fully encrypted.

Auditing systems (AS). These systems record and track events that occur in the organization's network. They help to discover a potential intruder before the intruder succeeds. It is indispensable that all corporate networks have a good AS in place.

Access control. This is the capability to control who accesses what on the network. It is related to user authentication whether local or remote. Security experts talk about three factors for authentication:

- What you know (username and password)
- What you have (a security key of some sort)
- Who you are (a fingerprint, signature verification, or retinal scan—physical authentication)

Most likely, the third option (physical authentication) is the best, but it is a very expensive solution to implement in most organizations. The most widely accepted way of making sure who is logging into a network is a combination of the first two options, also known as two-factor authentication. Requiring a digital signature, like the one provided by VeriSign Inc., in addition to username and password, provides some additional assurances. This type of key is being used largely for securing e-commerce and e-mail transmissions, but can also be used to verify intranet access rights. Yet, somebody could gain unauthorized access to the computer where the authentication key is stored. Therefore, a network log-in, in addition to the authentication provided, is a better choice. However, with more than 10 million people communicating with the office and wanting access to the corporate intranet, the authentication key needs to be a moving target. Several companies have developed and manufactured devices that can be embedded in a PC, PDA, or notebook that looks like a credit card or keychain and generates a new mathematical key every 60 s according to a formula that the company's security server recognizes (see Exhibit 24.6). By integrating a security service of this sort with the firewall, dial-up access and applications security are greatly improved.

Internet security products must be implemented at multiple levels within an organization. Corporation security policies should include continuous monitoring at each security layer. Although many companies have implemented firewalls, virus protection, and user authentication technologies for the Internet, other technology and techniques are being used in combination with other security measures on the intranet (see Exhibit 24.7). There has been additional development in authentication technologies, such as digital certificates, single sign-on, tunneling, VPNs, and key recovery systems.

Network Security Products

There are plenty of security applications available. What is selected depends on the company's security needs and what the vendor's product offers.

RSA SecurID SID800

Blackberry with
RSA SecurID software taken

Exhibit 24.6   Example of security tokens.

Technology/Technique
Authentication for users
Authentication for messages
Authentication for servers
Business contingency plan
Digital certificates
Disaster recovery plan
Encryption
Firewalls
Key recovery or escrow
Risk assessment/management
Single sign-on
Tunneling
Virtual private connections
Virus protection

Exhibit 24.7   Types of common Internet security technology and techniques.

Over the years, we have seen software security vendors pursuing partnership opportunities with server hardware and software manufacturers because customers in general do not perceive security as a separate product. The need for external access has driven the increased adoption of security products and the percentage of companies gaining access to the Internet.

There are also available tools that a network administrator can use to test the effectiveness of the security established at their companies. These tools can actually do little to catch any outsiders, but what they can do is highlight the security weaknesses in a company's network. The first one is SATAN for UNIX systems. SATAN collects data from each host in the specified network and creates reports for each host by type, service, vulnerability, and trust relationship. SATAN is free and available on the Internet, and for this reason many critics have argued that SATAN lets potential intruders take advantage of the information it contains to learn how to infiltrate systems more effectively. There are several packages available that run on the Windows environment. Some of the basic features of most packages are

Account restrictions. Evaluates password controls, use of log-on scripts, and password-expiration dates

Password strength. Rates password policies

Access control. Checks user rights and removable-drive allocations

System monitoring. Collects a set of security-related concerns

Data integrity. Checks uninterruptible power supply (UPS) installation and configuration

Data confidentiality. Tests to see if passwords are stored in cleartext or in encrypted form

Wireless Technology

Wireless technologies have become more popular in our everyday business and personal lives. New technologies, such as iPhone, iPad, and smartphones, allow individuals to access calendars, e-mail, phone number lists, and the Internet. Others offer capabilities that can pinpoint the location of the device anywhere in the world, such as global positioning system (GPS). Wireless technology enables devices to communicate without physical connections and utilizes radio frequency transmissions as a way to transmit data, whereas the traditional wired technology uses cables. Wireless networks serve as the means of transport between devices and among devices and wired networks such as the Internet. It is categorized into three groups based on the coverage range. They are wireless wide area networks (WWANs), WLANs, and wireless personal area networks (WPANs).

Several groups of computer security specialists have discovered security problems that let malicious users compromise the security of IEEE 802.11 WLAN's standard, such as passive attacks, to decrypt traffic, and trick the access point. Active attacks inject new traffic from unauthorized mobile stations to decrypt traffic. Also, there are well-known security vulnerabilities, including the use of static keys, where users in a wireless network share identical keys for long periods of time. If a computer, such as a laptop, were to be lost or stolen, the key could become compromised along with all the other computers sharing that key.

WEP is a weak security algorithm, intended to provide data confidentiality comparable to that of a traditional wired network. It was used for IEEE 802.11a and b wireless products. Wi-Fi Protected Access (WPA) encryption allows protection for data that are transmitted over a wireless network. WEP and WPA offer different levels of security for wireless communication. WPA is considered to be more secure than WEP because it uses dynamic key encryption. To protect the information as it passes over the airwaves, the highest level of encryption that is supported by your network equipment should be used.

WPA2 is the second generation of WPA. WPA2 was not formed to address any limitations in WPA, and is backward compatible with products that support WPA. The main difference between the original WPA and WPA2 is that WPA2 requires Advanced Encryption Standard (AES) for encryption of data, whereas the original WPA uses TKIP. AES provides enough security to meet the high-level standards of many federal government agencies.

For Wireless: Key Audit and Security Checkpoints

Indeed, many WLAN products include encryption features as a standard or optional component. The IEEE 802.11i standard, for example, includes security techniques known as WPA and WPA2, which is based on the use of 128-bit keys and a 48-bit initialization vector (IV). From March 2006, WPA2 certification is mandatory for all new devices wishing to be Wi-Fi certified.

IEEE 802.11i Robust Security Network Standard

The IEEE 802.11i data protocols provide confidentiality, data origin authenticity, and replay protection. This standard enables WLANs to be trusted within the architecture and infrastructure. It provides native per-user access control, strong authentication capability (e.g., smart badges, certificates, and token cards), and strong native encryption. This technology must be strategically incorporated into the organizational infrastructure and coexist with the corporation infrastructure strategies. These protocols require a fresh key on every session. The key management capability delivers keys used as authorization tokens, providing channel access is authorized. The architecture requires the key to the authentication process.

Identity Theft

Online identity theft is another major concern in e-commerce security. Striking millions of people every year, identity theft is carried out when someone uses another person's name or personal information (such as a credit card) in a fraudulent manner and without the other's consent. Such action can be carried out on purchasing products, taking out loans, accessing bank accounts, and much more. The most common way personal information is stolen is through stealing business records, but other ways such as "dumpster diving" or stealing information found in the trash, stealing mail, and simply snatching someone's wallet or purse have been exploited as ways to gain private information.

According to CyberSource survey, online revenue lost due to fraud is estimated at 2.7 billion in 2010, up from $1.5 billion in 2000, but down from $4 billion in 2008. There are various ethical, legal, and business issues, and each requires businesses to conduct specific levels of privacy protection while at the same time track changes to a consumer's personal information. One such tactic popular among businesses is to publicly declare their privacy policy. This is a way of assuring customers that their information is safe, and it also lets them know how the company will utilize their information. To be effective, these policies must be consistent throughout the company to ensure data integrity when it is being transmitted. The primary goal of the security is to provide access to specific information for those who request it and at the same time make sure that it only allows and ensures that the people who receive the information are the people who have the right level of access.

To encourage Internet growth and participation, a number of government and private organizations are trying to track and fight electronic crimes. However, because many businesses are reluctant to provide law enforcement officials with sufficient information to pursue possible criminals, legal action over Internet concerns have been limited. FBI officials believe companies "often fear that they will lose business if security breaches become public or that they will become the target of revenge attacks."

Regardless of advancements in security and encryption, consumer fears continue to hurt the ability of companies to conduct transactions and documentation via the Internet. According to the U.S. Federal Trade Commission, it received 250,854 complaints about identity theft during 2010—nearly one-fifth of the entire number of complaints received by the agency. For the eleventh year in succession, it was the subject most consumers complained about.

Conclusions

Internet security has had significant impacts on businesses worldwide. The emergence of new and more dangerous types of attacks from cyber-criminals continues to pose big challenges for businesses and security professionals. Cyber-attacks have caused huge monetary losses and other devastating damages to many companies.

Cyber-threats continue to present big challenges for businesses and security professionals. More sophisticated methods of attacks have become more common. The intruders have shown that they are moving from exploiting well-known vulnerabilities to exploring the weaknesses in software programs to launch the attacks.

Wireless networks have become more and more common. However, the wireless technology used in these networks, Wi-Fi, still has some serious security weaknesses. There are still many wireless networks so open or unprotected that confidential information from those can be easily intercepted and stolen. Many of these networks belong to major companies and to other organizations with significant investments in security their information systems.

The security professionals and IT auditor must understand that they play a very important role in battling cyber-crimes. Despite facing many difficulties that seem very frustrating and discouraging, these IT professionals must always try to overcome them, fully utilize their knowledge and talents, and do their best to fight security intrusion.

The risks from cyber-threats can be prevented or significantly minimized only when all involved parties, including the governments, understand and realize the potential dangers caused by cyber-criminals, fully cooperate, and do their best to fight against these hard-to-beat law breakers.

Review Questions

1. What are some of the major technology tactics used to protect networks?
2. What is CERT? Where is the CERT coordination center? What is FedCIRC?
3. What are scanners? What are password crackers? What are Trojan horses?
4. What are sniffers? And how can perpetrators use them?
5. What is DoS? Give an example.

6. Does TCP/IP have security holes? How can systems be protected?
7. What is a syn_flood attack?
8. What is IP spoofing?
9. What is hacking? In what four major areas are there security holes?
10. After reading this chapter, what is your opinion of today's state of IS security and privacy?

Multiple-Choice Questions

1. Which is the major attacking tool used by hackers?
   a. Scanners
   b. Trojan horses
   c. Sniffers
   d. All of the above
2. Destructive devices are
   a. E-mail bombs and worms
   b. Viruses
   c. DoS tools
   d. All of the above
3. IP spoofing is
   a. An e-mail bomb
   b. Where the attacker impersonates a value site for purposes of gaining information that may be used in identity fraud
   c. A virus
   d. None of the above
4. Which are technology tactics used to protect networks?
   a. Firewalls
   b. Proxy servers
   c. Auditing systems
   d. All of the above
5. One of the fastest-growing crimes on the Internet reported by the FTC and GAO is
   a. IP spoofing
   b. DoS
   c. Identity fraud
   d. None of the above
6. SATAN is
   a. A report-generation tool
   b. A computer language
   c. A security administrator tool for analyzing UNIX networks
   d. None of the above
7. If not protected, a WLAN can be vulnerable to
   a. Active attacks such as injecting new traffic from unauthorized mobile stations to decrypt traffic
   b. Passive attacks to decrypt traffic and trick the access point
   c. Rogue access points
   d. All of the above

8. WLANs are actually more secure than their wired counterparts because of
   a. Threats to the physical security of network
   b. A WLAN having all of the properties of a wired LAN
   c. An additional set of unique security elements
   d. Unauthorized access and eavesdropping
9. WPA and WPA2 are based on the use of
   a. 32-bit keys
   b. 64-bit keys
   c. 128-bit keys
   d. 256-bit keys
10. Which of the following is not true about the IEEE 802.11i data protocol?
   a. The protocol requires a fresh key every month
   b. The key management capability provides channel access as needed
   c. The architecture requires the key to the authentication process
   d. The protocol requires a 256-bit key

Exercises

1. List 10 GAO reports in the past 2 years that have identified information security weaknesses in federal agencies (www.gao.gov).
2. Using a Web browser, search for the term "CERT." List and describe what is available at five Websites.
3. Universities worldwide have done important research in the areas of computer security and privacy. Using the Internet, identify five that have done research or faculty who have published on this topic.

Answers to Multiple-Choice Questions

1—a; 2—d; 3—b; 4—d; 5—c; 6—c; 7—d; 8—c; 9—c; 10—c

Further Reading

1. 2011 CyberSecuirty Watch Survey: How Bad Is the Insider Threat? CSO Magazine, U.S. Secret Service, Software Engineering Institute CERT Program at Carnegie Mellon University and Deloitte, January 2011.
2. Agarwal, D., *The Need for and Implementation of Audit Trails*, ISACA, 2006.
3. Ashley, M., A network is threatened by its own endpoints, ISACA, *JournalOnline*, 2005.
4. Axelrod, W., Cybersecurity and the critical infrastructure: Looking beyond the perimeter, ISACA, *JournalOnline*, 2006.
5. Biggs, M., Invasion of the data snatchers, ComputerUser.com, May 2003, p. 24.
6. Birdi, T. and K. Jansen, Network intrusion detection: Know what you do (not) need, ISACA, *JournalOnline*, 2005.
7. Burr, B., T. Polk, and D. Dodson, NIST: Electronic Authentication Guideline, NIST Special Publication 800-63, April 2006.
8. Cilli, C., Identity theft: A new frontier for hackers and cybercrime, *ISACA*, 6, 39–42, 2005.

9. Cohen, G., The role of attack simulation in automating security risk management, *ISACA*, 1, 51–54, 2005.

10. CSPAN, Internet Identity Theft, Joint presentation by Earthlink, FBI, and FTC, 7/21/03.

11. Cerullo, M. and V. Cerullo, Threat assessment and security measures justification for advanced IT networks, *ISACA*, 1, 35–43, 2005.

12. Ferrera, G.R., M.E.K. Reder, R.C. Bird, J.J. Darrow, J.M. Aresty, J. Klosek, and S.D. Lichtenstein, *CyberLaw: Text and Cases*, 3rd Edition, Thomson/South-Western West, Cincinnati, OH, 2011.

13. Ford, W. and M.S. Baum, *Secure Electronic Commerce*, Prentice-Hall PTR, Englewood Cliffs, NJ, 2001.

14. Gallegos, F., *Security and Control over Intranets and Extranets: Part 1*, #75-10-35, Auerbach Publishers, Boca Raton, FL, 2002, pp. 1–12.

15. Gallegos, F., *Security and Control over Intranets and Extranets: Part 2*, #75-10-36, Auerbach Publishers, Boca Raton, FL, 2002, pp. 1–20.

16. Huang, S., Survivability strategies for the next generation network, ISACA, *JournalOnline*, 2006.

17. Hunter, J.M.D., *An Information Security Handbook*, Springer, New York, 2001.

18. Jasper, M.C., *Identity Theft and How to Protect Yourself*, Oceana Publications, New York, 2002.

19. McCarthy, L., *IT Security: Risking the Corporation*, Prentice-Hall PTR/Sun Microsystems Press, New Jersey, 2003.

20. Nachenberg, C., Generic exploit blocking: Prevention, not cure, ISACA, *JournalOnline*, 2005.

21. Olsen, G., Secure your Web services, *Net Magazine*, March 2003, p. 41.

22. Ross, S., Converging need, diverging response, ISACA, *JournalOnline*, 2006.

23. Saddat, M., *Network Security Principles and Practices*, Cisco Press, Indianapolis, IN, 2002, pp. 5–12.

24. Singleton, T., What every IT auditor should know about identity theft, ISACA, *JournalOnline*, 2006.

25. Synovate, *Federal Trade Commission—2006 Identity Theft Survey Report*, November 2007.

26. Tryfonals, T., P. Thomas, and P. Owen, ID theft: Fraudster techniques for personal data collection, the related digital evidence and investigation issues, ISACA, *JournalOnline*, 2006.

27. Tyson, J., How firewalls work, how stuff works, April 2003, http://computer.howstuffworks.com/firewall.htm/printable.

28. United States Government Accountability Office, Testimony before Congressional Subcommittees on Information Security, February 14, 2008.

29. United States Government Accountability Office, *Report to Congressional Requesters on Personal Information*, June 2007.

Internet References

1. Bradley, T., What is a Firewall? What you need to know about, April 13, 2003, http://netsecurity.about.com/library/weekly/aa030503b.htm.

2. Boutin, P., Slammed! *Wired Magazine*, July 2003, http://www.wired.com/wired/archive/11.07/slammer.html.

3. CERT, 2000–2003, Number of incidents reported, CERT/CC statistics 1988–2003, April 29, 2003, http://www.cert.org/stats/cert_stats.html.

4. Clyde, R., Exposing the future of Internet security, May 2003, http://www.extremetech.com/print_article/0,3998,a=39857,00.asp.

5. Costello, S., Internet attacks up 28 percent in 2002, *InfoWorld*, July 8, 2002; April 27, 2003, http://archive.infoworld.com/articles/hn/xml/02/07/08/020708hnriptech.xml.

6. McClearn, M., Firms wage war on industrial espionage, January 18, 1999; April 29, 2003, http://www.landfield.com/isn/mail-archive/1999/Jan/0083.html.

7. Mulpuru, S., US Online Retail, Forrester Research, Inc., March 13, 2007, http://www.forrester.com/Research/Document/Excerpt/0,7211,41752,00.html.

8. Mulpuru, S., US eCommerce: Five-Year Forecast and Data Overview, Forrester Research, Inc., October 12, 2006, http://www.forrester.com/Research/Document/Excerpt/0,7211,41752,00.html.

9. Ouellet, E. and R. McMillan, August 2010, http://www.gartner.com/technology/streamReprints. do?id=1-16XQWWD&ct=110810&st=sb.
10. Strickland, J., 10 Worst computer viruses of all time. HowStuffWorks.com, August 26, 2008, http:// computer.howstuffworks.com/worst-computer-viruses.htm.
11. Symantec Enterprise Solutions 2000, A comprehensive risk management guide, accessed October 15, 2002, http://enterprisesecurity.Symantec.com.
12. Testimony—FTC by Charles Harwood Deputy Dir FTC 7/26/2011, http://www.ftc.gov/os/testimony/ 110714internetprivacytestimony.pdf.
13. Tyson, J., How encryption works, how stuff works, May 7, 2003, http://computer.howstuffworks.com/ encryption.htm/printable.
14. Unknown, Visa USA pledges $20 million in incentives to protect cardholder data, Visa Inc. Press Release, San Francisco, December 12, 2006, http://corporate.visa.com/md/nr/press667.jsp.
15. Unknown, SoBig.F breaks virus speed records, CNN.com, August 22, 2003, http://www.cnn.com/ 2003/TECH/internet/08/21/sobig.virus/index.html.
16. Unknown, Sobig virus damage breaks world record, Help Net Security, August 30, 2003, http://www. net-security.org/secworld.php?id=1635.
17. Unknown, Blaster worm exploits Microsoft security hole and targets critical update Website, Sophos, August 12, 2003, http://www.sophos.com/pressoffice/news/articles/2003/08/va_blaster.html.
18. Unknown, W32.Sircam.Worm@mm, January 22, 2003; April 29, 2003, http://www.symantec.com/ security_response/writelip.jsp?docid=2001-071720-1640-99.
19. Unknown, Lawyers disagree over Blaster virus author sentencing, Sophos, January 26, 2005, http:// www.sophos.com/pressoffice/news/articles/2005/01/va_parson3.html.
20. Unknown, Cyber-Crime bleeds U.S. Corporations, Survey Shows; Financial Losses from Attacks Climb for Third Year in a Row, May 2003, http://www.gocsi.com/press/20020407.jhtml; jsessioni d=1MSCNTT5U4NWGQSNDLOSKH0CJUNN2JVN?_requestid=538392.
21. Unknown, What is Kerberos? October 2002, http://Web.mit.edu/kerberos/www/#what_is.
22. Unknown, The national strategy to secure cyberspace, May 2003, http://www.whitehouse.gov/pcipb/ cyberspace_strategy.pdf.
23. Unknown, Wi-Fi protected access, Wikipedia, March 2008, http://en.wikipedia.org/wiki/Wi-Fi_ Protected_Access.

Chapter 25

Virtual Application Security and Risks

E-commerce has become a way of life for many organizations and provided many benefits for individuals and organizations. e-commerce has continued to grow at ever-increasing rates. Forrester Research reported that e-commerce has grown to nearly $200 billion in 2010, up from less than $50 billion in 2002, and is expected to continue growing to nearly $300 billion by 2015. However, e-commerce is not without risk. This chapter discusses the security and risks associated with doing business on the Internet and controls that help mitigate these security and risks. This chapter addresses the security and risks associated with Web applications, transmitting confidential information over the Internet, practical security solutions, and changing business processes associated with e-commerce.

E-Commerce Application Security as a Strategic and Structural Problem

An effective security management system should be made an integral part of an organization's business strategy. The development and management of security should support the core business of the organization. Security management, therefore, consists of guidelines that are based on the security practices, which support the business strategy as a whole. These guidelines form the basic security policy to develop an information security management system. They are then monitored to assess their vulnerability to attack and misuse. The result is assurance that data confidentiality, integrity, and availability both inside and outside the organization are properly guarded.

In e-commerce businesses, information security should be seen as a strategic asset and not as a cost. The increase in a company's e-commerce investment will automatically decrease the system's vulnerability to attack; lack of security management measures and policies will result in a greater cost.

Information Security Management Systems

Information security management consists of an infrastructure and a set of procedures to provide assurance that confidentiality, integrity, and availability of data are maintained. Defining such a system is a very complicated task. Not only does the technology have to be secure but the surrounding security environment also has to be mature (see Chapters 20 and 24).

The complex nature of e-commerce companies' IT systems means that they are always at risk if they do not monitor internal and external security trends at all times. Financial damage caused by lack of security management can be very serious (e.g., denial of service, access to confidential information). Thus, e-commerce companies must implement security management system that is well designed and managed. The following steps need to be taken to identify and document the technical and organizational controls and their objectives:

Policy and procedures. Define IT security policy and procedures.

Scope. Define scope of Information Security Management Systems (ISMS). The environments should be defined in terms of an organization's characteristics, resources, technology, and location.

Risk assessment. Identify dangers to resources, vulnerabilities, and impacts on the organization, and determine the degree of risk.

Risk areas. Identify the risk areas to be managed based on the company's information security policy and the degree of protection required.

Controls. Apply necessary and appropriate controls for implementation by the company and justify their selection.

Documentation. Prepare documentation of the chosen technical and organizational measures/controls, their objectives, and the reasons for choosing them.

Planning and Control Approach to E-Commerce Security Management

The corporate approach to high-level security management involves different aspects within the organization. These planning and control areas are strategic, organizational, technical, financial, and legal. Each of these aspects involves specific activities, which will be discussed in the following paragraphs.

Strategic Aspect

Once the organization has realized and accepted security as of strategic value, the approach to security begins with analyzing the strategic aspect. The strategic aspect involves the following activities:

Planning corporate objectives. Define the company's e-commerce objectives clearly. This would help to form an effective security plan and give an adequate level of security for the e-commerce initiatives.

Defining budgets. Define budgets according to the required security to meet agreed-upon objectives.

Defining information security policy. Develop a policy that includes the corporate e-commerce objectives, actions, and methods required to protect the information and make every employee in the company aware of this policy.

Organizational Aspect

The next aspect involves developing and implementing organizational measures to support the security-related infrastructure. The organizational aspect involves the following activities:

Setting up a security team of managers and technical personnel. Assign responsibility for the development, management, and maintenance of the information security and corporate structure.

Defining responsibility. Specify responsibilities for each member of the security team and everyone with operational involvement in e-commerce.

Drawing up training programs in technology and methods. Train all staff in security-related issues and the use of the security systems. Make sure all the staff has access to security information, policies, and technical documentation. Update staff responsible for systems and network security through classes and conferences on the latest technology in security.

Documenting information security procedures. Document in detail all organizational procedures required to implement the security policy. Describe methods of doing every task, such as analyzing and managing information risk, physical security of hardware/software resources, software management, antivirus controls, backup, disaster recovery, secure use of IS, secure use of the Internet, secure use of e-mail, operating systems (OS) security, Web server security, and incident management.

Application of security procedures. Distribute security policies and procedures within the organization in the form of documentation, tools, and methods.

Compliance with security procedures. Conduct periodic audits to assess the adequacy of the policies and compliance. This will help the company to ensure that the systems continued to be adequately secured and the written policies and procedures still address the appropriate security needs.

Technical Aspect

Once the organizational aspect has been created, an appropriate technology infrastructure can be developed, which provides both physical and logical security for IT, as follows:

Firewall. It is a must for an e-commerce company to use firewall to protect the company's local networks against outside attacks.

Access control. The organization also needs to establish an access control system to information.

Authentication. Access authentication systems need to be established and implemented using technology according to the security classification assigned to data, systems, and networks.

Cryptography. The right cryptographic method needs to be chosen to protect transmitted information whether it is internal or external. This access must be secure both locally and remotely.

Virus protection. Antivirus systems must be implemented to protect data and critical information.

Backup. Backup systems will be required in case of accidents that would result in data loss.

Intrusion detection. Intrusion detection tools are necessary to monitor critical networks, identify any attacks or intrusions, and take immediate corrective action.

Operation systems and applications. Guidelines on how to protect OS and applications are necessary to prevent attacks.

Database and file systems. Appropriate security measures will be required to protect data and file systems against attacks.

Vulnerability management. Each element of the IT infrastructure will need to be systematically managed for vulnerability. Identify vulnerabilities from time to time by using software tools. Analyze and assess the risk. Finally, and most important, take corrective action to resolve the problem found in the vulnerability analysis.

Monitor threats. IT staff needs to be alert at all times about current threats. New threats and attacks are reported each day in security alerts on Websites and in newsgroups.

Financial Aspect

A financial evaluation must be carried out of the company resources requiring protection. Cost analysis should be carried out of the cost of the security solutions to be adopted. Remember that for an e-commerce company, lack of security would result in greater cost in the long run.

Legal Aspect

E-commerce organizations also need to consider the legal requirements in force in each country before the implementation of technical and organizational controls to ensure the security of company information. Security policies need to comply with national and international laws. For example, if you have operations in England, then the organization must comply with the Data Protection Act of 1998.

The preceding scenario represents the type of checkpoints IT auditors and management should typically look for in the planning and control phase. As covered later, it represents the action plan to accomplish the product and deliverable. The project plan is a controlling document with which deviations against the plan can be monitored, identified, and justified with supporting documentation.

Web Application Risks

The Internet has been around for years, but private industry became interested in its commercial possibilities only after the graphical World Wide Web emerged during the early 1990s. The Web version of the Internet offered a potentially inexpensive and platform-independent network over which business could be conducted and information disseminated. In addition, companies grew excited about the possibility of developing intranets (internal Internets) that would give them access to all of their legacy data via one simple Internet browser interface.

All of this was to be enabled by a Web application programming language (e.g., Java, Perl) that would work on any OS or computing platform. These languages can also be used to deliver to client machines the program and data elements that the client needed to use at any given time. Organizations envisioned desktops equipped with "Internet appliances" that would not need to contain expensive copies of application programs, such as word processors and spreadsheets. It is little wonder that organizations were ready to embrace both the Internet and Web programming languages for enterprise applications. Java became the most popular Web programming language as the technologies associated with Java allow control of the presentation, application, and data layers from a single language (albeit using different associated tools).

Perceived Risks

However, the Internet and Web programming languages present an interesting mix of opportunities and risks to organizations. On the one hand, organizations want to stay competitive and embrace technologies that provide so much promise. On the other, both organizations and individuals still perceive the Internet as risky. Organizations are wary of the very serious security threats from outside hackers to which a connection to the Internet might expose them. Individual users of the Internet are wary of the possible destructive devices that they download to their computers over the Internet.

Internet Security

Security tools and procedures exist to reduce risk when a company gives its customers access to business resources over the Internet. Security measures are available to provide "access security" to protect the company's own computers, disks, memory, and other computing equipment from outside interference and "transaction security" to ensure that two individuals or organizations on the Internet can privately and safely execute a transaction.

Properly implemented, these security mechanisms will

- Protect the company from intruders who attempt to enter the internal network through the Internet
- Provide authorized users with access to Internet services such as HTTP, FTP, Telnet, and Gopher
- Deliver required Internet applications from the internal network to the Internet
- Deliver SMTP and Netnews services to the internal network from the Internet
- Prevent unauthorized use of resources on the internal network
- Give users an easy way to understand network security status without being Internet security experts with the use of security tools that automate technical tasks
- Assure expert round-the-clock, seven-day-a-week (7×24) monitoring and response to security events
- Maximize protection from the Internet and minimize the cost of operating and monitoring protective devices such as the application proxy firewall

Security Tools and Technologies

Effective security solutions rely on several tools and technologies designed to protect information and computers from intrusion, compromise, or misuse, such as encryption technologies, security policies and procedures, and various types of firewalls.

Encryption Technologies

Encryption technologies electronically store information in an encoded form that can only be decoded by an authorized entity with the appropriate decryption technology and authorization to decrypt. Encryption provides a number of important security components to protect electronic information:

Identification. Who are you?
Authentication. Can you prove who you are?

Authorization. What can you do?
Auditing. What did you do?
Integrity. Is it tamperproof?
Privacy. Who can see it?
Nonrepudiation. Can I prove that you said what you said?

When information is encoded, it is first translated into a numerical form and then encrypted using a mathematical algorithm. The algorithm requires a number or message, called a key, to encode or decode the information. The algorithm cannot decode the encrypted information without a decode key. Exhibit 25.1 illustrates the need for Web protection levels.

Security Policies and Procedures

In the rush to establish an Internet presence, many organizations have overlooked perhaps the most important foundation piece in an effective security solution: a sound security policy that identifies who has access to a company's electronic resources and under what circumstances they have access. Thus, security policies in some organizations are almost nonexistent and in others not clearly defined. For example, the use of stateless filters means that the organization is relying on defaults set by the vendor of the security package, whereas the use of state-maintained filters means the organization is ensuring that certain types of activities or patterns are reviewed to prevent possible intrusion or loss.

Security policies fall along a continuum that ranges from promiscuous at one end to paranoid at the other. The promiscuous policy allows unchecked access between the Internet and the organization's internal network to everyone. The paranoid policy refuses access between these two networks to everyone. In between are two more palatable alternatives—the permissive and the prudent policy.

The permissive policy allows all traffic to flow between the internal network and the Internet except that which is explicitly disallowed. Permissive policies are implemented through packet filtering gateways, where stateless filters prevent individual packets of data from crossing the network boundary if the packet is coming from or going to a specific computer, network, or network port. However, there are two major drawbacks to a permissive policy. First, it requires an exhaustive set of filters to cover all possible addresses and ports that should be denied access. Second, it is virtually impossible to block certain undesirable packets without also blocking other desirable and necessary packets because network protocols are dynamic and often change network port numbers, depending on the protocol state.

A prudent policy, in contrast, selectively allows traffic that is explicitly allowed by the protocol and excludes any other. Prudent policies are implemented by a set of application proxies that understand the underlying application protocol and can implement a set of state-maintaining filters that allow specific application data to pass from one network to the next. Because the filters can follow the state of the protocol, they can change dynamically when the protocol changes state. This way, rules allow only properly authorized data to flow across the network boundary. Prudent policies are implemented through application proxy firewalls. Because prudent and permissive policies act as the network boundaries, they are referred to as "perimeter security solutions."

Once a company selects the appropriate security policy, it can be implemented according to a strict set of procedures with the support of software systems. These security procedures—which include a documented set of rules governing the management and administration of the security system and its generated events—record a trail of all modifications to the security system (auditing) and set off signal

Service Type	Threat								
	Destruction	Inter-ference	Modification or Replacement	Misrepresen-tation	Reputa-tion	Inadver-tent Misuse	Unauthor-ized Altering/ Down-loading	Unauthorized Transaction	Unauthorized Disclosure
Advertising	Basic	Basic	Strong	Basic	Basic	Strong/prevent			
IP spoofing	Basic	Basic	Strong[a]						
Secure Internet/ intranet/ extranet									
1. Informational	Basic	Basic	Strong	Basic	No level	Basic	Strong	Basic	Basic
2. Transactional basic	Strong	Strong	Basic	Basic	Basic	Strong	Basic	Basic	Strong[a]
Electronic commerce	Strong	Strong	Strong	Strong	Strong	Basic	Strong	Strong	Strong[a]

[a] See State of California SB 1386.

Exhibit 25.1   Need for Web protection levels (encrypted).

alarms when someone attempts to violate the policies. Properly followed, they protect an organization from all types of security violations, including accidental administrative mistakes and unauthorized modifications to the security policy. To reduce the risk of "inside" break-ins, many companies also require a background check of security systems personnel and separate security management and auditing to prevent an administrator from altering the audit of management actions.

To boost consumer confidence, some companies go through a certification process to obtain a "trust seal." Depending on the type of seal the company wishes to obtain (security, privacy, or business trust seal), for a fee, a third party will scan the company's e-commerce Website to evidence good security practices or secure method of transactions is used (e.g., seal by VeriSign Inc.) or provide verification of a company's existence (e.g., seal by BBB Online). Once the company passes the tests, they may display the third-party seal on the company's Website which links to a Webpage that describe the currency of the seal, last test performed, and the result of the test. Although it is not fool proof, more customers would choose an e-commerce Website with an active trust seal.

Internet Firewalls

Internet application proxy firewalls are a prudent perimeter security solution. These systems sit between the Internet and the organization's internal network (see Exhibit 25.2) and control the traffic flow between the Internet and a company's internal resources. A firewall provides application proxies for most popular Internet applications as well as support for a more restrictive prudent policy. This policy might restrict the establishment of network connections from within the company outward to the Internet. In addition, rather than forwarding packets between networks, the firewall can require the application client to establish an application service connection to the firewall. The firewall then maintains the connection with the outside server. The firewall will only pass data for applications that it currently supports, which eliminates most security "holes."

Security holes created by incorrectly configured computers on the internal network are not visible to the Internet and, therefore, cannot be exploited by external Internet users. The organization's

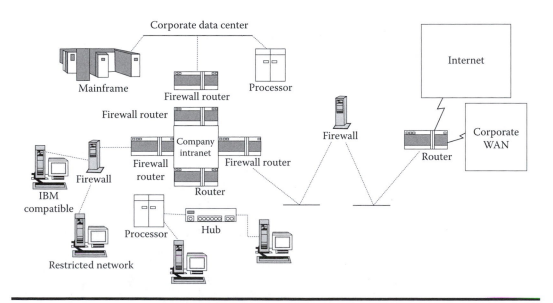

Exhibit 25.2   Firewall placement within an organization's intranet/WAN.

own Internet application servers then sit outside the firewall in what is called the "demilitarized zone" (or DMZ). This eliminates the need for outside traffic to travel through the firewall into the organization's internal network when it is using Web, FTP, or Telnet services.

To maintain the integrity of the perimeter, the firewall must be constantly monitored for potential security breaches. Should a breach occur, an Internet security expert must be available to survey the damage and recommend a solution.

Internet Firewall Configurations: Bastion Host

This is the only host on the customer's internal network that is visible to the Internet. It has no customer-accessible accounts for logging into it. Customer communications travel through the bastion host via proxy applications. This is the most secure method of performing perimeter security today.

In the popular "dual-homed bastion host" configuration, the toolkit software is installed on a host with two network interfaces. The toolkit software provides proxy services for common applications, such as FTP and Telnet, and security for SMTP mail. As the bastion host is a security-critical network strong point, it is important that the configuration of the software on that system be as secure as possible.

Dual-homed gateways provide an appealing firewall as they are simple to implement, require a minimum of hardware, and can be verified easily. Most Berkeley-based UNIX implementations have a kernel variable that can be set to indicate to the OS that it should not route traffic between networks even if it is connected to them (which would normally cause the system to act as a gateway router). By completely disabling routing, the administrator can have a high degree of confidence that any traffic between the protected network and any untrusted network has to occur through an application that is running on the firewall. As there is no traffic transferred directly between the internal and the untrusted network, it is not necessary to show any routes to the protected network over the untrusted network. This effectively renders the protected network "invisible" to any systems except the bastion host. The only disadvantage of this type of firewall is that it implicitly provides a firewall of the type in which "that which is not expressly permitted is prohibited." This means that it is impossible to weaken the firewall's security to let a service through should one later decide to do so. Instead, all services must be supported via proxies on the firewall.

Choke Router/Screened Host

The choke router reinforces the bastion host, enforces security policy, and isolates the internal network from the Internet. A "screened host gateway" relies on a router with some form of packet screening capacity to block off access between the protected and the untrusted network. A single host is identified as a bastion host and traffic is permitted only to that host. The software suite that is run on the bastion host is similar to a dual-homed gateway; the system must be as secure as possible, as it is the focal point for attack on the network. Screened host gateways are a very flexible solution because they offer the opportunity to selectively permit traffic through the screening router for applications that are considered trustworthy, or between mutually trusted networks.

The disadvantage of this configuration is that there are now two critical security systems in effect: the bastion host and the router. If the router has access control lists that permit certain services through, the firewall administrator has to manage an additional point of complexity.

Verifying the correctness of a screened host firewall is a bit more difficult. It becomes increasingly difficult as the number of services permitted through the router grows. Screened host firewalls also introduce management risks because it is possible to open holes in the firewall for special applications or influential users; the firewall administrator must be careful to resist pressure to modify the screening rules in the router.

In a "screened subnet firewall," a small isolated network is placed between the trusted and the untrusted network. Screening rules in routers protect access to this network by restricting traffic so that both networks can only reach hosts on the screened subnet. Conceptually, this is the dual-homed gateway approach applied to an entire network. The main utility of this approach is that it permits multiple hosts to exist on the "outside" network (again referred to as the demilitarized zone). An additional advantage to the screened host subnet is that the firewall administrator can configure network routing in a way that does not advertise routes to the private network from the Internet, or internal routes to the Internet. This is a powerful means to protect a large private network because it becomes very difficult for an outsider to direct traffic toward the hidden private network. If the routing is blocked, all traffic must pass through an application on the bastion host just as it must in the dual-homed gateway.

Firewalls in a Partitioned Network

Not every network is a single, isolated network attached to an untrusted network. As the use of large-scale networks continues to increase, businesses increasingly form business partnerships and transmit corporate-sensitive information over public networks. A business can effectively combine a firewall with network-level encryption hardware (or software) to produce a virtual network with a common security perimeter.

A company can establish a common security perimeter between two facilities over a public WAN. The encryption is separate from the router but need not be if integrated encrypting routers are available. Currently, there are several products that act as encrypting bridges at a frame level. These products work by examining the source and destination address of all packets arriving via one interface and retransmitting the packet out via another interface. If the encrypting bridge/router is configured to encrypt traffic to a specific network, the packet data are encrypted and a new checksum inserted into the "packet" header. Once the packet is received at the other "computer," the peer encrypting bridge/router determines that it is from a network with which the router is encrypting traffic and decrypts the packet, patches the checksum, and retransmits it.

Anyone intercepting traffic between the two encrypting networks would see only useless ciphertext. An additional benefit of this approach is that it protects against attempts to inject traffic by spoofing the source network address. Unless attackers know the cipher key that is in use, their packets will be encrypted into junk when they go through the encrypting bridge/router. If the encrypting bridge/router gets traffic for a network with which it does not have an encryption arrangement, traffic is transmitted normally. In this manner, a firewall can be configured with encrypted "tunnels" to other networks. For example, a company could safely share files via NFS or safely use weakly authenticated network log-in programs, such as rlogin over their encrypted link, and still have a strong firewall protecting access between the corporate perimeter and the rest of the world. Two companies that want to establish a business connection for proprietary information could apply a similar approach in which traffic between the firewall bastion host on one corporate network and the firewall bastion host on the other corporate network is automatically encrypted.

Web Programming Language Risks

Another area for management review in corporate use of the Internet is the use of Web programming languages. Web programming languages are object-oriented programming languages that can be compiled and run on any computing platform. Because of their capabilities, many developers have chosen to write applets/plug-ins that use Web programming languages. Applets/plug-ins can deliver software and data to client workstations only as needed. The applet/plug-in only needs to include the functions of a software application and the data that the client needs to accomplish a specific task. However, many individuals fear the destructive potential of applets/plug-ins from unknown sources. Current browsers allow users to refuse applets/plug-ins or accept them only from trusted sources.

Web programming languages provide benefits and cost-effective measures to organizations. Earlier versions of Web programming tools provided weak data validation and leaned too heavily on object linking and embedding (OLE). These older Java tools were geared too much toward Windows and often lacked some of the key features such as debuggers and compilers that are essential in a workbench. Web programming languages have matured significantly in the past 10 years to address the needs of corporate security. Java and other Web programming languages are used for building mission-critical e-commerce applications.

With regard to Web operational issues, some of the security tools and procedures that exist now to reduce risk when a company gives its customers access to business resources over the Internet have been discussed. Examples have been given of security measures available to provide access security to protect the company's own computers, disks, memory, and other computing equipment from outside interference, and transaction security to ensure that two individuals or organizations on the Internet can privately and safely execute a transaction.

Users also need to understand that they do not control applets/plug-ins once they are downloaded into the local environment. For example, users may not necessarily know that an applet/plug-in has been downloaded or may not have information on how many applets/plug-ins are in operation, unless they set up adequate security on their Internet browsers. A common form of malicious applet/plug-in can continue running on the client and force the user to restart the system.

There are other security problems as well. Today, compiler languages such as C or Ada can produce bytecode that looks like Java bytecode to the verifier. If the verifier erroneously accepts the non-Java bytecode, it is unlikely to follow Java's language restrictions and may allow performance of illegal procedures. For example, a hostile applet could be used to create a class loader containing unacceptable statements. The class loader, which is responsible for defining namespace seen by other classes, could then allow the attacking applet to customize the user's computer environment.

Finally, from an IT audit standpoint, Web programming language input/output object classes are public. Although this feature improves the usefulness of Web programming languages, it provides hackers with a way to deliver damage. This major weakness of Web programming languages makes the use of audit tools critical for the safe use of Web programs.

Practical Web Security Solutions

It is easy to see that businesses need not be intimidated into bypassing the opportunities available to them on the Internet. Several security solutions exist immediately to reduce or remove the risk involved in connecting to the Internet.

Backdoor Connection

This method connects the Internet server (Web server, list server, etc.) to other company computer systems through a dial-up link that is not made available anywhere on the Internet.

A backdoor data transfer method might include setting up a program, such as ProComm Plus (by Datastorm), on a computer connected to the Web server. The company's other computer systems periodically dial into that backdoor computer via ProComm to upload files that are then imported to the Web server's database via a custom import program. This same method works well for sending order or questionnaire data in batches from a Web server to other computers within the company.

In using this approach, the communications lines between the company's computers and its Internet presence are severed most of the time. Even when the link is established between computers, it does not use an insecure network protocol, such as TCP/IP, which is easy for hackers to penetrate. This prevents Internet hackers from drilling through to vital company systems and information.

Network Firewall

A network firewall connects the Internet server to the company's existing computer network system via a permanent firewall router. Firewall routers are sold by a growing number of network hardware and software companies. They serve as a security barrier between network systems. By placing such a barrier between the company's Web server and the rest of the company's network, a network administrator can restrict the flow of network data packets between these segments. The firewall could restrict all inbound packets to those generated by the Web server itself; thus, only the Web server can access internal information.

A good hacker can get through a firewall, although attempting to gain access beyond the firewall would require the use of sophisticated IP source-address spoofing techniques. These techniques fool the firewall into believing that the hacker's connection has the same network address as the Web server or some other privileged user. At this point, the hacker would need sufficient motivation to expend the effort and time to get through.

Any time a company plans to connect its in-house computer network directly to an Internet server, a firewall should be used to deter casual hacking and other less malicious security risks.

Pseudofirewall

A pseudofirewall connects the Internet server to the company's existing computer network system via standard router equipment but segregates network traffic with different network protocols (i.e., TCP/IP and Internet packet exchange [IPX] sequenced packet exchange [SPX]). The main security problem on the Internet exists due to certain flaws in the Internet network protocol (TCP/IP). Thus, using a different protocol to connect the company's internal computers to its Internet server solves this problem.

For example, if a company's Internet server used a PC running Microsoft SQL as its Web server over a leased line connected to an ISP, this method would entail running two network protocols on the Web server. The Web server must use TCP/IP to connect to the Internet. Yet, to access information on internal computer networks, that same Web server could be configured to use something else, such as IPX/SPX, which is native to Novell's NetWare. The hacker could spoof the TCP/IP address but would find no other network connections beyond the Web server.

This method is not proven to work more effectively than a firewall. However, its appeal is that it can provide a similar level of security to a firewall router at lower cost.

Case Example: GMA Business Overview and Profile

General Mercantile of America, also known as GMA, is the premier importer and distributor of chinaware in the United States. Founded in 1985, GMA has been able to secure, maintain, and grow its market share by offering the largest selection of products available from a single distributor resource to the various channels of distributors. By stocking more than 1100 individual items, GMA serves its dealers and suppliers by providing each of them with a virtually uninterrupted flow of well-designed, well-manufactured, and well-priced products. This is accomplished via its network of four strategically located warehouses whose total square footage exceeds 400,000. There are plans currently in place to add one new branch in New York in 2001.

GMA is headquartered in the Los Angeles suburb of City of Commerce, which has convenient access to several major freeways and the ports of Los Angeles and Long Beach. This location has the capacity to handle more than 5000 ocean containers annually, 3000 of which are piggybacked to branch locations. The commitment to depth and breadth of inventory makes GMA the logical, one-stop source for full-line chinaware dealers or specialty retailers who require a narrow selection of merchandise.

International trade is complex because it involves suppliers and importers, customer services, port storage companies, and transportation companies. GMA operates in a highly competitive environment along with hundreds of other chinaware importers and distributors in the United States. In this market, large amounts of information flow among several trading partners and support services. This information includes orders, billings, status query, contracts, and payments. The problem faced by GMA is how to effectively manage the information at competitive prices and utilize current IT to effectively support its business operation process and meet the business objective.

The external business operations actively involve parties from overseas manufacturers (suppliers), transportation forwarding companies, customs, and banks (see Exhibit 25.3).

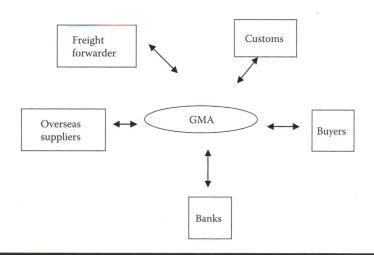

Exhibit 25.3   GMA business processes.

IT Solutions for GMA

Based on an evaluation of GMA's business process, trading partner preferences, and requirements, GMA launched e-commerce solutions for its international trading business. The company believes that e-commerce is the trend in doing business in the future and this is why it started its Website in 1998. At the same time, GMA started Web-based EDI to conduct its import business with overseas supplies and major vendors in the United States, such as Nordstrom Department Store and Sears. The management of GMA believes that the effective way of doing business equates potentially to saving time and money. Normal business transactions require large amounts of paper, phone calls, and printing among other things. All of these can be replaced with the use of Web-based EDI. By performing the same transactions done on paper electronically, not only is time saved but the chance of error is also reduced. Much of the error that occurs during such transactions includes human typographical errors. A user may enter in an extra zero, changing 10,000 to 100,000. With EDI, having to reenter data is no longer an issue. Moreover, EDI can reduce business expenses such as shipping and handling by providing added support to manufacturers in terms of Just-In-Time inventory and third-party warehousing.

At the same time, GMA is using the extranet to open their networks to provide access for business partners, distributors, and customers. When deploying extranets, transactions between companies become less and less complicated. The extranet has become the ideal medium for business-to-business (B2B) transactions. They are fast becoming vital business tools, providing a cross between the openness of the Internet and the security and privacy of the intranet. On a basic level, the extranet allows for routine transactions via the Internet within a trading community, assuring security through built-in measures appropriate to the user and the task at hand. A much broader perspective envisions collaborative communities where partnering companies readily share data, knowledge, systems, goals, and issues.

Major E-Commerce Security Implementation Issues at GMA

The issues of identification, privacy, and overall security are compounded within GMA as it engages in commerce on the Internet on a global basis. There are several main risks of utilizing e-commerce, which could impact GMA's business operations. For instance, extranets are not without caveats. For one thing, the security may be rudimentary. Most extranets, for instance, do not encrypt the passwords and the user IDs sent across the network. Customers may not protect their user IDs and passwords as well as they should. In each case, the result could be unauthorized use. Based on an awareness assessment before implementation in GMA, we can locate some crucial risks facing international trading companies that are deploying e-commerce. The most threatening risk facing organizations such as GMA is the leakage of business-sensitive data. Such sensitive data can be customer data, credit card data, contracts between supplier and vendor, supplier information, and so on. In addition, data inaccessibility and lack of data integrity are also major threats to organizations that conduct international trading business.

Awareness Assessment

The following questions are intended to gauge the level of data sensitivity involved in the e-commerce solution being deployed in international trading businesses. Data sensitivity is a vulnerability that must be addressed in a B2B and business-to-customer (B2C) solution.

1. Is there or will there be financial data being transmitted?
2. Is there or will there be customer information being transmitted?
3. Is there or will there be contract information being transmitted?

The following questions assess the level of communication that has taken place between trading partners using a B2B solution. It is critical to communicate and agree upon policies and procedures, as well as how and what business will be conducted in a B2B deployment.

1. Are there standards set and communicated between trading partners in regard to security architecture and policies?
2. Is there a recovery plan shared between partners if one or more systems' security is compromised?
3. Is there an agreed-upon access control policy between trading partners?

The following questions raise the issue of physical and logical security. Again, are the trading partners involved aware and comfortable with the others' security measures?

1. Is your enterprise systems' architecture protected with firewalls? At what levels are firewalls deployed and what risks have been identified but not addressed?
   a. WAN/LAN level
   b. OS level
   c. Server level (Domain Name System [DNS] servers)
   d. Application level
   e. Database level
2. What is the physical access level policy for your systems? Are all stakeholders aware and in agreement with this policy?

The following questions are intended to point out the importance of development standards within an organization and across trading organizations for the sake of security. It is important that all stakeholders understand the development process of B2B solutions in terms of security policy adherence at development, maintenance, and support.

1. Are your systems' solution development projects centralized or decentralized?
2. Do developers of B2B solutions in your organization and trading partners adhere to security and architecture standards? How are these policies communicated and enforced?
3. Will the development, support, or maintenance of the B2B solution be outsourced? If so, what are the security policies and controls deployed by the outsource partner?

The objective of the preceding assessment is not to measure the risks present in a current e-commerce solution in GMA but to get the business entities behind an e-commerce solution asking the right questions before implementation. The goal is awareness. The assessment is a gauge as to how aware the business entity is of the risks and controls that must be considered along with the return on investment analysis of an e-commerce solution. The assessment is composed of questions that are, also, intended to raise the level of awareness. Each question should be followed by a small explanation of the question's value.

Implementing Risk Analysis and Controls at GMA

Three main areas of concern to address the risks of compromising e-commerce solution securities involve the method of capturing and formatting data for Internet communication through XML, the data transport security involved in virtual private networks, and policies revolving around security measures for a B2B solution.

With the growth of B2B solutions, we cannot ignore the fundamental steps of the e-commerce solutions and the security risks they introduce. For the sake of this discussion, let us use an order entry in the GMA Website as our example. The GMA Company manufactures ceramic cups that are sold in department stores. These department stores enter their orders for the ceramic cups on the GMA Website, which is protected by a username and a password. The GMA Company does not extend credit to its customers, which means a VISA or MasterCard number must accompany each order. Payment for the orders is verified and transacted at the time the orders are confirmed by the GMA system.

The first thing a GMA customer must do is log on to the GMA Website, which requires a username and a password that are unique to each one of its customers. The authentication information is then verified by the GMA system and access is either granted or denied. Let us assume the customer is granted access. The order entry screen is shown with the customer's name, address, phone and shipping information, and compliments of the GMA system. Next, an order must be entered for the ceramic cups; again, a VISA or MasterCard number must accompany this order. The customer provides the information and clicks a button to submit the order. This information is transmitted to the GMA system for confirmation. Confirmation is granted when the GMA inventory has been checked for product availability and the customer credit card transaction is successful. Again, let us assume the order is confirmed, which allows for the GMA system to send a confirmation message back to the waiting customer. The cups are then picked, packed, and shipped to the customer. All this business was performed paper free and just in time. This scenario is the ideal behind a B2B solution. What are the concerns?

Were risks involved in that scenario? Yes. The GMA Company and customer systems were opened to the worldwide network and the customer's financial data was transmitted across open lines. From a business perspective, the main risks here are the risks that an attack from an intruder could take the ordering system down and customer information confidentiality could be compromised, causing the loss of a potentially large amount of business. Before we begin the discussion of how to address these risks, let us state the scope of this discussion. As stated, the risks involved extend across the entire network of systems connected to the systems involved in the e-commerce solution as well as the data being transmitted across the systems. The three overriding concerns are confidentiality, authenticity, and data integrity. This section concentrates on the preservation of the data confidentiality and the authenticity. Again, the loss of business can be attributed to an intruder who gains access to the systems via capturing of authentication information and "takes down" the systems, or by an intruder capturing customer financial information for malicious use. Both vulnerabilities are exposed when the data passes from one system to another via untrusted transport. The scope of the controls to combat or manage these risks will revolve around the securing of the transport of this confidential data rather than the deploying of firewalls that can be deployed to either detect intruders or slow them down.

What controls are available for improving the security of vulnerable data passing through the open pipes of the network? Before we can answer this question, we must understand where and how the data are vulnerable. Let us take data entry as an example. In the case of our example, this would be at the order entry screen. The problem with this is that it depends on further standards development to ensure security. Key security issues include authentication and nonrepudiation of XML documents.

Cloud Computing Security

Cloud computing is a relatively new concept. It is not the same as outsourcing, but has some similarities. To manage security and risks, organizations may leverage best practices from vendor management, as well as lessons learned from outsourcing. In a cloud environment, security is even more important because the boundaries may not be clear. In a traditional IT environment, the physical infrastructure and access to data is maintained internally by the organization that owns the data. In a cloud environment, the physical location of the servers may not be known to the (client) organizations, several organizations data may be stored in the same server, and security and privacy standards may not be in-line with organization's policy. Several possible types of attacks against cloud computing services include

- Compromises to the confidentiality and integrity of data in transit to and from a cloud provider
- Wide-scale attacks which take advantage of the homogeneity and power of cloud computing environments
- Unauthorized access by a consumer (through improper authentication or authorization, or vulnerabilities introduced during maintenance) to software, data, and resources in use by an authorized cloud service consumer
- Increased levels of network-based attacks, such as denial–of-service attacks, which exploit software not designed for an Internet threat model and vulnerabilities in resources which were formerly accessed through private networks
- Limited ability to encrypt data at rest in a multitenancy environment
- Portability constraints resulting from nonstandard application programming interfaces (APIs) which make it difficult for a cloud consumer to change to a new cloud service provider when SLAs are not met
- Attacks which exploit the physical abstraction of cloud resources and exploit a lack of audit procedures or logging
- Attacks due to delay in patching security vulnerabilities
- Attacks which exploit inconsistencies in global privacy policies and regulations

The NIST suggested that major security objectives for a cloud computing implementation should include the following:

- Protect customer data from unauthorized access, disclosure, modification, or monitoring. This includes supporting identity management such that the customer has the capability to enforce identity and access control policies on authorized users accessing cloud services. This includes the ability of a customer to make access to its data selectively available to other users.
- Protect from supply chain threats. This includes ensuring the trustworthiness and reliability of the service provider as well as the trustworthiness of the hardware and software used.
- Prevent unauthorized access to cloud computing infrastructure resources. This includes implementing security domains that have logical separation between computing resources

(e.g., logical separation of customer workloads running on the same physical server by VM monitors [hypervisors] in a multitenant environment) and using secure-by-default configurations.

- Design Web applications deployed in a cloud for an Internet threat model and embedding security into the software development process.
- Protect Internet browsers from attacks to mitigate end-user security vulnerabilities. This includes taking measures to protect Internet-connected personal computing devices by applying security software, personal firewalls, and patch maintenance.
- Deploy access control and intrusion detection technologies at the cloud provider, and conduct an independent assessment to verify that they are in place. This includes (but does not rely on) traditional perimeter security measures in combination with the domain security model. Traditional perimeter security includes restricting physical access to network and devices; protecting individual components from exploitation through security patch deployment; setting as default most secure configurations; disabling all unused ports and services; using role-based access control; monitoring audit trails; minimizing the use of privilege; using antivirus software; and encrypting communications.
- Define trust boundaries between service provider(s) and consumers to ensure that the responsibility for providing security is clear.
- Support portability such that the customer can take action to change cloud service providers when needed to satisfy availability, confidentiality, and integrity requirements. This includes the ability to close an account on a particular date and time, and to copy data from one service provider to another.

Several not-for-profit organizations and government agencies, such as ISACA and CSA, have been developing guidelines to help cloud computing technology adoption. For example, vendor management in a cloud environment may be similar to managing outsourcing relationships. Therefore, existing best practices and standards may be applicable, such as ISACA IT Assurance Framework (ITAF) section 3630.6 (Outsourced and Third-Party Activities). ITAF is designed to provide IT audit and assurance professionals with a single source for IT audit and assurance standards, guidelines, and tools and techniques. ITAF section 3630.6 (Outsourced and Third-Party Activities) discusses the various types of outsourcing (outsourcing, insourcing, offshoring, facilities management, etc.) and the issues about each, of which the IT assurance professional must be aware. The guidance in this section also identifies the risks associated with the various outsourcing options and provides information on how management can minimize or mitigate the risks. This guidance also provides helpful hints regarding contracting, reducing outsourced risks, legal remedies, and other protection devices. Mapping to COBIT control objectives is included. ISACA publications, such as *IT Control Objectives for Cloud Computing: Controls and Assurance in the Cloud*, further describes the cloud computing landscape and how to build the relevant controls and governance mechanisms around it.

Other resources include publications by CSA, such as *Security Guidance for Critical Areas of Focus in Cloud Computing and Cloud Controls Matrix*. For the European community, the European Network and Information Security Agency (ENISA) is working on developing a risk assessment for cloud computing. The paper is expected to provide an assessment of key risks and their mitigation strategies in cloud computing.

To minimize risks, organizations should ask hard questions during information gathering phase of cloud implementation. Some of the questions that should be asked before selecting a cloud vendor include the following:

Application and Data

- How will the data be stored? In a public cloud model, a single machine may host several client organizations applications and data. How will the data be separated from among clients, especially, competitors' data?
- Who have access to the data? What type of access to the data will the employees of the cloud provider have? What assurance would the client organization have?
- How many copies of customer's data do the vendors keep and are they stored in geographically separated regions? If they are stored in geographically diverse regions, what are the countries where the data resides, and what are the laws governing security and privacy of user data in those countries?
- When data are deleted by the customer, are they deleted completely from their Web service, or would they still be accessible?

Legal and Compliance-Related Questions

- Where do the applications reside? There may be legal implications, such as legal requirements in Europe and China to maintain data within the country's physical boundaries.
- What are the vendor's policies and procedures? How do they comply with HIPAA, SOX, and other regulations?
- What is the cloud provider's policy when law enforcement sends a subpoena to access the customer data?

Cloud Provider's Going Concerns

- What is the cloud provider's reputation and sustainability? What is the likelihood for the cloud provider to remain in business in the long term? In case of cloud provider's failure to stay in business, how will the client organization gain access to its application and data?
- What are the cloud provider's business continuity and disaster recovery plans? What additional preventative measures will the client organization need to plan for?
- What are the SLAs (e.g., availability, confidentiality, and timeliness)? What are the remedies if SLAs are not met?

Security-Related Questions

- What are the cloud provider's security capabilities to mitigate threats? Would the cloud provider have sufficient technology to meet the client organization's regulatory, privacy, and compliance responsibilities? What influence would the client organization have on the security selection to protect against external threats?
- What are the encryption technologies used by the vendors to authenticate users to the services? What level of encryption do vendors offer to their customers to protect their data?
- How secure are their SaaS applications and do they work with any independent security group to establish the security of their app code?
- What type of third-party security and/or certification does the vendor have? How often does the company get recertification? What is the scope of the certification?

Infrastructure-Related Questions

- How are multitenanted applications isolated from each other? Request a high-level description of containment and isolation measures.
- What is vendor's approach to the security of their infrastructure? How are data in the data center being protected?
- How easy is it to export the data from their service in order to move to a new service? Are there any extra charges for exporting the data out of a cloud vendor's service?

Although an application or data may now be hosted at a cloud provider's location, client organizations are "relief" from responsibilities. For example, in an IaaS delivery model, while the physical support of the organization's infrastructure (facilities, rack space, power, cooling, cabling, etc.) may be fully outsourced to a cloud provider, the security responsibility is not completely transferred to the vendor. The vendor may be responsible for maintaining physical and logical security; however, since the customer managed the applications that run within this infrastructure, the customer is responsible for securing their cloud-deployed applications. Thus, clearly defined roles and responsibilities from the beginning of a relationship are vital.

Mobile Computing Security

The business risks of mobile computing are significant. Specific risks associated with mobile computing include

- Unauthorized access risks
- Physical security risks
- Mobile data storage device risk
- Operating system or application risk
- Network risk

Many of these mobile devices have sizable storage capability, but most of them lack encrypted software. Data are essentially exposed to unauthorized users. In the event that the device is stolen or misplaced, sensitive and proprietary information are at risk and may be compromised. Mobile devices have numerous vulnerabilities that are susceptible to malicious and nonmalicious attacks. Vulnerabilities may be exploited to gain control of the device or access to its data. The devices may carry malware, viruses, and worms unknown to the user and could negatively impact the systems within the organization's network.

As mobile computing benefits both management and the business users, management should embrace the technology by developing appropriate security policy. The policy should define the following:

- Allowable device types (enterprise-issued only vs. allowing personal devices and types of devices such as BlackBerry, iPhone, iPad, or other tablets)
- The type of authentication and encryption (logical security)
- The required software and configuration standards
- The types of services that will be accessible through the devices
- The type of data that may be stored in the mobile device (e.g., no trade secret, customer-sensitive data)

- The tasks for which employees may use the devices for and the types of applications that are allowable
- The minimally required prevention and detection software to defend against malware and other forms of attack
- User responsibility for the physical security of the mobile device (physical security)
- Reporting requirement when a device is lost or stolen
- Reporting requirement of security breach or any incident involving potential compromise to organization's confidential information

Conclusion

For CIOs and CEOs, the twenty-first century promises many exciting opportunities and risks in IT. As unsettling and unnerving as many of these changes are, managers must employ common sense and informed business judgment to understand both risks and benefits. Managers should understand the technical complexities and encourage decision makers to carefully weigh the investment in security against the potential risks. There are answers and solutions for many of the security issues discussed. Effective measures exist to protect both access security and transaction security over the Internet. As improvements are made to Java and as the programming language matures, it can be expected that Java will incorporate more and better security measures because Java language developers realize that security is critical to the acceptance and success of the language.

Java provides an entirely new kind of cross-platform computing environment that can be used to integrate and work with an organization's existing systems and networks. As Java matures, it may well replace costlier, less efficient elements in existing computing systems and make feasible the continued use of existing legacy systems. This is especially important today, when multiple incompatible platforms and legacy systems are typical in global corporate and private IS infrastructures. Web and Java hold great promise for organizations that want to integrate their existing, incompatible applications and make them available through one common user interface—an Internet browser.

Web platforms and application platforms are incredibly complex and resource intensive, expensive to buy and maintain, and costly to update or expand. But, as troublesome as these systems may be, the CEO and the CIO have to consider whether they can afford to scrap huge corporate investments in such IS. It is very costly to replace systems, convert databases that contain invaluable information, and retrain workers in new computing environments and techniques.

Throughout the business and personal computing world, industry leaders, software vendors, and software developers are showing utmost support for Java, the programming language that they believe will transcend all barriers. Most business organizations will benefit by using adaptable application architecture. This new technology can save a company millions of corporate dollars per fiscal year on hardware, software, and systems development by converting a "custom fat client" into a "thin client."

Identification of risks and controls in e-commerce is not intended to defer the deployment of a B2B and B2C solution. It is this technology that will catapult a business into competitiveness in tomorrow's market. The intent of this is to provide an understanding that will lead to proper deployment of security technology and policy to provide a safe environment for conducting business in the E-commerce realm. To what extent does a company or client have to deploy the available solutions or be concerned about the risks involved? Is cloud computing technology the right solution? Again, the answer is that it depends.

Review Questions

1. What are some of the perceived risks of using the Internet and the Web programming languages?
2. List the reasons to implement Internet security tools.
3. List and discuss Internet tools and technologies.
4. What is an Internet firewall?
5. How should an organization manage its cloud computing risks?

Multiple-Choice Questions

1. Properly implemented, Internet security mechanisms will
   a. Protect the company from inside employees who attempt to enter the internal network from the Internet
   b. Provide unauthorized users with access to Internet services such as HTTP, FTP, Telnet, and Gopher
   c. Deliver unneeded Internet applications from the internal network
   d. Prevent unauthorized use of resources on the internal network
2. Encryption technologies electronically store information in an encoded form that can only be decoded by an authorized individual who has the appropriate decryption technology and
   a. Private key
   b. Public key
   c. Authorization to decrypt
   d. Ability to decrypt
3. Internet security policies fall along a continuum that ranges from promiscuous to
   a. Permissive
   b. Undocumented
   c. Informal
   d. Paranoid
4. Internet application proxy firewalls are
   a. A prudent perimeter security solution
   b. A sufficient defense against hackers
   c. An inadequate use of firewall technology
   d. A way to avoid using network connections from within the company
5. A network firewall connects the Internet server to the company's existing computer network system via a permanent firewall
   a. Router
   b. Hub
   c. Bridge
   d. Port

6. According to the 2007 CSI Computer Crime and Statistics Survey, the average annual loss reported
    a. Decreased 40% from the previous year
    b. More than doubled from the previous year
    c. Stayed about the same as the previous year
    d. None of the above
7. Over the past 6 years, the total annual loss due to cyber-crime has
    a. Decreased 40%
    b. Quadrupled
    c. Increased 50%
    d. None of the above
8. The planning and control areas for security management are
    a. Strategic and organizational
    b. Legal and technical
    c. Financial
    d. All of the above
9. Organizational measure to support the security-related infrastructure include
    a. Setting up a security team
    b. Training programs in technology and methods
    c. Documenting information security procedures
    d. All of the above
10. Technical infrastructure that provides physical and logical security includes
    a. Cryptography
    b. Authentication
    c. Vulnerability management
    d. All of the above

Exercises

1. Your organization is performing an evaluation of security tools to be used to provide protection for your company intranet from unauthorized use by employees and outside intruders. Write a list of evaluation criteria for security software and hardware to be used, including client software, server software, network software, and firewall hardware and software.
2. You have been asked to audit your company security plan as it applies to acceptable employee use of the Internet and e-mail. Write a preliminary audit plan; include scope, objectives, and audit steps.
3. The CIO is proposing to move the management of sales force data to the cloud to reduce costs and improve agility. The CEO/CFO asked you to help them assess the risks and whether to approve this proposal. Outline your risk assessment and recommendation in business terms. Prevent using audit and IT jargons.

Answers to Multiple-Choice Questions

1—c; 2—c; 3—d; 4—a; 5—a; 6—b; 7—b; 8—d; 9—d; 10—d

Further Reading

1. Badger, L., T. Grance, R. Patt-Corner, and J. Voa, *NIST: Draft Cloud Computing Synopsis and Recommendations; Recommendations of the National Institute of Standards and Technology*, Special Publication 800-146, May 2011.
2. Bank for International Settlements and Basel Committee on Banking Supervision, Consultative Document Operational Risk, 2001, updated July 2002, http://www.bis.org/publ/bcbsca/07.pdf.
3. Bartels, A., *Global IT Spending and Investment Forecast, 2006 to 2007*, Forrester Research, Inc., Cambridge, MA, 2006.
4. Basel II mandates a nest egg for banks, *U.S. Banker*, July 1, 2002, p. 48, http://www.accessmy library. com/coms2/summary_0286-25582710_ITM.
5. Berson, A. and G. Anderson, *Sybase and Client/Server Computing, 1996*, BITS Technology Risk Transfer Gap Analysis Tool, BITS, Washington DC, 2002.
6. Department of the Premier and Cabinet, A security management framework for online services, Government of Western Australia, 2003, http://www.egov.dpc.wa.gov.au/documents/security_ management.pdf.
7. ENISA, http://www.enisa.europa.eu/publications.
8. ENISA, *Cloud Computing Information Assurance Framework*, 2009.
9. Federal Cloud Security Guidelines: Guidelines for Secure Use of Cloud Computing by Federal Departments and Agencies, June 2010.
10. Ford, W. and M.S. Baum, *Secure Electronic Commerce*, Prentice Hall PTR, Englewood Cliffs, NJ, 2001.
11. ISACA, *Securing Mobile Devices*, 2010.
12. ISACA, *IT Control Objectives for Cloud Computing: Controls and Assurance in the Cloud*, 2011.
13. ISACA, *Cloud Computing Management Audit/Assurance Program*, 2010.
14. ISACA, *Mobile Computing Security Audit/Assurance Program*, 2010.
15. Jensen, W. and K. Scarfone, *NIST: Guidelines on Cell Phone and PDA Security*, Special Publication 800-124, October 2008.
16. Marks, N., The New Age of internal auditing, *The Internal Auditor*, December 2001, http:// findarticles. com/p/articles/mi_m4153/is_6_58/ai_82886228?tag=artBody;call.
17. Symantec Enterprise Solutions 2000, A comprehensive risk management guide, http://enterprise security, Symantec.com, accessed October 15, 2002.
18. U.S. General Accounting Office, Assessing the Reliability of Computer-Processed Data [Supplement to the Government Auditing Standards (Yellow Book)—External Version], GAO-03-273G, October 2002.

Chapter 26

Enterprise Resource Planning

This chapter includes an overview of control and audit of ERP systems and operational approaches in reviewing system application products (SAP) in a client/server environment. SAP is a revolutionary support product being acquired and implemented by many companies worldwide. An important role for today's information systems auditor is in the design of internal controls and the definition of security measures. Issues of implementation and control of SAP must be addressed by the management, user, and auditor. This chapter provides general guidelines and suggested approaches to achieving both teamwork and success.

ERP Solutions

ERP is a software that provides standard business functionality in an integrated system. Typical functionality includes procurement, inventory, accounting, and human resources (HR). Many ERPs allow multiple functions to access a common database—reducing storage costs and increasing consistency and accuracy of data from a single source. The primary ERP suppliers are Oracle, PeopleSoft, and SAP.

Benefits of ERP Solutions

Historically, organizations either developed or purchased individual applications for each of the back-office functions (e.g., inventory). For the most part, the functionality for accounting, inventory, and HR applications are the same for most organizations. In addition, information is shared across back-office applications. Human information and inventory information is needed for accounting. The cost and complexity of integrating and modifying these applications gave rise to the need for an integrated application package. ERP solutions began in the manufacturing industry and slowly spread to the service industry. ERP solutions provide the following benefits:

Integrated financial systems. A fully integrated ERP system captures the information needed to prepare financial statements from the source (e.g., sales), making it easier to report on real-time transactions with fewer errors. This feature also increases the auditability of transactions as it is easier to track transactions from the source to the financial statements.

Standardized processes. An ERP system provides standard methods for automating processes. In a fully integrated solution, the information in the HR system can be used by payroll, help desk, and so on. Standardized processes are more efficient for business processes and computer processing. The more complex a system, the more programming, processing power, and data storage is required.

Shared, real-time information. An ERP system enables information from sales to production, increasing the accuracy of demand-forecasting models. Fully implemented, an ERP system can create financial statements on a daily basis. Drill-down capabilities allow for faster analysis to find exceptional items that may impact trends and forecasting.

Key Risks of ERP Solutions

ERP solutions are not without risks. The same risks apply from any purchased application. A packaged application may not meet all of the business needs, resulting in extensive modification or changes to business processes. Also, any future releases of this software may require extensive programming to retrofit all of the organization-specific code. Because packaged systems are generic by nature, the organization may need to modify its business operations to match the vendor's method of processing. Changes in business operations may be costly due to training and the new processes may not fit into the organization's culture or other processes. In addition, some integration may be required for functionality that is not part of the ERP, but provides integral information to the ERP functions.

As ERP solutions are offered by a single vendor, all of the risks associated with a single supplier apply. The organization will be dependent on a single supplier for maintenance and support, specific hardware or software requirements, and limitations on the use or customization of the software. When selecting a vendor package, organizations should consider the following:

- Stability of the vendor company
- Volatility of system upgrades
- Existing customer base
- Vendor's ability to provide support
- Required hardware or software in support of the vendor application
- Required modifications of the base software

The other risk with ERP applications is the specialized nature of the resources required to customize and implement. In most organizations, these specialized resources must be procured from high-priced consulting firms. To decrease the dependency on high-priced consultants, organizations need to invest in educating their own staff to take over responsibility for maintaining the ERP system. As these resources are in high-demand, the challenge is to keep these resources once they are fully trained.

ERP solutions can be quite complex with the underlying database, application modules, and interfaces with third-party and legacy applications. The cost and complexity of ERP solutions may actually cost more than the multiple application environments it was intended to replace. There are more advantages for implementing an ERP solution than cost savings. Having a single database should improve the quality and timeliness of financial information. However, processing errors can quickly impact multiple functions as the information is shared but sourced from the same database.

Implementing ERP Systems

Enterprise-integrated systems may be the answer to the needs of many organizations. The process of achieving successful implementation, although, has often been painful. After recognizing the threats, accurately assessing the ramifications and developing ways to mitigate the risks associated with ERP, organizations will be ready to begin implementation. The implementation of ERP should be performed with its unique characteristics in mind. The key areas for IT auditors to understand and monitor, where integration and implementation issues often pop up in these projects, include

- Corporate culture
- Process change
- Enterprise communication
- Management support
- ERP project manager competence
- The ERP team
- Project methodology
- Training
- Institutional commitment to change

Corporate Culture

The first factor involves understanding the corporate culture of the company in relation to its readiness and capability for change. There is a difference between seeing the necessity for change and being able to actually make the change. An ERP system using SAP, PeopleSoft, or Oracle is an enterprise-wide implementation that will affect many, if not all, of the departments. Thus, understanding each department and its concerns is important. Many decentralized organizations may find that their divisions do not welcome change that affects their territory. Resistance to change is common. The implementation team will need to "unfreeze the organization" or prepare the organization for change. By educating the users about the ERP system and involving user departments in the decision-making process, project teams can develop stronger acceptance of the system change.

Process Change

The second critical success factor requires the completion of all business process changes. These changes must occur before implementation. Thus, difficult decision making can be done early. Each company should perform some level of business process reevaluation or redesign before implementing ERP. With ERP comes cost, and changing the way the packaged system is configured after implementation is far more difficult than making the most informed decisions early. It is important to understand the structural and policy decisions that must be made. In addition, controls need to be reevaluated in the newly designed processes. Emphasis should be placed on the new risks associated with the new objectives. Because the controls available in the new system will differ from the previous environment, exposures inherent in the new system need to be addressed during the design phase.

Enterprise Communication

The third factor deals with communication. It is important to communicate continuously with new users at all levels in the organization. Employees who are affected by the new system need to be informed of its progress so their expectations will be set accurately. People need to be notified many times about change. Communication is the key to managing expectations. When expectations are set too high, people tend to become frustrated, upset, and disappointed with the results. When they are set too low, people may have difficulty adapting or be surprised with the extent of the change. Thus, to allow people time to accept and fully use the new system, a rigorous communication program should be adopted.

Auditors evaluating the system development phase of ERPs can ensure that the team is performing communication activities appropriately by reviewing minutes from meetings and workshops, interviewing users, and watching for behavioral problems. Lack of communication will create tension and resistance to the system change. By helping employees see their work as part of the whole and how it fits into the final product, the team can help communicate that the success of the project depends on the efforts of all employees.

Management Support

Acquiring executive support for the project is essential from the beginning. Executive management must spearhead the effort to conform to the ERP structure. The champion of this effort must be someone who is respected and can provide an objective point of view. Executives need to provide active leadership and commitment during the implementation of their ERP system. Their efforts to personally engage in the change process will provide the support needed to gain success in this project. Many companies or divisions within an organization will be reluctant to change their business to fit the ERP framework. Some may become territorial and want to sabotage the project. Many executives find that this phase is the hardest part of implementation. Aligning their policies and processes with the ERP system, perhaps giving up operational control and territorial control of their areas can be difficult.

ERP Project Manager Competence

If the critical factors above are working, another relevant critical success factor deals with project management and leadership. The ERP project manager should be capable of negotiating on even terms with the technical, business, and change management requirements. Integrated change blends the organizational and technical solutions into one large-scale change to avoid past systems development efforts where many concerns fell through the cracks. With an enterprise-wide-integrated information system, there is a need to address issues from all perspectives. Thus, the project manager and the project team must be sensitive to the impact of the new technology, new business processes, and changes in organization structures, standards, and procedures on the project as a whole. This will help keep the project manager from becoming overwhelmed by the potentially conflicting requirements of the project.

ERP Team

The ERP project team includes IT and business personnel. After defining project roles up front, team members should be reminded that they may be expected to shift to nontraditional roles. With ERP systems, many IT roles shift to the users. Configuring the ERP software to fit the requirements of a particular function becomes a user responsibility. Users configure the systems by using the tables and functions to run their business in the new way. The users modify tables and maintain systems. Thus, with many IT responsibilities shifting to the users, the project teams will be more effective when they are also composed of people from the business departments affected by the new systems. The people from the business departments become the champion from their respective areas, which usually help the adoption process. Many organizations are further strengthening their ERP project teams by adding outside consultants. These firms are able to provide project leadership support and ERP expertise that are not always readily available in-house.

Project Methodology

Another critical success factor relates to the project methodology. The selected project methodology should act as a road map to the project team. Objectives should be clear and measurable so that progress can be reviewed at intervals. Setting measurement goals is a key aspect of reengineering, and it demonstrates the effectiveness of actual improvements. System integration projects are complicated and require close attention. All interfaces should be documented so that any implication of change will be given the required attention. Whichever methodology is chosen, auditors must keep in mind that no single approach will work best at all times. The auditor must evaluate how a particular implementation approach was chosen and assess its appropriateness to the ERP project.

Training

It is also important to train users at all levels and provide support for all job changes. The ERP environment will change the roles of many employees. Current skills need to be reassessed and new skills need to be developed. The changing nature of the jobs means that management will need to provide support via new job definitions, rewards and recognition, and reevaluation of pay schedules. Education reflects a financial commitment to the effort and promotes problem-solving skills. Problem-solving skills empower employees to make effective changes.

It is also important to provide the project team members with the training to help them succeed in the project, such as training in technology, business, and change management issues. However, training is only the beginning with any ERP implementation. It is difficult to master all the modules because the system is complex. Experimentation is the only way to arrive at the best choice; it also locks in the learning. Users of the system have hundreds of ways to access the same data. They will need to understand what will and will not happen with certain parameters. For example, SAP encourages the "sandbox" approach, so users can understand in detail exactly what the system is designed to do. Even the team members need to try multiple options before they choose the configuration that works best for them.

Institutional Commitment to Change

Problems will definitely arise, and the project team should expect them. The project scale and complexity of ERP systems ensure that problems will surface throughout the implementation effort. The project leader and team, however, must continue to persevere and remain committed to the information system change. Thus, although the project team may run into resistance and problems, commitment to the change will help overcome the tides of reengineering. With management's persistence and consistency, the team will be able to overcome the pitfalls.

ERP Data Warehouse

Before ERP systems, organizations had separate systems and databases for finance, production, sales, and HR. There was often redundant and conflicting information contained in the separate databases and different uses with the separate systems. With the implementation of ERP systems, this information is now shared in a common data warehouse. In fact, this is one of the reasons for implementing an ERP solution. However, getting to the optimal position of using a common data warehouse requires a significant amount of up-front effort to define data elements, clean up the existing data, and convert the data to the new system/database.

Trends in Data Warehousing

"The data warehouse remains one of the largest—if not the largest—information repository in the enterprise," said Mark Beyer, research vice president at Gartner. "Only by being aware of the key market trends and how emerging technology solutions will blend with proven practices can the CIO avoid budget waste through 'misdirection' by the data warehouse management and delivery team" (January 2011). Gartner analysts said the data warehouse is set to remain a key component of the IT infrastructure and believe that, as the demand for business intelligence (BI) and the wider category of business analytics increases, optimization, flexible designs and alternative strategies will become more important.

SaaS ERP sees growing interest, but adoption has been limited. Most companies that Gartner spoke with are using their ERP systems in a traditional on-premises model. Where cloud-based offerings are used, they are primarily in adjacent areas, like collaboration and Web conferencing, CRM, e-mail, and HR.

Backup and Recovery of the Data Warehouse

The warehouse databases must be available and up to date during business hours and even for a while after hours. Business hours for many large global companies could be close to 24 hours to accommodate the various time zones around the world. Availability in this context means that the users must be able to access the data stored in the databases. Many factors threaten the availability of the data warehouse databases. These include natural disasters (such as floods and earthquakes), hardware failures (such as power failure or disk crash), software failures (such as DBMS malfunctions), and people failures (such as operator errors and user misunderstanding).

Recovery is the corrective process to restore the database to usable state from an erroneous state. The basic recovery process consists of the following steps:

- Identifying that the database is in an erroneous, damaged, or crashed state
- Suspending normal processing
- Determining the source and extent of the damage
- Taking corrective action such as:
  - Restoring the system resources to a usable state
  - Correcting the damage or removing invalid data
  - Restarting or continuing the interrupted process, including the reexecution of interrupted transactions
- Resuming normal processing

To cope with failures, additional components and algorithms are usually added to the system. Most techniques use recovery data or redundant data, which makes recovery possible. When taking corrective action, the effects of some transactions must be removed, whereas other transactions must be reexecuted; some transactions must even be undone and redone. The recovery data must make it possible to perform these steps.

A last, but extremely important, aspect of backup and recovery is testing. Test the backup and recovery procedures in a test environment before deploying them in the production environment.

Data Warehouse Integrity Checklist

Data warehouse integrity should be the concern of all those who will be designing and using the warehouse. There are three areas of integrity that should be considered throughout the life of the data warehouse system. Exhibits 26.1 and 26.2 illustrate this point.

Data integrity ⟹ Metadata integrity ⟹ Data warehouse integrity

Exhibit 26.1 Phases of data integrity.

How *stable* was the data when it was transferred?
  At what point in time should the data migrate to the data warehouse?
    Too close to the transaction and it is still in flux and subject to change.
    Too far away and the detail is lost in an aggregation.

What is the *basis* of its quantitative value?
  What operational unit holds the keys to the data's storage and definition?
    When is a "sale" considered to be completed?
    Sales: when the customer signs the order.
    Marketing: when it is invoiced.
    Finance: when the accounting period closes.
    Production: when it is ready to ship.
    Distribution: when it is shipped.
    Accounts receivable: when the check clears.
  All of these positions are valid from the perspective of each operational unit. When they are finished working with a sale, they consider it complete.

What is the *state* of the data value?
    Inventory, for example, changes its state as it moves through the firm from raw material to work-in-process to finished goods.
  Different material control policies have a diverse effect on the state of these values.
    Does the material get pushed through the system? Is the material "kited" for production and moved in lots?
    Does the material get pulled through the system? Does each operation in the cycle pull the material as needed?
    Does the material get "flushed" through the system? Is work-in-process only debited on an explosion of the bill-of-material, based on units completed at the end of the run?

Exhibit 26.2 Data warehouse integrity checklist.

Although these are basic questions of business policy, database design, and audit procedures, they take on a new meaning when asked in the environment of a data warehouse. As we are all too aware, policies change. The historical nature of a data warehouse precludes the assumption that all pieces of data have been gathered under the same policies that are in effect today or that will be in the future. IT auditors and managers will have to make certain that not only will they need to understand the impacts, but decision makers using the data will also have to have access to an expanded understanding of these potential anomalies in the data.

Example of Security and Controls in SAP ERP

SAP continues to be one of the market leaders in ERP even during economic downturn in 2009–2010. In late 2010, Gartner Inc. confirmed that SAP is one of the broadest and deepest solutions in the market, and its best practices and the fast-start program reduce the effort needed for the early phases of an implementation. The following is a discussion of establishing security and controls in SAP ERP.

Establishing Security and Controls in SAP ERP

SAP ERP imposes on an organization a changed computer environment and a stronger reliance on networked computers. Thus, there is a need for the reassessment of the information security architecture. The information security architecture is the foundation of all diverse computing and networking elements of an organization. It is imperative that information security architectures provide for consistent administration and monitoring tools and techniques, common identification and authentication processes, and an alerting capability that meets realistic needs. Lastly, we will discuss the impact of EDI and Internet capabilities on security.

Security Features of the Basis Component

Auditors are challenged with ensuring that adequate controls are in place in information systems. Controls should reduce business risks and security exposures. Fortunately, the SAP Business Connection Module has built-in security features. They provide for security-related concerns of applications, data, and resources. SAP's security and control capabilities support identification, authentication, and authorization of system users to ensure that only authorized users are able to access specific transactions, tables, modules, or the entire ERP system. In addition, SAP programs and data are internally protected from other applications and utilities. Thus, with SAP's security and control features, the complex SAP ERP environment can be adequately safeguarded.

The effectiveness of the security system depends on the combination of the security measures implemented. Security measures should uniquely define individual users to the system and prove or confirm their identity. In addition, they should determine whether users are allowed access to certain resources. The IT auditor needs to review the major areas below. These are SAP's unique security components and how they work together to support the identification, authentication, and authorization of the ERP users.

- Log-on process
- User master records

- SAP
- TSTC table (Internal Sorted Table [TS] Table Control [TC] SAP Instructions)
- Authorization objects
- Authorization value sets
- Authorization profiles
- Additional authorization checks
- Changes

Summary of Access Control

To summarize, the ERP process for user access is very detailed. Before a user can initiate a transaction, SAP performs an access-checking process. When the user enters the user ID and password, the system checks the user ID and only allows valid users with the appropriate password to gain access. After gaining access, the user can initiate a transaction. However, if the transaction is not defined or locked in the TSTC table, it is rejected. Furthermore, if an additional authorization check has been defined, the user's authorization value set for the object is tested. It is rejected if the user is not authorized for the additional check. Lastly, the other detailed authorizations of the user (that are stored in profiles and in authorization value sets) are checked by the system to determine whether the user is authorized for the object.

In SAP ERP, user access capabilities are managed by the user master records, authorization profiles, and authorization value sets. To ensure that all user access is consistent with management policies, procedures, and guidelines, control must be exercised over changes to user master records, profiles, and authorization value sets. The SAP ERP system provides standard authorization objects specifically for this purpose. Thus, they can be used to control the actions of the administrator in relation to different user groups. They can also specify the profiles an administrator is able to maintain, and the profiles a user is able to add to a user master record. Furthermore, the authorization value sets that an administrator is able to maintain and enter into a profile can also be restricted.

Administrative Controls

Administrative controls are implemented via documented policies and procedures and are exercised by people rather than the system. These controls address access to data, system development, customization and modification, and maintenance processes. The automated control procedures offered through the SAP system are more effective when reinforced with control procedures. Business-based policies and procedures should be established to address accountability, access control, confidentiality, integrity, and security management issues.

Accountability

As users become developers of the SAP ERP system, they will be customizing the system through changes to the tables. Segregation of duties between the users and the IT department will become imperative to ensure accountability. Thus, policies should address and monitor segregation of duties. For example, customization should be separated from the production environment and procedures should allow only properly tested and approved changes to be copied into production. Similarly, access to customization functions should be prevented in the production environment and all changes should require approval and require sign-off by users and IT management. In addition, a detailed security policy should specify the ownership of the system and data and require the documentation of all system changes. Management should review system logs for unauthorized table changes and follow up and investigate any unauthorized use of the system. Lastly, physical access to the servers and workstations should be restricted to authorized personnel.

Access Control

Access to SAP data and transactions are restricted by the SAP security system. However, standards and procedures will ensure that management has authorized access rights, users' accesses are relevant to their duties, and that access rights are not incompatible. Thus, the following segregation of duty procedures should be established:

■ Users' direct access capability should be restricted by the operating system and database.
■ Users' access rights should be approved and documented by management.
■ User master records should be assigned for each user to prevent sharing of IDs and passwords.
■ Passwords should be kept confidential and should be difficult to divulge.
■ Passwords should be changed regularly.
■ Management should regularly review and follow up on any access violations.
■ Access to the SAP system during nonworking hours should be minimized and adequately controlled.

Confidentiality, Integrity, and Security Management

The environmental controls within SAP can be compromised if access or changes to SAP programs and data from other applications and utilities are not properly restricted. Thus, the following issues should be reviewed to ensure that the security system is not negated:

■ The ability to change the system and start-up profiles should be appropriately restricted.
■ The SAP user master record should not be deleted and users should not be able to delete this record.
■ DYNPROs changes should be prohibited in the production environment and should be restricted to appropriate authorized users. The DYNPRO flow logic are the dialog modules of the Advanced Business Application Programming (ABAP) program itself are called. The program flow can differ from execution to execution. You can even assign different dialog transaction codes to one program.
■ Additional authorization checks for potentially dangerous transactions should be defined in the TSTC and should not be changed or deleted.
■ Review of users given access as batch administrators should be performed periodically because these users can perform any operations on all background jobs in the SAP ERP system.
■ Batch input session files that have been created by an interface program or an internal SAP program should not be modified before the release stage.
■ Changes to the ABAP/4 Dictionary should be adequately tested and authorized.
■ Standard table entries should be removed when not intended to be used for a particular installation.
■ ABAPs should be assigned to appropriate authorization groups so that users cannot execute ABAPs that are not relevant to their work functions.

EDI and Internet Security

SAP ERP is not immune to intrusion and exploitation from outsiders. SAP ERP supports EDI; EDI and the Internet make security issues more critical because external intruders can degrade the integrity of the system and jeopardize company assets. Thus, security policies should accommodate the unique needs of EDI and the Internet.

Dangers threatening EDI messages include the compromise of message integrity, message repudiation, disclosure of confidential data, misrouting of messages, and delaying of messages. To ensure that EDI messages arrive at appropriate destinations and are only accessed by authorized users, security mechanisms and procedures must be employed. EDI security mechanisms available include encryption, digital signatures, key management, and sealing. Auditors must ensure that the overall security architecture includes security mechanisms that support EDI. In addition, procedures to ensure that information transferred via EDI is complete and accurate should be established.

With the advent of the Internet, computer hackers are becoming more sophisticated. As companies combine SAP with the advantages of the Internet, security threats will continue to multiply. In an integrated system such as SAP ERP, a hacker may be able to compromise not only a small section of the system but all the systems connected to the basic component. Thus, it is even more crucial to ensure that basic Internet security measures are applied. Examples of Internet security measures include installing internal and external firewalls, using security tools to find well-known security problems and holes, and making safe computing practices a condition for employment. Although SAP provides Internet capabilities, they do not yet provide for the encryption or encoding of TCP/IP packets over the Internet.

Conclusion

In today's client–server environment, success with ERP requires diligence for all the critical success factors. There is little tolerance for mediocre performance. Control breakdowns and financial losses to the organization often occur when these areas are not closely monitored and corrective action is not taken. Auditors and project teams that encourage the consideration of these critical success factors will set a winning course for the implementation of the enterprise resource system.

With regard to ERP systems, such as SAP, people and passwords can become the weakest link in most information systems. Both must be managed effectively to ensure the protection of the ERP system. Thus, system security features can only be effective when reinforced with policies and procedures that prevent the compromise of security in the ERP system.

Review Questions

1. How does ERP impact corporate culture? How does it impact business processes?
2. If ERP is being considered for implementation in your company, list the control points you would look for in its implementation.
3. What security features does SAP BC have? List and explain five of them.
4. What security features does SAP have with regard to EDI and the Internet?
5. What are some of the control concerns in backup and recovery of data warehousing?

Multiple-Choice Questions

1. Communication is the key to managing expectations because
   a. When expectations are set too low, people tend to become frustrated, upset, and disappointed with the results
   b. When expectations are set too high, people may have difficulty adapting or are surprised with the extent of the change
   c. A rigorous communications program is needed to allow people time to accept and fully use the new system
   d. People need to be notified once or twice about change

2. In SAP ERP, user access capabilities are managed by all of the following except
   a. Encryption
   b. Authorization value sets
   c. Authorization profiles
   d. User master records

3. Benefits of implementing an ERP solution includes
   a. Integrated financial systems
   b. Standardized processes
   c. Shared, real-time information
   d. All of the above

4. Key risks of ERP solutions includes
   a. Cost to implement
   b. Shortage of trained personnel
   c. Reliance on a single supplier
   d. All of the above

5. Implementing and ERP solution is challenging because
   a. The organization must adapt to the system
   b. The project methodology is different from other projects
   c. The organization is dependent on consultants
   d. None of the above

6. Staffing an ERP project is unique in that
   a. Users take on greater responsibility for configuring the system
   b. Consultants may be required for their expertise
   c. Job descriptions may change
   d. All of the above

7. Using a common data warehouse requires a significant amount of up-front effort to
   a. Define data elements
   b. Clean up existing data
   c. Convert data to the new database
   d. All of the above

8. Business process changes are critical for the success of an ERP solution because
   a. The organization will need to adapt to the ERP solution
   b. Controls in the new system will differ from the previous environment
   c. Processes must be redesigned before implementation
   d. All of the above

9. Management support of the ERP project is essential because of
   a. Organizations reluctant to change

    b. Lack of management commitment

    c. Negative organizational climate

    d. None of the above

10. Database recovery processes consist of the following:

    a. Determining the source and extent of damage

    b. Restoring the system to a usable state

    c. Restarting or continuing the interrupted process

    d. All of the above

Exercises

1. You are asked to perform an audit of an ERP implementation in your company. Design an audit program for reviewing key steps or control points in this process.
2. Develop an audit program to validate the security controls implemented in SAP ERP.

Answers to Multiple-Choice Questions

1—c; 2—a; 3—d; 4—d; 5—a; 6—d; 7—d; 8—d; 9—a; 10—d

Further Reading

1. Gallegos, F., *Reviewing Focus Database Applications*, EDP Auditing Series, #74-10-23, Auerbach Publishers, Boca Raton, FL, 2001, pp. 1–24.
2. Gallegos, F., *Security and Control over Intranets and Extranets*, Part 1, Auerbach Publishers, Boca Raton, FL, 2002.
3. Gallegos, F., *Security and Control Over Intranets and Extranets*, Part 2, Auerbach Publishers, Boca Raton, FL, 2002.
4. Gallegos, F., IT auditor careers: IT governance provides new roles and opportunities, *Inf. Syst. Control J.*, 3, 40–43, 2003.
5. Gallegos, F., IT governance: IT audit role, *Inf. Syst. Control J.*, 4(3), 25–27, 2003.
6. Gallegos, F. and C. Liam, Securing clinical information systems: Accessing health care in the information age, *J. Assoc. HealthCare Internal Auditors: New Perspect. HealthCare Risk Manage., Control Gov.*, 23(4), 30–37, 2004.
7. Gallegos, F. and D. Manson, *Auditing DBMS Recover Procedures*, Auerbach Publishers, Boca Raton, FL, 2002.
8. Gallegos, F. and L. Preiser-Houy, *Auditing Prototypes: Approaches and Techniques*, #74-30-60, Auerbach Publishers, Boca Raton, FL, 2001, pp. 1–8.
9. Gallegos, F. and L. Tyson-Dualan, Electronic funds transfer: Control issues in a cashless, checkless society, *Info. Strategy—The Executives J.*, 17(2), 36–39, 2001.
10. Hesterman, C., C. Pang and N. Montgomery, *Gartner: Magic Quadrant for ERP for Product-Centric Midmarket Companies*, December 17, 2010.
11. Musaji, Y., The SAP landscape that warrants audit, *Inf. Syst. Audit Control Assoc.*, 2006. Available at: http://www.isaca.org/Journal/Past-Issues/2006/Volume-1/Documents/jopdf0601-sap-landscape-that-warrants-audit.pdf
12. SAP Global, SAP leads enterprise software market worldwide, June 29, 2006, http://www.sap.com/about/press/press.epx?pressid=6449.

Appendix I

Information Technology Audit Cases

Computer-Assisted Audit Cases

Case 1: Wooback City

Part 1

The computerized human resource system of Wooback City is undergoing an audit. Audry Wilson is the senior member of the audit team reviewing the payroll component of this system. Audry has heard how helpful computer-assisted audit procedures can be, and she has asked you to suggest how some of these procedures can be used in the audit.

Wooback has two types of payroll disbursements: employee, which is part of the human resources system, and welfare, which is maintained on a separate system. Audry has been informed by the IT manager that transactions for the last three years are available; however, the programmer/analyst responsible for this area was terminated, and funding was not budgeted for a replacement.

Your assignment: identify and describe potential computer-assisted audit procedures that could be used in this situation.

Part 2

On examination of files, you find that no transaction files exist for either the welfare or employee distributions for the last year. However, updated master files of the employee payroll exist for each pay period for the last year. Master files for prior periods can be obtained from the International Revenue Service (IRS) on multifile backup tapes retained under a record retention agreement. Per discussion with the IT manager, the record layout for the file was last revised in 2001. Print files were found on the welfare payments for the last three years. These files are used to print the actual checks.

Your assignment: What do you do now?

Case 2: Ready or Not Auto Insurance

As an IT auditor for the state insurance commission, you have been asked to assist field auditors. The commission's audit team would like to verify the company's total revenue from policy premiums by direct confirmation with policyholders. However, the company's computer records do not show cumulative premiums by customers. The president of the company does not want to use his staff to regenerate this information, stating that their time is valuable.

The company retains all transactions for one year on their client/server. Each transaction is recorded in an Access database, one per record, with the customer number being the primary key. There are close to three million records in the file, and backup copies of the record are made in random order and copied to a Zip drive. The insurance company also keeps another Access file that contains the name, address, and customer number for each policyholder. The senior auditor would like you to assist in obtaining the transaction data for a sample of policyholders and preparing the confirmations.

Your assignment: Describe the steps you would take to generate the data and produce the desired confirmations. You may either write a narrative or use a flow diagram to describe the process.

Case 3: Holt Valley Hospital Services, Inc.

Holt Valley Hospital Services, Inc., is a large healthcare services company that acquired W. Wilson Hospital, an acute-care hospital, this past year. This is a large facility with a typically long collection cycle for its patients' accounts receivable. During the annual audit, the "Big Four" auditors supplied a year-end aged accounts receivable trial balance to the internal audit staff. Now, three months later, the internal audit team needs to determine subsequent collections on 22,567 patient accounts.

Your assignment:

1. State the audit objective in determining subsequent collections, and discuss two functions in which the use of a computer would be helpful to the auditors in meeting that objective.
2. Describe the process, using transaction files that are also available, in narrative or flowchart form to summarize subsequent activity on each account.
3. Determine if the hospital is in compliance with the Health Insurance Portability and Accountability Act (HIPAA) of 1996. How do you approach this?

Case 4: Acme Insurance Corporation

The Acme Insurance Corporation is presently undergoing an audit by the state insurance commission. The commissioner's audit team would like to verify the company's total revenue. The revenue transaction file contains 30 million transactions. Each transaction is recorded individually with a summary field indicating premium paid year to date. Their tax year ends 12/31, and the file is sequentially arranged by account number.

They also have another file that contains the names, addresses, and account numbers of active and inactive policyholders. The senior auditor would like you to assist in obtaining transaction data for a random sample of policyholders and preparing the confirmations.

1. The auditors, before sampling, would like a profile of the number of transactions that occurred during each month of the tax year as well as the range and frequency of dollar value. How would you meet this requirement?

2. Describe in detail the steps you would take to generate the transaction data, produce the desired confirmations, and meet the auditors' additional requests.
3. Flowchart the solution to this problem.

Controls

Case 5: OnTheRise Corporation

The OnTheRise Corporation wants to automate its decision support model for organizational change. To obtain inputs for the model, the corporate managers wish to download information directly from the corporate personnel files. Personnel files are maintained on the corporate human resources system. The basic worksheet for this application is the Organizational Change Model Calculation Sheet (see Exhibit A1.1). They are considering using Excel and importing data from the human resources system, which is in Oracle.

Your assignment:

1. What type of a decision support model do we have?
2. List and describe the major controls to look for in this type of model.
3. What computer-assisted audit tools and techniques (CATTs) can be used in auditing this application? List and explain in detail at least three techniques and three tools that could be used.

Age	Start	Losses	Hires	Hires Rate	Part-Time Hires	Turnover Rate	Final Group
(1)	(2)	(3)	(4)	(5)	(6)	(7)	(8)
20–27							
28–35							
36–45							
46–50							
51–55							
56–60							
61–65							
Total							

Column # instructions projection processing.
1. For age groups Step Column #.
2. Number of employees by age group at beginning year.
3. Employees who left company, calculate T/O.
4. Employees who entered company, calculate hiring rate.
5. Derived for past year, a constant in projection.
6. Hires part-time.
7. Derived from past year, a constant in projections.
8. Column 2 plus column 4 minus (total × column 7).

Exhibit A1.1 All degreed employees: Year 1.

Case 6: Wedco Electronics

As a result of an inventory audit, it was found that electronic supplies worth over $1 million were stolen from the company due to control weaknesses in the equipment ordering system. Also, employee information was compromised. The perpetrator was able to access the inventory budget data, economic order quantities, and the equipment ordering system via the network. This corporation is located in California, and the state recently passed SB 1386.

Your assignment:

1. How would you conduct the audit of this system and the event?
2. What controls would you test in this situation?
3. What key steps would you look for to see if they are in compliance with SB 1386?

Case 7: Amazon Industries

As a Certified Public Accountant (CPA), Certified Internal Auditor (CIA), and Certified Information Systems Auditor (CISA) you have been asked to perform an audit of company records in support of the Attest function to verify the annual statements. The inventory balances from the computerized system are reported to be $121 million, but reports from field auditors show that balances are severely overstated. In discussions with employees and managers you find some overlap in functions with certain personnel authorized to perform functions in other departments. Also, several personnel have not taken vacations in over three years. In compliance with the Sarbanes–Oxley Act of 2002, what do you do?

Your assignment:

1. How would you deal with this situation as an internal auditor?
2. How would you deal with this situation as an external auditor?
3. What general control weaknesses might you test and examine? And what audit evidence would you gather?
4. What application tests might you perform?

Legal Issues

Case 8: OhMY Corporation

Your company, OhMY Corporation, hires a Big Four firm to recommend a turnkey system. Your company states that it does not want to go through the hassle of customizing a system or invest in extensive training of employees to run a system. It wants a system that is ready to run. Your company has specified this in written contractual terms signed by the CPA firm's partner. The system you got is difficult to operate and does not meet your company's needs. The president of the company would like internal audit and legal counsel input to the following questions:

1. What evidence must your company provide to prove negligence on the part of the CPA firm?
2. How did the CPA firm owe duty of care?
3. How could the "reasonable person" test enter into the outcome of a potential lawsuit?
4. Where could you go to determine who is liable for damages?

Case 9: Ideal Financial

You have been asked to audit the development of Ideal Financial Integrated Systems (IFIS). In reviewing background information about the system, you find the contract, which has an integration clause written by your company's president that the contractor, AZ Consulting Services, would honor the target budget. It was signed by the AZ representative. Six weeks into the contract and systems development, the contractor appears to be overrunning his initial estimates by 50%. The overrun appears to be due to requirement changes, which both the contractor and your company have agreed to, and technology issues. The project is approximately 24 weeks away from the completion date.

Your report is due. What do you report?

It is now 15 weeks into the project and the contractor is still 50% over budget and demands that the contract be renegotiated. The system is desperately needed for replacing systems that have Year 2000 problems. It will cause significant problems to customers being promised these new services and may cost the company at least $20 million in new sales. What is the likely outcome of this situation?

If the decision for renegotiations was given, what additional clauses would you recommend be added to the contract to protect your company?

Security Issues

Case 10: Real-Wire

Real-Wire is a public electronic funds transfer (EFT) network with its head office and major computer switch based in Chicago. It is currently under contract to the Department of Treasury to assist in e-commerce and EFT initiatives when federal systems are overloaded. They have handled overload processing, which has increased their workload by 15–20% on occasions. The company has computer switches in each capital city throughout the United States, including Alaska and Hawaii, which are linked into a national communications network. Approximately 200 financial institutions (banks, building societies, and credit unions) use the network to provide automatic teller machine and point-of-sale services to their customers.

Real-Wire has only been in operation for 15 years, but during that time it has been very successful. When the United States began to deregulate its financial markets in 1985 and foreign banks began to enter the marketplace, Real-Wire obtained substantial new business because it could offer these financial institutions immediate EFT services.

As a consultant specializing in computer controls and audit, you have been hired by the managing director of Real-Wire to examine the state of controls within the EFT system. She explains to you that an increasing number of potential customers are requesting some type of independent assurance that controls within the system are reliable. Accordingly, she has decided to initiate a controls review of the entire system so that a third-party "letter of comfort" can be provided to potential customers.

The initial part of your controls review focuses on the main switch in Chicago. As part of your review, you examine the status of disaster recovery planning for the switch. In terms of short-term recovery, controls appear to be in place and working. Backup tapes for all data and programs are stored both on- and off-site to enable recovery if programs and data are lost for some reason. In addition, protocols for short-term recovery are well documented, and operators seem familiar with and well trained in these protocols. From time to time they have to exercise these protocols because some temporary system failure occurs. Real-Wire claims to offer its customers 24-hour service. The director states that its personnel recognize the criticality of being able to perform efficient, effective system recovery in a timely manner.

When you examine controls over long-term disaster recovery, however, the situation is different. There is no long-term disaster recovery plan, nor are there operators and other personnel trained in recovery protocols for a major disaster. For example, it is uncertain how Real-Wire would recover from a fire that destroyed the switch or an event that caused major structural damage to the switch.

As a result of your findings, you meet with the managing director to find out why controls in this area are so weak when controls in other areas seem strong. She is surprised by your concern about long-term disaster recovery. She argues that it is not cost effective to prepare a long-term disaster recovery plan and practice recovery protocols on a regular basis for three reasons. First, she believes a plan is useless because, in the event of a major disaster, timely recovery is impossible anyway. She points out that it would take several days for the telephone company to reconfigure all the data communications lines to another site. Even if Real-Wire had another switch available immediately, it could not operate during this period. Second, she argues that Real-Wire's customers would not tolerate a decrease in their service levels while disaster recovery exercises were carried out. Unless the recovery protocols are practiced regularly, she argues, they are useless. Third, she contends that eventual recovery will not be a problem anyway. Operations can simply be transferred to another switch in one of the other capital cities. While the telephone company reconfigures data communications lines to the other switch, backup files can be flown to the site with plenty of time to spare. She argues that the customers of Real-Wire recognize they will not be able to use their EFT facilities during the recovery period, but they accept this situation as a risk of doing business. The only other alternative, she argues, is to replicate all switching facilities in each capital city, and this clearly is not cost effective.

Required

1. Outline how you intend to respond to the managing director's comments in your report to the board of directors on the state of controls in Real-Wire computer operations.
2. What federal laws apply to Real-Wire? List and explain each applicable law and describe how it could be used to support your audit.
3. Do they have an intranet that uses Transmission Control Protocol/Internet Protocol (TCP/IP) heavily? Do they have any security software installed? What would be your major security concerns?
4. The office of the comptroller of the currency plans to review them next year. What would you recommend?

Cloud and Mobile Computing

Case 11: Silver Lining Investments Company

The Chief Investments Officer of Silver Lining Investments Company would like to improve the management of agents/brokers data without incurring additional costs. He is hoping that with a more streamlined process, the agents and brokers would be more inclined to do business with Silver Lining Corporation.

The three main goals are

1. Provide the ability to pay different commission rate for different products sold
2. Provide agents/brokers access to their earned commissions information and potential bonus payouts
3. Lower internal maintenance costs

The IT department performed analysis of potential solutions, including modifying existing systems, developing a new system internally, and engaging a cloud provider. Based on the Return on Investment (ROI) analysis, engaging a cloud provider appears to be the most cost efficient. The CEO has been reading about security and risks of cloud computing and is not sure if this is the right solution, Hence, he called the Chief Audit Executive (CAE) to help him with the decision. You, the IT Auditor, are assigned to work on this project.

1. How would you accomplish this task?
2. What would you present to the CAE? CEO? Write your proposed recommendations.
3. If the company decided to move forward with Request for Proposal, what type of questions and information would you want the potential vendors to provide?

Case 12: Mobile-Work Inc.

You have been asked to audit the "Bring-Your-Own-Device" program at Mobile-Work Inc.

1. Develop a detailed audit program.
2. What type of issues do you expect to encounter? What would be your recommendations to remediate those issues or to mitigate the risks?

Appendix II

Bibliography of Selected Publications for Information Technology Auditors

Today's IT auditor is often confronted with situations in which accurate information is needed urgently. This updated bibliography lists many of these publications and identifies significant works released since 2000. It comprises publications from government agencies and professional associations as well as relevant textbooks and reference books.

Government Publications

During the past seven years, various governmental organizations have published a variety of studies and reports on IT audit-related topics. Publications can be ordered directly from the governmental agencies for a nominal fee. Most of them can also be ordered through the Internet or accessed online.

Department of Justice of the United States

Publications can be ordered from the Department of Justice of the United States, 950 Pennsylvania Avenue, NW, Washington, DC 20530-0001. They can also be ordered, and some retrieved, through the Web at http://www.justice.gov/publications/publications_a.html.

From the Computer Crime and Intellectual Property Section:

Computer Crime Legal Resources, http://www.usdoj.gov/criminal/cybercrime/cclaws.html.
Frequently Asked Questions and Answers about the Council of Europe Convention on Cybercrime (Draft 24REV2), http://www.usdoj.gov/criminal/cybercrime/COEFAQs.htm.

Intellectual Property Policy and Programs, Cases, and Legal Resources, http://www.usdoj.gov/criminal/cybercrime/ippolicy.html.

International Aspects of Computer Crime, http://www.usdoj.gov/criminal/cybercrime/intl.html.

Privacy Issues in the High-Tech Context, http://www.usdoj.gov/criminal/cybercrime/privacy.html.

Prosecuting Crimes Facilitated by Computers and by the Internet, http://www.justice.gov/criminal/cybercrime/crimes.html.

Searching and Seizing Computers, http://www.usdoj.gov/criminal/cybercrime/searching.html.

Speech Issues in the High-Tech Context, http://www.usdoj.gov/criminal/cybercrime/speech.html.

The Electronic Frontier: The Challenge of Unlawful Conduct Involving the Use of the Internet—A Report of the President's Working Group on Unlawful Conduct on the Internet, http://www.usdoj.gov/criminal/cybercrime/unlawful.htm.

From the Civil Rights Division:

Information Technology and People with Disabilities: The Current State of Federal Accessibility, http://www.usdoj.gov/crt/508/report/content.htm.

From the Federal Bureau of Investigation Division:

A Parent's Guide to Internet Safety, http://www.fbi.gov/publications/pguide/pguidee.htm.

From the Justice Management Division:

The Department of Justice Systems Development Life Cycle Guidance Document, http://www.usdoj.gov/jmd/irm/lifecycle/table.htm.

Government Accountability Office of the United States

Publications can be ordered from the U.S. Government Accountability Office (GAO), PO Box 37050, Washington, DC 20013. They can also be ordered through the Web at http://www.gao.gov.

1. Although Progress Reported, Federal Agencies Need to Resolve Significant Deficiencies, GAO-08-496T, February 14, 2008.
2. Protecting Personally Identifiable Information, GAO-08-343, January 25, 2008.
3. Improvements for Acquisition of Customs Trade Processing System Continue, but Further Efforts Needed to Avoid More Cost and Schedule Shortfalls, GAO-08-46, October 25, 2007.
4. Challenges in Developing a Public/Private Recovery Plan, GAO-08-212T, October 23, 2007.
5. Further Improvements Needed to Identify and Oversee Poorly Planned and Performing Projects, GAO-07-1211T, September 20, 2007.
6. Areas for Improvement in Information Security Controls, GAO-07-899R, June 14, 2007.
7. Data Breaches Are Frequent, but Evidence of Resulting Identity Theft Is Limited; However, the Full Extent Is Unknown, GAO-07.737, June 4, 2007.
8. Areas for Improvement in Information Security Controls, GAO-06-522R, March 16, 2006.
9. Responsibilities and Information Technology Governance at Leading Private-Sector Companies, GAO-05-986, September 9, 2005.
10. Implementation of the Freedom of Information Act, GAO-05-648T, May 11, 2005.
11. Emerging Cybersecurity Issues Threaten Federal Information Systems, GAO-05-231, May 13, 2005.
12. Areas for Improvement in Information Security Controls, GAO-05-467R, April 18, 2005.
13. Assessing the Reliability of Computer-Processed Data, GAO-02-15G, September 1, 2002.
14. Contracting for Information Technology Services, GAO-03-384R, February 14, 2003.

15. A Framework for Assessing and Improving Enterprise Architecture Management (Version 1.1), GAO-03-584G, April 1, 2003.
16. Challenges to the Adoption of Smart Card Technology, GAO-03-1108T, September 9, 2003.
17. Effective Patch Management Is Critical to Mitigating Software Vulnerabilities, GAO-03-1138T, September 10, 2003.
18. A Framework for Assessing and Improving Process Maturity, GAO-04-394G, March 1, 2004.
19. Technologies to Secure Federal Systems, GAO-04-467, March 9, 2004.
20. Cybersecurity for Critical Infrastructure Protection, GAO-04-321, May 28, 2004.
21. Information Resource Management Internal Control Issues, GAO-05-288R, March 10, 2005.
22. Protecting Information Systems Supporting the Federal Government's and the Nation's Critical Information, GAO High Risk Series, GAO-03-121, January 2003.
23. Federal Information System Controls Audit Manual, GAO-09-232G, 2009.
24. Government Auditing Standards (Yellow Book), Preliminary Edition, GAO-03-673G, June 2003.
25. Financial Management Service: Significant Weaknesses in Computer Controls Continue, GAO-02-317, http://www.gao.gov/new.items/d02317.pdf, January 31, 2002.
26. European Security: U.S. and European Contributions to Foster Stability and Security in Europe, GAO-02-174, http://www.gao.gov/new.items/d02174.pdf, November 28, 2001.
27. Computer Security: Improvements Needed to Reduce Risk to Critical Federal Operations and Assets, GAO-02-231T, http://www.gao.gov/new.items/d02231t.pdf, November 9, 2001.
28. Homeland Security: Challenges and Strategies in Addressing Short- and Long-Term National Needs, GAO-02-160T, http://www.gao.gov/new.items/d02160t.pdf, November 7, 2001.
29. Homeland Security: A Risk Management Approach Can Guide Preparedness Efforts, GAO-02-208T, http://www.gao.gov/new.items/d02208t.pdf, October 31, 2001.
30. Critical Infrastructure Protection: Significant Challenges in Safeguarding Government and Privately Controlled Systems from Computer-Based Attacks, GAO-01-1168T, http://www.gao.gov/new.items/d011168t.pdf, September 26, 2001.
31. Education Information Security: Improvements Made but Control Weaknesses Remain, GAO-01-1067, http://www.gao.gov/new.items/d011067.pdf, September 12, 2001.
32. Information Security: Code Red, Code Red II, and SirCam Attacks Highlight Need for Proactive Measures, GAO-01-1073T, http://www.gao.gov/new.items/d011073t.pdf, August 29, 2001.
33. Information Technology Management: Social Security Administration Practices Can Be Improved, GAO-01-961, http://www.gao.gov/new.items/d01961.pdf, August 21, 2001.
34. Information Security: Weaknesses Place Commerce Data and Operations at Serious Risk, GAO-01-751, http://www.gao.gov/new.items/d01751.pdf, August 13, 2001.
35. Information Security: Weaknesses Place Commerce Data and Operations at Serious Risk, GAO-01-1004T, http://www.gao.gov/new.items/ d011004t.pdf, August 3, 2001.
36. Information Systems: Opportunities Exist to Strengthen SEC's Oversight of Capacity and Security, GAO-01-863, http://www.gao.gov/new.items/d01863.pdf, July 25, 2001.
37. Information Security: Weak Controls Place Interior's Financial and Other Data at Risk, GAO-01-615, http://www.gao.gov/new.items/d01615.pdf, July 3, 2001.
38. Social Security Administration: Information Systems Could Improve Processing Attorney Fee Payments in Disability Program, GAO-01-796, http://www.gao.gov/new.items/d01796.pdf, June 29, 2001.
39. Computer-Based Patient Records: Better Planning and Oversight by VA, DOD, and IHS Would Enhance Health Data Sharing, GAO-01-459, http://www.gao.gov/new.items/d01459.pdf, April 30, 2001.
40. Computer Security: Weaknesses Continue to Place Critical Federal Operations and Assets at Risk, GAO-01-600T, http://www.gao.gov/archive/2000/d01600t.pdf, April 5, 2001.
41. Information Security: Challenges to Improving DOD's Incident Response Capabilities, GAO-01-341, http://www.gao.gov/new.items/d01341.pdf, March 29, 2001.
42. Information Security: Safeguarding of Data in Excessed Department of Energy Computers, GAO-01-469, http://www.gao.gov/new.items/d01469.pdf, March 29, 2001.
43. Information Security: Advances and Remaining Challenges to Adoption of Public Key Infrastructure Technology, GAO-01-277, http://www.gao.gov/new.items/d01277.pdf, February 26, 2001.

44. Information Security: IRS Electronic Filing Systems, GAO-01-306, http://www.gao.gov/new.items/d01306.pdf, February 16, 2001.

45. Information Security: Weak Controls Place DC Highway Trust Fund and Other Data at Risk, GAO-01-155, http://www.gao.gov/new.items/d01155.pdf, January 31, 2001.

46. FAA Computer Security: Actions Needed to Address Critical Weaknesses that Jeopardize Aviation Operations, T-AIMD-00-330, http://www.gao.gov/archive/2000/ai00330t.pdf, September 27, 2000.

47. Information Security: Progress Made but Challenges Remain to Protect Federal Systems and the Nation's Critical Infrastructures, GAO-03-564T, http://www.gao.gov/new.items/d03564t.pdf, April 8, 2003.

48. Technology Assessment: Using Biometrics for Border Security, GAO-03-174, November 14, 2002.

49. Border Security: Challenges in Implementing Border Technology, GAO-03-546T, http://www.gao.gov/new.items/d03546t.pdf, March 12, 2003.

50. Homeland Security: Information Sharing Activities Face Continued Management Challenges, GAO-02-1122T, http://www.gao.gov/new.items/d021122t.pdf, October 1, 2002.

51. Homeland Security: OMB's Temporary Cessation of Information Technology Funding for New Investments, GAO-03-186T, http://www.gao.gov/new.items/d03186t.pdf, October 1, 2002.

52. Mass Transit: Challenges in Securing Transit Systems, GAO-02-1075T, http://www.gao.gov/new.items/d021075t.pdf, September 18, 2002.

53. Critical Infrastructure Protection: Significant Homeland Security Challenges Need to Be Addressed, GAO-02-918T, http://www.gao.gov/new.items/d02918t.pdf, July 9, 2002.

54. National Preparedness: Integrating New and Existing Technology and Information Sharing into an Effective Homeland Security Strategy, GAO-02-811T, http://www.gao.gov/new.items/d02811t.pdf, June 7, 2002.

55. Security Breaches at Federal Buildings in Atlanta, Georgia, GAO-02-668T, http://www.gao.gov/cgi-bin/ordtab.pl?Item0=GAO-02-668T, April 30, 2002.

56. National Preparedness: Technologies to Secure Federal Buildings, GAO-02-687T, http://www.gao.gov/new.items/d02687t.pdf, April 25, 2002.

57. Diffuse Security Threats: Technologies for Mail Sanitization Exist, but Challenges Remain, GAO-02-365, http://www.gao.gov/new.items/d02365.pdf, April 23, 2002.

58. Homeland Security: A Framework for Addressing the Nation's Efforts, GAO-01-1158T, http://www.gao.gov/new.items/d011158t.pdf, September 21, 2001.

59. Critical Infrastructure Protection: Significant Challenges in Protecting Federal Systems and Developing Analysis and Warning Capabilities, GAO-01-1132T, http://www.gao.gov/new.items/d011132t.pdf, September 12, 2001.

60. Critical Infrastructure Protection: Significant Challenges in Developing Analysis, Warning, and Response Capabilities, GAO-01-1005T, http://www.gao.gov/new.items/d011005t.pdf, July 25, 2001.

61. Critical Infrastructure Protection: Significant Challenges in Developing National Capabilities, GAO-01-323, http://www.gao.gov/new.items/d01323.pdf, April 25, 2001.

62. FAA Computer Security: Recommendations to Address Continuing Weaknesses, GAO-01-171, http://www.gao.gov/new.items/d01171.pdf, December 6, 2000.

63. Assessing the Reliability of Computer-Processed Data (Supplement to the Government Auditing Standards [Yellow Book]—External Version), GAO-03-273G, October 2002.

64. Electronic Law Enforcement: Introduction to Investigations in an Electronic Environment, GAO-01-121G, February 2001.

65. Executive Guide: Maximizing the Success of Chief Information Officers: Learning from Leading Organizations, GAO-01-376G, February 2001.

66. Human Services Integration: Results of a GAO Cosponsored Conference on Modernizing Information Systems, GAO-02-121, January 2002.

67. Electronic Law Enforcement: Introduction to Investigations in an Electronic Environment, GAO-01-121G, February 2001.

68. Critical Infrastructure Protection: Challenges for Selected Agencies and Industry Sectors, GAO-03-233, February 2003.

69. U.S. General Accounting Office, Government Auditing Standards, Exposure Draft, 2010 available at http://www.gao.gov/yellowbook.

National Institute of Standards and Technology

Publications can be ordered from the National Institute of Standards and Technology (NIST), Information Technology Laboratory, Building 820, Room 562, Gaithersburg, MD 20899-0001. They can also be ordered through the Web at http://www.nist.gov/.

1. Bace, R. and P. Mell, *Intrusion Detection Systems (IDS)*, NIST Special Publication 800-31, November 2001.
2. Black, P.E. et al., *Model Checkers for Software Testing*, NISTIR 6777, February 2002.
3. Bowen, P., J. Hash, and M. Wilson, *Information Security Handbook: A Guide for Managers*, NIST Special Publication 800-100, October 2006.
4. Chernick, M., *Federal S/MIME V3 Client Profile*, NIST Special Publication 800-49, November 2002.
5. Cugini, J., *The FLUD Format: Logging Usability Data from Web-Based Applications*, NIST Special Publication 500-247, January 2001.
6. Cugini, J. and S. Laskowski, *Design of a File Format for Logging Website Information*, NIST Special Publication 500-248, April 2001.
7. Dray, J., A. Goldfine, M. Iorga, T. Schwarzhoff, and J. Wack, *Government Smart Card Interoperability Specification (GSC-IS), v2.0*, NIST IR 6887, June 2002.
8. Dworkin, M., *Recommendation for Block Cipher Modes of Operation—Methods and Techniques*, NIST Special Publication 800-38A, December 2001.
9. Frankel, S., B. Eydt, L. Owens, and K. Scarfone, *Establishing Wireless Robust Security Networks: A Guide to IEEE 802.11i*, NIST Special Publication 800-97, February 2007.
10. Grance, T., J. Hash, S. Peck, J. Smith, and K. Korow-Diks, *Security Guide for Interconnecting Information Technology Systems*, NIST Special Publications 800-47, September 2002.
11. Grance, T., T. Nolan, K. Burke, R. Dudley, G. White, and T. Good, *Guide to Test, Training, and Exercise Programs for IT Plans and Capabilities*, NIST Special Publication 800-85, September 2006.
12. Grance, T., J. Hash, and M. Stevens, *Security Considerations in the Information Systems Development Life Cycle*, NIST Special Publication 800-64, June 2004.
13. Jansen, W., *Guidelines on Active Content and Mobile Code*, NIST Special Publications 800-28, October 2001.
14. Jansen, W. and R. Ayers, *Guidelines on Cell Phone Forensics*, NIST Special Publication 800-101, May 2007.
15. Kent, K., S. Chevalier, T. Grance, and H. Dang, *Guide to Integrating Forensic Techniques into Incident Response*, NIST Special Publication 800-86, August 2006.
16. Karygiannis, T. and L. Owens, *Wireless Network Security: 802.11, Bluetooth, and Handheld Devices*, NIST Special Publication 800-48, November 2002.
17. Kuhn, R., *PBX Vulnerability Analysis: Finding Holes in Your PBX before Someone Else Does*, NIST Special Publication 800-24, August 2000.
18. Kuhn, R., M. Tracy, and S. Frankel, *Security for Telecommuting and Broadband Communications*, NIST Special Publication 800-46, September 2002.
19. Kuhn, R., V. Hu, T. Polk, and S.-J. Chang, *Introduction to Public Key Technology and the Federal PKI Infrastructure*, NIST Special Publication 800-32, February 2001.
20. Lee, A., *Guideline for Implementing Cryptography in Federal Government*, NIST Special Publication 800-21, November 1999.
21. Lyons-Burke, K., *Federal Agency Use of Public Key Technology for Digital Signatures and Authentication*, NIST Special Publication 800-25, October 2000.
22. MacGregor, W., T. Schwarzhoff, and K. Mehta, *A Scheme for PIV Visual Card Topography*, NIST Special Publication 800-104, June 2007.
23. Mell, P. and T. Grance, *Use of the Common Vulnerabilities and Exposures (CVE) Vulnerability Naming Scheme*, NIST Special Publication 800-51, September 2002.
24. Mell, P. and M. Tracy, *Procedures for Handling Security Patches*, NIST Special Publication 800-40, September 2002.

25. Mell, P., K. Kent, and J. Nusbaum, *Guide to Malware Incident Prevention and Handling*, NIST Special Publication 800-83, November 2005.

26. Polk, W., D. Dodson, and W. Burr, *Cryptographic Algorithms and Key Sizes for Personal Identity Verification*, NIST Special Publication 800-78-1, August 2007.

27. Roback, E., *Guideline to Federal Organizations on Security Assurance and Acquisition/Use of Tested/ Evaluated Products*, NIST Publication 800-23, August 2000.

28. Rukhin, A., J. Soto, J. Nechvatal, M. Smid, E. Barker, S. Leigh, M. Levenson, M. Vangel, D. Banks, A. Heckert, J. Dray, and S. Vo, *A Statistical Test Suite for Random and Pseudorandom Number Generators for Cryptographic Applications*, NIST Special Publication 800-22, October 2000.

29. Scarfone, K., T. Grance, and K. Masone, *Computer Security Incident Handling Guide*, NIST Special Publication 800-61, March 2008.

30. Scarfone, K. and M. Souppaya, *User's Guide to Securing External Devices for Telework and Remote Access*, NIST Special Publication 800-114, November 2007.

31. Scarfone, K., M. Souppaya, and M. Sexton, *Recommendations of the National Institute of Standards and Technology*, NIST Special Publication 800-111, November 2007.

32. Scarfone, K. and P. Mell, *Recommendations of the National Institute of Standards and Technology*, NIST Special Publication 800-84, February 2007.

33. Scarfone, K. and P. Mell, *Guide to Intrusion Detection and Prevention Systems (IDPS)*, NIST Special Publication 800-94, February 2007.

34. Singhal, A., T. Winograd, and K. Scarfone, *Guide to Secure Web Services*, NIST Special Publications 800-95, August 2007.

35. Snoufeer, R., A. Lee, and A. Oldehoeft, *A Comparison of the Security Requirements for Cryptographic Modules in FIPS 140-1 and FIPS 140-2*, NIST Special Publication 800-29, June 2001.

36. Soto, J. and L. Basham, *Randomness Testing of the Advanced Encryption Standard Finalist Candidates*, NIST IR 6483, March 2000.

37. Stoneburner, G., CSSP. *Underlying Models for Information Technology Security*, NIST Special Publication 800-33, December 2001.

38. Stoneburner, G. et al., *Risk Management Guide for Information Technology Systems*, NIST Special Publication 800-30, January 2002.

39. Stoneburner, G., C. Hayden, and A. Feringa, *Engineering Principles for Information Technology Security (A Baseline for Achieving Security)*, NIST Special Publication 800-27, June 2001.

40. Swanson, M., A. Wohl, L. Pope, L. Grance, J. Hash, and R. Thomas, *Contingency Planning Guide for Information Technology Systems*, NIST Special Publication 800-34, June 2002.

41. Swanson, M., *Security Self-Assessment Guide for Information Technology Systems*, NIST Special Publications 800-26, November 2001.

42. Wack, J. et al., *Guidelines on Firewall and Firewall Policy*, NIST Special Publication 800-41, January 2002.

43. Wilson, C., P. Grother, and R. Chandramouli, *Biometric Data Specification for Personal Identity Verification*, NIST Special Publication 800-76-1, January 2007.

National Technical Information Service

Publications can be ordered from the National Technical Information Service (NTIS), 5285 Port Royal Road, Springfield, VA 22161. They can also be ordered through the Web at http://www.ntis.gov/.

Publications Available from Professional Associations

Many professional associations are very active in the publication and distribution of IT audit and security literature. Some of these associations are based in the United States but many are international in concept and scope. Most groups are willing to share their information for a nominal fee even with nonmembers of their association.

American Institute of Certified Public Accountants

Publications can be ordered from the American Institute of Certified Public Accountants (AICPA), 1211 Avenue of the Americas, New York, NY 10036. They can also be ordered through the Web at http://www.cpa2biz.com/CS2000/Home/default.htm.

Association for Computing Machinery

Publications can be ordered from the Association for Computing Machinery, One Astor Plaza, 1515 Broadway, New York, NY 10036. They can also be ordered through the Web at http://www.acm.org/catalog/books/homepage.html.

Canadian Institute of Chartered Accountants

Publications can be ordered from the Canadian Institute of Chartered Accountants (CICA), 277 Wellington Street West, Toronto, ON M5V 3H2, Canada. They can also be ordered through the Web at http://www.cica.ca/cica/cicaWebsite.nsf/public/ServicesProducts.

Institute of Internal Auditors

Publications can be ordered from the Institute of Internal Auditors (IIA), 249 Maitland Avenue, Altamonte Springs, FL 32701-4201. They can also be ordered through the Web at http://www.theiia.org/.

International Federation for Information Processing

Publications can be ordered from Kluwer Academic Publishers, 101 Philip Drive, Assinippi Park, Norwell, MA 02061. They can also be ordered through the International Federation for Information Processing Website at http://www.ifip.org/homeintro.html.

International Federation of Accountants

Publications can be ordered from the International Federation of Accountants (IFAC), 535 Fifth Avenue, 26th Floor, New York, NY 10017. They can also be ordered through the Web at http://www.ifac.org/.

Quality Assurance Institute

Publications can be ordered from the Quality Assurance Institute, 7575 Dr. Phillips Boulevard, Suite 350, Orlando, FL 32819. They can also be ordered through the Web at http://www.qaiworld-wide.org/.

Other Publications

This section provides selected references from various publishers categorized according to current topics of interest to IT auditors. Some publications can be ordered directly from the publishers. Most of them can also be ordered through the Internet at http://www.amazon.com.

Best Practices in Information Technology

1. Aspatore Books Staff, *Technology Benchmarks for Success: Leading Executives on Establishing Best Practices, Improving Return on Investment, and Creating a Benchmarking Structure*, 2006.
2. Curley, M., *Managing Information Technology for Business Value: Practical Strategies for IT and Business Managers*, 2004.
3. IBM, *ILM Library: Information Lifecycle Management Best Practices Guide*, 2007.
4. Krafzig, D., K. Banke, and D. Slama, *Enterprise SOA: Service-Oriented Architecture Best Practices*, 2004.
5. Schwalbe, K., *Information Technology Project Management*, Fifth Edition, 2007.
6. Stenzel, J., G. Cokins, B. Flemming, and A. Hill, *CIO Best Practices: Enabling Strategic Value with Information Technology*, 2007.
7. Thompson, P., *Maximizing 'IT' Value through Operational Excellence: A Definitive Guide to Twelve Best Practices in Application Support and Maintenance*, 2006.
8. Turban, E., D. Leidner, E. McLean, and J. Wetherbe, *Information Technology for Management: Transforming Organizations in the Digital Economy*, 2007.
9. Robertson, B. and V. Sribar, *The Adaptive Enterprise: IT Infrastructure Strategies to Manage Change and Enable Growth*, 2004.
10. Van den Berg, M. and M. Van Steenbergen, *Building an Enterprise Architecture Practice: Tools, Tips, Best Practices, Ready-to-Use Insights*, 2006.
11. The Open Group Architecture Framework (TOGAF), The Open Group, www.opengroup.org/architecture.

Information Security

1. Cretaro, P., *Lab Manual and for Security Guide to Network Security Fundamentals*, 2003.
2. Calbrese, T., *Information Security Intelligence: Cryptographic Principles & Applications*, 2003.
3. Holden, G., *Guide to Network Defense and Countermeasures*, 2003.
4. Holden, G., *Guide to Firewalls and Network Security*, 2004.
5. Humphreys, E., *Implementing the ISO/IEC 27001 Information Security Management System Standard*, 2007.
6. Killmeyer, J., *Information Security Architecture: An Integrated Approach to Security in the Organization*, Second Edition, 2006.
7. Nelson, S., *Information Security for Lawyers and Law Firms*, 2007.
8. Panko, R.R., *Corporate Computer and Network Security*, 2004.
9. Peltier, T., *Information Security Risk Analysis*, Second Edition, 2005.
10. Penfold, R.R.C., *Computer Security: Business at Risk*, June 1999.
11. Stallings, W., *Cryptography and Network Security*, 2003.
12. Stamp, M., *Information Security: Principles and Practice*, 2005.
13. Tipton, H. and M. Krause, *Information Security Management Handbook*, Fifth Edition, 2006.
14. Whitman, M. and H. Mattord, *Management of Information Security*, Second Edition, 2007.

Enterprise Resource Planning (ERP) Systems

1. Anderson, G., *SAP Planning: Best Practices in Implementation*, 2003.
2. Carroll, B., *Lean Performance ERP Project Management: Implementing the Virtual Supply Chain*, February 2002.
3. Carter, J., *The Expert Guide to PeopleSoft Security*, 2004.
4. Clott, J. and S. Raff, *PeopleSoft Application Development Tools*, September 1999.
5. Deloite Touche Tohmatsu Research Team; ISACA, *Security, Audit & Control Features PeopleSoft: A Technical and Risk Management Reference Guide*, Second Edition, 2006.
6. Franz, M., *Project Management with SAP Project System*, 2007.
7. Hamilton, S., *Maximizing Your ERP System: A Practical Guide for Managers*, October 2002.

8. IBM Business Consulting, *SAP Authorization Systems: Design and Implementation of Authorization Concepts for SAP R/3 and SAP Enterprise Portals*, 2003.
9. Linkies, M., *SAP Security and Authorizations*, 2006.
10. McDonald, K., A. Wilmsmeier, D. Dixon, and W. Inmon, *Mastering the SAP Business Information Warehouse: Leveraging the Business Intelligence Capabilities of SAP NetWeaver*, 2006.
11. Monk, E. and B. Wagner, *Concepts in Enterprise Resource Planning*, Second Edition, 2005.
12. Murray, M., *SAP MM-Functionality and Technical Configuration*, Second Edition, 2008.
13. Norris, G. et al., *E-Business and ERP: Transforming the Enterprise*, May 2000.
14. Norris, G., *E-Business and ERP: Transforming the Enterprise*, July 2000.
15. O-Leary, D., *Enterprise Resource Planning Systems: Systems, Life Cycle, Electronic Commerce, and Risk*, January 2000.
16. Shields, M., *E-Business and ERP: Rapid Implementation and Project Planning*, April 2001.
17. Snevely, R., *Enterprise Data Center Design and Methodology, 1e*, 2002.
18. Wallace, T. and M. Kremzar, *ERP: Making it Happen: The Implementer's Guide to Success with Enterprise Resource Planning*, July 2001.

Information Technology and Accounting Systems

1. Gelinas, U. and R. Dull, *Accounting Information Systems*, 2007.
2. Gelinas, U., S. Sutton, and A. Orma, *Accounting Information Systems*, May 2001.
3. Jones, F. and D. Rama, *Accounting Information Systems: A Business Process Approach*, 2005.
4. Romney, M. and P. Steinbart, *Accounting Information Systems*, Eleventh Edition, 2008.
5. Turner, L. and A. Weickgenannt, *Accounting Information Systems: Controls and Processes*, 2008.
6. Vaassen, E.H., *Accounting Information Systems: A Managerial Approach*, April 2002.

Internet, E-Commerce, and Web Security

1. Allamaraju, S., *Professional Java E-Commerce*, February 2001.
2. Campbell, D., *E-Commerce and the Law of Digital Signatures*, 2005.
3. Cheeseman, H., *Contemporary Business and E-Commerce Law: The Legal, Global, Digital, and Ethical Environment*, Fourth Edition, 2002.
4. Smith, G., *E-Commerce: A Control and Security Guide*, 2003.
5. Warner, R., G. Dinwoodie, H. Krent, and M. Stewart, *E-Commerce, the Internet and the Law, Cases and Materials*, 2006.
6. Chissick, M. and A. Kelman, *E-Commerce: Law and Practice*, March 2000.
7. Convery, S., *Network Security Architectures*, 2004.
8. Cranor, L., *Web Privacy with P3P*, September 2002.
9. Dustin, E., J. Rashka, D. McDiarmid, and J. Mielson, *Quality Web Systems: Performance, Security, and Usability*, August 2001.
10. Faulkner Information Services. *Alternatives for Secure Online Transactions*, May 2001.
11. Ferrera, G.R. et al., *CyberLaw: Texts and Cases*, Second Edition, 2004.
12. Ferrari, E. and B. Thuraisingham, *Web and Information Security*, 2005.
13. Ford, W. and M.S. Baum, *Secure Electronic Commerce*, Second Edition, 2001.
14. Greenstein, M. and M. Vasarhelyi, *Electronic Commerce: Security, Risk Management, and Control with PowerWeb Passcode Card (E-Commerce)*, July 2001.
15. Graff, J., *Cryptography and E-Commerce: A Wiley Tech Brief*, December 2000.
16. Hardjono, T. and L. Dondeti, *Security in Wireless LANS and MANS*, 2005.
17. Held, J. and J. Bowers, *Securing E-Business Applications and Communications*, June 2001.
18. Jennings, C. et al., *The Hundredth Window: Protecting Your Privacy and Security in the Age of the Internet*, May 2000.
19. Killelea, P., *Web Performance Tuning*, Second Edition, March 2002.
20. McClure, S., S. Shah, and S. Shah, *Web Hacking: Attacks and Defense*, August 2002.

21. O'Neill, M., *Web Services Security*, January 2003.
22. Phaltankar, K.M., *Practical Guide for Implementing Secure Intranets and Extranets*, December 1999.
23. Scambray, J. and M. Shema, *Hacking Exposed™ Web Applications*, June 2002.
24. Schetina, E., K. Green, and J. Carlson, *Internet Site Security*, March 2002.
25. Smith, G., *E-Commerce: A Control and Security Guide*, December 2001.
26. Splaine, S., *Testing Web Security: Assessing the Security of Web Sites and Applications*, October 2002.
27. Trevedi, R., D. Whitney, B. Galbraith, D.V. Prasad, M. Janakiramin, A. Hiotis, and W. Hnakison, *Professional Web Services Security*, December 2002.
28. Oppliger, R., *Internet and Intranet Security*, 2007.
29. Rhee, M., *Internet Security: Cryptographic Principles, Algorithms and Protocols*, 2003.
30. Stuttard, D. and M. Pinto, *The Web Application Hacker's Handbook: Discovering and Exploiting Security Flaws*, 2007.
31. Shoniregun, C., *Impacts and Risk Assessment of Technology for Internet Security: Enabled Information Small-Medium Enterprises*, 2005.
32. Badger, L. et al., NIST: Draft Cloud Computing Synopsis and Recommendations; Recommendations of the National Institute of Standards and Technology. Special Publication 800-146, May 2011.

IT Auditing and Control Systems

1. Arter, D., *Quality Audits for Improved Performance*, December 2002.
2. Bourn, J., *Public Sector Auditing: Is It Value for Money?* 2008.
3. Cangemi, M. and T. Singleton, *Managing the Audit Function: A Corporate Audit Department Procedures Guide*, April 2003.
4. Dayton, D., *Information Technology Audit Handbook*, April 1997.
5. Gallegos, F. et al., *Information Technology Control and Audit*, July 1999.
6. Hunton, J., M. Bryant, and A. Nancy, *Core Concepts of Information Technology Auditing*, 2003.
7. IT Governance Institute, *Managing Enterprise Information Integrity: Security, Control and Audit Issues*, 2004.
8. Kimbell, L., *Audit*, May 2003.
9. Marcella, A.J., *EDI Security, Control, and Audit*, March 2003.
10. Russell, J.P., *After the Quality Audit: Closing the Loop on the Audit Process*, May 2000.
11. Weber, R., *Information Systems Control and Audit*, 1999.

Privacy of Information

1. Bloustein, E.J. and N.J. Pallone, *Individual and Group Privacy*, December 2002.
2. Cady, G.H., P. McGregor, and J. Beverley, *Protect Your Digital Privacy! Survival Skills for the Information Age*, December 2001.
3. Caloyannides, M.A., *Computer Forensics and Privacy*, December 2001.
4. Chesbro, M., *Freeware Encryption and Security Programs: Protecting Your Computer and Your Privacy*, September 2001.
5. Cobb, S., *Privacy for Business: Web Sites and Email*, October 2002.
6. Committee on Privacy in the Information Age and National Research Council, *Engaging Privacy and Information Technology in a Digital Age*, 2007.
7. Electronic Privacy Information Center, *Privacy and Human Rights Report 2006: An International Survey of Privacy Laws and Developments*, 2007.
8. Erbschloe, M., *The Executives Guide to Privacy Management*, 2001.
9. Erbschloe, M. and J. Vaca, *Net Privacy: A Guide to Developing and Implementing an Ironclad Ebusiness Privacy Plan*, 2001.
10. Fischer-Hubner, S. and G. Fisher-Hubner, *IT-Security and Privacy*, September 2001.
11. Garfinkel, S., *Web Security, Privacy, and Commerce*, Second Edition, January 2002.
12. Garfinkel, S., *Database Nation: The Death of Privacy in the 21st Century*, January 2001.

13. Hunter, R., *World without Secrets: Business, Crime, and Privacy in the Age of Ubiquitous Computing*, April 2002.
14. Hyatt, M.S. and M. Hyatt, *Invasion of Privacy: How to Protect Yourself in the Digital Age*, April 2001.
15. Kahin, B. and C. Nesson, *Borders in Cyberspace: Information Policy and the Global Information Infrastructure*, March 1997.
16. Klosek, J., *Data Privacy in the Information Age*, August 2000.
17. Marcella, A.J., *Privacy Handbook: Guidelines, Exposures, Policy Implementation, and International Issues*, April 2003.
18. Melanson, P.H. and A. Summers, *Secrecy Wars: National Security, Privacy, and the Public's Right to Know*, January 2002.
19. Miller, M., *Absolute PC Security and Privacy*, August 2002.
20. Pfleeger, C., *Security in Computing*, Third Edition, December 2002.
21. Schwartz, P. and D. Solove, *Information Privacy: Statutes and Regulations*, 2008–2009 Supplement, 2008.
22. Solove, D., M. Rotenberg, and P. Schwartz, *Privacy, Information and Technology*, 2006.
23. Solove, D., M. Rotenberg, and P. Schwartz, *Information Privacy Law*, 2005.

Quality Assurance

1. Bernowski, K. and B. Stratton, *101 Good Ideas: How to Improve Just About Any Process*, February 1999.
2. Bradley, V.J., *Quality Assurance in a Rapidly Changing World: Challenges and Opportunities in a Changing World*, March 2003.
3. Godbole, N., *Software Quality Assurance: Principles and Practice*, 2004.
4. Hoyle, D., *Quality Management Essentials*, 2007.
5. Lewis, W.E., *Software Testing and Continuous Quality Improvement*, April 2000.
6. Peach, R.W., *The ISO 9000 Handbook*, 2002.
7. Ratliff, T.A., *The Laboratory Quality Assurance System: A Manual of Quality Procedures and Forms*, March 2003.
8. Regal, T. and J.P. Russell, *After the Quality Audit: Closing the Loop on the Audit Process*, May 2000.
9. Schulmeyer, G., *Handbook of Software Quality Assurance*, 2007.
10. Stamelos, I. and P. Sfetsos, *Agile Software Development Quality Assurance*, 2007.
11. Tian, J., *Software Quality Engineering: Testing, Quality Assurance, and Quantifiable Improvement*, 2005.
12. U.S. CERT Software Assurance Community, https://buildsecurityin.us-cert.gov/swa/measwg.html, September 2011.

Risk Management

1. Barton, T.L., W.G. Shenkir, and P.L. Walker, *Making Enterprise Risk Management Pay Off: How Leading Companies Implement Risk Management*, February 2002.
2. Basel Committee on Banking Supervision. Sound Practices for the Management and Supervision of Operational Risk. Consultative Document issued December 2010. http://www.bis.org/publ/bcbs183.pdf
3. Crouhy, M., R. Mark and D. Galai, *Risk Management*, April 2001.
4. Erbschloe, M., *Guide to Disaster Recovery*, 2003.
5. Grunendahl, R. and P. Will, *Beyond Compliance: 10 Practical Actions on Regulation, Risk, and IT Management*, 2006.
6. Harris, M., D. Herron, and S. Iwanicki, *The Business Value of IT: Managing Risks, Optimizing Performance and Measuring Results*, 2008.
7. Hoffman, D.G., *Managing Operational Risk: 20 Firmwide Best Practice Strategies*, January 2002.
8. IT Goverance Institute, *IT Control Objectives for Basel II—The Importance of Governance and Risk Management for Compliance*, 2007.
9. Janczewski, L., *Internet and Intranet Security Management: Risks and Solutions*, July 2000.

10. Lochhead, D., *Shifting Realities: Information Technology and the Church*, January 2000.
11. McCumber, J., *Assessing and Managing Security Risk in IT Systems: A Structured Methodology*, 2004.
12. Moynihan, T., *Coping with IS/IT Risk Management: The Recipes of Experienced Project Managers*, April 2002.
13. O'Bryan, S., *IT Outsourcing Risk Management*, 2008.
14. Pritchard, C., *Risk Management: Concepts and Guidance*, Second Edition, November 2001.
15. Peltier, T.R., *Information Security Risk Analysis*, January 2001.
16. Quarterman, J., *Risk Management Solutions for Sarbanes–Oxley Section 404 IT Compliance*, 2006.
17. Taylor, I., *Procurement of Information Systems: Getting Value from Suppliers in High Risk, Hi Tech, and Highly Competitive Markets*, March 2001.
18. Walker, P., W. Shenkir, and T. Barton, *Enterprise Risk Management: Pulling It All Together*, 2002.
19. Westerman, G. and R. Hunter, *IT Risk: Turning Business Threats into Competitive Advantage*, 2007.

Appendix III

Professional Standards That Apply to Information Technology (Audit, Security, and Privacy Issues)

The purpose of this appendix is to identify, review, and categorize both standards and guidelines related to IT established by professional organizations in the fields of accounting, audit, and technology. Upon review, the standards and guidelines relating to IT have been categorized into three areas: audit, security, and privacy issues.

In addition to categorizing these professional organizations, other information was also collected for those readers interested in contacting the professional organizations for additional information and updates. This information includes contact address, contact telephone, contact facsimile, contact Internet home page, and contact e-mail address.

The information sources used to collect information relevant for this research project have been noted in each of the corresponding professional organizations following the contact information.

With the exception of the *CICA Handbook*, dated 1991 (revised), the majority of the information collected was taken from the professional organization's main Internet home page (Website).

American Institute of Certified Public Accountants

The AICPA and its predecessors have a history dating back to 1887, when the American Association of Public Accountants was formed. In 1916, the American Association was succeeded by the Institute of Public Accountants at which time there were 1150 members. The name was changed to the American Institute of Accountants in 1917 and remained so until 1957, when the name was again changed to the American Institute of Certified Public Accountants. The American Society of Certified Public Accountants was formed in 1921 and acted as a federation of state societies. The society was merged into the institute in 1936 and, at that time, the institute agreed to restrict its future members to CPAs.

American Institute of Certified Public Accountants
1211 Avenue of the Americas
New York, NY 10036-8775
Telephone: (212) 596-6200
Facsimile: (212) 596-6213
Website: http://www.aicpa.org

Authoritative Guide

Statements on Audit Standards (SASs) are issued by the Auditing Standards Board (ASB) of the AICPA and are recognized as interpretations of the 10 generally accepted auditing standards (AUSs). SASs usually apply only in situations where auditing services are being performed.

Institute of Internal Auditors

Established in 1941, the IIA serves more than 170,000 members in internal auditing; governance and internal control; and IT audit, education, and security from more than 100 countries. As the world's leader in certification, education, research, and technological guidance for the profession, the institute serves as the profession's watchdog and resource on significant auditing issues around the globe. Presenting important conferences and seminars for professional development, producing leading-edge educational products, certifying qualified auditing professionals, providing quality assurance reviews and benchmarking, and conducting valuable research projects through the IIA Research Foundation are just a few of the institute's many activities. The IIA also provides internal auditing practitioners, executive management, boards of directors, and audit committees with standards, guidance, and information on internal auditing best practices. The institute is a dynamic international organization that meets the needs of a worldwide body of internal auditors. The history of internal auditing has been synonymous with that of the IIA and its motto, "Progress through Sharing."

The Institute of Internal Auditors (IIA)
247 Maitland Avenue
Altamonte Springs, FL 32701-4201
Telephone: (407) 937-1100
Facsimile: (407) 937-1101
E-mail: iia@theiia.org

Information Source

http://www.theiia.org/

Authoritative Guide

The International Standards for the Professional Practice of Internal Auditing are issued by the Professional Standards and Responsibilities Committee, the senior technical committee (TC) designated by the Institute of Internal Auditors, Inc., to issue pronouncements on AUSs. These statements are authoritative interpretations of the Standards for the Professional Practice of Internal Auditing. Organizations, internal auditing departments, directors of internal auditing, and internal auditors should strive to comply with the standards. The implementation of the standards and related statements will be governed by the environment in which the internal auditing department carries out its assigned responsibilities. The adoption and implementation of the standards and related statements will assist internal auditing professionals in accomplishing their responsibilities. The standards are divided into two areas: performance and attribute.

Information Systems Audit and Control Association

A worldwide not-for-profit member association of more than 95,000 IS professionals, it is dedicated to IS audit, control, and security practitioners through a commitment to education, certification, and standards and an associated not-for-profit foundation committed to expanding the knowledge base of the profession through a commitment to research. ISACA provides practical guidance, benchmarks and other effective tools for all enterprises that use information systems. Through its comprehensive guidance and services, ISACA defines the roles of information systems governance, security, audit and assurance professionals worldwide. The COBIT, Val IT and Risk IT governance frameworks and the CISA, CISM, CGEIT and CRISC certifications are ISACA brands respected and used by these professionals for the benefit of their enterprise.

> Information Systems Audit and Control Association (ISACA)
> 3701 Algonquin Road, Suite 1010
> Rolling Meadows, IL 60008
> Telephone: (847) 253-1545
> Facsimile: (847) 253-1443
> Website: http://www.isaca.org
> E-mail: membership@isaca.org, education@isaca.org, publication@isaca.org, certification@isaca.org, conference@iscaa.org, bookstore@isaca.org, research@isaca.org

Authoritative Guide

Information System Auditing Standards is issued by the Standards Board of the ISACA and is recognized as the information systems auditing standard.

The *guidelines* provide examples of different types of IS audit work and set requirements for the work and its reporting. They are standards to the extent that an IS auditor should be prepared to justify departures from them but is not required to follow them. The *standards* define mandatory requirements for IS auditing and reporting.

Canadian Institute of Chartered Accountants

The CISA, like the profession it serves, reflects the national character of Canada; its members work in virtually all streams of Canadian life. The CICA serves not only the accounting profession at the national and international level, but it provides significant input to the public and private sectors through Canada regarding business practices and government legislation. In its organization, the profession reflects the federalism of Canada. Through a system of interlocking membership, chartered accountants automatically become members of CICA upon admission to a provincial institute. The institute was established in 1972 and is governed by the 23-member board of governors. Chartered Accountants (CAs) are Canada's most valued, internationally recognized profession of leaders in senior management, advisory, financial, tax and assurance roles. Through their integrity, expertise, and internationally recognized qualification standards, Canada's 78,000 CAs sustain their influence and leadership position both in Canada and globally. As trusted business advisors to Canadian organizations of all sizes, Canada's CAs foster confidence in Canadian business and contribute to the health and sustainability of Canada's capital markets and economy. The Canadian Institute of Chartered Accountants (CICA) represents Canada's CA profession both nationally and internationally. The CICA is a founding member of the International Federation of Accountants (IFAC) and the Global Accounting Alliance (GAA).

> The Canadian Institute of Chartered Accountants (CICA)
> 277 Wellington Street West
> Toronto, ON, M5V 3H2
> Canada
> Telephone: (416)977-3222
> Facsimile: (416)977-8585
> Website: http://www.cica.ca
> E-mail: customer.service@cica.ca

Authoritative Guide

The Accounting Research and Auditing Standards Committees were established in 1973 when the board of governors decided to split its predecessor, the Accounting and Auditing Research Committee, into two separate committees. By far, the most important responsibility of both committees is the issuance of accounting and auditing recommendations for the *CICA Handbook (Accounting and Assurance)*. Only these committees have been given the authority to issue pronouncements without reference to the board of governors. Information about the *CICA Handbook* can be obtained by the members at http://handbook.cica.ca/.

International Federation of Accountants

The IFAC is an organization of national professional accountancy organizations that represent accountants employed in public practice, business and industry, the public sector, and education, as well as some specialized groups that interface frequently with the profession. Currently, IFAC is comprised of 164 members and associates in 125 countries and jurisdictions, representing approximately 2.5 million accountants in public practice, education, government service, industry, and commerce. IFAC members are professional accountancy organizations recognized by law or general consensus within their countries as substantial national organizations. National organizations may apply to become an IFAC associate where the organization is working toward membership. Full membership in IFAC automatically includes membership in the International Accounting Standards Committee (IASC).

International Federation of Accountants
535 Fifth Avenue, 26th Floor
New York, NY 10017
Telephone: (212) 286-9344
Facsimile: (212) 286-9570
Website: http://www.ifac.org
Email: Communications@ifac.org

Authoritative Guides

Auditing, Assurance and Related Services. International Standards on Auditing—Codified Introductory Matters (ISA) is issued by the IFAC and gives recognized standards or guidelines.

Education. International Education Guidelines (IEG) are issued by the IFAC and are recognized as standards or guidelines.

Financial and Management Accounting. International Management Accounting Practice Statements and International Management Accounting Studies Statements are issued by the IFAC and are recognized as standards or guidelines.

Information Technology. International Information Technology Guidelines are issued by the IFAC and are recognized as standards or guidelines. The Information Technology Committee is in the process of developing a series of international guidelines to assist management in both understanding and ultimately managing the risks associated with information technology.

Public Sector. International Public Sector Guidelines are issued by the IFAC and are recognized as standards or guidelines.

Information System Security Association

The Information Systems Security Association (ISSA) is an international organization of information security professionals and practitioners. It provides education forums, publications, and peer interaction opportunities that enhance the knowledge, skill, and professional growth of its members. The ISSA is a not-for-profit, international organization of information security professionals and practitioners. It provides educational forums, publications, and peer interaction opportunities that enhance the knowledge, skill, and professional growth of its members. The primary goal of the ISSA is to promote management practices that will ensure the confidentiality, integrity, and availability of information resources. The ISSA facilitates interaction and education to create a more successful environment for global information systems security and for the professionals involved. Members include practitioners at all levels of the security field in a broad range of industries such as communications, education, healthcare, manufacturing, financial, and government.

Information System Security Association (ISSA)
9220 SW Barbur Blvd #119–333

Portland, OR 97219
Phone: +1 866 349 5818 (USA toll-free)
Seattle: +1 206 388 4584 (local/international)
Fax: +1 206 299 3366 (local/international)
Website: https://www.issa.org/

Authoritative Guide

Guideline for Information Valuation (GIV) publication—has been created exclusively by a knowledgeable task force of ISSA members, and these guidelines provide the tools necessary for assigning value to an organization's information assets.

Society for Information Management

The Society for Information Management (SIM) comprises 3500 senior executives who are corporate and divisional heads of IT organizations and their management staff, leading academicians, consultants, and other leaders who shape and influence the management and use of IT.

Society for Information Management (SIM)
401 North Michigan Avenue
Chicago, IL 60611-4267
Telephone: (312) 527-6734
Facsimile: (800) 387-9746
Website: http://www.simnet.org
Email: SIM_Central@simnet.org

Authoritative Guide

The SIM has not issued authoritative guides to date. However, the SIM has issued several press releases on technology-related topics and may be found at http://www.simnet.org/public/aboutsim/pressrls/.

Association of Information Technology Professionals

The AITP is the professional association consisting of career-minded individuals who look to expand their talents—employers, employees, managers, and programmers who share an enthusiasm for knowledge. The organization aims to provide avenues for all members to become teachers, as well as students, and to open doors to exchange ideas with other professionals in an effort to become more marketable. For over six decades, AITP has championed the human element of the IT profession and remains focused on providing a community of knowledge, education and resources that will empower its members to reach their true potential as an IT business professional.

Association of Information Technology Professionals (AITP)
401 North Michigan Avenue, Suite 2200
Chicago, IL 60622-4267
Telephone: (800) 224-9371/(312) 245-1070
Facsimile: (312) 673-6659

Website: http://www.aitp.org/
Email: aitp_hq@aitp.org

Authoritative Guide

The AITP has not issued authoritative guides to date. However, the AITP has two publications.

Information Executive

Each monthly issue of the *Information Executive* focuses on current industry topics from technical and managerial viewpoints to help IS and data processing individuals understand and meet the most important challenges of the IS industry. Contributions from industry experts, practitioners, and educators are regular features of *Information Executive* topics, which cover a full range of industry issues, including client/server management, project management, online services, downsizing, rightsizing, local area networks (LANs), microcomputers, workstations, security, disaster recover, systems integration, and total quality management.

The Nanosecond

This newsletter is published for the AITP student members and faculty advisors. Published six times a year, each issue contains articles that are contributed by AITP student members, student advisors, and professionals within the industry. In addition to student chapter information, articles that address the key topics of interest to students are also featured.

International Federation for Information Processing

The IFIP is a nongovernmental, nonprofit umbrella organization for national societies working in the field of information processing. It was established in 1960 under the auspices of UNESCO as an aftermath of the first World Computer Congress held in Paris in 1959. Today, IFIP has several types of members and maintains friendly connections with specialized agencies of the U.N. system and nongovernmental organizations. Technical work, which is the heart of IFIP's activity, is managed by a series of TCs. The leading multinational, apolitical organization in Information & Communications Technologies and Sciences. It is recognized by United Nations and other world bodies and IFIPS represents IT Societies from 56 countries/regions, covering five continents with a total membership of over half a million. Today, it has links of more than 3500 scientists from Academia & Industry and over 100 Working Groups and 13 Technical Committees.

IFIP Secretariat
Hofstrasse 3,
A-2361 Laxenburg
Austria
Telephone: +43 2236 73616
Facsimile: +43 2236 736169
Website: http://www.ifip.org/
E-mail: ifip@ifip.or.at

Authoritative Guide

IFIP Technical Committee and Working Group: Aims and Scopes

There are aims shared by all or most committees that are not subject specific. They are as follows:

■ Establish and maintain liaison with national and international organizations with allied interests and foster cooperative action, collaborative research, and information exchange
■ Identify subjects and priorities for research, stimulate theoretical work on fundamental issues, and foster fundamental research that will underpin future development
■ Provide a forum for professionals with a view to promote the study, collection, exchange, and dissemination of ideas, information, and research findings, and thereby promote the state-of-the-art
■ Seek and use the most effective ways of disseminating information about our work including the organization of conferences, workshops, and symposia, and the timely production of relevant publications
■ Have special regard for the needs of developing countries and seek practical ways of working with them
■ Encourage communication and promote interaction between users, practitioners, and researchers
■ Foster interdisciplinary work and, in particular, collaborate with other TCs and working groups

Association for Computing Machinery

The ACM, is an international scientific and educational organization dedicated to advancing the arts, sciences, and applications of IT. The ACM functions as a locus for computing professionals and students working in the various fields of IT. The ACM is the world's oldest and largest educational and scientific computing society. Since 1947, the ACM has provided a vital forum for the exchange of information, ideas, and discoveries. Today, the ACM, the Association for Computing Machinery is the world's largest educational and scientific computing society, uniting educators, researchers and professionals to inspire dialogue, share resources and address the field's challenges. The ACM strengthens the computing profession's collective voice through strong leadership, promotion of the highest standards, and recognition of technical excellence. The ACM supports the professional growth of its members by providing opportunities for life-long learning, career development, and professional networking.

With over 100,000 members from over 100 countries, the ACM works to advance computing as a science and a profession in all areas of industry, academia, and government.

Association for Computing Machinery (ACM)
2 Penn Plaza, Suite 701
New York, NY 10121-0701
Phone: +1 800 342 6626 (US/Canada)
     +1 212 626 0500 (Global)
Fax: +1 212 944 1318 (Global)
Email: acmhelp@acm.org
Website: http://www.acm.org

Authoritative Guide

As the push for standardization becomes international in scope, understanding the development and use of standards is critical. Producers and users of standards in business, government research, and academia will benefit from StandardView's practical and theoretical information on all aspects of standardization with an emphasis on how standards affect the daily work of all IT professionals.

Institute of Chartered Accountants in Australia

The ICAA was established by the Royal Charter in 1928 following antecedent bodies dating from 1885. It currently operates under a Supplemental (amending) Charter granted by the governor-general on March 17, 1988. The institute sets the technical and ethical standards for members and provides leadership for the profession. The ethical rulings issued by the institute, along with current accounting and AUSs, are binding on members. A major part of the institute's activities involves representing members at the highest levels with governments, business and professional organizations, academic institutions, and the news media.

The Institute of Chartered Accountants in Australia (ICAA)
Level 14
37 York Street
Sydney, NSW 2000
Australia
Telephone: 61-2-9290 1344
Facsimile: 61-2-9262 1512
Website: www.charteredaccountants.com.au
Email: rebekah@icaa.org.au

Authoritative Guide

The purpose of this AUS is to establish standards and provide guidance on obtaining an understanding of the internal control structure and on audit risk and its components: inherent risk, control risk, and detection risk. Auditing Guidance Statements (AGS) are issued by the ASB when the board wishes to provide guidance on procedural matters, guidance on entity or industry-specific issues, or believes an underlying principle in an auditing standard requires clarification, explanation, or elaboration. AGS do not establish new auditing standards, do not amend existing auditing standards, and are not mandatory.

National Institute of Standards and Technology

The National Institute of Standards and Technology is an agency of the U.S. Department of Commerce, was founded in 1901 as the nation's first federal physical science research laboratory. Over the years, the scientists and technical staff at NIST have made solid contributions to image processing, DNA diagnostic "chips," smoke detectors, and automated error-correcting software for machine tools. Just a few of the other areas in which NIST has had major impact include atomic clocks, x-ray standards for mammography, scanning tunneling microscopy, pollution-control technology, computer security resources/guidance and high-speed dental drills. The major focus of NIST activities in IT is developing tests, measurements, proofs of concept, reference data, and other technical tools to support the development of pivotal, forward-looking technology. Under Section 512 of the Information Technology Reform Act of 1996 and the Computer Security Act of 1987, Public Law 104-106, NIST develops standards, guidelines, and associated methods and techniques for federal computer systems.

National Institute of Standards and Technology
Conformance Testing Group
Building 820, Room 562
Gaithersburg, MD 20899-0001
Telephone: (301) 975-3283
Facsimile: (301) 948-6213
Website: http://www.itl.nist.gov
Computer security resource center: http://csrc.nist.gov/
E-mail: itlab@nist.gov

Authoritative Guide

Under the Information Technology Management Reform Act (Public Law 104–106), the Secretary of Commerce approves standards and guidelines that are developed by the NIST for federal computer systems. These standards and guidelines are issued by NIST as Federal Information Processing Standards (FIPS) for government-wide use. NIST develops FIPS when there are compelling federal government requirements such as security and interoperability, and there are no acceptable industry standards or solutions.

Government Accountability Office

The GAO is a nonpartisan agency within the legislative branch of the government. GAO conducts audits, surveys, investigations, and evaluations of federal programs. This work is done at the request of congressional committees or members, or to fulfill GAO's specifically mandated or basic legislative requirements. GAO's findings and recommendations are published as reports to congressional members or delivered as testimony to congressional committees.

U.S. General Accounting Office
PO Box 37050
Washington, DC 20013
Telephone: (202) 512-6000
Facsimile: (202) 512-6061
Website: http://www.gao.gov
E-mail: documents@gao.gov

A substantial portion of the general guidance issued by GAO to executive agencies was first codified into the GAO *Policy and Procedures Manual for Guidance of Federal Agencies* in 1957. Over the years, the manual was updated to incorporate current changes in laws, regulations, and practices.

However, in the recent past changes in certain laws; the creation of the Federal Accounting Standards Advisory Board (FASAB); the establishment of the Advisory Council on Government Auditing Standards; and the different medium GAO has published guidance (e.g., the Yellow Book and the Green Book on internal control standards); their most current guidance to federal agencies and programs was issued in February 2009. *Federal Information System Controls Audit Manual (FISCAM)* GAO-09-232G February 2, 2009. FISCAM presents a methodology for performing IS control audits of federal and other governmental entities in accordance with professional standards. This exposure draft (ED) reflects the current computing environment and other changes affecting IS audits.

International Organization of Supreme Audit Institutions

The INTOSAI is the professional organization of Supreme Audit Institutions (SAIs) in countries that belong to the United Nations or its specialized agencies. SAIs play a major role in auditing government accounts and operations and promoting sound financial management and accountability in their governments. The INTOSAI supports its members in this task by providing opportunities to share information and experiences about the auditing and evaluation challenges facing them in today's changing and increasingly interdependent world. The INTOSAI was founded in 1953 and has grown from the original 34 countries to a membership of 175 SAIs.

INTOSAI—Austrian Court of Audit
Rechnungshof, Fach 240
A-1033 Vienna
Austria
Telephone: +43 (1) 711 71 8456
Facsimile: +43 (1) 718 94 25
Website: http://www.intosai.org

Authoritative Guide

INTOSAI offers two guidelines and their Committee on IT Audit has issued two IT Audit Guides.

Committee on IT Audit

- Information System Security Review Methodology—A Guide for Reviewing Information System Security in Government Organisations (ISSA 5310)
- Guide to Developing IT Strategies in Supreme Audit Institutions

Auditing Standards

Auditing Standards Committee, Chair: Riksrevisionsverket (The Swedish National Audit Office), Sweden.

Issued by the Auditing Standards Committee at the XIVth Congress of INTOSAI in 1992 in Washington, DC, as amended by the XVth Congress of INTOSAI 1995 in Cairo, Egypt, as amended by the XVIIth Congress of INTOSAI in Seoul 2001.

Guidelines for Internal Control Standards for the Public Sector

Internal Control Standards Committee, Chair: Állami Számvevöszék (State Audit Office), Hungary.

Issued by Internal Control Standards Committee, INTOSAI, June 1992, as amended by the XVIIth Congress of INTOSAI in Seoul 2001, as amended by the XVIII INCOSAI in Budapest 2004. The 17th INCOSAI (Seoul, 2001) agreed to rely on the Committee on Sponsoring Organisations of the Treadway Commission's (COSO) integrated framework for internal controls.

Appendix IV

Glossary

Abend: The abnormal termination of a computer application or job because of a nonsystematic condition or a failure that causes a program to halt.

Acceptance confidence level: The degree of certainty in a statement of probabilities that a conclusion is correct. In sampling, a specified confidence level is expressed as a percentage of certainty.

Acceptance testing: The formal testing conducted to determine whether a software system satisfies its acceptance criteria. It enables the customer to determine whether to accept the system or not.

Access: The ability and the means necessary to approach, store, or retrieve data, or to communicate with or make use of any resources of a computer information system.

Access category: An authorization that defines the resources in a computer-based system to which a user, program, or process is granted access.

Access control: The process of allowing only authorized users, programs, or other computer systems (i.e., networks) to access the resources of a computer system.

Access control mechanisms: Hardware, software, or firmware features, and operating and management procedures in various combinations designed to detect and prevent unauthorized access and to permit authorized access to a computer system.

Access list: A catalog of users, programs, or processes and the specifications of the access categories to which each is assigned.

Access period: A segment of time, generally expressed on a daily or weekly basis, during which access rights prevail.

Access type: The nature of access granted to a particular device, program, or file (e.g., read, write, execute, append, modify, delete, or create).

Accountability: The quality or state that enables attempted and committed violations of computer systems security to be traced to individuals who may then be held responsible.

Accumulator: An area of storage in memory used to develop totals of units or items being computed.

Active wiretapping: The attachment of an unauthorized device (e.g., a computer terminal) to a communications circuit to gain access to data by generating false messages or control signals, or by altering the communications of legitimate users.

651

Ada: A programming language that allows use of structured techniques for program design; a concise but powerful language designed to fill government requirements for real-time applications.

Adaptive filter: Prompts user to rate products or situations and also monitors your actions over time to find out what you like and dislike.

Adaptivity: The ability of intelligent agents to discover, learn, and take action independently.

Add-on security: The retrofitting of protection mechanisms, implemented by hardware, firmware, or software, on a computer system that has become operational.

Administrative security: The management constraints, operational procedures, accountability procedures, and supplemental controls established to provide an acceptable level of protection for sensitive data.

Adware: Software to generate ads that installs itself on your computer when you download some other (usually free) program from the Web.

Affiliate programs: Arrangements made between e-commerce sites that direct users from one site to the other and by which, if a sale is made as a result, the originating site receives a commission.

Agent: In the client/server model, the part of the system that performs information preparation and exchange on behalf of a client or server application.

Aging: The identification, by date, of unprocessed or retained items in a file. This is usually done by date of transaction and classifying items according to ranges of data.

Alphabetic test: The check on whether an element of data contains only alphabetic or blank characters.

Alphanumeric: A character set that includes numeric digits, alphabetic characters, and other special symbols.

American National Standards Institute (ANSI): The agency that recommends standards for computer hardware, software, and firmware design and use.

American Standard Code for Information Interchange (ASCII): A byte-oriented coding system based on an 8-bit code and used primarily to format information for transfer in a data communications environment.

Analysis and design phase: The phase of the SDLC in which an existing system is studied in detail and its functional specifications are generated.

Annual loss expectancy (ALE): In risk assessment, the average monetary value of losses per year.

Anonymous Web browsing (AWB): Services hide your identity from the Websites you visit.

Antivirus software: Detects and removes or quarantines computer viruses.

Application: Computer software used to perform a distinct function. Also used to describe the function itself.

Application architects: IT professionals who can design creative technology-based business solutions.

Application generation subsystem: Contains facilities to help you develop transaction-intensive applications.

Application layer: The top-most layer in the OSI Reference Model providing such data communication service is invoked through a software package.

Application programming interface (API): A set of calling conventions defining how a service is invoked through a software package.

Application service provider (ASP): Provides an outsourcing service for business software applications.

Application software: Software that enables you to solve specific problems or perform specific tasks.

Architecture: The structure and organization of IT hardware, software, and information.

Arithmetic logic unit (ALU): A component of the computer's processing unit in which arithmetic and matching operations are performed.

Arithmetic operator: In programming activities, a symbol representing an arithmetic calculation or process.

Array: Consecutive storage areas in memory that are identified by the same name. The elements (or groups) within these storage areas are accessed through subscripts.

Artificial intelligence (AI): A field of study involving techniques and methods under which computers can simulate human intellectual activities such as learning.

Artificial neural network (ANN): Also called a neural network; an AI system that is capable of finding and differentiating patterns.

ASCII: See "American Standard Code for Information Interchange."

Assembler language: A computer programming language in which alphanumeric symbols represent computer operations and memory addresses. Each assembler instruction translates into a single machine-language instruction.

Assembler program: A program language translator that converts assembler programs into machine code.

Assertion: A logical expression specifying a program state that must exist or a set of conditions that program variables must satisfy at a particular point during program execution.

Association control service element (ACSE): Part of the application layer of the OSI Model. ASCE provides the means to exchange authentication information coming from the Specific Application Service Element (SASE) of the OSI Model.

Asynchronous transfer mode (ATM): A transfer mode in which data are transmitted in the form of 53 byte units called "cells." Each cell consists of a 5-byte header and a 48-byte payload. The term "asynchronous" in this context refers to the fact that cells from any one particular source need not be periodically spaced within the overall cell stream. In other words, users are not assigned a set position in a recurring frame as is common in circuit switching.

Audio output: Voice synthesizers that create audible signals resembling a human voice out of computer-generated output.

Audio response system: The method of delivering output by using audible signals and transmitters that simulate a spoken language.

Audit: An independent review and examination of system records and activities that test for the adequacy of system controls, ensure compliance with established policy and operational procedures, and recommend any indicated changes in controls, policies, and procedures.

Audit risk: The probable unfavorable monetary effect related to the occurrence of an undesirable event or condition.

Audit trail: A chronological record of system activities that is sufficient to enable the reconstruction, review, and examination of each event in a transaction from inception to output of final results.

Authentication: The act of identifying or verifying the eligibility of a station, originator, or individual to access specific categories of information. Typically, a measure designed to protect against fraudulent transmissions by establishing the validity of a transmission, message, station, or originator.

Authorization: The granting of right of access to a user, program, or process.

Autofilter function: Filters a list and allows you to hide all the rows in a list except those that match criteria you specify.

Automated security monitoring: The use of automated procedures to ensure that the security controls implemented within a computer system or network are not circumvented or violated.

Automatic speech recognition (ASR): A system that not only captures spoken words, but also distinguishes word groupings to form sentences.

Autonomy: The ability of an intelligent agent to act without your telling it every step to take.

B2B marketplace: An Internet-based service that brings together many buyers and sellers.

Backbone: The primary connectivity mechanism of a hierarchical distributed system. All systems that have connectivity to an intermediate system on the backbone are assured of connectivity to each other. This does not prevent systems from setting up private arrangements with each other to bypass the backbone for reasons of cost, performance, or security.

Backbone network: A network that interconnects various computer networks and mainframe computers in an enterprise. The backbone provides the structure through which computers communicate.

Back-propagation neural network: A neural network trained by someone.

Backup operation: A method of operation used to complete essential tasks (as identified by risk analysis) subsequent to the disruption of the information processing facility and continuing to do so until the facility is sufficiently restored.

Backup procedures: Provisions made for the recovery of data files and program libraries, and for the restart or replacement of computer equipment after the occurrence of a system failure or disaster.

Backward chaining: A process related to an expert system inference engine that starts with a hypothesis and attempts to confirm that the hypothesis is consistent with information in the knowledge base.

Balanced scorecard: Performance measures and reporting tied to the achievement of stated objectives.

Bandwidth: The range of frequencies assigned to a channel or circuit. The difference expressed in hertz (cycles per second) between the highest and lowest frequencies of the transmission band.

Banner ad: A small ad on one Website that advertises the products and services of another business.

Bar-code: A series of solid bars of different widths used to encode data. Special OCR devices can read these data.

Bar-code reader: Captures information that exists in the form of vertical bars whose width and distance from each other determine a number.

Baseband: Characteristic of any network technology that uses a single carrier frequency and requires all stations attached to the network to participate in every transmission. See "broadband."

BASIC: See "Beginner's All-Purpose Symbolic Instruction Code."

Basic text formatting tag: HTML tags that allow you to specify formatting for text.

Batch control: A computer information processing technique in which numeric fields are totaled and records are tabulated to provide a comparison check for subsequent processing results.

Baud: Signal or state change during data transmission. Each state change can be equal to multiple bits, so the actual bit rate during data transmission may exceed the baud rate.

Beginner's All-Purpose Symbolic Instruction Code (BASIC): A programming language designed in the 1960s to teach students how to program and to facilitate learning. The powerful language syntax was designed especially for time-sharing systems.

Benchmark test: A simulation evaluation conducted before purchasing or leasing equipment to determine how well hardware, software, and firmware perform.

Between-the-lines entry: Access obtained through the use of active wiretapping by an unauthorized user to a momentarily inactive terminal of a legitimate user assigned to a communications channel.

Binary digit: A state of function represented by the digit 0 or 1.

Biometrics: The use of one's physical characteristics such as fingerprints, blood vessels in the retina of the eye, and the sound of one's voice to provide identification.

Bit: A binary value represented by an electronic component that has a value of 0 or 1.

Bits per second (bps): The speed at which bits are sent during data transmission.

Blackhat hackers: Cyber vandals.

Blocking factor: The number of records appearing between interblock gaps on magnetic storage media.

Block structure: In programming, a segment of code that can be treated as an independent module.

Bluetooth: Technology that provides entirely wireless connections for all kinds of communication devices.

Bounds checking: The testing of computer program results for access to storage outside its authorized limits.

Bounds register: A hardware or firmware register that holds an address specifying a storage boundary.

Branch: An alteration of the normal sequential execution of program statements.

Brevity lists: A coding system that reduces the time required to transmit information by representing long, stereotyped sentences with only a few characters.

Bridge: A device that connects two or more physical networks and forwards packets between them. Bridges can usually be made to filter packets, that is, to forward only certain traffic.

Broadband: Characteristic of any network that multiplexes multiple, independent network carriers onto a single cable.

Broadcast: A packet delivery system where a copy of a given packet is given to all hosts attached to the network, for example, Ethernet.

Browser-safe colors: A range of 216 colors that can be represented using 8 bits and are visible in all browsers.

Browsing: The searching of computer storage to locate or acquire information without necessarily knowing whether it exists or in what format.

Buffer: A storage location used to compensate for differences in the rate of speed of data being transferred between devices.

Bug: A coded program statement containing a logical or syntactical error.

Burst: The separation of multiple-copy printout forms into individual sheets.

Bus: A data path that connects the CPU, input, output, and storage devices.

Business intelligence: Knowledge about customers, competitors, partners, and own internal operations. Business intelligence from information.

Business process: A standardized set of activities that accomplishes a specific task such as processing a customer's order.

Business process reengineering (BPR): The reinventing of a process within a business.

Business requirement: A detailed knowledge worker request that the system must meet to be successful.

Business-to-business (B2B): Companies whose customers are primarily other businesses.

Business-to-consumer (B2C): Companies whose customers are primarily individuals.

Buyer agent or shopping bot: An intelligent agent or application on a Website that helps customers find the products and services they want.

Byte: The basic unit of storage for many computers; typically, one configuration consists of 8 bits used to represent data plus a parity bit for checking the accuracy of representation.

Byte–digit portion: Usually, the four rightmost bits in a byte.

C: A third-generation computer language used for programming on microcomputers. Most microcomputer software products such as spreadsheets and DBMS programs are written in C.

Cable modem: A device that uses a television (TV) cable to deliver an Internet connection.

Callback: A procedure that identifies a terminal dialing into a computer system or network by disconnecting the calling terminal, verifying the authorized terminal against the automated control table, and then, if authorized, reestablishing the connection by having the computer system dial the telephone number of the calling terminal.

Capacity planning: Determining the future IT infrastructure requirements for new equipment and additional network capacity.

Cathode-ray tube (CRT): The display device for computer terminals, typically a TV-like electronic vacuum tube.

Cave (cave automatic virtual environment): A special 3-D virtual reality room that can display images of other people and objects located in other cave's all over the world.

CCITT: See "Telecommunications Standardization Sector of the International Telecommunications Union (TSS-ITU)."

CD-R (compact disk-recordable): An optical or laser disk that offers one-time writing capability with about 700 MB or greater of storage.

CD-ROM: A compact disk (CD), similar to an audio CD, which is used to store computer information (e.g., programs, data, or graphics).

CD-RW (compact disk-rewritable): A CD that offers unlimited writing and updating capabilities.

Central processing unit (CPU): The part of the computer system containing the control and ALUs.

Certification: The acceptance of software by an authorized agent, usually after the software has been validated by the agent or its validity has been demonstrated to the agent.

Channel: A magnetic track running along a length of tape that can be magnetized in bit patterns to represent data.

Character: A single numeric digit, special symbol, or letter.

Check digit: A numeric digit that is used to verify the accuracy of a copied or transcribed number. The numeric digit is typically appended to the end of a number.

Chief information officer (CIO): The title for the highest-ranking MIS officer in the organization.

Chip: A wafer containing miniature electronic imprinted circuits and components.

Choice: The third step in the decision-making process where you decide on a plan to address the problem or opportunity.

Class: Contains information and procedures and acts as a template to create objects.

Clickstream: A stored record of a Web surfing session containing information such as Websites visited, how long the user was there, what ads were looked at, and the items purchased.

Click-throughs: A count of the number of people who visit one site and click on an ad, and are taken to the site of the advertiser.

Client: A workstation in a network that is set up to use the resources of a server.

Client/server: A network in which several PC-type systems (clients) are connected to one or more powerful central computers (servers). In databases, this term refers to a model in which a client system runs a database application (front end) that accesses information in DBMSs situated on a server (back end).

Client/server architecture: A LAN in which microcomputers called servers provide specialized service on behalf of the user's computers which are called clients.

Client/server model: A common way to describe network services and the model user processes (programs) of those services. Examples include the name–serve/name–resolver paradigm of the DNS and file–server/file–client relationships such as NFS and diskless hosts.

Cloud computing: The delivery of computing as a service rather than a product over the Internet.

Cipher system: A system in which cryptography is applied to plaintext elements of equal length.

Ciphertext: Encoded text or signals produced through the use of cipher systems.

Coaxial cable: A medium used for telecommunications. It is similar to the type of cable used for carrying TV signals.

COBOL: See "Common Business-Oriented Language."

Code generator: A precompiler program that translates fourth-generation language-like code into the statements of a third-generation language code.

Code system: Any system of communication in which groups of symbols represent plaintext elements of varying length.

Coder: The individual who translates program design into executable computer code.

Coding: The activity of translating a set of computer processing specifications into a formal language for execution by a computer.

Cold site: A separate facility that does not have any computer equipment, but is a place where the knowledge workers can move after the disaster.

Collaboration system: A system that is designed specifically to improve the performance of teams by supporting the sharing and flow of information.

Collaborative filtering: A method of placing you in an affinity group of people with the same characteristics.

Collaborative planning, forecasting, and replenishment (CPFR): A concept that encourages and facilitates collaborative processes between members of a supply chain.

Collaborative processing enterprise information portal: Provides knowledge workers with access to workgroup information such as e-mails, reports, meeting minutes, and memos.

Colocation: A vendor that rents space and telecommunications equipment to other companies.

COM: See "computer output microfilm."

Common Business-Oriented Language (COBOL): A high-level programming language for business computer applications.

Common carrier: An organization or company that provides data or other electronic communication services for a fee.

Communications medium: The path or physical channel in a network over which information travels.

Communications Protocol (protocol): A set of rules that every computer follows to transfer information.

Communications satellite: A microwave repeater in space.

Communications security: The level of protection that ensures the authenticity of telecommunications. The application of measures taken to deny unauthorized persons' access to valuable information that might be acquired from the network.

Communications service provider: A third party who furnishes the conduit for information.

Communications software: Helps you communicate with other people.

Community cloud: A cloud infrastructure that is shared by several organizations and supports a specific community, such as healthcare, that has shared concerns around mission, policy and compliance considerations.

Compare: A computer-applied function that examines two elements of data to determine their relationship to each other.

Compartmentalization: The isolation of the OS, user programs, and data files from one another in main storage to protect them against unauthorized or concurrent access by other users or programs. This also includes the division of sensitive data into small, isolated blocks to reduce risk to the data.

Competitive advantage: Providing a product or service in a way that customers value more than what the competition is able to do.

Compiler: A program that translates high-level computer language instruction into machine code.

Complementor: Provides services that complement the offerings of the enterprise and thereby extend its value-adding capabilities to its customers.

Completeness: The property that all necessary parts of an entity are included. Completeness of a product often means that the product has met all requirements.

Composite primary key: The primary key fields from two intersecting relations.

Compromise: Unauthorized disclosure or loss of sensitive information.

Compromising emanations: Electromagnetic emanations that convey data and, if intercepted and analyzed, could compromise sensitive information being processed by a computer system.

Computer-aided design (CAD): A term used to describe the use of computer technology as applied to the design of problems and opportunities.

Computer-aided instruction (CAI): The interactive use of a computer for instructional purposes. Software provides educational content to students and adjusts its presentation to the responses of the individual.

Computer-aided manufacturing (CAM): The use of computer technology as applied to the manufacturing of computer technology as applied to the manufacturing of goods and services.

Computer-aided software engineering (CASE): Tools that automate the design, development, operation, and maintenance of software.

Computer crime: The act of using IT to commit an illegal act.

Computer ethics: The issues and standards that support the proper use of IT which are not criminal or threatening to another person or organization.

Computer Fraud and Abuse Act (P.L. 99-474): The Computer Fraud and Abuse Act of 1986 strengthens and expands the 1984 Federal Computer Crime Legislation. Law extended to computer crimes in private enterprise and anyone who willfully disseminates information for the purpose of committing a computer crime (i.e., distribute phone numbers to hackers from a Bulletin Board System [BBS]).

Computer Matching Act (P.L. 100-503): The Computer Matching and Privacy Act of 1988 ensures privacy, integrity, and verification of data disclosed for computer matching and establishes data integrity boards within federal agencies.

Computer network: Two or more computers connected so that they can communicate with one another and share information, software, peripheral devices, and processing power.

Computer output microfilm (COM): The production of computer output on a photographic film.

Computer program: A series of operations that perform a task when executed in a logical sequence.

Computer security: The practice of protecting a computer system against internal failures, human error, attacks, and natural catastrophes, which might cause improper disclosure, modification, destruction, or DoS.

Computer Security Act (P.L. 100-235): The Computer Security Act of 1987 directs the U.S. National Bureau of Standards (NBS), now known as the National Institute of Standards and Technology (NIST), to establish a computer security standards program for federal computer systems.

Computer system: An interacting assembly of elements, including at least computer hardware and usually software, data procedures, and people.

Computer system security: All of the technological safeguards and managerial procedures established and applied to computers and their networks (including related hardware, firmware, software, and data) to protect organizational assets and individual privacy.

Computer virus: Software that is written with malicious intent to cause annoyance or damage.

Concealment systems: A method of keeping sensitive information confidential by embedding it in irrelevant data.

Concentrator: A computer that consolidates the signals from any slower-speed transmission lines into a single faster line or performs the reverse function.

Concurrent processing: The capability of a computer to share memory with several programs and simultaneously execute the instructions provided by each.

Conditional branch: The alteration of the normal sequence of program execution following the text of the contents of a memory area.

Conditional formatting: Highlights the information in a cell that meets some specified criteria.

Condition test: A comparison of two data items in a program to determine whether one value is equal to, less than, or greater than the second value.

Conference on Data Systems Languages (CODASYL): A Department of Defense-sponsored group that studies the requirements and design specifications for a common business programming language.

Confidentiality: A concept that applies to data that must be held in confidence and describes that status or degree of protection that must be provided for such data about individuals as well as organizations.

Configuration management: The use of procedures appropriate for controlling changes to a system's hardware, software, or firmware structure to ensure that such changes will not lead to a weakness or fault in the system.

Connectivity software: Enables a computer to "dial up" or connect to another computer.

Consistency: Logical coherency among all integrated parts; also, adherence to a given set of instructions or rules.

Console operator: Someone who works at a computer console to monitor operations and initiate instructions for efficient use of computer resources.

Constant: A value in a computer program that does not change during program execution.

Contingency plans: Plans for emergency response, backup operations, and postdisaster recovery maintained by a computer information processing facility as a part of its security program.

Control: Any protective action, device, procedure, technique, or other measure that reduces exposures.

Control break: A point during program processing at which some special processing event takes place. A change in the value of a control field within a data record is characteristic of a control break.

Control field: A field of data within a record used to identify and classify a record.

Controllable isolation: Controlled sharing in which the scope or domain of authorization can be reduced to an arbitrarily small set or sphere of activity.

Controlled sharing: The condition that exists when access control is applied to all users and components of a resource-sharing computer system.

Control logic: The specific order in which processing functions are carried out by a computer.

Control signals: Computer-generated signals for the automatic control of machines and processes.

Control statement: A command in a computer program that establishes the logical sequence of processing operations.

Control structure: A program that contains a logical construct of sequences, repetitions, and selections.

Control totals: Accumulations of numeric data fields that are used to check the accuracy of the input, processing, or output data.

Control unit: A component of the CPU that evaluates and carries out program processing and execution.

Control zone: The space surrounding equipment that is used to process sensitive information and that is under sufficient physical and technical control to preclude an unauthorized entry or compromise.

Conversational program: A program that permits interaction between a computer and a user.

Conversion: The process of replacing a computer system with a new one.

Conversion rate: The percentage of customers who visit a Website and actually buy something.

Cookie: A small record deposited on the hard disk by a Website containing information about users and their Web activities.

Copyright: The legal protection afforded to the expression of an idea, such as a song or a game and some types of proprietary documents.

Correctness: The extent to which software is free from design and coding defects (i.e., fault-free). Also, the extent to which software meets its specified requirements and user objectives.

Cost/benefit analysis: Determination of the economic feasibility of developing a system on the basis of a comparison of the projected costs of the proposed system and the expected benefits from its operation.

Cost-risk analysis: The assessment of the cost of potential risk of loss or compromise of data in a computer system without data protection versus the cost of providing data protection.

Counterfeit software: Software that is manufactured to look like the real thing and sold as such.

Courseware: Computer programs used to deliver educational materials within computer-assisted instruction systems.

Cracker: A hacker for hire; a person who engages in electronic corporate espionage.

Crash-proof software: Utility software that helps save information if the system crashes and the user is forced to turn it off and then back on.

Critical success factor (CSF): A factor simply critical to the organization's success.

Crossover: The process within a genetic algorithm where portions of the good outcome are combined in the hope of creating an even better outcome.

Cross talk: An unwanted transfer of energy from one communications channel to another.

CRT: A monitor that looks like a TV set.

CRUD (create, read, update, delete): The four primary procedures or ways a system can manipulate information.

Cryptanalysis: The deciphering of encrypted messages into plaintext without initial knowledge of the key employed in the encryption algorithm.

Cryptographic system: The documents, devices, equipment, and associated techniques that are used as a unit to provide a single means of encryption.

Cryptography: The art or science that applies the principles, means, and methods for producing encrypted text and converting encrypted messages into plaintext.

Cryptology: The field of study that encompasses both cryptography and cryptanalysis.

Culture: The collective personality of a nation, society, or organization, encompassing language, traditions, currency, religion, history, music, and acceptable behavior, among others.

Custom auto filter function: Allows one to hide all the rows in a list except those that match the criteria specified.

Customer-integrated system: An extension of a TPS that places technology in the hands of an organization's customers and allows them to process their own transactions.

Customer relationship management (CRM) system: Uses information about customers to gain insights into their needs, wants, and behaviors to serve them better.

Cyber-terrorist: One who seeks to cause harm to people or destroy critical systems or information.

Data: Raw facts and figures that are meaningless by themselves. Data can be expressed in characters, digits, and symbols, which can represent people, things, and events.

Data administration: The function in an organization that plans for, oversees the development of, and monitors the information resource.

Data administration subsystem: Helps manage the overall database environment by providing facilities for backup and recovery, security management, query optimization, concurrency control, and change management.

Database: An integrated aggregation of data usually organized to reflect logical or functional relationships among data elements.

Database administrator: A person who is in charge of defining and managing the contents of the database.

Database-based workflow system: Stores the document in a central location and automatically asks the knowledge workers to access the document when it is their turn to edit the document.

Database management system (DBMS): The software that directs and controls data resources.

Data communications: The transmission of data between two or more Websites through the use of public and private communications channels or lines.

Data contamination: A deliberate or accidental process or act that compromises the integrity of the original data.

Data Definition Language (DDL): A set of instructions or commands used to define data for the data dictionary.

Data-dependent protection: The protection of data at a level that is commensurate with the sensitivity of the entire file.

Data dictionary: A document or listing defining all items or processes represented in a data flow diagram or used in a system.

Data diddling: A type of computer crime where information and data flowing in or out of a computer is being altered.

Data element: The smallest unit of data accessible to a DBMS or a field of data within a file processing system.

Data Encryption Standard (DES): A cipher standardized by the NBS. DES is a symmetric block cipher with a block length of 64 bits and effective key length of 56 bits.

Data flow analysis: A graphic analysis technique to trace the behavior of program variables as they are initialized, modified, or referenced during program execution.

Data flow diagram: A descriptive modeling tool providing a graphic and logical description of a system.

Data integrity: The state that exists when automated information or data are the same as that in the source documents and has not been exposed to accidental or malicious modification, alteration, or destruction.

Data link layer: The OSI layer that is responsible for data transfer across a single physical connection or series of bridged connections between two network entities.

Data management system: System software that supervises the handling of data required by programs during execution.

Data mart: Subset of a data warehouse in which only a focused portion of the data warehouse is stored.

Data mining: A methodology used by organizations to better understand their customers, products, markets, or any other phase of the business.

Data-mining agent: An intelligent agent or application that operates in a data warehouse discovering information.

Data-mining tool: Software tool used to query information in a data warehouse.

Data protection engineering: The methodology and tools used to design and implement data protection mechanisms.

Data representation: The manner in which data are characterized in a computer system and its peripheral devices.

Data security: The protection of data from accidental or malicious modification, destruction, or disclosure.

Data segment: A collection of data elements accessible to a DBMS; a record in a file processing system.

Data warehouse: A logical collection of information, gathered from many different operational databases, used to create business intelligence that supports business analysis activities and decision-making tasks.

Deadlock: A condition that occurs when two users invoke conflicting locks in trying to gain access to a specific record or records.

Debugging: The process of correcting static and logical errors detected during coding. With the primary goal of obtaining an executable piece of code, debugging shares certain techniques and strategies with testing but differs in its usual ad hoc application and scope.

Decentralized computing: An environment in which an organization splits computing power and locates it in functional business areas as well as on the desktops of knowledge workers.

Decipher: The ability to convert, by use of the appropriate key, enciphered text into its equivalent plaintext.

Decision processing enterprise information portal: Provides knowledge workers with corporate information for making key business decisions.

Decision support system (DSS): A computer information system that helps executives and managers formulate policies and plans. This support system enables the users to access information and assess the likely consequences of their decisions through scenario projections.

Decrypt: Synonymous with decipher.

Dedicated mode: The operation of a computer system such that the central computer facility, connected peripheral devices, communications facilities, and all remote terminals are used and controlled exclusively by the users or groups of users for the processing of particular types and categories of information.

Dedicated server: A microcomputer used exclusively to perform a specific service, such as to process the network OS.

Degauss: To erase or demagnetize magnetic recording media (usually tapes) by applying a variable, alternating current (AC) field.

Demand aggregation: Combines purchase requests from multiple buyers into a single large order, which justifies a discount from the business.

Denial-of-service (DoS) attack: The attacker floods a Website with many electronic message requests for service that it slows down or crashes the network or computer targeted.

Design: Considering possible ways of solving the problem, filling the need, or taking advantage of the opportunity.

Design and implementation: A phase of the SDLC in which a set of functional specifications produced during systems analysis is transformed into an operational system for hardware, software, and firmware.

Desktop computer: The most popular choice for personal computing needs.

Desktop publishing: The use of computer technology equipped with special hardware, firmware, and software features to produce documents that look equivalent to those printed by a professional print company.

Digit: A single numeral representing an arithmetic value.

Digital cash: An electronic representation of cash. Also called e-cash.

Digital divide: The fact that different peoples, cultures, and areas of the world or within a nation do not have the same access to information and telecommunications technologies.

Digital economy: Marked by the electronic movement of all types of information, not limited to numbers, words, graphs, and photos, but also including physiological information such as voice recognition and synthesization, biometrics (e.g., a person's retina scan and breath), and 3-D holograms.

Digital Subscriber Line (DSL): A high-speed Internet connection using phone lines that allows the use of phone for voice communications at the same time.

Direct access: The method of reading and writing specific records without having to process all preceding records in a file.

Direct organization: A method of file organization under which records are located on the basis of their keys and associated addresses on the storage media.

Directory engine search: Organizes listings of Websites into hierarchical lists.

Disaster recovery cost curve: Charts (1) the cost to the organization due to the unavailability of information and technology, and (2) the cost to the organization of recovering from a disaster over time.

Disaster recovery plan: A detailed process for recovering information or an IT system in the event of a catastrophic disaster such as a fire or flood.

Disintermediation: The use of the Internet as a delivery vehicle whereby intermediate players in a distribution channel can be bypassed.

Disk address: The positioned location of a data record on magnetic disk storage.

Diskette: A flexible disk storage medium most often used with microcomputers; also called a floppy disk.

Disk optimization software: Utility software that organizes information on the hard disk in the most efficient way.

Distributed computing environment (DCE): An architecture of standard programming interfaces, conventions, and server functionalities (e.g., naming, distributed file system, and RPC) for distributing applications transparently across networks of heterogeneous computers.

Promoted and controlled by the Open Software Foundation (OSP), a consortium led by Hewlett-Packard, Digital Equipment Corp, and IBM.

Distributed denial-of-service (DDoS) attack: Multiple computers flooding a Website with so many requests for service that it slows down or crashes.

Documentation: The written narrative of the development, workings, and operation of a program or system.

Domain: A part of the naming hierarchy in the Internet. Syntactically, an Internet domain name consists of a sequence of names (labels) separated by periods (dots), for example, tundra. mpk.ca.us. In OSI, domain is generally used as an administrative partition of a complex distributed system, as in MHS Private Management Domain (PRMD) and Directory Management Domain (DMD).

Domain name system (DNS): The distributed name and address mechanism used in the Internet.

Downtime: A period of time in which the computer is not available for operation.

DSS shell: A set of programs that can be used for constructing a DSS.

Dump: The contents of a file or memory that are output as listings. These listings may be formatted.

Dynamic analysis: The execution of program code to detect errors by analyzing the code's response to input.

Dynamic processing: The technique of swapping jobs in and out of computer memory. This technique can be controlled by the assignment priority and the number of time slices allocated to each job.

Eavesdropping: The unauthorized interception of information-bearing emanations through methods other than wiretapping.

ebXML: A set of technical specifications for business documents built around XML designed to permit enterprises of any size and in any geographical location to conduct business over the Internet.

Echo: The display of characters on a terminal output device as they are entered into the system.

Edit: The process of inspecting a data field or element to verify the correctness of its content.

EDP auditor: A professional whose responsibility is to certify the validity, reliability, and integrity of all aspects of the computer information system environment of an organization, a.k.a. information system (IS) auditor, CIS auditor, or IT auditor.

E-government: The application of e-commerce technologies in government agencies.

Electromagnetic emanations: Signals transmitted as radiation through the air or conductors.

Electronic bill presentation and payment (EBPP): A system that sends people their bills over the Internet and gives them an easy way to pay.

Electronic bulletin board: An application program that lets users contribute messages via e-mail that can be routed or shared with users.

Electronic business XML: See "ebXML."

Electronic catalog: Designed to present products to customers via the Internet.

Electronic Communications Privacy Act (P.L. 99-508): The Electronic Communication Privacy Act of 1986 extends the Privacy Act of 1974 to all forms of electronic communication, including e-mail.

Electronic data interchange (EDI): A process whereby such specially formatted documents as an invoice can be transmitted from one organization to another.

Electronic document file: A magnetic storage area that contains electronic images of papers and other communications documents.

Electronic job market: Consists of employers using the Internet to advertise for and screen potential employees.

Electronic journal: A computerized log file summarizing, in chronological sequence, the processing activities and events performed by a system. The log file is usually maintained on magnetic storage media.

Electronic mail (e-mail): Formal or informal communications electronically transmitted or delivered.

Electronic office: An office that relies on word processing, computer systems, and communications technologies to support its operations.

Electronic portfolio: Collection of Web documents used to support a stated purpose such as writing skills.

E-mail software (electronic mail software): Enables people to electronically communicate with other people by sending and receiving e-mail.

Emanation security: The protection that results from all measures designed to deny unauthorized persons access to valuable information that might be derived from interception and analysis of compromising emanations.

Encapsulation: The technique used by layered protocols in which a layer adds header information to the PDU from the layer above.

Encipher: The process of converting plaintext into unintelligible form by means of a cipher system.

Encryption: The use of algorithms to encode data to render a message or a file readable only for the intended recipient.

Encryption algorithm: A set of mathematically expressed rules for encoding information, which renders it unintelligible to those who do not have the algorithm decoding key.

End-to-end encryption: The encryption of information at the point of origin within the communications network and postponing of decryption to the final destination point.

Enterprise application integration (EAI): The process of developing an IT infrastructure that enables employees to implement new or changing business processes.

Enterprise application integration middleware (EAI middleware): Allows organizations to develop different levels of integration from the information level to the business process level.

Enterprise information portal (EIP): Allows knowledge workers to access company information via a Web interface.

Enterprise resource planning (ERP): The method of getting and keeping an overview of every part of the business, so that production and selling of goods and services will be coordinated to contribute to the company's goals.

Enterprise risk management (ERM): Enterprise risk management is a process designed to identify potential events that may affect the entity, and manage risks to be within its risk appetite, to provide reasonable assurance regarding the achievement of entity objectives.

Enterprise software: A suite of software that includes (1) a set of common business applications, (2) tools for modeling how the organization works, and (3) development tools for building applications unique to the organization.

Entity barrier: A product or service feature that customers have come to expect from companies.

Entity class: A concept—typically people, places, or things—about which information can be stored and then identified with a unique key called the primary key.

Entity-relationship (ER) diagram: A graphic method of representing entity classes and their relationships.

Entrapment: The deliberate planting of apparent flaws in a system to detect attempted penetrations or confuse intruders about which flaws to exploit.

Erasable programmable read-only memory (EPROM): A memory chip that can have its circuit logic erased and reprogrammed.

E-tailor: An Internet retail site.

Ethernet card: The most common type of network interface card.

Ethical (whitehat) hacker: A computer security professional who is hired by a company to break into its computer system.

Ethics: The principles and standards that guide people's behavior toward others.

Evolution checking: Testing to ensure the completeness and consistency of a software product at different levels of specification when that product is a refinement or elaboration of another.

Exception report: A manager report that highlights abnormal business conditions. Usually, such reports prompt management action or inquiry.

Executive information system (EIS): A very interactive IT system that allows the user to first view highly summarized information and then choose how to see greater detail, which may be an alert to potential problems or opportunities.

Expandability: Refers to how easy it is to add features or functions to a system.

Expansion bus: Moves information from the CPU and RAM to all other hardware devices such as a microphone or printer.

Expansion card: A circuit board that is inserted into an expansion slot.

Expansion slot: A long skinny pocket on the motherboard into which an expansion card can be inserted.

Expert system: The application of computer-based AI in areas of specialized knowledge.

Explanation module: The part of an expert system where the "why" information, supplied by the domain expert, is stored to be accessed by knowledge workers who want to know why the expert systems asked a question or reached a conclusion.

Exposure: A form of possible loss or harm (e.g., erroneous record keeping, unmaintainable applications, or business interruptions) that affects the profitability of the going concern.

Extended binary-coded decimal interchange code (EBCDIC): A data representation and code system based on the use of an 8-bit byte.

External information: Describes the environment surrounding the organization.

Extraction engine: Smart software with a vocabulary of job-related skills that allows it to recognize and catalog terms in a scannable resume.

Extranet: An intranet that is restricted to an organization and certain outsiders, such as customers and suppliers.

Facsimile (fax): A technology used to send document images over telecommunications lines.

Fail safe: The automatic termination and protection of programs or other processing operations when a hardware, software, or firmware failure is detected in a computer system.

Fail soft: The selective termination of nonessential processing affected by a hardware, software, or firmware failure in a computer system.

Failure access: Unauthorized and usually inadvertent access to data resulting from a hardware, software, or firmware failure in the computer system.

Failure control: The methodology used to detect and provide fail-safe or fail-soft recovery from hardware, software, or firmware failure in a computer system.

Fair Credit Reporting Act (P.L. 91-508): A federal law that gives individuals the right of access to credit information pertaining to them and the right to challenge such information.

Fair Use Doctrine: Allows the use of copyrighted material in certain situations.

Fault: A weakness of the system that allows circumventing protective controls.

Feasibility study: An investigation of the legal, political, social, operational, technical, economic, and psychological effects of developing and implementing a system.

Feature analysis: The step of ASR in which the system captures the users' words as spoken into a microphone, eliminates any background noise, and converts the digital signals of speech into phonemes (syllables).

Feature creep: Occurs when developers add extra features that were not part of the initial requirements.

Federal Computer Fraud Act: The Counterfeit Access Device and Computer Fraud and Abuse Act of 1986 outlaws unauthorized access to the federal government's computers and financial databases as protected under the Right to Financial Privacy Act of 1978 and the Fair Credit Reporting Act of 1971. This act is an amendation of the 1984 Federal Computer Fraud Act.

Fetch protection: A system-provided restriction to prevent a program from accessing data in another user's segment of storage.

Fiber distributed data interface (FDDI): A standard for a 100-Mbps token-passing ring network operating over fiber optics.

Fiche: A sheet of photographic film containing multiple microimages; a form of computer output microfilm.

Field: A basic unit of data, usually part of a record that is located on an input, storage, or output microfilm.

File: A basic unit of data records organized on a storage medium for convenient location, access, and updating.

File creation: The building of master or transaction files.

File inquiry: The selection of records from files and immediate display of their contents on a terminal output device.

File maintenance: The changing of master file by changing the contents of existing records, adding new records, or deleting old records.

File protection: The aggregate of all processes and procedures established in a computer system and designed to inhibit unauthorized access, contamination, or elimination of a file.

File Transfer Protocol (FTP): The IP (and program) used to transfer files between hosts.

File updating: The posting of transaction data to master files or maintenance of master files through record additions, changes, or deletions.

Financial cybermediaries: Internet-based companies that make it easy for one person to pay another over the Internet.

Financial EDI (FEDI): The use of EDI for payments.

Firewall: Hardware or software that protects a computer or network from intruders.

Firmware: Software or computer instructions that have been permanently encoded into the circuits of semiconductor chips.

Flame: To express strong opinion or criticism of something, usually as a frank inflammatory statement in an electronic message.

Flat-panel display: Thin lightweight monitor that takes up much less space than a CRT.

Floppy disk: A flexible removable disk used for magnetic storage of data, programs, or information.

Foreign Corrupt Practices Act: The act covers an organization's system of internal accounting control and requires public companies to make and keep books, records, and accounts that, in reasonable detail, accurately and fairly reflect the transactions and disposition of company assets and to devise and maintain a system of sufficient internal accounting controls. This act was amended in 1988.

Foreign key: A primary key of one file (relation) that appears in another file (relation).

Forensic image copy: An exact copy or snapshot of the contents of an electronic medium.

Formal analysis: The use of rigorous mathematical techniques to analyze a solution. The algorithms may be analyzed for numerical properties, efficiency, and correctness.

Format: The physical arrangement of data characters, fields, records, and files.

Formula translator programming language (Fortran): A high-level programming language developed primarily to translate mathematical formulas into computer code.

Formulary: A technique for permitting the decision to grant or deny access to be determined dynamically at access time rather than at the time the access list is created.

Fortran: See "Formula translator programming language."

Fourth-generation language (4GL): A computer language that is easy to learn and use and often associated with rapid applications development.

Front-end computer: A computer that off-loads input and output activities from the central computer so it can operate primarily in a processing mode; sometimes called a front-end processor.

Front office space: The primary interface to customers and sales channels.

FTP (File Transfer Protocol) server: Maintains a collection of files that can be downloaded.

Function: In computer programming, a processing activity that performs a single, identifiable task.

Functional specification: The main product of systems analysis, which presents a detailed logical description of the new system. It contains sets of input, processing, storage, and output requirements specifying what the new system can do.

Functional testing: The application of test data derived from the specified functional requirements without regard to the final program structure.

Gateway: A product that enables two dissimilar networks to communicate or interface with each other.

General-purpose computer: A computer that can be programmed to perform a wide variety of processing tests.

Genetic algorithm: An AI system that mimics the evolutionary, survival-of-the-fittest process to generate increasingly better solutions to a problem.

Geographic information system (GIS): A DSS designed specifically to work with spatial information.

Gigabyte (G byte): The equivalent of 1 billion bytes.

Gigahertz: The number of billions of CPU cycles per second.

Global digital divide: The term used specifically to describe differences in IT access and capabilities between different countries or regions of the world.

Global economy: One in which customers, businesses, suppliers, distributors, and manufacturers operate without regard to physical and geographical boundaries.

Global positioning system: A collection of 24 earth-orbiting satellites that continuously transmit radio signals to determine an object or target's current longitude, latitude, speed, and direction of movement.

Global reach: The ability to extend a company's reach to customers anywhere through an Internet connection and at a lower cost.

Glove: An input device that captures and records the shape, movement, and strength of the users' hands and fingers.

Governance: A series of processes and procedures that identify who can make decisions, what decisions can be made, how decisions are made, how investments are managed, and how results are measured.

Government OSI Profile (GOSIP): A U.S. government procurement specification for OSI protocols.

Government-to-business (G2B): The e-commerce activities performed between a government and its business partners for purposes such as purchasing materials or soliciting and accepting bids for work.

Government-to-consumer (G2C): The e-commerce activities performed between a government and its citizens or consumers, including paying taxes and providing information and services.

Government-to-government (G2G): The e-commerce activities limited to a single nation's government focusing on vertical integration (local, city, state, and federal) and horizontal integration (within the various branches and agencies).

Graphical user interface (GUI): An interface (e.g., in Macintosh, Microsoft Windows, or Motif) in which the user can manipulate icons, windows, pop-down menus, or other related constructs.

Graphics output: Computer-generated output in the form of pictures, charts, and line drawings.

Graphics software: Helps the user create and edit photos and art.

Graphics terminal: An output device that displays pictures, charts, and line drawings, typically a high-resolution CRT.

Grid computing: Harnesses computers together by way of the Internet or a virtual network to share CPU power, databases, and storage.

Group document databases: A powerful storage facility for organizing and managing all documents relayed to specific teams.

Groupware: Software designed to function over a network to allow several people to work together on documents and files.

GUI (graphical user interface) screen design: The ability to model the information system screens for an entire system.

Hacking: A computer crime in which a person breaks into an information system simply for the challenge of doing so.

Hacktivist: A politically motivated hacker who uses the Internet to send a political message of some kind.

Handshaking procedure: Dialogue between a user and a computer, two computers, or two programs to identify the user and authenticate the identity. This is done through a sequence of questions and answers that are based on information either previously stored in the computer or supplied to the computer by the initiator of the dialogue.

Handspring: A type of PDA that runs on the Palm Operating System (Palm OS).

Hard disk: A fixed or removable disk mass storage system permitting rapid direct access to data, programs, or information.

Hardware: The physical equipment or devices included in computer systems.

Hardware key logger: A hardware device that captures keystrokes on their way from the keyboard to the motherboard.

Heading tag: HTML tag that puts certain information, such as the title, at the top of the page.

Headset: It combines input and output devices that (1) capture and record the movements of the user's head, and (2) contains a screen that covers the user's field of vision and displays various views of an environment based on the head's movements.

Help desk: Responds to knowledge workers' questions.

Hertz: One cycle per second.

High-capacity floppy disk: Storage device that holds between 100 and 250 MB of information. Superdisks and Zip disks are examples.

High-level language: The class of procedure-oriented language.

HIPAA Act of 1996: The Administrative Simplification provisions of the Health Insurance Portability and Accountability Act of 1996 (HIPAA) (Title II) require the Department of Health and Human Services to establish national standards for electronic healthcare transactions and national identifiers for providers, health insurers, and employers. It also addresses the security and privacy of health data. Adopting these standards will improve the efficiency and effectiveness of the nation's healthcare system by encouraging the widespread use of EDI in healthcare.

Holographic device: A device that creates, captures, and displays images in true 3-D form.

Home PNA (home phoneline networking alliance): Allows one to network home computer using telephone wiring.

Homeland Security Act of 2002: The act restructures and strengthens the executive branch of the federal government to better meet the threat to the United States posed by terrorism. In establishing a new department of Homeland Security, the act for the first time creates a federal department whose primary mission will be to help prevent, protect against, and respond to acts of terrorism on the U.S. soil.

Horizontal market software: Application software that is general enough to be suitable for use in a variety of industries.

Hot site: A separate and fully equipped facility where the company can move after a disaster and resume business.

HTML document: A file made from the HTML language.

HTML tag: Specifies the formatting and presentation of information in an HTML document.

Hypertext Markup Language (HTML): A language created by programmers at the European Organization for Nuclear Research (CERN) in Switzerland to create Web pages.

Hypertext Transfer Protocol (HTTP): The communications protocol that supports the movement of information over the Web, essentially from a Web server to the user.

Humanware: Computer programs that interface or communicate with users by means of voice-integrated technology, interpret user-specified command, and execute or translate commands into machine-executable code.

Hybrid cloud: A combination of two or more clouds (private, community, or public) that remain unique entities, but are bound together by standardized or proprietary technology that enables data and application portability (e.g., cloud bursting for load balancing between clouds).

Hypermedia: An extension to hypertext in which frames contain graphics, illustrations, images, audio, animation, text, and other forms of information or knowledge.

Hypertext: Text that is held in frames; authors develop or define the linkage between frames.

Icon: A pictorial symbol used to represent data, information, or a program on a GUI screen.

Ida (infrared date association) port: A port for wireless devices that works in essentially the same way as the remote control on TV.

Identification: The process, generally employing unique machine-readable names, that enables recognition of users or resources as identical to those previously described to the computer system.

Identity theft: Identity theft occurs when someone uses someone else's personally identifying information, like name, Social Security number, or credit card number, without the person's permission, to commit fraud or other crimes.

Impact printer: A hard-copy device on which a print mechanism strikes against a ribbon to create imprints on paper. Some impact printers operate one character at a time; others strike an entire line at a time.

Impersonation: An attempt to gain access to a system by posing as an authorized user.

Implant chip: A technology-enabled microchip implanted into the human body.

Implementation: The specific activities within the SDLC through which the software portion of the system is developed, coded, debugged, tested, and integrated with existing or new penetration.

Implementation phase: Distributes the system to the knowledge workers who begin using the system in their everyday jobs.

Incomplete parameter checking: A system fault that exists when all parameters have not been fully checked for correctness and consistency by the OS, leaving the system vulnerable to penetration.

Indexed sequential filing: A file organization method in which records are maintained in logical sequence and indices (or tables) are used to reference their storage addresses. The method allows direct and serial access to records.

Indirect material: Material that is necessary for running a modern corporation, but does not relate to the company's primary business activities. Commonly called Maintenance Repair and Operation (MRO) materials.

Inference engine: A system of computer programs in an expert systems application that uses expert experience as a basis for conclusions.

Information: Meaningful data; the result of processing data by computer or other means.

Information age: A time when knowledge is power.

Information decomposition: Breaking down the information for ease of use and understandability.

Information float: The amount of time it takes to get information from its source into the hands of the decision makers.

Information granularity: The extent of detail within the information.

Information-literate knowledge workers: Can define what information they need, know how to obtain that information, understand the information once they receive it, and act appropriately to help the organization achieve the greatest advantage.

Information partnership: Two or more companies that cooperate by integrating their IT systems, thereby providing customers with the best of what each has to offer.

Information resource management: A concept or practice in which information is recognized as a key asset to be appropriately managed as a vital resource.

Information technology (IT): Any computer-based tool that people use to work with the information processing needs of an organization.

Information view: Includes all of the information stored within a system.

Infrared: A wireless communications medium that uses light waves to transmit signals or information.

Infrastructure as a Service (IaaS): A service provided by a vendor that supplies hardware and middleware.

Inheritance: The ability to define superclass and subclass relationships among classes.

Inkjet printer: Makes images by forcing ink droplets through nozzles.

Input controls: Techniques and methods for verifying, validating, and editing data to ensure that only correct data enter a system.

Input device: A tool used to capture information and commands by the user.

Inquiry processing: The process of selecting a record from a file and immediately displaying its contents.

Insourcing: It means that IT specialists within the organization will develop the system.

Inspection: A manual analysis technique that examines the program requirements, design, or code in a formal and disciplined manner to discover errors.

Instance: An occurrence of an entity class that can be uniquely described.

Instrumental input: The capture of data and their placement directly into a computer by machines.

Integrated circuit: A miniature microchip incorporating circuitry and semiconductor components. The circuit elements and components are created as a part of the same manufacturing process.

Integrated Services Digital Network (ISDN): An emerging technology that is being offered by the telephone carriers of the world. ISDN combines voice and digital network services in a single medium making it possible to offer customers digital data services as well as voice connections through a single wire. The standards that define ISDN are specified by ITU-TSS.

Integration: Allows separate systems to communicate directly with each other by automatically exporting data files from one system and importing them into another.

Integration testing: The orderly progression of testing in which software, hardware, or both are combined and tested until all intermodule communication links have been integrated.

Integrity checking: The testing of programs to verify the soundness of a software product at each phase of development.

Intellectual property: Intangible creative work that is embodied in physical form.

Intelligence: The first step in the decision-making process where a problem, need, or opportunity is found or recognized. Also called the diagnostic phase of decision making.

Intelligent agent: Software that assists the user in performing repetitive computer-related tasks.

Interactive chat: Lets the user engage in real-time exchange of information with one or more individuals over the Internet.

Interactive video: A system in which video segments are integrated via a menu-based processing application.

Interblock gap (IBG): A blank space appearing between records or groups of records on magnetic storage media.

Interdiction: Impeding or denying someone the use of system resources.

Interface analysis: The checking and verification process that ensures intermodule communications links are performed correctly.

Interleaving: The alternating execution of programs residing in the memory of a multiprogramming environment.

Intermediary: A specialist company that provides services better than its client companies.

Internal accounting control: The process of safeguarding the accounting functions and processes of a business. This process includes validating that the accounting system complies with the appropriate, generally accepted accounting principles and that audit trails exist for verification of all processes.

Internal control: The method of safeguarding business assets, including verifying the accuracy and reliability of accounting data, promoting operational efficiency, and encouraging adherence to prescribed organizational policies and procedures.

Internal controls: The policies, plans and procedures, and organizational structures designed to provide reasonable assurance that business objectives will be achieved and undesired events will be prevented or detected and corrected.

Internal information: Information that describes specific operational aspects of the organization.

International government-to-government (IG2G): The e-commerce activities performed between two or more governments, including foreign aid.

International Standards Organization (ISO): Best known for the seven-layer OSI Reference Model and ISO 17799 and ISO 9000. See "OSI."

International virtual private network (IVPN): Virtual private networks that depend on services offered by phone companies of various nationalities.

Internet: The Internet consists of large national backbone networks (such as MILNET, NSFNET, and CREN) and a myriad of regional and local campus networks all over the world. The Internet uses the IP suite. To be on the Internet the user must have IP connectivity, that is, be able to Telnet to or ping other systems. Networks with only e-mail connectivity are not actually classified as being on the Internet.

Internet address: A 32-bit address assigned to hosts using TCP/IP.

Internet backbone: The major set of connections for computers on the Internet.

Internet Protocol (IP): The network layer protocol for the IP suite.

Internet server computer: Computer that provides information and services on the Internet.

Internet service provider (ISP): A company that provides individuals, organizations, and businesses access to the Internet.

Internet telephony: A combination of hardware and software that uses the Internet as the medium for transmission of telephone calls in place of traditional telephone networks.

Interorganizational System (IOS): Automates the flow of information between organizations to support the planning, design, development, production, and delivery of products and services.

Intersection relation: A relation the user creates to eliminate a many-to-many relationship. Also called a composite relation.

Intranet: An internal organizational Internet that is guarded against outside access by a special security feature called a firewall.

Intrusion-detection software: Looks for unauthorized users on the Internet.

Investigation: The phase of the SDLC in which the problem or need is identified and a decision made on whether to proceed with a full-scale study.

IRC (Internet Relay Chat) server: Supports the use of discussion groups or chat rooms.

IT infrastructure: The hardware, software, and telecommunications equipment that when combined provides the underlying foundation to support the organization's goal.

ISO 9000: A certification program that demonstrates an organization adheres to steps that ensure quality of goods and services.

Isolation: The separation of users and processes in a computer system from one another as well as from the protection controls of the OS.

Java: An object-oriented programming language that was developed by Sun Microsystems and is used in developing applications on the Web and other environments.

Job: A complete set of programs to be executed in a sequence on a computer.

Job accounting system: A set of systems software that can track the services and resources used by computer system account holders.

Job queue: A set of programs held in temporary storage and awaiting execution.

Joint application development (JAD): Occurs when knowledge workers and IT specialists meet, sometimes for several days, to define or review the business requirements for the system.

Just in Time (JIT): An approach that produces or delivers a product or service just at the time the customer wants it.

Kermit: A popular file transfer and terminal emulation program.

Key: A control field in a record that uniquely identifies the record or classifies it as a member of a segment of records within a file. In cryptography, a sequence of symbols that controls encryption and decryption.

Keyboard: Today's most popular input technology.

Key generation: The origination of a key or a set of distinct keys.

Key logger (or key trapper) software: A program that, when installed on a computer, records every keystroke and mouse click.

Key-to-disk device: A keyboard unit that records data as patterns of magnetic spots onto magnetic disks.

Key-to-tape device: A keyboard unit that records data as patterns of magnetic spots onto magnetic tape.

Kilobyte (K byte): The equivalent of 1024 bytes.

Knowledge acquisition: The component of the expert system that the knowledge engineer uses to enter the rules.

Knowledge base: The part of an expert system that contains specific information and facts about the expert area. Rules that the expert system uses to make decisions are derived from this source.

Knowledge-based system: An AI system that applies reasoning capabilities to reach a conclusion. Also known as an expert system.

Knowledge engineer: The person who formulates the domain expertise of an expert system.

Knowledge worker: Works with and produces information as a product.

Language processing: The step of ASR in which the system attempts to analyze and make sense of the user's verbal instructions by comparing the word phonemes generated in step 2 with a language model database.

Language translator: Systems software that converts programs written in assembler or a higher-level language into machine code.

Laser printer: An output unit that uses intensified light beams to form an image on an electrically charged drum and then transfers the image to paper.

Last mile bottleneck problem: Occurs when information is traveling on the Internet over a very fast line for a certain distance and then comes near the user where it must travel over a slower line.

Legacy system: A previously built system using older technologies such as mainframe computers and programming languages such as COBOL.

Limit check: An input control text that assesses the value of a data field to determine whether values fall within set limits.

Line printer: An output unit that prints alphanumeric characters one line at a time.

Linkage: The purposeful combination of data or information from one information system with that from another system in the hope of deriving additional information.

Link encryption: The application of online crypto-operations to a link of a communications system so that all information passing over the link is encrypted in its entirety.

Linux: An open source OS that provides a rich operating environment for high-end workstations and network servers.

List: A collection of information arranged in columns and rows in which each column displays one particular type of information.

List definition table: A description of a list by column.

Local area network (LAN): The physical connection of microcomputers with communication media (e.g., cable and fiber optics) that allows the sharing of information and peripherals among those microcomputers.

Lock/key protection system: A protection system that involves matching a key or a password with a specified access requirement.

Logical error: A programming error that causes the wrong processing to take place in a syntactically valid program.

Logical file organization: The sequencing of data records in a file according to their key.

Logical Link Control (LLC): The portion of the link level protocol in the 802 standards that is in direct contact with higher-level layers.

Logical operation: A comparison of data values within the ALU. These comparisons show when one value is greater than, equal to, or less than a second value.

Logical operator: A symbol used in programming that initiates a comparison operation of two or more data values.

Logical organization: Data elements organized in a manner that meets human and organizational processing needs.

Loophole: An error of omission or oversight in software, hardware, or firmware that permits circumventing the access control process.

Machine language: Computer instructions or code representing computer operations and memory addresses in a numeric form that is executable by the computer without translation.

Mac OS: The OS for today's Apple computers.

Macro virus: A computer virus that spreads by binding itself to software such as Word or Excel.

Magnetic disk: A storage device consisting of metallic platters coated with an oxide substance that allows data to be recorded as patterns of magnetic spots.

Magnetic ink character recognition (MICR): An input method under which data are encoded in special ink containing iron particles. These particles can be magnetized and sensed by special machines and converted into computer input.

Magnetic tape: A storage medium consisting of a continuous strip of coated plastic film wound onto a reel and on which data can be recorded as defined patterns of magnetic spots.

Mail gateway: A machine that connects two or more e-mail systems (especially dissimilar mail systems on two different networks) and transfers messages between them. Sometimes the mapping and translation can be quite complex, and generally it requires a store-and-forward scheme whereby the message is received from one system completely before it is transmitted to the next system after suitable translations.

Mail server: Provides e-mail services and accounts.

Mailing list: Discussion groups organized by area of interest.

Mainframe computer: A computer designed to meet the computing needs of hundreds of people in a large business environment.

Maintenance phase: Monitors and supports the new system to ensure it continues to meet the business goals.

Maintenance programmer: An applications programmer responsible for making authorized changes to one or more computer programs and ensuring that the changes are tested, documented, and verified.

Management information systems (MIS): Deals with the planning, development, management, and use of IT tools to help people perform tasks related to information processing and management.

Marketing mix: The set of marketing tools that a firm uses to pursue its marketing objectives in the target market.

Mass customization: When a business gives its customers the opportunity to tailor its product or service to the customer's specifications.

Master file: An automated file that contains semipermanent or permanent information and is maintained over a time period required by organizational policy.

Matrix display: The alphanumeric representation of characters as patterns of tiny dots in specific positions on a display terminal.

Matrix printer: A hard-copy printing device that forms alphanumeric characters with small pins arranged in a matrix of rows and columns.

Mature system: A fully operational system that performs all the functions it was designed to accomplish.

M-commerce: The term used to describe e-commerce conducted over a wireless device such as a cell phone or personal digital assistant.

md5 hash value: A mathematically generated string of 32 letters and digits that is unique for an individual storage medium at a specific point in time.

Media: The various physical forms (e.g., disk, tape, and diskette) on which data are recorded in machine-readable formats.

Megabyte (M byte): The equivalent of 1,048,576 bytes.

Megahertz (MHz): The number of millions of CPU cycles per second.

Memory: The area in a computer that serves as a temporary storage for programs and data during program execution.

Memory bounds: The limits in the range of storage addresses for a protected region in memory.

Memory chips: A small integrated circuit chip with a semiconductor matrix used as computer memory.

Menu: A section of the computer program—usually the top-level module—that controls the order of execution of other program modules. Also, online options displayed to a user prompting the user for specific input.

Message handling system (MHS): The system of message user agents, MTAs, message stores, and access units that together provide OSI e-mail. MHS is specified in the ITU-TSS X.400 series of recommendations.

Message transfer agent (MTA): An OSI application process used to store and forward messages in the X.400 MHS. Equivalent to Internet mail agent.

Messaging-based workflow system: Sends work assignments through an e-mail system.

Metatag: A part of a Website text not displayed to users, but accessible to browsers and search engines for finding and categorizing Websites.

Metrics: A systematic measurement to evaluate something. A complete metric defines the unit used, frequency, ideal target value, the procedure to carry out the measurement, and the procedure for the interpretation of the assessment.

Microcomputer: A small microprocessor-based computer built to handle input, output, processing, and storage functions.

Microfilm: A film for recording alphanumeric and graphics output that has been greatly reduced in size.

Micro-payment: A technique to facilitate the exchange of small amounts of money for an Internet transaction.

Microphone: For capturing live sounds, such as human voice.

Microprocessor: A single small chip containing circuitry and components for arithmetic, logical, and control operations.

Microsoft SharePoint: A collaboration software developed by Microsoft.

Microsoft Windows 2000 Millennium (Windows 2000 Me): An OS for a home computer featuring utilities for setting up a home network and performing video, photo, and music editing and cataloging.

Microsoft Windows 2000 Professional (Windows 2000 Pro): An OS for people who have a PC connected to a network of other computers at work or at school.

Microsoft Windows XP: Home Microsoft's latest upgrade to Windows 2000 Me, with enhanced features for allowing multiple users to use the same computer.

Microsoft Windows XP Professional (Windows XP Pro): Microsoft's latest upgrade to Windows 2000 Pro.

Microwave: A type of radio transmission used to transmit information.

Millions of instructions per second (MIPS): Used as a measure for assessing the speed of mainframe computers.

Minicomputer: Typically a word-oriented computer whose memory size and processing speed falls between that of a microcomputer and a medium-sized computer. Sometimes called mid-range computer.

MIPS: See "millions of instructions per second."

Mobile computing: The ability to remain connected and access enterprise data while being mobile or away from the office.

Mobile device: A lightweight computer. It may be a smartphone or a tablet computer.

Model management: Component of a DSS that consists of the DSS models and the DSS model management system.

Modeling: The activity of drawing a graphical representation of a design.

Modem (modulator/demodulator): A device that converts the digital language of the PC to a series of high- and low-pitched tones for transmission over analog telephone lines.

Monitoring and surveillance agents (or predictive agents): Intelligent agents that observe and report on equipment.

Mouse: A hardware device used for moving a display screen cursor.

Multiaccess rights terminal: A terminal that may be used by more than one class of users, for example, users with different access rights to data or files.

Multidimensional analysis (MDA) tools: Slice and dice techniques that allow viewing multidimensional information from different perspectives.

Multifunction printer: Scans, copies, and faxes as well as prints.

Multiprocessing: A computer operating method under which two or more processors are linked and execute multiple programs simultaneously.

Multiprogramming: A computer operating environment in which several programs can be placed in memory and executed concurrently.

Multitasking: Allows the user to work with more than one piece of software at a time.

Municipal area network (MAN): A network that covers a metropolitan area.

Mutation: The process within a genetic algorithm of randomly trying combinations and evaluating the success or failure of the outcome.

Mutually suspicious: Pertaining to a state that exists between interactive processes (systems or programs), each of which contains sensitive data and is assumed to be designed to extract data from the other and to protect its own data.

NAK attack: A penetration technique that capitalizes on an OS's inability to handle asynchronous interrupts properly.

National Science Foundation (NSF): Sponsors of the NSFNET.

National Science Foundation Network (NSFNET): A collection of local, regional, and mid-level networks in the United States tied together by a high-speed backbone. NSFNET provides scientists access to a number of supercomputers across the country.

Natural language: A language that is used in communication with computers and that closely resembles English syntax.

Need-to-know basis: A term used to describe restrictions put on something, such as access to sensitive data.

Netbook: A small laptop computer that is smaller than a notebook, with little processing power, designed primarily for accessing Internet-based applications.

Network: An integrated, communicating aggregation of computers and peripherals linked through communications facilities.

Network access point (NAP): A point on the Internet where several connections converge.

Network Basic Input Output System (NetBIOS): The standard interface to networks on IBM PC and compatible system.

Network File System (NFS): A distributed file system developed by Sun Microsystems which allows a set of computers to cooperatively access each other's files in a transparent manner.

Network hub: A device that connects multiple computers into a network.

Network Information Center (NIC): Originally there was only one, located at SRI International and tasked to serve the ARPANET (and later DDN) community. Today, there are many NICs, operated by local, regional, and national networks all over the world. Such centers provided user assistance, document service, training, and much more.

Network layer: The OSI layer that is responsible for routing, switching, and subnetwork access across the entire OSI environment.

Network Service Provider (NSP): Owns and maintains routing computers at NAPs and even the lines that connect the NAPs to each other. For example, MCI and AT&T.

Networking: A method of linking distributed data processing activities through communications facilities.

Neural network (NN): A type of system developed by AI researchers used for processing logic.

Nonprocedural language: A programming language with fixed logic, which allows the programmer to specify processing operations without concern for processing logic.

Nonrecurring (ad hoc) decision: One that is made infrequently and may have different criteria for determining the best solution each time.

Nonstructured decision: A decision for which there may be several right answers and there is no precise way to get a right answer.

Normalization: A process of assuring that a relational database structure can be implemented as a series of two-dimensional relations.

Notebook computer: A highly portable, battery-powered microcomputer with a display screen, carried easily in a briefcase, and used away from a user's workplace.

Numeric test: An input control method to verify that a field of data contains only numeric digits.

Object: An instance of a class.

Object program: A program that has been translated from a higher-level source code into machine language.

Objective information: Quantifiably describes something that is known.

Object-oriented approach: Combines information and procedures into a single view.

Object-oriented database: Works with traditional database information and also complex data types such as diagrams, schematic drawings, videos, and sound and text documents.

Object-oriented programming language: A programming language used to develop object-oriented systems. The language groups together data and instructions into manipulative objects.

Office automation: The application of computer and related technologies to office procedure.

Online analytical processing (OLAP): The manipulation of information to support decision making.

Online processing: Often called interactive processing. An operation in which the user works at a terminal or other device that is directly attached or linked to the computer.

Online training: Runs over the Internet or off a CD-ROM.

Online transaction processing (OLTP): The gathering of input information, processing that information, and updating.

Open network computing (ONC): A distributed applications architecture promoted and controlled by a consortium led by Sun Microsystems.

Open Network Management (ONM): The administration, monitoring, and supervision over Open Systems Interconnection Networks and infrastructure.

Open Systems Interconnection (OSI): An international standardization program to facilitate communications among computers from different manufactures. See "ISO."

Operand: The portion of a computer instruction that references the memory address of an item to be processed.

Operating system (OS): The various sets of computer programs and other software that monitor and operate the computer hardware and the firmware to facilitate use of the hardware.

Operating system software: System software that controls the application software and manages how the hardware devices work together.

Operation code: The portion of the computer instruction that identifies the specific processing operation to be performed.

Operational database: A database that supports OLTP.

Operational level agreement: Define the underlying services required by application development and maintenance groups to deliver the end-to-end application services to customers.

Operational management: Manages and directs the day-to-day operations and implementations of the goals and strategies.

Operational risk: The risk of loss resulting from inadequate or failed internal processes, people and systems, or from external events.

Optical character recognition (OCR): An input method in which handwritten, typewritten, or printed text can be read by photosensitive devices for input to a computer.

Optical disk: A disk that is written to or read from by optical means.

Optical fiber: A form of transmission medium that uses light to encode signals and has the highest transmission rate of any medium.

Optical mark recognition (OMR): Detects the presence of or absence of a mark in a predetermined place (popular for multiple choice exams).

Output controls: Techniques and methods for verifying that the results of processing conform to expectations and are communicated only to authorized users.

Output device: A tool used to see, hear, or otherwise accept the results of information-processing requests.

Outsourcing: The delegation of specific work to a third party for a specified length of time, cost, and level of service.

Overlapped processing: The simultaneous execution of input, processing, and output functions by a computer system.

Overwriting: The obliteration of recorded data by recording different data on the same surface.

Packet Internet Groper (PING): A program used to test reachability of destinations by sending them an Internet Control Messaging Protocol (ICMP) echo request and waiting for a reply. The term is used as a verb: "Ping host X to see if it is up."

Packet switching: A switching procedure that breaks up messages into fixed length units (called packets) at the message source. These units may travel along different routes before reaching their intended destination.

Paging: A method of dividing a program into parts called pages and introducing a given page into memory as the processing on the page is required for program execution.

Palm: A type of PDA that runs on the Palm Operating System (Palm OS).

Palm Operating System: The OS for Palm and Handspring PDAs.

Parallel connector: Has 25 pins that fit into the corresponding holes in the port. Most printers use parallel connectors.

Parallel conversion: The concurrent use of new system by its users.

Parity bit: A bit attached to a byte that is used to check the accuracy of data storage.

Partition: A memory area assigned to a computer program during its execution.

Pascal: A computer programming language designed especially for writing structured programs. This language is based on the use of a minimum set of logical control structures.

Passive wiretapping: The monitoring or recording of data while it is being transmitted over a communications link.

Password: A protected word or string of characters that identifies or authenticates a user, a specific resource, or an access type.

Pattern classification: The step of ASR in which the system matches the user's spoken phonemes to a phoneme sequence stored in an acoustic model database.

Peer-to-peer network: A network in which a small number of computers share hardware (such as a printer), software, and information.

Penetration: A successful unauthorized access to a computer system.

Penetration profile: A delineation of the activities required to effect penetration.

Penetration signature: The description of a situation or set of conditions in which a penetration might occur.

Penetration testing: The use of special programmer or analyst teams to attempt to penetrate a system to identify security weaknesses.

Performance: Measures how quickly an IT system performs a certain process.

Performance monitor: A set of systems software that tracks service levels provided by a computer system.

Permission marketing: When a person has given a merchant permission to send special offers.

Personal agent (or user agent): An intelligent agent that takes action on the user's behalf.

Personal computer: A commonly used term that refers to a microcomputer. Often called a PC.

Personal digital assistant (PDA): A small handheld computer that helps surf the Web and perform simple tasks such as note taking, calendaring, appointment scheduling, and maintaining an address book.

Personal finance software: Helps the user maintain a checkbook, prepare a budget, track investments, monitor credit card balances, and pay bills electronically.

Personal information management (PIM) software: Helps create and maintain (1) lists, (2) appointments and calendars, and (3) points of contact.

Personalization: When a Website can know enough about the user's likes and dislikes that it can fashion offers that are more likely to appeal to the user.

Personal productivity software: Helps the user perform personal tasks—writing a memo, creating a graph, and creating a slide presentation—that can usually be done even if the user does not own a computer.

Phased conversion: The system installation procedure that involves a step-by-step approach for the incremental installation of one portion of a new system at a time.

Physical layer: The OSI layer that provides the means to activate and use physical connections for bit transmission. In simple terms, the physical layer provides the procedures for transferring a single bit across a physical media.

Physical organization: The packaging of data into fields, records, files, and other structures to make them accessible to a computer system.

Piggyback entry: Unauthorized access to a computer system that is gained through another user's legitimate connection.

Pirated software: The unauthorized use, duplication, distribution, or sale of copyrighted software.

Pivot table: Enables to group and summarize information.

Plaintext: Intelligible text or signals that have meaning and can be read or acted on without being decrypted.

Planning phase: Involves determining a solid plan for developing information system.

Platform as a Service (PaaS): A service provided by a vendor which enables companies to develop applications more quickly and efficiently in a cloud environment using programming languages and tools supported by the provider.

Plotter: A graphics output device in which the computer drives a pen that draws on paper.

PNA adapter card: An expansion card that is put into the user's computer to act as a doorway for information flowing in and out.

Pocket PC: A type of PDA that runs on Pocket PC OS that used to be called Windows CE.

Pocket PC OS (or Windows CE): The OS for the Pocket PC PDA.

Pointing stick: Small rubberlike pointing device that causes the pointer to move on the screen as the user applies directional pressure. Popular on notebooks.

Point-of-sale (POS): Applications in which purchase transactions are captured in machine-readable form at the point of purchase.

Point-to-Point Protocol (PPP): The successor to SLIP, PPP provides router-to-router and host-to-network connections over both synchronous and asynchronous circuits.

Policies: A set of specific statements of guiding actions or intent that provide a basis for consistent decision making.

Polling: A procedure by which a computer controller unit asks terminals and other peripheral devices in a serial fashion if they have any messages to send.

Polymorphism: Having many forms.

Port: An outlet, usually on the exterior of a computer system, that enables peripheral devices to be connected and interfaced with the computer.

Portable Document Format (PDF): The standard electronic distribution file format for heavily formatted documents such as a presentation resume because it retains the original document formatting.

Postscript: A language used to describe the printing of images and text and typically used with laser printing capability. Word processor or desktop publishing applications generate postscript code for higher-quality laser products.

Preprocessors: Software tools that perform preliminary work on a draft computer program before it is completely tested on the computer.

Presentation layer: The OSI layer that determines how application information is represented (i.e., encoded) while in transit between two end systems.

Presentation resume: A format-sensitive document created in a word processor to outline job qualifications in one to two printed pages.

Presentation software: Helps create and edit information that will appear in electronic slides.

Primary key: A field (or group of fields) that uniquely describes each record.

Principle of least privilege: A security procedure under which users are granted only the minimum access authorization they need to perform required tasks.

Print suppress: The elimination of the printing of characters to preserve their secrecy—for example, the characters of a password as they are keyed by a user at a terminal or station on the network.

Privacy: The right of people to be left alone when they want to be, to have control over their own personal possessions, and not to be observed without their consent.

Privacy Act of 1974: The federal law that allows individuals to know what information about them is on file and how it is used by all government agencies and their contractors. The Electronic Communication Act of 1986 is an extension of the Privacy Act.

Privacy protection: The establishment of appropriate administrative, technical, and physical safeguards to protect the security and confidentiality of data records against anticipated threats or hazards that could result in substantial harm, embarrassment, inconvenience, or unfairness to any individual about whom such information is maintained.

Private branch exchange (PBX): A central telecommunications switching station that an organization uses for its own purposes.

Private cloud: A system or collection of systems that provide hosted access to systems and applications, where the resources are dedicated to one organization.

Privileged instructions: A set of instructions generally executable only when the computer system is operating in the executive state (e.g., while handling interrupts). These special instructions are typically designed to control such protection features as the storage protection features.

Procedural language: A computer programming language in which the programmer must determine the logical sequence of program execution as well as the processing required.

Procedure: Manipulates or changes information.

Procedure division: A section of a COBOL program that contains statements that direct computer processing operations.

Procedure view: Contains all of the procedures within a system.

Process: The steps taken to implement principles and provide services.

Process description: A narrative that describes in sequence the processing activities that take place in a computer system and the procedures for completing each activity.

Processing controls: Techniques and methods used to ensure that processing produces correct results.

Processor: The hardware unit containing the functions of memory and the CPU.

Profile filtering: Requires that the user choose terms or enter keywords to provide a more personal picture of preferences.

Program analyzers: Software tools that modify or monitor the operation of an application program to allow information about its operating characteristics to be collected automatically.

Program development process: The activities involved in developing computer programs, including problem analysis, program design, process design, program coding, debugging, and testing.

Program maintenance: The process of altering program code or instructions to meet new or changing requirements.

Programmable read-only memory (PROM): Computer memory chips that can be programmed permanently to carry out a defined process.

Programmer: The individual who designs and develops computer programs.

Programmer/analyst: The individual who analyzes processing requirements and then designs and develops computer programs to direct processing.

Programming language: A language with special syntax and style conventions for coding computer programs.

Programming Language/1 (PL/1): A general-purpose, high-level language that combines business and scientific processing features. The language contains advanced features for experienced programmers yet can be easily learned by novice programmers.

Programming specifications: The complete description of input, processing, output, and storage requirements necessary to code a computer program.

Project manager: An individual who is an expert in project planning and management, defines and develops the project plan, and tracks the plan to ensure all key project milestones are completed on time.

Project milestone: Key date by which a certain group of activities needs to be performed.

Project plan: Defines the what, when, and who questions of system development including all activities to be performed, the individuals or resources who will perform the activities, and the time required to complete each activity.

Project scope: Clearly defines the high-level system requirements.

Project scope document: A written definition of the project scope and usually no longer than a paragraph.

Project team: A team designed to accomplish specific one-time goals, which is disbanded once the project is complete.

Prolog: A language widely used in the field of AI.

Proof-of-concept prototype: A prototype used to prove the technical feasibility of a proposed system.

Proof of correctness: The use of mathematical logic to infer that a relation between program variables assumed true at the program entry implies that another relation between program variables holds at program exit.

Protection ring: A hierarchy of access modes through which a computer system enforces the access rights granted to each user, program, and process, ensuring that each operates only within the authorized access mode.

Protocol: A set of instructions required to initiate and maintain communication between sender and receiver devices.

Protocol data unit (PDU): This is OSI terminology for "packet." A PDU is a data object exchanged by protocol machines (entities) within a given layer. PDUs consist of both protocol control information (PCI) and user data.

Prototype: A usable system or subcomponent that is built inexpensively or quickly with the intention of modifying or replacing it.

Pseudocode: Program processing specifications that can be prepared as structured English-like statements which can then be easily converted into source code.

Pseudoflow: An apparent loophole deliberately implanted in an OS program as a trap for intruders.

Psychographic filtering: Anticipates the user's preferences based on the answers given to a questionnaire.

Public cloud: A Web service that is made available to the general public or a large industry group.

Public key encryption (PKE): An encryption system that uses two keys: a public key that everyone can have and a private key for only the recipient.

Public network: A network on which the organization competes for time with others.

Purging: The orderly review of storage and removal of inactive or obsolete data files.

Push technology: An environment in which businesses and organizations come to the user with information, services, and product offerings based on the user profile.

Quality assurance: A systematic process of checking to see whether a product or service being developed is meeting specified requirements.

Query and reporting tools: Similar to QBE tools, SQL, and report generators in the typical database environment.

Query-by-example tools (QBE): Helps the user graphically design the answer to a question.

Queue: A waiting line in which a set of computer programs is in secondary storage awaiting processing.

Random access: A method that allows records to be read from and written to disk media without regard to the order of their record key.

Random-access memory (RAM): Computer memory chips used to store programs and data temporarily during processing, a technology that is used heavily in microcomputers.

Read-only access: A method to limit access to data so that the user cannot make any changes (add, delete, or modify) to data.

Read-only memory (ROM): Computer memory chips with preprogrammed circuits for storing software such as word processors and spreadsheets.

Real-time processing: Computer processing that generates output fast enough to support multiple activities being performed concurrently.

Real-time reaction: A response to a penetration attempt that can prevent actual penetration because the attempt is detected and diagnosed in time.

Record block: A group or collection of records appearing between interblock gaps on magnetic storage media. This group of records is handled as a single entity in computer processing.

Record blocking: A technique of writing several records to magnetic storage media in between interblock gaps or spaces.

Recovery: The restoration of the information processing facility or other related assets following physical destruction or damage.

Recovery procedures: The action necessary to restore a system's computational capability and data files after system failure or penetration.

Recurring decision: A decision that you have to make repeatedly and often periodically, whether weekly, monthly, quarterly, or yearly.

Reduced instruction set computing (RISC): A method of processing by which the set of instructions available to the computer is a subset of that found on conventional computers.

Regression testing: The rerunning of test cases that a program has previously executed correctly to detect errors created during software correction or modification.

Regulatory risk: The risk of changes in laws and regulations or the failure to comply with existing laws and regulations.

Relation: Describes each two-dimensional table or file in the relation model (hence its name relational database model).

Relational database: Uses a series of logically related two-dimensional tables or files to store information in the form of a database.

Remanence: The residual magnetism that remains on magnetic storage media after degaussing.

Remote File System (RFS): A distributed file system, similar to NFS, developed by AT&T and distributed with their UNIX System V OS. See "Network File System."

Remote procedure call (RPC): An easy and popular paradigm for implementing the client/server model of distributed computing. A request is sent to a remote system to execute a designated procedure using arguments supplied and the result returned to the caller.

Repeater: A device that propagates electrical signals from one cable to another without making routing decisions or providing packet filtering. In OSI terminology, a repeater is a physical layer intermediate system. See "bridge and router."

Report: Printed or displayed output that communicates the content of files and other activities. The output is typically organized and easily read.

Report Program Generator (RPG): A nonprocedural programming language used for many business applications.

Report writing: The process of accessing data from files and generating it as information in the form of output.

Request for comments (RFCs): The document series begun in 1969, which describes the Internet suite of protocols and related experiments. Not all (in fact very few) RFCs describe Internet standards, but all Internet standards are written up as RFCs.

Request for proposal (RFP): A formal document that describes in detail logical requirements for a proposed system and invites outsourcing organizations (vendors) to submit bids for its development.

Requirement definition document: Defines all of the business requirements, prioritizes them in order of business importance, and places them in a formal comprehensive document.

Residue: Data left in storage after processing operations and before degaussing or rewriting has occurred.

Resolution of a printer: The number of dots per inch (dpi) a printer produces, which is the same principle as the resolution in a monitor.

Resolution of a screen: The number of pixels a screen has. Pixels (picture elements) are the dots that make up an image on the screen.

Resource: In a computer system, any function, device, or data collection that can be allocated to users or programs.

Resource sharing: In a computer system, the concurrent use of a resource by more than one user, job, or program.

Risk analysis: An analysis that examines an organization's information resources, its existing controls, and its remaining organization and computer system vulnerabilities. It combines the loss potential for each resource or combination of resources with an estimated rate of occurrence to establish a potential level of damage in dollars or other assets.

Risk assessment: Synonymous with risk analysis.

Risk management: Consists of the identification of risks or threats, the implementation of security measures, and the monitoring of those measures for effectiveness.

Rlogin: A service offered by Berkeley UNIX that allows users of one machine to log into other UNIX systems (for which they are authorized) and interact as if their terminals were connected directly. Similar to Telnet.

Robot: A mechanical device equipped with simulated human senses and the capability of taking action on its own.

Robotics: The use of automated equipment for production work and other mechanical tasks.

Router: A system responsible for making decisions about which of several paths will be followed by network (or Internet) traffic. To do this, it uses a routing protocol to gain information about the network, and algorithms to choose the best route based on several criteria known as "routing metrics." In OSI terminology, a router is a network layer intermediate system. See "gateway, bridge, and repeater."

Rule-based expert: The type of expert system that expresses the problem-solving process as rules.

Safeguard: Synonymous with control.

Safe Harbor Principles: The set of rules to which U.S. businesses that want to trade with the European Union (EU) must adhere.

Sales force automation (SFA) system: Automatically tracks all of the steps in the sales process.

Sanitizing: The degaussing or overwriting of sensitive information in magnetic or other storage media.

Sarbanes–Oxley Act of 2002: The most dramatic change to federal securities laws since the 1930s, the act radically redesigns federal regulation of public company corporate governance and reporting obligations. It also significantly tightens accountability standards for directors and officers, auditors, securities analysts, and legal counsel.

Satellite modem: A modem that allows Internet access from a satellite dish.

Scalability: Refers to how well a system can adapt to increased demands.

Scannable resume (ASCII resume, plaintext resume): Designed to be evaluated by skills-extraction software and typically contains all resume content without any formatting.

Scanner: Captures images, photos, and artwork that already exist on paper.

Scavenging: The searching of residue for the purpose of unauthorized data acquisition.

Scheduling program: A systems program that schedules and monitors the processing of production jobs in the computer system.

Scope creep: Occurs when the scope of the project increases.

Script bunny (or script kiddie): Someone who would like to be a hacker but does not have much technical expertise.

Search engine: A facility on the Web that helps the user find sites with the information the user wants.

Secure operating system: An operating system that effectively controls hardware, software, and firmware functions to provide the level of protection appropriate to the value of the data resources managed by the operating system.

Security audit: An examination of data security procedures and measures to evaluate their adequacy and compliance with established policy.

Security controls: Techniques and methods to ensure that only authorized users can access the computer information system and its resources.

Security filter: A set of software or firmware routines and techniques employed in a computer system to prevent automatic forwarding of specified data over unprotected links or to unauthorized persons.

Security kernel: The central part of a computer system (hardware, software, or firmware) that implements the fundamental security procedures for controlling access to system resources.

Security program: A systems program that controls access to data in files and permits only authorized use of terminals and other related equipment. Control is usually exercised through various levels of safeguards assigned on the basis of the user's need to know.

Seepage: The accidental flow of data or information to unauthorized individuals that is presumed to be protected by computer security safeguards.

Selection: A program control structure created in response to a condition test in which one of two or more processing paths can be taken.

Self-organizing neural network: A network that finds patterns and relationships in vast amounts of data by itself.

Self-sourcing (or knowledge worker/end-user development): The development and support of IT systems by knowledge workers with little or no help from IT specialists.

Selling prototype: A prototype used to convince people of the worth of a proposed system.

Semiconductor: Material used in electronic components that possesses electrical conducting qualities of conductors and resistors.

Sensitive information: Any information that requires protection and that should not be made generally available.

Sequential organization: The physical arrangement of records in a sequence that corresponds with their logical key.

Serial connector: Usually has 9 holes but may have 25 that fit into the corresponding number of pins in the port. Serial connectors are often used for monitors and certain types of modems.

Serial Line IP (SLIP): An IP used to run over serial lines such as telephone circuits or RS-232 cables interconnecting two systems. SLIP is now being replaced by Point-to-Point Protocol. See "Point-to-Point Protocol."

Serial organization: The physical arrangement of records in a sequence.

Serial processing: The processing of records in the physical order in which they appear in a file or on an input device.

Server farm: A location that stores a group of servers in a single place.

Service-level agreement (SLA): Defines the specific responsibilities of the service provider and sets the customer expectations.

Service-oriented architecture (SOA): An IT architecture strategy based on a service orientation where business processes are packaged as individual services that can be reused.

Service program: An OS program that provides a variety of common processing services to users (e.g., utility programs, librarian programs, and other software).

Session layer: The OSI layer that provides means for dialogue control between end systems.

Shared information: An organization's information is in one central location allowing anyone to access and use it as they need it.

Sign-off: The knowledge workers' actual signatures indicating they approve all of the business requirements.

Simple Mail Transfer Protocol (SMTP): The Internet e-mail protocol.

Simple Network Management Protocol (SNMP): The network management protocol of choice for TCP/IP-based Internets.

Simulation: The use of an executable model to represent the behavior of an object. During testing, the computational hardware, the external environment, and even the coding segments may be simulated.

Simultaneous processing: The execution of two or more computer program instructions at the same time in a multiprocessing environment.

Skill words: Nouns and adjectives used by organizations to describe job skills that should be woven into the text of applicants' resumes.

Slack space: The space left over from the end of the file to the end of the cluster.

Slave computer: A front-end processor that handles input and output functions for a host computer.

Smart cards: Plastic cards the size of a credit card that contain an embedded chip on which digital information can be stored.

Smartphone: A phone with advanced computing ability.

Sociability: The ability of intelligent agents to confer with each other.

Social engineering: A person conning his way into acquiring information that the person has no right to.

Software: Computer programs, procedures, rules, and possibly documentation and data pertaining to the operation of the computer system.

Software as a Service (SaaS): On-demand software provided by a vendor through an online service.

Software development life cycle (SDLC): The systematic systems building process consisting of specific phases—for example, preliminary investigation, requirements determination, systems analysis, systems design, systems development, systems implementation, and systems operation and maintenance.

Software life cycle: The period of time beginning when a software product is conceived and ending when the product is no longer available for use. The software life cycle is typically broken into phases (e.g., requirements, design, programming, testing, conversion, operations, and maintenance).

Software suite: Bundled software that comes from the same publisher and costs less than buying all the software pieces individually.

Sort: The arrangement of data in ascending or descending, alphabetic or numeric order.

Source document: The form that is used for the initial recording of data before system input.

Source program: The computer program that is coded in an assembler or higher-level programming language.

Spam: Unsolicited e-mail.

Spoofing: The deliberate inducement of a user or resource to take incorrect action, such as forging the return address on an e-mail message so the message appears to come from someone other than the actual sender.

Spooling: A technique that maximizes processing speed through the temporary use of high-speed storage devices. Input files are transferred from slower, permanent storage and queued in the high-speed devices to await processing, or output files are queued in high-speed devices to await transfer to slower storage devices.

Spreadsheet software: Computer software that divides a display screen into a large grid. This grid allows the user to enter labels and values that can be manipulated or analyzed.

Spyware (or sneakware or stealthware): Software that comes hidden in free downloadable software and tracks the user's online movements.

SQL: See "Structure Query Language."

Stacked-job processing: A computer processing technique in which programs and data awaiting processing are placed into a queue and executed sequentially.

Standards: Documented agreements containing technical specifications or other precise criteria to be used consistently as rules, guidelines or definitions of characteristics, to ensure consistent materials, products, processes.

Standards audit: The check to ensure that applicable standards are properly used.

Statement testing: A test method of satisfying the criterion that each statement in a program be executed at least once during the program testing.

Static analysis: The direct analysis of the form and structure of a product that does not require its execution. It can be applied to the requirements, design, or code.

Steganography: The hiding of information inside other information.

Storage media: Physical hardware on which programs and data are maintained in machine-readable format.

Strategic management: Provides an organization with overall direction and guidance.

Structure Query Language (SQL): The international standard language for defining and accessing relational database.

Structured design: A methodology for designing systems and programs through a top-down, hierarchical segmentation.

Structured programming: The process of writing computer programs using logical, hierarchical control structures to carry out processing.

Subjective information: Attempts to describe something that is unknown.

Subroutine: A segment of code that can be called up by a program and executed at any time from any point.

Subscript: A value used in programming to reference an item of data stored in a table.

Supercomputer: The fastest, most powerful, and expensive type of computer.

Supply chain: The paths reaching out to all of a company's suppliers of parts and services.

Supply-chain management (SCM) system: Tracks inventory and information among business processes and across companies.

Swapping: A method of computer processing in which programs not actively being processed are held on special storage devices and alternated in and out of memory with other programs according to priority.

Switch: A device that connects multiple computers into a network in which multiple communications links can be in operation simultaneously.

Switching costs: Costs that can make customers reluctant to switch to another product or service.

Symbolic evaluation: The process of analyzing the path of program execution through the use of symbolic expressions.

Symbolic execution: The analytical technique of dissecting each program path.

Syntax: The statement formats and rules for the use of a programming language.

System bus: The electronic pathways that move information between basic components on the motherboard, including the pathway between the CPU and RAM.

System integrity: The state that exists when there is complete assurance that under all conditions a computer system is based on the logical correctness and reliability of the OS and the logical completeness of the hardware, software, and firmware that implement the protection mechanisms and data integrity.

System integrity procedures: Procedures established to ensure that hardware, software, firmware, and data in a computer system maintain their state of original integrity and are not tampered with by unauthorized personnel.

Systems analysis: The process of studying information requirements and preparing a set of functional specifications that identify what a new or replacement system should accomplish.

Systems design: The development of a plan for implementing a set of functional requirements as an operational system.

Systems Network Architecture (SNA): IBM's proprietary network architecture.

Systems software: The programs and other processing routines that control and activate the computer hardware facilitating its use.

System test: The process of testing an integrated hardware/software system to verify that the system meets its specified requirements.

Table: An area of computer memory containing multiple storage locations that can be referenced by the same name.

Table driven: An indexed file in which tables containing record keys (i.e., disk addresses) are used to retrieve records.

Tablet computer: A mobile computer that uses touch screen technology.

Tactical management: Develops the goals and strategies outlined by strategic management.

Tape management system: Systems software that assesses the given information on jobs to be run and produces information for operators and librarians regarding which data resources (e.g., tapes and disks) are needed for job execution.

Task management system: It allocates the processor unit resources according to priority scheme or other assignment methods.

TCP/IP (Transmission Control Protocol): See "Internet Protocol."

Technical architecture: Defines the hardware, software, and telecommunications equipment required to run the system.

Technological attack: An attack that can be perpetrated by circumventing or nullifying hardware, software, and firmware access control mechanisms rather than by subverting system personnel or other users.

Technology-literate knowledge worker: A person who knows how and when to apply technology.

Telecommunications: Any transmission, emission, or reception of signs, signals, writing, images, sounds, or other information by wire, radio visual, satellite, or electromagnetic systems.

Telecommunications device: A tool used to send information to and receive it from another person or location.

Telecommunications Standardization Sector of the International Telecommunications Union (TSS-ITU): A unit of the International Telecommunications Union (ITU) of the United Nations. An organization with representatives from the post office, telegraph, and telecommunications (PTT) agencies of the world. The ITU-TSS produces technical standards, known as recommendations, for all internationally controlled aspects of analog and digital communications.

Telecommuting: The use of communications technologies (such as the Internet) to work in a place other than a central location.

Teleprocessing: Information processing and transmission performed by an integrated system of telecommunications, computers, and person-to-machine interface equipment.

Teleprocessing security: The protection that results from all measures designed to prevent deliberate, inadvertent, or unauthorized disclosure or acquisition of information stored in or transmitted by a teleprocessing system.

Telnet: The virtual terminal protocol in the Internet suite of protocols. Allows users of one host to log into a remote host and interact as normal terminal users of that host.

Temporary advantage: An advantage that, sooner or later, the competition duplicates or leap frogs with a better system.

Terabyte (TB): Approximately 1 trillion bytes.

Terminal identification: The means used to establish the unique identification of a terminal by a computer system or network.

Test condition: A detailed step the system must perform along with the expected result of the step.

Test data: Data that simulate actual data to form and content and are used to evaluate a system or program before it is put into operation.

Test data generators: Computer software tools that help generate files of data that can be used to test the execution and logic of application programs.

Testing: The examination of the behavior of a program through its execution on sample datasets.

Thick client: A full-powered workstation.

Thin client: A workstation with a small amount of processing power and costing less than a full-powered workstation.

Threat monitoring: The analysis, assessment, and review of audit trails and other data collected to search out system events that may constitute violations or precipitate incidents involving data privacy.

Three-dimensional (3-D) technology: Presentations of information that give the user the illusion that the object viewed is actually in the room with the user.

Three generic strategies: Cost leadership, differentiation, and a focused strategy.

Thrill-seeker hacker: A hacker who breaks into computer systems for fun.

Throughput: The process of measuring the amount of work that a computer system can execute within a specified period of time.

Time-dependent password: A password that is valid only for a certain period of time of the day or during a specified time interval.

Top-level domain: Three-letter extension of a Website address that identifies its type.

Touchpad: Popular on notebook computers, a stationary mouse that is touched with the finger.

Touch screen: Special screen the user touches to perform a particular function.

Trackball: An upside-down, stationary mouse in which the ball is moved instead of the device. Used mainly for notebooks.

Traditional technology approach: Has two primary views of any system—information and procedures—and it keeps these two views separate and distinct at all times.

Traffic flow security: The protection that results from those features in some cryptography equipment that conceal the presence of valid messages on a communications circuit, usually by causing the circuit to appear busy at all times or by encrypting the source and destination addresses of valid messages.

Transactional processing system (TPS): The processing of transactions as they occur rather than in batches.

Transaction file: A collection of records containing data generated from the current business activity.

Transmission Control Protocol (TCP): The major transport protocol in the Internet suite of protocols providing reliable, connect-oriented, full duplex streams.

Transceiver: The physical device that connects a host interface to a LAN, such as Ethernet. Ethernet transceivers contain electronics that apply signals to the cable and sense collisions.

Transnational firm: A firm that produces and sells products and services all over the world.

Transport layer: The OSI layer that is responsible for reliable end-to-end data transfer between end systems.

Trapdoor: A breach created intentionally in a computer system to collect, alter, or destroy data.

Trojan horse: A computer program that is apparently or actually useful and contains a trap door.

Trojan horse software: Software the user does not want that is hidden inside software the user wants.

Trojan horse virus: Hides inside other software. Usually an attachment or download.

True search engine: Uses software agent technologies to search the Internet for keywords and then places them into indices.

Trust seal: A seal awarded by proprietary companies to businesses to display on their Website to boost customer confidence.

Trusted Computer Security Evaluation Criteria (TCSEC): A security development standard for system manufacturers and a basis for comparing and evaluating different computer systems. Also known as the Orange Book.

Turnkey system: A complete, ready-to-operate system that is purchased from a vendor as opposed to a system developed in-house.

Twisted-pair wire: A communication medium that consists of pairs of wires that are twisted together and bound into cable.

Unallocated space: The set of clusters that has been marked as available to store information but has not yet received a file, or still contains some or all of a file marked as deleted.

Uninstaller software: Utility software that can be used to remove software that the user no longer wants from the hard disk.

Unit testing: The testing of a module for typographic, syntactic, and logical errors and for correct implementation of its design and satisfaction of its requirements.

Universal product code (UPC): An array of varied width lines that can be read by special machines (e.g., OCR devices) and converted into alphanumeric data. This method is used to mark merchandise for direct input of sales transactions.

UNIX: An OS initially developed by Bell Labs. Used primarily on engineering workstations and computers, and networked systems. UNIX is difficult for nontechnical people to use but is becoming increasingly popular in the business environment in supporting GUI applications.

Update: The file processing activity in which master records are altered to reflect the current business activity reflected in transaction files.

URL (uniform resource locator): An address for a specific Web page or document within a Website.

USB (Universal Serial Bus): It is becoming the most popular means of connecting devices to a computer. Most standard desktops today have at least two USB ports, and most standard notebooks have at least one.

User acceptance testing (UAT): Determines if the system satisfies the business requirements and enables the knowledge workers to perform their jobs correctly.

User agent: An intelligent agent that takes action on the user's behalf.

User documentation: Highlights how to use the system.

User interface management: The component of the expert system that is used to run a consultation.

Utility software: Software that provides additional functionality to the OS.

Validation: The determination of correctness with respect to the user's needs and requirements of the final program or software produced from a development effort.

Validation, verification, and testing: Used as an entity to define a procedure of review, analysis, and testing to discover errors throughout the software life cycle. Determines that functions operate as specified and ensures the production of quality software.

Value-added network (VAN): A semipublic network that provides services beyond the movement of information from one place to another.

Value chain: A tool that views the organization as a chain or series of processes, each of which adds value to the product or service for the customer.

Value network: All the resources behind the click on a Web page that the customer does not see, but that together create the customer relationship service, order fulfillment, shipping, financing, information brokering, and access to other products.

Verification: A demonstration of the consistency, completeness, and correctness of the software at and between each stage of the development life cycle.

Verify: The process of ensuring that transcribed data have been accurately keyboarded.

Vertical market software: Application software that is unique to a particular industry.

Video disk: An optical disk that can store images.

Videotext: Generic text that refers to a computer information system that uses TV, telecommunication, and computer technologies to access and manipulate large, graphics-oriented databases.

Virtual marketing: Encourages users of a product or service supplied by a B2C (buyer-to-customer) company to ask friends to join.

Virtual memory: A method of extending computer memory by using secondary storage devices to store program pages that are not being executed at the time.

Virtual private network (VPN): Uses software to establish a secure channel on the Internet for transmitting data.

Virtual reality: A 3-D computer simulation in which the user actively and physically participates.

Virtual workplace: A technology-enabled workplace—no walls, no boundaries, work anytime, anyplace. Linked to other people and information the user needs.

Virus: Software that is written with malicious intent to cause annoyance or damage.

Voice mail: An e-mail system that allows a regular voice message to be digitally stored at the receiving location and converted back into voice form when it is accessed.

Voice over Internet Protocol (VoIP): A technology that allows telephone calls to be made overcomputer networks like the Internet. VoIP converts analog voice signals into digital data packets and supports real-time, two-way transmission of conversations using Internet Protocol (IP).

Voice synthesizer: An input and output device that can either interpret and convert human speech into digital signals for computer processing or convert digital signals into audible signals that resemble human speech.

Walker: An input device that captures and records the movement of the feet as the user walks or turns in different directions.

Walk-through: A manual analysis technique in which the module author or developer describes the module's structure and logic to colleagues.

Wearable computer: A fully equipped computer that is worn just like a piece of clothing or attached to a piece of clothing similar to the way the cell phone is carried on the belt.

Web authoring software: Helps design and develop Websites and pages that are published on the Web.

Web browser software: Enables the user to surf the Web.

Web farm: Either a Website that has multiple servers or an ISP that provides Website outsourcing services using multiple servers.

Web log: Consists of one line of information for every visitor to a Website and is usually stored on a Webserver.

Web page: A specific portion of a Website that deals with a certain topic.

Web portal: A site that provides a wide range of services including search engines, free e-mail, chat rooms, discussion boards, and links to hundreds of different sites.

Web server: Provides information and services to Web surfers.

Web services: Software applications that talk to other software applications over the Internet using XML as a key enabling technology.

Website: A specific location on the Web where the user can visit, gather information, and order products.

Website address: A unique name that identifies a specific site on the Web.

Web space: A storage area where the user's Website can be kept.

Whitehat (or ethical) hacker: A computer security professional who is hired by a company to break into its computer system.

Wide area network (WAN): A communications network that covers a broad geographic area.

Wi-Fi (wireless fidelity): A way of transmitting information in a waveform that is reasonably fast and is often used for notebooks. Also known as IEEE 802.11b.

Wired communications: Media that transmit information over a closed connected path.

Wireless communications: Media that transmit information through the air.

Wireless Internet service provider (wireless ISP): A company that provides the same services as a standard Internet service provider except that the user does not need a wired connection for access.

Wireless local area network (WLAN): A LAN using wireless communication protocol.

Wireless network access point: A device that allows computers to access a network using radio waves.

Word: In computer memory, a contiguous set of bits used as a basic unit of storage. Words are usually 8, 16, 32, or 64 bits long.

Word processing: The use of computers or other technology for storage, editing, correction, revision, and production of textual files in the form of letters, reports, and documents.

Workflow: Defines all of the steps or business rules, from beginning to end, required for a process to run correctly.

Workgroup: A group of people who can work together to achieve a common set of goals, linked together via technological tools and hardware.

Workshop training: Held in a classroom environment and led by an instructor.

World Wide Web or Web: A multimedia-based collection of information, services, and Websites supported by the Internet.

Worm: A type of virus that spreads itself not just from file to file but from computer to computer via e-mail and other Internet traffic.

X.500: A ITU-TSS international standard that binds a public key to a directory name.

X.400: A ITU-TSS international standard for reformatting and sending Internet work via e-mail.

XML (eXtensible Markup Language): A coding language for the Web that lets computers interpret the meaning of information in Web documents.

X-Open: A group of computer manufacturers who promote the development of portable applications based on UNIX. They publish a document called the X-Open Portability Guide.

X/recommendations: The ITU-TSS documents that describe data communication network standards. Well-known ones include X.25 Packet Switching Standard, X.400 Message Handling System, and X.500 Directory Services.

Zip drive: A high-capacity, removable diskette drive that typically uses 100 MB Zip disks or cartridges.

Appendix V

Sample Audit Programs

Example A5.1

Audit program for systems maintenance review.

1. Systems Maintenance
   Objective: Determine that all maintenance activity is performed and documented according to installation standards and procedures by reviewing documentation related to systems maintenance.
   Audit steps
   a. Determine whether standards have been established for the documentation of systems maintenance.
   b. Evaluate existing standards to determine whether they are comprehensive enough and cover issues such as compliance with International Standards Organization (ISO) 17799.
   c. Review a sample of existing documentation to determine whether it complies with installation standards.
   d. Ascertain whether systems maintenance documentation is maintained in a secure environment and protected against tampering.
2. Change Procedures
   Objective: Determine whether all changes to the system are completely documented and tested to ensure the desired results by reviewing documentation related to system changes (maintenance) and evaluating its adequacy.
   Audit steps
   a. Interview appropriate personnel to determine
      Documentation standards that relate to system changes
      Testing standards that relate to system changes
   b. Select a sample of completed system changes and determine whether
      Documentation is in accordance with installation standards
      Documentation provides a clear explanation of the change made and the reason for the change

Documentation has been appropriately reviewed and approved

Test plans for the change are in compliance with installation standards

The test plan thoroughly tested the implemented change

The test plan and the results of the test were reviewed and approved

c. Evaluate the review process related to system changes and determine whether

A peer review of system changes is done before they are submitted for approval

Operations management reviews and approves system changes before implementation

Errors were identified, corrected, retested, documented, and reviewed for approval before release for use

d. Assess whether the controls over documentation and test results are adequate to prevent tampering

3. Implementation of System Changes

Objective: The implementation of system changes should be performed by a group other than the group responsible for the system (e.g., systems software changes should be implemented by someone other than a systems programmer). All procedures related to the implementation of system changes should be reviewed.

Audit steps

a. Identify the personnel responsible for implementing system changes and determine whether an adequate separation of duties exists.

b. Determine whether adequate communication links exist between the change implementation group and the other data processing and user groups involved in the change process.

c. Determine the adequacy of documentation supplied to the change implementation group to support the change.

d. Determine whether the change documentation includes the date and time at which changes will be installed.

e. Determine that documentation similar to that given to the change implementation group has been released to system users to inform them of the impending changes.

f. Determine whether system changes have been installed in an orderly manner (i.e., in compliance with standards and procedures).

g. Determine whether system changes are evaluated and accepted after installation.

h. Determine whether computer operators cannot reverse system changes without assistance from the change implementation group.

4. System Change Log

Objective: Determine whether a chronological record of all system changes is maintained by reviewing records of all system changes.

Audit steps

a. Determine whether a log exists to record all changes made to the system.

b. Review the log for completeness and for evidence of management approval.

ISO 9001 Review: Conclusion and Documents

In this section, a New York company's ISO 9001 review is examined in terms of lessons learned, which can be applied to similar audits. The initial National Standards Authority of Ireland (NSAI) audit was conducted over a 3-day period. The net result was a total of 52 Corrective Action Requests (CARs) written, of which one was deleted, two were issued to the corporate phase review process, and eight were issued to software. The site was certified pending a resolution of issues within 90 days.

Notes on audits for use by guides:

First and most important in this NSAI review was beginning each new piece of an audit with a manager. Allowing the upper management to answer the broad questions and paint an overview of their projects, processes, and interdependencies made it easier for the auditor to isolate and identify the appropriate project and the next layer of management to approach. (The auditor's questions are best answered by management; at the lowest technical level, the answers are generally too focused and detailed and served only to confuse the audit.)

The more the guide knows about all the processes used as well as the history of the processes, the better. There were many times in this audit when it appeared that a process not known to the guide was being followed or that the process had actually been changed during the course of the project. If a project passes through many different people during its cycle, this is not always obvious to the person being audited (who is usually the last to touch the project). In some instances in this audit, the guide could help point the person being audited to the process or procedure that the auditor was looking for or to the person who really knew where specific information was kept.

The more the guide knows about the projects and their history, the better. For example, avoid, if possible, projects that may be associated with CARs or other nonstandard processes or projects that have been through numerous changes in personnel, management, or processes. Such projects can pose a challenge as an auditor tries to trace their development against the company's current processes. They may also pose a challenge in finding someone who remembers what happened during an early phase. (Of course, this is less of a problem if record keeping has been maintained in good shape throughout the life of the project.) Care must be taken, however, to ensure the auditor has a choice of projects so as to avoid creating the belief that he was directed to the "perfect" project.

At least in this audit, the guide was not only welcomed but also asked by the auditor to feel free to interject comments or questions that would help the audit. It is one role of the guide to help translate the auditor's questions into local terminology. The guide was not prevented from making suggestions to the person being audited such as "Why don't you show item X?" or "Why don't you pull out procedure X and we'll follow that?"

The NSAI auditor in this review was very disturbed by the company's untidy offices. The feeling was "How can you produce a controlled product out of an uncontrolled environment." Even so, because the staff did produce the items needed for the audit, there was nothing in this area that could be cited. This pointed out a need for the company to examine its quality records procedures and the audit guide anticipated producing future recommendations in this area.

A breakdown of the 52 CARs cited in the audit is as follows:

Document Control (4). Documents that were current and in use but lacked information such as page numbers, approval, and so on.

Quality System (2). Portions of the company's quality procedures were not completely documented.

Design Verification (1). The company was requested to add and document a step in one of the product initiation processes.

Process Control (1). No evidence was found of a documented and controlled process for a significant step in the product cycle.

Example A5.2

Lessons learned: 9001 review.

The staff associated with the New York City review and the ISO certification effort was asked for their reaction to the process. Following are excerpted quotes summarizing their comments:

Expect to be challenged. You will not get complete buy-in because people are being asked to go beyond the scope of what they believe they were hired to do. It is important that employees have a forum to vent their frustrations. Such comments can be a good indicator of the attitude and commitment employees are making and how well they understand why the company has chosen specific approaches to meeting its business needs.

It was very poor planning to let another group within our facility have its own ISO certification in the same plant with the rest of us. It increases Commercial-Off-The-Shelf Hardware or Software (COTS) and duplicates services.

It is much harder to achieve and maintain certification for a site which does not have a single site manager . . . . If we could change the world we would have all orgs in New York City report up to one manager who is located here.

We did too much work when we first started. We had people with backgrounds in product quality assurance running the program and they make it a major effort. Perhaps if we had known, we would not have had these same people calling the shots. We might have more quickly gone to the streamlined internal auditing system.

. . . A sitewide document control system and team . . . . Common numbering and formats would have helped. More document templates would have helped. Developing our own on-line document control system has been a tragedy of errors. Don't do it.

Conclusion

In terms of the description, experience, and examples given earlier regarding ISO certification, the IS auditor can contribute to the training and development of internal staff in performing the audit process. There are a number of questions the organization must ask itself in performing this function. It is an intensive effort and process that must be followed and performed to the letter. There must be a commitment to training, learning, and education if it is to succeed. Management and corporate must support the process.

Document 1. Audit Analysis

Analysis Date:	Analyzed By:	
Audit Date:	Audit Number:	
OUTCOME		
ISO 9001 Clause Number	*P = Passed* *N = Not Covered* *# = No. of CARs*	*ISO 9001 CLAUSE Name*
4.1	_____	Management responsibility
4.2	_____	Quality system

4.3	_____	Contract review
4.4	_____	Design control
4.5	_____	Document control
4.6	_____	Purchasing
4.7	_____	Purchaser supplied product
4.8	_____	Product identification and traceability
4.9	_____	Process control
4.10	_____	Inspection and testing
4.11	_____	Inspection, measuring, and test equipment
4.12	_____	Inspection and test status
4.13	_____	Control of nonconforming product
4.14	_____	Corrective action
4.15	_____	Handling, storage, packaging, and delivery
4.16	_____	Quality records
4.17	_____	Internal quality audits
4.18	_____	Training
4.19	_____	Servicing
4.20	_____	Statistical techniques

Document 2. ISO 9000 Reference Card

Orange County Software Engineering
ISO 9001 Reference Card
Orange County Quality Policy

Unisys Quality Policy

We are committed to quality and excellence in all endeavors. We have set our goals to achieve customer satisfaction—to deliver error-free, competitive products and customer solutions on time with service second to none.

Seven Quality Beliefs

1. Quality is the responsibility of every employee.
2. Quality improvement results from management leadership.
3. Quality attributes should be viewed from the customer's view.
4. Focus for improvement must be on each job at each step of the process.
5. No level of defect is acceptable.
6. Commitment to continuous improvement.
7. Quality improvement reduces costs.

Orange County Quality System

OC Quality System Manual [QSM]
Global Policies, Processes, and Procedures
[Phase Review SMM], Process Guides
Local Policies, Processes, and Procedures
[Work Instructions, Handbooks, and Guides]
Checklists and Forms
OC Software Engineering ISO 9001 Reference Card

Document 3. ISO 9001 Principle Themes

Documentation:	Record what you do.
Practices:	Do what you have documented.
Records:	Keep evidence of what you have done.
Audits:	Check what you do.
Corrective Action:	Correct discrepancies that are found.

Phase Review Phases

Phase 1: Study [Feasibility]
Phase 2: Design [Design Review]
Phase 3: Develop [Coding, Inspection, Unit Test, Integration Test]
Phase 4: Quality [System & Field Test]
Phase 5: Evaluate [Continuation]
Phase 6: Withdraw [Terminate Support]

Software Engineering Organization

ISO 9001 News

Check A-Mail Newsgroup WC.QIT for latest news on ISO 9001 status and issues. The Software Engineering ISO 9001 Review Board is also available to address questions on ISO 9001.

What do I say to an auditor?
1. *Listen to the questions.*
2. *Give answers that are brief and to the point.*
3. *Be truthful.*
4. *Focus on facts not opinions.*
5. *If you don't know the answer, say so (it's ok!).*
6. *You may refer the auditor to someone who will know the answer.*
7. *Remember—the auditor is looking at your group's processes, not you.*

What questions might an auditor ask?

1. *What is your job?*
2. *What processes and procedures do you follow to do your job?*
3. *How do these processes and procedures relate to the Phase Review or other processes?*
4. *What are your qualifications to do this job?*
5. *How do you know that the specification you are working to is still current?*
6. *Are you familiar with the Orange County Quality Policy?*
7. *How were you trained to do your job?*
8. *Can you show me the process document you use for process "x?"*

Document 4. Sample CAR Forms

Software House	*New York City*
CORRECTIVE ACTION REQUEST *QUALITY SYSTEM AUDIT*	
CAR Number:	
Area Audited: Area Manager:	Audit Date:
Responsible Manager: Reference No:	Audit Number:
NONCOMPLIANCE has been identified as defined below. Please respond to this noncompliance by indicating the nature of corrective action you are planning and the date it will become effective. Per the referenced DI, your response is required within five working days.	
Process Being Audited: Local Reference: Procedure Name:	QSM Ref:
Finding:	
Recommendation:	
Audited By: Observed By:	Car Date:
Approved By:	Approval Date:
Reference: DI 34700047	Side 1 of 2 Sides	Form: F-3470S020 1/01

CORRECTIVE ACTION REQUEST

Closing Meeting Date:	CAR Number:

Planned Corrective Action: Addressee	To be completed by CAR

Committed Completion Date:

Closure Criteria:	To be completed by Auditor

Commitment:

Responsible Manager Signature:	Date Signed:

Status Update:

Item Changed:	To be completed by Auditor
Date:	By:

Corrective Action Verified:	To be completed by Auditor
Signature:	Date:

Distribution: Controlled Copy: Auditor until closure, then Quality System Coordinator Copies: Manager of the area audited Responsible Manager Quality System Coordinator until closure, then Auditor	To be completed by Auditor

Note: Redistribute copies each time information content is updated

Reference: DI 34700047	Side 2 of 2 Sides	Form: F-34705020 1/01

Document 5. Corrective Action Request Form

Software House INTERNAL ISO 9001/9002 QUALITY AUDIT IAF-03 *CORRECTIVE ACTION REQUEST FORM   REV B*   *PAGE 1 OF _____*

Issued to:	Issued by:	Date Issued:
Audit#:		CAR#:

Nonconformity with Description:

Nonconformity with Paragraph:

Auditee Concurrence with Nonconformity Description and Corrective Action Commitment:

Date for Completion of CAR:		
Signed:	Position:	Date:

Follow-Up/Close-Out Action:	
Correction Action Verified	Signed:
Date CAR Closed:	Position:
Date:	

Detroit Facility Procedure #43578921-00

Audit Program for Operating System Security Evaluation		
	Location:	Date:

Initial Checklist

Before beginning the audit, the auditor should locate the following documents for easy access:

1. A list of all hardware configurations showing all devices, communication lines, and operating systems   _____

2. A list of operating systems being used or planned, with version and release levels, brief descriptions, target dates for implementation, and management approvals   _____

3. A list of application systems in production with a brief description of each   _____

4. A list of utilities for each operating system, detailing utility name, purpose, approvals required to use the utility, names or classes of individuals authorized to use each utility, levels of access control over each utility, and monitoring policies and procedures   _____

5. An organizational chart of the IT department showing names and position titles   _____

1.		*Systems Documentation Review*	
		Objective: To ensure that current documentation is available, adequate, and safeguarded for each operating system version. Recommendations resulting from the systems documentation review should cite appropriate control objectives, reference numbers, and applicable workpapers.	
Audit Test No.		*Action*	*Source of Information or Documentation*
1.1		**Vendor-Supplied Systems Documentation**	
1.1.1		Identify the vendor-supplied documentation for each operating system.	
1.1.2		Determine whether vendor-supplied documentation is complete and current for each operating system in use.	
1.2		**System Documentation for Internal Modifications**	
1.2.1		Identify the documentation for operating system modifications.	
1.2.2		Confirm that the following documentation is available for each operating system modification: Detailed description of the operating system Security features Detailed description of system utilities Control or command language requirements User error messages Error detection and correction features A list of all files and modules used by the operating system	
1.2.3		Verify that documentation is complete and current for each operating system modification.	

1.2.4	Review the procedures that restrict operating system documentation to authorized personnel.	
1.2.5	Confirm that backup copies of operating system and utility documentation are available.	
2.	**Utilities Review**	
	Objective: To ensure that all utilities are adequately restricted to authorized users. Recommendations resulting from the utilities review should cite appropriate control objectives, reference numbers, and applicable workpapers.	
Audit Test No.	*Action*	*Source of Information or Documentation*
2.1	Determine whether all users are restricted from copying or renaming utility programs.	
2.2	Confirm that all programming, debugging, and file-altering utilities are restricted from unauthorized personnel.	
2.3	Determine whether necessary approvals are obtained before utilities are used.	
2.4	Determine whether any utilities can bypass controls in the operating system or security software.	
2.5	Determine whether any utilities can be used when the operating system or security software is not running.	
2.6	When the operating system is not running, determine whether operating system modules are protected from access.	
2.7	Confirm that utility use is monitored by management.	
3.	**System Security Review**	
	Objective: To determine whether controls adequately prevent the unauthorized modification or use of the operating system. Recommendations resulting from the system security review should cite appropriate control objectives, reference numbers, and applicable workpapers.	

Audit Test No.	Action	Source of Information or Documentation
3.1	**Privileges and Quotas**	
3.1.1	Identify which user and system privileges should not be restricted.	
3.1.2	Identify which user and system privileges should be restricted.	
3.1.3	Determine whether management periodically reviews the user authorization file for accounts with unnecessary privileges or quotas or unusual attributes and determine whether this review is documented.	
3.1.4	Obtain a listing of the user authorization file for all on-site computer systems. This listing should show all privileges and quotas assigned to each user.	
3.1.5	Identify all users with privileges that should be restricted and determine whether they require all the assigned privileges to perform their job functions.	
3.1.6	Identify all users with quotas in excess of those necessary to perform their functions.	
3.2	**File Protection**	
3.2.1	Describe the universal file-protection schemes for operating system files for all systems.	
3.2.2	Evaluate the file-protection schemes for adequacy and appropriateness.	
3.2.3	Determine whether user groupings are appropriate.	
3.2.4	Obtain directory listings indicating owner, protection, size, backup date, and creation date for all system and user files.	
3.2.5	Identify all system directories.	
3.2.6	Confirm that all files in system directories are authorized.	
3.2.7	Determine whether the online system files are adequately protected.	
3.2.8	Confirm that application users are assigning appropriate file protections.	

3.2.9	Verify that application command files do not contain embedded passwords or sensitive materials.	
3.2.10	Compare file sizes from the directory listings with file records to determine whether any unauthorized modifications have been made to the system or security software. Hash totals, byte counts, and so on may be used.	
3.2.11	If operating system source code is present at this location, determine whether it is licensed.	
3.2.12	Determine whether operating system source code is adequately safeguarded (i.e., off-line, backed up, and restricted to authorized personnel).	
3.3	**Sysgen**	
3.3.1	Identify all command files used in system start-up.	
3.3.2	Determine that start-up command files do not undermine privileges or file-protection controls by granting terminals, users, or processes added abilities.	
3.3.3	Identify all processes created at system start-up.	
3.3.4	Verify that all processes created at system start-up (i.e., control programs) are approved by management and perform only authorized functions.	
4.	**System Environment Control Review**	
	Objective: To determine whether the operating system holds all users and processes in a controlled environment. Recommendations resulting from the system environment control review should cite appropriate control objectives, reference numbers, and applicable workpapers.	
Audit Test No.	*Action*	*Source of Information or Documentation*
4.1	**Access Procedures**	
4.1.1	Identify the methods that the operating system uses to control access to the computer system and its resources.	

4.1.2	Determine whether all users are uniquely identified to the system by at least one of the following: 　　User identification and password 　　Key or badge 　　Physical characteristics	
4.1.3	Confirm that automatic log-ons are not enabled on the system. (Note: the Digital Equipment Corporation VMS specifies automatic terminal log-ons in the file sysalf.dat.)	
4.1.4	Verify that a user cannot circumvent the defined and authorized access procedures.	
4.1.5	Confirm that log-ons are disabled when the operating system is not functioning or partially functioning.	
4.1.6	Determine whether passwords are changed regularly.	
4.1.7	Confirm that the ability to change passwords is restricted to authorized personnel.	
4.1.8	Verify that passwords are arbitrary and difficult to compromise.	
4.1.9	Determine whether all terminals connected to the system are positively identified, preferably by unique hardwired terminal IDs.	
4.1.10	Verify that the operating system or security software notifies operations of all unauthorized access attempts.	
4.1.11	Discover whether a line or terminal is disabled after a predetermined number of unauthorized access attempts.	
4.1.12	Confirm that procedures are documented for, and followed by, operations for the identification of individuals responsible for unauthorized access attempts.	
4.1.13	Determine whether users are restricted to specific days and hours of computer resource use.	
4.1.14	Identify which log-on flags are available under the operating system and security software at this site.	
4.1.15	Verify that appropriate log-on flags are set for each user.	

4.1.16	Determine whether users are restricted to specific computer resources (e.g., specific terminals and printers).	
4.1.17	If operating system source code is available, review the modules controlling access to computer resources for any control weaknesses.	
4.2	**Users**	
4.2.1	Confirm that a formal procedure has been established for authorizing the use of computer resources and creating user accounts.	
4.2.2	Review the process by which management approves user accounts, user identification codes, privileges, and quotas.	
4.2.3	Determine whether the name, address, telephone number, and reason for using a computer account is documented for all users.	
4.2.4	Verify that every user account is used solely by the individual it is assigned to.	
4.2.5	Confirm that it is not possible for any user to emulate the operating system of other users.	
4.2.6	Determine whether the operating system restricts users to their own work area.	
4.2.7	Verify that applications users are limited to applications-controlled environments.	
4.2.8	Review the procedures for ensuring that the system does not provide information on the bypassing of operating system or security software controls (e.g., online help procedures that show how to log on and bypass log-on or application command files).	
4.2.9	Confirm that users are automatically logged off when activity ceases for a predetermined length of time.	
4.2.10	Determine whether all dormant user accounts are removed from the user authorization file.	
4.2.11	Verify that log-ons are disabled for all field service and system default accounts when they are not in use.	
4.2.12	Review the formal procedures for authorization, authentication, and monitoring of field service personnel.	

4.3	**Operations**	
4.3.1	Determine whether operators are required to use hard-copy terminals or whether their terminal sessions are logged.	
4.3.2	Verify that access as a system console is restricted to authorized operations personnel.	
4.3.3	Confirm that unauthorized personnel cannot take logical control of the system console or become as powerful as the system console without the knowledge of operations personnel.	
4.3.4	Determine whether the uses of all operator and special functions are logged.	
4.3.5	Verify that the operating system or security software prevents operators from modifying application data or programs while online.	
4.3.6	Review the operating system controls to prevent computer operators from modifying applications data or processes in main storage.	
4.3.7	Determine whether the computer system's clock is protected from unauthorized access or modification.	
5.	**Remote Access and Communications Review**	
	Objective: To determine whether dial-up and network users are properly controlled. Recommendations resulting from the remote access and communications review should cite appropriate control objectives, reference numbers, and applicable workpapers	
Audit Test No.	*Action*	*Source of Information or Documentation*
5.1	Determine whether all lines of communication are disabled when not in use.	
5.2	Review how dial-up users are identified to the system.	
5.3	Confirm that the operating system or security software access controls cannot be bypassed by dial-up or network users.	
5.4	Verify that all dial-up and network sessions are prearranged with computer operations and preauthorized.	

5.5	Review the call-in/dial-back procedure used and confirm that all dial-out accesses use prearranged telephone numbers and terminals.	
6.	**Review of Interfaces with Other Operating Systems**	
	Objective: To ensure that when more than one operating system is used concurrently, the appropriate operating system retains control over system resources and that the operating systems do not undermine the controls of each other. Recommendations resulting from the review of interfaces with other operating systems should cite appropriate control objectives, reference numbers, and applicable workpapers.	
Audit Test No.	*Action*	*Source of Information or Documentation*
6.1	Determine whether two or more operating systems can run concurrently on the computer system.	
6.2	Identify the relationship between the operating systems.	
6.3	Identify which operating system controls which system resources.	
6.4	Confirm that neither operating system undermines controls of the other.	
7.	**Software Modifications Review**	
	Objective: To determine whether operating system modifications are tested, documented, and performed according to established procedures. Recommendations resulting from the software modifications review should cite appropriate control objectives, reference numbers, and applicable workpapers.	
Audit Test No.	*Action*	*Source of Information or Documentation*
7.1	**Testing**	
7.1.1	Review the adequacy of procedures used for testing operating system modifications for program bugs.	
7.1.2	Review the adequacy of procedures used for testing utility modifications for program bugs.	

7.1.3	Determine whether the systems supervisor or systems staff, other than the original system programmer, reviews all system and utility testing before cataloging for production.	
7.1.4	Review the procedures by which environmental testing is authorized before being performed.	
7.1.5	Review system test documentation for adequacy of the tests that were performed.	
7.2	**Production Update**	
7.2.1	Identify the formal procedures established for initiation and implementation of operating system and utility changes.	
7.2.2	Confirm that there is an authorization procedure for all operating systems and utility changes, and that the procedure requires the approval of system management before cataloging.	
7.2.3	Verify that computer operations require formal approval before implementing any new or changed operating system software or utilities.	
7.2.4	Determine whether full consideration is given to security requirements before the implementation of new system software, module updates, or utilities in accordance with organizational policies.	
7.2.5	Review the system modification history log that records changes to the operating system and utilities.	
7.2.6	Determine whether all modifications to system software are logged in the system modification history log.	
7.3	**Maintenance**	
7.3.1	Record the number of systems programmers assigned to system maintenance; all required maintenance of the existing operating systems and utilities should be able to be performed promptly.	
7.3.2	Review the controls over emergency changes and patches made by system programmers.	
7.3.3	Confirm that formal system maintenance requests must fully explain the change to be made, the reason for the change, and the cost justification.	

8.	**Automated Logs Review**	
	Objective: To determine whether automated logs are produced, reviewed, and stored as appropriate to record significant system events. Recommendations resulting from the automated logs review should cite appropriate control objectives, reference numbers, and applicable workpapers.	
Audit Test No.	*Action*	*Source of Information or Documentation*
8.1	Determine whether automated logs are produced for 　　Operating system accesses 　　Utilities accesses 　　Network accesses 　　System halts and restarts 　　Software modifications 　　Accesses to the system clock	
8.2	Confirm that automated logs cannot be turned off by unauthorized users.	
8.3	Verify that automated logs are reviewed for any unusual activity.	
8.4	Determine whether a retention schedule is available for automated logs.	
8.5	Review the procedures by which the operations division follows the retention schedule.	
9.	**Error Handling Review**	
	Objective: To ensure that the operating system maintains control of users and processes during error handling and provides information on error resolution Recommendations resulting from the error handling review should cite appropriate control objectives, reference numbers, and applicable workpapers.	
Audit Test No.	*Action*	*Source of Information or Documentation*
9.1	Determine whether system error traps are sufficient to control all users upon error detection.	
9.2	Verify that the operating system produces error messages for all system errors.	

9.3	Review operating system and utility error messages to ensure that they accurately describe the cause of the error and suggest any corrective actions required.	
10.	**System Backup Review**	
	Objective: To ensure that all necessary versions of the operating systems and utilities in use are properly backed up. Recommendations resulting from the system backup review should cite appropriate control objectives, reference numbers, and applicable workpapers.	
Audit Test No.	*Action*	*Source of Information or Documentation*
10.1	Review the procedures by which operators periodically back up the operating system.	
10.2	Determine whether the backup procedures are adequate.	
10.3	Confirm that previous versions of the operating system are retained intact until new versions or modifications are completely tested and accepted by all affected users.	
11.	**Administrative Controls Review**	
	Objective: To ensure that separation of duties is adequate and that personnel policies are properly adhered to. Recommendations resulting from the administrative controls review should cite appropriate control objectives, reference numbers, and applicable workpapers.	
Audit Test No.	*Action*	*Source of Information or Documentation*
11.1	Verify that only systems programmers write operating system software.	
11.2	Verify that systems programmers do not write application programs.	
11.3	Ensure that applications programmers and operations staff are not allowed to make direct program calls to operating system modules but must instead use the command language provided by the operating system.	

12.	**Security Software Review**	
	Objective: To determine whether the security software used provides an adequate level of control over system resources. Recommendations resulting from the security software review should cite appropriate control objectives, reference numbers, and applicable workpapers.	
Audit Test No.	*Action*	*Source of Information or Documentation*
12.1	Determine whether security software is used to control applications, functions, and other bank resources.	
12.2	Identify the specific resources that the security software protects or monitors.	
12.3	Determine whether security software is transparent to all users.	
12.4	Review the procedures for preventing and detecting hostage situations involving users without the knowledge of the perpetrators (e.g., special log-on ID or password).	
12.5	Verify that the security software features cannot be bypassed or overridden.	
12.6	Determine whether output from the security software is reviewed periodically by supervisory personnel.	
12.7	Confirm that security breaches are followed up by appropriate security personnel.	

Data Center Audit Program

Administration of IT Activities

Audit Steps

1. Review the organization chart and evaluate the established procedures for adequacy in defining responsibilities in the security administration area. Implement general control (provision for general authorization over the execution of transactions, for example, prohibiting the IT department from initiating or authorizing transactions) and COBIT objective (position descriptions clearly and delineate both authority and responsibility).

2. Determine who is responsible for control and administration of security. Verify that adequate security exists in the security administration function. Implement general control (prevents or detects deliberate or accidental errors caused by improper use) and COBIT objective (information services function is in compliance with security standards).

3. Determine whether adequate direction is maintained for each IT functional area within a policy and procedures manual. Evaluate whether the manual is kept up to date by IT management. Implement general control (written manuals in support of systems and procedures) and COBIT objective (operations staff have operations manuals for all systems and processing within their responsibility).

4. Determine if written personnel policies for the IT administration personnel exist, and if these policies stress adequate qualification and level of training and development.

5. Determine if long-range (two to five) years' system planning is maintained by IT management and is adequately considered in the fiscal budgeting process.

6. Assess the adequacy of inventory procurement and control pertaining to the administration of the LAN environment. Review available inventory documentation to determine if it is adequately maintained and complete in description and location. Compare the serial numbers on the computer software with inventory records to determine if illegal copies of system and application software are being supported.

Operating Systems Software and Data

Audit Steps

1. Determine through interviews with data center personnel whether any significant modifications or upgrades were implemented during this audit year. Review authorization documentation to ensure that adequate IT management approval is obtained before the implementation.

2. Determine through interviews with the IT personnel the procedures implemented to ensure that adequate IT management approval is obtained before the implementation.

3. Evaluate access restrictions over critical system operation areas.

Computer Operations/Business Resumption

Audit Steps

1. Review the IT policies and procedures manual to determine if written operating instructions adequately define recovery procedures in the event of processing disruption, shutdown and restart procedures, procedures for restoration of file server data from backups, and procedures for reporting incidents.

2. Determine through interviews with IT personnel the use of tape management software or other mechanism used to prevent the erasure of data.

3. Determine through interviews with IT personnel the rotation of tapes used in storing backup data. Determine if adequate off-site storage facilities are used and that tapes are rotated to the facility daily.

4. Evaluate procedures in place to control inventory of tapes maintained both on- and off-site.

5. Determine through observation the physical security of the consoles supporting backup procedures. If the console is not adequately secure, inquire as to the mechanisms used to prevent unauthorized tampering during backup processing.

6. Determine through the observation of computer operations facility the use of security mechanisms to provide access to authorized personnel only.

7. Evaluate procedures in place to monitor the activities of noncomputer operations personnel having access to the operations facility. Entry of unauthorized personnel should be supervised, and a log maintained and regularly reviewed by IT management.
8. Determine through observation the installation and maintenance of an automated fire-suppression system, raised-floor water sensors below floors, installation of power conditioning units, and backup power supply.

Security Administration

Audit Steps

1. Determine through interviews with IT personnel if a separate security administration function has been established.
2. Determine through interviews with IT personnel, review of IT policies and procedures manuals, and IT job descriptions if training programs have been established for all personnel for areas such as
   Organizational security policies
   Disclosure of sensitive data
   Access privileges to IT resources
   Reporting of security incidents
   Naming conventions for user passwords
3. Determine if formal policies define the organization's information security objectives and the responsibilities of employees with respect to the protection and disclosure of informational resources. Agreement to these policies should be evidenced by the signature of employees.
4. Determine if procedures and responsibility for the maintenance of user IDs and access privileges in the case of termination or transfer are defined and performed on a regular basis.

Cloud Computing Consulting Engagement

Due Diligence before Selecting a Cloud Service Provider (CSP)

1. Understand business requirements.
2. Research potential CSP.
3. Engage analysts from research companies, such as Gartner Research, to help focus on CSPs whose product offerings match closest to the business requirements.
4. Request demo of the product offering. Involve appropriate stakeholders, including who might use the data for other purposes, such as financial reporting.
5. Develop metrics to objectively measure CSP's offerings. Determine through interviews or questionnaire:
   - General information about the CSP
   - CSP's general capabilities/solutions offerings
   - Adaptability to business/configuration changes
   - Systems development methodology
   - Solution design and architecture
   - Audit, security, and compliance (e.g., SSAE 16, ISO27001 certification, SOX compliance)
   - Built-in application controls

- Monitoring tools
- Training requirements and support
- Support and maintenance
- Licensing and pricing structure

6. Based on the results of the demos and questionnaires, develop the appropriate recommendations for senior management's considerations.

Index